The Inequality Reader

The Inequality Reader

Contemporary and Foundational Readings in

Race, Class, and Gender

Edited by

David B. Grusky
Szonja Szelényi

Westview Press

A Member of the Perseus Books Group

Designed by Brent Wilcox

Library of Congress Cataloging-in-Publication Data
    The inequality reader : contemporary and foundational readings in race, class, and gender /
edited by David B. Grusky and Szonja Szelényi.
        p.   cm.
    Includes bibliographical references and index.
    ISBN-13: 978-0-8133-4345-7 (pbk. : alk. paper)
    ISBN-10: 0-8133-4345-3 (pbk. : alk. paper)
    1. Equality.   2. Social stratification.   3. Social classes.   4. Race.   5. Sex role.   I. Grusky,
David B.   II. Szelényi, Szonja, 1960-
    HM821.I54 2007
    305.01—dc22

                                                                                        2006017299

07 08 09 / 10 9 8 7 6 5 4 3 2 1

‖ To our fathers ‖

Contents

PART IV

Inequality at the Extremes

PART V

Racial and Ethnic Inequality

CONSTRUCTING RACIAL CATEGORIES

MODES OF INCORPORATION

CHANGE AND PERSISTENCE IN RACIAL
AND ETHNIC INEQUALITY

PART VI

Gender Inequality

CONSTRUCTING CATEGORIES

LABOR FORCE PARTICIPATION

DISCRIMINATION

SEX SEGREGATION

PART VII

Generating Inequality

PART VIII

The Consequences of Inequality

POLITICS

PART IX

Globalization and Inequality

Preface and Acknowledgments

Why publish yet another anthology of research on poverty and inequality? Although it wouldn't serve us well to draw too much attention to our many high-quality competitors, it surely can't come as a surprise that the market is rather well-stocked with other anthologies, a few of which have even been edited by us. The potential reader of the present anthology might reasonably ask why we have reentered a market so dense with competitors.

In addressing that question, our main response is that new developments in the field demand a new type of anthology that is quite unlike existing ones, even our own. There are three developments, in particular, that have transformed the field in important ways and have motivated us to assemble a new anthology for introductory students of poverty and inequality. These new developments, which we list below, are part of the ongoing transformation of sociology as it refashions a place for itself within an increasingly competitive social science landscape.

Rise of a multidisciplinary inequality field: For better or worse, there is no longer a consensual, interdisciplinary division of labor that has economists studying the total output of goods and sociologists studying how goods and resources are unequally distributed. Although such a simple division of labor never obtained even in the past, clearly economists have turned to the study of poverty and inequality, once the special province of sociologists, with unprecedented vigor. As a result, sociology is no longer a dominant force in the field, and "head-in-the-sand anthologies" that continue to pretend otherwise by relying exclusively on contributions by sociologists clearly do not prepare our students well. We have sought to incorporate into our reader some of the most important contributions by economists and other social scientists, contributions that have in many cases already entered into sociological discourse and have accordingly become, in effect, part of sociology.

Public intellectuals and inequality: As poverty and inequality increasingly become mainstream concerns, public intellectuals have emerged as yet another new group of "practicing sociologists," although in this case they have contributed mainly to the qualitative side of inequality research. Whereas economists are making headway, then, on the quantitative model-building front, public intellectuals and journalists are working mainly on the qualitative ethnographic front. The latter research has taken not only the usual small-scale form characteristic of qualitative research in sociology but also a more heavily-funded "big journalism" form in which cadres of investigators address a well-defined sociological question as part of a long-term research project. If one wants a searing expose or a provocative hypothesis, it often pays to turn to these journalists and public intellectuals. Although some of our readers might have wanted us to turn even more frequently to them (if only for their pleasing writing style), it bears emphasizing that sociologists still hold a distinct advantage in rigorous hypothesis-testing, an advantage that implies a somewhat circumscribed role for "public-intellectual sociology," at least as it is currently practiced.

The new post-survey world: Over the last decade, the standard survey instrument has come to be appreciated as but one useful approach to studying poverty and inequality, while other approaches, especially quasi-experimental ones, have clearly gained in prominence. We are referring, for example, to quasi-experimental studies of hiring discrimination, neighborhood effects, and returns to schooling. It is important, we think, to feature this quasi-experimental turn in our anthology, as it has been exceedingly influential in many subfields of poverty and inequality research. We have also drawn far more heavily than in prior anthologies on ethnographic and mixed-method studies. In many cases, these qualitative studies have attracted much attention and become widely celebrated, and not just among a narrow academic audience.

We would argue, therefore, that the disciplinary and methodological foundations of the poverty and inequality field have changed in such fundamental ways as to warrant assembling a new anthology. Moreover, the conceptual and empirical advances in the field have also been very substantial, again reason enough for assembling a new anthology. We have reviewed these advances in our introductory chapter (Ch. 1) and won't attempt to review them here as well. It should suffice to note that recent scholarship has turned to (a) examining recent dramatic increases in inequality (e.g., the spectacular growth in income inequality) as well as recent slowdowns in the rate of change (e.g., the slowing rate of decline in the gender pay gap), (b) exploring new types of inequality that were either ignored in the past or have been spawned by new technologies or institutions (e.g., the "digital divide"), and (c) teasing out the implications of inequality for both individual-level (e.g., health) and macro-level (e.g., terrorism, GNP) outcomes.

The editing rules adopted throughout this anthology are in most cases conventional. For example, brackets are used to mark off a passage that has been inserted for the purpose of clarifying meaning, whereas ellipses are used whenever a passage appearing in the original contribution has been excised altogether. The ellipses have been omitted when the excised text was a footnote, a minor reference to a table or passage (e.g., "see table 1"), or simply quite short in length. When necessary, tables and footnotes are renumbered without so indicating in the text, and all articles that were cited in excised passages are likewise omitted, without indication, from the list of references appearing at the end of each chapter. We were obliged for reasons of space to omit all footnotes (or endnotes) that were not strictly necessary. In the lead footnotes for each article, we have detailed any of the potentially controversial editing decisions, including resequencing paragraphs and smoothing out transitional prose between adjacent sections. We have also inserted references to the source article whenever it seemed appropriate to remind the reader that more detail is available in that source.

The spelling, grammatical, and stylistic conventions of the original contributions have otherwise been preserved. In this respect, the reader should be forewarned that some of the terms appearing in the original contributions would now be regarded as inappropriate (e.g., *Negro*), whereas others have passed out of common usage and will possibly be unfamiliar. While a strong argument could clearly be made for eliminating all language that is no longer acceptable, this type of sanitizing would not only exceed usual editorial license but would also generate a final text that contained inconsistent, and possibly confusing, temporal cues.

The selections reproduced here have all been pre-tested in graduate and undergraduate inequality classes at the University of Chicago, Stanford University, and Cornell University. We are indebted to the many students in these classes who shared their reactions to the selections and thereby shaped the final product more than they may realize. The anonymous reviewers of a proposal for this book also provided unusually constructive criticisms that were helpful in assembling the final book.

We are no less grateful for the market research carried out by Karl Yambert, for Michelle Trader's careful work securing permissions to reprint, and for Carol Smith's patient overseeing of a complicated, fast, and high-pressure production process. Finally, we must of course thank our Westview Press Editor, Steve Catalano, not just for conceiving of the project but also for his unusually sage advice throughout the long and hard process of realizing that conception.

David B. Grusky & Szonja Szelényi
Palo Alto, California 2006

The Rise and Fall of
Benign Narratives About Inequality

DAVID B. GRUSKY
SZONJA SZELÉNYI

There is a growing consensus among academics, policy makers, and even politicians that poverty and inequality should no longer be treated as soft "social issues" that can safely be subordinated to more fundamental interests in maximizing total economic output. The most important sources of this newfound concern with poverty and inequality are (1) the spectacular increase in economic inequality and other forms of disadvantage in many late-industrial countries (the *takeoff account*); (2) the striking persistence of many noneconomic forms of inequality despite decades of quite aggressive egalitarian reform (the *persistence account*); (3) an emerging concern that poverty and inequality may have negative macro-level effects on terrorism, total economic production, and ethnic unrest (the *macro-level externalities account*); (4) a growing awareness of the negative individual-level effects of poverty on health, political participation, and a host of other life conditions (the *micro-level externalities account*); (5) the rise of a "global village" in which regional disparities in the standard of living have become more widely visible and hence increasingly difficult to ignore (the *visibility account*); (6)

the ongoing tendency to expose and delegitimate new types of inequalities (based on sexual orientation, disability, or citizenship) that, not so long ago, were taken for granted, rarely discussed, and barely seen (the *new inequalities account*); and (7) a growing commitment to a conception of human entitlements that includes, at minimum, the right to seek or secure employment and thereby be spared extreme deprivation (the *social inclusion account*).

The foregoing list is remarkable in two ways. First, only two of the seven reasons for this newfound interest are about the brute empirics of inequality (i.e., its growth or intransigence), while all others are about changes in how we have come to view, study, and evaluate those empirics. When scholars now argue, for example, that inequality has multifarious effects (i.e., an *externalities account*), they presumably don't mean to suggest that such effects suddenly multiplied in the contemporary period. Rather, we are to understand that inequality was always rife with externalities, however inadequately we may have appreciated them in the past. Although changes in empirics hardly exhaust, then, the sources of

---

Original article prepared for this book.

our growing concern with inequality, this is not to gainsay the equally important point that such changes, especially the takeoff in income inequality, are likely a core reason why inequality has come to be understood as a fundamental social problem of our time.

The above list is no less remarkable for the relatively minor role that normative concerns play. To be sure, there appears to be a growing sentiment that, at minimum, contemporary social systems should guarantee an opportunity to all citizens to participate in economic life and hence avoid the most extreme forms of social and economic exclusion (i.e., the *social inclusion account*). It would nonetheless be a mistake to understand the rising interest in poverty and inequality as principally fueled by some sudden realization that social inclusion is a fundamental social good. Indeed, far from treating inequality as a moral problem in itself, the contemporary tendency is to emphasize its profound consequences and threats for the world community as a whole (i.e., the *macro-level externalities account*). The rhetoric of "sustainability," although more frequently featured in discussions of environmental problems, is increasingly taken as relevant to discussions of inequality as well. In adopting this rhetoric, the claim is that extreme inequality is counterproductive not just because it reduces total economic output, but also because other very legitimate objectives, such as reducing mortality rates, might also be compromised. By this logic, social policy must simultaneously be oriented to increasing economic output *and* restraining the rise of debilitating and counterproductive forms of inequality, a rather more complicated maximization problem than those conventionally taken on in economics (see Ch. 3, Fischer et al.; Ch. 4, Krueger).

The Role of Benign Narratives in Past Scholarship

The foregoing orientation to poverty and inequality should be understood as a sea change relative to the sensibilities that prevailed after World War II and even into the 1960s and 1970s. To be sure, the standard-issue sociologist of the past also embraced the view that inequality was an important social problem, but overlaid on this sensibility was an appreciation of various "logics of history" that operated in the main to reduce inequality, if only gradually and fitfully. The problem of inequality was understood, then, as a tractable moral problem, an unfortunate side-circumstance of capitalism (and even socialism) that would become yet more manageable with the transition into the increasingly affluent forms of advanced industrialism. This orientation to inequality, which we characterize throughout our essay as "benign," is expressed in the standard postwar narratives about three types of outcomes: (1) the distribution of income, power, and other valued resources; (2) the distribution of opportunities for securing income, power, and other valued resources; and (3) the formation of social classes and other institutionalized groups (e.g., racial groups, gender groups). We review each of these three types of benign narratives below.

Long-Term Trend in Inequality

The dominant inequality narrative of the postwar period featured the emergence of egalitarian ideologies and the consequent delegitimation of the extreme forms of inequality found in agrarian systems (e.g., Bell 1973; Kerr et al. 1964; Parsons 1970). The Enlightenment was understood as fostering a critical rhetoric of equality that unleashed one of the most profound revolutions in human history. The resulting decline in inequality can be seen, for example, in (1) the European revolutions of the eighteenth and nineteenth centuries against the privileges of rank (honorific equality); (2) the gradual elimination of inequalities in the right to vote, own property, and speak and assemble (civil equality); (3) the abolition of slavery and the establishment of the radically egalitarian principle of self-ownership (equality of human assets); and (4) the equalization of economic assets via the rise of socialism, welfare capitalism, and their many institutions (economic equality).[1]

As is well known, the latter commitment to equalizing economic assets was rather weaker than the commitment to other forms of equalization, with the result that economic inequalities remained extreme in all market economies. There was nonetheless a gradual decline in economic inequality throughout the postwar period in the United States. According to the classic Kuznets curve (Kuznets 1955), the initial stages of capitalist development bring about an increase in income inequality as capital is increasingly concentrated among a small number of investors, whereas more advanced forms of capitalism entail a growth in the size of the middle class and a consequent reversal of the upward trend. The causal dynamics behind the resulting inverted-U pattern remain unclear (see Acemoglu and Robinson 2002), but most sociologists attribute the late-industrial decline in inequality to the increasingly crucial role that the skilled working class played in production, the associated growth in working-class productivity, and the leverage that this growth in skills and productivity conferred on skilled workers.

The careful reader might inquire as to the mechanisms by which cultural egalitar-

ianism of this sort diffuses and takes hold. The conventional view in this regard is that a series of crucial historical events after the Enlightenment (e.g., the defeat of Nazism, the civil rights movement) served to define equality as one of our core cultural commitments. Absent some revolutionary event that changes this cultural trajectory, the course of human history then becomes the "working out" of this commitment, a task that involves shedding subsidiary values that sometimes come into conflict with our deeper commitment to egalitarianism. The core mechanism that drives this cultural diffusion may therefore be understood as the gradual reconciling of competing values to a new value, that of equality, that has been elevated by one or more historical events to a position of prominence.

Long-Term Trend in Inequality of Opportunity

The second narrative of interest rests on a sharp distinction between the distribution of social rewards (e.g., income) and the distribution of opportunities for securing these rewards. In liberal welfare regimes, extreme inequalities in rewards may be tolerated, but only insofar as opportunities for attaining these rewards are understood to be equally distributed. It is inequalities of opportunity that are regarded, then, as especially illegitimate in the context of liberal welfare regimes.

The dominant narratives of the postwar period have these inequalities of opportunity gradually weakening. The narratives of this period may be understood as benign because they describe the withering away of precisely those types of inequalities (i.e., inequalities of opportunity) that are regarded as problematic or illegitimate. The trademark of the benign narrative is this simple correspondence between what we want and what we think will likely happen. We describe below four benign subnarratives that characterize some of the processes by which inequalities of opportunity come to be weakened.

The most famous such subnarrative pertains to the discrimination-reducing effects of competitive market economies. In his original formulation of the "taste for discrimination" model, Becker (1957) argued that discrimination would be eroded by competitive market forces because it requires employers to pay a premium to hire members of the preferred class of labor, whether these be males, whites, or any other ascriptively defined classes. This taste is "discriminatory" because it rests on exogenous preferences for a certain category of labor that cannot be understood as arising from some larger concern for maximizing profitability or market share. When managers make hiring decisions in accord with such tastes, their firms will not be competitive with nondiscriminating firms because they must pay extra to secure labor from the preferred class (without any compensating increase in productivity). In standard renditions of this account, it is presumed that discriminating firms will gradually be selected out by the market, although it is also possible that some discriminating firms will change their hiring practices to remain competitive.

This economic subnarrative works in tandem with a second, "organizational" one that emphasizes the diffusion of modern personnel practices in the form of universalistic hiring practices (e.g., open hiring, credentialism) and bureaucratized pay scales and promotion procedures (see Ch. 5, Weber; Ch. 38, Charles and Grusky; Reskin and McBrier 2000). The essence of such bureaucratic personnel practices is a formal commitment to universalism (i.e., treating all workers equally) and to meritocratic hiring and promotion (i.e., hiring and promoting on the basis of credentials). In its ideal-typical form, the spread of bureaucracy becomes an organizational process with its own dynamic, a process of diffusion that rests not on actual efficiencies, as with the economic subnarrative, but simply on the *presumption* that bureaucratic practices are efficient and that "modern firms" must therefore adopt them. This subnarrative, like the economic one, implies that firms will gradually come to embrace organizational procedures that reduce inequalities of opportunity.

The third subnarrative of interest is the political one. Whereas the economic and organizational subnarratives treat change in inequality as an unintended by-product of macro-level forces (i.e., competition and bureaucratization), the political subnarrative is about instrumental action explicitly oriented towards effecting a decline in inequality. In theory, such political action could be oriented toward reducing either inequalities of opportunity or outcome, but historically a main emphasis within liberal welfare regimes has been legislation aimed at reducing inequality of opportunity (e.g., antidiscrimination legislation, early education programs, educational loans). The distinctive assumption of the political subnarrative is that straightforward "social engineering" is an important source of change and that the unintended or unanticipated consequences of such engineering are too often overemphasized.

The final subnarrative, a simple cultural one, rests on the argument that Western ideals of justice and equality continue to be endogenously worked out through a logic that diffuses independently of the economic efficiency of such ideals. The cultural subnarrative can be straightforwardly distinguished from the economic one because the growing "taste" for equality is presumed to be an exogenous shift rather than some accommodation to the rising economic cost of exercising discriminatory tastes. Likewise, the cultural subnarrative is distinct from the organizational subnarrative by virtue of focusing on the spread of tastes for equality and equality-enhancing practices, not the spread of organizational forms (e.g., bureaucratization) that are deemed efficient, normatively desirable, or both. Finally, the cultural and political subnarratives are closely related because political commitments to equal opportunity, antidiscrimination legislation, and school reform may be partly or even largely motivated by these newfound tastes for equal opportunity. At the same time, the cultural commitment to equal opportunity is not expressed exclusively in such political terms but is additionally expressed in the attitudes, behaviors, and personnel practices of employers. Most obviously, employers may gradually shed their preferences for certain categories of labor and instead develop tastes for equality in hiring, firing, and promotion, tastes that might at the limit be exercised in the labor market even with some loss in profits or efficiency.

The spread of such tastes for equal opportunity may again be viewed as part of our Enlightenment legacy, albeit a particular "liberal" variant of that legacy that emphasizes equalizing opportunities, not outcomes. This commitment is expressed not only at the individual level (e.g., changes in attitudes) but also at the collective level through various types of political reform (e.g., antidiscrimination legislation) as well

as the diffusion of bureaucratic personnel policies (e.g., open hiring).

Long-Term Trend in Class Formation

The final benign narrative of interest describes the gradual transition from "lumpy" class-based labor markets to more purely gradational ones (see Ch. 9, Hauser and Warren). Within this narrative, the early-industrial economy is represented as deeply balkanized into partly-independent labor markets defined by detailed occupations (e.g., economist, carpenter), big social classes (e.g., manager, farmer), or yet more aggregated factors of production (e.g., worker, capitalist) (Wright 2005). For our purposes, what is principally of interest is our collective fascination with arguments describing how these classes, however they may be defined (see Wright 2005), tend to gradually dissipate and leave us with gradational labor markets that increasingly approximate the seamless neoclassical ideal. The first step in this transition, as described most famously by Dahrendorf (1959), is the gradual "institutionalization" of class conflict, a regularization of labor–capital relations achieved through the establishment of unions, collective bargaining agreements, and other laws defining how labor and capital should negotiate (also see Parsons 1970). The second step in this transition involves the dismantling of unions and other institutionalized residues of classes as the liberal welfare ideals of "deregulation" and flexibility are increasingly pursued.

This line of argumentation is somewhat differently expressed in more recent postmodernist narratives. Although the postmodern literature is itself notoriously fragmented, most variants have proceeded from the assumption that class identities, ideologies, and organization are attenuating and that "new theories, perhaps more cultural than structural, [are] in order" (Davis 1982, p. 585). The core claim is that politics, lifestyles, and consumption practices are no longer class-determined and increasingly become a "function of individual taste, choice, and commitment" (Crook, Pakulski, and Waters 1992, p. 222; Ch. 8, Pakulski and Waters; Pakulski 2005).

In more ambitious variants of postmodernism, the focus shifts away from simply claiming that attitudes and practices are less class-determined, and the older class-analytic objective of understanding macro-level stratificational change is resuscitated. This ambition underlies, for example, all forms of postmodernism that seek to represent "new social movements" (e.g., environmentalism) as the vanguard force behind future stratificatory change. As argued by Eyerman (1992) and others (e.g., Touraine 1981), the labor movement can be seen as a fading enterprise rooted in the old conflicts of the workplace and industrial capitalism, whereas new social movements provide a more appealing call for collective action by virtue of their emphasis on issues of lifestyle, personal identity, and normative change. With this formulation, the proletariat is stripped of its privileged status as a universal class, and new social movements emerge as an alternative and far more benign force "shaping the future of modern societies" (Haferkamp and Smelser 1992, p. 17).

New Approaches to Studying Inequality

The foregoing narratives, all of which were fixtures of the postwar intellectual landscape, describe the emergence of a world in which inequalities are less profound, opportunities are more equally distributed, and class conflicts and interclass differences become attenuated. These narratives are benign in the sense that they push us toward equilibria that most commentators, even neo-Marxian ones, might well regard as appealing. The benign narrative is accordingly built on the happy correspondence between what should be and what will be.

If there is any theme to contemporary analyses of inequality, it is that the benign narrative has fallen largely out of fashion. We have nonetheless laid out these narratives in some detail because they provide an important backdrop to current theorizing and are often used as foils by contemporary scholars seeking to motivate their own analyses. The benign narrative is in this sense lurking in the background of contemporary discussions of inequality. We turn now to a closer discussion of how contemporary analyses of inequality have developed partly in reaction to the benign narratives of the postwar period.

Multidimensionalism and New Inequalities

As a natural starting point for this discussion, we note that contemporary inequality scholarship is increasingly concerned with new forms of inequality, forms that were either ignored in the past or have been spawned by new technologies or institutions. This growing emphasis on new inequalities is consistent with the now fashionable view that inequality is "multidimensional" and that conventional studies of economic, socioeconomic, or cultural inequality hardly exhaust its many forms (e.g., Sen 2006).

If a multidimensional approach is taken, one might usefully distinguish between the eight forms of inequality listed in Table 1.1,

Table 1.1   Types of Assets and Examples of Advantaged and Disadvantaged Groups

Assets		Examples	
Asset group	Examples of types	Advantaged	Disadvantaged
1. Economic	Wealth	Billionaire	Bankrupt worker
	Income	Professional	Laborer
	Ownership	Capitalist	Worker (i.e., employed)
2. Power	Political power	Prime minister	Disenfranchised person
	Workplace authority	Manager	Subordinate worker
	Household authority	Head of household	Child
3. Cultural	Knowledge	Intelligentsia	Uneducated
	Digital culture	Silicon Valley resident	Residents of other places
	"Good" manners	Aristocracy	Commoner
4. Social	Social clubs	Country club member	Nonmember
	Workplace associations	Union member	Nonmember
	Informal networks	Washington A-list	Social unknown
5. Honorific	Occupational	Judge	Garbage collector
	Religious	Saint	Excommunicate
	Merit-based	Nobel Prize winner	Nonwinner
6. Civil	Right to work	Citizen	Illegal immigrant
	Due process	Citizen	Suspected terrorist
	Franchise	Citizen	Felon
7. Human	On-the-job	Experienced worker	Inexperienced worker
	General schooling	College graduate	High school dropout
	Vocational training	Law school graduate	Unskilled worker
8. Physical (i.e., health)	Mortality	Person with long life	A "premature" death
	Physical disease	Healthy person	Person with AIDS, asthma
	Mental health	Healthy person	Depressed, alienated

each such form pertaining to a type of good that is intrinsically valuable (as well as possibly an investment). The multidimensional space formed by these variables may be labeled the "inequality space." We can characterize the social location of an individual within this inequality space by specifying her or his constellation of scores on each of the eight classes of variables in this table.

This framework allows scholars to examine how individuals are distributed among the less conventionally studied dimensions of the inequality space. Are "new" assets as unequally distributed as old ones? Is inequality becoming more of an "all or nothing" affair in which upper-class workers are advantaged on all dimensions of interest and lower-class workers are disadvantaged on all dimensions of interest? Are new assets sometimes distributed in ways that compensate for shortfalls in older ones? In the present volume, multidimensionalist questions of this kind are posed for such "new" outcomes as health (Ch. 55, Scott; Ch. 56, Mullahy, Robert, and Wolfe), computer literacy (Ch. 59, DiMaggio et al.), imprisonment or capital punishment (Ch. 21, Western), and networks and social capital (Ch. 52, Granovetter; Ch. 53, Lin; Ch. 54, Burt). These new types of inequality may be understood in some cases as truly new divides generated by new technologies (e.g., the digital divide) or new social institutions (e.g., modern mass prisons). More typically, the "new" outcomes are just increasingly popular topics of study among academics, not truly new forms (e.g., health inequalities).

The Intransigence of Poverty and Inequality

The foregoing line of research typically takes the form of an exposé of the extent to which seemingly basic human entitlements, such as living outside of prison, freely participating in "digital" culture, or living a long and healthy life, are unequally distributed in ways that sometimes amplify well-known differentials of income or education. The continuing attraction of such exposés (at least among academics) may be attributed to our collective discomfort with an economic system that generates rather more inequality than is palatable under contemporary cultural standards. Although the equalizing reforms of social democracy have historically been a main solution to this tension, the declining legitimacy of such reform (especially in Europe and the United States) leaves the tension an increasingly unresolved one.

Whereas the old narratives focused, then, on the forces making for decline in inequality, a more pessimistic assessment of the trajectory of late industrialism has now taken

hold, and much scholarship accordingly focuses on documenting that inequality has persisted at higher levels than had been anticipated. This sensibility underlies, for example, contemporary research showing that residential segregation in the United States is so extreme as to constitute a modern form of "apartheid" (Ch. 18, Massey and Denton), that racial discrimination in labor markets likewise remains extreme (Ch. 28, Bertrand and Mullainathan), that the occupational structure is "hypersegregated" by gender (Ch. 38, Charles and Grusky), that income inequality has increased markedly in many countries over the last thirty-five years (Ch. 10, Morris and Western), that poverty rates in the United States remain strikingly high (Ch. 16, Smeeding, Rainwater, and Burtless), that African Americans are routinely harassed, slighted, and insulted in public places (Ch. 27, Feagin), that working-class and middle-class children tend to be raised in profoundly different ways (Ch. 58, Lareau), that political behavior continues to be strongly shaped by class-based politics (Ch. 60, Hout and Moodie), and that massive class disparities in access to health services persist (Ch. 55, Scott; Ch. 56, Mullahy, Robert, and Wolfe).

The cynic might ask whether this new muckraking tradition is really all that necessary. Is there truly a large public that doesn't already appreciate the persistence of many of these inequalities? We live, after all, in a market society in which virtually everything is commodified, meaning that almost all goods and services (e.g., health care, housing) are allocated on the basis of our ability to pay for them. Because we are so deeply and (seemingly) irrevocably marketized, the real intellectual challenge would be to find a good, service, or outcome that is somehow untouched by class, one that is perfectly and equally distributed to all.

We suspect that our contributors would react to such (hypothetical) criticism by emphasizing that only some inequalities may be understood as the inevitable outcome of our collective decision to allocate resources on the basis of a market. It is at least possible to imagine markets that do not entail racial discrimination, that do not entail gender discrimination, and that encompass institutions that have a substantial inequality-moderating effect. It is likewise possible to imagine that class differences in politics, culture, and child rearing practices would have by now abated. The benign narratives of the postwar period in fact laid out precisely such imaginings. If it is now clear that these imagined futures have not been realized, surely we need to document that conclusion with all the rigor that can possibly be mustered. To be sure, many of us well know that the world is a massively unequal one, but even so the force of the known can be readily lost when we live with profound inequality on a day-to-day basis. This commitment to remind us of what comes to be taken for granted is the cornerstone, we suspect, of the renewed interest in the inequality-documenting function.

The Rise of New and Less Benign Narratives

The rise of this muckraking exposé of inequality has been coupled, moreover, with increasing interest in developing narratives that explain why inequality has persisted or grown more extreme. These narratives are typically less grand than the quite encompassing narratives of the postwar period; that is, rather specialized narratives have recently developed around many of the various unit trends of interest (e.g., the ex-

pansion of income inequality, the stalling decline in the gender wage gap), and rather little attention has been paid to developing some grand meta-narrative that links these specialized narratives together. The signature, then, of the contemporary narrative is this highly delimited focus, a commitment to developing a rigorously empirical foundation, and a special interest in identifying those more insidious social forces that undermine the benign narratives of the past.

By way of example, consider the historic rise in income inequality, a development that has spawned one of the most sustained efforts at narrative-building of our time (see Ch. 10, Morris and Western). As noted above, the classic Kuznets curve aligns nicely with the facts of inequality up to the early 1970s, but then a dramatic, unprecedented upswing in inequality in the post-1970 period made it clear that inequality history had not ended. We have since witnessed one of the most massive research efforts in the history of social science as scholars sought to identify the "smoking gun" that accounted for this dramatic increase in inequality.

Initially, the dominant hypothesis was that deindustrialization (i.e., the relocation of manufacturing jobs to offshore labor markets) brought about a decline in demand for less-educated manufacturing workers, a decline that generated increases in inequality by hollowing out the middle class and sending manufacturing workers into unemployment or into the ranks of poorly paid service work. Although this line of argumentation still has its advocates, it cannot easily be reconciled with evidence suggesting that the computerization of the workplace and related technological change has been at least one force behind a heightened demand for highly educated workers.

Because of this result (and other supporting evidence), the deindustrialization story has now been largely supplanted by the converse hypothesis that "skill-biased technological change" has increased the demand for high-skill workers beyond the increase in supply, thus inducing a short-term disequilibrium and a correspondingly increased payoff for high-skill labor. At the same time, most scholars acknowledge that this story is at best an incomplete one and that other accounts, especially more narrowly political ones, must additionally be entertained (e.g., Card and DiNardo 2002). Most notably, some of the rise in income inequality in the United States was clearly attributable to the declining minimum wage (in real dollars), a decline that in turn has to be understood as the outcome of political processes that increasingly favor pro-inequality forces (Ch. 10, Morris and Western). The same conclusion applies yet more obviously to the recent round of tax cuts in the United States.

The future of income inequality depends on which of these underlying mechanisms is principally at work. The silver lining of the deindustrialization story is that within-country increases in inequality should be offset by between-country declines (as poor countries profit from new manufacturing jobs), whereas the silver lining of skill-biased technological change is that the heightened demand for high-skill workers is presumably a one-time, short-term disequilibrium that will, by virtue of the higher payoff to high-skill jobs, trigger a compensating growth in the supply of high-skill workers. There is, unfortunately, no shortage of competing stories that imply more disturbing futures, even futures consistent with a classical Marxian account in which low-skill workers are emiserated within some

countries by virtue of a globalization-induced "race to the bottom." Indeed, accounts that focus on the political sources of rising inequality often take on this more disturbing character, given that social democratic ideologies have fallen largely out of fashion and no longer provide capitalists with a viable high road of "enlightened self-interest" (e.g., support for labor unions, redistribution). As social democratic agendas come to be viewed with suspicion, political support for the minimum wage and other inequality-reducing institutions may increasingly falter, and market-generated inequality may no longer be much restrained by premarket or after-market interventions.

We have focused on the rise of income inequality and the various narratives it has generated only because this literature is especially well known and central to the field. The larger point that we seek to make is that, no matter the subfield, there appears to be much interest in developing narratives that explain why long-standing declines in inequality have slowed down, stalled altogether, or even reversed themselves. We are referring, for example, to (1) narratives of "globalization" that describe how the liberalization of financial and capital markets has harmed poor countries (Ch. 61, Stiglitz); (2) narratives of "deindustrialization" that describe the loss of inner-city jobs and the associated rise of an urban underclass (Ch. 17, Wilson); (3) narratives of "segmented assimilation" that describe the relatively bleak prospects for at least some new immigrant groups (Ch. 24, Portes and Zhou); (4) narratives of "opting out" that have highly trained women eschewing stressful careers in favor of recommitting to their children, spouses, and domestic responsibilities (Ch. 34, Belkin; cf. Boushey 2005); and (5) narratives of "essentialist segregation" that describe how sex-typed occupational ghettos continue to be built around presumed differences in male and female aptitudes (Ch. 38, Charles and Grusky). Although counternarratives of the more optimistic sort are also being developed (e.g., Alba and Nee 2003; Ch. 62, Firebaugh), these seem not to be as frequently generated or as readily embraced; and the proponents of such narratives find themselves beleaguered, outnumbered, and on the defensive.

Conclusions

We have fashioned our review and introduction around the revolutionary changes over the last half-century in the types of narratives that sociologists and other social scientists have applied to make sense of trends in inequality. The narratives of the postwar period took on a strikingly benign form in which the dominant logics of history were understood as operating in the main to reduce inequality. These benign narratives, which now mainly seem naive and quaint, have been supplanted by a host of new narratives that give far greater weight to the forces making for inequality.

Has the pendulum swung too far? It is of course child's play to posit any number of nonempirical sources of our fascination, some might say obsession, with the pessimistic narrative. The following are perhaps the most obvious of such accounts:

1. *The newsworthiness account.* If the postwar era of the benign narrative was indeed one of across-the-board declines in inequality, then a special incentive presumably emerged to ferret out results that were inconsistent with the prevailing wisdom and hence would

be regarded as newsworthy. It is surely difficult to market analyses and forge careers on the basis of business-as-usual evidence. We might ask, for example, whether the "digital divide" emerged as a newsworthy topic because of early evidence of a substantial divide. If instead access to computing was found to be equal, would we have quickly discarded the topic and set off to find some other more unequal outcome? This type of selection on the dependent variable (i.e., inequality) will create a research literature that exaggerates how unequal the world is.

2. *The "moral credentials" account.* It is well to bear in mind that the contemporary academic, far from taking a vow of poverty, is now firmly ensconced in the middle class, often the upper middle class. When relatively privileged scholars study poverty and disadvantage, they often feel a special obligation to demonstrate a strong commitment to amelioration and to display political sentiments that are liberal, progressive, or even radical. In some cases, this pressure may motivate them to downplay any evidence of decline in inequality or disadvantage, presumably out of concern that undue emphasis on the progress achieved so far will make it appear that the remaining disadvantage is taken as acceptable or unproblematic.

3. *The "obsession with small differences" account.* The continuing diffusion of egalitarian values renders any departures from equality, no matter how small, as problematic and newsworthy. By this logic, even increasingly small intergroup differences will attract much attention, especially because ever more

powerful models and statistical methods now make it possible to tease them out (see Nisbet 1959, p. 12).

These nonempirical interpretations shouldn't be dismissed out of hand, nor should they be taken too seriously. It is relevant in this regard that many of the pessimistic narratives involve indisputably dramatic changes in outcomes (e.g., income) that were frequently studied well before any reversal in the trendline was detected. Although some of the pessimistic narratives featured in this volume are still in incipient form and are not yet well-researched (especially Ch. 34, Belkin), it will of course be difficult to continue to maintain these narratives should strong disconfirming evidence turn up. The implication, then, is that our exaggerated taste for pessimism might conceivably lead us to cycle through a great many pessimistic stories (and fail to develop enough benign ones), but at least the usual rules of evidence will have us excise egregiously flawed narratives, no matter how benign or pessimistic they may be.

NOTE

1. This is not to suggest that *all* postwar sociologists and social scientists emphasized forces making for a decline in inequality. However, even when a benign narrative was not adopted, there was usually some effort to engage with it and to explain or defend the decision not to take it up. This defensiveness was especially apparent in neo-Marxian analyses of the postwar era. Although such analyses were based on deeply pessimistic subnarratives about the trajectory of capitalism, these subnarratives were typically attached to larger and more benign narratives about the post-capitalist trajectory (see Ch. 5, Marx; Ch. 7, Wright).

REFERENCES

Acemoglu, Daron, and James A. Robinson. 2002. "The Political Economy of the Kuznets Curve." *Review of Development Economics* 6: 183–203.

Alba, Richard, and Victor Nee. 2003. *Remaking the American Mainstream: Assimilation and Contemporary Immigration.* Cambridge: Harvard University Press.

Becker, Gary S. 1957. *The Economics of Discrimination.* Chicago: University of Chicago Press.

Bell, Daniel. 1973. *The Coming of Post-Industrial Society.* New York: Basic Books.

Boushey, Heather. 2005. *Are Women Opting Out? Debunking the Myth.* Washington, DC: Center for Economic and Policy Research.

Card, D., and J. E. DiNardo. 2002. "Skill-Biased Technological Change and Rising Wage Inequality: Some Problems and Puzzles." *Journal of Labor Economics* 20: 733–83.

Charles, Maria, and David B. Grusky. 2004. *Occupational Ghettos: The Worldwide Segregation of Women and Men.* Stanford: Stanford University Press.

Crook, Stephen, Jan Pakulski, and Malcolm Waters. 1992. *Postmodernization.* London: Sage Publications.

Dahrendorf, Ralf. 1959. *Class and Class Conflict in Industrial Society.* Stanford: Stanford University Press.

Davis, James. 1982. "Achievement Variables and Class Cultures: Family, Schooling, Job, and Forty-nine Dependent Variables in the Cumulative GSS." *American Sociological Review* 47: 569–86.

Eyerman, Ron. 1992. "Modernity and Social Movements." In *Social Change and Modernity*, edited by Hans Haferkamp and Neil J. Smelser. Berkeley: University of California Press.

Haferkamp, Hans, and Neil J. Smelser. 1992. "Introduction." In *Social Change and Modernity*, edited by Hans Haferkamp and Neil J. Smelser. Berkeley: University of California Press.

Kerr, Clark, John T. Dunlop, Frederick H. Harbison, and Charles A. Myers. 1964. *Industrial-*

ism and Industrial Man. New York: Oxford University Press.

Kuznets, Simon. 1955. "Economic Growth and Income Inequality (Presidential Address)." *American Economic Review* 45: 1–28.

Nisbet, Robert A. 1959. "The Decline and Fall of Social Class." *Pacific Sociological Review* 2: 11–17.

Pakulski, J. 2005. "Foundations of a Post-Class Analysis." In *Approaches to Class Analysis*, edited by E. Wright. Cambridge: Cambridge University Press.

Parsons, Talcott. 1970. "Equality and Inequality in Modern Society, or Social Stratification Revisited." In *Social Stratification: Research and Theory for the 1970s*, edited by Edward O. Laumann. Indianapolis: Bobbs-Merrill.

Reskin, Barbara F., and Debra Branch McBrier. 2000. "Why Not Ascription? Organizations' Employment of Male and Female Managers." *American Sociological Review* 65: 210–33.

Sen, A. 2006. "Conceptualizing and Measuring Poverty." In *Inequality and Poverty*, edited by D. Grusky and R. Kanbur. Stanford: Stanford University Press.

Touraine, Alain. 1981. *The Voice and the Eye: An Analysis of Social Movements.* Cambridge: Cambridge University Press.

Wright, Erik O. 2005. *Approaches to Class Analysis.* Cambridge: Cambridge University Press.

2

Some Principles of Stratification

KINGSLEY DAVIS

WILBERT E. MOORE

In a previous paper some concepts for handling the phenomena of social inequality were presented.[1] In the present paper a further step in stratification theory is undertaken—an attempt to show the relationship between stratification and the rest of the social order.[2] Starting from the proposition that no society is "classless," or unstratified, an effort is made to explain, in functional terms, the universal necessity which calls forth stratification in any social system.

Throughout, it will be necessary to keep in mind one thing—namely, that the discussion relates to the system of positions, not to the individuals occupying those positions. It is one thing to ask why different positions carry different degrees of prestige, and quite another to ask how certain individuals get into those positions. Although, as the argument will try to show, both questions are related, it is essential to keep them separate in our thinking.

Most of the literature on stratification has tried to answer the second question (particularly with regard to the ease or difficulty of mobility between strata) without tackling the first. The first question, however, is logically prior and, in the case of any particular individual or group, factually prior.

The Functional Necessity of Stratification

Curiously the main functional necessity explaining the universal presence of stratification is precisely the requirement faced by any society of placing and motivating individuals in the social structure. As a functioning mechanism a society must somehow distribute its members in social positions and induce them to perform the duties of these positions. It must thus concern itself with motivation at two different levels: to instill in the proper individuals the desire to fill certain positions, and, once in these positions, the desire to perform the duties attached to them. Even though the social order may be relatively static in form, there is a continuous process of metabolism as new individuals are born into it, shift with age, and die off. Their absorption into the positional system must somehow be arranged and motivated. This is true whether the sys-

Kingsley Davis and Wilbert E. Moore, "Some Principles of Stratification," *American Sociological Review* 10 (April 1945), pp. 242–249.

tem is competitive or non-competitive. A competitive system gives greater importance to the motivation to achieve positions, whereas a non-competitive system gives perhaps greater importance to the motivation to perform the duties of the positions; but in any system both types of motivation are required.

If the duties associated with the various positions were all equally pleasant to the human organism, all equally important to societal survival, and all equally in need of the same ability or talent, it would make no difference who got into which positions, and the problem of social placement would be greatly reduced. But actually it does make a great deal of difference who gets into which positions, not only because some positions are inherently more agreeable than others, but also because some require special talents or training and some are functionally more important than others. Also, it is essential that the duties of the positions be performed with the diligence that their importance requires. Inevitably, then, a society must have, first, some kind of rewards that it can use as inducements, and, second, some way of distributing these rewards differentially according to positions. The rewards and their distribution become a part of the social order, and thus give rise to stratification.

One may ask what kind of rewards a society has at its disposal in distributing its personnel and securing essential services. It has, first of all, the things that contribute to sustenance and comfort. It has, second, the things that contribute to humor and diversion. And it has, finally, the things that contribute to self-respect and ego expansion. The last, because of the peculiarly social character of the self, is largely a function of the opinion of others, but it nonetheless

ranks in importance with the first two. In any social system all three kinds of rewards must be dispensed differentially according to positions.

In a sense the rewards are "built into" the position. They consist in the "rights" associated with the position, plus what may be called its accompaniments or perquisites. Often the rights, and sometimes the accompaniments, are functionally related to the duties of the position. (Rights as viewed by the incumbent are usually duties as viewed by other members of the community.) However, there may be a host of subsidiary rights and perquisites that are not essential to the function of the position and have only an indirect and symbolic connection with its duties, but which still may be of considerable importance in inducing people to seek the positions and fulfill the essential duties.

If the rights and perquisites of different positions in a society must be unequal, then the society must be stratified, because that is precisely what stratification means. Social inequality is thus an unconsciously evolved device by which societies insure that the most important positions are conscientiously filled by the most qualified persons. Hence every society, no matter how simple or complex, must differentiate persons in terms of both prestige and esteem, and must therefore possess a certain amount of institutionalized inequality.

It does not follow that the amount or type of inequality need be the same in all societies. This is largely a function of factors that will be discussed presently.

The Two Determinants of Positional Rank

Granting the general function that inequality subserves, one can specify the two factors that determine the relative rank of different positions. In general those positions convey the best reward, and hence have the highest rank, which (a) have the greatest importance for the society and (b) require the greatest training or talent. The first factor concerns function and is a matter of relative significance; the second concerns means and is a matter of scarcity.

Differential Functional Importance.   Actually a society does not need to reward positions in proportion to their functional importance. It merely needs to give sufficient reward to them to insure that they will be filled competently. In other words, it must see that less essential positions do not compete successfully with more essential ones. If a position is easily filled, it need not be heavily rewarded, even though important. On the other hand, if it is important but hard to fill, the reward must be high enough to get it filled anyway. Functional importance is therefore a necessary but not a sufficient cause of high rank being assigned to a position.[3]

Differential Scarcity of Personnel.   Practically all positions, no matter how acquired, require some form of skill or capacity for performance. This is implicit in the very notion of position, which implies that the incumbent must, by virtue of his incumbency, accomplish certain things.

There are, ultimately, only two ways in which a person's qualifications come about: through inherent capacity or through training. Obviously, in concrete activities both are always necessary, but from a practical standpoint the scarcity may lie primarily in one or the other, as well as in both. Some positions require innate talents of such high degree that the persons who fill them are bound to be rare. In many cases, however, talent is fairly abundant in the population but the training process is so long, costly, and elaborate that relatively few can qualify. Modern medicine, for example, is within the mental capacity of most individuals, but a medical education is so burdensome and expensive that virtually none would undertake it if the position of the M.D. did not carry a reward commensurate with the sacrifice.

If the talents required for a position are abundant and the training easy, the method of acquiring the position may have little to do with its duties. There may be, in fact, a virtually accidental relationship. But if the skills required are scarce by reason of the rarity of talent or the costliness of training, the position, if functionally important, must have an attractive power that will draw the necessary skills in competition with other positions. This means, in effect, that the position must be high in the social scale—must command great prestige, high salary, ample leisure, and the like.

How Variations Are to Be Understood.   In so far as there is a difference between one system of stratification and another, it is attributable to whatever factors affect the two determinants of differential reward—namely, functional importance and scarcity of personnel. Positions important in one society may not be important in another, because the conditions faced by the societies, or their degree of internal development, may be different. The same conditions, in turn, may affect the question of scarcity; for in some societies the stage of development, or the external situation, may wholly obviate the necessity of certain kinds of skill or talent. Any particular system of stratification, then, can be understood as a product of the special conditions affecting the two afore-mentioned grounds of differential reward.

NOTES

1. Kingsley Davis, "A Conceptual Analysis of Stratification," *American Sociological Review.* 7:309–321, June, 1942.

2. The writers regret (and beg indulgence) that the present essay, a condensation of a longer study, covers so much in such short space that adequate evidence and qualification cannot be given and that as a result what is actually very tentative is presented in an unfortunately dogmatic manner.

3. Unfortunately, functional importance is difficult to establish. To use the position's prestige to establish it, as is often unconsciously done, constitutes circular reasoning from our point of view. There are, however, two independent clues: (a) the degree to which a position is functionally unique, there being no other positions that can perform the same function satisfactorily; (b) the degree to which other positions are dependent on the one in question. Both clues are best exemplified in organized systems of positions built around one major function. Thus, in most complex societies the religious, political, economic, and educational functions are handled by distinct structures not easily interchangeable. In addition, each structure possesses many different positions, some clearly dependent on, if not subordinate to, others. In sum, when an institutional nucleus becomes differentiated around one main function, and at the same time organizes a large portion of the population into its relationships, the *key* positions in it are of the highest functional importance. The absence of such specialization does not prove functional unimportance, for the whole society may be relatively unspecialized; but it is safe to assume that the more important functions receive the first and clearest structural differentiation.

3

Inequality by Design

CLAUDE S. FISCHER, MICHAEL HOUT,
MARTÍN SÁNCHEZ JANKOWSKI, SAMUEL R. LUCAS,
ANN SWIDLER, AND KIM VOSS

Why do some Americans have a lot more than others? Perhaps, inequality follows inevitably from human nature. Some people are born with more talent than others; the first succeed while the others fail in life's competition. Many people accept this explanation, but it will not suffice. Inequality is not fated by nature, nor even by the "invisible hand" of the market; it is a social construction, a result of our historical acts. *Americans have created the extent and type of inequality we have, and Americans maintain it.*

To answer the question of what explains inequality in America, we must divide it in two. First, who gets ahead and who falls behind in the competition for success? Second, what determines how much people get for being ahead or behind? To see more clearly that the two questions are different, think of a ladder that represents the ranking of affluence in a society. Question one asks why this person rather than that person ended up on a higher or lower rung. Question two asks why some societies have tall and narrowing ladders—ladders that have huge distances between top and bottom

rungs and that taper off at the top so that there is room for only a few people—while other societies have short and broad ladders—ladders with little distance between top and bottom and with lots of room for many people all the way to the top.

The answer to the question of who ends up where is that people's social environments largely influence what rung of the ladder they end up on.[1] The advantages and disadvantages that people inherit from their parents, the resources that their friends can share with them, the quantity and quality of their schooling, and even the historical era into which they are born boost some up and hold others down. The children of professors, our own children, have substantial head starts over children of, say, factory workers. Young men who graduated from high school in the booming 1950s had greater opportunities than the ones who graduated during the Depression. Context matters tremendously.

The answer to the question of why societies vary in their structure of rewards is more political. In significant measure, societies choose the height and breadth of their "ladders." By loosening markets or regulating them, by providing services to all citizens or rationing them according to income, by subsidizing some groups more than others, societies, through their politics, build their ladders. To be sure, historical and external constraints deny full freedom of action, but a substantial freedom of action remains. In a democracy, this means that the inequality Americans have is, in significant measure, the historical result of policy choices Americans—or, at least, Americans' representatives—have made. In the United States, the result is a society that is distinctively *un*equal. Our ladder is, by the standards of affluent democracies and even by the standards of recent American history, unusually extended and narrow—and becoming more so.

To see how policies shape the structure of rewards (i.e., the equality of outcomes), consider these examples: Laws provide the ground rules for the marketplace—rules covering incorporation, patents, wages, working conditions, unionization, security transactions, taxes, and so on. Some laws widen differences in income and earnings among people in the market; others narrow differences. Also, many government programs affect inequality more directly through, for example, tax deductions, food stamps, social security, Medicare, and corporate subsidies.

To see how policies also affect which particular individuals get to the top and which fall to the bottom of our ladder (i.e., the equality of opportunity), consider these examples: The amount of schooling young Americans receive heavily determines the jobs they get and the income they make. In turn, educational policies—what sorts of schools are provided, the way school re-

sources are distributed (usually according to the community in which children live), teaching methods such as tracking, and so on—strongly affect how much schooling children receive. Similarly, local employment opportunities constrain how well people can do economically. Whether and where governments promote jobs or fail to do so will, in turn, influence who is poised for well-paid employment and who is not.

Claiming that intentional policies have significantly constructed the inequalities we have and that other policies could change those inequalities may seem a novel idea in the current ideological climate. So many voices tell us that inequality is the result of individuals' "natural" talents in a "natural" market. Nature defeats any sentimental efforts by society to reduce inequality, they say; such efforts should therefore be dropped as futile and wasteful. Appeals to nature are common and comforting. As Kenneth Bock wrote in his study of social philosophy, "We have been quick to seek explanations of our problems and failures in what we *are* instead of what we *do*. We seem wedded to the belief that our situation is a consequence of our nature rather than of our historical acts."[2] In this case, appeals to nature are shortsighted.

Arguments from nature are useless for answering the question of what determines the structure of rewards because that question concerns differences in equality *among societies*. Theories of natural inequality cannot tell us why countries with such similar genetic stocks (and economic markets) as the United States, Canada, England, and Sweden can vary so much in the degree of economic inequality their citizens experience. The answer lies in deliberate policies.

Appeals to nature also cannot satisfactorily answer even the first question: Why do some *individuals* get ahead and some fall behind? Certainly, genetic endowment helps. Being tall, slender, good-looking, healthy, male, and white helps in the race for success, and these traits are totally or partly determined genetically. But these traits matter to the degree that society makes them matter—determining how much, for example, good looks or white skin are rewarded. More important yet than these traits are the social milieux in which people grow up and live.

Realizing that intentional policies account for much of our expanding inequality is not only more accurate than theories of natural inequality; it is also more optimistic. We are today more unequal than we have been in seventy years. We are more unequal than any other affluent Western nation. Intentional policies could change those conditions, could reduce and reverse our rush to a polarized society, could bring us closer to the average inequality in the West, could expand both equality of opportunity and equality of result.

Still, the "natural inequality" viewpoint is a popular one. Unequal outcomes, the best-selling *Bell Curve* argues, are the returns from a fair process that sorts people out according to how intelligent they are.[3] But *The Bell Curve*'s explanation of inequality is inadequate. The authors err in assuming that human talents can be reduced to a single, fixed, and essentially innate skill they label intelligence. They err in asserting that this trait largely determines how people end up in life. And they err in imagining that individual competition explains the structure of inequality in society. . . .

Disparities in income and wealth, [other] analysts argue, encourage hard work and saving. The rich, in particular, can invest their capital in production and thus create

jobs for all.[4] This was the argument of "supply-side" economics in the 1980s, that rewarding the wealthy—for example, by reducing income taxes on returns from their investments—would stimulate growth to the benefit of all. The 1980s did not work out that way, but the theory is still influential. We *could* force more equal outcomes, these analysts say, but doing so would reduce living standards for all Americans.

Must we have so much inequality for overall growth? The latest economic research concludes *not;* it even suggests that inequality may *retard* economic growth. In a detailed statistical analysis, economists Torsten Persson and Guido Tabellini reported finding that, historically, societies that had more inequality of earnings tended to have lower, not higher, subsequent economic growth. Replications by other scholars substantiated the finding: More unequal nations grew less quickly than did more equal societies.[5] . . .

This recent research has not demonstrated precisely how greater equality helps economic growth,[6] but we can consider a few possibilities. Increasing resources for those of lower income might, by raising health, educational attainment, and hope, increase people's abilities to be productive and entrepreneurial. Reducing the income of those at the top might reduce unproductive and speculative spending. Take, as a concrete example, the way American corporations are run compared with German and Japanese ones. The American companies are run by largely autonomous managers whose main responsibility is to return short-term profits and high stock prices to shareholders and—because they are often paid in stock options—to themselves as well. Japanese and German managers are more like top employees whose goals largely focus on keeping the company a thriving enterprise. The latter is more conducive to reinvesting profits and thus to long-term growth.[7] Whatever the mechanisms may be, inequality appears to undermine growth. Americans certainly need not feel that they must accept the high levels of inequality we currently endure in order to have a robust economy.

A related concern for Americans is whether "leveling" stifles the drive to get ahead. Americans prefer to encourage Horatio Alger striving and to provide opportunities for everyone. Lincoln once said "that some would be rich shows that others may become rich."[8] Many, if not most, Americans believe that inequality is needed to encourage people to work hard.[9] But, if so, *how much* inequality is needed?

For decades, sociologists have been comparing the patterns of social mobility across societies, asking: In which countries are people most likely to overcome the disadvantages of birth and move up the ladder? In particular, does more or less equality encourage such an "open" society? The answer is that Western societies vary little in the degree to which children's economic successes are constrained by their parents' class positions. America, the most unequal Western society, has somewhat more fluid intergenerational mobility than do other nations, but so does Sweden, the most equal Western society.[10] There is no case for encouraging inequality in this evidence, either.

In sum, the assumption that considerable inequality is needed for, or even encourages, economic growth appears to be false. We do not need to make a morally wrenching choice between more affluence and more equality; we can have both. But even if such a choice were necessary, both sides of the debate, the "altruists" who favor intervention for equalizing and the supposed "realists" who resist it, agree that inequality can be shaped by policy decisions: Wittingly or unwittingly, we choose our level of inequality.

NOTES

1. We know that in statistical models of individual status attainment much, if not most, of the variance is unaccounted for. Of the explained variance, however, the bulk is due to social environment broadly construed. Also, we believe that much of the residual, unexplained variance is attributable to unmeasured social rather than personal factors.

2. Kenneth Bock, *Human Nature Mythology* (Urbana 1994), p. 9.

3. Richard J. Herrnstein and Charles Murray, *The Bell Curve: Intelligence and Class Structure in American Life* (New York 1994).

4. See, for example, Rich Thomas, "Rising Tide Lifts the Yachts: The Gap Between Rich and Poor Has Widened, but There Are Some Comforting Twists," *Newsweek*, May 1, 1995. See also George Will, "What's Behind Income Disparity," *San Francisco Chronicle*, April 24, 1995.

5. Torsten Persson and Guido Tabellini, "Is Inequality Harmful for Growth?," *American Economic Review* 84, 1994; Roberto Chang, "Income Inequality and Economic Growth: Evidence and Recent Theories," *Economic Review* 79, 1994; George R. G. Clarke, "More Evidence on Income Distribution and Growth," *Journal of Development Economics* 47, 1995. See also Peter H. Lindert, "The Rise of Social Spending," *Explorations in Economic History* 31, 1994.

6. Persson and Tabellini's explanation ("Is Inequality Harmful?") for their results is that in societies with greater earnings inequality, there is less political pressure for government redistribution; such redistribution impairs growth. However, their evidence for the explanation is thin, and Clarke's results ("More Evidence") are inconsistent with that argument. Chang ("Income Inequality") suggests that with more equality, lower-income families could make longer-term investment decisions. In any event, the statistical

results suggest that government intervention on behalf of equality in the market, rather than after the market, would be beneficial.

7. See, for example, Michael Porter, *Capital Choices: Changing the Way America Invests in Industry* (Washington 1992).

8. Quoted by Alan Trachtenberg, *The Incorporation of America: Culture and Society in the Gilded Age* (New York 1982), p. 75.

9. See, for example, Lee Rainwater, *What Money Buys: Inequality and the Social Meanings of Income* (New York 1974); James R. Kluegel and E. R. Smith, "Beliefs About Stratification," *Annual Review of Sociology* 7, 1981.

10. Harry B. G. Ganzeboom, Donald J. Treiman, and Wout C. Ultee, "Comparative Intergenerational Stratification Research," *Annual Review of Sociology* 17, 1991.

4

Inequality,
Too Much of a Good Thing

ALAN B. KRUEGER

As the title of this essay suggests, I believe inequality has both positive and negative effects. On the positive side, differential rewards provide incentives for individuals to work hard, invest, and innovate. On the negative side, differences in rewards that are unrelated to productivity—those that result from racial discrimination, for example—are corrosive to civil society and cause resources to be misallocated. Even if discrimination did not exist, however, income inequality is problematic in a democratic society if those who are privileged use their economic muscle to curry favor in the political arena and thereby secure monopoly rents or other advantages. Moreover, for several reasons discussed in the next section, poverty and income inequality create negative externalities.[1] Consequently, it can be in the interest of the wealthy as well as the poor to raise the incomes of the poor, especially by using education and training as a means for redistribution.

The term *inequality* is often used rather loosely and can be a lightning rod. Some have argued that only extreme poverty is a concern. Others have argued that the gap in income or wealth between the well off and the poor is a concern. Yet others have argued that the rapid growth in income disparity between the richest of the rich and everyone else is an issue. I will argue that, for various reasons elaborated below, all of these forms of inequality are of concern to contemporary American society, and that America has reached a point at which, on the margin, efficiently redistributing income from rich to poor is in the nation's interest.

A theme of my contribution to this debate is that societies must strike a *balance* between the beneficial incentive effects of inequality and the harmful welfare-decreasing effects of inequality. The optimal balance will differ across societies and time, but too much inequality can be harmful in any society, just as too much equality can suppress innovation and drive. . . .

Why Care about Rising Inequality?

Philosophers have argued about income inequality and social justice for centuries. I will sidestep most of that debate. What follows is a thumbnail sketch of reasons why I think it is in our interest for U.S. public policy to try to restore a more balanced distribution of income in the country. Because such a conclusion fundamentally rests on one's values as well as an empirical view of the world, I will touch lightly on these reasons. Suffice it to say that I hope there are enough arguments here to persuade the reader that it is worth considering using education and training as part of an overall strategy to reduce income inequality in America.

Philosophy

As Atkinson (1983) observes, "different principles of justice lead to quite different views about inequality" (p. 5). Principles of justice provide guidelines for society's welfare function, and with a welfare function for a particular society, economists could judge the distribution of inequality in that society against the optimal level. The rub, of course, is that the welfare function in a society is *not* observable and depends on philosophical arguments that are not testable. In addition, one has the Arrow impossibility theorem[2] with which to contend. Consequently, appealing to philosophical arguments can never be universally dispositive.

Principles of social justice can be divided into those that focus on fair exchange starting from a just distribution of endowments, and those that focus on the equality of outcomes. Rawls invites readers to arrive at a theory of justice by selecting the principles they would desire if they were choosing such principles in an original position behind a veil of ignorance, unaware of their standing in society or initial endowment of talents. He argues that in this case the social justice that would be desired would involve two principles: one protecting liberties and the other providing for an egalitarian distribution of opportunities and material goods. This leads him to a maximin welfare function in which the well-being of the worst off in society should be as high as possible. Interestingly, Adam Smith arrived at a somewhat similar conclusion nearly two hundred years earlier, positing that "[n]o society can surely be flourishing and happy, of which the far greater part of the members are poor and miserable. It is but equity, besides, that they who feed, clothe and lodge the whole body of the people, should have such a share of the produce of their own labour as to be themselves tolerably well fed, clothed and lodged" (Smith 1776, 110–111).

Nozick (1974) questions whether a theory of justice can be based on the distribution of outcomes. Using the analogy of fans who are willing to pay a fee to watch Wilt Chamberlain play basketball—an updated analogy might substitute Shaquille O'Neal—Nozick argues that "no end-state principle or distributional patterned principle of justice can be continuously realized without continuous interference with people's lives" (p. 163). Who could complain about Wilt Chamberlain's exorbitant salary if it results from rational choices? Nozick also raises the issue of the adverse incentive effects Rawls's theory of justice would have on the acquisition of talent.

Religion

I would argue that religious beliefs provide as strong (or weak) a justification for views toward society's implicit welfare function as do philosophical reflections behind a veil of ignorance. Indeed, I would go further and say that religious tenets reflect the demand for equality among the public. If people did not adhere to the basic tenets of their religion, they would not practice or would eventually change faiths. Thus, long-standing religious views toward inequality provide something of a revealed-preference argument.[3] And with regard to wealth inequality, the world's major religions are united in favoring redistribution of wealth toward the poor. Robert Nelson (1991), for example, observes that "Roman Catholicism has traditionally instilled a strong concern for the poor; in the Middle Ages the church itself provided much of the care for the indigent. The welfare state today similarly accomplishes substantial internal redistribution with the approval of many of the wealthier contributing members of the community" (p. 326). The Jewish *Siddur* advises followers to "Be just to the poor and the orphan; Deal righteously with the afflicted and the destitute" and comments, "Happy are they who are thoughtful of the needy; In time of trouble may the Lord Keep them from harm." And the Koran criticizes the egoism of the rich inhabitants of Mecca and urges believers in Islam to support poor people, orphans, and captives. Islam requires five major obligations of its followers, including *zakat,* an obligatory contribution to the needy (which today is implemented in the form of a tax).

Enlightened Self-Interest

Another line of argument for achieving and maintaining a minimum level of equality rests on self-interest. If wide disparities in income or education create negative externalities for a majority of people, then it clearly is in the self-interest of members of society to reduce those disparities. Individuals acting on their individual preferences (e.g., paying to see Shaquille O'Neal play basketball) will not internalize these externalities. What might such exter-

nalities be? An incomplete list would involve the following.

- More-educated voters make the democratic process work better. First, people with more education are more likely to be informed and more likely to participate in democracy. Second, more-informed citizens are likely (though not guaranteed) to make better decisions. For the latter reason, even a devout defender of free markets like Milton Friedman (1982) can be found supporting a minimum compulsory level of education.
- Available evidence suggests a link between crime and inequality (e.g., Ehrlich 1973; Freeman 1983, 1995; and Imrohoroglu, Merlo, and Rupert 2001). Other things being equal, the incentive for those with limited market opportunities to commit property crimes rises as inequality increases. From the criminal's perspective, the potential gain from crime is higher if inequality is higher, and the opportunity cost is lower. Society can devote more resources to crime prevention and incarceration, or to reducing inequality.
- Society is not willing to allow citizens to be totally destitute, to fall below some minimum level of basic consumption when it comes to food or health care (see, e.g., Pauly 1971). By providing those likely to have low incomes with skills, therefore, and thereby raising their future earnings, society can reduce the cost of providing transfer payments later on. . . .
- Nelson and Phelps (1966) and Romer (1990) model the level of education in a society as generating positive externalities for economic growth, although

empirical support for this model is mixed (see Krueger and Lindahl 2001).

Low Wages, Imperfect Monitoring, and Public Safety

In an advanced economy, people are connected via markets in a myriad of ways. Employee performance can be monitored only imperfectly. If an employee performs poorly because he or she feels poorly compensated, others may suffer as a result of his or her poor performance. The tragic events of September 11th, for example, highlighted the importance of paying baggage screeners better wages.

Market Failure

More generally, market failures could lead the distribution of income in a society to be suboptimal. Credit constraints, for example, might prevent children from poor families from investing adequately in education. Monopsony power on the part of employers might enable firms to pay workers less than the value of their marginal products.[4] Statistical discrimination might lead to lower-than-optimal investment in education for discriminated-against groups (e.g., Lundberg and Startz 1983).

Efficient Policy Changes

Another type of externality could arise in the political arena in a society if income inequality in that society is viewed as excessive. Treaties to reduce international trade barriers offer an example. A policy that reduces trade barriers undoubtedly will increase national income in the society that enacts it. However, there will be winners and losers from such a policy. If some segments of society feel that they have not benefited from developments in the economy, then they are unlikely to support efforts to

reduce trade barriers. I am not talking here just about the losers from the trade barrier reduction policy specifically, who are usually few in number and concentrated in a handful of industries. Instead, views toward free trade seem to be class related. For example, Blendon et al. (1997) find that 72 percent of those with less than a college education say one reason the U.S. economy is not doing better is that "companies are sending jobs overseas," whereas only 53 percent of college graduates agree with the same statement, and just 6 percent of American Economic Association members. Less-educated people are also less likely than those with more education to respond in the survey that trade agreements are good for the economy. I suspect that one reason Presidents (George W.) Bush and Clinton had difficulty securing fast-track authority for the passage of trade agreement is that large segments of the public perceived that they would lose from free trade, an inference that they drew because they had seen their real incomes stagnate or decline over the previous twenty years while trade expanded. Although I suspect trade has had little to do with rising wage inequality in the United States, it is understandable why so many people would draw such an inference.

Unless the public perceives that it will benefit from more efficient policies, there is little reason to suspect it will support such policies, and with 94 percent of income growth accruing to the top 1 percent of the U.S. population since 1973, it is understandable why the American public might be a little skeptical that it gained from past changes such as expanded trade.

Money Buys Influence

Economists at least since Adam Smith have fretted that wealthy merchants and manufacturers would be led by self-interest to seek government regulation and privilege to protect their monopoly position, thereby preventing the invisible hand from working its magic. Money buys access and influence in politics. It also buys influence through think tanks. A negative consequence of the skewed distribution of income in the United States is that some individuals have much more political influence than others.

Benabou (2000) develops a formal model in which the progressivity of educational funding and taxation is endogenous. He shows that the political influence of the wealthy interacts with income inequality to block efficient progressive policies or impose inefficient regressive ones. When income inequality is high, he finds, the wealthy are more likely to block *efficiency-enhancing* programs that would improve educational opportunities for the less well off.

Growth and Income Inequality

Persson and Tabellini (1994) develop a model of economic growth in which income inequality negatively influences growth through the political process. In their model, income inequality leads to policies that do not protect property rights and therefore do not allow full private appropriation of the returns from investment. A growing body of cross-country and cross-state studies have estimated the relationship between initial income inequality and subsequent GDP growth.[5] Although attributing causality is difficult in these studies, the correlation between income inequality and growth is negative, conditional on variables like initial GDP per capita and average education. Two-stage least-squares estimates that use variables such as initial literacy and infant mortality as instruments for income

inequality also show an inverse relationship between GDP growth and such inequality.

Health and Income Inequality

One common argument I will *not* make concerns health and income inequality. Wilkenson (1996), for example, argues that average health is negatively affected by the societal level of income inequality. The evidence in support of this view, however, is far from compelling (see, e.g., Smith 1999 and Deaton 2001), although Eibner and Evans (2002) provide evidence that relative deprivation affects health, and a large body of evidence finds that a person's own income level is related to his or her health.

Winner-Take-All Inefficiency in Superstar Markets

Frank and Cook (1996) argue that technological changes have facilitated a shift to superstar markets in many top-paying professions. The reward received by the one who finishes first is much greater than the reward received by the also-rans. They lament that this shift is inefficient and inequitable, causing too many students to pursue careers in law, finance, and consulting at the expense of more socially beneficial fields such as engineering, manufacturing, civil service, and teaching. The winner-take-all society engendered by this shift may create the same type of misallocation of talent that Murphy, Shleifer, and Vishny (1991) attribute to rent seeking. To some extent, income inequality probably leads to legions of tax lawyers and lobbyists who look for ways to help wealthy clients avoid taxation. Frank and Cook believe that superstar markets have led to inefficient investment and wasteful competition. Although I think we are at little risk of becoming a nation of Tonya Hardings, there may be something to the argument that superstar salaries provide perverse incentives and unnecessary competition in some sectors and divert some workers from pursuing more socially rewarding careers.

Public Preference

Last but not least, I would surmise that a majority of the public demands a certain amount of equality and is particularly supportive of using education and training to achieve more equality of outcomes. A survey of 1,001 adults by Lake, Snell, Perry & Associates in July 2000 posed the following request to respondents: "I am going to read some different ways the government can help poor Americans find and keep good jobs. For each, please tell me if you strongly support, somewhat support, somewhat oppose, or strongly oppose this idea." Fully 90 percent supported "helping to pay for education and job training for people leaving welfare." Similarly, a Gallup poll sponsored by General Motors in May 1998 asked the following free-form question: "Just your opinion, in what ways do you think the government should help the poor?" By far, the top two responses were providing better/more affordable education (38 percent) and providing job training/skills training (29 percent). The next-highest response was providing more jobs/job opportunities, at 16 percent. Only 5 percent of those surveyed cited lowering taxes as a way the government might assist poor people.

Even when given an explicit choice of lower taxes, the public prefers education and training. A CBS News poll in September 1999, for example, asked 1,376 respondents, "Which comes closer to your view? Government should provide tools to help families better their lives, such as education and job training programs. The best thing that government can do for families is to cut taxes and allow individual families to decide for themselves how to allocate their money." Fifty-five percent of respondents said the first statement more closely reflected their views, whereas only 42 percent replied that the second statement came closer to what they believed.

Wrapping Up

In supporting minimum schooling, Milton Friedman (1982) argued that "[a] stable and democratic society is impossible without a minimum degree of literacy and knowledge on the part of most citizens and without widespread acceptance of some common set of values" (p. 86). I would argue that inequality could grow so extreme that it eventually jeopardizes any type of "widespread acceptance" of a democratic capitalist society that might be established. This leads me to agree with Victor Fuchs (1979): "For me the key word is *balance,* both in the goals that we set and in the institutions that we nourish in order to pursue these goals. I value freedom *and* justice *and* efficiency, and economics tells me that I may have to give up a little of one goal to insure the partial achievement of others" (p. 180).

Targeted Education and Training: Part of the Solution

In a perfect world, children from all families would invest in educational resources up to the point that their marginal return equaled their discount rate, and all families would have equal access to credit and discount investments at the same prevailing rate. The evidence suggests, however, that education decisions are not made in a perfect world. Children from poor families *behave* as if they have higher discount rates.

The most plausible explanations for this phenomenon are that poor families are credit constrained (i.e., cannot borrow at the same rate as everyone else), or that they discount future benefits of human capital investments at a higher than market rate because they are impatient, have a greater disutility of schooling, or fail to appreciate the benefits of education. Of these possible explanations, credit constraints have received the most attention in the literature, because students cannot easily use the return on their future human capital as collateral to borrow for human capital investments. This may be a reason for discount rates to vary. Poor families face different borrowing costs than rich ones.

The following five observations are consistent with the view that low-income families face credit constraints when it comes to education. First, Ellwood and Kane (2000) find that when the return to college education increased in the 1980s, four-year college enrollment increased for children from all quartiles of the income distribution except the bottom one. Second, Behrman and Taubman (1990) find that the timing of parental income matters for children's educational attainment. Using data from the Panel Study of Income Dynamics (PSID), they find that father's income earned when children are teenagers has a stronger effect on children's educational attainment than income earned later on. Third, Shea (2000) looks at the effect on children's human capital of differences in parental income emanating from non-competitive factors, such as employment in a high-paying union job or industry. Wage differences for reasons such as these arguably are independent of parents' ability. Shea finds that family income matters for children's human capital investment in a

sample of low-income families, but not for the broader population. He concludes that this finding is consistent with the idea that the accumulation of observable skills by poverty sample fathers may have been sub-optimal due to liquidity constraints. Fourth, Björklund and Jantti (1997) find stronger family income effects on children's outcomes in the United States than in Sweden, which provides much more generous educational subsidies than the United States. Fifth, the reaction of college enrollment to changes in tuition, especially at the two-year-college level, is substantially larger than the reaction of college enrollment to equivalent, present-value changes in the payoff to education (see Kane 1999).

Although it is possible to construct complicated explanations of the above findings that are consistent with all families' having equal access to credit—and I suspect part of the association between education and parental income reflects intergenerational transmission of ability and motivation for schooling, as Cameron and Heckman (2001) argue—Occam's razor and common sense suggest that families have different access to credit. For example, some families borrow for college costs by accumulating debt on their credit cards at exorbitant rates, whereas others tap into their family finances or take out home equity loans that are given tax-preferred treatment.

One does not have to resort to theoretical assumptions or indirect tests of credit constraints, however, to support the view that redistribution of wealth via targeted education and training is desirable. *It is clear that returns to education and training are at least as big at the bottom of the income distribution as at the top.* I have presented evidence elsewhere (Krueger 2003) that the *social return* from investment in education and training for poor children, from infancy through early adulthood, is at least as great as the social return from investments in education and training in the general public.

A theme that emerges from my survey of the evidence (see Krueger 2003) is that the real rate of return from investment in various education and training programs for the disadvantaged is 6 to 11 percent. This range applies to a diverse set of programs, ranging from preschool to Job Corps to conventional K–12 public schools. To put this figure in perspective, note that the historical real rate of return on the stock market has been calculated at 6.3 percent (Burtless 1999). So investment in human capital for the disadvantaged seems to yield at least as great a return as investment in the equity market. Also, because there is not currently universal access to most of the educational and training programs, and many willing participants are thus turned away, I would argue that the returns estimated from various evaluations reviewed below would approximately apply if the programs were greatly expanded to accommodate more participants. . . .

I would emphasize that I do not envision investment in human capital development as the sole component of a program to address the adverse consequences of income inequality. It is part of the solution, not the whole solution. In principle, the optimal government policy regarding income inequality would employ multiple instruments, up to the point at which the social benefit per additional dollar of cost of each instrument is equal across the instruments.

NOTES

1. In referring to "negative externalities," Krueger is claiming that decisions resulting in poverty and inequality are made without taking into account the full costs of those decisions, just as decisions by firms to pollute are often made without those firms having to bear the full costs of such decisions (e.g., the social costs of the resulting asthma).—EDS.

2. The Arrow impossibility theorem refers in this context to the impossibility of devising a "fair" procedure for translating individual preferences about how much inequality should be allowed into a collective decision about how much inequality should be allowed.—EDS.

3. The simple point that Krueger is making here is that consumers of religion are, by virtue of their decision to consume, revealing a taste for the egalitarian doctrines of most major religions.—EDS.

4. When workers face a single employer to whom they can sell their labor, that employer has "monopsony power" that makes it possible to offer wages that are lower than would be predicted in competitive markets.—EDS.

5. The GDP (Gross Domestic Product) is the total value of the final goods and products produced in a year within a country.—EDS.

REFERENCES

Atkinson, Anthony. 1983. *The Economics of Inequality,* 2d ed. Oxford: Oxford University Press.

Behrman, Jere, and Paul Taubman. 1990. "The Intergenerational Correlation between Children's Adult Earnings and Their Parents' Income: Results from the Michigan Panel Survey of Income Dynamics." *Review of Income and Wealth* 36, no. 2: 115–127.

Benabou, Roland. 2000. "Unequal Societies: Income Distribution and the Social Contract." *American Economic Review* 90, no. 1 (March): 96–129.

Björklund, Anders, and Markus Jantti. 1997. "Intergenerational Income Mobility in Sweden Compared to the United States." *American Economic Review* 87, no. 5 (December): 1009–1018.

Blendon, Robert, John Benson, Mollyann Brodie, Richard Morin, Drew Altman, Daniel Gitterman, Mario Brossard, and Matt James. 1997. "Bridging the Gap between the Public's and Economists' Views of the Economy." *Journal of*

Economic Perspectives 11, no. 3 (Summer): 105–118.

Burtless, Gary. 1999. "Risk and Returns of Stock Market Investments Held in Individual Retirement Accounts." Testimony before the House Budget Committee Task Force on Social Security Reform, May 11.

Cameron, Stephen, and James Heckman. 2001. "The Dynamics of Educational Attainment for Black, Hispanic, and White Males." *Journal of Political Economy* 109, no. 3 (June): 455–499.

Deaton, Angus. 2001. "Health, Inequality, and Economic Development." Research Program in Development Studies working paper, Princeton University.

Ehrlich, Isaac. 1973. "Participation in Illegitimate Activities: A Theoretical and Empirical Investigation." *Journal of Political Economy* 81, no. 3 (May): 521–565.

Eibner, Christine, and William Evans. 2002. "Relative Deprivation, Poor Health Habits and Mortality." University of Maryland, College Park, mimeo.

Ellwood, David, and Thomas Kane. 2000. "Who Is Getting a College Education? Family Background and the Growing Gaps in Enrollment." In *Securing the Future: Investing in Children from Birth to College,* Sheldon Danziger and Jane Waldfogel, eds. New York: Russell Sage.

Frank, Robert H., and Philip J. Cook. 1996. *The Winner Take All Society.* New York: Free Press.

Freeman, Richard. 1983. "Crime and the Labor Market." In *Crime and Public Policy,* James Wilson, ed. San Francisco: Institute for Contemporary Studies.

Freeman, Richard. 1995. "The Labor Market." In *Crime,* James Wilson and Joan Petersilia, eds. San Francisco: Institute for Contemporary Studies.

Friedman, Milton. 1982. *Capitalism and Freedom.* Chicago: University of Chicago Press.

Fuchs, Victor. 1979. "Economics, Health, and Post-Industrial Society." *Health and Society* 57, no. 2 (Spring): 153–182.

Imrohoroglu, Ayse, Antonio Merlo, and Peter Rupert. 2001. "What Accounts for the Decline in Crime?" Penn Institute for Economic Research working paper no. 01–012.

Kane, Thomas. 1999. *The Price of Admission: Rethinking How Americans Pay for College.* Washington, D.C.: Brookings Institution Press.

Krueger, Alan. 2003. "Economic Considerations and Class Size." *Economic Journal,* forthcoming.

Krueger, Alan, and Mikael Lindahl. 2001. "Education and Growth: Why and for Whom?" *Journal of Economic Literature* 39, no. 4 (December): 1101–1136.

Lundberg, Shelly, and Richard Startz. 1983. "Private Discrimination and Social Intervention in Competitive Labor Markets." *American Economic Review* 73, no. 3 (June): 340–347.

Murphy, Kevin M., Andrei Shleifer, and Robert Vishny. 1991. "The Allocation of Talent: Implications for Growth." *Quarterly Journal of Economics* 106, no. 2 (May): 503–530.

Nelson, Richard, and Edmund Phelps. 1966. "Investment in Humans, Technological Diffusion, and Economic Growth." *American Economic Review* 56, no. 2 (March): 69–75.

Nelson, Robert. 1991. *Reaching for Heaven on Earth.* Savage, Md.: Rowman & Littlefield.

Nozick, Robert. 1974. *Anarchy, State, and Utopia.* New York: Basic.

Pauly, Mark V. 1971. *Medical Care at Public Expense: A Study in Applied Welfare Economics.* New York: Praeger.

Persson, Torsten, and Guido Tabellini. 1994. "Is Inequality Harmful for Growth?" *American Economic Review* 84, no. 3 (June): 600–621.

Rawls, John. 1971. *A Theory of Justice.* Cambridge: Belknap Press of Harvard University Press.

Romer, Paul. 1990. "Endogenous Technological Change." *Journal of Political Economy* 98, no. 5 (October): 71–102.

Shea, John. 2000. "Does Parents' Money Matter?" *Journal of Public Economics* 77, no. 2 (August): 155–184.

Smith, Adam. [1776]. *The Wealth of Nations.* New York: Random House.

Smith, James P. 1999. "Healthy Bodies and Thick Wallets: The Dual Relation between Health and Economic Status." *Journal of Economic Perspectives* 13, no. 2 (Spring): 145–166.

Wilkenson, Richard. 1996. *Unhealthy Societies: The Afflictions of Inequality.* London: Routledge.

5

Classes in Capitalism and Pre-capitalism

KARL MARX

The history of all hitherto existing society[1] is the history of class struggles.

Freeman and slave, patrician and plebeian, lord and serf, guild-master[2] and journeyman, in a word, oppressor and oppressed, stood in constant opposition to one another, carried on an uninterrupted, now hidden, now open fight, a fight that each time ended, either in a revolutionary re-constitution of society at large, or in the common ruin of the contending classes.

In the earlier epochs of history, we find almost everywhere a complicated arrangement of society into various orders, a manifold gradation of social rank. In ancient Rome we have patricians, knights, plebeians, slaves; in the Middle Ages, feudal lords, vassals, guild-masters, journeymen, apprentices, serfs; in almost all of these classes, again, subordinate gradations.

The modern bourgeois society that has sprouted from the ruins of feudal society has not done away with class antagonisms. It has but established new classes, new conditions of oppression, new forms of struggle in place of the old ones.

Our epoch, the epoch of the bourgeoisie, possesses, however, this distinctive feature: it has simplified the class antagonisms. Society as a whole is more and more splitting up into two great hostile camps, into two great classes directly facing each other: Bourgeoisie and Proletariat.

From the serfs of the Middle Ages sprang the chartered burghers of the earliest towns. From these burgesses the first elements of the bourgeoisie were developed.

The discovery of America, the rounding of the Cape, opened up fresh ground for the rising bourgeoisie. The East-Indian and Chinese markets, the colonisation of America, trade with the colonies, the increase in the means of exchange and in commodities generally, gave to commerce, to navigation, to industry, an impulse never before known, and thereby, to the revolutionary element in the tottering feudal society, a rapid development.

Karl Marx, "The Communist Manifesto," in *Selected Works*, vol. 1 (Moscow: Progress Publishers, 1964), pp. 108–119. Reprinted by permission of Progress Publishers. *The Poverty of Philosophy* (New York: International Publishers, 1963), pp. 172–175. Reprinted by permission of International Publishers. "The Eighteenth Brumaire of Louis Bonaparte," in *Selected Works*, vol. 1 (Moscow: Progress Publishers, 1963), pp. 478–479. Reprinted by permission of Progress Publishers. *Capital*, vol. 3 (Moscow: Progress Publishers, 1967), pp. 885–886. Reprinted by permission of Progress Publishers.

The feudal system of industry, under which industrial production was monopolised by closed guilds, now no longer sufficed for the growing wants of the new markets. The manufacturing system took its place. The guild-masters were pushed on one side by the manufacturing middle class; division of labour between the different corporate guilds vanished in the face of division of labour in each single workshop.

Meantime the markets kept ever growing, the demand ever rising. Even manufacture no longer sufficed. Thereupon, steam and machinery revolutionised industrial production. The place of manufacture was taken by the giant, Modern Industry, the place of the industrial middle class, by industrial millionaires, the leaders of whole industrial armies, the modern bourgeois.

Modern industry has established the world-market, for which the discovery of America paved the way. This market has given an immense development to commerce, to navigation, to communication by land. This development has, in its turn, reacted on the extension of industry; and in proportion as industry, commerce, navigation, railways extended, in the same proportion the bourgeoisie developed, increased its capital, and pushed into the background every class handed down from the Middle Ages.

We see, therefore, how the modern bourgeoisie is itself the product of a long course of development, of a series of revolutions in the modes of production and of exchange.

Each step in the development of the bourgeoisie was accompanied by a corresponding political advance of that class. An oppressed class under the sway of the feudal nobility, an armed and self-governing association in the mediaeval commune;[3] here independent urban republic (as in Italy and Germany), there taxable "third estate" of the monarchy (as in France), afterwards, in the period of manufacture proper, serving either the semi-feudal or the absolute monarchy as a counterpoise against the nobility, and, in fact, cornerstone of the great monarchies in general, the bourgeoisie has at last, since the establishment of Modern Industry and of the world-market, conquered for itself, in the modern representative State, exclusive political sway. The executive of the modern State is but a committee for managing the common affairs of the whole bourgeoisie.

The bourgeoisie, historically, has played a most revolutionary part. The bourgeoisie, wherever it has got the upper hand, has put an end to all feudal, patriarchal, idyllic relations. It has pitilessly torn asunder the motley feudal ties that bound man to his "natural superiors," and has left remaining no other nexus between man and man than naked self-interest, than callous "cash payment." It has drowned the most heavenly ecstasies of religious fervour, of chivalrous enthusiasm, of philistine sentimentalism, in the icy water of egotistical calculation. It has resolved personal worth into exchange value, and in place of the numberless indefeasible chartered freedoms, has set up that single, unconscionable freedom—Free Trade. In one word, for exploitation, veiled by religious and political illusions, it has substituted naked, shameless, direct, brutal exploitation.

The bourgeoisie has stripped of its halo every occupation hitherto honoured and looked up to with reverent awe. It has converted the physician, the lawyer, the priest, the poet, the man of science, into its paid wage-labourers.

The bourgeoisie has torn away from the family its sentimental veil, and has reduced the family relation to a mere money relation.

The bourgeoisie has disclosed how it came to pass that the brutal display of vigour in the Middle Ages, which Reactionists so much admire, found its fitting complement in the most slothful indolence. It has been the first to show what man's activity can bring about. It has accomplished wonders far surpassing Egyptian pyramids, Roman aqueducts, and Gothic cathedrals; it has conducted expeditions that put in the shade all former Exoduses of nations and crusades.

The bourgeoisie cannot exist without constantly revolutionising the instruments of production, and thereby the relations of production, and with them the whole relations of society. Conservation of the old modes of production in unaltered form, was, on the contrary, the first condition of existence for all earlier industrial classes. Constant revolutionising of production, uninterrupted disturbance of all social conditions, everlasting uncertainty and agitation distinguish the bourgeois epoch from all earlier ones. All fixed, fast-frozen relations, with their train of ancient and venerable prejudices and opinions, are swept away, all new-formed ones become antiquated before they can ossify. All that is solid melts into air, all that is holy is profaned, and man is at last compelled to face with sober senses, his real conditions of life, and his relations with his kind.

The need of a constantly expanding market for its products chases the bourgeoisie over the whole surface of the globe. It must nestle everywhere, settle everywhere, establish connexions everywhere.

The bourgeoisie has through its exploitation of the world-market given a cosmopolitan character to production and consumption in every country. To the great chagrin of Reactionists, it has drawn from under the feet of industry the national ground on which it stood. All old-established national industries have been destroyed or are daily being destroyed. They are dislodged by new industries, whose introduction becomes a life and death question for all civilised nations, by industries that no longer work up indigenous raw material, but raw material drawn from the remotest zones; industries whose products are consumed, not only at home, but in every quarter of the globe. In place of the old wants, satisfied by the productions of the country, we find new wants, requiring for their satisfaction the products of distant lands and climes. In place of the old local and national seclusion and self-sufficiency, we have intercourse in every direction, universal inter-dependence of nations. And as in material, so also in intellectual production. The intellectual creations of individual nations become common property. National one-sidedness and narrow-mindedness become more and more impossible, and from the numerous national and local literatures, there arises a world literature.

The bourgeoisie, by the rapid improvement of all instruments of production, by the immensely facilitated means of communication, draws all, even the most barbarian, nations into civilisation. The cheap prices of its commodities are the heavy artillery with which it batters down all Chinese walls, with which it forces the barbarians' intensely obstinate hatred of foreigners to capitulate. It compels all nations, on pain of extinction, to adopt the bourgeois mode of production; it compels them to introduce what it calls civilisation into their midst, *i.e.,* to become bourgeois themselves. In one word, it creates a world after its own image.

The bourgeoisie has subjected the country to the rule of the towns. It has created enormous cities, has greatly increased the urban population as compared with the rural, and has thus rescued a considerable part of the population from the idiocy of rural life. Just as it has made the country dependent on the towns, so it has made barbarian and semi-barbarian countries dependent on the civilised ones, nations of peasants on nations of bourgeois, the East on the West.

The bourgeoisie keeps more and more doing away with the scattered state of the population, of the means of production, and of property. It has agglomerated population, centralised means of production, and has concentrated property in a few hands. The necessary consequence of this was political centralisation. Independent, or but loosely connected provinces, with separate interests, laws, governments and systems of taxation, became lumped together into one nation, with one government, one code of laws, one national class-interest, one frontier and one customs-tariff.

The bourgeoisie, during its rule of scarce one hundred years, has created more massive and more colossal productive forces than have all preceding generations together. Subjection of Nature's forces to man, machinery, application of chemistry to industry and agriculture, steam-navigation, railways, electric telegraphs, clearing of whole continents for cultivation, canalisation of rivers, whole populations conjured out of the ground—what earlier century had even a presentiment that such productive forces slumbered in the lap of social labour?

We see then: the means of production and of exchange, on whose foundation the bourgeoisie built itself up, were generated in feudal society. At a certain stage in the development of these means of production and of exchange, the conditions under which feudal society produced and exchanged, the feudal organisation of agriculture and manufacturing industry, in one word, the feudal relations of property became no longer compatible with the already developed productive forces; they became so many fetters. They had to be burst asunder; they were burst asunder.

Into their place stepped free competition, accompanied by a social and political constitution adapted to it, and by the economical and political sway of the bourgeois class.

A similar movement is going on before our own eyes. Modern bourgeois society with its relations of production, of exchange and of property, a society that has conjured up such gigantic means of production and of exchange, is like the sorcerer, who is no longer able to control the powers of the nether world whom he has called up by his spells. For many a decade past the history of industry and commerce is but the history of the revolt of modern productive forces against modern conditions of production, against the property relations that are the conditions for the existence of the bourgeoisie and of its rule. It is enough to mention the commercial crises that by their periodical return put on its trial, each time more threateningly, the existence of the entire bourgeois society. In these crises a great part not only of the existing products, but also of the previously created productive forces, are periodically destroyed. In these crises there breaks out an epidemic that, in all earlier epochs, would have seemed an absurdity—the epidemic of over-production. Society suddenly finds itself put back into a state of momentary barbarism; it appears as if a famine, a universal war of devastation had cut off the supply of every means of subsistence; industry and commerce seem to be destroyed; and why? Because there is too much civilisation, too much means of subsistence, too much industry, too much commerce. The productive forces at the disposal of society no longer tend to further the development of the conditions of bourgeois property; on the contrary, they have become too powerful for these conditions, by which they are fettered, and so soon as they overcome these fetters, they bring disorder into the whole of bourgeois society, endanger the existence of bourgeois property. The conditions of bourgeois society are too narrow to comprise the wealth created by them. And how does the bourgeoisie get over these crises? On the one hand by enforced destruction of a mass of productive forces; on the other, by the conquest of new markets, and by the more thorough exploitation of the old ones. That is to say, by paving the way for more extensive and more destructive crises, and by diminishing the means whereby crises are prevented.

The weapons with which the bourgeoisie felled feudalism to the ground are now turned against the bourgeoisie itself.

But not only has the bourgeoisie forged the weapons that bring death to itself; it has also called into existence the men who are to wield those weapons—the modern working class—the proletarians.

In proportion as the bourgeoisie, *i.e.,* capital, is developed, in the same proportion is the proletariat, the modern working class, developed—a class of labourers, who live only so long as they find work, and who find work only so long as their labour increases capital. These labourers, who must sell themselves piecemeal, are a commodity, like every other article of commerce, and are consequently exposed to all the vicissitudes of competition, to all the fluctuations of the market.

Owing to the extensive use of machinery and to division of labour, the work of the proletarians has lost all individual character, and, consequently, all charm for the workman. He becomes an appendage of the machine, and it is only the most simple, most monotonous, and most easily acquired knack, that is required of him. Hence, the cost of production of a workman is restricted, almost entirely, to the means of subsistence that he requires for his maintenance, and for the propagation of his race. But the price of a commodity, and therefore also of labour, is equal to its cost of production. In proportion, therefore, as the repulsiveness of the work increases, the wage decreases. Nay more, in proportion as the use of machinery and division of labour increases, in the same proportion the burden of toil also increases, whether by prolongation of the working hours, by increase of the work exacted in a given time or by increased speed of the machinery, etc.

Modern industry has converted the little workshop of the patriarchal master into the great factory of the industrial capitalist. Masses of labourers, crowded into the factory, are organised like soldiers. As privates of the industrial army they are placed under the command of a perfect hierarchy of officers and sergeants. Not only are they slaves of the bourgeois class, and of the bourgeois State; they are daily and hourly enslaved by the machine, by the overlooker, and, above all, by the individual bourgeois manufacturer himself. The more openly this despotism proclaims gain to be its end and aim, the more petty, the more hateful and the more embittering it is.

The less the skill and exertion of strength implied in manual labour, in other words, the more modern industry becomes developed, the more is the labour of men superseded by that of women. Differences of age and sex have no longer any distinctive social validity for the working class. All are instruments of labour, more or less expensive to use, according to their age and sex.

No sooner is the exploitation of the labourer by the manufacturer, so far, at an end, and he receives his wages in cash, than he is set upon by the other portions of the bourgeoisie, the landlord, the shopkeeper, the pawnbroker, etc.

The lower strata of the middle class—the small tradespeople, shopkeepers, and retired tradesmen generally, the handicraftsmen and peasants—all these sink gradually into the proletariat, partly because their diminutive capital does not suffice for the scale on which Modern Industry is carried on, and is swamped in the competition with the large capitalists, partly because their specialised skill is rendered worthless by new methods of production. Thus the proletariat is recruited from all classes of the population.

The proletariat goes through various stages of development. With its birth begins its struggle with the bourgeoisie. At first the contest is carried on by individual labourers, then by the workpeople of a factory, then by the operatives of one trade, in one locality, against the individual bourgeois who directly exploits them. They direct their attacks not against the bourgeois conditions of production, but against the instruments of production themselves: they destroy imported wares that compete with their labour, they smash to pieces machinery, they set factories ablaze, they seek to restore by force the vanished status of the workman of the Middle Ages.

At this stage the labourers still form an incoherent mass scattered over the whole country, and broken up by their mutual competition. If anywhere they unite to form more compact bodies, this is not yet the consequence of their own active union, but of the union of the bourgeoisie, which class, in order to attain its own political ends, is compelled to set the whole proletariat in motion, and is moreover yet, for a time, able to do so. At this stage, therefore, the proletarians do not fight their enemies, but the enemies of their enemies, the remnants of absolute monarchy, the landowners, the nonindustrial bourgeois, the petty bourgeoisie. Thus the whole historical movement is concentrated in the hands of the bourgeoisie; every victory so obtained is a victory for the bourgeoisie.

But with the development of industry the proletariat not only increases in number; it becomes concentrated in greater masses, its strength grows, and it feels that strength more. The various interests and conditions of life within the ranks of the proletariat are more and more equalised, in proportion as machinery obliterates all distinctions of labour, and nearly everywhere reduces wages to the same low level. The growing competition among the bourgeois, and the resulting commercial crises, make the wages of the workers ever more fluctuating. The unceasing improvement of machinery, ever more rapidly developing, makes their livelihood more and more precarious; the collisions between individual workmen and individual bourgeois take more and more the character of collisions between two classes. Thereupon the workers begin to form combinations (Trades' Unions) against the bourgeois; they club together in order to keep up the rate of wages; they found permanent associations in order to make provision beforehand for these occasional revolts. Here and there the contest breaks out into riots.

Now and then the workers are victorious, but only for a time. The real fruit of their battles lies, not in the immediate result, but in the ever-expanding union of the workers. This union is helped on by the improved means of communication that are created by modern industry and that place the workers of different localities in contact with one another. It was just this contact that was needed to centralise the numerous local struggles, all of the same character, into one national struggle between classes. But every class struggle is a political struggle. And that union, to attain which the burghers of the Middle Ages, with their miserable highways, required centuries, the modern proletarians, thanks to railways, achieve in a few years.

This organisation of the proletarians into a class, and consequently into a political party, is continually being upset again by the competition between the workers themselves. But it ever rises up again, stronger, firmer, mightier. It compels legislative recognition of particular interests of the workers, by taking advantage of the divisions among the bourgeoisie itself. Thus the ten-hours' bill in England was carried.

Altogether collisions between the classes of the old society further, in many ways, the course of development of the proletariat. The bourgeoisie finds itself involved in a constant battle. At first with the aristocracy; later on, with those portions of the bourgeoisie itself, whose interests have become antagonistic to the progress of industry; at all times, with the bourgeoisie of foreign countries. In all these battles it sees itself compelled to appeal to the proletariat, to ask for its help, and thus, to drag it into the political arena. The bourgeoisie itself, therefore, supplies the proletariat with its own elements of political and general education, in other words, it furnishes the proletariat with weapons for fighting the bourgeoisie.

Further, as we have already seen, entire sections of the ruling classes are, by the advance of industry, precipitated into the proletariat, or are at least threatened in their conditions of existence. These also supply the proletariat with fresh elements of enlightenment and progress.

Finally, in times when the class struggle nears the decisive hour, the process of dissolution going on within the ruling class, in fact within the whole range of old society, assumes such a violent, glaring character, that a small section of the ruling class cuts itself adrift, and joins the revolutionary class, the class that holds the future in its hands. Just as, therefore, at an earlier period, a section of the nobility went over to the bourgeoisie, so now a portion of the bourgeoisie goes over to the proletariat, and in particular, a portion of the bourgeois ideologists, who have raised themselves to the level of comprehending theoretically the historical movement as a whole.

Of all the classes that stand face to face with the bourgeoisie today, the proletariat alone is a really revolutionary class. The other classes decay and finally disappear in the face of Modern Industry; the proletariat is its special and essential product.

The lower middle class, the small manufacturer, the shopkeeper, the artisan, the peasant, all these fight against the bourgeoisie, to save from extinction their existence as fractions of the middle class. They are therefore not revolutionary, but conservative. Nay more, they are reactionary, for they try to roll back the wheel of history. If by chance they are revolutionary, they are so only in view of their impending transfer into the proletariat, they thus defend not their present, but their future interests, they desert their own standpoint to place themselves at that of the proletariat.

The "dangerous class," the social scum, that passively rotting mass thrown off by the lowest layers of old society, may, here and there, be swept into the movement by a proletarian revolution, its conditions of life, however, prepare it far more for the part of a bribed tool of reactionary intrigue.

In the conditions of the proletariat, those of old society at large are already virtually swamped. The proletarian is without property; his relation to his wife and children has no longer anything in common with the bourgeois family-relations; modern, industrial labour, modern subjection to capital, the same in England as in France, in America as in Germany, has stripped him of every trace of national character. Law, morality, religion, are to him so many bourgeois prejudices, behind which lurk in ambush just as many bourgeois interests.

All the preceding classes that got the upper hand, sought to fortify their already acquired status by subjecting society at large to their conditions of appropriation. The proletarians cannot become masters of the productive forces of society, except by abolishing their own previous mode of appropriation, and thereby also every other previous mode of appropriation. They have nothing of their own to secure and to fortify; their mission is to destroy all previous securities for, and insurances of, individual property.

All previous historical movements were movements of minorities, or in the interests of minorities. The proletarian movement is the self-conscious, independent movement of the immense majority, in the interests of the immense majority. The proletariat, the lowest stratum of our present society, cannot stir, cannot raise itself up, without the whole superincumbent strata of official society being sprung into the air.

Though not in substance, yet in form, the struggle of the proletariat with the bourgeoisie is at first a national struggle. The proletariat of each country must, of course, first of all settle matters with its own bourgeoisie.

In depicting the most general phases of the development of the proletariat, we traced the more or less veiled civil war, raging within existing society, up to the point where that war breaks out into open revolution, and where the violent overthrow of the bourgeoisie lays the foundation for the sway of the proletariat.

Hitherto, every form of society has been based, as we have already seen, on the antagonism of oppressing and oppressed classes. But in order to oppress a class, certain conditions must be assured to it under which it can, at least, continue its slavish existence. The serf, in the period of serfdom, raised himself to membership in the commune, just as the petty bourgeois, under the yoke of feudal absolutism, managed to develop into a bourgeois. The modern labourer, on the contrary, instead of rising with the progress of industry, sinks deeper and deeper below the conditions of existence of his own class. He becomes a pauper, and pauperism develops more rapidly than population and wealth. And here it becomes evident, that the bourgeoisie is unfit any longer to be the ruling class in society, and to impose its conditions of existence upon society as an overriding law. It is unfit to rule because it is incompetent to assure an existence to its slave within his slavery, because it cannot help letting him sink into such a state, that it has to feed him, instead of being fed by him. Society can no longer live under this bourgeoisie, in other words, its existence is no longer compatible with society.

The essential condition for the existence, and for the sway of the bourgeois class, is the formation and augmentation of capital; the condition for capital is wage-labour. Wage-labour rests exclusively on competition between the labourers. The advance of industry, whose involuntary promoter is the bourgeoisie, replaces the isolation of the labourers, due to competition, by their revolutionary combination, due to association. The development of Modern Industry, therefore, cuts from under its feet the very foundation on which the bourgeoisie produces and appropriates products. What the bourgeoisie, therefore, produces, above all, is its own grave-diggers. Its fall and the victory of the proletariat are equally inevitable.

NOTES

1. That is, all *written* history. In 1847, the pre-history of society, the social organisation existing previous to recorded history, was all but unknown. [*Note by Engels to the English edition of 1888.*]

2. Guild-master, that is, a full member of a guild, a master within, not a head of a guild. [*Note by Engels to the English edition of 1888.*]

3. "Commune" was the name taken, in France, by the nascent towns even before they had conquered from their feudal lords and masters local self-government and political rights as the "Third Estate." Generally speaking, for the economical development of the bourgeoisie, England is here taken as the typical country; for its political development, France. [*Note by Engels to the English edition of 1888.*]

This was the name given their urban communities by the townsmen of Italy and France, after they had purchased or wrested their initial rights of self-government from their feudal lords. [*Note by Engels to the German edition of 1890.*]

The Communist Manifesto, pp. 108–119

The first attempts of workers to *associate* among themselves always take place in the form of combinations.

Large-scale industry concentrates in one place a crowd of people unknown to one another. Competition divides their interests. But the maintenance of wages, this common interest which they have against their boss, unites them in a common thought of resistance—*combination*. Thus combination always has a double aim, that of stopping competition among the workers, so that they can carry on general competition with the capitalist. If the first aim of resistance was merely the maintenance of wages, combinations, at first isolated, constitute themselves into groups as the capitalists in their turn unite for the purpose of repression, and in face of always united capital, the maintenance of the association becomes more necessary to them than that of wages. This is so true that English economists are amazed to see the workers sacrifice a good part of their wages in favour of associations, which, in the eyes of these economists, are established solely in favour of wages. In this struggle—a veritable civil war—all the elements necessary for a coming battle unite and develop. Once it has reached this point, association takes on a political character.

Economic conditions had first transformed the mass of the people of the country into workers. The combination of capital has created for this mass a common situation, common interests. This mass is thus already a class as against capital, but not yet for itself. In the struggle, of which we have noted only a few phases, this mass becomes united, and constitutes itself as a class for itself. The interests it defends become class interests. But the struggle of class against class is a political struggle.

In the bourgeoisie we have two phases to distinguish: that in which it constituted itself as a class under the regime of feudalism and absolute monarchy, and that in which, already constituted as a class, it overthrew feudalism and monarchy to make society into a bourgeois society. The first of these phases was the longer and necessitated the greater efforts. This too began by partial combinations against the feudal lords.

Much research has been carried out to trace the different historical phases that the bourgeoisie has passed through, from the commune up to its constitution as a class.

But when it is a question of making a precise study of strikes, combinations and other forms in which the proletarians carry out before our eyes their organization as a class, some are seized with real fear and others display a *transcendental* disdain.

An oppressed class is the vital condition for every society founded on the antagonism of classes. The emancipation of the oppressed class thus implies necessarily the creation of a new society. For the oppressed class to be able to emancipate itself it is necessary that the productive powers already acquired and the existing social relations should no longer be capable of existing side by side. Of all the instruments of production, the greatest productive power is the revolutionary class itself. The organization of revolutionary elements as a class supposes the existence of all the productive forces which could be engendered in the bosom of the old society.

Does this mean that after the fall of the old society there will be a new class domination culminating in a new political power? No.

The condition for the emancipation of the working class is the abolition of every class, just as the condition for the liberation of the third estate, of the bourgeois order, was the abolition of all estates[1] and all orders.

The working class, in the course of its development, will substitute for the old civil society an association which will exclude classes and their antagonism, and there will be no more political power properly so-called, since political power is precisely the official expression of antagonism in civil society.

Meanwhile the antagonism between the proletariat and the bourgeoisie is a struggle of class against class, a struggle which carried to its highest expression is a total revolution. Indeed, is it at all surprising that a society founded on the opposition of classes should culminate in brutal *contradiction,* the shock of body against body, as its final *dénouement?*

Do not say that social movement excludes political movement. There is never a political movement which is not at the same time social.

It is only in an order of things in which there are no more classes and class antagonisms that *social evolutions* will cease to be *political revolutions.* Till then, on the eve of every general reshuffling of society, the last word of social science will always be:

"Le combat ou la mort; la lutte sanguinaire ou le néant. C'est ainsi que la question est invinciblement posée." [2]

NOTES

1. Estates here in the historical sense of the estates of feudalism, estates with definite and

limited privileges. The revolution of the bourgeoisie abolished the estates and their privileges. Bourgeois society knows only *classes*. It was, therefore, absolutely in contradiction with history to describe the proletariat as the "fourth estate." [*Note by F. Engels to the German edition, 1885.*]

2. "Combat or death; bloody struggle or extinction. It is thus that the question is inexorably put." George Sand, *Jean Ziska*.

The Poverty of Philosophy, pp. 172–175

The small-holding peasants form a vast mass, the members of which live in similar conditions but without entering into manifold relations with one another. Their mode of production isolates them from one another instead of bringing them into mutual intercourse. The isolation is increased by France's bad means of communication and by the poverty of the peasants. Their field of production, the small holding, admits of no division of labour in its cultivation, no application of science and, therefore, no diversity of development, no variety of talent, no wealth of social relationships. Each individual peasant family is almost self-sufficient; it itself directly produces the major part of its consumption and thus acquires its means of life more through exchange with nature than in intercourse with society. A small holding, a peasant and his family; alongside them another small holding, another peasant and another family. A few score of these make up a village, and a few score of villages make up a Department. In this way, the great mass of the French nation is formed by simple addition of homologous magnitudes, much as potatoes in a sack form a sack of potatoes. In so far as millions of families live under economic conditions of existence that separate their mode of life, their interests and their culture from those of the other classes, and put them in hostile opposition to the latter, they form a class. In so far as there is merely a local interconnection among these small-holding peasants, and the identity of their interests begets no community, no national bond and no political organisation among them, they do not form a class. They are consequently incapable of enforcing their class interests in their own name, whether through a parliament or through a convention. They cannot represent themselves, they must be represented. Their representative must at the same time appear as their master, as an authority over them, as an unlimited governmental power that protects them against the other classes and sends them rain and sunshine from above. The political influence of the small-holding peasants, therefore, finds its final expression in the executive power subordinating society to itself.

The Eighteenth Brumaire of Louis Bonaparte, pp. 478–479

The owners merely of labour-power, owners of capital, and landowners, whose respective sources of income are wages, profit and ground-rent, in other words, wage-labourers, capitalists and landowners, constitute then three big classes of modern society based upon the capitalist mode of production.

In England, modern society is indisputably most highly and classically developed in economic structure. Nevertheless, even here the stratification of classes does not appear in its pure form. Middle and intermediate strata even here obliterate lines of demarcation everywhere (although incomparably less in rural districts than in the cities). However, this is immaterial for our analysis. We have seen that the continual tendency and law of development of the capitalist mode of production is more and more to divorce the means of production from labour, and more and more to concentrate the scattered means of production into large groups, thereby transforming labour into wage-labour and the means of production into capital. And to this tendency, on the other hand, corresponds the independent separation of landed property from capital and labour, or the transformation of all landed property into the form of landed property corresponding to the capitalist mode of production.

The first question to be answered is this: What constitutes a class?—and the reply to this follows naturally from the reply to another question, namely: What makes wage-labourers, capitalists and landlords constitute the three great social classes?

At first glance—the identity of revenues and sources of revenue. There are three great social groups whose members, the individuals forming them, live on wages, profit and ground-rent respectively, on the realisation of their labour-power, their capital, and their landed property.

However, from this standpoint, physicians and officials, e.g., would also constitute two classes, for they belong to two distinct social groups, the members of each of these groups receiving their revenue from one and the same source. The same would also be true of the infinite fragmentation of interest and rank into which the division of social labour splits labourers as well as capitalists and landlords—the latter, e.g., into owners of vineyards, farm owners, owners of forests, mine owners and owners of fisheries.

[Here the manuscript breaks off.]

Capital, Vol. III, pp. 885–886

6

Class, Status, Party

MAX WEBER

Economically Determined Power and the Social Order

Law exists when there is a probability that an order will be upheld by a specific staff of men who will use physical or psychical compulsion with the intention of obtaining conformity with the order, or of inflicting sanctions for infringement of it.[1] The structure of every legal order directly influences the distribution of power, economic or otherwise, within its respective community. This is true of all legal orders and not only that of the state. In general, we understand by 'power' the chance of a man or of a number of men to realize their own will in a communal action even against the resistance of others who are participating in the action.

'Economically conditioned' power is not, of course, identical with 'power' as such. On the contrary, the emergence of economic power may be the consequence of power existing on other grounds. Man does not strive for power only in order to enrich himself economically. Power, including economic power, may be valued 'for its own sake.' Very frequently the striving for power is also conditioned by the social 'honor' it entails. Not all power, however, entails social honor: The typical American Boss, as well as the typical big speculator, deliberately relinquishes social honor. Quite generally, 'mere economic' power, and especially 'naked' money power, is by no means a recognized basis of social honor. Nor is power the only basis of social honor. Indeed, social honor, or prestige, may even be the basis of political or economic power, and very frequently has been. Power, as well as honor, may be guaranteed by the legal order, but, at least normally, it is not their primary source. The legal order is rather an additional factor that enhances the chance to hold power or honor; but it cannot always secure them.

The way in which social honor is distributed in a community between typical groups participating in this distribution we may call the 'social order.' The social order and the economic order are, of course, similarly related to the 'legal order.' However, the social and the economic order are not identical. The economic order is for us merely the way in which economic goods and services are distributed and used. The social order is of course conditioned by the economic order to a high degree, and in its turn reacts upon it.

Now: 'classes,' 'status groups,' and 'parties' are phenomena of the distribution of power within a community.

Determination of Class-Situation by Market-Situation

In our terminology, 'classes' are not communities; they merely represent possible, and frequent, bases for communal action. We may speak of a 'class' when (1) a number of people have in common a specific causal component of their life chances, in so far as (2) this component is represented exclusively by economic interests in the possession of goods and opportunities for income, and (3) is represented under the conditions of the commodity or labor markets. [These points refer to 'class situation,' which we may express more briefly as the typical chance for a supply of goods, external living conditions, and personal life experiences, in so far as this chance is determined by the amount and kind of power, or lack of such, to dispose of goods or skills for the sake of income in a given economic order. The term 'class' refers to any group of people that is found in the same class situation.]

It is the most elemental economic fact that the way in which the disposition over material property is distributed among a plurality of people, meeting competitively in the market for the purpose of exchange, in itself creates specific life chances. According to the law of marginal utility this mode of distribution excludes the non-owners from competing for highly valued goods; it favors the owners and, in fact, gives to them

a monopoly to acquire such goods. Other things being equal, this mode of distribution monopolizes the opportunities for profitable deals for all those who, provided with goods, do not necessarily have to exchange them. It increases, at least generally, their power in price wars with those who, being propertyless, have nothing to offer but their services in native form or goods in a form constituted through their own labor, and who above all are compelled to get rid of these products in order barely to subsist. This mode of distribution gives to the propertied a monopoly on the possibility of transferring property from the sphere of use as a 'fortune,' to the sphere of 'capital goods'; that is, it gives them the entrepreneurial function and all chances to share directly or indirectly in returns on capital. All this holds true within the area in which pure market conditions prevail. 'Property' and 'lack of property' are, therefore, the basic categories of all class situations. It does not matter whether these two categories become effective in price wars or in competitive struggles.

Within these categories, however, class situations are further differentiated: on the one hand, according to the kind of property that is usable for returns; and, on the other hand, according to the kind of services that can be offered in the market. Ownership of domestic buildings; productive establishments; warehouses; stores; agriculturally usable land, large and small holdings—quantitative differences with possibly qualitative consequences—ownership of mines; cattle; men (slaves); disposition over mobile instruments of production, or capital goods of all sorts, especially money or objects that can be exchanged for money easily and at any time; disposition over products of one's own labor or of others' labor differing according to their various distances from consumability; disposition over transferable monopolies of any kind—all these distinctions differentiate the class situations of the propertied just as does the 'meaning' which they can and do give to the utilization of property, especially to property which has money equivalence. Accordingly, the propertied, for instance, may belong to the class of rentiers or to the class of entrepreneurs.

Those who have no property but who offer services are differentiated just as much according to their kinds of services as according to the way in which they make use of these services, in a continuous or discontinuous relation to a recipient. But always this is the generic connotation of the concept of class: that the kind of chance in the *market* is the decisive moment which presents a common condition for the individual's fate. 'Class situation' is, in this sense, ultimately 'market situation.' The effect of naked possession *per se,* which among cattle breeders gives the nonowning slave or serf into the power of the cattle owner, is only a forerunner of real 'class' formation. However, in the cattle loan and in the naked severity of the law of debts in such communities, for the first time mere 'possession' as such emerges as decisive for the fate of the individual. This is very much in contrast to the agricultural communities based on labor. The creditor-debtor relation becomes the basis of 'class situations' only in those cities where a 'credit market,' however primitive, with rates of interest increasing according to the extent of dearth and a factual monopolization of credits, is developed by a plutocracy. Therewith 'class struggles' begin.

Those men whose fate is not determined by the chance of using goods or services for themselves on the market, e.g. slaves, are not, however, a 'class' in the technical sense of the term. They are, rather, a 'status group.'

Communal Action Flowing from Class Interest

According to our terminology, the factor that creates 'class' is unambiguously economic interest, and indeed, only those interests involved in the existence of the 'market.' Nevertheless, the concept of 'class-interest' is an ambiguous one: even as an empirical concept it is ambiguous as soon as one understands by it something other than the factual direction of interests following with a certain probability from the class situation for a certain 'average' of those people subjected to the class situation. The class situation and other circumstances remaining the same, the direction in which the individual worker, for instance, is likely to pursue his interests may vary widely, according to whether he is constitutionally qualified for the task at hand to a high, to an average, or to a low degree. In the same way, the direction of interests may vary according to whether or not a *communal* action of a larger or smaller portion of those commonly affected by the 'class situation,' or even an association among them, e.g. a 'trade union,' has grown out of the class situation from which the individual may or may not expect promising results. [Communal action refers to that action which is oriented to the feeling of the actors that they belong together. Societal action, on the other hand, is oriented to a rationally motivated adjustment of interests.] The rise of societal or even of communal action from a common class situation is by no means a universal phenomenon.

The class situation may be restricted in its effects to the generation of essentially *similar* reactions, that is to say, within our terminology, of 'mass actions.' However, it may not have even this result. Furthermore, often merely an amorphous communal action emerges. For example, the 'murmuring' of the workers known in ancient oriental ethics: the moral disapproval of the workmaster's conduct, which in its practical significance was probably equivalent to an increasingly typical phenomenon of precisely the latest industrial development, namely, the 'slow down' (the deliberate limiting of work effort) of laborers by virtue of tacit agreement. The degree in which 'communal action' and possibly 'societal action,' emerges from the 'mass actions' of the members of a class is linked to general cultural conditions, especially to those of an intellectual sort. It is also linked to the extent of the contrasts that have already evolved, and is especially linked to the *transparency* of the connections between the causes and the consequences of the 'class situation.' For however different life chances may be, this fact in itself, according to all experience, by no means gives birth to 'class action' (communal action by the members of a class). The fact of being conditioned and the results of the class situation must be distinctly recognizable. For only then the contrast of life chances can be felt not as an absolutely given fact to be accepted, but as a resultant from either (1) the given distribution of property, or (2) the structure of the concrete economic order. It is only then that people may react against the class structure not only through acts of an intermittent and irrational protest, but in the form of rational association. There have been 'class situations' of the first category (1), of a specifically naked and transparent sort, in the urban centers of Antiquity and during the Middle Ages; especially then, when great fortunes were accumulated by factually monopolized trading in industrial products of these localities or in foodstuffs. Furthermore, under certain circumstances, in the rural economy of the most diverse periods, when agriculture was increasingly exploited in a profit-making manner. The most important historical example of the second category (2) is the class situation of the modern 'proletariat.'

Types of 'Class Struggle'

Thus every class may be the carrier of any one of the possibly innumerable forms of 'class action,' but this is not necessarily so: In any case, a class does not in itself constitute a community. To treat 'class' conceptually as having the same value as 'community' leads to distortion. That men in the same class situation regularly react in mass actions to such tangible situations as economic ones in the direction of those interests that are most adequate to their average number is an important and after all simple fact for the understanding of historical events. Above all, this fact must not lead to that kind of pseudo-scientific operation with the concepts of 'class' and 'class interests' so frequently found these days, and which has found its most classic expression in the statement of a talented author, that the individual may be in error concerning his interests but that the 'class' is 'infallible' about its interests. Yet, if classes as such are not communities, nevertheless class situations emerge only on the basis of communalization. The communal action that brings forth class situations, however, is not basically action between members of the identical class; it is an action between members of different classes. Communal actions that directly determine the class situation of the worker and the entrepreneur are: the labor market, the commodities market, and the capitalistic enterprise. But, in its turn, the existence of a capitalistic enterprise presupposes that a very specific communal action exists and that it is specifically structured to protect the possession of goods *per se,* and especially the power of individuals to dispose, in principle freely, over the means of production. The existence of a capitalistic enterprise is preconditioned by a specific kind of 'legal order.' Each kind of class situation, and above all when it rests upon the power of property *per se,* will become most clearly efficacious when all other determinants of reciprocal relations are, as far as possible, eliminated in their significance. It is in this way that the utilization of the power of property in the market obtains its most sovereign importance.

Now 'status groups' hinder the strict carrying through of the sheer market principle. In the present context they are of interest to us only from this one point of view. Before we briefly consider them, note that not much of a general nature can be said about the more specific kinds of antagonism between 'classes' (in our meaning of the term). The great shift, which has been going on continuously in the past, and up to our times, may be summarized, although at the cost of some precision: the struggle in which class situations are effective has progressively shifted from consumption credit toward, first, competitive struggles in the commodity market and, then, toward price wars on the labor market. The 'class struggles' of antiquity—to the extent that they were genuine class struggles and not struggles between status groups—were initially carried on by indebted peasants, and perhaps also by artisans threatened by debt bondage and struggling against urban creditors. For debt bondage is the normal result

of the differentiation of wealth in commercial cities, especially in seaport cities. A similar situation has existed among cattle breeders. Debt relationships as such produced class action up to the time of Cataline. Along with this, and with an increase in provision of grain for the city by transporting it from the outside, the struggle over the means of sustenance emerged. It centered in the first place around the provision of bread and the determination of the price of bread. It lasted throughout antiquity and the entire Middle Ages. The propertyless as such flocked together against those who actually and supposedly were interested in the dearth of bread. This fight spread until it involved all those commodities essential to the way of life and to handicraft production. There were only incipient discussions of wage disputes in antiquity and in the Middle Ages. But they have been slowly increasing up into modern times. In the earlier periods they were completely secondary to slave rebellions as well as to fights in the commodity market.

The propertyless of antiquity and of the Middle Ages protested against monopolies, pre-emption, forestalling, and the withholding of goods from the market in order to raise prices. Today the central issue is the determination of the price of labor.

This transition is represented by the fight for access to the market and for the determination of the price of products. Such fights went on between merchants and workers in the putting-out system of domestic handicraft during the transition to modern times. Since it is quite a general phenomenon we must mention here that the class antagonisms that are conditioned through the market situation are usually most bitter between those who actually and directly participate as opponents in price wars. It is not the rentier, the share-holder, and the banker who suffer the ill will of the worker, but almost exclusively the manufacturer and the business executives who are the direct opponents of workers in price wars. This is so in spite of the fact that it is precisely the cash boxes of the rentier, the share-holder, and the banker into which the more or less 'unearned' gains flow, rather than into the pockets of the manufacturers or of the business executives. This simple state of affairs has very frequently been decisive for the role the class situation has played in the formation of political parties. For example, it has made possible the varieties of patriarchal socialism and the frequent attempts—formerly, at least—of threatened status groups to form alliances with the proletariat against the 'bourgeoisie.'

Status Honor

In contrast to classes, *status groups* are normally communities. They are, however, often of an amorphous kind. In contrast to the purely economically determined 'class situation' we wish to designate as 'status situation' every typical component of the life fate of men that is determined by a specific, positive or negative, social estimation of *honor*. This honor may be connected with any quality shared by a plurality, and, of course, it can be knit to a class situation: class distinctions are linked in the most varied ways with status distinctions. Property as such is not always recognized as a status qualification, but in the long run it is, and with extraordinary regularity. In the subsistence economy of the organized neighborhood, very often the richest man is simply the chieftain. However, this often means only an honorific preference. For example, in the so-called pure modern 'democracy,' that is, one devoid of any expressly ordered status privileges for individuals, it may be that only the families coming under approximately the same tax class dance with one another. This example is reported of certain smaller Swiss cities. But status honor need not necessarily be linked with a 'class situation.' On the contrary, it normally stands in sharp opposition to the pretensions of sheer property.

Both propertied and propertyless people can belong to the same status group, and frequently they do with very tangible consequences. This 'equality' of social esteem may, however, in the long run become quite precarious. The 'equality' of status among the American 'gentlemen,' for instance, is expressed by the fact that outside the subordination determined by the different functions of 'business,' it would be considered strictly repugnant—wherever the old tradition still prevails—if even the richest 'chief,' while playing billiards or cards in his club in the evening, would not treat his 'clerk' as in every sense fully his equal in birthright. It would be repugnant if the American 'chief' would bestow upon his 'clerk' the condescending 'benevolence' marking a distinction of 'position,' which the German chief can never dissever from his attitude. This is one of the most important reasons why in America the German 'clubby-ness' has never been able to attain the attraction that the American clubs have.

Guarantees of Status Stratification

In content, status honor is normally expressed by the fact that above all else a specific *style of life* can be expected from all those who wish to belong to the circle. Linked with this expectation are restrictions on 'social' intercourse (that is, intercourse which is not subservient to economic or any other of business's 'functional' purposes). These restrictions may confine normal marriages to within the status circle and may lead to complete endogamous closure. As soon as there is not a mere individual and socially irrelevant imitation of another style of life, but an agreed-upon communal action of this closing character, the 'status' development is under way.

In its characteristic form, stratification by 'status groups' on the basis of conventional styles of life evolves at the present time in the United States out of the traditional democracy. For example, only the resident of a certain street ('the street') is considered as belonging to 'society,' is qualified for social intercourse, and is visited and invited. Above all, this differentiation evolves in such a way as to make for strict submission to the fashion that is dominant at a given time in society. This submission to fashion also exists among men in America to a degree unknown in Germany. Such submission is considered to be an indication of the fact that a given man *pretends* to qualify as a gentleman. This submission decides, at least *prima facie,* that he will be treated as such. And this recognition becomes just as important for his employment chances in 'swank' establishments, and above all, for social intercourse and marriage with 'esteemed' families, as the qualification for dueling among Germans in the Kaiser's day. As for the rest: certain families resident for a long time, and, of course, correspondingly wealthy, e.g. 'F. F. V., i.e. First Families of Virginia,' or the actual or alleged descendants of the 'Indian Princess' Pocahontas, of the Pilgrim fathers, or of the Knickerbockers, the members of almost inaccessible sects and all sorts of circles setting themselves apart by means of any other characteristics

and badges . . . all these elements usurp 'status' honor. The development of status is essentially a question of stratification resting upon usurpation. Such usurpation is the normal origin of almost all status honor. But the road from this purely conventional situation to legal privilege, positive or negative, is easily traveled as soon as a certain stratification of the social order has in fact been 'lived in' and has achieved stability by virtue of a stable distribution of economic power.

'Ethnic' Segregation and 'Caste'

Where the consequences have been realized to their full extent, the status group evolves into a closed 'caste.' Status distinctions are then guaranteed not merely by conventions and laws, but also by *rituals.* This occurs in such a way that every physical contact with a member of any caste that is considered to be 'lower' by the members of a 'higher' caste is considered as making for a ritualistic impurity and to be a stigma which must be expiated by a religious act. Individual castes develop quite distinct cults and gods.

In general, however, the status structure reaches such extreme consequences only where there are underlying differences which are held to be 'ethnic.' The 'caste' is, indeed, the normal form in which ethnic communities usually live side by side in a 'societalized' manner. These ethnic communities believe in blood relationship and exclude exogamous marriage and social intercourse. Such a caste situation is part of the phenomenon of 'pariah' peoples and is found all over the world. These people form communities, acquire specific occupational traditions of handicrafts or of other arts, and cultivate a belief in their ethnic community. They live in a 'diaspora' strictly segregated from all personal intercourse, except that of an unavoidable sort, and their situation is legally precarious. Yet, by virtue of their economic indispensability, they are tolerated, indeed, frequently privileged, and they live in interspersed political communities. The Jews are the most impressive historical example.

A 'status' segregation grown into a 'caste' differs in its structure from a mere 'ethnic' segregation: the caste structure transforms the horizontal and unconnected coexistences of ethnically segregated groups into a vertical social system of super- and subordination. Correctly formulated: a comprehensive societalization integrates the ethnically divided communities into specific political and communal action. In their consequences they differ precisely in this way: ethnic coexistences condition a mutual repulsion and disdain but allow each ethnic community to consider its own honor as the highest one; the caste structure brings about a social subordination and an acknowledgment of 'more honor' in favor of the privileged caste and status groups. This is due to the fact that in the caste structure ethnic distinctions as such have become 'functional' distinctions within the political societalization (warriors, priests, artisans that are politically important for war and for building, and so on). But even pariah people who are most despised are usually apt to continue cultivating in some manner that which is equally peculiar to ethnic and to status communities: the belief in their own specific 'honor.' This is the case with the Jews.

Only with the negatively privileged status groups does the 'sense of dignity' take a specific deviation. A sense of dignity is the precipitation in individuals of social honor and of conventional demands which a positively privileged status group raises for the deportment of its members. The sense of dignity that characterizes positively privileged status groups is naturally related to their 'being' which does not transcend itself, that is, it is to their 'beauty and excellence.' Their kingdom is 'of this world.' They live for the present and by exploiting their great past. The sense of dignity of the negatively privileged strata naturally refers to a future lying beyond the present, whether it is of this life or of another. In other words, it must be nurtured by the belief in a providential 'mission' and by a belief in a specific honor before God. The 'chosen people's' dignity is nurtured by a belief either that in the beyond 'the last will be the first,' or that in this life a Messiah will appear to bring forth into the light of the world which has cast them out the hidden honor of the pariah people. This simple state of affairs, and not the 'resentment' which is so strongly emphasized in Nietzsche's much admired construction in the *Genealogy of Morals,* is the source of the religiosity cultivated by pariah status groups. In passing, we may note that resentment may be accurately applied only to a limited extent; for one of Nietzsche's main examples, Buddhism, it is not at all applicable.

Incidentally, the development of status groups from ethnic segregations is by no means the normal phenomenon. On the contrary, since objective 'racial differences' are by no means basic to every subjective sentiment of an ethnic community, the ultimately racial foundation of status structure is rightly and absolutely a question of the concrete individual case. Very frequently a status group is instrumental in the production of a thoroughbred anthropological type. Certainly a status group is to a high degree effective in producing extreme types, for they select personally qualified individuals (e.g. the Knighthood selects those who

are fit for warfare, physically and psychi-
cally). But selection is far from being the
only, or the predominant, way in which status groups are formed: political membership
or class situation has at all times been at
least as frequently decisive. And today the
class situation is by far the predominant factor, for of course the possibility of a style of
life expected for members of a status group
is usually conditioned economically.

Status Privileges

For all practical purposes, stratification by
status goes hand in hand with a monopolization of ideal and material goods or opportunities, in a manner we have come to know as
typical. Besides the specific status honor,
which always rests upon distance and exclusiveness, we find all sorts of material monopolies. Such honorific preferences may consist
of the privilege of wearing special costumes,
of eating special dishes taboo to others, of
carrying arms—which is most obvious in its
consequences—the right to pursue certain
non-professional dilettante artistic practices,
e.g. to play certain musical instruments. Of
course, material monopolies provide the
most effective motives for the exclusiveness
of a status group; although, in themselves,
they are rarely sufficient, almost always they
come into play to some extent. Within a status circle there is the question of intermarriage: the interest of the families in the
monopolization of potential bridegrooms is
at least of equal importance and is parallel to
the interest in the monopolization of daughters. The daughters of the circle must be provided for. With an increased inclosure of the
status group, the conventional preferential
opportunities for special employment grow
into a legal monopoly of special offices for
the members. Certain goods become objects

for monopolization by status groups. In the
typical fashion these include 'entailed estates'
and frequently also the possessions of serfs or
bondsmen and, finally, special trades. This
monopolization occurs positively when
the status group is exclusively entitled to
own and to manage them; and negatively
when, in order to maintain its specific way
of life, the status group must *not* own and
manage them.

The decisive role of a 'style of life' in status 'honor' means that status groups are the
specific bearers of all 'conventions.' In whatever way it may be manifest, all 'stylization'
of life either originates in status groups or is
at least conserved by them. Even if the principles of status conventions differ greatly,
they reveal certain typical traits, especially
among those strata which are most privileged. Quite generally, among privileged
status groups there is a status disqualification that operates against the performance
of common physical labor. This disqualification is now 'setting in' in America against
the old tradition of esteem for labor. Very
frequently every rational economic pursuit,
and especially 'entrepreneurial activity,' is
looked upon as a disqualification of status.
Artistic and literary activity is also considered as degrading work as soon as it is exploited for income, or at least when it is
connected with hard physical exertion. An
example is the sculptor working like a
mason in his dusty smock as over against
the painter in his salon-like 'studio' and
those forms of musical practice that are acceptable to the status group.

Economic Conditions and Effects of Status Stratification

The frequent disqualification of the gain-
fully employed as such is a direct result of

the principle of status stratification peculiar to the social order, and of course, of this principle's opposition to a distribution of power which is regulated exclusively through the market. These two factors operate along with various individual ones, which will be touched upon below.

We have seen above that the market and its processes 'knows no personal distinctions': 'functional' interests dominate it. It knows nothing of 'honor.' The status order means precisely the reverse, viz.: stratification in terms of 'honor' and of styles of life peculiar to status groups as such. If mere economic acquisition and naked economic power still bearing the stigma of its extra-status origin could bestow upon anyone who has won it the same honor as those who are interested in status by virtue of style of life claim for themselves, the status order would be threatened at its very root. This is the more so as, given equality of status honor, property *per se* represents an addition even if it is not overtly acknowledged to be such. Yet if such economic acquisition and power gave the agent any honor at all, his wealth would result in his attaining more honor than those who successfully claim honor by virtue of style of life. Therefore all groups having interests in the status order react with special sharpness precisely against the pretensions of purely economic acquisition. In most cases they react the more vigorously the more they feel themselves threatened. Calderon's respectful treatment of the peasant, for instance, as opposed to Shakespeare's simultaneous and ostensible disdain of the *canaille* illustrates the different way in which a firmly structured status order reacts as compared with a status order that has become economically precarious. This is an example of a state of affairs that recurs everywhere. Precisely be-

cause of the rigorous reactions against the claims of property *per se,* the 'parvenu' is never accepted, personally and without reservation, by the privileged status groups, no matter how completely his style of life has been adjusted to theirs. They will only accept his descendants who have been educated in the conventions of their status group and who have never besmirched its honor by their own economic labor.

As to the general *effect* of the status order, only one consequence can be stated, but it is a very important one: the hindrance of the free development of the market occurs first for those goods which status groups directly withheld from free exchange by monopolization. This monopolization may be effected either legally or conventionally. For example, in many Hellenic cities during the epoch of status groups, and also originally in Rome, the inherited estate (as is shown by the old formula for indication against spendthrifts) was monopolized just as were the estates of knights, peasants, priests, and especially the clientele of the craft and merchant guilds. The market is restricted, and the power of naked property *per se,* which gives its stamp to 'class formation,' is pushed into the background. The results of this process can be most varied. Of course, they do not necessarily weaken the contrasts in the economic situation. Frequently they strengthen these contrasts, and in any case, where stratification by status permeates a community as strongly as was the case in all political communities of antiquity and of the Middle Ages, one can never speak of a genuinely free market competition as we understand it today. There are wider effects than this direct exclusion of special goods from the market. From the contrariety between the status order and the purely economic order mentioned above, it follows that in most instances the notion of honor peculiar to status absolutely abhors that which is essential to the market: higgling. Honor abhors higgling among peers and occasionally it taboos higgling for the members of a status group in general. Therefore, everywhere some status groups, and usually the most influential, consider almost any kind of overt participation in economic acquisition as absolutely stigmatizing.

With some over-simplification, one might thus say that 'classes' are stratified according to their relations to the production and acquisition of goods; whereas 'status groups' are stratified according to the principles of their *consumption* of goods as represented by special 'styles of life.'

An 'occupational group' is also a status group. For normally, it successfully claims social honor only by virtue of the special style of life which may be determined by it. The differences between classes and status groups frequently overlap. It is precisely those status communities most strictly segregated in terms of honor (viz. the Indian castes) who today show, although within very rigid limits, a relatively high degree of indifference to pecuniary income. However, the Brahmins seek such income in many different ways.

As to the general economic conditions making for the predominance of stratification by 'status,' only very little can be said. When the bases of the acquisition and distribution of goods are relatively stable, stratification by status is favored. Every technological repercussion and economic transformation threatens stratification by status and pushes the class situation into the foreground. Epochs and countries in which the naked class situation is of predominant significance are regularly the pe-

riods of technical and economic transformations. And every slowing down of the shifting of economic stratifications leads, in due course, to the growth of status structures and makes for a resuscitation of the important role of social honor.

Parties

Whereas the genuine place of 'classes' is within the economic order, the place of 'status groups' is within the social order, that is, within the sphere of the distribution of 'honor.' From within these spheres, classes and status groups influence one another and they influence the legal order and are in turn influenced by it. But 'parties' live in a house of 'power.'

Their action is oriented toward the acquisition of social 'power,' that is to say, toward influencing a communal action no matter what its content may be. In principle, parties may exist in a social 'club' as well as in a 'state.' As over against the actions of classes and status groups, for which this is not necessarily the case, the communal actions of 'parties' always mean a societalization. For party actions are always directed toward a goal which is striven for in planned manner. This goal may be a 'cause' (the party may aim at realizing a program for ideal or material purposes), or the goal may be 'personal' (sinecures, power, and from these, honor for the leader and the followers of the party). Usually the party action aims at all these simultaneously. Parties are, therefore, only possible within communities that are societalized, that is, which have some rational order and a staff of persons available who are ready to enforce it. For parties aim precisely at influencing this staff, and if possible, to recruit it from party followers.

In any individual case, parties may represent interests determined through 'class situation' or 'status situation,' and they may recruit their following respectively from one or the other. But they need be neither purely 'class' nor purely 'status' parties. In most cases they are partly class parties and partly status parties, but sometimes they are neither. They may represent ephemeral or enduring structures. Their means of attaining power may be quite varied, ranging from naked violence of any sort to canvassing for votes with coarse or subtle means: money, social influence, the force of speech, suggestion, clumsy hoax, and so on to the rougher or more artful tactics of obstruction in parliamentary bodies.

The sociological structure of parties differs in a basic way according to the kind of communal action which they struggle to influence. Parties also differ according to whether or not the community is stratified by status or by classes. Above all else, they vary according to the structure of domination within the community. For their leaders normally deal with the conquest of a community. They are, in the general concept which is maintained here, not only products of specially modern forms of domination. We shall also designate as parties the ancient and medieval 'parties,' despite the fact that their structure differs basically from the structure of modern parties. By virtue of these structural differences of domination it is impossible to say anything about the structure of parties without discussing the structural forms of social domination *per se*. Parties, which are always structures struggling for domination, are very frequently organized in a very strict 'authoritarian' fashion. . . .

Concerning 'classes,' 'status groups,' and 'parties,' it must be said in general that they necessarily presuppose a comprehensive societalization, and especially a political framework of communal action, within which they operate. This does not mean that parties would be confined by the frontiers of any individual political community. On the contrary, at all times it has been the order of the day that the societalization (even when it aims at the use of military force in common) reaches beyond the frontiers of politics. This has been the case in the solidarity of interests among the Oligarchs and among the democrats in Hellas, among the Guelfs and among Ghibellines in the Middle Ages, and within the Calvinist party during the period of religious struggles. It has been the case up to the solidarity of the landlords (international congress of agrarian landlords), and has continued among princes (holy alliance, Karlsbad decrees), socialist workers, conservatives (the longing of Prussian conservatives for Russian intervention in 1850). But their aim is not necessarily the establishment of new international political, i.e. *territorial,* dominion. In the main they aim to influence the existing dominion.[2]

NOTES

1. *Wirtschaft und Gesellschaft,* part III, chap. 4, pp. 631–40. The first sentence in paragraph one and the several definitions in this chapter which are in brackets do not appear in the original text. They have been taken from other contexts of *Wirtschaft und Gesellschaft.*

2. The posthumously published text breaks off here. We omit an incomplete sketch of types of 'warrior estates.'

7

Class Counts

ERIK OLIN WRIGHT

A story from the *Li'l Abner* comic strips from the late 1940s will help to set the stage for the discussion of the concept of class structure. Here is the situation of the episode: Li'l Abner, a resident of the hillbilly community of Dogpatch, discovers a strange and wonderful creature, the "shmoo," and brings a herd of them back to Dogpatch. The shmoo's sole desire in life is to please humans by transforming itself into the material things human beings need. They do not provide humans with luxuries, but only with the basic necessities of life. If you are hungry, they can become ham and eggs, but not caviar. What's more, they multiply rapidly so you never run out of them. They are thus of little value to the wealthy, but of great value to the poor. . . .

In the episode from *Li'l Abner* reproduced here, a manager working for a rich capitalist, P.U., does a study to identify the poorest place in America in order to hire the cheapest labor for a new factory. The place turns out to be Dogpatch. P.U. and the manager come to Dogpatch to recruit employees for the new factory. The story unfolds in a sequence of comic strips from 1948 (Al Capp 1992: 134–136).

The presence of shmoos is a serious threat to class relations. Workers are more difficult to recruit for toilsome labor and no longer have to accept "guff" and indignities from their bosses. . . .

The saga of the shmoo helps to clarify the sense in which the interests of workers and capitalists are deeply antagonistic, one of the core ideas of Marxist class analysis. How do shmoos affect the material interests of people in these two classes? This depends upon the level of generosity of the shmoo. If the shmoo provides less than bare physical subsistence, it probably has a positive effect on the material interests of both workers and capitalists. For workers it makes their lives a little bit less precarious; for capitalists, such sub-subsistence shmoos could be considered a subsidy to the wage bill. All other things being equal, capitalists can pay lower wages if part of the subsistence of workers is provided outside of the market. At the other extreme, if shmoos provide for superabundance, gratifying every material desire of humans from basic necessities to the most expensive luxuries, then they would also positively serve the material interests of capitalists. Between these two extremes, however, the impact of the shmoo on the material interests of the two classes diverges. The welfare of workers is continuously improved as the generosity of shmoos increases, whereas for capitalists, after a point, their material interests are adversely affected. Once shmoos provide workers with a respectable standard of living, workers no longer have to work in order to live at an acceptable standard. As P.U.'s manager states in panic, "Do you realize what the shmoo means? Nobody'll have to work hard any more!!" This does not mean, of course, that no workers would be willing to work for an employer. Work fills many needs for people besides simply providing earnings, and in any case, so long as the shmoo does not provide superabundance, many people will have consumption desires beyond the shmoo level of provision. Nevertheless, workers would be in a much more powerful bargaining position with modestly generous shmoos at home, and it will be more difficult, in P.U.'s words, to get them to "do the long, dreary, backbreaking labor at our canning factories.". . .

What the story of the shmoo illustrates is that the deprivations of the propertyless in a capitalist system are not simply an unfortunate by-product of the capitalist pursuit of profit; they are a necessary condition for that pursuit. This is what it means to claim that capitalist profits depend upon "exploitation." Exploiting classes have an interest in preventing the exploited from acquiring the means of subsistence even if, as in the case of the shmoo story, that acquisition does not take the form of a redistribution of wealth or income from capitalists to workers.

The Concept of Exploitation

The story of the shmoo revolves around the linkage between class divisions, class interests and exploitation. There are two main classes in the story—capitalists who own the means of production and workers who do not. By virtue of the productive assets which they own (capital and labor power) they each face a set of constraints on how they can best pursue their material interests. The presence of shmoos fundamen-

tally transforms these constraints and is a threat to the material interests of capitalists. Why? Because it undermines their capacity to exploit the labor power of workers. "Exploitation" is thus the key concept for understanding the nature of the *interests* generated by the class relations.

Exploitation is a loaded theoretical term, since it suggests a moral condemnation of particular relations and practices, not simply an analytical description. To describe a social relationship as exploitative is to condemn it as both harmful and unjust to the exploited. Yet, while this moral dimension of exploitation is important, the core of the concept revolves around a particular type of *antagonistic interdependence of material interests* of actors within economic relations, rather than the injustice of those relations as such. As I will use the term, class exploitation is defined by three principal criteria:

A. *The material welfare of one group of people causally depends on the material deprivations of another.*

B. *The causal relation in (A) involves the asymmetrical exclusion of the exploited from access to certain productive resources.* Typically this exclusion is backed by force in the form of property rights, but in special cases it may not be.

C. *The causal mechanism which translates exclusion (B) into differential welfare (A) involves the appropriation of the fruits of labor of the exploited by those who control the relevant productive resources.*

This is a fairly complex set of conditions. Condition (A) establishes the antagonism of material interests. Condition (B) establishes that the antagonism is rooted in the way people are situated within the social organization of production. The expression "asymmetri-cal" in this criterion is meant to exclude "fair competition" from the domain of possible exploitations. Condition (C) establishes the specific mechanism by which the interdependent, antagonistic material interests are generated. The welfare of the exploiter depends upon the *effort* of the exploited, not merely the deprivations of the exploited.

If only the first two of these conditions are met we have what can be called "nonexploitative economic oppression," but not "exploitation." In nonexploitative economic oppression there is no transfer of the fruits of labor from the oppressed to the oppressor; the welfare of the oppressor depends simply on the exclusion of the oppressed from access to certain resources, but not on their effort. In both instances, the inequalities in question are rooted in ownership and control over productive resources.

The crucial difference between exploitation and nonexploitative oppression is that in an exploitative relation, the exploiter *needs* the exploited since the exploiter depends upon the effort of the exploited. In the case of nonexploitative oppression, the oppressors would be happy if the oppressed simply disappeared. Life would have been much easier for the European settlers in North America if the continent had been uninhabited by people. Genocide is thus always a potential strategy for nonexploitative oppressors. It is not an option in a situation of economic exploitation because exploiters require the labor of the exploited for their material well-being. It is no accident that culturally we have the abhorrent saying, "the only good Indian is a dead Indian," but not the saying "the only good worker is a dead worker" or "the only good slave is a dead slave." It makes sense to say "the only good worker is an obedient and conscien-

tious worker," but not "the only good worker is a dead worker." The contrast between North America and South Africa in the treatment of indigenous peoples reflects this difference poignantly: in North America, where the indigenous people were oppressed (by virtue of being coercively displaced from the land) but not exploited, genocide was the basic policy of social control in the face of resistance; in South Africa, where the European settler population heavily depended upon African labor for its own prosperity, this was not an option.

Exploitation, therefore, does not merely define a set of *statuses* of social actors, but a pattern of on-going *interactions* structured by a set of social relations, relations which mutually bind the exploiter and the exploited together. This dependency of the exploiter on the exploited gives the exploited a certain form of power, since human beings always retain at least some minimal control over their own expenditure of effort. Social control of labor which relies exclusively on repression is costly and, except under special circumstances, often fails to generate optimal levels of diligence and effort on the part of the exploited. As a result, there is generally systematic pressure on exploiters to moderate their domination and in one way or another to try to elicit some degree of consent from the exploited, at least in the sense of gaining some level of minimal cooperation from them. Paradoxically perhaps, exploitation is thus a constraining force on the practices of the exploiter. This constraint constitutes a basis of power for the exploited. . . .

Class and Exploitation

In capitalist society, the central form of exploitation is based on property rights in the means of production. These property rights generate three basic classes: *capitalists* (exploiters), who own the means of production and hire workers; *workers* (exploited), who do not own the means of production and sell their labor power to capitalists; and *petty bourgeois* (neither exploiter nor exploited), who own and use the means of production without hiring others. The Marxist account of how the capital-labor relation generates exploitation is a familiar one: propertyless workers, in order to acquire their means of livelihood, must sell their labor power to people who own the means of production. In this exchange relation, they agree to work for a specified length of time in exchange for a wage which they use to buy their means of subsistence. Because of the power relation between capitalists and workers, capitalists are able to force workers to produce more than is needed to provide them with this subsistence. As a result, workers produce a surplus which is owned by the capitalist and takes the form of profits. Profits, the amount of the social product that is left over after the costs of producing and reproducing all of the inputs (both labor power inputs and physical inputs) have been deducted, constitute an appropriation of the fruits of labor of workers.

Describing this relation as exploitative is a claim about the basis for the inherent conflict between workers and capitalists in the employment relation. It points to the crucial fact that the conflict between capitalists and workers is not simply over the *level of wages,* but over the *amount of work effort* performed for those wages. Capitalists always want workers to expend more effort than workers willingly want to do. . . .

For some theoretical and empirical purposes, this simple image of the class structure may be sufficient. For example, if the main purpose of an analysis is to explore the basic differences between the class structures of feudalism and capitalism, then an analysis which revolved entirely around the relationship between capitalists and workers might be adequate. However, for many of the things we want to study with class analysis, we need a more nuanced set of categories. In particular, we need concepts which allow for two kinds of analyses: first, the analysis of the variation across time and place in the class structures of concrete capitalist societies, and second, the analysis of the ways individual lives are affected by their location within the class structure. The first of these is needed if we are to explore macro-variations in a fine-grained way; the second is needed if we are to use class effectively in micro-analysis.

Both of these tasks involve elaborating a concept of class structure in capitalist societies that moves beyond the core polarization between capitalists and workers. More specifically, this involves solving two general problems in class structural analysis: first, the problem of locating the "middle class" within the class structure, and second, locating people not in the paid labor force in the class structure.

The Problem of the "Middle Class" Among Employees

If we limit the analysis of class structure in capitalism to the ownership of, and exclusion from, the means of production, we end up with a class structure in which there are only three locations—the capitalist class, the working class and the petty bourgeoisie (those who own means of production but do not hire workers)—and in which around 85–90% of the population in most developed capitalist countries falls into a single class. While this may in some sense reflect a profound truth about capitalism—that the large majority of the population are separated from the means of production and must sell their labor power on the labor market in order to survive—it does not provide us with an adequate conceptual framework for explaining many of the things we want class to help explain. In particular, if we want class structure to help explain class consciousness, class formation and class conflict, then we need some way of understanding the class-relevant divisions within the employee population.

In ordinary language terms, this is the problem of the "middle class"—people who do not own their own means of production, who sell their labor power on a labor market, and yet do not seem part of the "working class." The question, then, is on what basis can we differentiate class locations among people who share a common location of nonownership within capitalist property relations? In my analyses, I divide the class of employees along two dimensions: first, their relationship to authority within production, and second, their possession of skills or expertise.

Authority

There are two rationales for treating authority as a dimension of class relations among employees. The first concerns the role of *domination* within capitalist property relations. In order to insure the performance of adequate effort on the part of workers, capitalist production always involves an apparatus of domination involving surveillance, positive and negative sanctions and varying forms of hierarchy. Capitalists do not simply *own* the means of

production and *hire* workers; they also *dominate* workers within production.

In these terms, managers and supervisors can be viewed as exercising delegated capitalist class powers in so far as they engage in the practices of domination within production. In this sense they can be considered *simultaneously* in the capitalist class *and* the working class: they are like capitalists in that they dominate workers; they are like workers in that they are controlled by capitalists and exploited within production. They thus occupy what I have called *contradictory locations within class relations*. The term "contradictory" is used in this expression rather than simply "dual" since the class interests embedded in managerial jobs combine the inherently antagonistic interests of capital and labor. The higher one moves in the authority hierarchy, the greater will be the weight of capitalist interests within this class location. Thus upper managers, and especially Chief Executive Officers in large corporations will be very closely tied to the capitalist class, while the class character of lower level supervisor jobs will be much closer to that of the working class.

The second rationale for treating the authority dimension as a criterion for differentiating class locations among employees centers on the relationship between their earnings and the appropriation of surplus. The strategic position of managers within the organization of production enables them to make significant claims on a portion of the social surplus (defined in the counterfactual manner discussed above) in the form of relatively high earnings. In effect this means that the wages and salaries of managerial labor power are above the costs of producing and reproducing their labor power (including whatever skills they might have).. . .

Skills and Expertise

The second axis of class differentiation among employees centers on the possession of skills or expertise. Like managers, employees who possess high levels of skills/expertise are potentially in a privileged appropriation location within exploitation relations. There are two primary mechanisms through which this can happen. First, skills and expertise are frequently scarce in labor markets, not simply because they are in short supply, but also because there are systematic obstacles in the way of increasing the supply of those skills to meet the requirements of employing organizations. One important form of these obstacles is credentials, but rare talents could also constitute the basis for sustained restrictions on the supply of a particular form of labor power. The result of such restrictions on supply is that owners of the scarce skills are able to receive a wage above the costs of producing and reproducing their labor power.

Second, the control over knowledge and skills frequently renders also the labor effort of skilled workers difficult to monitor and control. The effective control over knowledge by such employees means that employers must rely to some extent on loyalty enhancing mechanisms in order to achieve desired levels of cooperation and effort from employees with high levels of skills and expertise, just as they have to do in the case of managers. Employees with high levels of expertise, therefore, are able to appropriate surplus both because of their strategic location within the organization of production (as controllers of knowledge), and because of their strategic location in the organization of labor markets (as controllers of a scarce form of labor power).. . .

A Map of Middle-Class Class Locations

Adding position within authority hierarchies and possession of scarce skills and expertise to the fundamental dimension of capitalist property relations generates the map of class locations presented in Figure 7.1. It is important to stress that this is a map of class *locations*. The cells in the typology are not "classes" as such; they are locations within class relations. Some of these

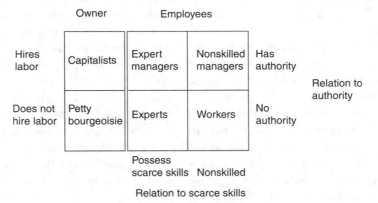

Figure 7.1 Basic Class Typology

are contradictory locations within class relations, others are privileged appropriation locations within exploitation relations and still others are polarized locations within capitalist property relations. By convention the polarized locations—"capitalists" and "workers" in capitalism—are often called "classes," but the more precise terminology would be to describe these as the fundamental locations within the capitalist class structure. The typology is thus not a proposal for a six-class model of the class structure of capitalism, but rather a model of a class structure which differentiates six locations within class relations.

REFERENCES

Capp, Al. 1992. *Li'L Abner,* vol 14: 1948. Princeton, WI: Kitchen Sink Press.

|| 8 ||

The Death of Class

JAN PAKULSKI
MALCOLM WATERS

"Class" has always been a contentious concept. In its most famous Marxian version, it is an explanatory term linking the economic sphere of production with the political and ideological superstructure. Here it is also a label for collective social actors, especially for that new historical subject, the proletariat, whose destiny was to transform social consciousness and to turn class society into a classless one. This mixture of sociology and eschatology proved exceptionally potent in propelling the concept to celebrity status. Class became a master term for both sociology and political analysis. With the formation of class parties of the left, the concept was further implicated within the global and national, political and ideological confrontations that became particularly acute during the hot and cold wars of the first three-quarters of the twentieth century. This was especially true in Europe where class became an ideological icon, a battle standard for the left and a bogey for the right. The intellectual left became preoccupied in identifying class divisions and condemning class inequalities, providing the central dogma of radicalized social science throughout the 1960s and 1970s. By contrast, denying the centrality of class became the hallmark of "bourgeois" sociology. Even if the term was used in an ideologically neutral context, the semantic-ideological halo it acquired made it inherently contentious and prone to political appropriation.

The degree of political appropriation has reduced in recent years. With the declining commitment to Marxism, the collapse of Soviet communism and the waning appeal of socialist ideologies in the West, class is losing its ideological significance and its political centrality. Both the right and the left are abandoning their preoccupation with class issues. The right is turning its attention to morality and ethnicity while the critical left is becoming increasingly concerned about issues of gender, ecology, citizenship and human rights. This rearrangement of political concerns coincides with a shift in intellectual fashion and a growing scepticism about the compatibility of class models with contemporary social reality. Class divisions are losing their self-evident and perva-

Jan Pakulski and Malcolm Waters, *The Death of Class,* pp. 1–5, 24–26, 153–158, 160–164, 166–168. Copyright © 1996 by Sage Publications, Ltd. Reprinted with the permission of Sage Publications, Ltd., and the authors.

sive character. Class identities are challenged by "new associations" and new social movements. Class radicalism is no longer the flavour of the month in the intellectual salons and on university campuses. Like beads and Che Guevara berets, class is *passé*, especially among advocates of the postmodernist avant-garde and practitioners of the new gender-, eco- and ethno-centred politics.

Naturally, these shifts in public attention and intellectual fashion cannot be decisive in debates about the objective significance of class. However, they are important because they create an auspicious climate for reaching conclusions on its relevance. For the first time in over half a century, such a debate can be conducted outside the trenches of the Cold War and in a spirit of impartiality and mutual respect. In this new climate, arguments about the declining salience of class can no longer be dismissed as symptoms of ideological bias, intellectual weakness or moral corruption. . . .

The debate about classes combines issues of semantics and substance. Although our focus is firmly on the latter we must also pay some attention to the former. This is quite natural in a situation where a concept has been so stretched that it can be used to mean almost any identifiable collectivity ranging from occupational position to political association, and any theoretical object from structural location to collective actor. It is impossible simultaneously to give justice to this semantic diversity and to present a consistent argument against the class paradigm. We therefore focus on analytic usages of "class" rather than the confused and vague applications of the term in popular discourse. In the context of the latter, "class" is bound to remain a routinized and vague classificatory term because it is a useful shorthand for a wide range of social entities and divisions. We respect this popular usage but refuse to accept it as evidence of, or an argument for, the relevance of class. We will also avoid defining class in such a restrictive way that it becomes a straw person, on one hand, or can be used to designate any structured inequality or conflict, on the other. The latter strategy transforms the class thesis into a virtual tautology because no known society is egalitarian and free of conflict. However, we do admit that there is a range of legitimate meanings of the term, each of which can be examined independently in terms of its theoretical utility and empirical relevance.

In the analytic vocabulary of contemporary sociology, "class" refers to a specific social location and causality, a specific pattern of groupness, and a specific form of identification. In the hands of some authors, as in classical Marxism, these aspects are combined, while for others, mainly those who subscribe to Weberian and action approaches, they are separated. However, we subscribe to the broad consensus that class is primarily about *economic-productive* location and determination; that is, it is based on property and/or market relations. People participate in class as producers rather than, say, as consumers, members of gender categories or organizational position-holders, although the impact of class may extend far beyond production roles. When stripped of this economic connotation and detached from its classical Marxist and Weberian roots, "class" loses most of its explanatory power.

It is equally untenable to treat class as a mere substructure or as a statistical category, without at least drawing some implications for social relationships, social distance, patterns of interaction and patterns of association. Class is sociologically important as a social entity, as *social* class, and as such must transpire in detectable patterns of exploitation, struggle, domination and subordination, or closure. The number of classes, the extent of polarization, the clarity of class boundaries and the extent of conflict between classes may vary because they are not definitional elements. However, a minimum level of detectable clustering or groupness is essential if we are to say that classes exist. A society in which such economically caused social clustering occurs, and where these clusters are the backbone of the social structure, is a *class society.*

Lastly, a fully formed class involves a measure of self-recognition and self-identification on the part of participants, although this identification need not involve explicit class terminology or imply a consciousness of antagonism and struggle. Minimally, the members of a class have to be aware of their commonality and employ some recognized terms for collective self-description. A sense of difference between "them" and "us" is a necessary condition for the formation of class actors that marks the most developed examples of class articulation.

All of this implies that the articulation of class is a matter of degree. Its strength, and the extent to which it structures society, can vary from a minimal level, where economically based social clustering is weak but still predominant, to an advanced level. Here classes are well articulated in the social, cultural, and political-ideological domains, class identifications predominate, class consciousness is acute, and politics is dominated by struggles between class-based groups and organizations. Few historical instances of whole societies approximate a fully fledged class configuration. More typically only a degree of "classness" can be observed. Moreover, the strength and the

pattern of classness can vary historically and between contemporaneous societies.

The issue of the degree of classness of a society is linked to the issue of the relevance of "class analysis", a type of social analysis that seeks to identify classes and to trace their social, cultural and political-ideological consequences. Class analysis makes sense only when applied to a class society. Its utility is proportional to the degree of classness. At one extreme, in a fully fledged class society, class analysis can be a legitimate substitute for social analysis. However, if classes are dissolving, a form of analysis that privileges class as an explanatory category has to give way to a more open-ended social analysis.

Historically there have been numerous examples of non-class societies. We embrace the convention that societies based on slave labour, such as ancient Rome and Greece, the estate societies of feudal Europe and modern state-socialist societies are non-class societies. In none of these societies are property and market relations the skeleton of the social structure or the predominant grid of social power. They are all unequal, stratified and conflictual but not made so predominantly by class. Class and class society are, in our vocabulary, distinctly modern phenomena inseparably linked to the market and its institutionalization within the early and mature forms of industrial capitalism.

This leads us to the central argument of this chapter, that classes are dissolving and that the most advanced societies are no longer class societies. The most important aspect is an attenuation of the class identities, class ideologies, and class organizations that framed West European corporatist politics in the middle of this century. Equally, the communal aspects of class, class subcultures and milieux, have long since disappeared. The issue of the decomposition of economic class mechanisms is more controversial. We cite the following developments: a wide redistribution of property; the proliferation of indirect and small ownership; the credentialization of skills and the professionalization of occupations; the multiple segmentation and globalization of markets; and an increasing role for consumption as a status and lifestyle generator.

We must stress our concentration on the advanced societies of the capitalist West and, to a lesser extent, on the "newly industrializing countries" (NICs) of East and South East Asia and the rapidly democratizing and marketizing societies of Russia and Eastern Europe. Quite clearly, class remains salient in the "less developed countries" (LDCs) of Asia, Africa and Latin America that have not reached an advanced social, political and economic stage. In so far as such societies are structured by productive industrial property they clearly remain class societies.

The historical side of the argument charts the process of class decomposition in the industrialized West over the last century and a half. We argue that class societies are specific historical entities. They were born with industrial capitalism, changed their form under the impact of organized or corporate capitalism, and are disappearing in the face of post-industrialization and postmodernization. The early forms of class were chronicled in England by generations of social observers from Engels (1892) to Thompson (1980). They arose in parallel with a gradual decline of such pre-industrial collectivities as village communities and estates and the strengthening of nation-states. From the early twentieth century onward the fate of classes, nation-states and parties became in-

timately linked. While localized communities of fate were gradually marginalized, politically organized national classes were gradually institutionalized mainly as class parties and trade unions. These national classes were quite different from their predecessors. They were politically generated rather than spontaneous, occupationally heterogeneous, and reconstructed as imagined communities on a national level. Participation in these national classes involved little by way of interaction and communication. Their constitutive common interests were abstract political constructs developed by elites. What such classes lacked in social bonding and cultural cohesion, they compensated for in political organization and strategic coherence. It was these politically organized national classes, the power of which peaked with the establishment of corporatist structures, that became the most powerful social actors and agents of social transformation of the twentieth century. . . .

In summary, the stratification order of capitalist societies can be traced as a succession of three periods roughly demarcated by the nineteenth century, the first three-quarters of the twentieth century, and the contemporary period. In highly formalized and abstracted terms they are as follows.

Economic-class Society. This is a society arranged into patterns of domination and struggle between interest groups that emerge from the economic realm. In the familiar terms of Marx, the classes will be property owners and sellers of labour power, but they can be conceptualized as employers and employees. The dominant class can control the state and maintain itself as a ruling class either by capturing its apparatuses, or by rendering them weak. In so far as the subordinate class undertakes collective action, it will be rebellious or rev-olutionary in character, aimed at dislodging this ruling class by the abolition of private property. Culture is divided to match class divisions, into dominant and subordinate ideologies and into high and low cultures.

Organized-class Society.   This type of society is dominated by a political or state sphere. The state is typically ruled by a single unified bloc, a political-bureaucratic elite, that exercises power over subordinated masses. The bloc may be factionalized horizontally into formally opposed parties. The elite will comprise either a party leadership or a corporatized leadership integrating party leaders with the leaders of other organized interest groups including economic and cultural ones. The elite uses the coercive power of the state to regulate economics and culture. The state can dominate the economy by redistribution or by the conversion of private into public property, although this need not be a complete accomplishment. Masses, in turn, reorganize themselves in national-political classes rather than in industrial terms by establishing links with milieu parties. Meanwhile, the cultural realm can be unified under the state umbrella or under the aegis of state-sponsored monopolies. It can thus be turned into an industrialized or mass culture.

Status-conventional Society.   In this type of society stratification emerges from the cultural sphere. The strata are lifestyle-and/or value-based status configurations. They can form around differentiated patterns of value commitment, identity, belief, symbolic meaning, taste, opinion or consumption. Because of the ephemeral

and fragile nature of these resources, a stratification system based on conventional status communities appears as a shifting mosaic which can destabilize the other two spheres. The state is weakened because it cannot rely on mass support, and the economy is weakened (in its capacity for social structuring) because of the critical importance of symbolic values. Each order is de-concentrated by a prevailing orientation to values and utilities that are established conventionally rather than by reference to collective interests.

In failing to recognize these developments the class paradigm has made two errors that have seriously damaged the capacity of sociology to generate public debate about social and economic inequality. First, it has offered continued credence and legitimacy to class theory as a vehicle for the analysis of twentieth-century developments. In an important but not absolutely critical sense, class died somewhere between the beginning of the twentieth century and the end of the Great Depression. It died with the absorption of class struggle into the democratic arena, with the emergence of the fascist and socialist states that so dominated civil society, with the institutionalization of corporatist deals that linked government, capital and labour into common projects, with the mitigation of the effects of the market through such institutions as citizenship and welfare, and with the domination of the planet by superpower politics. The development was not entirely critical because the effects of what we can call "organized class", the successor to true economic class, could still be analysed sociologically. As a successor to class theory, class analysis is indeed therefore an appropriate and impressive intellec-

Axial principle	System level							
	World	Society	Politics	Economy	Community	Domesticity	Gender	Individual
Economic class	Colonialism	Laissez-faire state	Plutocratic and revolutionary parties	Owner capitalism	Property order	Reproduction site	Patriarchy	Worker
Organized class	Imperialism	Corporatism	Mass parties	Fordism	Occupational order	Consumer sphere	Reorganized patriarchy (viriarchy)	Citizen
Conventional status	Globalization	Nation	Niche parties	Flexible specialization	Value order	Significant lifeworld	Hyperdifferentiation	Human

Figure 8.1 The Registration of Stratification Orders Through System Levels

tual development in which sociology can take just pride. However, we are now contemplating a second and more critical error. Sociology is continuing to offer class analysis as its main vehicle for the discovery of social inequality and struggle in the transmillennial period. It is failing to recognize that oppression, exploitation, and conflict are being socially constructed around transcendent conceptions of individual human rights and global values that identify and empower struggles around such diverse focuses as postcolonial racism, sexual preferences, gender discrimination, environmental degradation, citizen participation, religious commitments and ethnic self-determination. These issues have little or nothing to do with class. In the contemporary period of history, the class paradigm is intellectually and morally bankrupt. . . .

Figure 8.1 is a kind of master diagram that summarizes the substantive argument of this chapter. It shows that the historical transformation from economic-class society to organized-class society to status-conventional society is not merely an issue of stratification but one of wide-ranging societal transformation. The argument offered here

is therefore part of the general theoretical effort that focuses on post-industrialization (Bell 1976), detraditionalization (Beck 1992; Giddens 1991), postmodernization (Crook et al. 1992; Harvey 1989; Lyotard 1984), societal disorganization (Lash and Urry 1987; 1994; Offe 1985), and globalization (Featherstone 1990; Robertson 1992; Waters 1995).

The emerging stratificational picture is represented in such work as that of Kornblum (1974) on Chicago steelworkers that reveals anything but structural and cultural homogeneity. He shows that dense social networks of primary groups cross-cut old class boundaries and establish salient non-class divisions along regional-residential, ethnic, racial and status lines. These are the main focuses for identity formation and local politics. A similar picture is emerging from British studies of communities (e.g. Pahl and Wallace 1985; Williams 1975), political behaviour (e.g. Rose and McAllister 1985; Dunleavy and Husbands 1985), and consumption (Saunders 1990; Featherstone 1991). Here, gender divisions, market fragmentation, housing and consumption-sector cleavages, and state dependency are the main influences on political identities and voting patterns.

Equally Phizacklea's study (1990) of the fashion industry in Britain reveals deep divisions created by combinations of economic inequality, race, gender and locality. She argues that a dual labour market is generated in the garment industry by an intersection between organizational factors (relations between large corporations and small subcontractors), racial and ethnic divisions and a gendered-labour pattern exerted by domestic norms and relations. Recession and cheap imports have pushed "ethnic entrepreneurs", mainly of Asian extraction, into family businesses that rely on low-paid female labour. These women workers are vulnerable to exploitative conditions by dint of gendered social norms, i.e. notions of "women's work", modes of migration that often subject female dependants to indebtedness, and social discrimination that restricts their employment options. Such studies of multiple segmentation at the local level are becoming increasingly common.

This multiple socioeconomic and sociocultural fragmentation is very distant from the kind of class differentiation identified by Lockwood (1958) or Goldthorpe et al. (1969) a generation earlier. They proposed differentiated sub-types of working-class and lower-middle-class orientation that created locally concentrated and culturally homogeneous class communities. By contrast contemporary studies emphasize cultural diversity, especially among younger people. According to Willis (1990), this is the consequence not only of the decline in class-communal ties, but also of a drift away from the institutions that have engendered class identities in the past including community associations, trade unions, and schools. The

mass unemployment of the 1980s that placed many young people beyond the class-formational impact of work situation and increasingly under the individualizing effects of commercialized consumer culture also contributed to the process.

We can now theorize this transformation more formally. The four propositions that class theory makes are: economism; groupness; behavioural linkage; and transformative capacity. A status-conventional theory would offer the following parallel propositions:

- The proposition of *culturalism*. Status-conventional stratification is primarily a cultural phenomenon. It is based on subscription to lifestyles that form around consumption patterns, information flows, cognitive agreements, aesthetic preferences and value commitments. Material and power phenomena are reducible to these symbolically manifested lifestyle and value phenomena.
- The proposition of *fragmentation*. Conventional statuses, like classes, are real phenomena. However they consist of a virtually infinite overlap of associations and identifications that are shifting and unstable. Status-conventional society is a fluid matrix of fragile formations that cycle and multiply within a globalized field.
- The proposition of *autonomization*. The subjective orientation and behaviour of any individual or aggregate of individuals are very difficult to predict by virtue of stratificational location. There is no central cleavage or single dimension along which preferences can be ordered. Such attributes as po-

litical preference, access to educational opportunity, patterns of marriage and income are self-referential rather than externally constrained.

- The proposition of *resignification* based on subjective interests. The stratification process is continuously fluid. Its openness allows a constant respecification and invention of preferences and symbolic dimensions that provide for continuous regeneration. The source of novelty is a process of restless subjective choice that seeks to gratify churning and unrepressed emotions that include anxiety and aggression as well as desire.

The proposition of culturalism specifies that symbolic dimensions will compete with each other in the field of social structure. This will produce the phenomenon of multiple status cleavages. The stratificational categories of status-conventional society constitute a complex mosaic of taste subcultures, "new associations", civic initiatives, ethnic and religious revolutionary groups, generational cohorts, community action groups, new social movements, gangs, alternative lifestyle colonies, alternative production organizations, educational alumni, racial brotherhoods, gender sisterhoods, tax rebels, fundamentalist and revivalist religious movements, internet discussion groups, purchasing co-ops, professional associations, and so on. Many are ephemeral, some are continuous and stable.

A key feature of these multiple status cleavages is that because they are specialized and intersecting, membership in any one does not necessarily contradict membership in any other. From the subjective point of view the proposition of fragmentation en-

sures that individuals apprehend the stratification system as a status bazaar. Individuals can operate simultaneously as members of several status groups and have the potential to be members of any others. Their identities are reflexively self-composed as they move between status adherences. However, the fact of a status market does not imply an absolute voluntarism, and indeed the freedoms in most cases are relevant to exit from status groups rather than entry. Closure processes remain effective in status-conventional society.

The proposition of autonomization nevertheless allows individuals to be profligate in their behaviour. They will tend to spend their resources of time, energy, money, influence, and power in the pursuit of symbolic attachments that tend to advance the interests, identities, values and commitments to which they subscribe and aspire. The very act of doing this will, by the proposition of resignification, tend to redefine and reorder the symbolic dimensions that reference the system. Indeed, a particular effect is the redefinition of some traditional status-membership dimensions, especially education, religion, and ethnicity, into a more ephemeral and conventional regime. So education becomes a marketplace for credentials, religion becomes a vehicle for handling this week's anxieties as one is born again and again and again, and ethnicity is something one rediscovers through community action and involvement.

We must stress that we are not arguing for a decline in inequality and conflict but for a decline in *class* inequality and conflict. One last illustration can confirm the point. The available research shows that, even allowing for recent reversals, during the twentieth century household wealth has become more widely distributed. This is an indicator of the decomposition of class, as normally defined in relation to property. However, at the present time there is also an increasing inequality of income (*The Economist* 5 November 1994). This is not evidence of increasing class inequality but it is evidence of increasing inequality of sumptuary capacity and this links directly with the kind of status-conventional stratification that is theorized here. The income-poor so-called "underclass" is not class defined but is rather status defined by the symbolizations attached to postcolonial migration, race, ethnicity, gender, age and pattern of family support. Exclusionary closure based on these status attributes consigns people to an "underclass". The stigmatization that attaches to the "underclass" is a function not of its members' exploitation but of their incapacity to consume. An earlier generation of social scientists wrote of poverty as a culture (Lewis 1961; 1966; Valentine 1968). Perhaps it is time to do so once again.

All of this means that complexity is likely to increase. This calls for a theoretical stance that rejects any notion that there is a single conceptual or theoretical crowbar or even a magic word that can open the treasure cave of stratification, inequality and conflict. Contemporary sociology needs to be sensitive to and appreciative of diversity. It must be humble in the face of complexity and ready to accept contingency in relation to social attitudes and behaviours. It must not force a lively, engaging and ethically fraught reality into an inherited and stultifying conceptual straitjacket. If it continues on its procrustean path it will lose its audience.

REFERENCES

Beck, U (1992) *Risk Society.* London: Sage.

Bell, D (1976) *The Coming of Post-Industrial Society.* New York: Basic/Harper Torchbook (first published 1973).

Crook, S, J Pakulski and M Waters (1992) *Postmodernization.* London: Sage.

Dunleavy, P and C Husbands (1985) *British Democracy at the Crossroads.* London: Allen & Unwin.

Engels, F (1892) *The Condition of the Working Class in England in 1844.* London: Hamden.

Featherstone, M (1990) *Global Culture.* London: Sage.

Featherstone, M (ed) (1991) *Consumer Culture and Postmodernism.* London: Sage.

Giddens, A (1991) *Modernity and Self-Identity.* Cambridge: Polity.

Goldthorpe, J, D Lockwood, F Bechhofer and J Platt (1969) *The Affluent Worker in the Class Structure.* Cambridge: CUP.

Harvey, D (1989) *The Condition of Postmodernity.* Oxford: Blackwell.

Kornblum, W (1974) *Blue Collar Community.* Chicago: Chicago UP.

Lash, S and J Urry (1987) *The End of Organised Capitalism.* Cambridge: Polity.

Lash, S and J Urry (1994) *Economies of Signs and Space.* London: Sage.

Lewis, O (1961) *The Children of Sanchez.* New York: Random House.

Lewis, O (1966) *La Vida: A Puerto Rican Family in the Culture of Poverty.* New York: Random House.

Lockwood, D (1958) *The Blackcoated Worker.* London: Allen & Unwin.

Lyotard, J (1984) *The Postmodern Condition.* Manchester: Manchester UP.

Offe, C (1985) "New Social Movements: Challenging the Boundaries of Institutional Politics." *Social Research* 52(4): 817–68.

Ossowski, S (1963) *Class Structure in the Social Consciousness.* London: Routledge (first published 1958).

Pahl, R and C Wallace (1985) "Household Work Strategies in Economic Recession" in N Redclift and E Mingione (eds) *Beyond Employment.* Oxford: Blackwell.

Phizacklea, A (1990) *Unpacking the Fashion Industry: Gender, Racism and Class in Production.* London: Routledge.

Robertson, R (1992) *Globalization.* London: Sage.

Rose, R and I McAllister (1985) *Voters Begin to Choose.* London: Sage.

Saunders, P (1990) *A Nation of Home Owners.* London: Unwin Hyman.

Thompson, E (1980) *The Making of the English Working Class* (2nd edn). Harmondsworth: Penguin (first edn 1968).

Valentine, C (1968) *Culture and Poverty.* Chicago: Chicago UP.

Waters, M (1995) *Globalization.* London: Routledge.

Williams, R (1975) *The Country and the City.* London: Paladin.

Willis, P (1990) *Common Culture.* Milton Keynes: Open UP.

9

Socioeconomic Indexes for Occupations
A Review, Update, and Critique

ROBERT M. HAUSER
JOHN ROBERT WARREN

There are several reasons to focus more attention on the collection, scaling, and analysis of occupational data than has recently been the case. First, job-holding is the most important social role held by most adults outside their family or household. When we meet someone new, often our first question is, "What do you do?" and that is a very good question. Job-holding defines how we spend much of our time, and it provides strong clues about the activities and circumstances in which that time is spent. Second, job-holding tells us about the technical and social skills that we bring to the labor market, and for most people job-holding delimits current and future economic prospects. Thus, even for persons who are not attached to the labor market, past jobs or the jobs held by other members of the same family or household provide information about economic and social standing. Third, as market labor has become nearly universal among adult women as well as men, it is increasingly possible to characterize individuals in terms of their own current or past jobs. Fourth, once we have a good job description, it is possible to map jobs into many classifications, scales, and measures. Fifth, measurement of jobs and occupations does not entail the same problems of refusal, recall, reliability, and stability as occur in the measurement of income or wealth. Job descriptions—contemporary or retrospective, from job-holders or from their family members—are imperfect, but the reliability and validity of carefully collected occupational data are high enough to support sustained analysis (Hauser, Sewell, and Warren 1994). Thus, even if we are limited to retrospective questions, we can confidently trace occupational trajectories across the adult years. The same cannot be said of earnings trajectories, let alone other components of personal or household income or wealth.

Conceptual Issues

It is important to distinguish between jobs and occupations. A job is a specific and

---

This is a commissioned chapter that draws heavily on material in a previous publication (Robert M. Hauser and John Robert Warren, "Socioeconomic Indexes of Occupational Status: A Review, Update, and Critique," *Sociological Methodology, 1997*, edited by Adrian Raftery. Copyright © 1997 by Blackwell Publishers. Used by permission of Blackwell Publishers.).

sometimes unique bundle of activities carried out by a person in the expectation of economic remuneration. An occupation is an abstract category used to group and classify similar jobs. Such abstractions are often heterogeneous and idiosyncratic in construction, but they usually involve determinations of similarity in typical activities, in the sites where work is performed, in the form of job tenure, in the skill requirements of the job, or in the product or service that results from the job. There are multiple systems for the classification of jobs and complex interdependencies between occupational and industrial classifications. Most social scientific uses of occupational data are based either on (a) the classification systems of the U.S. Bureau of the Census, which are revised each decade at the time of the census, or (b) the *Dictionary of Occupational Titles,* which is produced by the Employment and Training Administration of the U.S. Department of Labor.

Some measures of social class reflect job or personal characteristics, whereas others depend on occupation. For example, consider two widely used conceptions of "social class." Wright's (1985, 88) class typology combines concepts of ownership, authority, and expertise. It requires information about a person's educational attainment as well as ownership, authority, supervision, and occupational classification. On the other hand, Erikson and Goldthorpe's (1992, 38–39) "class schema" is ultimately a grouping of occupational categories based upon Goldthorpe and Hope's (1974) study of occupational prestige in Great Britain (Goldthorpe 1980). Each author sees his scheme as a theoretically refined basis for identifying the membership of real and discrete social classes. In Wright's neo-Marxian classification, the aim is to identify modes of labor exploitation in the relations of production. In Erikson and Goldthorpe's neo-Weberian classification, the class categories are designed to identify distinct combinations of occupational function and employment status.

In our opinion, differences between the two class schemes and between them and our occupational status measures lie more in the proximity of constituent variables to jobs and persons than in other theoretical or conceptual distinctions that have been debated by their authors. Other things being equal, we should expect a classification based partly upon personal and job characteristics to be more direct and powerful in its influence than a classification based on occupational characteristics would be alone. Rather than relying on a predetermined combination of occupation and other social or economic characteristics, we suggest that investigators should use data on individual education and income, and on other job characteristics, as well as on occupational standing (see Jencks, Perman, and Rainwater 1988).

In working with measures of occupational social standing, we emphasize the social and economic grading of the occupational structure, rather than a priori constructions of distinct social classes. People are linked to jobs, not only through job-holding, but also through their relationships with others who hold or have held jobs. Jobs can be mapped into standard occupational classifications, and the categories of those classifications may be linked to occupational characteristics. By working back through this series of linkages, we can describe people in terms of occupational characteristics. Such characteristics will be valid as descriptions of jobs only to the degree that occupations are homogeneous and the intervening maps and linkages are sound. In our view, the remarkable thing about this way of measuring social and economic characteristics is not that it is error prone, which would seem obvious, but that it has such high reliability and validity. That it does so is a social fact, which rests both on skill and care in classification and coding but also on strong uniformities in social structure.

Occupational Prestige and Socioeconomic Indexes of Occupational Status

What are the relevant status characteristics of occupations? Many discussions of occupations in the stratification system begin with the concept of occupational prestige, the general level of social standing enjoyed by the incumbents of an occupation. In the United States there have been three major national surveys of occupational prestige, the most recent of which was carried out in conjunction with the 1989 General Social Survey (GSS) of the National Opinion Research Center (NORC; Nakao and Treas 1994). The main problem with all of these occupational prestige ratings is that they lack criterion validity. Prestige is not as highly correlated with other variables as are other measures of occupational social standing, specifically, measures of the socioeconomic status of occupations, as indicated by the average educational attainment and income of occupational incumbents.

Duncan (1961) created the first socioeconomic index (SEI) of occupational status. For forty-five census occupation lines, he ran the linear regression of the percentage of "good" or "excellent" ratings on measures of both occupational education and occupational income (see Duncan 1961 for details). This regression yielded roughly equal weights for the two regressors, a result that motivated some sociologists to characterize socioeconomic scales as a hybrid of "social status" (as indexed by occupational education) and economic status (see Hodge 1981).

The Duncan SEI has been updated or elaborated in several ways, and researchers should be cautious in using the updates because of their potential lack of comparability. Most recently, as part of their work with prestige scores obtained in the 1989 GSS, Nakao and Treas (1994) created socioeconomic scores for 1980-basis census occupational lines by regressing their prestige ratings on the characteristics of male and female occupational incumbents in the 1980 census. The obvious next step is to create another set of socioeconomic scores, using the 1989 prestige scores as a criterion, but based upon characteristics of the work force in the 1990 census.

In an earlier paper (see Hauser and Warren 1997), we made a special extract of occupational education and earnings from the 1990 census 5 percent public use sample. Throughout our analyses, we used the same definition of occupational education as Nakao and Treas (1994), namely, the percentage of people in an occupation who had completed one or more years of college. After experimenting with alternative treatments of earnings and income, we constructed the new socioeconomic indexes using occupational wage rates, whereas Duncan (1961) used the percentage of occupational incumbents who had reported incomes of $3500 or more. Our prestige criterion was the percentage of prestige ratings above a fixed threshold. However, for statistical reasons, we used a logistic transformation of the prestige criterion and of the educational level and wage rate of each occupation (see Hauser and Warren 1997, 203–17).

We then constructed socioeconomic indexes for the total work force and, separately, for men and for women. Our purpose in creating gender-specific indexes was to compare the behavior of occupational characteristics between men and women, especially in relation to occupational prestige. We do not recommend routine use of the gender-specific indexes in research. Although the indexes for all workers, men, and women have roughly the same range and are in the same metric, their statistical properties differ. Findings based on the total, male, and female indexes are not strictly comparable (Warren, Sheridan, and Hauser 1998), and, where researchers choose to use a composite socioeconomic index, we recommend the index based on the characteristics of all workers.

Chastened and instructed by the example of Fox's (1991) and Friendly's (1991) reanalyses of Duncan's data, we also paid a good deal of attention to issues of fit and functional form. In the final set of regression analyses, we used several types of residual plots to identify influential outliers. Based on these findings, we deleted several occupations from the regression analyses used to estimate weights for the socioeconomic scores. Several of the largest and most influential exceptions to typical relationships among occupational education, wage rates, and prestige occur in common and visible jobs: business owners, farmers, clergy, secretaries, teachers, waiters and waitresses, janitors, and truck drivers. This finding reminds us that occupational prestige is by no means the same as occupational socioeconomic status, and we should respect both the theoretical and empirical distinctions between them.

Using estimates from our preferred models, we computed total-based, male-based, and female-based SEI scores for all occupations. The combined three sets of scores were transformed to range between 0 and 100. Our 1990-basis and 1980-basis total (TSEI), male (MSEI), and female (FSEI) scores for all occupation lines, the socioeconomic components of those scores, and the 1989 Nakao-Treas prestige scores and ratings are available elsewhere (Hauser and Warren 1997; http://www.ssc.wisc.edu/cde/cdewp/1996papers.htm).

Structural Models of the Socioeconomic Index

Subsequent analyses—presented in detail in Hauser and Warren (1997)—reveal three potential weaknesses in composite socioeconomic indexes of occupational standing. First, gender differences appear both in the relationships between occupational socioeconomic standing and prestige and in the socioeconomic characteristics of occupational incumbents. Second, occupational wage rates appear to be far less highly correlated, both within and across generations, than occupational education. Third, the latter finding led us to wonder whether the use of prestige-validated socioeconomic indexes may overestimate the importance of the economic standing of occupations in the stratification process. Thus, we developed structural equation models in which the construction of socioeconomic indexes was embedded in the stratification process. These models were estimated using data for men and women in the 1994 GSS.

For example, one of our models considered relationships among father's occupational status, the status of a man or woman's first occupation, and the status of his or her current or last occupation. In this rudimentary model, we specified that the

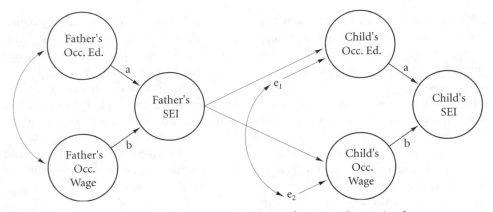

Figure 9.1   Illustrative Model of Intergenerational Stratification in Occupational
Socioeconomic Status

status of first occupation depends on that
of father's occupation, whereas the status of
current or last occupation depends upon father's occupation and first occupation. To
be sure, this is scarcely a complete model of
the stratification process, but it is sufficient
to generate new estimates of the weights of
the socioeconomic index components. At
each of the three stages of the model—father's occupation, first occupation, and current or last occupation—we assume that an
SEI composite is completely determined by
measures of occupational education and occupational wages (Hauser and Warren
1997, 236). Figure 9.1 illustrates part of
this model with measures of father's and
child's occupational education and occupational wage. The effects of father on child
identify the weights of occupational education, a, and occupational wage, b, in the
SEI. To our surprise, we found that the
weight of the wage rate is negligible, that is,
b = 0. Thus, in the GSS data the process of
occupational stratification is best described
by relationships among occupation-based
measures of educational attainment, not
the combination of occupation-based measures of educational attainment and wage

rates. Our findings from the socioeconomic
model point to occupational differentiation
by education as a central feature of the
stratification process.

Discussion

We are thus led to question the value of traditional socioeconomic indexes of occupational standing, including those that we
constructed. If the 1994 GSS data are a reliable guide, we would do better—in studies
of the stratification process—to index occupations by their educational level alone than
by any of the usual, weighted combinations
of educational level and earnings. However,
given the modest sensitivity of occupational
status correlations to differences in model
specification, we would not suggest any
wholesale effort to reevaluate previous findings about levels, trends, and differentials in
occupational stratification. It would be sufficient, we think, to suggest that previously estimated levels of correlation are slightly too
low. Finally, we would caution that our findings about the relative importance of occupational education and occupational wage
rates are specific to models of the stratifica-

tion process. Just as the relative weights of occupational education and wage rates differ between prestige and socioeconomic outcomes, so they may also differ across other outcomes (e.g., health, wellbeing, social participation, or political choice). If there is any general conclusion to be drawn from our analysis, it is that we ought to move toward a more specific and disaggregated appraisal of the effects of occupational characteristics on social, psychological, economic, political, and health outcomes. Although composite measures of occupational status may have heuristic uses, the global concept of occupational status is scientifically obsolete.

REFERENCES

Duncan, Otis Dudley. 1961. "A Socioeconomic Index for All Occupations." Pages 109–138 in *Occupations and Social Status*, edited by Albert J. Reiss, Jr. New York: Free Press.

Erikson, Robert, and John H. Goldthorpe. 1992. *The Constant Flux: A Study of Class Mobility in Industrial Societies*. Oxford: Clarendon Press.

Fox, John. 1991. *Regression Diagnostics*, edited by Michael S. Lewis-Beck. Quantitative Applications in the Social Sciences, Vol. 07–079. Newbury Park, CA: Sage.

Friendly, Michael. 1991. *SAS System for Statistical Graphics*. SAS Series in Statistical Applications. Cary, NC: SAS Institute.

Goldthorpe, John H. 1980. *Social Mobility and Class Structure in Modern Britain*. Oxford: Clarendon Press.

Goldthorpe, John, and Keith Hope. 1974. *The Social Grading of Occupations: A New Approach and Scale*. Oxford: Clarendon Press.

Hauser, Robert M., and John Robert Warren. 1997. "Socioeconomic Indexes of Occupational Status: A Review, Update, and Critique." Pages 177–298 in *Sociological Methodology, 1997*, edited by Adrian Raftery. Cambridge: Blackwell Publishers.

Hauser, Robert M., William H. Sewell, and John Robert Warren. 1994. "Education, Occupation, and Earnings in the Long Run: Men and Women from Adolescence to Midlife." Paper presented at the 1994 Meeting of the American Sociological Association. University of Wisconsin-Madison.

Hodge, Robert W. 1981. "The Measurement of Occupational Status." *Social Science Research* 10:396–415.

Jencks, Christopher, Lauri Perman, and Lee Rainwater. 1988. "What is a Good Job? A New Measure of Labor-Market Success." *American Journal of Sociology* 93:1322–57.

Nakao, Keiko, and Judith Treas. 1994. "Updating Occupational Prestige and Socioeconomic Scores: How the New Measures Measure Up." Pages 1–72 in *Sociological Methodology, 1994*, edited by Peter Marsden. Washington, D.C.: American Sociological Association.

Warren, John Robert, Jennifer T. Sheridan, and Robert M. Hauser. 1998. "Choosing a Measure of Occupational Standing: How Useful are Composite Measures in Analyses of Gender Inequality in Occupational Attainment?" *Sociological Methods and Research* 27:3–76.

Wright, Erik Olin. 1985. *Classes*. London: Verso.

10

Inequality in Earnings

Trends and Implications

MARTINA MORRIS
BRUCE WESTERN

Ironically, as some sociologists were debating whether social classes had finally withered away (e.g., Clark and Lipset 1991), earnings inequality in the United States quietly started to grow again. Median income declined and the distribution of income grew markedly more unequal during the last three decades of the twentieth century, reversing a long trend of earnings growth and equalization. Writers in economics and the popular press described, analyzed, and debated this new trend. Sociologists, on the other hand, were, and to a large extent remain, remarkably silent about it. We have continued to address trends in the earnings "gaps" (by gender and race) or focus on poverty alone, leaving the broader trends—stagnation in earnings levels and growing polarization in earnings distributions—to others. We have continued to study how people are allocated to positions in the earnings distribution, rather than the structure of those positions. If the structure had been stable, a narrow focus on allocation might be justifiable. But this has been a period of pervasive economic restructuring, and the impact on earnings distributions both within and between groups has been profound. Sociological theory provides a rich framework for understanding the broad changes now underway, and we offer this essay as a challenge to the field to critically evaluate the evidence and provide a sociologically informed response.

According to Simon Kuznets (1955), inequality should not be rising in late twentieth-century United States. The Kuznets curve predicts that economic development has an inverted U-shaped relationship to inequality. Inequality first rises as capital is concentrated in the hands of investors, then falls as economic development generates widespread prosperity. For much of this century, in fact, inequality followed the Kuznets path. Earnings inequality peaked on the eve of the Great Depression, then began a long secular decline.[1] Postwar prosperity was marked by a rise in median earnings and stability in earnings inequality. The annual income of the median worker

---

Figure 10.1   The lines trace the real value of wages at each decile relative to its value in 1973. Sample is all workers, from the CPS Outgoing Rotation Group File. The data can be obtained online at http//www.epinet.org/datazone/data/orghourlyxoffs_all.xls. For more analysis of these data see Bernstein and Mishel (1997).

more than doubled from 1950 to 1970, with those at the bottom of the earnings scale making even greater progress. It was, as many observed in chastened hindsight, a rising tide that lifted all boats. These trends reversed in the early 1970s. Median earnings stabilized in 1973 and then began to decline. In 1980 earnings inequality began to rise rapidly. The net result of these two trends was that by the early 1990s, nearly 80 percent of workers earned less than their counterparts in the 1960s.[2] Although there appeared to be a small uptick in median wages in the last years of the 1990s, it will take decades to make up the losses.

Data from the Current Population Survey (CPS) show these trends in terms of hourly wages (Figure 10.1).[3] Each line in the figure represents the dollar value of the wage decile cutoff indexed to its value in 1973. The line for decile 1, for example,

represents the relative wage earned by the worker at the tenth percentile of the wage distribution over time. If we follow it across the graph, we can see that workers in this decile saw their real wages rise slightly from the mid-1970s to the beginning of the 1980s, fall precipitously during the 1980s, and continue to decline at a lower rate during the 1990s. By 1996, wages for these workers had fallen about 13 percent in real terms (and by 20 percent if the sample is restricted to men). Wages at the median (fifth decile) stagnated through most of the 1970s and 1980s, then fell sharply in the 1990s, losing a total of about 10 percent over the two decades. Only those at the top (ninth decile) experienced some wage gains, a rise of about 5 percent, with most of the increase coming in the late 1980s.

Comparative data suggest that among industrialized countries, only the United

Kingdom experienced a similar growth in wage inequality. In France, Germany, and Italy, the earnings ratio of the first to the fifth decile among men declined or remained stable. And while British wage inequality grew, it was driven by gains at the top, not losses at the bottom.[4] The broad stagnation of living standards coupled with a collapse of wages at the bottom is thus a peculiarly American disease, at least in the industrialized democracies.

So the American story since the 1970s is not that the rich got richer and the poor got poorer, but that virtually everyone lost ground, and those at the bottom lost the most. Although mean trends differ by race and sex, all groups experienced a rise in within-group inequality. This leads to a set of research questions that breaks out of the usual "wage-gap" framework and begins to address the general issue of changes in labor market dynamics. We review below supply side, demand side, and institutional accounts of change.

Supply Side Accounts

On the supply side, the labor force expanded by more than 44 million workers from 1950 to 1980, a 70 percent increase. The baby boom, rising women's labor force participation, and growing immigration all increased the share of workers with little work experience, tenure or education. Although a rising supply of "unskilled" workers seems like a natural explanation for falling wages at the bottom of the distribution, the evidence suggests little role for most of these supply side changes:

1. The baby boom generation, born between 1946 and 1964, entered the workforce from 1964 to 1982, a pe-riod when earnings of low-wage workers held relatively steady. The dramatic decline in wages at the bottom occurred during the entry of the subsequent "baby bust" cohort, which should instead have benefited from the shrinking labor supply.

2. From 1950 to 1994, the fraction of women working for pay increased from 34 percent to 59 percent. Despite this increase in supply, women's wages rose at every decile of the distribution. Occupational segregation also remained high, indicating the persistence of largely separate labor markets for men and women and suggesting that the impact of women's entry on men's wages was probably small.

3. Immigration, and in particular the rapid influx of Asians and Latin Americans following the 1965 Amendments to the Immigration and Nationality Act, is the one supply side effect that finds some support in the data. Studies find a substantial impact of immigration on the rise in the wage differential between high school dropouts and graduates.

On the boundary between supply and demand explanations lies the debate over the role of education and "skill." Despite a rising supply of workers with a college education,[5] their relative wages began to rise in the mid-1980s. This came to be called a "rise" in the college premium, but it was almost entirely driven by the *collapse* in the earnings of high school graduates and dropouts. Initially, the growth in the education wage gap was attributed to a trade-induced decline in domestic demand for high-school educated workers driven by the relocation of manufacturing to less-developed countries. However, conflicting findings led to the rise of an alternative hypothesis: a rising demand for skill driven by "skill-biased technological change." The proponents of this argument claim that computerization of the workplace and other technological advances increased the demand for high-skill workers well beyond the increase in supply. One study reported that computer use at work raised earnings by as much as 19 percent. Critics countered with an analysis showing that the use of pencils and "sitting while working" had similarly strong effects. Despite the continuing weakness of the empirical evidence, skill-biased technological change remains the dominant explanation among labor economists for the increase in earnings inequality.

Demand Side Accounts

The structure of the labor market also changed substantially during the postwar boom years. Restructuring took two forms: continuing decline in manufacturing employment leading to the rise of a "service economy" and an increase in market-mediated employment relations that featured outsourcing, subcontracting, and temporary, contingent, and part-time work contracts. The trend toward growing employment in the service sector and shrinking employment in manufacturing has continued almost linearly since the 1940s, and by the mid-1990s the service sector accounted for more than 80 percent of total employment. Service sector jobs have traditionally paid less, offered fewer benefits, and relied more on part-time employment. Still, there was no sharp increase in deindustrialization in the 1970s or 1980s that would account for the sharp changes in earnings during these decades. In addition, inequality is growing within the sectors, not simply between them, and declines in manufacturing wages were also substantial. So the simpler versions of the deindustrialization thesis have been discarded.

The "good jobs-bad jobs" debate has therefore been refocused in recent years, noting that high- and low-road employment strategies are being used together, not only within industries, but even within firms. This shifts attention to the trends in the system of employment relations often referred to as the "internal labor market." Cost reduction became an important basis of competition during the 1970s, and internal labor markets became a prime target because they are inflexible and expensive to maintain. The wave of "downsizing" that took place during the late 1980s and 1990s heralded this change. Still, the size of the shift to market-mediated employment is unclear. One study finds that contingent work rose from about 25 percent of employment in 1980 to 35 percent by the end of the decade. Other estimates have been more conservative, ranging from 5 percent to 17 percent of the labor force by the end of the decade. Although the shift to market-mediated employment may not be as rapid or revolutionary as some scholars have suggested, the rise in job instability is well documented now, and it has been linked to the declining wages of workers who are not college educated.

Institutional Accounts

Market explanations have dominated research on rising inequality, but supply and demand are clearly mediated by institutional constraints. Relatively fewer studies have examined the role of institutional changes, and those that have focus chiefly on the minimum wage and unions. Both appear to explain part of the decline in wages at the bottom of the distribution. The federal minimum wage was frozen at $3.35/hour from 1980 to 1990. Although less than 10 percent of the working population typically makes the minimum wage, one estimate attributes about 17 percent of the growth in the gap between the wages of college graduates and high-school dropouts to the freeze. The 1990 increase is estimated to have reduced the previous decade's growth in wage inequality by about 30 percent. The decline in unionization may also have played a role. In 1970 unions represented about 27 percent of all wage and salary earners in the United States; by 1993 only 15 percent. When a job change is accompanied by the loss of union status, the wage penalty is on the order of 20 percent after controlling for other worker characteristics. Some studies suggest that the decline in union density may account for about 20 percent of the overall rise in male wage inequality and as much as 50 percent of the rise for male blue-collar workers. As with other potential explanatory factors, however, there is also evidence of increasing earnings inequality among union members.

An increasingly "globalized" economy provides the context in which all of these trends have emerged. Imports from less developed countries (LDCs) are typically produced by low-skill labor, and LDC imports increased by 75 percent between 1978 and 1990. Low-wage imports may be an important cause of declining demand for low-skill U.S. workers, but here again the empirical evidence is mixed. Capital mobility may also raise inequality by diverting investment to countries with low-wage labor, thus reducing labor demand in higher wage countries. In contrast to the theory, however, spending on new plants and equipment overseas by U.S. multinationals has been a declining proportion of total U.S. economic activity.

The Future of Inequality

What does the future hold for earnings inequality in America? That will depend in part on the underlying causal factors and in part on the public response to the current trends. As the review above suggests, the trends are at least now well-documented, but there is little consensus on the causal forces. What is clear is that the simplistic Kuznets curve cannot adequately represent the trends in contemporary inequality, if, indeed, it ever was adequate. Local earnings dynamics increasingly reflect the intersection of national political forces and the growing global reach of capital. At the most basic level, it is a question of whether markets or politics will have the upper hand in earnings determination. If market forces dominate, we would expect that the lower and middle classes will continue to lose the benefits of unionization, internal labor markets, and minimum wage laws, thus producing an increasingly bipolar society as the inequality-reducing institutional reforms of New Deal capitalism erode. Under this scenario, the United States is not becoming like Western Europe, which is likely to bear the continuing imprint of its more deeply institutionalized welfare capitalism, but rather like South America and Eastern Europe, with their (sometimes militarily enforced) laissez-faire systems.

The relocation of manufacturing jobs to less industrialized and lower wage countries has led some to predict that the United States and other highly industrialized countries will evolve into homogeneously high-skill (and, presumably, low inequality) labor markets.

However, this view could only be seen from an ivory tower. Over 80 percent of the U.S. labor force is already employed in the service sector. If this sector holds the clues to our future, then wage stagnation and polarization will clearly continue. Many of the lowest paid, least challenging jobs—cashiers, sales persons, truck drivers, receptionists, and information clerks—are in the service sector. They will never be exported. These particular jobs are also in the top 10 in terms of projected employment growth, led, at number one, by cashiers.

Cross-national variation in earnings inequality, however, makes it clear that distributional trends are not driven by a single logic of, say, capitalist development or post-industrialism. Other countries face similar pressures from global markets and structural change, but have maintained a level of equality that is unknown in the United States. The difference is in politics, not markets. It is possible, therefore, to use political institutions to reverse the trends in wage decline and polarization. To the extent that rising inequality in U.S. earnings can be traced to institutional change, and these are the explanations with the most consistent empirical support, inequality is likely to persist. Institutional change tends to be slow, and trends in institutional change are reversed even more slowly. The prospects for a reversal in declining union organization, for example, are dim. Job growth in the nonunion sector of the economy is so rapid that the maintenance of current levels of private sector unionization would require organizing efforts unprece-

dented in the postwar period. Despite the massive redistribution of income and wealth to those at the top, there seems to be little political support for institutional changes that would reverse these trends.

Why is it, then, that the decline and polarization of earnings has occasioned so little political response among the population at large? There are many possible reasons. One is that most people now rely on two incomes to support a family, so that individual earnings losses are masked by income pooling. Another is the explosion of consumer credit, which makes it possible for many to buy what they can no longer afford. Finally, political apathy may be one of the by-products of a high level of inequality. As those at the bottom of the income distribution feel increasingly remote from the mainstream, alienation from politics grows, election turnout declines, and the public sphere shrinks to include just the affluent. The consistuency for redistribution vanishes. In this scenario, graphically detailed by Massey in his provocative 1996 presidential address to the Population Association of America, the persistence of high inequality seems especially likely. The analysis may seem bleak, but it is supported by research that shows that political participation, political information, membership in voluntary associations, and a host of other indicators of political efficacy depend closely on income. The rise in inequality could thus become self-sustaining.

Sociology clearly has an important role to play in understanding the recent trends in economic inequality. It is not just a question of earnings, but of fundamental changes in politics, markets, and life chances. The current earnings trends challenge us to rethink our disciplinary perspective and reintegrate our theoretical and empirical agenda, or else lose the heart of our field to other disciplines.

NOTES

1. Here and throughout, detailed keys to the literature are provided by Morris and Western (1999). Other summaries of the literature include Levy and Murnane (1992) and Danziger and Gottschalk (1993; 1995). Comparative trends in earnings inequality are described in OECD (1996, ch. 6).

2. The precise figure depends on the measure used to adjust for inflation, and this is a hotly contested issue.

3. There are at least four different measures of economic well-being that can be examined here: hourly wages, annual earnings, household total earnings, and wealth. All show the same basic pattern, with pronounced rises in inequality. We show hourly wages here because they do not confound labor supply components, such as hours worked and income pooling, with labor pricing. Wages thus better represent the job structure.

4. Inequality does appear to be on the rise in post-socialist economies, although the quantitative evidence here is less reliable. The forces making for such change are, at least on the surface, very different than those at work in the United States, except insofar as one understands them as proceeding from "marketization" in its various forms (e.g., de-unionization, deregulation of wages).

5. About 25 percent of the 25–34-year-old population had a four-year college degree in 1995.

REFERENCES

Bernstein, Jared, and Lawrence Mishel. 1997. "Has Wage Inequality Stopped Growing?" *Monthly Labor Review* 120:3–16.

Clark, Terry N., and Seymour M. Lipset. 1991. "Are Social Classes Dying?" *International Sociology* 6:397–410.

Danziger, Sheldon, and Peter Gottschalk, eds. 1993. *Uneven Tides: Rising Inequality in America.* New York.

Danziger, Sheldon, and Peter Gottschalk. 1995. *America Unequal.* Cambridge: Harvard University Press.

Kuznets, Simon. 1955. "Economic Growth and Income Inequality (Presidential Address)." *American Economic Review* 45:1–28.

Levy, Frank, and Robert Murnane. 1992. "U.S. Earnings Levels and Earnings Inequality: A Review of Recent Trends and Proposed Explanations." *Journal of Economic Literature* 30: 1333–81.

Massey, Douglas S. 1996. "The Age of Extremes: Concentrated Affluence and Poverty in the Twenty-First Century." *Demography* 33:395–412.

Morris, Martina, and Bruce Western. 1999. "Inequality in Earnings at the Close of the Twentieth Century." *Annual Review of Sociology* 25:623–57.

Organisation for Economic Cooperation and Development (OECD). 1996. *Employment Outlook.* Paris: OECD.

11

The Power Elite

C. WRIGHT MILLS

The powers of ordinary men are circumscribed by the everyday worlds in which they live, yet even in these rounds of job, family, and neighborhood they often seem driven by forces they can neither understand nor govern. 'Great changes' are beyond their control, but affect their conduct and outlook none the less. The very framework of modern society confines them to projects not their own, but from every side, such changes now press upon the men and women of the mass society, who accordingly feel that they are without purpose in an epoch in which they are without power.

But not all men are in this sense ordinary. As the means of information and of power are centralized, some men come to occupy positions in American society from which they can look down upon, so to speak, and by their decisions mightily affect, the everyday worlds of ordinary men and women. They are not made by their jobs; they set up and break down jobs for thousands of others; they are not confined by simple family responsibilities; they can escape. They may live in many hotels and houses, but they are bound by no one community. They need not merely 'meet the demands of the day and hour'; in some part, they create these demands, and cause others to meet them. Whether or not they profess their power, their technical and political experience of it far transcends that of the underlying population. What Jacob Burckhardt said of 'great men,' most Americans might well say of their elite: 'They are all that we are not.'[1]

The power elite is composed of men whose positions enable them to transcend the ordinary environments of ordinary men and women; they are in positions to make decisions having major consequences. Whether they do or do not make such decisions is less important than the fact that they do occupy such pivotal positions: their failure to act, their failure to make decisions, is itself an act that is often of greater consequence than the decisions they do make. For they are in command of the major hierarchies and organizations of modern society. They rule the big corporations. They run the machinery of the state and claim its prerogatives. They direct the military establishment. They occupy the strategic command posts of the social structure, in which are now centered the effective means of the power and the wealth and the celebrity which they enjoy.

The power elite are not solitary rulers. Advisers and consultants, spokesmen and opinion-makers are often the captains of their higher thought and decision. Immediately below the elite are the professional politicians of the middle levels of power, in the Congress and in the pressure groups, as well as among the new and old upper classes of town and city and region. Mingling with them in curious ways are those professional celebrities who live by being continually displayed but are never, so long as they remain celebrities, displayed enough. If such celebrities are not at the head of any dominating hierarchy, they do often have the power to distract the attention of the public or afford sensations to the masses, or, more directly, to gain the ear of those who do occupy positions of direct power. More or less unattached, as critics of morality and technicians of power, as spokesmen of God and creators of mass sensibility, such celebrities and consultants are part of the immediate scene in which the drama of the elite is enacted. But that drama itself is centered in the command posts of the major institutional hierarchies.

1

The truth about the nature and the power of the elite is not some secret which men of affairs know but will not tell. Such men hold quite various theories about their own roles in the sequence of event and decision. Often they are uncertain about their roles, and even more often they allow their fears and their hopes to affect their assessment of their own power. No matter how great their actual power, they tend to be less acutely aware of it than of the resistances of others to its use. Moreover, most American men of affairs have learned well the rhetoric of public relations, in some cases even to the point of using it when they are alone, and thus coming to believe it. The personal awareness of the actors is only one of the several sources one must examine in order to understand the higher circles. Yet many who believe that there is no elite, or at any rate none of any consequence, rest their argument upon what men of affairs believe about themselves, or at least assert in public.

There is, however, another view: those who feel, even if vaguely, that a compact and powerful elite of great importance does now prevail in America often base that feeling upon the historical trend of our time. They have felt, for example, the domination of the military event, and from this they infer that generals and admirals, as well as other men of decision influenced by them, must be enormously powerful. They hear that the Congress has again abdicated to a handful of men decisions clearly related to the issue of war or peace. They know that the bomb was dropped over Japan in the name of the United States of America, although they were at no time consulted about the matter. They feel that they live in a time of big decisions; they know that they are not making any. Accordingly, as they consider the present as history, they infer that at its center, making decisions or failing to make them, there must be an elite of power.

On the one hand, those who share this feeling about big historical events assume that there is an elite and that its power is great. On the other hand, those who listen carefully to the reports of men apparently involved in the great decisions often do not believe that there is an elite whose powers are of decisive consequence.

Both views must be taken into account, but neither is adequate. The way to understand the power of the American elite lies neither solely in recognizing the historic scale of events nor in accepting the personal awareness reported by men of apparent decision. Behind such men and behind the events of history, linking the two, are the major institutions of modern society. These hierarchies of state and corporation and army constitute the means of power; as such they are now of a consequence not before equaled in human history—and at their summits, there are now those command posts of modern society which offer us the sociological key to an understanding of the role of the higher circles in America.

Within American society, major national power now resides in the economic, the political, and the military domains. Other institutions seem off to the side of modern history, and, on occasion, duly subordinated to these. No family is as directly powerful in national affairs as any major corporation; no church is as directly powerful in the external biographies of young men in America today as the military establishment; no college is as powerful in the shaping of momentous events as the National Security Council. Religious, educational, and family institutions are not autonomous centers of national power; on the contrary, these decentralized areas are increasingly shaped by the big three, in which developments of decisive and immediate consequence now occur. . . .

Within each of the big three, the typical institutional unit has become enlarged, has become administrative, and, in the power of its decisions, has become centralized. Behind these developments there is a fabulous technology, for as institutions, they have incorporated this technology and guide it, even as it shapes and paces their developments.

The economy—once a great scatter of small productive units in autonomous balance—has become dominated by two or three hundred giant corporations, administratively and politically interrelated, which together hold the keys to economic decisions.

The political order, once a decentralized set of several dozen states with a weak spinal cord, has become a centralized, executive establishment which has taken up into itself many powers previously scattered, and now enters into each and every cranny of the social structure.

The military order, once a slim establishment in a context of distrust fed by state militia, has become the largest and most expensive feature of government, and, although well versed in smiling public relations, now has all the grim and clumsy efficiency of a sprawling bureaucratic domain.

In each of these institutional areas, the means of power at the disposal of decision-makers have increased enormously; their central executive powers have been enhanced; within each of them modern administrative routines have been elaborated and tightened up.

As each of these domains becomes enlarged and centralized, the consequences of its activities become greater, and its traffic with the others increases. The decisions of a handful of corporations bear upon military and political as well as upon economic developments around the world. The decisions of the military establishment rest upon and grievously affect political life as well as the very level of economic activity. The decisions made within the political domain determine economic activities and military programs. There is no longer, on the one hand, an economy, and, on the other hand, a political order containing a military establishment unimportant to politics and to money-making. There is a political economy linked, in a thousand ways, with military institutions and decisions. On each side of the world-split running through central Europe and around the Asiatic rimlands, there is an ever-increasing interlocking of economic, military, and political structures.[2] If there is government intervention in the corporate economy, so is there corporate intervention in the governmental process. In the structural sense, this triangle of power is the source of the interlocking directorate that is most important for the historical structure of the present.

The fact of the interlocking is clearly revealed at each of the points of crisis of modern capitalist society—slump, war, and boom. In each, men of decision are led to an awareness of the interdependence of the major institutional orders. In the nineteenth century, when the scale of all institutions was smaller, their liberal integration was achieved in the automatic economy, by an autonomous play of market forces, and in the automatic political domain, by the bargain and the vote. It was then assumed that out of the imbalance and friction that followed the limited decisions then possible a new equilibrium would in due course emerge. That can no longer be assumed, and it is not assumed by the men at the top of each of the three dominant hierarchies.

For given the scope of their consequences, decisions—and indecisions—in any one of these ramify into the others, and hence top decisions tend either to become co-ordinated or to lead to a commanding indecision. It has not always been like this.

When numerous small entrepreneurs made up the economy, for example, many of them could fail and the consequences still remain local; political and military authorities did not intervene. But now, given political expectations and military commitments, can they afford to allow key units of the private corporate economy to break down in slump? Increasingly, they do intervene in economic affairs, and as they do so, the controlling decisions in each order are inspected by agents of the other two, and economic, military, and political structures are interlocked.

At the pinnacle of each of the three enlarged and centralized domains, there have arisen those higher circles which make up the economic, the political, and the military elites. At the top of the economy, among the corporate rich, there are the chief executives; at the top of the political order, the members of the political directorate; at the top of the military establishment, the elite of soldier-statesmen clustered in and around the Joint Chiefs of Staff and the upper echelon. As each of these domains has coincided with the others, as decisions tend to become total in their consequence, the leading men in each of the three domains of power—the warlords, the corporation chieftains, the political directorate—tend to come together, to form the power elite of America.

2

The higher circles in and around these command posts are often thought of in terms of what their members possess: they have a greater share than other people of the things and experiences that are most highly valued. From this point of view, the elite are simply those who have the most of what there is to have, which is generally held to include money, power, and prestige—as well as all the ways of life to which these lead.[3] But the elite are not simply those who have the most, for they could not 'have the most' were it not for their positions in the great institutions. For such institutions are the necessary bases of power, of wealth, and of prestige, and at the same time, the chief means of exercising power, of acquiring and retaining wealth, and of cashing in the higher claims for prestige.

By the powerful we mean, of course, those who are able to realize their will, even if others resist it. No one, accordingly, can be truly powerful unless he has access to the command of major institutions, for it is over these institutional means of power that the truly powerful are, in the first instance, powerful. Higher politicians and key officials of government command such institutional power; so do admirals and generals, and so do the major owners and executives of the larger corporations. Not all power, it is true, is anchored in and exercised by means of such institutions, but only within and through them can power be more or less continuous and important. . . .

If we took the one hundred most powerful men in America, the one hundred wealthiest, and the one hundred most celebrated away from the institutional positions they now occupy, away from their resources of men and women and money, away from the media of mass communication that are now focused upon them— then they would be powerless and poor and uncelebrated. For power is not of a man. Wealth does not center in the person of the wealthy. Celebrity is not inherent in any personality. To be celebrated, to be wealthy, to have power requires access to major institutions, for the institutional positions

men occupy determine in large part their chances to have and to hold these valued experiences.

3

The people of the higher circles may also be conceived as members of a top social stratum, as a set of groups whose members know one another, see one another socially and at business, and so, in making decisions, take one another into account. The elite, according to this conception, feel themselves to be, and are felt by others to be, the inner circle of 'the upper social classes.'[4] They form a more or less compact social and psychological entity; they have become self-conscious members of a social class. People are either accepted into this class or they are not, and there is a qualitative split, rather than merely a numerical scale, separating them from those who are not elite. They are more or less aware of themselves as a social class and they behave toward one another differently from the way they do toward members of other classes. They accept one another, understand one another, marry one another, tend to work and to think if not together at least alike.

Now, we do not want by our definition to prejudge whether the elite of the command posts are conscious members of such a socially recognized class, or whether considerable proportions of the elite derive from such a clear and distinct class. These are matters to be investigated. Yet in order to be able to recognize what we intend to investigate, we must note something that all biographies and memoirs of the wealthy and the powerful and the eminent make clear: no matter what else they may be, the people of these higher circles are involved in a set of overlapping 'crowds' and intricately connected 'cliques.' There is a kind of mutual attraction among those who 'sit on the same terrace'—although this often becomes clear to them, as well as to others, only at the point at which they feel the need to draw the line; only when, in their common defense, they come to understand what they have in common, and so close their ranks against outsiders.

The idea of such ruling stratum implies that most of its members have similar social origins, that throughout their lives they maintain a network of informal connections, and that to some degree there is an interchangeability of position between the various hierarchies of money and power and celebrity. We must, of course, note at once that if such an elite stratum does exist, its social visibility and its form, for very solid historical reasons, are quite different from those of the noble cousinhoods that once ruled various European nations.

That American society has never passed through a feudal epoch is of decisive importance to the nature of the American elite, as well as to American society as a historic whole. For it means that no nobility or aristocracy, established before the capitalist era, has stood in tense opposition to the higher bourgeoisie. It means that this bourgeoisie has monopolized not only wealth but prestige and power as well. It means that no set of noble families has commanded the top positions and monopolized the values that are generally held in high esteem; and certainly that no set has done so explicitly by inherited right. It means that no high church dignitaries or court nobilities, no entrenched landlords with honorific accouterments, no monopolists of high army posts have opposed the enriched bourgeoisie and in the name of

birth and prerogative successfully resisted its self-making.

But this does *not* mean that there are no upper strata in the United States. That they emerged from a 'middle class' that had no recognized aristocratic superiors does not mean they remained middle class when enormous increases in wealth made their own superiority possible. Their origins and their newness may have made the upper strata less visible in America than elsewhere. But in America today there are in fact tiers and ranges of wealth and power of which people in the middle and lower ranks know very little and may not even dream. There are families who, in their well-being, are quite insulated from the economic jolts and lurches felt by the merely prosperous and those farther down the scale. There are also men of power who in quite small groups make decisions of enormous consequence for the underlying population.

The American elite entered modern history as a virtually unopposed bourgeoisie. No national bourgeoisie, before or since, has had such opportunities and advantages. Having no military neighbors, they easily occupied an isolated continent stocked with natural resources and immensely inviting to a willing labor force. A framework of power and an ideology for its justification were already at hand. Against mercantilist restriction, they inherited the principle of *laissez-faire;* against Southern planters, they imposed the principle of industrialism. The Revolutionary War put an end to colonial pretensions to nobility, as loyalists fled the country and many estates were broken up. The Jacksonian upheaval with its status revolution put an end to pretensions to monopoly of descent by the old New England families. The Civil War broke the power, and so in due course the prestige, of the antebellum South's claimants for the higher esteem. The tempo of the whole capitalist development made it impossible for an inherited nobility to develop and endure in America.

No fixed ruling class, anchored in agrarian life and coming to flower in military glory, could contain in America the historic thrust of commerce and industry, or subordinate to itself the capitalist elite—as capitalists were subordinated, for example, in Germany and Japan. Nor could such a ruling class anywhere in the world contain that of the United States when industrialized violence came to decide history. Witness the fate of Germany and Japan in the two world wars of the twentieth century; and indeed the fate of Britain herself and her model ruling class, as New York became the inevitable economic, and Washington the inevitable political capital of the western capitalist world.

4

The elite who occupy the command posts may be seen as the possessors of power and wealth and celebrity; they may be seen as members of the upper stratum of a capitalistic society. They may also be defined in terms of psychological and moral criteria, as certain kinds of selected individuals. So defined, the elite, quite simply, are people of superior character and energy.

The humanist, for example, may conceive of the 'elite' not as a social level or category, but as a scatter of those individuals who attempt to transcend themselves, and accordingly, are more noble, more efficient, made out of better stuff. It does not matter whether they are poor or rich, whether they hold high position or low, whether they are

acclaimed or despised; they are elite because of the kind of individuals they are. The rest of the population is mass, which, according to this conception, sluggishly relaxes into uncomfortable mediocrity.[5]

This is the sort of socially unlocated conception which some American writers with conservative yearnings have recently sought to develop. But most moral and psychological conceptions of the elite are much less sophisticated, concerning themselves not with individuals but with the stratum as a whole. Such ideas, in fact, always arise in a society in which some people possess more than do others of what there is to possess. People with advantages are loath to believe that they just happen to be people with advantages.

They come readily to define themselves as inherently worthy of what they possess; they come to believe themselves 'naturally' elite; and, in fact, to imagine their possessions and their privileges as natural extensions of their own elite selves. In this sense, the idea of the elite as composed of men and women having a finer moral character is an ideology of the elite as a privileged ruling stratum, and this is true whether the ideology is elite-made or made up for it by others.

In eras of equalitarian rhetoric, the more intelligent or the more articulate among the lower and middle classes, as well as guilty members of the upper, may come to entertain ideas of a counter-elite. In western society, as a matter of fact, there is a long tradition and varied images of the poor, the exploited, and the oppressed as the truly virtuous, the wise, and the blessed. Stemming from Christian tradition, this moral idea of a counter-elite composed of essentially higher types condemned to a lowly station, may be and has been used by the underlying population to justify harsh criticism of ruling elites and to celebrate utopian images of a new elite to come.

The moral conception of the elite, however, is not always merely an ideology of the overprivileged or a counter-ideology of the underprivileged. It is often a fact: having controlled experiences and select privileges, many individuals of the upper stratum do come in due course to approximate the types of character they claim to embody. Even when we give up—as we must—the idea that the elite man or woman is born with an elite character, we need not dismiss the idea that their experiences and trainings develop in them characters of a specific type. . . .

5

These several notions of the elite, when appropriately understood, are intricately bound up with one another, and we shall use them all in this examination of American success. We shall study each of several higher circles as offering candidates for the elite, and we shall do so in terms of the major institutions making up the total society of America; within and between each of these institutions, we shall trace the interrelations of wealth and power and prestige. But our main concern is with the power of those who now occupy the command posts, and with the role which they are enacting in the history of our epoch.

Such an elite may be conceived as omnipotent, and its powers thought of as a great hidden design. Thus, in vulgar Marxism, events and trends are explained by reference to 'the will of the bourgeoisie'; in Nazism, by reference to 'the conspiracy of the Jews'; by the petty right in America today, by reference to 'the hidden force' of Communist spies. According to such notions of the omnipotent elite as historical cause, the elite is never an entirely visible agency. It is, in fact, a secular substitute for the will of God, being realized in a sort of providential design, except that usually non-elite men are thought capable of opposing it and eventually overcoming it.

The opposite view—of the elite as impotent—is now quite popular among liberal-minded observers. Far from being omnipotent, the elites are thought to be so scattered as to lack any coherence as a historical force. Their invisibility is not the invisibility of secrecy but the invisibility of the multitude. Those who occupy the formal places of authority are so checkmated—by other elites exerting pressure, or by the public as an electorate, or by constitutional codes—that, although there may be upper classes, there is no ruling class; although there may be men of power, there is no power elite; although there may be a system of stratification, it has no effective top. In the extreme, this view of the elite, as weakened by compromise and disunited to the point of nullity, is a substitute for impersonal collective fate; for, in this view, the decisions of the visible men of the higher circles do not count in history.

Internationally, the image of the omnipotent elite tends to prevail. All good events and pleasing happenings are quickly imputed by the opinion-makers to the leaders of their own nation; all bad events and unpleasant experiences are imputed to the enemy abroad. In both cases, the omnipotence of evil rulers or of virtuous leaders is assumed. Within the nation, the use of such rhetoric is rather more complicated: when men speak of the power of their own party or circle, they and their leaders are, of course, impotent; only 'the people' are omnipotent. But, when they speak of the power of their opponent's party or circle, they impute to them omnipotence; 'the people' are now powerlessly taken in.

More generally, American men of power tend, by convention, to deny that they are powerful. No American runs for office in order to rule or even govern, but only to serve; he does not become a bureaucrat or even an official, but a public servant. And nowadays, as I have already pointed out, such postures have become standard features of the public-relations programs of all men of power. So firm a part of the style of power-wielding have they become that conservative writers readily misinterpret them as indicating a trend toward an 'amorphous power situation.'

But the 'power situation' of America today is less amorphous than is the perspective of those who see it as a romantic confusion. It is less a flat, momentary 'situation' than a graded, durable structure. And if those who occupy its top grades are not omnipotent, neither are they impotent. It is the form and the height of the gradation of power that we must examine if we would understand the degree of power held and exercised by the elite.

If the power to decide such national issues as are decided were shared in an absolutely equal way, there would be no power elite; in fact, there would be no *gradation* of power, but only a radical homogeneity. At the opposite extreme as well, if the power to decide issues were absolutely monopolized by one small group, there would be no gradation of power; there would simply be this small group in command, and below it, the undifferentiated, dominated masses. American society today represents neither the one nor the other of these extremes, but a conception of them is

none the less useful: it makes us realize more clearly the question of the structure of power in the United States and the position of the power elite within it.

Within each of the most powerful institutional orders of modern society there is a gradation of power. The owner of a roadside fruit stand does not have as much power in any area of social or economic or political decision as the head of a multi-million-dollar fruit corporation; no lieutenant on the line is as powerful as the Chief of Staff in the Pentagon; no deputy sheriff carries as much authority as the President of the United States. Accordingly, the problem of defining the power elite concerns the level at which we wish to draw the line. By lowering the line, we could define the elite out of existence; by raising it, we could make the elite a very small circle indeed. In a preliminary and minimum way, we draw the line crudely, in charcoal as it were: By the power elite, we refer to those political, economic, and military circles which as an intricate set of overlapping cliques share decisions having at least national consequences. In so far as national events are decided, the power elite are those who decide them. . . .

6

It is not my thesis that for all epochs of human history and in all nations, a creative minority, a ruling class, an omnipotent elite, shape all historical events. Such statements, upon careful examination, usually turn out to be mere tautologies,[6] and even when they are not, they are so entirely general as to be useless in the attempt to understand the history of the present. The minimum definition of the power elite as those who decide whatever is decided of major consequence, does not imply that the members of this elite are always and necessarily the history-makers; neither does it imply that they never are. We must not confuse the conception of the elite, which we wish to define, with one theory about their role: that they are the history-makers of our time. To define the elite, for example, as 'those who rule America' is less to define a conception than to state one hypothesis about the role and power of that elite. No matter how we might define the elite, the extent of its members' power is subject to historical variation. If, in a dogmatic way, we try to include that variation in our generic definition, we foolishly limit the use of a needed conception. If we insist that the elite be defined as a strictly coordinated class that continually and absolutely rules, we are closing off from our view much to which the term more modestly defined might open to our observation. In short, our definition of the power elite cannot properly contain dogma concerning the degree and kind of power that ruling groups everywhere have. Much less should it permit us to smuggle into our discussion a theory of history.

During most of human history, historical change has not been visible to the people who were involved in it, or even to those enacting it. Ancient Egypt and Mesopotamia, for example, endured for some four hundred generations with but slight changes in their basic structure. That is six and a half times as long as the entire Christian era, which has only prevailed some sixty generations; it is about eighty times as long as the five generations of the United States' existence. But now the tempo of change is so rapid, and the means of observation so accessible, that the interplay of event and decision seems often to be quite historically visible, if we will only look carefully and from an adequate vantage point.

When knowledgeable journalists tell us that 'events, not men, shape the big decisions,' they are echoing the theory of history as Fortune, Chance, Fate, or the work of The Unseen Hand. For 'events' is merely a modern word for these older ideas, all of which separate men from history-making, because all of them lead us to believe that history goes on behind men's backs. History is drift with no mastery; within it there is action but no deed; history is mere happening and the event intended by no one.[7]

The course of events in our time depends more on a series of human decisions than on any inevitable fate. The sociological meaning of 'fate' is simply this: that, when the decisions are innumerable and each one is of small consequence, all of them add up in a way no man intended—to history as fate. But not all epochs are equally fateful. As the circle of those who decide is narrowed, as the means of decision are centralized and the consequences of decisions become enormous, then the course of great events often rests upon the decisions of determinable circles. This does not necessarily mean that the same circle of men follow through from one event to another in such a way that all of history is merely their plot. The power of the elite does not necessarily mean that history is not also shaped by a series of small decisions, none of which are thought out. It does not mean that a hundred small arrangements and compromises and adaptations may not be built into the going policy and the living event. The idea of the power elite implies nothing about the process of decision-making as such: it is an attempt to delimit the social areas within which that process, whatever its character, goes on. It is a conception of who is involved in the process.

The degree of foresight and control of those who are involved in decisions that count may also vary. The idea of the power elite does not mean that the estimations and calculated risks upon which decisions are made are not often wrong and that the consequences are sometimes, indeed often, not those intended. Often those who make decisions are trapped by their own inadequacies and blinded by their own errors.

Yet in our time the pivotal moment does arise, and at that moment, small circles do decide or fail to decide. In either case, they are an elite of power. The dropping of the A-bombs over Japan was such a moment; the decision on Korea was such a moment; the confusion about Quemoy and Matsu, as well as before Dienbienphu were such moments; the sequence of maneuvers which involved the United States in World War II was such a 'moment.' Is it not true that much of the history of our times is composed of such moments? And is not that what is meant when it is said that we live in a time of big decisions, of decisively centralized power?

Most of us do not try to make sense of our age by believing in a Greek-like, eternal recurrence, nor by a Christian belief in a salvation to come, nor by any steady march of human progress. Even though we do not reflect upon such matters, the chances are we believe with Burckhardt that we live in a mere succession of events; that sheer continuity is the only principle of history. History is merely one thing after another; history is meaningless in that it is not the realization of any determinate plot. It is true, of course, that our sense of continuity, our feeling for the history of our time, is affected by crisis. But we seldom look beyond the immediate crisis or the crisis felt to be just ahead. We believe neither in fate nor providence; and we assume, without talking about it, that 'we'—as a nation—can decisively shape the future but that 'we' as individuals somehow cannot do so.

Any meaning history has, 'we' shall have to give to it by our actions. Yet the fact is that although we are all of us within history we do not all possess equal powers to make history. To pretend that we do is sociological nonsense and political irresponsibility. It is nonsense because any group or any individual is limited, first of all, by the technical and institutional means of power at its command; we do not all have equal access to the means of power that now exist, nor equal influence over their use. To pretend that 'we' are all history-makers is politically irresponsible because it obfuscates any attempt to locate responsibility for the consequential decisions of men who do have access to the means of power.

From even the most superficial examination of the history of the western society we learn that the power of decision-makers is first of all limited by the level of technique, by the *means* of power and violence and organization that prevail in a given society. In this connection we also learn that there is a fairly straight line running upward through the history of the West; that the means of oppression and exploitation, of violence and destruction, as well as the means of production and reconstruction, have been progressively enlarged and increasingly centralized.

As the institutional means of power and the means of communications that tie them together have become steadily more efficient, those now in command of them have come into command of instruments of rule quite unsurpassed in the history of mankind. And we are not yet at the climax of their development. We can no longer lean upon or take soft comfort from the historical ups and downs of ruling groups of previous epochs. In that sense, Hegel is correct: we learn from history that we cannot learn from it.

NOTES

1. Jacob Burckhardt, *Force and Freedom* (New York: Pantheon Books, 1943), pp. 303 ff.

2. Cf. Hans Gerth and C. Wright Mills, *Character and Social Structure* (New York: Harcourt, Brace, 1953), pp. 457 ff.

3. The statistical idea of choosing some value and calling those who have the most of it an elite derives, in modern times, from the Italian economist, Pareto, who puts the central point in this way: 'Let us assume that in every branch of human activity each individual is given an index which stands as a sign of his capacity, very much the way grades are given in the various subjects in examinations in school. The highest type of lawyer, for instance, will be given 10. The man who does not get a client will be given 1—reserving zero for the man who is an out-and-out idiot. To the man who has made his millions—honestly or dishonestly as the case may be—we will give 10. To the man who has earned his thousands we will give 6; to such as just manage to keep out of the poor-house, 1, keeping zero for those who get in. . . . So let us make a class of people who have the highest indices in their branch of activity, and to that class give the name of *elite*.' Vilfredo Pareto, *The Mind and Society* (New York: Harcourt, Brace, 1935), par. 2027 and 2031. Those who follow this approach end up not with one elite, but with a number corresponding to the number of values they select. Like many rather abstract ways of reasoning, this one is useful because it forces us to think in a clear-cut way. For a skillful use of this approach, see the work of Harold D. Lasswell, in particular, *Politics: Who Gets What, When, How* (New York: McGraw-Hill, 1936); and for a more systematic use, H. D. Lasswell and Abraham Kaplan, *Power and Society* (New Haven: Yale University Press, 1950).

4. The conception of the elite as members of a top social stratum, is, of course, in line with the prevailing common-sense view of stratification. Technically, it is closer to 'status group' than to 'class,' and has been very well stated by Joseph A. Schumpeter, 'Social Classes in an Ethically Homogeneous Environment,' *Imperialism and Social Classes* (New York: Augustus M. Kelley, Inc., 1951), pp. 133 ff., especially pp. 137–47. Cf. also his *Capitalism, Socialism and Democracy,* 3rd ed. (New York: Harper, 1950), Part II. For the distinction between class and status groups, see *From Max Weber: Essays in Sociology* (trans. and ed. by Gerth and Mills (New York: Oxford University Press, 1946). For an analysis of Pareto's conception of the elite compared with Marx's conception of classes, as well as data on France, see Raymond Aron, 'Social Structure and Ruling Class,' *British Journal of Sociology,* vol. I, nos. 1 and 2 (1950).

5. The most popular essay in recent years which defines the elite and the mass in terms of a morally evaluated character-type is probably José Ortega y Gasset's, *The Revolt of the Masses,* 1932 (New York: New American Library, Mentor Edition, 1950), esp. pp. 91 ff.

6. As in the case, quite notably, of Gaetano Mosca, *The Ruling Class* (New York: McGraw-Hill, 1939). For a sharp analysis of Mosca, see Fritz Morstein Marx, 'The Bureaucratic State,' *Review of Politics,* vol. I, 1939, pp. 457 ff. Cf. also Mills, 'On Intellectual Craftsmanship,' April 1952, mimeographed, Columbia College, February 1955.

7. Cf. Karl Löwith, *Meaning in History* (Chicago: University of Chicago Press, 1949), pp. 125 ff. for concise and penetrating statements of several leading philosophies of history.

12

Who Rules America?

Power and Politics

G. WILLIAM DOMHOFF

Do corporations have far too much power in the United States? Does the federal government ignore the interests of everyday people? The great majority of Americans—70 to 75 percent in some surveys—answer "yes" to both questions.[1] This chapter explains why their answers are accurate even though there is freedom of speech, the possibility of full political participation, and increasing equality of opportunity due to the civil rights and women's movements. In other words, it attempts to resolve a seeming paradox that has bedeviled social scientists and political activists for a long time: How is it possible to have such extreme corporate domination in a democratic country?

This paradox is made all the more striking because corporations do not have as much power in most other democratic countries. The wealth and income differences between people at the top and the bottom are not as great, and the safety net for those who are poor, ill, or elderly is stronger. Why does the richest nation in the world also have the most poverty compared to any other democratic country?

Using a wide range of systematic empirical findings, this chapter shows how the owners and top-level managers in large companies work together to maintain themselves as the core of the dominant power group. Their corporations, banks, and agribusinesses form a *corporate community* that shapes the federal government on the policy issues of interest to it, issues that have a major impact on the income, job security, and well-being of most other Americans. At the same time, there is competition within the corporate community for profit opportunities, which can lead to highly visible policy conflicts among rival corporate leaders that are sometimes fought out in Congress. Yet the corporate community is cohesive on the policy issues that affect its general welfare, which is often at stake when political challenges are made by organized workers, liberals, or strong environmentalists. The chapter therefore deals with another seeming paradox: How can a highly competitive group of corporate leaders cooperate enough to work their common will in the political and policy arenas?. . .

Partly because the owners and high-level managers within the corporate community share great wealth and common economic interests, but also due to political opposition to their interests, they band together to develop their own social institutions—gated neighborhoods, private schools, exclusive social clubs, debutante balls, and secluded summer resorts. These social institutions create social cohesion and a sense of group belonging, a "we" feeling, and thereby mold wealthy people into a *social upper class*. In addition, the owners and managers supplement their small numbers by financing and directing a wide variety of nonprofit organizations—e.g., tax-free foundations, think tanks, and policy-discussion groups—to aid them in shaping public policy. The highest-ranking employees in these nonprofit organizations become part of a general leadership group for the corporate community and the upper class. . . .

The Corporate Community and the Upper Class

Why does it matter whether or not the corporate community and the upper class are intertwined? If the corporate community and the upper class are essentially one and the same in terms of people and objectives, then it is more likely that they have the wealth, social cohesion, and awareness of their common interests to organize themselves well enough to dominate government. If they are separate, the wealth and status of the upper class might form a rival power base and make the power structure more open.

The nationwide social upper class has its own exclusive social institutions and is based in the ownership of great wealth. The social cohesion that develops among members of the upper class . . . is based in the two types

of relationships found in a membership network: common membership in specific social institutions and friendships based on social interactions within those institutions. Research on small groups in laboratory settings suggests that social cohesion is greatest when (1) the social groups are seen to be exclusive and of high status; and (2) when the interactions take place in relaxed and informal settings.[2] Many of the social institutions of the upper class fit these specifications very well. From the viewpoint of social psychology, the people who make up the upper class can be seen as members of numerous small groups that meet at private schools, social clubs, retreats, and resorts. . . .

Prepping for Power

From infancy through young adulthood, members of the upper class receive a distinctive education. This education begins early in life in preschools that sometimes are attached to a neighborhood church of high social status. Schooling continues during the elementary years at a local private school called a day school. The adolescent years may see the student remain at day school, but there is a strong chance that at least one or two years will be spent away from home at a boarding school in a quiet rural setting. Higher education is obtained at one of a small number of prestigious private universities. Although some upper-class children may attend public high school if they live in a secluded suburban setting, or go to a state university if there is one of great esteem and tradition in their home state, the system of formal schooling is so insulated that many upper-class students never see the inside of a public school in all their years of education. This separate educational system is important evidence for the distinctiveness of the mentality and lifestyle that exists within the upper class, because schools play a large role in transmitting the class structure to their students.

The linchpins in the upper-class educational system are the dozens of boarding schools developed in the last half of the nineteenth and the early part of the twentieth centuries, coincident with the rise of a nationwide upper class whose members desired to insulate themselves from an inner city that was becoming populated by lower-class immigrants. They become surrogate families that play a major role in creating an upper-class subculture on a national scale in America.[3] The role of boarding schools in providing connections to other upper-class social institutions is also important. . . .

Virtually all graduates of private secondary schools go on to college, and most do so at prestigious universities. Graduates of the New England boarding schools, for example, historically found themselves at three or four large Ivy League universities: Harvard, Yale, Princeton, and Columbia. However, that situation changed somewhat after World War II as the universities grew and provided more scholarships. An analysis of admission patterns for graduates of 14 prestigious boarding schools between 1953 and 1967 demonstrated this shift by showing that the percentage of their graduates attending Harvard, Yale, or Princeton gradually declined over those years from 52 to 25 percent. Information on the same 14 schools for the years 1969 to 1979 showed that the figure had bottomed out at 13 percent in 1973, 1975, and 1979, with some schools showing very little change from the late 1960s and others dropping even more dramatically.[4] Now many upper-class students attend a select handful of smaller private colleges, most of which are in the East, but a few in the South and West as well.

Graduates of private schools outside of New England most frequently attend a prominent state university in their area, but a significant minority go to eastern Ivy League and top private universities in other parts of the country. For example, the Cate School, a boarding school near Santa Barbara, California, is modeled after its New England counterparts and draws most of its students from California and other western states. In the four years between 1993 and 1996, 35 percent of the 245 graduates went to one of fifteen prestigious Ivy League schools, with Middlebury (12), Harvard (10), and Brown (7) topping the list. The other leading destinations for Cate graduates were the University of California (27), Stanford (9), University of Colorado (9), Georgetown (8), Duke (7), Vanderbilt (6), and University of Chicago (5). Or, to take another example, St. John's in Houston is a lavishly endowed day school built in the Gothic architecture typical of many universities. From 1992 through 1996, 22 percent of its 585 graduates went to the fifteen Ivy League schools used in the Cate analysis, with Princeton (27), the University of Pennsylvania (15), Cornell (13), Harvard (12), and Yale (12) the most frequent destinations. As might be expected, 105 graduates went to the University of Texas (18 percent), but Rice (49), Vanderbilt (33), and Stanford (15) were high on the list. Few graduates of either Cate or St. John's went to less prestigious state schools.[5]

Most private school graduates pursue careers in business, finance, or corporate law, which is the first evidence for the intertwining of the upper class and the corporate community. Their business-oriented preoccupations are demonstrated in the greatest detail in a study of all those who graduated from Hotchkiss between 1940 and 1950. Using the school's alumni files, the researcher followed the careers of 228 graduates from their date of graduation until 1970.[6] Fifty-six percent of the sample are either bankers or business executives, with 80 of the 91 businessmen serving as president, vice-president, or partner in their firms. Another 10 percent of the sample are lawyers, mostly as partners in large firms closely affiliated with the corporate community.

The involvement of private school graduates on boards of directors is demonstrated in a study of all alumni over the age of 45 from one of the most prestigious eastern boarding schools, St. Paul's. Using *Poor's Register of Corporations, Directors and Executives,* and *Who's Who in America,* one finds that 303 of these several thousand men are serving as officers or directors in corporations in general, and that 102 are directors of 97 corporations in the *Fortune* 800. Their involvement is especially great in the financial sector. Most striking of all, 21 graduates of St. Paul's are either officers or directors at J. P. Morgan Bank, which for a time was one of the five largest banks in the country until it merged with Chase Manhattan Bank in late 2000. This finding suggests that the alumni of particular schools may tend to cluster at specific banks or corporations.

Social Clubs

Private social clubs are a major point of orientation in the lives of upper-class adults. These clubs also have a role in differentiating members of the upper class from other members of society. The clubs of the upper class are many and varied, ranging from family-oriented country clubs and downtown men's and women's clubs to highly specialized clubs for yachtsmen, sportsmen, gardening enthusiasts, and fox hunters. Downtown men's clubs originally were places for having lunch and dinner, and occasionally for attending an evening performance or a weekend party. As upper-class families deserted the city for large suburban estates, a new kind of club, the country club, gradually took over some of these functions. The downtown club became almost entirely a luncheon club, a site to hold meetings, or a place to relax on a free afternoon. The country club, by contrast, became a haven for all members of the family. It offered social and sporting activities ranging from dances, parties, and banquets to golf, swimming, and tennis. Special group dinners were often arranged for all members on Thursday night, the traditional maid's night off across the United States.

Initiation fees, annual dues, and expenses vary from a few thousand dollars in downtown clubs to tens of thousands of dollars in some country clubs, but money is not the primary barrier in gaining membership to a club. Each club has a very rigorous screening process before accepting new members. Most require nomination by one or more active members, letters of recommendation from three to six members, and interviews with at least some members of the membership committee. Negative votes by two or three members of what is typically a 10- to 20-person committee often are enough to deny admission to the candidate. The carefulness with which new members are selected extends to a guarding of club membership lists, which are usually available only to club members. Research on clubs therefore has to be based on out-of-date membership lists that have been given to historical libraries by members or their surviving spouses.

Men and women of the upper class often belong to clubs in several cities, creating a nationwide pattern of overlapping memberships. These overlaps provide evidence for social cohesion within the upper class. An indication of the nature and extent of this overlapping is revealed in a study of membership lists for 20 clubs in several major cities across the country, including the Links in New York, the Duquesne in Pittsburgh, the Chicago in Chicago, the Pacific Union in San Francisco, and the California in Los Angeles. There is sufficient overlap among 18 of the 20 clubs to form three regional groupings and a fourth group that provides a bridge between the two largest regional groups. The several dozen men who are in three or more of the clubs, most of them very wealthy people who also sit on several corporate boards, are especially important in creating the overall pattern.[7]

The overlap of this club network with corporate boards of directors provides important evidence for the intertwining of the upper class and corporate community. In one study, the club memberships of the chairpersons and outside directors of the 20 largest industrial corporations were counted. The overlaps with upper-class clubs in general are ubiquitous, but the concentration of directors in a few clubs is especially notable. At least one director from 12 of the 20 corporations is a member of the Links Club, which is the New York meeting grounds of the national corporate establishment. Seven of General Electric's directors are members, as are four from Chrysler, four from Westinghouse, and three from IBM. In addition to the Links, several other clubs have directors from four or more corporations. Another study, using membership lists from 11 prestigious clubs in different parts of the country, confirms and extends these findings. A majority of the top 25 corporations in every major sector of the economy have directors in at least one of these clubs, and several have many more. For example, all of the 25 largest industrials have one or more directors in these 11 clubs. The Links in New York, with 79 connections to 21 industrial corporations, has the most.[8] . . .

Continuity and Upward Mobility

Americans always have believed that anyone can rise from rags to riches if they try hard enough, but in fact a rise from the bottom to the top is very rare and often a matter of luck—being at the right place at the right time. In the late nineteenth century, a wealthy upper-class Bostonian with a Harvard education, Horatio Alger, became a best-selling author by writing short fictional books on young boys who had gone from penniless adversity to great wealth. In real life, the commentators of his day pointed to three or four actual examples. Subsequent research showed that most of the business leaders of that era did not fit the Horatio Alger myth. As one historian put it, Horatio Algers appeared more frequently in magazines and textbooks than they did in reality.[9]

Since 1982, the Horatio Alger story line has been taken up by *Forbes,* a business magazine that publishes an annual list of the allegedly 400 richest Americans. "Forget old money," says the article that introduces the 1996 list. "Forget silver spoons. Great fortunes are being created almost monthly in the U.S. today by young entrepreneurs who hadn't a dime when we created this list 14 years ago."[10] But the Horatio Alger story is no less rare today than it was in the 1890s. A study of all those on the *Forbes* lists for 1995 and 1996 showed that at least 56 percent of them came from millionaire families and that another 14 percent came from the top 10 percent of the income ladder.[11]. . .

Class Awareness:
A Capitalist Mentality

The institutions that establish the owners and high-level executives of corporations as a national upper class transcend the presence or absence of any given person or family. Families can rise and fall in the class structure, but the institutions of the upper class persist. Not everyone in this nationwide upper class knows everyone else, but everybody knows somebody who knows someone in other areas of the country, thanks to a common school experience, a summer at the same resort, membership in the same social club, or membership on the same board of directors. The upper class at any given historical moment consists of a complex network of overlapping social circles knit together by the members they have in common and by the numerous signs of equal social status that emerge from a similar lifestyle. Viewed from the standpoint of social psychology, the upper class is made up of innumerable face-to-face small groups that are constantly changing in their composition as people move from one social setting to another.

Involvement in these institutions usually instills a class awareness that includes feelings of superiority, pride, and justified privilege. Deep down, most members of the upper class think they are better than other people, and therefore fully deserving of their station in life. This class awareness is based in corporate ownership, but it is reinforced by the shared social identities and interpersonal ties created through participation in the social institutions of the upper class.

The fact that the upper class is based in the ownership and control of profit-producing investments in stocks, bonds, and real estate shows that it is a capitalist class as well as a social class. Its members are not concerned simply with the interests of one corporation or business sector, but with such matters as the investment climate, the rate of profit, and the overall political climate. That is, they have a capitalist mentality.

NOTES

1. Aaron Bernstein, "Too Much Corporate Power?," *BusinessWeek*, 11 September 2000, 145–149.

2. Michael Hogg, *The Social Psychology of Group Cohesiveness* (New York: New York University Press, 1992).

3. Peter W. Cookson and Caroline Hodges Persell, *Preparing for Power: America's Elite Boarding Schools* (New York: Basic Books, 1985).

4. Michael Gordon, "Changing Patterns of Upper-Class Prep School College Placements," *Pacific Sociological Review* 12, no. 1 (1969): 23–26.

5. These figures were obtained from the admissions offices at Cate and St. John's in 1997.

6. Christopher Armstrong, "Privilege and Productivity: The Cases of Two Private Schools and Their Graduates," Ph.D. Dissertation, University of Pennsylvania, 1974.

7. G. William Domhoff, "Social Clubs, Policy-Planning Groups, and Corporations: A Network Study of Ruling-Class Cohesiveness," *Insurgent Sociologist* 5, no. 3 (1975): 173–184.

8. G. William Domhoff, "Social Clubs, Policy-Planning Groups, and Corporations: A Network Study of Ruling-Class Cohesiveness," *Insurgent Sociologist* 5, no. 3 (1975): 173–184; G. William Domhoff, *Who Rules America?*, 1st ed. (Englewood Cliffs, N.J.: Prentice-Hall, 1967).

9. William Miller, "American Historians and the Business Elite," *Journal of Economic History* 9 (1949): 184–208.

10. Ann Marsh, "The Forbes Four Hundred," *Forbes*, 14 October 1996, 100.

11. Chuck Collins, *Born on Third Base: The Sources of Wealth of the 1996 Forbes 400* (Boston: United for a Fair Economy, 1997).

13

The Future of Intellectuals and the Rise of the New Class

ALVIN W. GOULDNER

In all countries that have in the twentieth century become part of the emerging world socioeconomic order, a New Class composed of intellectuals and technical intelligentsia—not the same—enters into contention with the groups already in control of the society's economy, whether these are businessmen or party leaders. A new contest of classes and a new class system is slowly arising in the third world of developing nations, in the second world of the USSR and its client states, and in the first world of late capitalism of North America, Western Europe, and Japan.

The early historical evolution of the New Class in Western Europe, its emergence into the public sphere as a structurally differentiated and (relatively) autonomous social stratum, may be defined in terms of certain critical episodes. What follows is only a synoptic inventory of some episodes decisive in the formation of the New Class.

1. A process of secularization in which most intelligentsia are no longer trained by, living within, and subject to close supervision by a churchly organization, and thus separated from the everyday life of society.[1]

Secularization is important because it desacralizes authority-claims and facilitates challenges to definitions of social reality made by traditional authorities linked to the church. Secularization is important also because it is an infrastructure on which there develops the modern grammar of rationality, or culture of critical discourse, with its characteristic stress on self-groundedness—in Martin Heidegger's sense of the "mathematical project."[2]

2. A second episode in the emergence of the New Class is the rise of diverse vernacular languages, the corresponding decline of Latin as the language of intellectuals, and especially of their scholarly production. Latin becomes a ritual, rather than a technical language. This development further dissolves the membrane between everyday life and the intellectuals—whether clerical or secular.

3. There is a breakdown of the feudal and old regime system of personalized *patronage* relations between the old hegemonic elite and individual members of the New Class as cultural producers; and

Alvin W. Gouldner, *The Future of Intellectuals and the Rise of the New Class*. (New York: Continuum Publishing Service, 1979), pp. 1–8, 18–20, 28–29, 83–85, 102–4, 106, 110, 112–13. Reprinted by permission of Continuum International Publishing Group.

4. A corresponding growth of an anonymous *market* for the products and services of the New Class, thus allowing them to make an independent living apart from close supervision and *personalized controls by patrons*. Along with secularization, this means that the residence and work of intellectuals are both now less closely supervised by others.

They may now more readily take personal initiatives in the public, political sphere, while also having a "private" life.

5. The character and development of the emerging New Class also depended importantly on the multi-national structure of European polities. That Europe was not a single empire with a central authority able to impose a single set of norms throughout its territory, but a system of competing and autonomous states with diverse cultures and religions, meant that dissenting intellectuals, scientists, and divines could and did protect their own intellectual innovations by migrating from their home country when conditions there grew insupportable and sojourning in foreign lands. Even the enforced travel of exiled intellectuals also enabled them to enter into a European-wide communication network. In an article (as yet unpublished), Robert Wuthnow has suggested that their often extensive travel led many intellectuals to share a cosmopolitan identity transcending national limits and enhancing their autonomy from local elites.

6. A sixth episode in the formation of the New Class is the waning of the extended, patriarchical family system and its replacement by the smaller, nuclear family. As middle class women become educated and emancipated, they may increasingly challenge paternal authority and side with their children in resisting it. With declining pa-

ternal authority and growing maternal influence, the autonomy strivings of children are now more difficult to repress; hostility and rebellion against paternal authority can become more overt. There is, correspondingly, increasing difficulty experienced by paternal authority in imposing and reproducing its social values and political ideologies in their children.

7. Following the French Revolution, there is in many parts of Europe, especially France and Germany, a profound reformation and extension of *public, non*-church controlled, (relatively more) *multi-class* education, at the lower levels as well as at the college, polytechnical, and university levels. On the one hand, higher education in the public school becomes the institutional basis for the *mass* production of the New Class of intelligentsia and intellectuals. On the other hand, the expansion of primary and secondary public school teachers greatly increases the jobs available to the New Class.

As teachers, intellectuals come to be defined, and to define themselves, as responsible for and "representative" of society as a *whole,*[3] rather than as having allegiance to the class interests of their students or their parents. As teachers, they are not defined as having an *obligation* to reproduce parental values in their children. Public teachers supersede private tutors.

8. The new structurally differentiated educational system is increasingly insulated from the family system, becoming an important source of values among students divergent from those of their families. The socialization of the young by their families is now mediated by a *semi*-autonomous group of teachers.

9. While growing public education limits family influence on education, it also

increases the influence of the state on education. The public educational system thus becomes a major *cosmopolitanizing* influence on its students, with a corresponding distancing from *localistic* interests and values.

10. Again, the new school system becomes a major setting for the intensive linguistic conversion of students from casual to reflexive speech, or (in Basil Bernstein's terms) from "restricted" linguistic codes to "elaborated" linguistic codes,[4] to a culture of discourse in which claims and assertions may *not* be justified by reference to the speaker's social status. This has the profound consequence of making all *authority-referring* claims potentially problematic.

11. This new culture of discourse often diverges from assumptions fundamental to everyday life, tending to put them into question even when they are linked to the upper classes. These school-inculcated modes of speech are, also, (relatively) situation-free language variants. Their situation-freeness is further heightened by the "communications revolution" in general, and by the development of printing technology, in particular. With the spread of printed materials, definitions of social reality available to intellectuals may now derive increasingly from *distant* persons, from groups geographically, culturally, and historically distant and even from dead persons, and may therefore diverge greatly from any local environment in which they are received. Definitions of social reality made by local elites may now be invidiously contrasted (by intellectuals) with definitions made in other places and times.

12. With the spread of public schools, literacy spreads; humanistic intellectuals lose their exclusiveness and privileged market position, and now experience a status disparity between their "high" culture, as they see it, and their lower deference, repute, income and social power. The social position of humanistic intellectuals, *particularly in a technocratic and industrial society,* becomes more marginal and alienated than that of the technical intelligentsia. The New Class becomes internally differentiated.

13. Finally, a major episode in the emergence of the modern intelligentsia is the changing form of the revolutionary *organization.* Revolution itself becomes a technology to be pursued with "instrumental rationality." The revolutionary organization evolves from a ritualistic, oath-bound secret society into the modern "vanguard" party. When the *Communist Manifesto* remarks that Communists have nothing to hide,[5] it is exactly a proposed emergence into *public* life which is implied. The *Communist Manifesto* was written by Marx and Engels for the "League of Communists," which was born of the "League of the Just" which, in turn, was descended from the "League of Outlaws." This latter group of German emigrants in Paris had a pyramidal structure, made a sharp distinction between upper and lower members, blindfolded members during initiation ceremonies, used recognition signs and passwords, and bound members by an oath.[6] The vanguard organization, however, de-ritualizes participation and entails elements of both the "secret society" and of the public political party. In the vanguard organization, public refers to the public availability of the *doctrine* rather than the availability of the organization or its membership to public scrutiny. Here, to be "public" entails the organization's rejection of "secret doctrines" known only to an elite in the organization—as, for instance, Bakunin's doctrine of an elite dictatorship of anarchists.[7] The

modern vanguard structure is first clearly encoded in Lenin's *What Is to Be Done?* Here it is plainly held that the proletariat cannot develop a *socialist* consciousness by itself, but must secure this from a scientific theory developed by the intelligentsia.[8] The "vanguard" party expresses the *modernizing* and elite ambitions of the New Class as well as an effort to overcome its political limitations. Lenin's call for the development of "professional" revolutionaries, as the core of the vanguard, is a rhetoric carrying the tacit promise of a *career*-like life which invites young members of the New Class to "normalize" the revolutionary existence. . . .

There are several distinguishable conceptions of the New Class:

1. *New Class as Benign Technocrats:* Here the New Class is viewed as a new historical elite already entrenched in institutional influence which it uses in benign ways for society; it is more or less inevitable and trustworthy: e.g., Galbraith,[9] Bell,[10] Berle and Means.[11]

(*Sed contra:* This obscures the manner in which the New Class egoistically pursues its own special vested interests. Moreover, the power of the New Class today is scarcely entrenched. This view also ignores the limits on the rationality of the New Class.)

2. *New Class as Master Class:* Here the New Class is seen as another moment in a long-continuing circulation of historical elites, as a socialist intelligentsia that brings little new to the world and continues to exploit the rest of society as the old class had, but now uses education rather than money to exploit others: Bakunin,[12] Machajski.[13]

(*Sed contra:* The New Class is more historically unique and discontinuous than

this sees; while protecting its own special interests, it is not bound by the same *limits* as the old class and, at least transiently, contributes to collective needs.)

3. *New Class as Old Class Ally:* The New Class is here seen as a benign group of dedicated "professionals" who will uplift the old (moneyed) class from a venal group to a collectivity-oriented elite and who, fusing with it, will forge a new, genteel elite continuous with but better than the past: Talcott Parsons.[14]

(*Sed contra:* Neither group is an especially morally bound agent; the old class is constrained to protect its profits, the New Class is cashing in on its education. Immersed in the present, this view misses the fact that each is ready to exploit the other, if need be, and shows little understanding of the profound (if different) limits imposed on the rationality and morality of each of these groups, and of the important tensions between them.)

4. *New Class as Servants of Power:* Here the New Class is viewed as subservient to the old (moneyed) class which is held to retain power much as it always did, and is simply using the New Class to maintain its domination of society: Noam Chomsky[15] and Maurice Zeitlin.[16]

(*Sed contra:* This ignores the revolutionary history of the twentieth century in which radicalized elements of the New Class played a major leadership role in the key revolutions of our time. It greatly overemphasizes the common interests binding the New and old class, systematically missing the tensions between them; it ignores the fact that elimination of the old class is an historical option open to the New Class. This static conception underestimates the growth in the numbers and influence of the New Class. The view is also unexpectedly Marcusean in overstressing the prospects of old class continuity; it really sees the old class as having no effective opponents, either in the New Class or in the old adversary class, the proletariat. It thus ends as seeing even less social change in prospect than the Parsonian view [#3 above].)

5. *New Class as Flawed Universal Class* (*my own view*): The New Class is elitist and self-seeking and uses its special knowledge to advance its own interests and power, and to control its own work situation. Yet the New Class may also be the best card that history has presently given us to play. The power of the New Class is growing. It is substantially more powerful and independent than Chomsky suggests, while still much less powerful than is suggested by Galbraith who seems to conflate present reality with future possibility. The power of this morally ambiguous New Class is on the ascendent and it holds a mortgage on at least *one* historical future.

In my own left Hegelian sociology, the New Class bearers of knowledge are seen as an embryonic new "universal class"—as the prefigured embodiment of such future as the working class still has. It is that part of the working class which will survive cybernation. At the same time, a left Hegelian sociology also insists that the New Class is profoundly flawed as a universal class. Moreover, the New Class is not some unified subject or a seamless whole; it, too, has its own internal contradictions. It is a class internally divided with tensions between (technical) intelligentsia and (humanistic) intellectuals. No celebration, mine is a critique of the New Class which does not view its growing power as inevitable, which sees

it as morally ambivalent, embodying the collective interest but partially and transiently, while simultaneously cultivating its own guild advantage. . . .

The New Class as a Cultural Bourgeoisie

1. The New Class and the old class are at first undifferentiated; the New Class commonly originates in classes with property advantages, that is, in the old class, or is sponsored by them. The New Class of intellectuals and intelligentsia are the relatively more *educated* counterpart—often the brothers, sisters, or children—of the old moneyed class. Thus the New Class contest sometimes has the character of a *civil war within the upper classes*. It is the differentiation of the old class into contentious factions. To understand the New Class contest it is vital to understand how the *privileged* and advantaged, not simply the suffering, come to be alienated from the very system that privileges them.

2. The "non-negotiable" objectives of the old moneyed class are to reproduce their capital, at a minimum, but, preferably, to make it accumulate and to appropriate profit: M-C-M′, as Marx said. This is done within a structure in which all of them must compete with one another. This unrelenting competition exerts pressure to rationalize their productive and administrative efforts and unceasingly to heighten efficiency. (Marx called it, "revolutionizing" production.) But this rationalization is dependent increasingly on the efforts of the New Class intelligentsia and its expert skills. It is inherent in its structural situation, then, that the old class must bring the New Class into existence.

3. Much of the New Class is at first trained under the direct control of the old class's firms or enterprises. Soon, however, the old class is separated from the reproduction of the New Class by the emergence and development of a public system of education whose costs are "socialized."[17]

4. The more that the New Class's reproduction derives from specialized systems of public education, the more the New Class develops an ideology that stresses its *autonomy,* its separation from and presumable independence of "business" or political interests. This autonomy is said to be grounded in the specialized knowledge or cultural capital transmitted by the educational system, along with an emphasis on the obligation of educated persons to attend to the welfare of the collectivity. In other words, the *ideology* of "professionalism" emerges.

5. Professionalism is one of the public *ideologies* of the New Class, and is the genteel subversion of the old class by the new. Professionalism is a phase in the historical development of the "collective consciousness" of the New Class. While not overtly a critique of the old class, professionalism is a tacit claim by the New Class to *technical and moral superiority* over the old class, implying that the latter lack technical credentials and are guided by motives of commercial venality. Professionalism silently installs the New Class as the paradigm of virtuous and legitimate authority, performing with technical skill and with dedicated concern for the society-at-large. Professionalism makes a focal claim for the legitimacy of the New Class which tacitly deauthorizes the old class.

On the one side, this is a bid for prestige *within* the established society; on the other, it tacitly presents the New Class as an *alternative* to the old. In asserting its own claims

to authority, professionalism in effect *devalues the authority of the old class.*

6. The special privileges and powers of the New Class are grounded in their *individual* control of special cultures, languages, techniques, and of the skills resulting from these. The New Class is a cultural bourgeoisie who appropriates privately the advantages of a historically and collectively produced cultural capital. Let us be clear, then: the New Class is not just *like* the old class; its special culture is not just *like* capital. No metaphor is intended. The special culture of the New Class *is* a stock of capital that generates a stream of income (some of) which it appropriates privately.

7. The fundamental objectives of the New Class are: to increase its own share of the national product; to produce and reproduce the special social conditions enabling them to appropriate privately larger shares of the incomes produced by the special cultures they possess; to control their work and their work settings; and to increase their political power partly in order to achieve the foregoing. The struggle of the New Class is, therefore, to *institutionalize a wage system,* i.e., a social system with a distinct principle of distributive justice: "from each according to his ability, to each according to his work," which is also the norm of "socialism." Correspondingly, the New Class may oppose other social systems and their different systems of privilege, for example, systems that allocate privileges and incomes on the basis of controlling stocks of money (i.e., old capital). The New Class, then, is prepared to be egalitarian so far as the privileges of the *old* class are concerned. That is, under certain conditions it is prepared to remove or restrict the special incomes of the old class: profits, rents, interest. The New Class is anti-egalitarian,

however, in that it seeks special guild advantages—political powers and incomes—on the basis of its possession of cultural capital. . . .

The New Class as a Speech Community

1. The culture of critical discourse (CCD)[18] is an historically evolved set of rules, a grammar of discourse, which (1) is concerned to *justify* its assertions, but (2) whose *mode* of justification does not proceed by invoking authorities, and (3) prefers to elicit the *voluntary* consent of those addressed solely on the basis of arguments adduced. CCD is centered on a specific speech act: justification. It is a culture of discourse in which there is nothing that speakers will on principle permanently refuse to discuss or make problematic; indeed, they are even willing to talk about the value of talk itself and its possible inferiority to silence or to practice. This grammar is the deep structure of the common ideology shared by the New Class. *The shared ideology of the intellectuals and intelligentsia is thus an ideology about discourse.* Apart from and underlying the various technical languages (or sociolects) spoken by specialized professions, intellectuals and intelligentsia are commonly committed to a culture of critical discourse (CCD). CCD is the latent but mobilizable infrastructure of modern "technical" languages.

2. The culture of critical discourse is characterized by speech that is *relatively* more *situation-free*, more context or field "independent." This speech culture thus values expressly legislated meanings and devalues tacit, context-limited meanings. Its ideal is: "one word, one meaning," for everyone and forever.

The New Class's special speech variant also stresses the importance of particular modes of *justification,* using especially explicit and articulate rules, rather than diffuse precedents or tacit features of the speech context. The culture of critical speech requires that the validity of claims be justified without reference to the speaker's *societal position or authority.* Here, good speech is speech that can make its own principles *explicit* and is oriented to conforming with them, rather than stressing context-sensitivity and context-variability. Good speech here thus has *theoreticity.*[19]

Being pattern-and-principle-oriented, CCD implies that that which is said may *not* be correct, and may be *wrong.* It recognizes that "What Is" may be mistaken or inadequate and is therefore open to alternatives. CCD is also relatively more *reflexive,* self-monitoring, capable of more metacommunication, that is, of talk about talk; it is able to make its own speech problematic, and to edit it with respect to its lexical and grammatical features, as well as making problematic the validity of its assertions. CCD thus requires considerable "expressive discipline," not to speak of "instinctual renunciation."

3. Most importantly, the culture of critical speech forbids reliance upon the speaker's person, authority, or status in society to justify his claims. As a result, CCD de-authorizes all speech grounded in traditional societal authority, while it authorizes itself, the elaborated speech variant of the culture of critical discourse, as the standard of *all* "serious" speech. From now on, persons and their social positions must not be visible in their speech. Speech becomes impersonal. Speakers hide behind their speech. Speech seems to be dis-embodied, de-contextualized and self-grounded. (This is especially so for the speech of intellectuals and somewhat less

so for technical intelligentsia who may not invoke CCD except when their paradigms break down.) The New Class becomes the guild masters of an invisible pedagogy.

4. The culture of critical discourse is the common ideology shared by the New Class, although technical intelligentsia sometimes keep it in latency. The skills and the social conditions required to reproduce it are among the common *interests* of the New Class. Correspondingly, it is in the common interest of the New Class to prevent or oppose all censorship of its speech variety and to install it as the standard of good speech. *The New Class thus has both a common ideology in CCD and common interests in its cultural capital....*

The Flawed Universal Class

1. The New Class is the most progressive force in modern society and is a center of whatever human emancipation is possible in the foreseeable future. It has no motives to curtail the forces of production and no wish to develop them solely in terms of their profitability. The New Class possesses the scientific knowledge and technical skills on which the future of modern forces of production depend. At the same time, members of the New Class also manifest increasing sensitivity to the ecological "side effects" or distant diseconomies of continuing technical development. The New Class, further, is a center of opposition to almost all forms of censorship, thus embodying a universal societal interest in a kind of rationality broader than that invested in technology. Although the New Class is at the center of nationalist movements throughout the world, after that phase is secured, the New Class is also the most internationalist and most universalist of all social

strata; it is the most cosmopolitan of all elites. Its control over ordinary "foreign" languages, as well as of technical sociolects, enable it to communicate with other nationalities and it is often a member of a technical guild of international scope.

2. For all that, however, the New Class is hardly the end of domination. While its ultimate significance is the end of the old moneyed class's domination, the New Class is also the nucleus of a *new* hierarchy and the elite of a new form of cultural capital.

The historical limits of the New Class are inherent in both the nature of its own characteristic rationality, and in its ambitions as a cultural bourgeoisie. Its culture of critical discourse fosters a purely "theoretical" attitude toward the world. Speakers are held competent to the degree that they know and can *say* the rules, rather than just happening to follow them. The culture of critical discourse thus values the very theoreticity that the "common sense" long suspected was characteristic of intellectuals.

Intellectuals have long believed that those who know the rule, who know the theory by which they act, are superior because they lead an "examined" life. They thus exalt theory over practice, and are concerned less with the success of a practice than that the practice should have submitted itself to a reasonable rule. Since intellectuals and intelligentsia are concerned with doing things in the right way and for the right reason—in other words, since they value doctrinal conformity for its own sake—they (we) have a native tendency toward ritualism and *sectarianism*.

3. The culture of the New Class exacts still other costs: since its discourse emphasizes the importance of carefully edited speech, this has the vices of its virtues: in its *virtuous* aspect, self-editing implies a com-

mendable circumspection, carefulness, self-discipline and "seriousness." In its negative modality, however, self-editing also disposes toward an unhealthy self-consciousness, toward stilted convoluted speech, an inhibition of play, imagination and passion, and continual pressure for expressive discipline. The new rationality thus becomes the source of a new alienation.

Calling for watchfulness and self-discipline, CCD is productive of intellectual reflexivity *and* the loss of warmth and spontaneity. Moreover, that very reflexivity stresses the importance of adjusting action to some pattern of propriety. There is, therefore, a structured inflexibility when facing changing situations; there is a certain disregard of the differences in situations, and an insistence on hewing to the required rule.

This inflexibility and insensitivity to the force of differing contexts, this inclination to impose one set of rules on different cases also goes by the ancient name of "dogmatism." Set in the context of human relationships, the vulnerability of the New Class to dogmatism along with its very *task*-centeredness, imply a certain insensitivity to *persons,* to their feelings and reactions, and open the way to the disruption of human solidarity. Political brutality, then, finds a grounding in the culture of critical discourse; the new rationality may paradoxically allow a new darkness at noon.

4. The paradox of the New Class is that it is both emancipatory *and* elitist. It subverts all establishments, social limits, and privileges, including its own. The New Class bears a culture of critical and careful discourse which is an historically emancipatory rationality. The new discourse (CCD) is the grounding for a critique of established forms of domination and provides an escape from tradition, but it also bears the seeds of a new domination. Its discourse is a lumbering machinery of argumentation that can wither imagination, discourage play, and curb expressivity. The culture of discourse of the New Class seeks to *control* everything, its topic and itself, believing that such domination is the only road to truth. The New Class begins by monopolizing truth and by making itself its guardian. It thereby makes even the claims of the old class dependent on it. The New Class sets itself above others, holding that its speech is better than theirs; that the examined life (*their* examination) is better than the unexamined life which, it says, is sleep and no better than death. Even as it subverts old inequities, the New Class silently inaugurates a new hierarchy of the knowing, the knowledgeable, the reflexive and insightful. Those who talk well, it is held, excel those who talk poorly or not at all. It is now no longer enough simply to be good. Now, one has to explain it. The New Class is the universal class in embryo, but badly flawed.

NOTES

1. It is not my intention to suggest that modern intellectuals are merely the secular counterpart of clericals. Indeed, my own stress (as distinct, say, from Edward Shils who does appear to view intellectuals as priests *manqués*) is on the discontinuity of the two.

2. For full development of this, see chapter 2, especially p. 42, of my *Dialectic of Ideology and Technology* (New York, 1976).

3. Doubtless some will insist this is a "false consciousness." But this misses the point. My concern here is with their own definitions of their social role, precisely because these influence the manner in which they perform their roles. As W. I. Thomas and Florian Znaniecki long ago (and correctly) insisted, a thing defined as real is real in its consequences. Moreover, the state who employs most of these teachers is itself interested in having

teachers consolidate the tie between students and it itself, rather than with the students' parents.

4. See Basil Bernstein, *Class, Codes and Control,* vol. 1, *Theoretical Studies Towards a Sociology of Language* (London, 1971), vol. 2, *Applied Studies Towards a Sociology of Language* (London, 1973), vol. 3, *Towards a Theory of Educational Transmission* (London, 1975). Bernstein's theory is used here in a critical appropriation facilitated by the work of Dell Hymes and William Labov. My own critique of Bernstein emerges, at least tacitly, in the discussion of [the "Flawed Universal Class"] in the text. It is developed explicitly in my *Dialectic of Ideology and Technology,* pp. 58–66. While Labov has sharply criticized Bernstein, he himself also stresses the general importance of self-monitored speech and of speech *reflexivity* in general (i.e., not only of careful pronunciation) thus converging with Bernstein's focus on reflexivity as characterizing the elaborated linguistic variant and distinguishing it from the restricted variant. See William Labov, *Sociolinguistic Patterns* (Philadelphia, 1972), p. 208.

5. For example: "The Communists disdain to conceal their views and aims. They openly declare . . ." (*Communist Manifesto* [Chicago, 1888], authorized English edition edited by Engels, p. 58).

6. See E. Hobsbawm, *Primitive Rebels* (Manchester, 1959), p. 167 ff.

7. A secret doctrine is one which, because it is reserved only for the organization elite, can be made known only after persons join organizations and reach a certain membership position in it. A secret doctrine thus is never one which can have been a *motive* for joining the organization in the first instance.

8. Lenin's *What Is to Be Done?* was originally published in 1902.

9. *The New Industrial State* (Boston, 1967).

10. *The Coming of Post-Industrial Society* (New York, 1973).

11. *The Modern Corporation and Private Property* (New York, 1932).

12. "It stands to reason that the one who knows more will dominate the one who knows less," M. Bakouinine, *Oeuvres,* Vol. 5 (Paris, 1911), p. 106.

13. See V. F. Calverton, *The Making of Society* (New York, 1937).

14. Talcott Parsons, *The Social System* (Glencoe, 1951), chapter 10; *Essays in Sociological Theory* (Glencoe, 1954), chapter 18; "The Professions," *International Encyclopedia of Social Sciences* (New York, 1968).

15. While Chomsky's position is exhibited in various of his writings, I shall rely here on his most recent statement in his Huizinga lecture, "Intellectuals and the State," delivered at Leiden, 9 October 1977. Citations will be from the manuscript copy. Cf. N. Chomsky, *American Power and the New Mandarins* (New York, 1969).

16. Maurice Zeitlin, "Corporate Ownership and Control: The Large Corporations and the Capitalist Class," *American Journal of Sociology* (March 1974), pp. 1073–1119.

17. Cf. James O'Connor, *Corporations and the State* (New York, 1974), pp. 126–28 for the argument that government financing of R & D and advanced education constitute a socialization of part of the costs of production whose net surplus is privately appropriated.

18. This section is indebted to Basil Bernstein and is based on a critical appropriation of his "elaborated and restricted linguistic codes," which have gone through various re-workings. That controversial classic was published in J. J. Gumperz and D. Hymes, *Directions in Sociolinguistics* (New York, 1972). A recent re-working is to be found in Bernstein's "Social Class, Language, and Socialization," in T. A. Sebeok, ed., *Current Trends in Linguistics* (The Hague, 1974). For full bibliographic and other details see note 4 above.

19. Cf. Peter McHugh, "A Common-Sense Perception of Deviance," in H. P. Dreitzel, ed., *Recent Sociology, Number 2* (London, 1970), pp. 165 ff. For good speech as "serious" speech see David Silverman, "Speaking Seriously," *Theory and Society* (Spring, 1974).

14

Bobos in Paradise

The New Upper Class and How They Got There

DAVID BROOKS

The Rise of the Educated Class

I'm not sure I'd like to be one of the people featured on the *New York Times* wedding page, but I know I'd like to be the father of one of them. Imagine how happy Stanley J. Kogan must have been, for example, when his daughter Jamie was admitted to Yale. Then imagine his pride when Jamie made Phi Beta Kappa and graduated summa cum laude. Stanley himself is no slouch in the brains department: he's a pediatric urologist in Croton-on-Hudson, with teaching positions at the Cornell Medical Center and the New York Medical College. Still, he must have enjoyed a gloat or two when his daughter put on that cap and gown.

And things only got better. Jamie breezed through Stanford Law School. And then she met a man—Thomas Arena—who appeared to be exactly the sort of son-in-law that pediatric urologists dream about. He did his undergraduate work at Princeton, where he, too, made Phi Beta Kappa and graduated summa cum laude. And he, too, went to law school, at Yale. After school they both went to work as assistant U.S. at-torneys for the mighty Southern District of New York.

These two awesome résumés collided at a wedding ceremony in Manhattan, and given all the school chums who must have attended, the combined tuition bills in that room must have been staggering. The rest of us got to read about it on the *New York Times* weddings page. The page is a weekly obsession for hundreds of thousands of *Times* readers and aspiring Balzacs. Un-abashedly elitist, secretive, and totally hon-est, the "mergers and acquisitions page" (as some of its devotees call it) has always pro-vided an accurate look at at least a chunk of the American ruling class. And over the years it has reflected the changing ingredi-ents of elite status.

When America had a pedigreed elite, the page emphasized noble birth and breeding. But in America today it's genius and genial-ity that enable you to join the elect. And when you look at the *Times* weddings page, you can almost feel the force of the min-gling SAT scores. It's Dartmouth marries Berkeley, MBA weds Ph.D., Fulbright hitches with Rhodes, Lazard Frères joins with CBS, and summa cum laude embraces summa cum laude (you rarely see a summa settling for a magna—the tension in such a marriage would be too great). The *Times* emphasizes four things about a person—college degrees, graduate degrees, career path, and parents' profession—for these are the markers of upscale Americans today. . . .

The Fifties

The *Times* weddings page didn't always pulse with the accomplishments of the Résumé Gods. In the late 1950s, the page projected a calm and more stately ethos. The wedding accounts of that era didn't emphasize jobs or advanced degrees. The profession of the groom was only sometimes mentioned, while the profession of the bride was almost never listed (and on the rare occasions when the bride's profession was noted, it was in the past tense, as if the marriage would obviously end her career). Instead, the *Times* listed pedigree and connections. Ancestors were frequently mentioned. The ushers were listed, as were the bridesmaids. Prep schools were invariably mentioned, along with colleges. The *Times* was also careful to list the groom's clubs—the Union League, the Cosmopolitan Club. It also ran down the bride's debutante history, where she came out, and whatever women's clubs she might be a member of, such as the Junior League. In short, the page was a galaxy of restricted organizations. . . .

The section from the late fifties evokes an entire milieu that was then so powerful and is now so dated: the network of men's clubs, country clubs, white-shoe law firms, oak-paneled Wall Street firms, and WASP patriarchs. Everybody has his or her own mental images of the old Protestant Establishment: lockjaw accents, the Social Regis-ter, fraternity jocks passing through Ivy League schools, constant rounds of martinis and highballs, bankers' hours, starched old men like Averell Harriman, Dean Acheson, and John J. McCloy, the local bigwigs that appear in John Cheever and John O'Hara stories. . . .

It really was possible to talk about an aristocratic ruling class in the fifties and early sixties, a national elite populated by men who had gone to northeastern prep schools like Groton, Andover, Exeter, and St. Paul's and then ascended through old-line firms on Wall Street into the boardrooms of the Fortune 500 corporations and into the halls of Washington power. The WASPs didn't have total control of the country or anything like it, but they did have the hypnotic magic of prestige. As Richard Rovere wrote in a famous 1962 essay entitled "The American Establishment," "It has very nearly unchallenged power in deciding what is and what is not respectable opinion in this country.". . .

This was the last great age of socially acceptable boozing. It was still an era when fox hunting and polo didn't seem antiquarian. But the two characteristics of that world that strike us forcefully today are its unabashed elitism and its segregation. Though this elite was nowhere near as restrictive as earlier elites—World War II had exerted its leveling influence—the 1950s establishment was still based on casual anti-Semitism, racism, sexism, and a thousand other silent barriers that blocked entry for those without the correct pedigree. Wealthy Jewish and Protestant boys who had been playing together from childhood were forced to endure "The Great Division" at age 17, when Jewish and Gentile society parted into two entirely separate orbits, with separate debutante seasons, dance schools, and social secretaries. A Protestant business executive may have spent his professional hours working intimately with his Jewish colleague, but he never would have dreamed of putting him up for membership in his club. When Senator Barry Goldwater attempted to play golf at the restricted Chevy Chase Club, he was told the club was restricted. "I'm only half Jewish, so can't I play nine holes?" he is said to have replied.

The WASP elite was also genially anti-intellectual. Its members often spoke of "eggheads" and "highbrows" with polite disdain. Instead, their status, as F. Scott Fitzgerald had pointed out a few decades before, derived from "animal magnetism and money." By contrast with today's ruling class, they had relatively uncomplicated attitudes about their wealth. They knew it was vulgar to be gaudy, they tended toward thriftiness, but they seem not to have seen their own money as an affront to American principles of equality. On the contrary, most took their elite status for granted, assuming that such position was simply part of the natural and beneficent order of the universe. There was always going to be an aristocracy, and so for the people who happened to be born into it, the task was to accept the duties that came along with its privileges. . . .

The Hinge Years

Then came the change. By 1960 the average verbal SAT score for incoming freshmen at Harvard was 678, and the math score was 695—these are stratospheric scores. The average Harvard freshman in 1952 would have placed in the bottom 10 percent of the Harvard freshman class of 1960. Moreover, the 1960 class was drawn from a much wider socioeconomic pool. Smart kids from Queens or Iowa or California, who wouldn't have thought of applying to Harvard a decade earlier, were applying and getting accepted. Harvard had transformed itself from a school catering mostly to the northeastern social elite to a high-powered school reaching more of the brightest kids around the country. And this transformation was replicated in almost all elite schools. . . .

History, as Pareto once remarked, is the graveyard of aristocracies, and by the late fifties and early sixties the WASP Establishment had no faith in the code—and the social restrictions—that had sustained it. Maybe its members just lost the will to fight for their privileges. As the writer David Frum theorizes, it had been half a century since the last great age of fortune making. The great families were into at least their third genteel generation. Perhaps by then there wasn't much vigor left. Or perhaps it was the Holocaust that altered the landscape by discrediting the sort of racial restrictions that the Protestant Establishment was built on.

In any case, in 1964 Digby Baltzell astutely perceived the crucial trends. "What seems to be happening," he wrote in *The Protestant Establishment*, "is that a scholarly hierarchy of campus communities governed by the values of admissions committees is gradually supplanting the class hierarchies of local communities which are still governed by the values of parents. . . . Just as the hierarchy of the Church was the main avenue of advancement for the talented and ambitious youth from the lower orders during the medieval period, and just as the business enterprise was responsible for the nineteenth century rags-to-riches dream (when we were predominantly an Anglo-Saxon country), so the campus community has now become the principal guardian of our traditional opportunitarian ideals."

The campus gates were thus thrown open on the basis of brains rather than blood, and within a few short years the university landscape was transformed. Harvard, as we've seen, was changed from a school for the well-connected to a school for brainy strivers. The remaining top schools eliminated their Jewish quotas and eventually dropped their restrictions on women. Furthermore, the sheer numbers of educated Americans exploded. The portion of Americans going to college had been rising steadily throughout the 20th century, but between 1955 and 1974 the growth rate was off the charts. Many of the new students were women. Between 1950 and 1960 the number of female students increased by 47 percent. It then jumped by an additional 168 percent between 1960 and 1970. Over the following decades the student population kept growing and growing. In 1960 there were about 2,000 institutions of higher learning. By 1980 there were 3,200. In 1960 there were 235,000 professors in the United States. By 1980 there were 685,000. . . .

The Sixties

The educated-class rebellion we call "the sixties" was about many things, some of them important and related to the Civil Rights movement and Vietnam, some of them entirely silly, and others, like the sexual revolution, overblown (actual sexual behavior was affected far more by the world wars than by the Woodstock era). But at its core the cultural radicalism of the sixties was a challenge to conventional notions of success. It was not only a political effort to

dislodge the establishment from the seats of power. It was a cultural effort by the rising members of the privileged classes to destroy whatever prestige still attached to the WASP lifestyle and the WASP moral code, and to replace the old order with a new social code that would celebrate spiritual and intellectual ideals. The sixties radicals rejected the prevailing definition of accomplishment, the desire to keep up with the Joneses, the prevailing idea of social respectability, the idea that a successful life could be measured by income, manners, and possessions. . . .

And Then Comes Money

The hardest of the hard-core sixties radicals believed the only honest way out was to reject the notion of success altogether: drop out of the rat race, retreat to small communities where real human relationships would flourish. But that sort of utopianism was never going to be very popular, especially among college grads. Members of the educated class prize human relationships and social equality, but as for so many generations of Americans before them, achievement was really at the core of the sixties grads' value system. They were meritocrats, after all, and so tended to define themselves by their accomplishments. Most of them were never going to drop out or sit around in communes smelling flowers, raising pigs, and contemplating poetry. Moreover, as time went by, they discovered that the riches of the universe were lying at their feet.

At first, when the great hump of baby boom college graduates entered the workforce, having a college degree brought few financial rewards or dramatic life changes. As late as 1976, the labor economist Richard

Freeman could write a book called *The Overeducated American,* arguing that higher education didn't seem to be paying off in the marketplace. But the information age kicked in, and the rewards for education grew and grew. In 1980, according to labor market specialist Kevin Murphy of the University of Chicago, college graduates earned roughly 35 percent more than high school graduates. But by the mid-1990s, college graduates were earning 70 percent more than high school graduates, and those with graduate degrees were earning 90 percent more. The wage value of a college degree had doubled in 15 years.

The rewards for intellectual capital have increased while the rewards for physical capital have not. That means that even liberal arts majors can wake up one day and find themselves suddenly members of the top-income brackets. A full professor at Yale who renounced the capitalist rat race finds himself making, as of 1999, $113,100, while a professor at Rutgers pulls in $103,700 and superstar professors, who become the object of academic bidding wars, now can rake in more than $300,000 a year. Congressional and presidential staffers top out at $125,000 (before quintupling that when they enter the private sector), and the journalists at national publications can now count on six-figure salaries when they hit middle age, not including lecture fees. Philosophy and math majors head for Wall Street and can make tens of millions of dollars from their quantitative models. America has always had a lot of lawyers, and now the median income for that burgeoning group is $72,500, while income for the big-city legal grinds can reach seven figures. And super-students still flood into medicine— three-quarters of private practitioners net more than $100,000. Meanwhile, in Silicon Valley there are more millionaires than people. . . .

The Anxieties of Abundance

Those who want to win educated-class approval must confront the anxieties of abundance: how to show—not least to themselves—that even while climbing toward the top of the ladder they have not become all the things they still profess to hold in contempt. How to navigate the shoals between their affluence and their self-respect. How to reconcile their success with their spirituality, their elite status with their egalitarian ideals. Socially enlightened members of the educated elite tend to be disturbed by the widening gap between rich and poor and are therefore made somewhat uncomfortable by the fact that their own family income now tops $80,000. Some of them dream of social justice yet went to a college where the tuition costs could feed an entire village in Rwanda for a year. Some once had "Question Authority" bumper stickers on their cars but now find themselves heading start-up software companies with 200 people reporting to them. The sociologists they read in college taught that consumerism is a disease, and yet now they find themselves shopping for $3,000 refrigerators. They took to heart the lessons of *Death of a Salesman,* yet now find themselves directing a sales force. They laughed at the plastics scene in *The Graduate* but now they work for a company that manufactures . . . plastic. Suddenly they find themselves moving into a suburban house with a pool and uncomfortable about admitting it to their bohemian friends still living downtown. . . .

The Reconcilers

The grand achievement of the educated elites in the 1990s was to create a way of living that lets you be an affluent success and at the same time a free-spirit rebel. Founding design firms, they find a way to be an artist and still qualify for stock options. Building gourmet companies like Ben & Jerry's or Nantucket Nectars, they've found a way to be dippy hippies and multinational corporate fat cats. Using William S. Burroughs in ads for Nike sneakers and incorporating Rolling Stones anthems into their marketing campaigns, they've reconciled the antiestablishment style with the corporate imperative. Listening to management gurus who tell them to thrive on chaos and unleash their creative potential, they've reconciled the spirit of the imagination with service to the bottom line. Turning university towns like Princeton and Palo Alto into entrepreneurial centers, they have reconciled the highbrow with the high tax bracket. Dressing like Bill Gates in worn chinos on his way to a stockholders' meeting, they've reconciled undergraduate fashion with upper-crust occupations. Going on eco-adventure vacations, they've reconciled aristocratic thrill-seeking with social concern. Shopping at Benetton or the Body Shop, they've brought together consciousness-raising and cost control.

When you are amidst the educated upscalers, you can never be sure if you're living in a world of hippies or stockbrokers. In reality you have entered the hybrid world in which everybody is a little of both.

Marx told us that classes inevitably conflict, but sometimes they just blur. The values of the bourgeois mainstream culture and the values of the 1960s counterculture have merged. That culture war has ended, at least within the educated class. In its place that class has created a third culture, which is a reconciliation between the previous two. The educated elites didn't set out to create this reconciliation. It is the product of millions of individual efforts to have things both ways. But it is now the dominant tone of our age. In the resolution between the culture and the counterculture, it is impossible to tell who co-opted whom, because in reality the bohemians and the bourgeois co-opted each other. They emerge from this process as bourgeois bohemians, or Bobos.

The New Establishment

Today the *New York Times* weddings section is huge once again. In the early 1970s the young rebels didn't want to appear there, but now that their own kids are in college and getting married, they are proud to see their offspring in the Sunday paper. For a fee the *Times* will send you a reproduction of your listing, suitable for framing.

And the young people, the second-generation Bobos, are willing to see their nuptials recorded. Look at the newlyweds on any given Sunday morning, beaming out at you from the pages of the *Times*. Their smiles seem so genuine. They all look so nice and approachable, not dignified or fearsome, the way some of the brides on the 1950s pages did. Things are different but somehow similar. . . .

Today's establishment is structured differently. It is not a small conspiracy of well-bred men with interlocking family and school ties who have enormous influence on the levers of power. Instead, this establishment is a large, amorphous group of meritocrats who share a consciousness and who unself-consciously reshape institutions to accord with their values. They are not confined to a few East Coast institutions. In 1962, Richard Rovere could write, "Nor has the Establishment ever made much headway in such fields as advertising, television or motion pictures." Today's establishment is everywhere. It exercises its power subtly, over ideas and concepts, and therefore pervasively. There are no sure-fire demographic markers to tell who is a member of this establishment. Members tend to have gone to competitive colleges, but not all have. They tend to live in upscale neighborhoods, such as Los Altos, California, and Bloomfield, Michigan, and Lincoln Park, Illinois, but not all do. What unites them is their shared commitment to the Bobo reconciliation. People gain entry into the establishment by performing a series of delicate cultural tasks: they are prosperous without seeming greedy; they have pleased their elders without seeming conformist; they have risen toward the top without too obviously looking down on those below; they have achieved success without committing certain socially sanctioned affronts to the ideal of social equality; they have constructed a prosperous lifestyle while avoiding the old clichés of conspicuous consumption (it's OK to hew to the new clichés).

Obviously, none of this is to suggest that all members of the new Bobo establishment think alike, any more than it's true to say that all members of any establishment think alike. Some of the bourgeois bohemians are more on the bourgeois side; they are stockbrokers who happen to like artists' lofts. Some are on the bohemian side; they are art professors who dabble in the market. Nonetheless, if you look at some quintessential figures of the new establishment—such as Henry Louis Gates, Charlie Rose, Steven Jobs, Doris Kearns Goodwin, David

Geffen, Tina Brown, Maureen Dowd, Jerry Seinfeld, Stephen Jay Gould, Lou Reed, Tim Russert, Steve Case, Ken Burns, Al Gore, Bill Bradley, John McCain, George W. Bush—you can begin to sense a common ethos that mingles 1960s rebellion with 1980s achievement. You can feel the Bobo ethos, too, in the old institutions that have been taken over by the new establishment, such as the *New Yorker,* Yale University, the American Academy of Arts and Letters (which now includes people like Toni Morrison, Jules Feiffer, and Kurt Vonnegut among its members), or the *New York Times* (which now runs editorials entitled "In Praise of the Counterculture"). You can sense the ethos with special force in the new establishment institutions that would have been alien to the old elite: NPR, DreamWorks, Microsoft, AOL, Starbucks, Yahoo, Barnes & Noble, Amazon, and Borders.

And over the past few years, this new educated establishment has begun to assume the necessary role of an establishment. That is to say, it has begun to create a set of social codes that give coherent structure to national life. Today, America once again has a dominant class that defines the parameters of respectable opinion and taste—a class that determines conventional wisdom, that promulgates a code of good manners, that establishes a pecking order to give shape to society, that excludes those who violate its codes, that transmits its moral and etiquette codes down to its children, that imposes social discipline on the rest of society so as to improve the "quality of life," to use the contemporary phrase. . . .

Class Rank

This has got to be one of the most anxious social elites ever. We Bobos are not anxious because there is an angry mob outside the gates threatening to send us to the guillotine. There isn't. The educated elite is anxious because its members are torn between their drive to succeed and their fear of turning into sellouts. Furthermore, we are anxious because we do not award ourselves status sinecures. Previous establishments erected social institutions that would give their members security. In the first part of the 20th century, once your family made it into the upper echelons of society, it was relatively easy to stay there. You were invited on the basis of your connections to the right affairs. You were admitted, nearly automatically, to the right schools and considered appropriate for the right spouses. The pertinent question in those circles was not what do you do, but who are you. Once you were established as a Biddle or an Auchincloss or a Venderlip, your way was clear. But members of today's educated class can never be secure about their own future. A career crash could be just around the corner. In the educated class even social life is a series of aptitude tests; we all must perpetually perform in accordance with the shifting norms of propriety, ever advancing signals of cultivation. Reputations can be destroyed by a disgraceful sentence, a lewd act, a run of bad press, or a terrible speech at the financial summit at Davos.

And more important, members of the educated class can never be secure about their children's future. The kids have some domestic and educational advantages—all those tutors and developmental toys—but they still have to work through school and ace the SATs just to achieve the same social rank as their parents. Compared to past elites, little is guaranteed.

The irony is that all this status insecurity only makes the educated class stronger. Its members and their children must constantly be alert, working and achieving. Moreover, the educated class is in no danger of becoming a self-contained caste. Anybody with the right degree, job, and cultural competencies can join. Marx warned that "the more a ruling class is able to assimilate the most prominent men [or women] of the dominated classes, the more stable and dangerous its rule." And in truth it is hard to see how the rule of the meritocrats could ever come to an end. The WASP Establishment fell pretty easily in the 1960s. It surrendered almost without a shot. But the meritocratic Bobo class is rich with the spirit of self-criticism. It is flexible and amorphous enough to co-opt that which it does not already command. The Bobo meritocracy will not be easily toppled, even if some group of people were to rise up and conclude that it should be.

15

Nickel-and-Dimed

On (not) Getting by in America

BARBARA EHRENREICH

At the beginning of June 1998 I leave behind everything that normally soothes the ego and sustains the body—home, career, companion, reputation, ATM card—for a plunge into the low-wage workforce. There, I become another, occupationally much diminished "Barbara Ehrenreich"—depicted on job-application forms as a divorced homemaker whose sole work experience consists of housekeeping in a few private homes. I am terrified, at the beginning, of being unmasked for what I am: a middle-class journalist setting out to explore the world that welfare mothers are entering, at the rate of approximately 50,000 a month, as welfare reform kicks in. Happily, though, my fears turn out to be entirely unwarranted: during a month of poverty and toil, my name goes unnoticed and for the most part unuttered. In this parallel universe where my father never got out of the mines and I never got through college, I am "baby," "honey," "blondie," and, most commonly, "girl."

My first task is to find a place to live. I figure that if I can earn $7 an hour—which, from the want ads, seems doable—I can afford to spend $500 on rent, or maybe, with severe economies, $600. In the Key West area, where I live, this pretty much confines me to flophouses and trailer homes—like the one, a pleasing fifteen-minute drive from town, that has no air-conditioning, no screens, no fans, no television, and, by way of diversion, only the challenge of evading the landlord's Doberman pinscher. The big problem with this place, though, is the rent, which at $675 a month is well beyond my reach. . . .

So I decide to make the common trade-off between affordability and convenience, and go for a $500-a-month efficiency thirty miles up a two-lane highway from the employment opportunities of Key West, meaning forty-five minutes if there's no road construction and I don't get caught behind some sun-dazed Canadian tourists. . . .

I am not doing this for the anthropology. My aim is nothing so mistily subjective as to "experience poverty" or find out how it "really feels" to be a long-term low-wage worker. I've had enough unchosen encounters with poverty and the world of low-wage work to know it's not a place you want to visit for touristic purposes; it just smells too much like fear. And with all my

Barbara Ehrenreich, "Nickel and Dimed," *Harper's Magazine*, January 1999, pp. 37–52.

real-life assets—bank account, IRA, health insurance, multiroom home—waiting indulgently in the background, I am, of course, thoroughly insulated from the terrors that afflict the genuinely poor.

No, this is a purely objective, scientific sort of mission. The humanitarian rationale for welfare reform—as opposed to the more punitive and stingy impulses that may actually have motivated it—is that work will lift poor women out of poverty while simultaneously inflating their self-esteem and hence their future value in the labor market. Thus, whatever the hassles involved in finding child care, transportation, etc., the transition from welfare to work will end happily, in greater prosperity for all. Now there are many problems with this comforting prediction, such as the fact that the economy will inevitably undergo a downturn, eliminating many jobs. Even without a downturn, the influx of a million former welfare recipients into the low-wage labor market could depress wages by as much as 11.9 percent, according to the Economic Policy Institute (EPI) in Washington, D.C.

But is it really possible to make a living on the kinds of jobs currently available to unskilled people? Mathematically, the answer is no, as can be shown by taking $6 to $7 an hour, perhaps subtracting a dollar or two an hour for child care, multiplying by 160 hours a month, and comparing the result to the prevailing rents. According to the National Coalition for the Homeless, for example, in 1998 it took, on average nationwide, an hourly wage of $8.89 to afford a one-bedroom apartment, and the Preamble Center for Public Policy estimates that the odds against a typical welfare recipient's landing a job at such a "living wage" are about 97 to 1. If these numbers are right,

low-wage work is not a solution to poverty and possibly not even to homelessness. . . .

On the morning of my first full day of job searching, I take a red pen to the want ads, which are auspiciously numerous. Everyone in Key West's booming "hospitality industry" seems to be looking for someone like me—trainable, flexible, and with suitably humble expectations as to pay. I know I possess certain traits that might be advantageous—I'm white and, I like to think, well-spoken and poised—but I decide on two rules: One, I cannot use any skills derived from my education or usual work—not that there are a lot of want ads for satirical essayists anyway. Two, I have to take the best-paid job that is offered me and of course do my best to hold it; no Marxist rants or sneaking off to read novels in the ladies' room. . . .

Most of the big hotels run ads almost continually, just to build a supply of applicants to replace the current workers as they drift away or are fired, so finding a job is just a matter of being at the right place at the right time and flexible enough to take whatever is being offered that day. This finally happens to me at one of the big discount hotel chains, where I go for housekeeping and am sent, instead, to try out as a waitress at the attached "family restaurant," a dismal spot with a counter and about thirty tables that looks out on a parking garage and features such tempting fare as "Pollish [sic] sausage and BBQ sauce" on 95-degree days. Phillip, the dapper young West Indian who introduces himself as the manager, interviews me with about as much enthusiasm as if he were a clerk processing me for Medicare, the principal questions being what shifts can I work and when can I start. I mutter something about being woefully out of practice as a waitress, but he's already on to the uniform: I'm to show up tomorrow wearing black slacks and black shoes; he'll provide the rust-colored polo shirt with Hearthside embroidered on it, though I might want to wear my own shirt to get to work, ha ha. At the word "tomorrow," something between fear and indignation rises in my chest. I want to say, "Thank you for your time, sir, but this is just an experiment, you know, not my actual life."

So begins my career at the Hearthside, I shall call it, one small profit center within a global discount hotel chain, where for two weeks I work from 2:00 till 10:00 P.M. for $2.43 an hour plus tips. In some futile bid for gentility, the management has barred employees from using the front door, so my first day I enter through the kitchen, where a red-faced man with shoulder-length blond hair is throwing frozen steaks against the wall and yelling, "Fuck this shit!" "That's just Jack," explains Gail, the wiry middle-aged waitress who is assigned to train me. "He's on the rag again"—a condition occasioned, in this instance, by the fact that the cook on the morning shift had forgotten to thaw out the steaks. For the next eight hours, I run after the agile Gail, absorbing bits of instruction along with fragments of personal tragedy. All food must be trayed, and the reason she's so tired today is that she woke up in a cold sweat thinking of her boyfriend, who killed himself recently in an upstate prison. No refills on lemonade. And the reason he was in prison is that a few DUIs caught up with him, that's all, could have happened to anyone. Carry the creamers to the table in a monkey bowl, never in your hand. And after he was gone she spent several months living in her truck, peeing in a plastic pee bottle and reading by candlelight at night, but you can't live in a truck in

the summer, since you need to have the windows down, which means anything can get in, from mosquitoes on up.

At least Gail puts to rest any fears I had of appearing overqualified. From the first day on, I find that of all the things I have left behind, such as home and identity, what I miss the most is competence. Not that I have ever felt utterly competent in the writing business, in which one day's success augurs nothing at all for the next. But in my writing life, I at least have some notion of procedure: do the research, make the outline, rough out a draft, etc. As a server, though, I am beset by requests like bees: more iced tea here, ketchup over there, a to-go box for table fourteen, and where are the high chairs, anyway? Of the twenty-seven tables, up to six are usually mine at any time, though on slow afternoons or if Gail is off, I sometimes have the whole place to myself. There is the touch-screen computer-ordering system to master, which is, I suppose, meant to minimize server-cook contact, but in practice requires constant verbal fine-tuning: "That's gravy on the mashed, okay? None on the meatloaf," and so forth—while the cook scowls as if I were inventing these refinements just to torment him. Plus, something I had forgotten in the years since I was eighteen: about a third of a server's job is "side work" that's invisible to customers—sweeping, scrubbing, slicing, refilling, and restocking. If it isn't all done, every little bit of it, you're going to face the 6:00 P.M. dinner rush defenseless and probably go down in flames. I screw up dozens of times at the beginning, sustained in my shame entirely by Gail's support—"It's okay, baby, everyone does that sometime"—because, to my total surprise and despite the scientific detachment I am doing my best to maintain, I care. . . .

Sometimes I play with the fantasy that I am a princess who, in penance for some tiny transgression, has undertaken to feed each of her subjects by hand. But the non-princesses working with me are just as indulgent, even when this means flouting management rules—concerning, for example, the number of croutons that can go on a salad (six). "Put on all you want," Gail whispers, "as long as Stu isn't looking." She dips into her own tip money to buy biscuits and gravy for an out-of-work mechanic who's used up all his money on dental surgery, inspiring me to pick up the tab for his milk and pie. . . .

Ten days into it, this is beginning to look like a livable lifestyle. I like Gail, who is "looking at fifty" but moves so fast she can alight in one place and then another without apparently being anywhere between them. I clown around with Lionel, the teenage Haitian busboy, and catch a few fragments of conversation with Joan, the svelte fortyish hostess and militant feminist who is the only one of us who dares to tell Jack to shut the fuck up. I even warm up to Jack when, on a slow night and to make up for a particularly unwarranted attack on my abilities, or so I imagine, he tells me about his glory days as a young man at "coronary school"—or do you say "culinary"?—in Brooklyn, where he dated a knock-out Puerto Rican chick and learned everything there is to know about food. I finish up at 10:00 or 10:30, depending on how much side work I've been able to get done during the shift, and cruise home to the tapes I snatched up at random when I left my real home—Marianne Faithfull, Tracy Chapman, Enigma, King Sunny Ade, the Violent Femmes—just drained enough for the music to set my cranium resonating but hardly dead. Midnight snack is Wheat Thins and Monterey Jack, accompanied by cheap white wine on ice and whatever AMC has to offer. To bed by 1:30 or 2:00, up at 9:00 or 10:00, read for an hour while my uniform whirls around in the landlord's washing machine, and then it's another eight hours spent following Mao's central instruction, as laid out in the Little Red Book, which was: Serve the people.

I could drift along like this, in some dreamy proletarian idyll, except for two things. One is management. If I have kept this subject on the margins thus far it is because I still flinch to think that I spent all those weeks under the surveillance of men (and later women) whose job it was to monitor my behavior for signs of sloth, theft, drug abuse, or worse. Not that managers and especially "assistant managers" in low-wage settings like this are exactly the class enemy. In the restaurant business, they are mostly former cooks or servers, still capable of pinch-hitting in the kitchen or on the floor, just as in hotels they are likely to be former clerks, and paid a salary of only about $400 a week. But everyone knows they have crossed over to the other side, which is, crudely put, corporate as opposed to human. Cooks want to prepare tasty meals; servers want to serve them graciously; but managers are there for only one reason—to make sure that money is made for some theoretical entity that exists far away in Chicago or New York, if a corporation can be said to have a physical existence at all. . . .

Managers can sit—for hours at a time if they want—but it's their job to see that no one else ever does, even when there's nothing to do, and this is why, for servers, slow times can be as exhausting as rushes. You start dragging out each little chore, because if the manager on duty catches you in an idle moment, he will give you something far nastier to do. So I wipe, I clean, I consolidate ketchup bottles and recheck the cheesecake supply, even tour the tables to make sure the customer evaluation forms are all standing perkily in their places—wondering all the time how many calories I burn in these strictly theatrical exercises. When, on a particularly dead afternoon, Stu finds me glancing at a *USA Today* a customer has left behind, he assigns me to vacuum the entire floor with the broken vacuum cleaner that has a handle only two feet long, and the only way to do that without incurring orthopedic damage is to proceed from spot to spot on your knees. . . .

The other problem, in addition to the less-than-nurturing management style, is that this job shows no sign of being financially viable. You might imagine, from a comfortable distance, that people who live, year in and year out, on $6 to $10 an hour have discovered some survival stratagems unknown to the middle class. But no. It's not hard to get my co-workers to talk about their living situations, because housing, in almost every case, is the principal source of disruption in their lives, the first thing they fill you in on when they arrive for their shifts. After a week, I have compiled the following survey:

- Gail is sharing a room in a well-known downtown flophouse for which she and a roommate pay about $250 a week. Her roommate, a male friend, has begun hitting on her, driving her nuts, but the rent would be impossible alone.
- Claude, the Haitian cook, is desperate to get out of the two-room apartment he shares with his girlfriend and two other, unrelated, people. As far as I can

determine, the other Haitian men (most of whom only speak Creole) live in similarly crowded situations.
- Annette, a twenty-year-old server who is six months pregnant and has been abandoned by her boyfriend, lives with her mother, a postal clerk.
- Marianne and her boyfriend are paying $170 a week for a one-person trailer.
- Jack, who is, at $10 an hour, the wealthiest of us, lives in the trailer he owns, paying only the $400-a-month lot fee.
- The other white cook, Andy, lives on his dry-docked boat, which, as far as I can tell from his loving descriptions, can't be more than twenty feet long. He offers to take me out on it, once it's repaired, but the offer comes with inquiries as to my marital status, so I do not follow up on it.
- Tina and her husband are paying $60 a night for a double room in a Days Inn. This is because they have no car and the Days Inn is within walking distance of the Hearthside. When Marianne, one of the breakfast servers, is tossed out of her trailer for subletting (which is against the trailer-park rules), she leaves her boyfriend and moves in with Tina and her husband.
- Joan, who had fooled me with her numerous and tasteful outfits (hostesses wear their own clothes), lives in a van she parks behind a shopping center at night and showers in Tina's motel room. The clothes are from thrift shops.

It strikes me, in my middle-class solipsism, that there is gross improvidence in some of these arrangements. When Gail and I are wrapping silverware in napkins—the only task for which we are permitted to sit—she tells me she is thinking of escaping from her roommate by moving into the Days Inn herself. I am astounded: How can she even think of paying between $40 and $60 a day? But if I was afraid of sounding like a social worker, I come out just sounding like a fool. She squints at me in disbelief, "And where am I supposed to get a month's rent and a month's deposit for an apartment?" I'd been feeling pretty smug about my $500 efficiency, but of course it was made possible only by the $1,300 I had allotted myself for start-up costs when I began my low-wage life: $1,000 for the first month's rent and deposit, $100 for initial groceries and cash in my pocket, $200 stuffed away for emergencies. In poverty, as in certain propositions in physics, starting conditions are everything.

There are no secret economies that nourish the poor; on the contrary, there are a host of special costs. If you can't put up the two months' rent you need to secure an apartment, you end up paying through the nose for a room by the week. If you have only a room, with a hot plate at best, you can't save by cooking up huge lentil stews that can be frozen for the week ahead. You eat fast food, or the hot dogs and Styrofoam cups of soup that can be microwaved in a convenience store. If you have no money for health insurance—and the Hearthside's niggardly plan kicks in only after three months—you go without routine care or prescription drugs and end up paying the price. Gail, for example, was fine until she ran out of money for estrogen pills. She is supposed to be on the company plan by now, but they claim to have lost her application form and need to begin the paperwork all over again. So she

spends $9 per migraine pill to control the headaches she wouldn't have, she insists, if her estrogen supplements were covered. Similarly, Marianne's boyfriend lost his job as a roofer because he missed so much time after getting a cut on his foot for which he couldn't afford the prescribed antibiotic.

My own situation, when I sit down to assess it after two weeks of work, would not be much better if this were my actual life. The seductive thing about waitressing is that you don't have to wait for payday to feel a few bills in your pocket, and my tips usually cover meals and gas, plus something left over to stuff into the kitchen drawer I use as a bank. But as the tourist business slows in the summer heat, I sometimes leave work with only $20 in tips (the gross is higher, but servers share about 15 percent of their tips with the busboys and bartenders). With wages included, this amounts to about the minimum wage of $5.15 an hour. Although the sum in the drawer is piling up, at the present rate of accumulation it will be more than a hundred dollars short of my rent when the end of the month comes around. Nor can I see any expenses to cut. True, I haven't gone the lentil-stew route yet, but that's because I don't have a large cooking pot, pot holders, or a ladle to stir with (which cost about $30 at Kmart, less at thrift stores), not to mention onions, carrots, and the indispensable bay leaf. I do make my lunch almost every day—usually some slow-burning, high-protein combo like frozen chicken patties with melted cheese on top and canned pinto beans on the side. Dinner is at the Hearthside, which offers its employees a choice of BLT, fish sandwich, or hamburger for only $2. The burger lasts longest, especially if it's heaped with gutpuckering jalapeños, but by midnight my stomach is growling again.

So unless I want to start using my car as a residence, I have to find a second, or alternative, job. I call all the hotels where I filled out housekeeping applications weeks ago—the Hyatt, Holiday Inn, Econo Lodge, HoJo's, Best Western, plus a half dozen or so locally run guesthouses. Nothing. Then I start making the rounds again, wasting whole mornings waiting for some assistant manager to show up, even dipping into places so creepy that the front-desk clerk greets you from behind bulletproof glass and sells pints of liquor over the counter. But either someone has exposed my real-life housekeeping habits—which are, shall we say, mellow—or I am at the wrong end of some infallible ethnic equation: most, but by no means all, of the working housekeepers I see on my job searches are African Americans, Spanish-speaking, or immigrants from the Central European post-Communist world, whereas servers are almost invariably white and monolingually English-speaking. When I finally get a positive response, I have been identified once again as server material. Jerry's, which is part of a well-known national family restaurant chain and physically attached here to another budget hotel chain, is ready to use me at once. The prospect is both exciting and terrifying, because, with about the same number of tables and counter seats, Jerry's attracts three or four times the volume of customers as the gloomy old Hearthside. . . .

I start out with the beautiful, heroic idea of handling the two jobs at once, and for two days I almost do it: the breakfast/lunch shift at Jerry's, which goes till 2:00, arriving at the Hearthside at 2:10, and attempting to hold out until 10:00. In the ten minutes between jobs, I pick up a spicy chicken sandwich at the Wendy's drive-through window, gobble it down in the car, and change from khaki slacks to black, from Hawaiian to rust polo. There is a problem, though. When during the 3:00 to 4:00 P.M. dead time I finally sit down to wrap silver, my flesh seems to bond to the seat. I try to refuel with a purloined cup of soup, as I've seen Gail and Joan do dozens of times, but a manager catches me and hisses "No eating!" though there's not a customer around to be offended by the sight of food making contact with a server's lips. So I tell Gail I'm going to quit, and she hugs me and says she might just follow me to Jerry's herself.

But the chances of this are minuscule. She has left the flophouse and her annoying roommate and is back to living in her beat-up old truck. But guess what? she reports to me excitedly later that evening: Phillip has given her permission to park overnight in the hotel parking lot, as long as she keeps out of sight, and the parking lot should be totally safe, since it's patrolled by a hotel security guard! With the Hearthside offering benefits like that, how could anyone think of leaving?. . .

Management at Jerry's is generally calmer and more "professional" than at the Hearthside, with two exceptions. One is Joy, a plump, blowsy woman in her early thirties, who once kindly devoted several minutes to instructing me in the correct one-handed method of carrying trays but whose moods change disconcertingly from shift to shift and even within one. Then there's B. J., a.k.a. B. J.-the-bitch, whose contribution is to stand by the kitchen counter and yell, "Nita, your order's up, move it!" or, "Barbara, didn't you see you've got another table out there? Come on, girl!" Among other things, she is hated for having replaced the whipped-cream squirt cans with big plastic whipped-cream-filled baggies that have to be squeezed with both hands—because, reportedly, she saw or thought she saw employees trying to inhale the propellant gas from the squirt cans, in the hope that it might be nitrous oxide. On my third night, she pulls me aside abruptly and brings her face so close that it looks as if she's planning to butt me with her forehead. But instead of saying, "You're fired," she says, "You're doing fine." The only trouble is I'm spending time chatting with customers: "That's how they're getting you." Furthermore I am letting them "run me," which means harassment by sequential demands: you bring the ketchup and they decide they want extra Thousand Island; you bring that and they announce they now need a side of fries; and so on into distraction. Finally she tells me not to take her wrong. She tries to say things in a nice way, but you get into a mode, you know, because everything has to move so fast. . . .

I make friends, over time, with the other "girls" who work my shift: Nita, the tattooed twenty-something who taunts us by going around saying brightly, "Have we started making money yet?" Ellen, whose teenage son cooks on the graveyard shift and who once managed a restaurant in Massachusetts but won't try out for management here because she prefers being a "common worker" and not "ordering people around." Easy-going fiftyish Lucy, with the raucous laugh, who limps toward the end of the shift because of something that has gone wrong with her leg, the exact nature of which cannot be determined without health insurance. We talk about the usual girl things—men, children, and the sinister allure of Jerry's chocolate peanut-butter cream pie—though no one, I notice, ever brings up anything potentially expensive, like shopping or movies. As at the Hearthside, the only recreation ever referred to is partying, which requires little more than some beer, a joint, and a few close friends. Still, no one here is homeless, or cops to it anyway, thanks usually to a working husband or boyfriend. All in all, we form a reliable mutual-support group: If one of us is feeling sick or overwhelmed, another one will "bev" a table or even carry trays for her. If one of us is off sneaking a cigarette or a pee, the others will do their best to conceal her absence from the enforcers of corporate rationality. . . .

I make the decision to move closer to Key West. First, because of the drive. Second and third, also because of the drive: gas is eating up $4 to $5 a day, and although Jerry's is as high-volume as you can get, the tips average only 10 percent, and not just for a newbie like me. Between the base pay of $2.15 an hour and the obligation to share tips with the busboys and dishwashers, we're averaging only about $7.50 an hour. Then there is the $30 I had to spend on the regulation tan slacks worn by Jerry's servers—a setback it could take weeks to absorb. (I had combed the town's two downscale department stores hoping for something cheaper but decided in the end that these marked-down Dockers, originally $49, were more likely to survive a daily washing.) Of my fellow servers, everyone who lacks a working husband or boyfriend seems to have a second job: Nita does something at a computer eight hours a day; another welds. Without the forty-five-minute commute, I can picture myself working two jobs and having the time to shower between them.

So I take the $500 deposit I have coming from my landlord, the $400 I have earned toward the next month's rent, plus the $200 reserved for emergencies, and use the $1,100 to pay the rent and deposit on trailer number 46 in the Overseas Trailer Park, a mile from the cluster of budget hotels that constitute Key West's version of an industrial park. Number 46 is about eight feet in width and shaped like a barbell inside, with a narrow region—because of the sink and the stove—separating the bedroom from what might optimistically be called the "living" area, with its two-person table and half-sized couch. The bathroom is so small my knees rub against the shower stall when I sit on the toilet, and you can't just leap out of the bed, you have to climb down to the foot of it in order to find a patch of floor space to stand on. Outside, I am within a few yards of a liquor store, a bar that advertises "free beer tomorrow," a convenience store, and a Burger King—but no supermarket or, alas, laundromat. By reputation, the Overseas park is a nest of crime and crack, and I am hoping at least for some vibrant, multicultural street life. But desolation rules night and day, except for a thin stream of pedestrian traffic heading for their jobs at the Sheraton or 7-Eleven. There are not exactly people here but what amounts to canned labor, being preserved from the heat between shifts. . . .

When my month-long plunge into poverty is almost over, I finally land my dream job—housekeeping. I do this by walking into the personnel office of the only place I figure I might have some credibility, the hotel attached to Jerry's, and confiding urgently that I have to have a second job if I am to pay my rent and, no, it couldn't be front-desk clerk. "All right," the personnel lady fairly spits, "So it's housekeeping," and she marches me back to meet Maria, the housekeeping manager, a tiny, frenetic Hispanic woman who greets me as "babe" and hands me a pamphlet emphasizing the need for a positive attitude. The hours are nine in the morning till whenever, the pay is $6.10 an hour, and there's one week of vacation a year. I don't have to ask about health insurance once I meet Carlotta, the middle-aged African-American woman who will be training me. Carla, as she tells me to call her, is missing all of her top front teeth.

On that first day of housekeeping and last day of my entire project—although I don't yet know it's the last—Carla is in a foul mood. We have been given nineteen rooms to clean, most of them "checkouts," as opposed to "stay-overs," that require the whole enchilada of bed-stripping, vacuuming, and bathroom-scrubbing. When one of the rooms that had been listed as a stay-over turns out to be a checkout, Carla calls Maria to complain, but of course to no avail. "So make up the motherfucker," Carla orders me, and I do the beds while she sloshes around the bathroom. For four hours without a break I strip and remake beds, taking about four and a half minutes per queen-sized bed, which I could get down to three if there were any reason to. We try to avoid vacuuming by picking up the larger specks by hand, but often there is nothing to do but drag the monstrous vacuum cleaner—it weighs about thirty pounds—off our cart and try to wrestle it around the floor. Sometimes Carla hands me the squirt bottle of "BAM" (an acronym for something that begins, ominously, with "butyric"; the rest has been worn off the label) and lets me do the bathrooms. No service ethic challenges me here to new heights of performance. I just concentrate on removing the pubic hairs from the bathtubs, or at least the dark ones that I can see. . . .

When I request permission to leave at about 3:30, another housekeeper warns me that no one has so far succeeded in combining housekeeping at the hotel with serving at Jerry's: "Some kid did it once for five days, and you're no kid." With that helpful information in mind, I rush back to number 46, down four Advils, shower, stooping to fit into the stall, and attempt to compose myself for the oncoming shift. So much for what Marx termed the "reproduction of labor power," meaning the things a worker has to do just so she'll be ready to work again. . . .

Then it comes, the perfect storm. Four of my tables fill up at once. Four tables is nothing for me now, but only so long as they are obligingly staggered. As I bev table 27, tables 25, 28, and 24 are watching enviously. As I bev 25, 24 glowers because their bevs haven't even been ordered. Twenty-eight is four yuppyish types, meaning everything on the side and agonizing instructions as to the chicken Caesars. Twenty-five is a middle-aged black couple, who complain, with some justice, that the iced tea isn't fresh and the tabletop is sticky. But table 24 is the meteorological event of the century: ten British tourists who seem to have made the decision to absorb the American experience entirely by mouth. Here everyone has at least two drinks—iced tea and milk shake, Michelob and water (with lemon slice, please)—and a huge promiscuous orgy of breakfast specials, mozz sticks, chicken strips, quesadillas, burgers with cheese and without, sides of hash browns with cheddar, with onions, with gravy, seasoned fries, plain fries, banana splits. Poor Jesus (the cook)! Poor me! Because when I arrive with their first tray of food—after three prior trips just to refill bevs—Princess Di refuses to eat her chicken strips with her pancake-and-

sausage special, since, as she now reveals, the strips were meant to be an appetizer. Maybe the others would have accepted their meals, but Di, who is deep into her third Michelob, insists that everything else go back while they work on their "starters." Meanwhile, the yuppies are waving me down for more decaf and the black couple looks ready to summon the NAACP.

Much of what happened next is lost in the fog of war. Jesus starts going under. The little printer on the counter in front of him is spewing out orders faster than he can rip them off, much less produce the meals. Even the invincible Ellen is ashen from stress. I bring table 24 their reheated main courses, which they immediately reject as either too cold or fossilized by the microwave. When I return to the kitchen with their trays (three trays in three trips), Joy confronts me with arms akimbo: "What is this?" She means the food—the plates of rejected pancakes, hash browns in assorted flavors, toasts, burgers, sausages, eggs. "Uh, scrambled with cheddar," I try, "and that's. . ." "NO," she screams in my face. "Is it a traditional, a super-scramble, an eye-opener?" I pretend to study my check for a clue, but entropy has been up to its tricks, not only on the plates but in my head, and I have to admit that the original order is beyond reconstruction. "You don't know an eye-opener from a traditional?" she demands in outrage. All I know, in fact, is that my legs have lost interest in the current venture and have announced their intention to fold. I am saved by a yuppie (mercifully not one of mine) who chooses this moment to charge into the kitchen to bellow that his food is twenty-five minutes late. Joy screams at him to get the hell out of her kitchen, please, and then turns on Jesus in a fury, hurling an empty tray across the room for emphasis.

I leave. I don't walk out, I just leave. I don't finish my side work or pick up my credit-card tips, if any, at the cash register or, of course, ask Joy's permission to go. And the surprising thing is that you *can* walk out without permission, that the door opens, that the thick tropical night air parts to let me pass, that my car is still parked where I left it. There is no vindication in this exit, no fuck-you surge of relief, just an overwhelming, dank sense of failure pressing down on me and the entire parking lot. I had gone into this venture in the spirit of science, to test a mathematical proposition, but somewhere along the line, in the tunnel vision imposed by long shifts and relentless concentration, it became a test of myself, and clearly I have failed. . . .

When I moved out of the trailer park, I gave the key to number 46 to Gail and arranged for my deposit to be transferred to her. She told me that Joan is still living in her van and that Stu had been fired from the Hearthside. . . .

In one month, I had earned approximately $1,040 and spent $517 on food, gas, toiletries, laundry, phone, and utilities. If I had remained in my $500 efficiency, I would have been able to pay the rent and have $22 left over (which is $78 less than the cash I had in my pocket at the start of the month). During this time I bought no clothing except for the required slacks and no prescription drugs or medical care (I did finally buy some vitamin B to compensate for the lack of vegetables in my diet). Perhaps I could have saved a little on food if I had gotten to a supermarket more often, instead of convenience stores, but it should be noted that I lost almost four pounds in four weeks, on a diet weighted heavily toward burgers and fries.

How former welfare recipients and single mothers will (and do) survive in the low-wage workforce, I cannot imagine. Maybe they will figure out how to condense their lives—including child-raising, laundry, romance, and meals—into the couple of hours between full-time jobs. Maybe they will take up residence in their vehicles, if they have one. All I know is that I couldn't hold two jobs and I couldn't make enough money to live on with one. And I had advantages unthinkable to many of the long-term poor—health, stamina, a working car, and no children to care for and support. . . .

The thinking behind welfare reform was that even the humblest jobs are morally uplifting and psychologically buoying. In reality they are likely to be fraught with insult and stress. But I did discover one redeeming feature of the most abject low-wage work—the camaraderie of people who are, in almost all cases, far too smart and funny and caring for the work they do and the wages they're paid. The hope, of course, is that someday these people will come to know what they're worth, and take appropriate action.

16

United States Poverty in a
Cross-National Context

TIMOTHY SMEEDING, LEE RAINWATER, AND GARY BURTLESS

Policymakers in most industrialized countries share common concerns about family well-being and poverty, but *measuring* poverty is an exercise that has been largely confined to the English-speaking countries; few continental European nations routinely do so. The United States in particular has a long tradition of measuring income poverty and weighing the effectiveness of government policies aimed at poverty reduction. Yet U.S. analysis rests on an inherently parochial foundation, for it is based on the experiences of only one nation.

Until fairly recently, it has been extremely difficult to compare U.S. poverty rates and policies with those of other nations. It is still not particularly simple or straightforward, but data being assembled by the Luxembourg Income Study (LIS), an international cooperative research project, make such comparisons more feasible.[1] This article uses LIS data to compare absolute and relative rates of U.S. poverty with those of other industrialized nations, and considers some implications for U.S. antipoverty policy.

For American voters and policymakers, much can be learned about antipoverty policy from cross-national comparisons. Although per capita income in the United States is 30 percent higher than the average for the other nations in our study, its rate of absolute poverty is also very much higher— 13.6 percent, compared with the average of 8.1 percent for the other countries considered. The child poverty rates seem particularly troublesome. In most rich countries, that rate is 8 percent or less. In the United States, it was 14.7 percent in 1997, according to the criteria we have established in this article. (The official U.S. poverty rate for children under 18 was 19.9 percent in 1997.). . .

Absolute Poverty

Only a handful of cross-national studies have used an "absolute" poverty line. In the United States, a poverty threshold for an absolute measure was established by calculating the minimum resources needed to purchase a basket of goods that were considered "necessary" by an expert panel. The threshold is then adjusted only for changes in aggregate prices over time; thus it remains, in real terms, constant.

Timothy Smeeding, Lee Rainwater, and Gary Burtless, "United States Poverty in a Cross-National Context," *Focus* 21 (Spring 2001), pp. 50-54.

To estimate absolute poverty rates in different countries, researchers must convert national currencies into units of equal purchasing power, or "purchasing power parity" (PPP) exchange rates. In principle, the PPP rates permit us to estimate the amount of money needed in country A to purchase the same bundle of consumption goods in country B. Comparison is still problematic, because PPP rates were devised to permit accurate comparison of aggregate national output, rather than the disposable incomes or private consumption of lower-income families. PPP rates are appropriate for comparing market baskets of aggregate consumption, including health care, education, and housing. But these goods are paid for in different ways in different nations. In most countries, health care, some housing, child care, and education are more generously subsidized by government than they are in the United States, and household disposable incomes therefore reflect the fact that those costs have already been subtracted (as taxes). Since the United States provides lower than average amounts of noncash benefits, some might argue that U.S. rates of absolute poverty are understated, whereas poverty rates in Northern European countries which provide high levels of tax-financed health care and education benefits are likely to be always overstated.

"Absolute" poverty measures are always in some sense relative; they must be appropriate to the context in which they are used. For instance, the World Bank defines absolute poverty in Africa and Latin America using an income threshold of $1 or $2 a day; in Central Europe the Bank uses a threshold of $2 or $3 per day. The U.S. poverty line, in contrast, is 6 to 12 times higher. The World Bank poverty thresholds are obviously too low for use in rich countries in the Organisation for Economic Co-operation and Development (OECD). At the other extreme, Scandinavian countries have "minimum income standards" that are set at 60 percent of median national income, roughly 40 percent higher than the official U.S. poverty line.

In Table 16.1, we compare the U.S. household poverty rate to absolute poverty rates in other nations, using as our threshold the U.S. poverty line. We use PPP rates developed by the OECD for 1994 or 1995, and translate household incomes in countries for which we have reliable data into U.S. dollars. The United States has the third highest poverty rate, 13.6 percent, behind only Australia and the United Kingdom. Since these two countries have much lower per capita incomes, their higher poverty rates are hardly surprising. But nearly all the countries in Table 16.1 have per capita incomes and absolute poverty rates lower than the United States. This suggests that among rich nations the distribution of income is as important as average income in determining poverty rates. Poor countries can have lower poverty rates than rich ones if their income distribution is compressed; rich countries can have higher poverty rates than poor ones if their incomes are more unequally distributed.

Relative Poverty

Relative poverty can be simply enough defined as "having less than others in the society." In our analysis of relative poverty we use the most common threshold for within-country comparisons—50 percent of median income—but we also use a 40 percent

Table 16.1   Absolute Poverty Rates for OECD Nations in 1994 and 1995, Using the U.S. Poverty Line

Nation	Poverty Rate (%)	GDP Capita in 1995[a]
Australia	17.6	$21,459
United Kingdom 1995	15.7	18,743
United States	13.6	27,895
France	9.9	20,192
Canada	7.4	22,951
Germany[b]	7.3	21,357
Netherlands	7.1	21,222
Sweden 1995	6.3	19,949
Finland 1995	4.8	18,861
Norway 1995	4.3	23,316
Overall Average	9.4	$22,956

Sources: Authors' calculations from LIS; OECD, "Purchasing Power Parities for OECD Countries, 1970–1999," 2001, http://www.oecd.org/std/pppoecd.xls; T. Smeeding and L. Rainwater, "Comparing Living Standards across Nations: Real Incomes at the Top, the Bottom, and the Middle," unpublished paper, prepared for the Levy Institute Conference on the Quality of Life in America and Other Advanced Industrialized Nations, Annandale-on-Hudson, NY, June 6–7, 2001.

Notes: Poverty is measured using the official U.S. poverty line and equivalence scales. All country data are for 1994 unless otherwise indicated. OECD purchasing power parities are used to convert the U.S. poverty line. See OECD, *Social Expenditure Database* 1980–96 (Paris: OECD, 1999).

[a]Amount in 1995 U.S. dollars using OECD purchasing power parities.

[b]All of Germany, including western and eastern Länder.

threshold because, as noted above, it is comparable to the U.S. poverty line. Figure 16.1 shows relative poverty rates in 15 nations, using both thresholds. "Deep" poverty in the United States stands out very clearly even when the poverty threshold is set at 40 percent of median income. At this level, over 11 percent of the U.S. population is poor.

Higher poverty rates are found in countries with a high level of overall inequality (the United States, Italy), in geographically large and diverse countries (United States, Canada, Australia), and in countries with poorly developed national welfare states (Spain, Japan). Low poverty rates are more common in smaller, well-developed, and high-spending welfare states (the European Union, Scandinavia) and in countries with more generous unemployment insurance,

social policies supporting single mothers and working women, and high minimum social assistance payments. . . .

Relative poverty rates can vary across age groups within a nation as much as they do across nations (Figure 16.2). Overall, child poverty rates are about 0.5 of a percentage point higher than the national average, but in the United States and Italy, both high-poverty countries, they are 4–5 percentage points higher. In the low-poverty countries of the European Union and Scandinavia, they are usually equal to or less than adult rates. Using the 40 percent threshold, the child poverty rate is 14.7 percent in the United States versus 1.3 percent in Sweden.

The elderly stand in the greatest contrast to other groups (Figure 16.2). Using the 40 percent threshold, their rates are in general

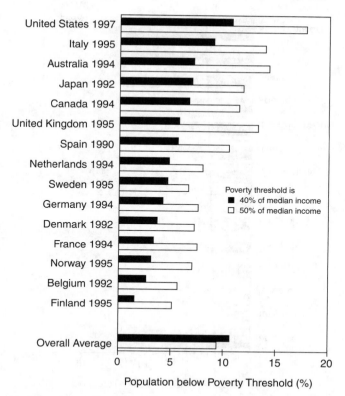

Figure 16.1   Relative Poverty Rates of Industrialized Nations in the 1990s.

Poverty is measured as a percentage of median adjusted disposable personal income (DPI) for individuals. Incomes are adjusted for household size (S) by a family size equivalence scale (E=0.5), where adjusted DPI = actual DPI/S^E.

Source: Authors' tabulations of LIS files.

lower than the average. Among the countries considered, only the United States and Australia have a poverty rate for the elderly higher than 10 percent. Poverty rates for the elderly in Canada, 1.2 percent, are far below the rates for children and working-age adults.

The poverty rate of the elderly is, however, particularly sensitive to the income cutoff used to determine poverty. If we raise the poverty threshold from 40 to 50 percent of median income, the average (un-weighted) poverty rate for the elderly rises from 4.5 to 11.6 percent in the countries considered in Figure 16.2. This increase is the largest for any group. It suggests that social protection systems for the elderly often provide income guarantees that are no more than 40–50 percent of median income and that many elderly fall into the "near-poor" category.

Some Correlates of Poverty

Poverty and inequality are higher in the United States than in some countries with

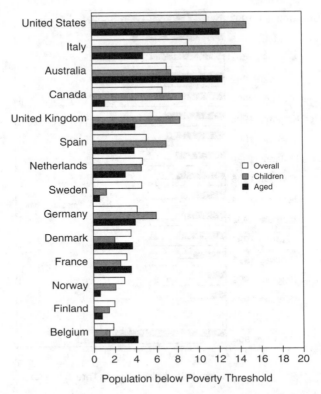

Figure 16.2   Poverty Rates of Industrialized Nations, by Age, in the 1990s.

Poverty is measured at 40 percent median adjusted disposable personal income (DPI) for individuals. Incomes are adjusted for household size (S) by a family size equivalence scale (E=0.5), where adjusted DPI = actual DPI/S^E. Germany includes both the western and the eastern Länder. Japan is not included because it does not have separate rates for children and the elderly.

Source: Author's tabulations of LIS files.

similar (and even with much lower) average incomes. An American citizen whose income is in the lowest 10 percent of the U.S. income distribution has an adjusted disposable income that is just 34–38 percent of U.S. median income. This is 5–7 percentage points lower than a similarly placed citizen in any other nation discussed here.

The low-income population is larger in the United States than in these other na-tions for two main reasons: low market wages for those with few skills and limited public benefits. Figure 16.3 shows a strong association between low pay and national poverty rates. A substantial fraction of the variation in poverty rates appears to be accounted for by the variation in the incidence of low pay. The United States has the highest proportion of workers in relatively poorly paid full-time jobs; it also has the

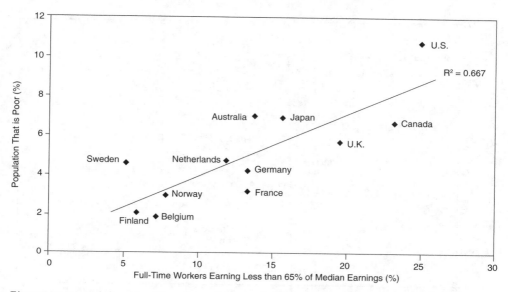

Figure 16.3   Relationship of Low Pay and Poverty Rates in Industrialized Countries in the 1990s.
Countries with values above the diagonal line have higher poverty rates than are predicted by the incidence of low relative wages; countries below the line have lower poverty rates.

Source: OECD, "Employment Outlook 1996," *OECD Employment Outlook* 59 and 60 (June and December 1996) and authors' tabulations of the LIS data files.

highest poverty rate. Canada, in contrast, has a lower poverty rate than its unequal wage distribution would lead us to expect.

Low pay, however, is not the only reliable predictor of poverty rates. Social spending clearly affects the prevalence of poverty. Figure 16.4 correlates child poverty rates with the fraction of each country's gross domestic product that is spent on cash and near-cash social transfers to the nonaged. Measured in this way, higher social spending is correlated with lower child poverty rates.

Different patterns of social spending can produce different effects—antipoverty and social insurance programs are in many respects unique to each country. The United States differs from most nations that achieve lower poverty rates because of its emphasis on work and self-reliance for

working-age adults, regardless of the wages workers must accept.

As long as the United States relies almost exclusively on the labor market to generate incomes for working-age families, changes in the wage distribution that affect the earnings of less-skilled workers will inevitably have a big effect on poverty among children and prime-age adults. For over a decade U.S. unemployment has been well below the OECD average. Continued tight labor markets can help reduce poverty as the wages received by less-skilled workers are bid up. The strong economy, coupled with a few specific antipoverty devices such as the expanded Earned Income Tax Credit and increases in the minimum wage, has produced most of the reduction in U.S. poverty over the last few years.

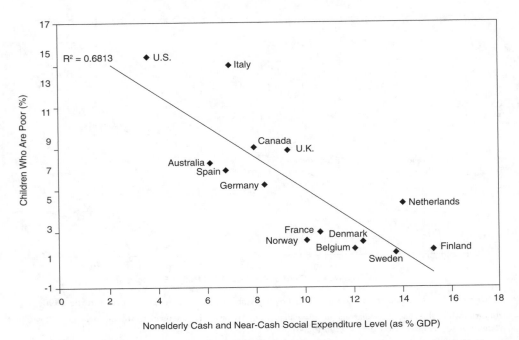

Figure 16.4   Relationship of Cash Social Expenditures and Child Poverty Rates in Industrialized Countries in the 1990s.

Countries with values above the diagonal line have higher poverty rates than are predicted by social expenditures; countries below the line have lower poverty rates.

Source: OECD, Social Expenditure Database 1980–96 (Paris: OECD, 1999), and authors' tabulations of the LIS data files. Cash and noncash social expenditures exclude health, education, and social services, but include all forms of cash benefits and near-cash housing subsidies, active labor market program subsidies, and other contingent cash and near-cash benefits. Nonelderly benefits include only those accruing to household heads under age 65.

But there are two important limits to reliance on the labor market only. First, not all of the poor can be expected to earn their way out of poverty. Through low wages alone, single parents with young children, disabled workers, and the unskilled will continue to face significant challenges in earning a comfortable income. Second, in recessions, declines in employment and hourly wages are likely to be particularly severe for low-wage workers. Many single mothers have become breadwinners as a result of the welfare reforms of the last

decade, but the same reforms make it possible that those who lose their jobs in the next recession will be ineligible for cash public assistance at the same time that most will be ineligible for unemployment compensation.

The relationship between antipoverty spending and poverty rates is complicated, so these simple correlations are at best suggestive. U.S. poverty rates are high, yet so is U.S. economic performance. Carefully crafted public policy can certainly reduce American poverty, yet it also has costs,

among them, perhaps, a higher unemployment rate and slower economic growth.
The direct and indirect costs of antipoverty
programs are now widely recognized, and
sometimes overstated, in public debate. Yet
in light of the low rates of poverty achieved
elsewhere it is hard to argue that the prosperous United States could not do more to
help the poor, particularly those who are
employed.

NOTE

1. The Luxembourg Income Study is described
in detail on the study's World Wide Web site,
http://www.lis.ceps.lu/. International bodies such
as the United Nations Children's Fund, the
OECD, and the European Statistical Office have
published cross-national studies of poverty in recent years. The large majority of these studies use
the LIS database, which now contains almost 100
household income data files for 25 nations covering the period 1967 to 1997.

17

Jobless Poverty

A New Form of Social Dislocation in the Inner-city Ghetto

WILLIAM JULIUS WILSON

In September 1996 my book, *When Work Disappears: The World of the New Urban Poor,* was published. It describes a new type of poverty in our nation's metropolises: poor, segregated neighborhoods in which a majority of adults are either unemployed or have dropped out of the labor force altogether. What is the effect of these "jobless ghettos" on individuals, families, and neighborhoods? What accounts for their existence? I suggest several factors and conclude with policy recommendations: a mix of public-and-private sector projects is more effective than relying on a strategy of employer subsidies.

The Research Studies

When Work Disappears was based mainly on three research studies conducted in Chicago between 1986 and 1993. The first of these three studies included a variety of data: a random survey of nearly 2,500 poor and nonpoor African American, Latino, and white residents in Chicago's poor neighborhoods; a more focused survey of 175 participants who were reinterviewed and answered open-ended questions; a survey of 179 employers selected to reflect distribution of employment across industry and firm size in the Chicago metropolitan areas; and comprehensive ethnographic research, including participant-observation research and life-history interviews by ten research assistants in a representative sample of inner-city neighborhoods.

The first of the two remaining projects also included extensive data: a survey of a representative sample of 546 black mothers and up to two of their adolescent children (aged eleven to sixteen—or 887 adolescents) in working-class, middle-class, and high-poverty neighborhoods; a survey of a representative sample of 500 respondents from two high-joblessness neighborhoods on the South Side of Chicago; and six focus-group discussions involving the residents and former residents of these neighborhoods.

Jobless Ghettos

The jobless poverty of today stands in sharp contrast to previous periods. In 1950, a substantial portion of the urban black population was poor but they were working. Urban poverty was quite extensive but people held jobs. However, as we entered the 1990s most adults in many inner-city ghetto neighborhoods were not working. For example, in 1950 a significant majority of adults held jobs in a typical week in the three neighborhoods that represent the historic core of the Black Belt in Chicago—Douglas, Grand Boulevard, and Washington Park. But by 1990, only four in ten in Douglas worked in a typical week, one in three in Washington Park, and one in four in Grand Boulevard.[1] In 1950, 69 percent of all males aged fourteen and older who lived in these three neighborhoods worked in a typical week, and in 1960, 64 percent of this group were so employed. However, by 1990 only 37 percent of all males aged sixteen and over held jobs in a typical week in these three neighborhoods.

The disappearance of work has had negative effects not only on individuals and families, but on the social life of neighborhoods as well. Inner-city joblessness is a severe problem that is often overlooked or obscured when the focus is mainly on poverty and its consequences. Despite increases in the concentration of poverty since 1970, inner cities have always featured high levels of poverty. But the levels of inner-city joblessness reached during the first half of the 1990s were unprecedented.

Joblessness versus Informal Work Activity

I should note that when I speak of "joblessness" I am not solely referring to official unemployment. The unemployment rate represents only the percentage of workers in the *official* labor force—that is, those who are *actively* looking for work. It does not include those who are outside of or have dropped out of the labor market, including the nearly six million males aged twenty-five to sixty who appeared in the census statistics but were not recorded in the labor market statistics in 1990 (Thurow 1990).

These uncounted males in the labor market are disproportionately represented in the inner-city ghettos. Accordingly, in *When Work Disappears,* I use a more appropriate measure of joblessness, a measure that takes into account both official unemployment and non–labor-force participation. That measure is the employment-to-population ratio, which corresponds to the percentage of adults aged sixteen and older who are working. Using the employment-to-population ratio we find, for example, that in 1990 only one in three adults aged sixteen and older held a job in the ghetto poverty areas of Chicago, areas representing roughly 425,000 men, women, and children. And in the ghetto tracts of the nation's one hundred largest cities, for every ten adults who did not hold a job in a typical week in 1990 there were only six employed persons (Kasarda 1993).

The consequences of high neighborhood joblessness are more devastating than those of high neighborhood poverty. A neighborhood in which people are poor but employed is much different than a neighborhood in which people are poor and jobless. *When Work Disappears* shows that many of today's problems in the inner-city ghetto neighborhoods—crime, family dissolution, welfare, low levels of social organization, and so on—are fundamentally a consequence of the disappearance of work.

It should be clear that when I speak of the disappearance of work, I am referring to the declining involvement in or lack of attachment to the formal labor market. It could be argued that, in the general sense of the term, "joblessness" does not necessarily mean "nonwork." In other words, to be officially unemployed or officially outside the labor market does not mean that one is totally removed from all forms of work activity. Many people who are officially jobless are nonetheless involved in informal kinds of work activity, ranging from unpaid housework to work that draws income from the informal or illegal economies.

Housework is work, baby-sitting is work, even drug dealing is work. However, what contrasts work in the formal economy with work activity in the informal and illegal economies is that work in the formal economy is characterized by, indeed calls for, greater regularity and consistency in schedules and hours. Work schedules and hours are formalized. The demands for discipline are greater. It is true that some work activities outside the formal economy also call for discipline and regular schedules. Several studies reveal that the social organization of the drug industry is driven by discipline and a work ethic, however perverse.[2] However, as a general rule, work in the informal and illegal economies is far less governed by norms or expectations that place a premium on discipline and regularity. For all these reasons, when I speak of the disappearance of work, I mean work in the formal economy, work that provides a framework for daily behavior because of the discipline, regularity, and stability that it imposes.

Effect of Joblessness on Routine and Discipline

In the absence of regular employment, a person lacks not only a place in which to work and the receipt of regular income but also a coherent organization of the present—that is, a system of concrete expectations and goals. Regular employment provides the anchor for the spatial and temporal aspects of daily life. It determines where you are going to be and when you are going to be there. In the absence of regular employment, life, including family life, becomes less coherent. Persistent unemployment and irregular employment hinder rational planning in daily life, a necessary condition of adaptation to an industrial economy (Bourdieu 1965).

Thus, a youngster who grows up in a family with a steady breadwinner and in a neighborhood in which most of the adults are employed will tend to develop some of the disciplined habits associated with stable or steady employment—habits that are reflected in the behavior of his or her parents and of other neighborhood adults. These might include attachment to a routine, a recognition of the hierarchy found in most work situations, a sense of personal efficacy attained through the routine management of financial affairs, endorsement of a system of personal and material rewards associated with dependability and responsibility, and so on. Accordingly, when this youngster enters the labor market, he or she has a distinct advantage over the youngsters who grow up in households without a steady breadwinner and in neighborhoods that are not organized around work—in other words, a milieu in which one is more exposed to the less disciplined habits associated with casual or infrequent work.

With the sharp recent rise of solo-parent families, black children who live in inner-city households are less likely to be socialized in a work environment for two main reasons. Their mothers, saddled with child-care responsibilities, can prevent a slide deeper into poverty by accepting welfare. Their fathers, removed from family responsibilities and obligations, are more likely to become idle as a response to restricted employment opportunities, which further weakens their influence in the household and attenuates their contact with the family. In short, the social and cultural responses to joblessness are reflected in the organization of family life and patterns of family formation; there they have implications for labor-force attachment as well.

Given the current policy debates that assign blame to the personal shortcomings of the jobless, we need to understand their behavior as responses and adaptations to chronic subordination, including behaviors that have evolved into cultural patterns. The social actions of the jobless—including their behavior, habits, skills, styles, orientations, attitudes—ought not to be analyzed as if they are unrelated to the broader structure of their opportunities and constraints that have evolved over time. This is not to argue that individuals and groups lack the freedom to make their own choices, engage in certain conduct, and develop certain styles and orientations; but I maintain that their decisions and actions occur within a context of constraints and opportunities that are drastically different from those in middle-class society.

Explanations of the Growth of Jobless Ghettos

What accounts for the growing proportion of jobless adults in inner-city communities? An easy explanation would be racial segregation. However, a race-specific argument is not sufficient to explain recent changes in such neighborhoods. After all, these historical Black Belt neighborhoods were *just as segregated by skin color in 1950* as they are today, yet the level of employment was much higher then. One has to account for the ways in which racial segregation interacts with other changes in society to produce the recent escalating rates of joblessness. Several factors stand out: the decreasing demand for low-skilled labor, the suburbanization of jobs, the social deterioration of ghetto neighborhoods, and negative employer attitudes. I discuss each of these factors next.

Decreasing Demand for Low-Skilled Labor

The disappearance of work in many inner-city neighborhoods is in part related to the nationwide decline in the fortunes of low-skilled workers. The sharp decline in the relative demand for unskilled labor has had a more adverse effect on blacks than on whites because a substantially larger proportion of African Americans are unskilled. Although the number of skilled blacks (including managers, professionals, and technicians) has increased sharply in the last several years, the proportion of those who are unskilled remains large, because the black population, burdened by cumulative experiences of racial restrictions, was overwhelmingly unskilled just several decades ago (Schwartzman 1997).[3]

The factors involved in the decreased relative demand for unskilled labor include changes in skill-based technology, the rapid growth in college enrollment that increased the supply and reduced the relative cost of skilled labor, and the growing internationalization of economic activity, including trade liberalization policies, which reduced the price of imports and raised the output of export industries (Schwartzman 1997). The increased output of export industries aids skilled workers, simply because they are heavily represented in export industries. But increasing imports, especially those from developing countries that compete with labor-intensive industries (for example, apparel, textile, toy, footwear, and some manufacturing industries), hurts unskilled labor (Schwartzman 1997).

Accordingly, inner-city blacks are experiencing a more extreme form of the economic marginality that has affected most unskilled workers in America since 1980. Unfortunately, there is a tendency among policy makers, black leaders, and scholars alike to separate the economic problems of the ghetto from the national and international trends affecting American families and neighborhoods. If the economic problems of the ghetto are defined solely in racial terms they can be isolated and viewed as only requiring race-based solutions as proposed by those on the left, or as only requiring narrow political solutions with subtle racial connotations (such as welfare reform), as strongly proposed by those on the right.

Overemphasis on Racial Factors

Race continues to be a factor that aggravates inner-city black employment problems as we shall soon see. But the tendency to overemphasize the racial factors obscures other more fundamental forces that have sharply increased inner-city black joblessness. As the late black economist Vivian Henderson put it several years ago, "[I]t is as if racism having put blacks in their economic place steps aside to watch changes in the economy destroy that place" (Henderson 1975, 54). To repeat, the concentrated joblessness of the inner-city poor represents the most dramatic form of the growing economic dislocations among the unskilled stemming in large measure from changes in the organization of the economy, including the global economy.

Suburbanization of Jobs

But inner-city workers face an additional problem: the growing suburbanization of jobs. Most ghetto residents cannot afford an automobile and therefore have to rely on public transit systems that make the connection between inner-city neighborhoods and suburban job locations difficult and time consuming.

Although studies based on data collected before 1970 showed no consistent or convincing effects on black employment as a consequence of this spatial mismatch, the employment of inner-city blacks relative to suburban blacks has clearly deteriorated since then. Recent research (conducted mainly by urban labor economists) strongly shows that the decentralization of employment is continuing and that employment in manufacturing, most of which is already suburbanized, has decreased in central cities, particularly in the Northeast and Midwest (Holzer 1996).

Blacks living in central cities have less access to employment (as measured by the ratio of jobs to people and the average travel time to and from work) than do central-city whites. Moreover, unlike most other groups of workers across the urban-suburban divide, less-educated central-city blacks receive lower wages than suburban blacks who have similar levels of education. And the decline in earnings of central-city blacks is related to the decentralization of employment—that is, the movement of jobs from the cities to the suburbs—in metropolitan areas (Holzer 1996).

Social Deterioration of Ghetto Neighborhoods

Changes in the class, racial, and demographic composition of inner-city neighborhoods have also contributed to the high percentage of jobless adults in these neighborhoods. Because of the steady out-migration of more advantaged families, the proportion of nonpoor families and prime-age working adults has decreased sharply in the typical inner-city ghetto since 1970 (Wilson 1987). In the face of increasing and prolonged joblessness, the declining proportion of nonpoor families and the overall depopulation has made it increasingly difficult to sustain basic neighborhood institutions or to achieve adequate levels of social organization. The declining presence of working- and middle-class blacks has also deprived ghetto neighborhoods of key structural and cultural resources. Structural resources include residents with income high enough to sustain neighborhood services, and cultural resources include conventional role models for neighborhood children.

On the basis of our research in Chicago, it appears that what many high jobless neighborhoods have in common is a relatively high degree of social integration (high levels of local neighboring while being relatively isolated from contacts in the broader mainstream society) and low levels of informal social control (feelings that they have little control over their immediate environment, including the environment's negative influences on their children). In such areas, not only are children at risk because of the lack of informal social controls, they are also disadvantaged because the social interaction among neighbors tends to be confined to those whose skills, styles, orientations, and habits are not as conducive to promoting positive social outcomes (academic success, pro-social behavior, employment in the formal labor market, etc.) as those in more stable neighborhoods. Although the close

interaction among neighbors in such areas may be useful in devising strategies, disseminating information, and developing styles of behavior that are helpful in a ghetto milieu (teaching children to avoid eye-to-eye contact with strangers and to develop a tough demeanor in the public sphere for self-protection), they may be less effective in promoting the welfare of children in society at large.

Despite being socially integrated, the residents in Chicago's ghetto neighborhoods shared a feeling that they had little informal social control over the children in their environment. A primary reason is the absence of a strong organizational capacity or an institutional resource base that would provide an extra layer of social organization in their neighborhoods. It is easier for parents to control the behavior of the children in their neighborhoods when a strong institutional resource base exists and when the links between community institutions such as churches, schools, political organizations, businesses, and civic clubs are strong or secure. The higher the density and stability of formal organizations, the less illicit activities such as drug trafficking, crime, prostitution, and the formation of gangs can take root in the neighborhood.

Few Community Institutions

A weak institutional resource base is what distinguishes high jobless inner-city neighborhoods from stable middle-class and working-class areas. As one resident of a high jobless neighborhood on the South Side of Chicago put it, "Our children, you know, seems to be more at risk than any other children there is, because there's no library for them to go to. There's not a center they can go to, there's no field house that they can go into. There's nothing.

There's nothing at all." Parents in high jobless neighborhoods have a much more difficult task controlling the behavior of their adolescents and preventing them from getting involved in activities detrimental to prosocial development. Given the lack of organizational capacity and a weak institutional base, some parents choose to protect their children by isolating them from activities in the neighborhood, including avoiding contact and interaction with neighborhood families. Wherever possible, and often with great difficulty when one considers the problems of transportation and limited financial resources, they attempt to establish contacts and cultivate relations with individuals, families, and institutions, such as church groups, schools, and community recreation programs, outside their neighborhood. A note of caution is necessary, though. It is just as indefensible to treat inner-city residents as super heroes who overcome racist oppression as it is to view them as helpless victims. We should, however, appreciate the range of choices, including choices representing cultural influences that are available to inner-city residents who live under constraints that most people in the larger society do not experience.

Effect of Joblessness on Marriage and Family

It is within the context of labor-force attachment that the public policy discussion on welfare reform and family values should be couched. The research that we have conducted in Chicago suggests that as employment prospects recede, the foundation for stable relationships becomes weaker over time. More permanent relationships such as marriage give way to temporary liaisons that result in broken unions, out-of-wedlock pregnancies, and, to a lesser extent,

separation and divorce. The changing norms concerning marriage in the larger society reinforce the movement toward temporary liaisons in the inner city, and therefore economic considerations in marital decisions take on even greater weight. Many inner-city residents have negative outlooks toward marriage, outlooks that are developed in and influenced by an environment featuring persistent joblessness.

The disrupting effect of joblessness on marriage and family causes poor inner-city blacks to be even more disconnected from the job market and discouraged about their role in the labor force. The economic marginality of the ghetto poor is cruelly reinforced, therefore, by conditions in the neighborhoods in which they live.

Negative Employer Attitudes

In the eyes of employers in metropolitan Chicago, the social conditions in the ghetto render inner-city blacks less desirable as workers, and therefore many are reluctant to hire them. One of the three studies that provided the empirical foundation for *When Work Disappears* included a representative sample of employers in the greater Chicago area who provided entry-level jobs. An overwhelming majority of these employers, both white and black, expressed negative views about inner-city ghetto workers, and many stated that they were reluctant to hire them. For example, a president of an inner-city manufacturing firm expressed a concern about employing residents from certain inner-city neighborhoods:

> If somebody gave me their address, uh, Cabrini Green I might unavoidably have some concerns.
> *Interviewer:* What would your concerns be?

That the poor guy probably would be frequently unable to get to work and . . . I probably would watch him more carefully even if it wasn't fair, than I would with somebody else. I know what I should do though is recognize that here's a guy that is trying to get out of his situation and probably will work harder than somebody else who's already out of there and he might be the best one around here. But I, I think I would have to struggle accepting that premise at the beginning. (Wilson 1996, field notes)

In addition to qualms about the neighborhood milieu of inner-city residents, the employers frequently mentioned concerns about applicants' language skills and educational training. An employer from a computer software firm in Chicago expressed the view "that in many businesses the ability to meet the public is paramount and you do not talk street talk to the buying public. Almost all your black welfare people talk street talk. And who's going to sit them down and change their speech patterns?" (Wilson 1996, field notes) A Chicago real estate broker made a similar point:

A lot of times I will interview applicants who are black, who are sort of lower class. . . . They'll come to me and I cannot hire them because their language skills are so poor. Their speaking voice for one thing is poor . . . they have no verbal facility with the language . . . and these . . . you know, they just don't know how to speak and they'll say "salesmens" instead of "salesmen" and that's a problem. . . . They don't know punctuation, they don't know how to use correct grammar, and they cannot spell. And I can't hire them. And I feel bad about

that and I think they're being very disadvantaged by the Chicago Public School system. (Wilson 1996, field notes)

Another respondent defended his method of screening out most job applicants on the telephone on the basis of their use of "grammar and English":

I have every right to say that that's a requirement for this job. I don't care if you're pink, black, green, yellow or orange, I demand someone who speaks well. You want to tell me that I'm a bigot, fine, call me a bigot. I know blacks, you don't even know they're black. (Wilson 1996, field notes)

Finally, an inner-city banker claimed that many blacks in the ghetto "simply cannot read. When you're talking our type of business, that disqualifies them immediately, we don't have a job here that doesn't require that somebody have minimum reading and writing skills" (Wilson 1996, field notes).

How should we interpret the negative attitudes and actions of employers? To what extent do they represent an aversion to blacks *per se* and to what degree do they reflect judgments based on the job-related skills and training of inner-city blacks in a changing labor market? I should point out that the statements made by the African American employers concerning the qualifications of inner-city black workers did not differ significantly from those of the white employers. Whereas 74 percent of all the white employers who responded to the open-ended questions expressed negative views of the job-related traits of inner-city blacks, 80 percent of the black employers did so as well.

This raises a question about the meaning and significance of race in certain situations—in other words, how race intersects with other factors. A key hypothesis in this connection is that given the recent shifts in the economy, employers are looking for workers with a broad range of abilities: "hard" skills (literacy, numerical ability, basic mechanical ability, and other testable attributes) and "soft" skills (personalities suitable to the work environment, good grooming, group-oriented work behaviors, etc.). While hard skills are the product of education and training—benefits that are apparently in short supply in inner-city schools—soft skills are strongly tied to culture, and are therefore shaped by the harsh environment of the inner-city ghetto. For example, our research revealed that many parents in the inner-city ghetto neighborhoods of Chicago wanted their children not to make eye-to-eye contact with strangers and to develop a tough demeanor when interacting with people on the streets. While such behaviors are helpful for survival in the ghetto, they hinder successful interaction in mainstream society.

Statistical Discrimination

If employers are indeed reacting to the difference in skills between white and black applicants, it becomes increasingly difficult to discuss the motives of employers: are they rejecting inner-city black applicants out of overt racial discrimination or on the basis of qualifications?

Nonetheless, many of the selective recruitment practices do represent what economists call "statistical discrimination": employers make assumptions about the inner-city black workers *in general* and reach decisions based on those assumptions before they have had a chance to review systematically the qualifications of an individual applicant. The net effect is that many black inner-city applicants are never given the chance to prove their qualifications on an individual level because they are systematically screened out by the selective recruitment process.

Statistical discrimination, although representing elements of class bias against poor workers in the inner city, is clearly a matter of race both directly and indirectly. Directly, the selective recruitment patterns effectively screen out far more black workers from the inner city than Hispanic or white workers from the same types of backgrounds. But indirectly, race is also a factor, even in those decisions to deny employment to inner-city black workers on the basis of objective and thorough evaluations of their qualifications. The hard and soft skills among inner-city blacks that do not match the current needs of the labor market are products of racially segregated communities, communities that have historically featured widespread social constraints and restricted opportunities.

Thus the job prospects of inner-city workers have diminished not only because of the decreasing relative demand for low-skilled labor in the United States economy, the suburbanization of jobs, and the social deterioration of ghetto neighborhoods, but also because of negative employer attitudes. This combination of factors presents a real challenge to policy makers. Indeed, considering the narrow range of social policy options in the "balance-the-budget" political climate, how can we immediately alleviate the inner-city jobs problem—a problem which will undoubtedly grow when the new welfare reform bill takes full effect and creates a situation that will be even more harmful to inner-city children and adolescents?

Public Policy Dilemmas

What are the implications of these studies on public policy? A key issue is public-sector employment. If firms in the private sector cannot hire or refuse to hire low-skilled adults who are willing to take minimum-wage jobs, then policy makers should consider a policy of public-sector employment-of-last-resort. Indeed, until current changes in the labor market are reversed or until the skills of the next generation of workers can be upgraded before they enter the labor market, many workers, especially those who are not in the official labor force, will not be able to find jobs unless the government becomes an employer-of-last-resort (Danziger and Gottschalk 1995). This argument applies especially to low-skilled inner-city black workers. It is bad enough that they face the problem of shifts in labor-market demand shared by all low-skilled workers; it is even worse that they confront negative employer perceptions about their work-related skills and attitudes.

For all these reasons, the passage of the 1996 welfare reform bill, which did not include a program of job creation, could have very negative social consequences in the inner city. Unless something is done to enhance the employment opportunities of inner-city welfare recipients who reach the time limit for the receipt of welfare, they will flood a pool already filled with low-skilled, jobless workers. . . .

West Virginia, a state that has been plagued with a severe shortage of work opportunities, has provided community service jobs to recipients of welfare for several years. In Wisconsin, Governor Thompson's welfare reform plan envisions community service jobs for many parents in the more depressed areas of the state, and the New Hope program in Milwaukee provides community service jobs for those unable to find employment in the private sector (Center on Budget and Policy Priorities 1996). It is especially important that this mixed strategy include a plan to make *adequate* monies available to localities or communities with high jobless and welfare dependency rates.

Obviously, as more people become employed and gain work experience, they will have a better chance of finding jobs in the private sector when jobs become available. The attitudes of employers toward inner-city workers could change, in part because they would be dealing with job applicants who have steady work experience and who could furnish references from their previous supervisors. Children are more likely to be socialized in a work-oriented environment and to develop the job readiness skills that are seen as important even for entry-level jobs.

Thus, given the recent welfare reform legislation, *adequate* strategies to enhance the employment opportunities of inner-city residents should be contemplated, strategies that would be adequately financed and designed to address the employment problems of low-skilled workers not only in periods of tight labor markets, but, even more important, in periods when the labor market is slack.

NOTES

1. The figures on adult employment are based on calculations from data provided by the 1990 U.S. Bureau of the Census (1993) and the *Local Community Fact Book for Chicago—1950* (1953) and the *Local Community Fact Book for Chicago—1960* (1963). The adult employment rates represent the number of employed individuals (aged fourteen and older in 1950 and sixteen

and older in 1990) among the total number of adults in a given area. Those who are not employed include both the individuals who are members of the labor force but are not working and those who have dropped out or are not part of the labor force.

2. See, for example, Bourgois (1995) and Venkatesh (1996).

3. The economist David Schwartzman defines "unskilled workers to include operators, fabricators, and laborers, and those in service occupations, including private household workers, those working in protective service occupations, food service, and cleaning and building service." On the basis of this definition he estimates that 80 percent of all black workers and 38 percent of all white workers were unskilled in 1950. By 1990, 46 percent of black workers and 27 percent of white workers were employed in unskilled occupations (Schwartzman 1997).

BIBLIOGRAPHY

Bourdieu, Pierre. 1965. *Travail et Travailleurs en Algerie.* Paris: Editions Mouton.

Bourgois, Philippe. 1995. *In Search of Respect: Selling Crack in El Barrio.* New York: Cambridge University Press.

Center on Budget and Policy Priorities. 1996. *The Administration's $3 Billion Jobs Proposal.* Washington, DC: Center on Budget and Policy Priorities.

Danziger, Sheldon H., and Peter Gottschalk. 1995. *America Unequal.* Cambridge, MA: Harvard University Press.

Henderson, Vivian. 1975. "Race, Economics, and Public Policy." *Crisis* 83 (Fall):50–55.

Holzer, Harry J. 1996. *What Employers Want: Job Prospects for Less-Educated Workers.* New York: Russell Sage.

Kasarda, John D. 1993. "Inner-City Concentrated Poverty and Neighborhood Distress: 1970–1990." *Housing Policy Debate* 4(3): 253–302.

Local Community Fact Book for Chicago—1950. 1953. Chicago: Community Inventory, University of Chicago.

Local Community Fact Book for Chicago—1960. 1963. Chicago: Community Inventory, University of Chicago.

Schwartzman, David. 1997. *Black Unemployment: Part of Unskilled Unemployment.* Westport, CT: Greenwood.

Thurow, Lester. 1990. "The Crusade That's Killing Prosperity." *American Prospect* March/April:54–59.

U.S. Bureau of the Census. 1993. *Census of Population: Detailed Characteristics of the Population.* Washington, DC: U.S. Government Printing Office.

Venkatesh, Sudhir. 1996. "Private Lives, Public Housing: An Ethnography of the Robert Taylor Homes." Ph.D. dissertation, University of Chicago.

Wilson, William Julius. 1987. *The Truly Disadvantaged: The Inner City, the Underclass, and Public Policy.* Chicago: University of Chicago Press.

———. 1996. *When Work Disappears: The World of the New Urban Poor.* New York: Alfred A. Knopf.

18

American Apartheid
Segregation and the Making of the Underclass

DOUGLAS S. MASSEY
NANCY A. DENTON

It is quite simple. As soon as there is a group area then all your uncertainties are removed and that is, after all, the primary purpose of this Bill [requiring racial segregation in housing].

—Minister of the Interior, Union of South Africa
legislative debate on the Group Areas Act of 1950

During the 1970s and 1980s a word disappeared from the American vocabulary.[1] It was not in the speeches of politicians decrying the multiple ills besetting American cities. It was not spoken by government officials responsible for administering the nation's social programs. It was not mentioned by journalists reporting on the rising tide of homelessness, drugs, and violence in urban America. It was not discussed by foundation executives and think-tank experts proposing new programs for unemployed parents and unwed mothers. It was not articulated by civil rights leaders speaking out against the persistence of racial inequality; and it was nowhere to be found in the thousands of pages written by social scientists on the urban underclass. The word was segregation.

Most Americans vaguely realize that urban America is still a residentially segregated society, but few appreciate the depth of black segregation or the degree to which it is maintained by ongoing institutional arrangements and contemporary individual actions. They view segregation as an unfortunate holdover from a racist past, one that is fading progressively over time. If racial residential segregation persists, they reason, it is only because civil rights laws passed during the 1960s have not had enough time to work or because many blacks still prefer to live in black neighborhoods. The residential segregation of blacks is viewed charitably as a "natural" outcome of impersonal social and economic forces, the same forces that produced Italian and Polish neighborhoods in the past and that yield Mexican and Korean areas today.

But black segregation is not comparable to the limited and transient segregation experienced by other racial and ethnic groups, now or in the past. No group in the history of the United States has ever experienced the sustained high level of residential segregation that has been imposed on blacks in large American cities for the past fifty years. This extreme racial isolation did not just happen; it was manufactured by whites through a series of self-conscious actions and purposeful institutional arrangements that continue today. Not only is the depth of black segregation unprecedented and utterly unique compared with that of other groups, but it shows little sign of change with the passage of time or improvements in socioeconomic status.

If policymakers, scholars, and the public have been reluctant to acknowledge segregation's persistence, they have likewise been blind to its consequences for American blacks. Residential segregation is not a neutral fact; it systematically undermines the social and economic well-being of blacks in the United States. Because of racial segregation, a significant share of black America is condemned to experience a social environment where poverty and joblessness are the norm, where a majority of children are born out of wedlock, where most families are on welfare, where educational failure prevails, and where social and physical deterioration abound. Through prolonged exposure to such an environment, black chances for social and economic success are drastically reduced.

Deleterious neighborhood conditions are built into the structure of the black community. They occur because segregation concentrates poverty to build a set of mutually reinforcing and self-feeding spirals of decline into black neighborhoods. When economic dislocations deprive a segregated group of employment and increase its rate of poverty, socioeconomic deprivation inevitably becomes more concentrated in neighborhoods where that group lives. The damaging social consequences that follow from increased poverty are spatially concentrated as well, creating uniquely disadvantaged environments that become progressively isolated—geographically, socially, and economically—from the rest of society.

The effect of segregation on black well-being is structural, not individual. Residential segregation lies beyond the ability of any individual to change; it constrains black life chances irrespective of personal traits, individual motivations, or private achievements. For the past twenty years this fundamental fact has been swept under the rug by policymakers, scholars, and theorists of the urban underclass. Segregation is the missing link in prior attempts to understand the plight of the urban poor. As long as blacks continue to be segregated in American cities, the United States cannot be called a race-blind society.

The Forgotten Factor

The present myopia regarding segregation is all the more startling because it once figured prominently in theories of racial inequality. Indeed, the ghetto was once seen as central to black subjugation in the United States. In 1944 Gunnar Myrdal wrote in *An American Dilemma* that residential segregation "is basic in a mechanical sense. It exerts its influence in an indirect and impersonal way: because Negro people do not live near white people, they cannot . . . associate with each other in the many activities founded on common neighborhood. Residential segregation . . . becomes reflected in uni-racial schools, hospitals, and other institutions" and creates "an artificial city . . . that permits any prejudice on the part of public officials to be freely vented on Negroes without hurting whites."[2]

Kenneth B. Clark, who worked with Gunnar Myrdal as a student and later applied his research skills in the landmark *Brown v. Topeka* school integration case, placed residential segregation at the heart of the U.S. system of racial oppression. In *Dark Ghetto,* written in 1965, he argued that "the dark ghetto's invisible walls have been erected by the white society, by those who have power, both to confine those who have *no* power and to perpetuate their powerlessness. The dark ghettos are social, political, educational, and—above all—economic colonies. Their inhabitants are subject peoples, victims of the greed, cruelty, insensitivity, guilt, and fear of their masters."[3]

Public recognition of segregation's role in perpetuating racial inequality was galvanized in the late 1960s by the riots that erupted in the nation's ghettos. In their aftermath, President Lyndon B. Johnson appointed a commission chaired by Governor Otto Kerner of Illinois to identify the causes of the violence and to propose policies to prevent its recurrence. The Kerner Commission released its report in March 1968 with the shocking admonition that the United States was "moving toward two societies, one black, one white—separate and unequal."[4] Prominent among the causes that the commission identified for this growing racial inequality was residential segregation.

In stark, blunt language, the Kerner Commission informed white Americans that "discrimination and segregation have long permeated much of American life; they now threaten the future of every American."[5] "Segregation and poverty have created in the racial ghetto a destructive environment totally unknown to most white Americans. What white Americans have never fully understood—but what the Negro can never forget—is that white society is deeply implicated in the ghetto. White institutions created it, white institutions maintain it, and white society condones it."[6]

The report argued that to continue present policies was "to make permanent the division of our country into two societies; one, largely Negro and poor, located in the central cities; the other, predominantly white and affluent, located in the suburbs."[7] Commission members rejected a strategy of ghetto enrichment coupled with abandonment of efforts to integrate, an approach they saw "as another way of choosing a permanently divided country."[8] Rather, they insisted that the only reasonable choice for America was "a policy which combines ghetto enrichment with programs designed to encourage integration of substantial numbers of Negroes into the society outside the ghetto."[9]

America chose differently. Following the passage of the Fair Housing Act in 1968, the problem of housing discrimination was declared solved, and residential segregation dropped off the national agenda. Civil rights leaders stopped pressing for the enforcement of open housing, political leaders increasingly debated employment and educational policies rather than housing integration, and academicians focused their theoretical scrutiny on everything from culture to family structure, to institutional racism, to federal welfare systems. Few people spoke of racial segregation as a problem or acknowledged its persisting consequences. By the end of the 1970s residential segregation became the forgotten factor in American race relations.[10]

While public discourse on race and poverty became more acrimonious and more focused on divisive issues such as school busing, racial quotas, welfare, and affirmative action, conditions in the nation's ghettos steadily deteriorated.[11] By the end of the 1970s, the image of poor minority families mired in an endless cycle of unemployment, unwed childbearing, illiteracy, and dependency had coalesced into a compelling and powerful concept: the urban underclass.[12] In the view of many middle-class whites, inner cities had come to house a large population of poorly educated single mothers and jobless men—mostly black and Puerto Rican—who were unlikely to exit poverty and become self-sufficient. In the ensuing national debate on the causes for this persistent poverty, four theoretical explanations gradually emerged: culture, racism, economics, and welfare.

Cultural explanations for the underclass can be traced to the work of Oscar Lewis, who identified a "culture of poverty" that he felt promoted patterns of behavior inconsistent with socioeconomic advancement.[13] According to Lewis, this culture originated in endemic unemployment and chronic social immobility, and provided an ideology that allowed poor people to cope with feelings of hopelessness and despair that arose because their chances for socioeconomic success were remote. In individuals, this culture was typified by a lack of impulse control, a strong present-time orientation, and little ability to defer gratifica-

tion. Among families, it yielded an absence of childhood, an early initiation into sex, a prevalence of free marital unions, and a high incidence of abandonment of mothers and children.

Although Lewis explicitly connected the emergence of these cultural patterns to structural conditions in society, he argued that once the culture of poverty was established, it became an independent cause of persistent poverty. This idea was further elaborated in 1965 by the Harvard sociologist and then Assistant Secretary of Labor Daniel Patrick Moynihan, who in a confidential report to the President focused on the relationship between male unemployment, family instability, and the intergenerational transmission of poverty, a process he labeled a "tangle of pathology."[14] He warned that because of the structural absence of employment in the ghetto, the black family was disintegrating in a way that threatened the fabric of community life.

When these ideas were transmitted through the press, both popular and scholarly, the connection between culture and economic structure was somehow lost, and the argument was popularly perceived to be that "people were poor because they had a defective culture." This position was later explicitly adopted by the conservative theorist Edward Banfield, who argued that lower-class culture—with its limited time horizon, impulsive need for gratification, and psychological self-doubt—was primarily responsible for persistent urban poverty.[15] He believed that these cultural traits were largely imported, arising primarily because cities attracted lower-class migrants.

The culture-of-poverty argument was strongly criticized by liberal theorists as a self-serving ideology that "blamed the victim."[16] In the ensuing wave of reaction, black families were viewed not as weak but, on the contrary, as resilient and well-adapted survivors in an oppressive and racially prejudiced society.[17] Black disadvantages were attributed not to a defective culture but to the persistence of institutional racism in the United States. According to theorists of the underclass such as Douglas Glasgow and Alphonso Pinkney, the black urban underclass came about because deeply imbedded racist practices within American institutions—particularly schools and the economy—effectively kept blacks poor and dependent.[18]

As the debate on culture versus racism ground to a halt during the late 1970s, conservative theorists increasingly captured public attention by focusing on a third possible cause of poverty: government welfare policy. According to Charles Murray, the creation of the underclass was rooted in the liberal welfare state.[19] Federal antipoverty programs altered the incentives governing the behavior of poor men and women, reducing the desirability of marriage, increasing the benefits of unwed childbearing, lowering the attractiveness of menial labor, and ultimately resulted in greater poverty.

A slightly different attack on the welfare state was launched by Lawrence Mead, who argued that it was not the generosity but the permissiveness of the U.S. welfare system that was at fault.[20] Jobless men and unwed mothers should be required to display "good citizenship" before being supported by the state. By not requiring anything of the poor, Mead argued, the welfare state undermined their independence and competence, thereby perpetuating their poverty.

This conservative reasoning was subsequently attacked by liberal social scientists, led principally by the sociologist William Julius Wilson, who had long been arguing for the increasing importance of class over race in understanding the social and economic problems facing blacks.[21] In his 1987 book *The Truly Disadvantaged,* Wilson argued that persistent urban poverty stemmed primarily from the structural transformation of the inner-city economy.[22] The decline of manufacturing, the suburbanization of employment, and the rise of a low-wage service sector dramatically reduced the number of city jobs that paid wages sufficient to support a family, which led to high rates of joblessness among minorities and a shrinking pool of "marriageable" men (those financially able to support a family). Marriage thus became less attractive to poor women, unwed childbearing increased, and female-headed families proliferated. Blacks suffered disproportionately from these trends because, owing to past discrimination, they were concentrated in locations and occupations particularly affected by economic restructuring.

Wilson argued that these economic changes were accompanied by an increase in the spatial concentration of poverty within black neighborhoods. This new geography of poverty, he felt, was enabled by the civil rights revolution of the 1960s, which provided middle-class blacks with new opportunities outside the ghetto.[23] The out-migration of middle-class families from ghetto areas left behind a destitute community lacking the institutions, resources, and values necessary for success in post-industrial society. The urban underclass thus arose from a complex interplay of civil rights policy, economic restructuring, and a historical legacy of discrimination.

Theoretical concepts such as the culture of poverty, institutional racism, welfare disincentives, and structural economic change have all been widely debated. None of these explanations, however, considers residential segregation to be an important contributing cause of urban poverty and the underclass. In their principal works, Murray and Mead do not mention segregation at all;[24] and Wilson refers to racial segregation only as a historical legacy from the past, not as an outcome that is institutionally supported and actively created today.[25] Although Lewis mentions segregation sporadically in his writings, it is not assigned a central role in the set of structural factors responsible for the culture of poverty, and Banfield ignores it entirely. Glasgow, Pinkney, and other theorists of institutional racism mention the ghetto frequently, but generally call not for residential desegregation but for race-specific policies to combat the effects of discrimination in the schools and labor markets. In general, then, contemporary theorists of urban poverty do not see high levels of black-white segregation as particularly relevant to understanding the underclass or alleviating urban poverty.[26]

The purpose of this book is to redirect the focus of public debate back to issues of race and racial segregation, and to suggest that they should be fundamental to thinking about the status of black Americans and the origins of the urban underclass. Our quarrel is less with any of the prevailing theories of urban poverty than with their systematic failure to consider the important role that segregation has played in mediating, exacerbating, and ultimately amplifying the harmful social and economic processes they treat.

We join earlier scholars in rejecting the view that poor urban blacks have an autonomous "culture of poverty" that explains their failure to achieve socioeconomic success in American society. We argue instead

that residential segregation has been instrumental in creating a structural niche within which a deleterious set of attitudes and behaviors—a culture of segregation—has arisen and flourished. Segregation created the structural conditions for the emergence of an oppositional culture that devalues work, schooling, and marriage and that stresses attitudes and behaviors that are antithetical and often hostile to success in the larger economy. Although poor black neighborhoods still contain many people who lead conventional, productive lives, their example has been overshadowed in recent years by a growing concentration of poor, welfare-dependent families that is an inevitable result of residential segregation.

We readily agree with Douglas, Pinkney, and others that racial discrimination is widespread and may even be institutionalized within large sectors of American society, including the labor market, the educational system, and the welfare bureaucracy. We argue, however, that this view of black subjugation is incomplete without understanding the special role that residential segregation plays in enabling all other forms of racial oppression. Residential segregation is the institutional apparatus that supports other racially discriminatory processes and binds them together into a coherent and uniquely effective system of racial subordination. Until the black ghetto is dismantled as a basic institution of American urban life, progress ameliorating racial inequality in other arenas will be slow, fitful, and incomplete.

We also agree with William Wilson's basic argument that the structural transformation of the urban economy undermined economic supports for the black community during the 1970s and 1980s.[27] We argue, however, that in the absence of segregation, these structural changes would not have produced the disastrous social and economic outcomes observed in inner cities during these decades. Although rates of black poverty were driven up by the economic dislocations Wilson identifies, it was segregation that confined the increased deprivation to a small number of densely settled, tightly packed, and geographically isolated areas.

Wilson also argues that concentrated poverty arose because the civil rights revolution allowed middle-class blacks to move out of the ghetto. Although we remain open to the possibility that class-selective migration did occur,[28] we argue that concentrated poverty would have happened during the 1970s with or without black middle-class migration. Our principal objection to Wilson's focus on middle-class out-migration is not that it did not occur, but that it is misdirected: focusing on the flight of the black middle class deflects attention from the real issue, which is the limitation of black residential options through segregation.

Middle-class households—whether they are black, Mexican, Italian, Jewish, or Polish—always try to escape the poor. But only blacks must attempt their escape within a highly segregated, racially segmented housing market. Because of segregation, middle-class blacks are less able to escape than other groups, and as a result are exposed to more poverty. At the same time, because of segregation no one will move into a poor black neighborhood except other poor blacks. Thus both middle-class blacks and poor blacks lose compared with the poor and middle class of other groups: poor blacks live under unrivaled concentrations of poverty and affluent blacks live in neighborhoods that are far less advanta-geous than those experienced by the middle class of other groups.

Finally, we concede Murray's general point that federal welfare policies are linked to the rise of the urban underclass, but we disagree with his specific hypothesis that generous welfare payments, by themselves, discouraged employment, encouraged unwed childbearing, undermined the strength of the family, and thereby caused persistent poverty.[29] We argue instead that welfare payments were only harmful to the socioeconomic well-being of groups that were residentially segregated. As poverty rates rose among blacks in response to the economic dislocations of the 1970s and 1980s, so did the use of welfare programs. Because of racial segregation, however, the higher levels of welfare receipt were confined to a small number of isolated, all-black neighborhoods. By promoting the spatial concentration of welfare use, therefore, segregation created a residential environment within which welfare dependency was the norm, leading to the intergenerational transmission and broader perpetuation of urban poverty.

Coming to Terms with American Apartheid

Our fundamental argument is that racial segregation—and its characteristic institutional form, the black ghetto—are the key structural factors responsible for the perpetuation of black poverty in the United States. Residential segregation is the principal organizational feature of American society that is responsible for the creation of the urban underclass. . . . It can be shown that any increase in the poverty rate of a residentially segregated group leads to an immediate and automatic increase in the geographic concentration of poverty. When the rate of minority poverty is increased under conditions of high segregation, all of the increase is absorbed by a small number of neighborhoods. When the same increase in poverty occurs in an integrated group, the added poverty is spread evenly throughout the urban area, and the neighborhood environment that group members face does not change much.

During the 1970s and 1980s, therefore, when urban economic restructuring and inflation drove up rates of black and Hispanic poverty in many urban areas, underclass communities were created only where increased minority poverty coincided with a high degree of segregation—principally in older metropolitan areas of the northeast and the midwest. Among Hispanics, only Puerto Ricans developed underclass communities, because only they were highly segregated; and this high degree of segregation is directly attributable to the fact that a large proportion of Puerto Ricans are of African origin.

The interaction of intense segregation and high poverty leaves black neighborhoods extremely vulnerable to fluctuations in the urban economy, because any dislocation that causes an upward shift in black poverty rates will also produce a rapid change in the concentration of poverty and, hence, a dramatic shift in the social and economic composition of black neighborhoods. The concentration of poverty, for example, is associated with the wholesale withdrawal of commercial institutions and the deterioration or elimination of goods and services distributed through the market.

Neighborhoods, of course, are dynamic and constantly changing, and given the high rates of residential turnover characteristic of contemporary American cities, their well-being depends to a great extent on the characteristics and actions of their residents. Decisions taken by one actor affect the subsequent decisions of others in the neighborhood. In this way isolated actions affect the well-being of the community and alter the stability of the neighborhood.

Because of this feedback between individual and collective behavior, neighborhood stability is characterized by a series of thresholds, beyond which various self-perpetuating processes of decay take hold. Above these thresholds, each actor who makes a decision that undermines neighborhood well-being makes it increasingly likely that other actors will do the same. Each property owner who decides not to invest in upkeep and maintenance, for example, lowers the incentive for others to maintain their properties. Likewise, each new crime promotes psychological and physical withdrawal from public life, which reduces vigilance within the neighborhood and undermines the capacity for collective organization, making additional criminal activity more likely.

Segregation increases the susceptibility of neighborhoods to these spirals of decline. During periods of economic dislocation, a rising concentration of black poverty is associated with the simultaneous concentration of other negative social and economic conditions. Given the high levels of racial segregation characteristic of American urban areas, increases in black poverty such as those observed during the 1970s can only lead to a concentration of housing abandonment, crime, and social disorder, pushing poor black neighborhoods beyond the threshold of stability.

By building physical decay, crime, and social disorder into the residential structure of black communities, segregation creates a harsh and extremely disadvantaged environment to which ghetto blacks must adapt. In concentrating poverty, moreover, segregation also concentrates conditions such as drug use, joblessness, welfare dependency, teenage childbearing, and unwed parenthood, producing a social context where these conditions are not only common but the norm. By adapting to this social environment, ghetto dwellers evolve a set of behaviors, attitudes, and expectations that are sharply at variance with those common in the rest of American society.

As a direct result of the high degree of racial and class isolation created by segregation, for example, Black English has become progressively more distant from Standard American English, and its speakers are at a clear disadvantage in U.S. schools and labor markets. Moreover, the isolation and intense poverty of the ghetto provides a supportive structural niche for the emergence of an "oppositional culture" that inverts the values of middle-class society. Anthropologists have found that young people in the ghetto experience strong peer pressure not to succeed in school, which severely limits their prospects for social mobility in the larger society. Quantitative research shows that growing up in a ghetto neighborhood increases the likelihood of dropping out of high school, reduces the probability of attending college, lowers the likelihood of employment, reduces income earned as an adult, and increases the risk of teenage childbearing and unwed pregnancy.

Segregation also has profound political consequences for blacks, because it so isolates them geographically that they are the only ones who benefit from public expenditures in their neighborhoods. The relative integration of most ethnic groups means that jobs or services allocated to them will generally benefit several other groups at the same time. Integration thus creates a basis for political coalitions and pluralist politics, and most ethnic groups that seek public resources are able to find coalition partners because other groups can anticipate sharing the benefits. That blacks are the only ones to benefit from resources allocated to the ghetto—and are the only ones harmed when resources are removed—makes it difficult for them to find partners for political coalitions. Although segregation paradoxically makes it easier for blacks to elect representatives, it limits their political influence and marginalizes them within the American polity. Segregation prevents blacks from participating in pluralist politics based on mutual self-interest.

Because of the close connection between social and spatial mobility, segregation also perpetuates poverty. One of the primary means by which individuals improve their life chances—and those of their children—is by moving to neighborhoods with higher home values, safer streets, higher-quality schools, and better services. As groups move up the socioeconomic ladder, they typically move up the residential hierarchy as well, and in doing so they not only improve their standard of living but also enhance their chances for future success. Barriers to spatial mobility are barriers to social mobility, and by confining blacks to a small set of relatively disadvantaged neighborhoods, segregation constitutes a very powerful impediment to black socioeconomic progress.

Despite the obvious deleterious consequences of black spatial isolation, policymakers have not paid much attention to segregation as a contributing cause of urban poverty and have not taken effective steps to dismantle the ghetto. Indeed, for most of

the past two decades public policies tolerated and even supported the perpetuation
of segregation in American urban areas. Although many political initiatives were
launched to combat discrimination and
prejudice in the housing and banking industries, each legislative or judicial act was
fought tenaciously by a powerful array of
people who believed in or benefited from
the status quo.

Although a comprehensive open housing
bill finally passed Congress under unusual
circumstances in 1968, it was stripped of its
enforcement provisions as its price of enactment, yielding a Fair Housing Act that was
structurally flawed and all but doomed to
fail. As documentation of the law's defects
accumulated in multiple congressional hear-
ings, government reports, and scholarly
studies, little was done to repair the situation until 1988, when a series of scandals
and political errors by the Reagan administration finally enabled a significant strengthening of federal antidiscrimination law.

Yet even more must be done to prevent
the permanent bifurcation of the United
States into black and white societies that are
separate and unequal. As of 1990, levels of
racial segregation were still extraordinarily
high in the nation's large urban areas, particularly those of the north. Segregation has
remained high because fair housing enforcement relies too heavily on the private
efforts of individual victims of discrimination. Whereas the processes that perpetuate
segregation are entrenched and institutionalized, fair housing enforcement is individual, sporadic, and confined to a small
number of isolated cases.

As long as the Fair Housing Act is enforced individually rather than systemically,
it is unlikely to be effective in overcoming
the structural arrangements that support
segregation and sustain the ghetto. Until the
government throws its considerable institutional weight behind efforts to dismantle
the ghetto, racial segregation will persist. . . .

Ultimately, however, dismantling the
ghetto and ending the long reign of racial
segregation will require more than specific
bureaucratic reforms; it requires a moral
commitment that white America has historically lacked. The segregation of American blacks was no historical accident; it was
brought about by actions and practices that
had the passive acceptance, if not the active
support, of most whites in the United
States. Although America's apartheid may
not be rooted in the legal strictures of its
South African relative, it is no less effective
in perpetuating racial inequality, and whites
are no less culpable for the socioeconomic
deprivation that results.

As in South Africa, residential segregation in the United States provides a firm
basis for a broader system of racial injustice.
The geographic isolation of Africans within
a narrowly circumscribed portion of the
urban environment—whether African
townships or American ghettos—forces
blacks to live under extraordinarily harsh
conditions and to endure a social world
where poverty is endemic, infrastructure is
inadequate, education is lacking, families
are fragmented, and crime and violence are
rampant.[30] Moreover, segregation confines
these unpleasant by-products of racial oppression to an isolated portion of the urban
geography far removed from the experience
of most whites. Resting on a foundation of
segregation, apartheid not only denies
blacks their rights as citizens but forces
them to bear the social costs of their own
victimization.

Although Americans have been quick to
criticize the apartheid system of South

Africa, they have been reluctant to acknowledge the consequences of their own institutionalized system of racial separation. The topic of segregation has virtually disappeared from public policy debates; it has vanished from the list of issues on the civil rights agenda; and it has been ignored by social scientists spinning endless theories of the underclass. Residential segregation has become the forgotten factor of American race relations, a minor footnote in the ongoing debate on the urban underclass. Until policymakers, social scientists, and private citizens recognize the crucial role of America's own apartheid in perpetuating urban poverty and racial injustice, the United States will remain a deeply divided and very troubled society.[31]

NOTES

1. Epigraph from Edgar H. Brookes, *Apartheid: A Documentary Study of Modern South Africa* (London: Routledge and Kegan Paul, 1968), p. 142.

2. Gunnar Myrdal, *An American Dilemma,* vol. 1 (New York: Harper and Brothers, 1944), p. 618; see also Walter A. Jackson, *Gunnar Myrdal and America's Conscience* (Chapel Hill: University of North Carolina Press, 1990), pp. 88–271.

3. Kenneth B. Clark, *Dark Ghetto: Dilemmas of Social Power* (New York: Harper and Row, 1965), p. 11.

4. U.S. National Advisory Commission on Civil Disorders, *The Kerner Report* (New York: Pantheon Books, 1988), p. 1.

5. Ibid.

6. Ibid., p. 2.

7. Ibid., p. 22.

8. Ibid.

9. Ibid.

10. A few scholars attempted to keep the Kerner Commission's call for desegregation alive, but their voices have largely been unheeded in the ongoing debate. Thomas Pettigrew has continued to assert the central importance of residential segregation, calling it the "linchpin" of American race relations; see "Racial Change and Social Policy," *Annals of the American Academy of Political and Social Science* 441 (1979):114–31. Gary Orfield has repeatedly pointed out segregation's deleterious effects on black prospects for education, employment, and socioeconomic mobility; see "Separate Societies: Have the Kerner Warnings Come True?" in Fred R. Harris and Roger W. Wilkins, eds., *Quiet Riots: Race and Poverty in the United States* (New York: Pantheon Books, 1988), pp. 100–122; and "Ghettoization and Its Alternatives," in Paul E. Peterson, ed., *The New Urban Reality* (Washington, D.C.: Brookings Institution, 1985), pp. 161–96.

11. See Thomas B. Edsall and Mary D. Edsall, *Chain Reaction: The Impact of Race, Rights, and Taxes on American Politics* (New York: Norton, 1991).

12. For an informative history of the evolution of the concept of the underclass, see Michael B. Katz, *The Undeserving Poor: From the War on Poverty to the War on Welfare* (New York: Pantheon, 1989), pp. 185–235.

13. Oscar Lewis, *La Vida: A Puerto Rican Family in the Culture of Poverty—San Juan and New York* (New York: Random House, 1965); "The Culture of Poverty," *Scientific American* 215 (1966): 19–25; "The Culture of Poverty," in Daniel P. Moynihan, ed., *On Understanding Poverty: Perspectives from the Social Sciences* (New York: Basic Books, 1968), pp. 187–220.

14. The complete text of this report is reprinted in Lee Rainwater and William L. Yancey, *The Moynihan Report and the Politics of Controversy* (Cambridge: MIT Press, 1967), pp. 39–125.

15. Edward C. Banfield, *The Unheavenly City* (Boston: Little, Brown, 1970).

16. William Ryan, *Blaming the Victim* (New York: Random House, 1971).

17. Carol Stack, *All Our Kin: Strategies of Survival in a Black Community* (New York: Harper and Row, 1974).

18. Douglas C. Glasgow, *The Black Underclass: Poverty, Unemployment, and Entrapment of Ghetto Youth* (New York: Vintage, 1981), p. 11; Alphonso Pinkney, *The Myth of Black Progress*

(Cambridge: Cambridge University Press, 1984), pp. 78–80.

19. Charles Murray, *Losing Ground: American Social Policy, 1950–1980* (New York: Basic Books, 1984).

20. Lawrence M. Mead, *Beyond Entitlement: The Social Obligations of Citizenship* (New York: Free Press, 1986).

21. William Julius Wilson, *The Declining Significance of Race: Blacks and Changing American Institutions* (Chicago: University of Chicago Press, 1978).

22. William Julius Wilson, *The Truly Disadvantaged: The Inner City, the Underclass, and Public Policy* (Chicago: University of Chicago Press, 1987), pp. 1–108.

23. Ibid., pp. 49–62.

24. The subject indices of *Losing Ground* and *Beyond Entitlement* contain no references at all to residential segregation.

25. The subject index of *The Truly Disadvantaged* contains two references to pre1960s Jim Crow segregation.

26. Again with the exception of Thomas Pettigrew and Gary Orfield.

27. We have published several studies documenting how the decline of manufacturing, the suburbanization of jobs, and the rise of low-wage service employment eliminated high-paying jobs for manual workers, drove up rates of black male unemployment, and reduced the attractiveness of marriage to black women, thereby contributing to a proliferation of female-headed families and persistent poverty. See Mitchell L. Eggers and Douglas S. Massey, "The Structural Determinants of Urban Poverty," *Social Science Research* 20 (1991): 217–55; Mitchell L. Eggers and Douglas S. Massey, "A Longitudinal Analysis of Urban Poverty: Blacks in U.S. Metropolitan Areas between 1970 and 1980," *Social Science Research* 21 (1992): 175–203.

28. The evidence on the extent of middle-class out-migration from ghetto areas is inconclusive. Because racial segregation does not decline with rising socioeconomic status, out-movement from poor black neighborhoods certainly has not been to white areas. When Kathryn P. Nelson measured rates of black out-migration from local "zones" within forty metropolitan areas, however, she found higher rates of out-movement for middle- and upper-class blacks compared with poor blacks; but her "zones" contained more than 100,000 inhabitants, making them considerably larger than neighborhoods (see "Racial Segregation, Mobility, and Poverty Concentration," paper presented at the annual meetings of the Population Association of America, Washington, D.C., March 19–23, 1991). In contrast, Edward Gramlich and Deborah Laren found that poor and middle-class blacks displayed about the same likelihood of out-migration from poor census tracts (see "Geographic Mobility and Persistent Poverty," Department of Economics, University of Michigan, Ann Arbor, 1990).

29. See Eggers and Massey, "A Longitudinal Analysis of Urban Poverty."

30. See International Defense and Aid Fund for Southern Africa, *Apartheid: The Facts* (London: United Nations Centre against Apartheid, 1983), pp. 15–26.

31. We are not the first to notice the striking parallel between the institutionalized system of racial segregation in U.S. cities and the organized, state-sponsored system of racial repression in South Africa. See John H. Denton, *Apartheid American Style* (Berkeley, Calif.: Diablo Press, 1967); James A. Kushner, "Apartheid in America: An Historical and Legal Analysis of Contemporary Racial Residential Segregation in the United States," *Howard Law Journal* 22 (1979):547–60.

19

Neighborhoods, Poverty, and Children's Well-Being

ANNE R. PEBLEY

NARAYAN SASTRY

Research on neighborhood effects suggests that neighborhood characteristics such as poverty, crime, and residential turnover influence several interrelated aspects of the neighborhood environment that, in turn, affect families and children. These mechanisms can be summarized in four categories: child and family-related institutions; social organization and interaction; normative environment; and labor and marriage markets. We will briefly describe each of these.

Child and family-related institutions include schools, child care providers, public libraries, recreational programs and activities (such as music lessons, youth organizations, sports activities, arts and theater activities, and mentoring programs), parks, religious institutions, and social service providers. These institutions play a vital role in the general process of socialization, but many also impart important skills and provide specific services. While the availability and quality of these institutions may be affected directly by public policy (for example, by school improvement pro-grams in poorer neighborhoods), they are also likely to be determined by neighborhood socioeconomic characteristics (Jencks and Mayer 1990; Aber et al. 1997). For example, child care centers and after-school programs may be more readily available, hire better staff, and provide better service in more affluent or well-educated neighborhoods, because residents demand it and can afford to pay for it. As described later, more socially organized neighborhoods may also be able to demand better institutions through collective action and the political process, even if income and educational levels are low. Poorer neighborhoods may be worse off than others not only because they have weaker institutions but also because the greater needs of families are likely to overtax the existing institutions (Aber et al. 1997).

Neighborhood *social organization and interaction* has recently received considerable attention in research on neighborhood effects. Social disorganization theory suggests that some neighborhood characteristics (such as poverty, ethnic heterogeneity,

Anne R. Pebley and Narayan Sastry, "Neighborhoods, Poverty, and Children's Well-Being," *Social Inequality*, edited by Kathryn M. Neckerman, pp. 120–123, 129–135, 138–145. Copyright © 2004 by Russell Sage Foundation.

high residential turnover rates, low home-ownership rates, and concentration of recent immigrants) make it harder for residents to establish social ties and agree on the values needed to exercise social control and work together on common goals. As a result, socially disorganized neighborhoods are more difficult, dangerous, and stressful places to live. Parents and children in these neighborhoods are both more likely to participate in deviant behavior (delinquency, crime, violence, substance abuse) and to suffer the consequences of this behavior in others (Shaw and McKay 1969; Sampson, Morenoff, and Gannon-Rowley 2002). Sampson and his colleagues (Sampson, Morenoff, and Earls 1999; Sampson, Morenoff, and Gannon-Rowley 2002) argue that neighborhood collective efficacy—that is, shared expectations and the involvement of neighborhood residents in active support and social control of children—is key to a positive neighborhood environment for children. In neighborhoods with higher collective efficacy, residents are more likely to monitor and, when necessary, correct children's behavior. They are also more likely to work together on neighborhood problems and to build and maintain strong local institutions.

Two other theoretical perspectives—William Julius Wilson's (1987, 1996) collective socialization model and James Coleman's (1988) social capital theory—suggest related ways in which neighborhood social interaction may be important for children. Collective socialization models posit that neighborhood adults play an important role by monitoring children's behavior (as Sampson and his colleagues emphasize) and by providing role models. For example, Wilson argues that the selec-tive out-migration of middle-class professionals from African American inner-city neighborhoods has resulted in fewer positive role models for the children in those neighborhoods. Social capital models suggest that the key elements are the dense and overlapping social ties among adults and children. In neighborhoods with more social capital, children know that they will be held accountable for their actions and that they can rely on neighborhood adults for support. However, as Wilson (1996) and Sampson, Morenoff, and Earls (1999) note, high levels of social capital can facilitate the enforcement of *both* negative and positive norms and behavior. Wilson (1996, 62) points out, for example, that in neighborhoods "characterized by high levels of individual and family involvement in aberrant behavior," a high degree of social integration among adults can in fact help to create and reinforce problem behavior among children.

Connections with the world outside the neighborhood may also be important. Especially in disadvantaged neighborhoods, extralocal social ties can provide access to information about, or assistance with, opportunities, services, or normative feedback from those who move in other social circles (Coleman 1988; Stack 1974; Edin 1991; Tigges, Browne, and Green 1998). Melvin Oliver's (1988) study of social networks in urban African American communities in Los Angeles shows that extralocal social ties vary considerably among neighborhoods. He concludes that in poor neighborhoods the lack of outside social ties may be a significant disadvantage. In recent decades urban sociologists have argued that despatialized social networks have displaced the role of neighborhoods in urban life; neighborhoods are increasingly *un*important, they argue, in individuals' lives (South 2001; Fischer 1984; Wellman 1999). However, Barry Wellman (1999, 27), a proponent of this view, admits that "communities have not totally lost their domestic roots. . . . Local relationships are necessary for domestic safety, controlling actual land use, and quickly getting goods and services." He shows, for example, that much of Toronto residents' telephone contact is with neighbors rather than with extralocal ties (Wellman 1996). As Sampson and his colleagues (2002) point out, social ties among neighbors do not need to be strong or close in order to be effective. In fact, social disorganization theory suggests that neighborhood environments depend on weak and limited ties among neighbors who share a minimum level of trust, agreement on basic standards, and willingness to live by and enforce those standards. Nonetheless, the relative importance for children's development of urban neighborhood environments versus social networks is an empirical question for which we do not yet have complete answers.

The economic models suggest that *labor and marriage markets* are key elements in neighborhood effects on families and children (Duncan and Hoffman 1990; Haveman and Wolfe 1994). Local labor markets, marriage markets, and, in some neighborhoods, the illicit economy provide constraints and opportunities for neighborhood residents. Market conditions affect adults and adolescents most directly. However, by affecting their *parents'* probabilities of employment and marriage, local markets may have indirect effects on younger children. For example, in neighborhoods with poor labor markets, higher rates of parental un-

employment may affect children by increasing stress on parents, depressing household income, and creating a more stressful home environment.

Neighborhood characteristics, such as high levels of marriage, are thought to affect children's well-being both directly, by providing a positive normative environment, strong institutions, effective monitoring and social control, and a supportive climate for children, and indirectly, through effects on parents and the home environment. As noted earlier, neighborhood labor market and marriage market conditions can affect parents' income, family structure, and the home environment. Neighborhoods may also directly affect parenting behavior and family dynamics (Aneshensel and Sucoff 1996; Klebanov et al. 1997; Coulton 1996; Korbin and Coulton 1997). For example, parents in extremely disadvantaged neighborhoods are more likely to exhibit more punitive, authoritarian, and coercive parenting styles and to use corporal punishment (McLoyd 1990; Sampson and Laub 1994) as well as to withdraw emotionally from their children (Klebanov, Brooks-Gunn, and Duncan 1994). These responses are likely to have detrimental consequences for children's emotional, cognitive, and social development, and those consequences may later be reinforced by other negative aspects of neighborhood life.

Several theorists emphasize the key role of the *normative environment* itself in linking neighborhood compositional characteristics (such as poverty or high turnover rates) and child outcomes. Neighborhood norms may be a consequence of the characteristics of the people who live in the neighborhood—their income level, ethnic background, education, or immigrant experience. Those norms may also be affected by the social organization and interaction and by marriage and labor markets, as described earlier. The central idea in this literature is that the greater the concentration of like-minded people, the stronger the normative climate and the greater the exposure of neighborhood residents to these norms. For example, black children in poor inner-city neighborhoods may be more likely to be exposed to social problems, because the extreme concentration of poverty in inner-city African American neighborhoods since 1970 has created negative normative environments in which behavior considered negative by the middle class is reinforced and valued (Massey, Gross, and Eggers 1991; Massey and Denton 1993; Wilson, 1987, 1996; Fordham and Ogbu 1986). However, this process is not necessarily limited to concentrated-poverty neighborhoods or to negative outcomes—for example, some observers have argued that concentrated immigrant communities in Los Angeles can provide supportive climates for social mobility (Waldinger 1996). The "epidemic" hypothesis (Crane 1991; Case and Katz 1991) is a specific version of theories about normative environments. Jonathan Crane (1991) argues that concentrated-poverty neighborhoods dramatically increase adolescents' exposure to problem behavior and negative norms through contacts with peers. Epidemics of social problems can occur once neighborhoods reach a critically high level of negative social behaviors. . . .

Neighborhood Selection

A serious problem in studying neighborhood effects on children's well-being is the potential endogeneity of neighborhood (and school) characteristics. Endogenous characteristics are independent variables that may be correlated with unobserved factors not included in the model. In the case of neighborhood selection, the problem is that parents can choose the neighborhood in which they live but they can also affect children's development in many other ways. Thus, parents' attitudes about child development may affect both the type of neighborhood their children grow up in and other factors that affect their children's development, such as parenting and the home environment. Parents who move to help their children escape the influences of gang activity, drug use, teenage pregnancy, or crime, or who choose a neighborhood for the quality of its schools, may also be better parents in other ways. Other neighborhood attributes that may influence both parents' choice of where to live and children's behavior and development include the strength of neighborhood ties and characteristics of other families and children in the neighborhood. To the extent that neighborhood of residence is a choice, all neighborhood characteristics should be treated as endogenous. It is important, however, to understand the source of the endogeneity in order to identify appropriate analytic strategies.

Neighborhood attributes may be endogenous because place of residence is a choice variable and is determined in part by factors that also influence children's behavior and development. Thus, a common set of parent and family characteristics determines both children's behavior and development *and* neighborhood choice. Some of these characteristics, such as household income and parents' education, are measurable and can be controlled in models of children's behavior and development. However, some are unobserved and hence are picked up in the random component of statistical models, where correlation with included regressors—neighborhood characteristics—leads to biased and inconsistent estimates of all model parameters. As Greg Duncan and his colleagues explain (see, for example, Duncan, Connell, and Klebanov 1997), the problem of neighborhood selection is thus really one of omitted variables. Specific unobserved (omitted) parent and family factors are the parents' cognitive ability and family motivation and aspirations, which may influence the degree to which a family values its children's behavior and development (as well as its choice of place of residence).. . .

Neighborhood-Effects Analyses

The extensive neighborhood-effects literature published since 1990 has generally sought to answer one or more of the following three questions:

1. Are children who grow up in poor neighborhoods worse off than other children?
2. Are disparities in children's welfare by neighborhood poverty level due to differences in their families' characteristics, or do neighborhood conditions themselves play a role?
3. What mechanisms link concentrated-poverty neighborhoods to poorer outcomes for children?

Studies addressing these questions have generally been of two types. The largest group is non-experimental or observational studies, generally based on sample survey data. More recently, several experimental studies have assessed the consequences for poor families of moving into nonpoor neighborhoods. Both types of studies have usually sought to investigate the first two questions—whether children's outcomes differ by neighborhood characteristics and whether this variation persists if family attributes are held constant. A smaller number of studies have attempted to answer the third question by exploring the mechanisms that may link the characteristics of concentrated-poverty neighborhoods to poorer outcomes for children.

Recent reviews by psychologists, economists, and sociologists have thoroughly cataloged and critiqued this literature (Leventhal and Brooks-Gunn 2000; Ginter, Haveman, and Wolfe 2000; Duncan and Raudenbush 1999, 2001; Sampson, Morenoff, and Gannon-Rowley 2002). In this section, we draw on these critiques and our own reading of the literature to summarize the results of non-experimental research on neighborhood effects. We then consider more recent experimental studies.

Observational Studies

Observational studies are typically based on individual and household data from sample surveys linked with census data on the local areas (usually census tracts) in which children and families live. These studies have employed a wide range of study designs, survey datasets, theoretical approaches, neighborhood, family, and outcome measures, and statistical methods. Here we summarize the results of this very diverse group of studies.

First, basic descriptive analyses have shown that many dimensions of children's well-being (including teen sexual behavior, substance abuse, mental health, cognitive and achievement scores, high school completion, youth violence, delinquency, and child abuse) vary significantly by neighborhood income levels and, less often, by other neighborhood characteristics such as residential stability, high school completion rate, female headship, social disorder, and social cohesion. Children and teens living in poorer neighborhoods generally have worse outcomes.

Second, a substantial part of the variation in children's outcomes by neighborhood income level is accounted for by differences in family income and other family characteristics. In other words, when family characteristics such as income, family structure, and parents' educational attainment are held constant, the relationship between children's outcomes and neighborhood income levels is substantially reduced. Moreover, Ginter and her colleagues (2000) show that the more complete the set of family characteristics that is held constant, the greater the decline in the size and significance of coefficients on neighborhood variables. They conclude that the results of many neighborhood-effects studies are likely due, at least in part, to omitted variables at the family level. Nonetheless, these researchers and others find that some neighborhood characteristics retain significant effects even after extensive controls for family and individual characteristics are introduced.

Third, the size of neighborhood effects on children's outcomes is generally modest and considerably smaller than the effects of family and individual characteristics. For example, in studies reviewed by Leventhal and Brooks-Gunn (2000), neighborhood characteristics accounted for 5 to 10 percent of the variance in children's outcomes. Duncan and Raudenbush (2001, 132) argue, however, that "the degree of neighborhood-based 'action' may still be large enough to be consistent with cost-effective, neighborhood based interventions."

Fourth, results from these studies, not surprisingly, suggest that the effects of neighborhood conditions (net of family SES) vary by type of child outcome investigated (behavior problems, school readiness, teen sex, delinquency) and by the child's age, ethnicity, and gender. For example, Brooks-Gunn, Duncan, and their colleagues examined an extensive set of child development indicators across a broader age range (Brooks-Gunn, Duncan, and Aber 1997). Duncan and Raudenbush (1999) summarize the results as follows: (1) neighborhood effects appear in the preschool years but are most consistent for school-age children; (2) neighborhood effects appear to be stronger for cognitive and achievement outcomes than for behavior and mental health measures; and (3) white children appear to be more affected by neighborhood conditions than African American children. Sampson and his colleagues (2002) argue that the evidence of neighborhood effects on crime rates is stronger than the evidence for other types of outcomes.

Fifth, several studies suggest that the presence of affluent neighbors has a greater impact on children's outcomes than neighborhood poverty (Brooks-Gunn, Duncan, and Aber 1997; Duncan and Raudenbush 1999; Sampson, Morenoff, and Earls 1999). However, Ginter and her colleagues (2000) dispute this conclusion. Their reanalysis of the PSID data includes variables indicating the percentage of households with high and low income as well as the income of the child's family relative to that of other families in the neighborhood. Their results suggest that "the income of the family relative to that of its neighbors—rather than the extent to which the neighborhood is populated by high (low) income families—may be the more relevant consideration" (628). This is an important topic for future neighborhood-effects research.

Sixth, reliable methods for assessing neighborhood social and physical environments are not well developed and tested. Those studies that have examined intervening processes have investigated a broad range of potential mechanisms. For example, Sampson and his colleagues (Sampson et al. 1997; Sampson and Raudenbush 1999; Morenoff, Sampson, and Raudenbush 2001) show that informal social control, collective efficacy, and social ties are significantly related to outcomes such as delinquency, crime, and homicide. Scott South and Eric Baumer's (2000; Baumer and South 2001) results suggest that peer attitudes and behaviors account for a substantial proportion of neighborhood effects on adolescents, particularly teen parenthood and sexual activity. Dawn Upchurch and her colleagues (1999) and Carol Aneshensel and Clea Sucoff (1996) show that perceived "ambient hazards" (for example, neighborhood disorder, disorganization, and threats) are an important mediating factor between neighborhood disadvantage and teen sexual behavior and mental health.

Finally, a few studies have tackled endogenous residential choice using non-experimental data and statistical models. William Evans, Wallace Oates, and Robert Schwab (1992), Anne Case and Lawrence Katz (1991), and Eric Foster and Sara McLanahan (1996) used instrumental variables to eliminate the correlation between unobserved parent attributes and neighborhood variables. However, finding credible and viable instruments is a very difficult task. Instead, Daniel Aaronson (1997, 1998) and Robert Plotnick and Saul Hoffman (1996) have used sibling fixed effects in analyses of educational attainment, adult economic status, and teen pregnancy in the PSID. While Aaronson found significant neighborhood effects once unobserved family characteristics were controlled, Plotnick and Hoffman did not. Aaronson (1998) suggests that the difference in results lies in the types of sibling pairs included and the measurement of neighborhood variables. Gary Solon, Marianne Page, and Greg Duncan (2000) take another approach: they compare correlations for sibling pairs with correlations among neighbors within sampling clusters in the PSID. Their results suggest that the size of neighborhood effects is small and considerably smaller than family effects.

Experimental Studies

More recently, several experimental or quasi-experimental studies have attempted to tackle the issue of endogenous neighborhood selection. The initial effort was the Gautreaux Program, in which low-income African American families from Chicago housing projects were given Section 8 housing vouchers that could be used only in predominantly white or multi-ethnic neighborhoods (typically in suburban areas). The control group was Section 8 voucher recipients who used their vouchers in the city of Chicago. James Rosenbaum (1991, 1995) shows that children who move to the suburbs rather than cities are less likely to drop out of school and more likely to attend college, have a job, and receive higher pay. However, the study has several methodological limitations, including self-selection into the study and substantial sample attrition.

The Moving To Opportunity (MTO) experiment was a more carefully designed outgrowth of the Gautreaux Program developed by the U.S. Department of Housing and Urban Development (HUD) and implemented by local public housing authorities and non-profits between 1994 and 1999 in Baltimore, Boston, Chicago, Los Angeles, and New York (Brennan 2002). Participants were volunteers from very low-income families with children in public housing or Section 8 project-based housing in inner-city, high-poverty neighborhoods. Each participant family was assigned randomly to one of three groups: the *experimental group,* which received vouchers that could be used only in low-poverty areas plus counseling and assistance locating housing; the *comparison group,* which received geographically unrestricted vouchers and standard housing authority briefings and assistance; and the *control group,* which continued to receive project-based assistance. The study sought to answer two questions: What impact does mobility counseling have on families' residential choices and housing and neighborhood conditions? And what are the effects of neighborhood conditions on the well-being of MTO families?

The follow-up design and analyses of MTO in each city have been conducted by separate groups of researchers using different data collection and analytic strategies. This approach has the disadvantage that it is harder to make comparisons across cities (and hence generalizations beyond each city). But it also has the advantage that the multiple research strategies used provide a richer picture of the experimental process and outcomes. The one commonality among all five sites is that HUD conducted a self-administered baseline survey of all families who volunteered to participate. Researchers in most study sites conducted follow-up telephone surveys two to three years after families were assigned to treatment groups. The Boston and Los Angeles projects also conducted qualitative studies with a sample of participants. In contrast, analyses of Boston participants have relied on baseline passive and active tracking of respondents and administrative data on arrests and school performance. Furthermore, the project in each city focused on a somewhat different set of children's outcomes.

As in almost all social experiments, the MTO project encountered significant problems in implementation of the experimental treatment (Matulef 1999). Large proportions of families who were offered vouchers did not move during the period when the vouchers were valid, and analyses comparing movers to nonmovers in the experimental and comparison groups show that movers are significantly different from nonmovers. As a result, most (but not all) MTO analyses adopt analytic strategies that account for this selection. For example, Jens Ludwig and his colleagues (Ludwig, Duncan, and Pinkston 2000; Ludwig, Ladd, and Duncan 2001) in Baltimore and Lawrence Katz and his colleagues (Katz, Kling, and Liebman 2001) in Boston produce both intent-to-treat (ITT) and treatment-on-treated (TOT) estimates. ITT analyses compare outcomes for families assigned to the two treatment groups whether or not they actually moved with outcomes for the control group. Thus, ITT results are "lower bounds" on the effects of the treatment because the two treatment groups include substantial proportions of families who never moved. These researchers also estimate an "effects of TOT" parameter, which is a measure of the effect of moving on those who actually moved during the program. The TOT analysis uses instrumental variables methods to estimate the difference between families in the treatment groups who moved with those in the control group who would have moved if offered the opportunity. In the New York study, Leventhal and Brooks-Gunn (2003) use a conceptually similar approach by comparing treatment group movers with both treatment group nonmovers and those who were assigned to the control group. . . .

In general, most studies show some improvements in children's outcomes in the treatment groups compared with the controls. In particular, the Boston and Baltimore studies show significant differences in behavior problems, including juvenile arrests and respondent-reported behavior problems. This result is particularly striking since both studies report that children in the experimental group were more likely than those in the other groups to be arrested prior to their move. Experimental group children in New York, especially boys, experienced fewer depressive and anxiety-related behaviors.

Baltimore children in the treatment groups also had better test scores. Compared with the control group, children in the experimental group had better test scores overall, while those in the comparison group had better reading scores. There is some evidence in the Baltimore results that experimental-group children were more likely to be suspended from and drop out of school. Ludwig, Ladd, and Duncan (2001) suggest that middle-income schools are less likely to tolerate behavior that is acceptable in schools in poor neighborhoods. Health outcomes were better for children in the experimental group in Boston. The Boston and Chicago studies also report significant declines in fears about safety and increases in feelings of safety, a point of view echoed in the Los Angeles and New York studies.

An important concern of the New York and Los Angeles studies was the impact of moving into middle-class neighborhoods on poor children's social adjustment, social capital, and friendship patterns. If children move to better neighborhoods but feel left out or are socially isolated, they may not be better off in the long run. In general, the results to date are reassuring. Children in all three groups were as likely to have a friend in the neighborhood. In some cases, children were less likely to participate in extracurricular activities in the experimental group. Maria Hanratty, Sara McLanahan, and Becky Pettit (1998) speculate that experimental group families may face more stringent financial situations because of higher rents and large security deposits compared with other groups.

In summary, the early results of the MTO experiments provide important new evidence that neighborhood social and physical conditions affect family life and at least some aspects of children's well-being. The results of these experimental studies are limited by implementation problems and unexpected events as well as by difficulties in generalizing to the rest of the population. Nonetheless, the results of experiments combined with those from observational studies will play an important role over the next several years in helping us understand the role of residential patterns in children's well-being.

Discussion

Despite the serious methodological problems that are only beginning to be addressed adequately, a review of previous experimental and observational studies suggests that growing up in a poor neighborhood negatively affects children's outcomes over and above the effects of family socioeconomic status. However, the effects may be complex and difficult to observe. For example, the MTO results suggest that a major effect of moving to a better neighborhood is feeling safer and less anxious and depressed. Although we might expect a greater sense of safety and lower anxiety and depression to have very important long-run effects on children's emotional development and outlook on life, the effects may be less immediately apparent on school performance, skills acquisition, and behaviors, outcomes that are more typically measured in surveys and administrative data.

Research to date also suggests that family effects on children's outcomes are significantly larger than neighborhood effects. However, it is important to keep in mind that the measurement of neighborhood characteristics is at a much more rudimentary stage of development than measurement of family processes in large-scale surveys. Because of their pervasive role in most children's lives, it makes sense that families would have a greater influence on children's well-being than neighborhoods or other social environments. However, public policy generally has considerably less ability to influence parents' behavior and attributes directly than to affect neighborhood quality. Hence, even modest neighborhood effects may be of considerable interest to policymakers.

Moreover, it is important to consider residential segregation and neighborhood and family effects on children's well-being in a larger context. The finding that neighborhood effects are more modest in size than family effects can be misleading to the extent that neighborhood conditions, and residential segregation more generally, have an important influence on families' socioeconomic status and family dynamics. Residential segregation has been implicated by many scholars as a key mechanism for the intergenerational transmission of inequality (Massey and Denton 1993; Wilson 1987, 1996; Jargowsky 1997). The argument is that restriction to concentrated-poverty neighborhoods compounds the difficulty that poor, minority families face in escaping poverty because in poor neighborhoods housing values remain low, the chances of criminal victimization remain higher, high-paying jobs are less available, exposure to disease and substance abuse is greater, and individuals are more socially isolated. Thus, residential segregation and residence in concentrated-poverty neighborhoods may be an important determinant of the family socioeconomic status and a major indirect influence on children's outcomes.

If residence in a poor and dangerous neighborhood affects parents' attitudes, mental health, and parenting practices (Furstenberg et al. 1999; Kling, Liebman, and Katz 2001; Brooks-Gunn, Duncan, and Aber 1997), it is even more difficult to disentangle "family" effects from "neighborhood" effects. Nonetheless, several recent experimental and observational studies promise to provide clearer answers than past research on the direct and indirect pathways through which residential segregation affects children growing up in poor neighborhoods.

REFERENCES

Aaronson, Daniel. 1997. "Sibling Estimates of Neighborhood Effects." In *Neighborhood Poverty: Policy Implications in Studying Neighborhoods,* vol. 2, edited by Jeanne Brooks-Gunn, Greg J. Duncan, and J. Lawrence Aber. New York: Russell Sage Foundation.

————. 1998. "Using Sibling Data to Estimate the Impact of Neighborhoods on Children's Educational Outcomes." *Journal of Human Resources* 33(4): 915–46.

Aber, J. Lawrence, Martha A. Gephart, Jeanne Brooks-Gunn, and James P. Connell. 1997. "Development in Context: Implications for Studying Neighborhood Effects." In *Neighborhood Poverty: Context and Consequences for Children,* vol. 1, edited by Jeanne Brooks-Gunn, Greg J. Duncan, and J. Lawrence Aber. New York: Russell Sage Foundation.

Aneshensel, Carol S., and Clea A. Sucoff. 1996. "The Neighborhood Context of Adolescent Mental Health." *Journal of Health and Social Behavior* 37: 293–310.

Baumer, Eric P., and Scott J. South. 2001. "Community Effects on Youth Sexual Activity." *Journal of Marriage and the Family* 63: 540–54.

Brennan, Brian. 2002. "Background on MTO." *Moving To Opportunity Research.* Created August 30, 2000; last modified August 22, 2002. Available at: www.princeton.edu/~kling/mto/background.htm.

Bronfenbrenner, Urie. 1986. "Ecology of the Family as Context for Human Development." *Developmental Psychology* 22(6): 723–42.

Brooks-Gunn, Jeanne, Greg J. Duncan, and J. Lawrence Aber, eds. 1997. *Neighborhood Poverty.* New York: Russell Sage Foundation.

Brooks-Gunn, Jeanne, Greg J. Duncan, Pamela K. Klebanov, and Naomi Sealand. 1993. "Do Neighborhoods Influence Child and Adolescent Development?" *American Journal of Sociology* 99(2): 353–95.

Case, Anne C., and Lawrence F. Katz. 1991. "The Company You Keep: The Effects of Family and Neighborhood on Disadvantaged Youth." Working paper. Cambridge, Mass.: National Bureau of Economic Research.

Coleman, James S. 1988. "Social Capital in the Creation of Human Capital." *American Sociological Review* 94 (supp.): S95–120.

Coulton, Claudia J. 1996. "Effects of Neighborhoods on Families and Children: Implications for Services." In *Children and Their Families in Big Cities: Strategies for Service Reform,* edited by A. J. Kahn and S. B. Kamerman. New York: Columbia University.

Crane, Jonathan. 1991. "The Epidemic Theory of Ghettos and Neighborhood Effects on Dropping Out and Teenage Childbearing." *American Sociological Review* 96(5): 1226–59.

Duncan, Greg J., James P. Connell, and Pamela K. Klebanov. 1997. "Conceptual and Methodological Issues in Estimating Causal Effects of Neighborhoods and Family Conditions on Individual Development." In *Neighborhood Poverty: Context and Consequences for Children,* vol. 1, edited by Jeanne Brooks-Gunn, Greg J. Duncan, and J. Lawrence Aber. New York: Russell Sage Foundation.

Duncan, Greg J., and Saul D. Hoffman. 1990. "Welfare Benefits, Economic Opportunities, and Out-of-Wedlock Births Among Black Teenage Girls." *Demography* 27(4): 519–35.

Duncan, Greg J., and Stephen W. Raudenbush. 1999. "Assessing the Effects of Context in Studies of Child and Youth Development." *Educational Psychologist* 34(1): 29–41.

————. 2001. "Neighborhoods and Adolescent Development: How Can We Determine the Links?" In *Does It Take a Village? Community Effects on Children, Adolescents, and Families,* edited by Alan Booth and Ann C. Crouter. Mahwah, N.J.: Lawrence Erlbaum Associates.

Edin, Kathryn. 1991. "Surviving the Welfare System: How AFDC Recipients Make Ends Meet in Chicago." *Social Problems* 38(4): 462–74.

Evans, William N., Wallace E. Oates, and Robert M. Schwab. 1992. "Measuring Peer Group Effects: A Study of Teenage Behavior." *Journal of Political Economy* 100(3): 966–91.

Fischer, Claude S. 1984. *The Urban Experience.* New York: Harcourt, Brace, Jovanovich.

Fordham, Signithia, and John U. Ogbu. 1986. "Black Students' School Success: Coping with the Burden of 'Acting White.'" *The Urban Review* 18: 176–206.

Foster, Eric M., and Sara McLanahan. 1996. "An Illustration of the Use of Instrumental Variables: Do Neighborhood Conditions Affect a Young Person's Chance of Finishing High School?" Unpublished paper. Princeton University.

Furstenberg, Frank F., Jr., Thomas D. Cook, Jacquelynne Eccles, Glen H. Elder Jr., and Arnold J. Sameroff. 1999. *Managing to Make It: Urban Families and Adolescent Success.* Chicago: University of Chicago Press.

Ginther, Donna, Robert Haveman, and Barbara Wolfe. 2000. "Neighborhood Attributes as Determinants of Children's Outcomes: How Robust Are the Relationships?" *Journal of Human Resources* 35(4): 603–42.

Hanratty, Maria, Sara McLanahan, and Becky Pettit. 1998. "The Impact of the Los Angeles Moving To Opportunity Program on Residential Mobility, Neighborhood Characteristics, and Early Child and Parent Outcomes." Working paper 98–18. Princeton, N.J.: Princeton University, Center for Research on Child Wellbeing.

Haveman, Robert, and Barbara Wolfe. 1994. *Succeeding Generations: On the Effects of Investments in Children.* New York: Russell Sage Foundation.

Jargwosky, Paul A. 1997. *Poverty and Place: Ghettos, Barrios, and the American City.* New York: Russell Sage Foundation.

Jencks, Christopher, and Susan E. Mayer. 1990. "The Social Consequences of Growing up in a Poor Neighborhood." In *Inner-City Poverty in the United States,* edited by Laurence E. Lynn Jr. and Michael G. H. McGeary. Washington, D.C.: National Academy Press.

Katz, Lawrence F., Jeffrey R. Kling, and Jeffrey B. Liebman. 2001. "Moving To Opportunity in Boston: Early Results of a Randomized Mobility Experiment." *Quarterly Journal of Economics* (May): 607–54.

Klebanov, Pamela K., Jeanne Brooks-Gunn, P. Lindsay Chase-Lansdale, and R. A. Gordon. 1997. "Are Neighborhood Effects on Young Children Mediated by Features of the Home Environment?" In *Neighborhood Poverty,* vol. 1, edited by Jeanne Brooks-Gunn, Greg J. Duncan, and J. Lawrence Aber. New York: Russell Sage Foundation.

Klebanov, Pamela K., Jeanne Brooks-Gunn, and Greg J. Duncan. 1994. "Does Neighborhood and Family Poverty Affect Mother's Parenting, Mental Health and Social Support?" *Journal of Marriage and the Family* 56: 441–55.

Kling, Jeffrey R., Jeffrey B. Liebman, and Lawrence F. Katz. 2001. "Bullets Don't Got No Name: Consequences of Fear in the Ghetto." Working paper 225. Chicago: Northwestern University and the University of Chicago, Joint Center for Poverty Research.

Korbin, Jill E., and Claudia J. Coulton. 1997. "Understanding the Neighborhood Context for Children and Families: Combining Epidemiological and Ethnographic Approaches." In *Neighborhood Poverty,* vol. 2, edited by Jeanne Brooks-Gunn, Greg J. Duncan, and J. Lawrence Aber. New York: Russell Sage Foundation.

Leventhal, Tama, and Jeanne Brooks-Gunn. 2000. "The Neighborhoods They Live In: The Effects of Neighborhood Residence on Child and Adolescent Outcomes." *Psychological Bulletin* 126(2): 309–37.

———. 2003. "The Early Impacts of Moving To Opportunity on Children and Youth in New York City." In *Choosing a Better Life: Evaluating the Moving To Opportunity Social Experiment,* edited by John Goering and Judith Feins. Washington, D.C.: Urban Institute Press.

Ludwig, Jens, Greg J. Duncan, and Joshua C. Pinkston. 2000. "Evidence from a Randomized Housing-Mobility Experiment." Unpublished paper. Georgetown University, Washington, D.C.

Ludwig, Jens, Helen F. Ladd, and Greg J. Duncan. 2001. "Urban Poverty and Educational Outcomes." *Brookings-Wharton Papers on Urban Affairs* 2001: 147–201.

Massey, Douglas S., and Nancy A. Denton. 1993. *American Apartheid: Segregation and the*

Making of the Underclass. Cambridge, Mass.: Harvard University Press.

Massey, Douglas S., and Mitchell L. Eggers. 1990. "The Ecology of Inequality: Minorities and the Concentration of Poverty, 1970 to 1980." *American Journal of Sociology* 95(5): 1153–88.

Massey, Douglas S., Andrew B. Gross, and M. L. Eggers. 1991. "Segregation, the Concentration of Poverty, and the Life Chances of Individuals." *Social Science Research* 20(4): 397–420.

Massey, Douglas S., Andrew B. Gross, and K. Shibuya. 1994. "Migration, Segregation, and the Concentration of Poverty." *American Sociological Review* 59: 425–45.

Matulef, Mark. 1999. "Moving To Opportunity (MTO) Demonstration for Fair Housing Program, Los Angeles Demonstration Site Interim Outcomes of Housing Search and Counseling Strategies: Early Lessons for Experimental Design and Implementation." Available at: www. wws.princeton.edu/~kling/mto/quick.htm.

McLoyd, Vonnie C. 1990. "The Impact of Economic Hardship on Black Families and Children: Psychological Distress, Parenting, and Socioemotional Development." *Child Development* 61: 311–46.

Morenoff, Jeffrey D., Robert J. Sampson, and Stephen W. Raudenbush. 2001. "Neighborhood Inequality, Collective Efficacy, and the Spatial Dynamics of Urban Violence." *Criminology* 39(3): 517–59.

Oliver, Melvin L. 1988. "The Urban Black Community as Network: Toward a Social Network Perspective." *Sociological Quarterly* 29(4): 623–45.

Rosenbaum, James E. 1991. "Black Pioneers: Do Their Moves to the Suburbs Increase Economic Opportunity for Mothers and Children?" *Housing Policy Debate* 2(4): 1179–1213.

———. 1995. "Changing the Geography of Opportunity by Expanding Residential Choice: Lessons from the Gautreaux Program." *Housing Policy Debate* 6(1): 231–70.

Sampson, Robert J., and John H. Laub. 1994. "Urban Poverty and the Family Context of Delinquency: A New Look at Structure and Process in a Classic Study." *Child Development* 65: 523–40.

Sampson, Robert J., Jeffrey D. Morenoff, and Felton Earls. 1999. "Beyond Social Capital: Spatial Dynamics of Collective Efficacy for Children." *American Sociological Review* 64(5): 633–60.

Sampson, Robert J., Jeffrey D. Morenoff, and Thomas Gannon-Rowley. 2002. "Assessing 'Neighborhood Effects': Social Processes and New Directions in Research." *Annual Review of Sociology* 28: 443–78.

Sampson, Robert J., and Stephen W. Raudenbush. 1999. "Systematic Social Observation of Public Spaces: A New Look at Disorder in Urban Neighborhoods." *American Journal of Sociology* 105(3): 603–51.

Sampson, Robert J., Stephen W. Raudenbush, and Felton Earls. 1997. "Neighborhoods and Violent Crime: A Multilevel Study of Collective Efficacy." *Science* 277 (August 15): 918–24.

Shaw, Clifford R., and McKay, Henry D. 1969. *Juvenile Delinquency and Urban Areas.* Chicago: The University of Chicago Press.

Solon, Gary, Marianne E. Page, and Greg J. Duncan. 2000. "Correlations Between Neighboring Children in Their Subsequent Educational Attainment." *Review of Economics and Statistics* 82(3): 383–92.

South, Scott J. 2001. "Issues in the Analysis of Neighborhoods, Families and Children." In *Does It Take A Village? Community Effects on Children, Adolescents, and Families,* edited by Alan Booth and Ann C. Crouter. Mahwah, N.J.: Lawrence Erlbaum Associates, Inc.

South, Scott J., and Eric P. Baumer. 2000. "Deciphering Community and Race Effects on Adolescent Premarital Childbearing." *Social Forces* 78: 1379–1407.

Stack, Carol. 1974. *All Our Kin: Survival Strategies.* New York: Harper Torchback.

Tigges, Leann M., Irene Browne, and Gary P. Green. 1998. "Social Isolation of the Urban Poor: Race, Class and Neighborhood Effects on Social Resources." *Sociological Quarterly* 39(1): 53–77.

Upchurch, Dawn M., Carol S. Aneshensel, Clea A. Sucoff, and Lene Levy-Storms. 1999. "Neighborhood and Family Contexts of Adolescent Sexual Activity." *Journal of Marriage and the Family* 61: 920–33.

Waldinger, Roger. 1996. "Ethnicity and Opportunity in the Plural City." In *Ethnic Los Angeles,* edited by Roger Waldinger and Mehdi Bozorgmehr. New York: Russell Sage Foundation.

Wellman, Barry. 1996. "Are Personal Communities Local? A Dumptarian Reconsideration." *Social Networks* 17(2): 423–36.

———. 1999. "Preface." In *Networks in the Global Village,* edited by Barry Wellman. Boulder, Colo.: Westview Press.

Wilson, William Julius. 1987. *The Truly Disadvantaged.* Chicago: University of Chicago Press.

———. 1996. *When Work Disappears: The World of the New Urban Poor.* New York: Alfred A. Knopf.

20

Flat Broke with Children
Women in the Age of Welfare Reform

SHARON HAYS

Money and Morality

A nation's laws reflect a nation's values. The 1996 federal law reforming welfare offered not just a statement of values to the thousands of local welfare offices across the nation, it also backed this up with something much more tangible. Welfare reform came with money. Lots of it. Every client and caseworker in the welfare office experienced this. New social workers and employment counselors were hired. New signs were posted. New workshops were set up. In Arbordale and Sunbelt City, the two welfare offices I studied, every caseworker found a new computer on her desk. (Arbordale and Sunbelt City are pseudonyms for the two towns where I studied the effects of welfare reform. I gave them these fictitious names to protect all the clients and caseworkers who shared with me their experiences of reform.) In small-town Arbordale, the whole office got a facelift: new carpets, new paint, a new conference room, new office chairs, and plush new office dividers. The reception area, completely remodeled with plants and posters and a children's play area, came to resemble the waiting room of an elite pediatrician's office more than the entrance to a state bureaucracy. Sunbelt City acquired new carpets, a new paint job, and new furniture as well. And all the public areas in that welfare office were newly decorated with images of nature's magnificence—glistening raindrops, majestic mountains, crashing waves, setting sun—captioned with inspirational phrases like "perseverance," "seizing opportunities," "determination," "success."

As I walked the halls of the Sunbelt City welfare office back in 1998, situated in one of the poorest and most dangerous neighborhoods of a western boom town, those scenes of nature's magnificence struck me as clearly out of place. But the inspirational messages they carried nonetheless seemed an apt symbolic representation of the new legislative strategy to train poor families in "mainstream" American values. Welfare reform, Congress had decreed, would "end the dependence of needy parents on government benefits by promoting job preparation, work, and marriage."[1] Welfare mothers, those Sunbelt signs implied, simply needed a *push*—to get them out to work, to keep them from having children they couldn't afford to raise, to get them married and safely embedded in family life. Seizing opportunities.

States were awash in federal funds. And the economy was booming in those early years of reform. Everyone was feeling it. There was change in the air. A sense of possibilities—with just a tinge of foreboding.

The Personal Responsibility and Work Opportunity Reconciliation Act of 1996, the law that ended 61 years of poor families' entitlement to federal welfare benefits—the law that asserted and enforced a newly reformulated vision of the appropriate values of work and family life—provided all that additional funding as a way of demonstrating the depth of the nation's commitment to change in the welfare system. It provided state welfare programs with federal grants in amounts matching the peak years of national welfare caseloads (1992 to 1995)—even though those caseloads had everywhere since declined. This meant an average budget increase of 10 percent, before counting the tremendous amount of additional federal funding coming in for new childcare and welfare-to-work programs. Even though there was lots more money, most states did not pass it on to poor mothers in the form of larger welfare checks. In fact, only two states raised their benefit amounts, while two others lowered theirs at the inception of reform.

Most of the welfare caseworkers I met were optimistic about the new law, at least in the first year of its enactment. "Welfare reform is the best thing that ever happened," was a phrase I heard frequently. A number of caseworkers, echoing popular sentiment, told me that "welfare had become a trap" and the clients had become

"dependent." Some focused on the tax money that would be saved. Others pointed out that lots of caseworkers are mothers too, and economic necessity forces them to come to work every day and leave their children in day care, so it seemed only fair that welfare mothers should be required to do the same. . . .

The purpose of this chapter is to explore the cultural norms, beliefs, and values embedded in welfare reform. While millions of dollars have been spent to track the outcomes of this legislation, and while scholars, politicians, and pundits have fiercely debated the effects of every policy contained within it, I want to focus attention on the broad *cultural* significance of this reform effort. What does the Personal Responsibility Act tell us about the values of our society? How have its moral prescriptions been translated into concrete practices? What message does it send to the poor and to the nation? In particular, I was interested from the start in determining just what welfare reform is saying about work and family life in American society today. . . .

Invisibility and Inclusion

Invisibility was a problem experienced by the majority of the welfare mothers I encountered. Most emphasized, in one way or another, that they were not "born to welfare" (as one put it), and almost all felt fairly certain that—time limits or no time limits—they would find some way to survive. These mothers did not, in other words, tell me their stories primarily to convince listeners that they were worthy of continued welfare receipt. Many did, on the other hand, share their tales because they wanted people to understand how they came to participate in one of the most universally despised social programs in U.S. history. They had heard more than once the stereotypes labeling them as lazy, dependent, ignorant, promiscuous, and manipulative cheats. They told their stories, therefore, with the hope that they would be recognized not simply as a composite of clichés, but as whole persons. . . .

Sheila's Downward Spiral

The spiral for Sheila began just after she finished high school. Sheila is white and was 29 years old at the time I met her in the old and notoriously dangerous housing project where she lived, not far from the Sunbelt City welfare office. From a working-class background, she was raised in a small town "with small town values." She was engaged to be married to her high school sweetheart. The summer after they graduated he was killed in an auto accident.

> I wish that then and there I had just said, "Okay, forward," instead of sitting and mourning and moping and weeping and thinking about what could have and should have and would have been. I should have just gone on ahead to college like I had intended. And I didn't do it. But you know what they say, hindsight is 20–20.

She moved to Sunbelt City with her parents and took a part-time job. Less than a year later her father left her mother.

> It was in February. He left a note on the kitchen table. It said, "I'm leaving you for good." And he left the keys to the car that was not paid for. He left one month owing in rent. My mom at the time was not working, and I was still mourning my boyfriend.

> Shortly after that me and my mom found jobs at a dry cleaners. We opened it in the morning, and we worked for 15 hours a day. We'd come home, go to sleep, get up, and go right back there. Six days a week. And we were doing good. We had paid up the back rent, and the car was being paid for.

> And then my mother got blood clots. She almost lost her leg. And the doctor said she shouldn't work any more. This meant we lost $1,500 a month in income and we were trying to make it on my little $1,200. With the medical bills and the car payments, I got a month behind on rent, and they evicted us.

> We were homeless. In all the hoopla and everything, I lost my job. It just kind of dominoed. We were actually homeless, living with friends and things like that. And I mean we went hungry—we ate the throwaways from McDonald's.

> A lot of people don't realize how close they live to being homeless. I mean, you're just one or two paychecks away from the street. And once you hit bottom, you're gonna hit and you're gonna hit hard. But you have to remember that once you hit bottom you're as low as you can go. There's only one way to go, and that's up.

Unfortunately for Sheila, the downward spiral had not yet reached its lowest point. It was while she and her mother were homeless that she met the man who was to become the father of her daughter. He was, at that moment, her savior, but only a temporary one:

> I met Sam, and I thought he was a very nice gentleman. Sam was living with a friend, and they took the two of us in. I found another job. We were hopeful; even

though my mom still couldn't work, we were beginning to get back on our feet.

Sam had told me he was divorced. I was still young; I was 21 at the time. And, like I said, I come from a small community. Well, after we'd been together for almost a year, I got a phone call one morning—and it was his wife! So I used the money I had to put him on a bus back to his wife in Florida. And that's the last I heard of him.

A month later I found out I was pregnant. Sam still doesn't know he's got a daughter. The child support people haven't found him yet.

Putting Sam on that bus meant that pregnant Sheila and her disabled mom were homeless again. And then Sheila was raped:

For a while I wasn't sure if Sam was the father. There was the small issue of the fact that three weeks almost to the day after he left I was raped. That's a part of living on the street; that's a danger for women who live on the street.

And that's how I came to find out I was pregnant—I went to the clinic to check a few weeks after the rape. So there were two possible identities to the father. I had a hard time knowing what to do. But as soon as she was born I saw what she looked like and I knew who she was; I knew who she belonged to. She looks too much like her dad.

Sheila was just 22 years old when she gave birth to her daughter. If things had gone as she had originally planned, she would have been starting her last year of college at that time.

Sheila first went to the welfare office in the last months of her pregnancy, hoping to get medical coverage for the birth.

I was a high-risk pregnancy all the way through my pregnancy. I went down to the welfare office and applied for medical assistance. My mother and I were still homeless. I worked a part-time job until things [with the pregnancy] got too bad. My mother had gotten a job [against her doctor's advice] and we managed, with my first welfare check, to finally get our very own small studio apartment. Just two weeks later my daughter was born.

Sheila's daughter (who was busy with her homework during most of my visit), was seven years old when I met her.

From the time she gave birth to the time of our interview, Sheila had a string of jobs. She went back to work when her daughter was just three months old. That job she described as a "really good one," where she worked her way up to a management position in a fast-food restaurant. The rest of the jobs were temporary or low-paying jobs, mainly entry-level fast foods and unskilled clerical work. She left every one. She quit the good one after more than two years, and she's still sorry about it, even though she remembers well all the time she spent agonizing over that decision. She left because the hours and the bus rides were so long that she was spending over 12 hours a day away from home, and she never had a chance to see her daughter. "My daughter was nearly three years old and she was calling my mother 'mom' and calling me 'Sheila.' It was just too hard. I just wanted to get to know her, to do her ABCs and her 1–2–3s. I wanted to be there."

She went back on welfare and spent almost a year getting to know her daughter before again seeking work. She spoke nostalgically of that time with her three-year-old, but she also emphasized that leaving that job was her "third big mistake," along-side mourning rather than continuing on to college, and getting involved with a married man.

Sheila left subsequent jobs because she hurt her back, loading boxes ("the doctors say I'm not allowed to lift over 15 pounds now"), because the pay was too poor, because the jobs were only temporary (through a "temp" agency), and most recently, because her mother was diagnosed as terminally ill and needed to be cared for. Her mother suffered respiratory failure first, then a massive heart attack and, by the time I met her, Sheila was afraid to leave her alone most of the time. "That's my greatest fear, that I'll go to work, and I'll be at work, and something will happen to my mom. I don't know what to do."

Sheila's combined time on welfare, including the time when her child was born, between jobs, and since her mother's illness, added up to about three and a half years, including the last year and a half since welfare reform. She'd been using the resources offered by the welfare office to train herself on computers and in accounting skills. She told me about the contacts she'd made with state agencies that might hire her, and she was feeling somewhat optimistic, though still quite worried about her mom. Her primary goal was to find an employer flexible enough to allow her to care for both her daughter and her mother.

The sheer number of tragedies in Sheila's young life—her fiancé's death, her father leaving, her homelessness, her affair with a married man, her rape, her high-risk pregnancy, and now her mother's terminal illness—testify to the unique circumstances that led her to go on welfare. But every mother I talked to had a story of hardship to tell. And every mother I met had experienced some version of the domino effect: one problem leading to another and compounding it, until too many dominoes fall and the situation becomes impossible to manage. In this, Sheila's story represents the most prominent pattern in the road to welfare.

A second, partially hidden, pattern that Sheila shares with many welfare mothers who have children out of wedlock involves the issue of birth control. Most observers of Sheila's life would agree that she has had some very tough luck. Yet many would also want to know why she allowed herself to get pregnant. After all, it is clear from this vantage point that the last thing Sheila needed was a child to support. She answered, "I did use birth control, but it must not have worked. I don't know what happened."

The truth is, it could very well be that Sheila simply did not use birth control faithfully enough, or that the methods she and her partner used were not sufficiently foolproof. The crucial point here, however, is that a substantial number of sexually active young men and women do not use birth control faithfully enough. This fact does not appear to vary significantly by one's race or economic status. About 50 percent of female teens are sexually active. About 70 percent of those say they used birth control the last time they had sex. But this percentage is based on self-reporting—in which case Sheila, for instance, would be included as a "yes." And equally important, having used birth control recently is not the same thing as using it consistently. There tends to be a good deal of variation in answers to the questions "used at most recent sex," and "used at first sex," for example, which confirms that "recently" is not the same as "always."[2] Putting all this together, it becomes clear that a large number of sexually active young people do not use foolproof birth control every time they have sex. Sheila, in this sense, is a member of the majority.

The central factor separating poor and working-class youth from the middle and upper classes on this score is that financially privileged young women who find themselves pregnant before they are ready are more likely to get an abortion.[3] I asked Sheila if she had thought about having an abortion.

> Oh no, no. Well, I can't say it didn't cross my mind. But I'm a person who believes if you're gonna play, you're gonna pay. And it's not her fault. I'm the kind of person who thinks that, as soon as they have that heartbeat, which is like ten days after conception, then that's a live human being. I just couldn't do it. I love my daughter.

No matter what we might think of the consequences of this choice in the context of Sheila's life, the vast majority of Americans agree that she has a right to make this decision. And few would argue that her problem, in this instance, is a problem of bad values.

There is a third important pattern that Sheila shares with the majority of welfare mothers—the pushes toward work and the pulls toward home. The stress associated with those pushes and pulls is something welfare mothers have in common with parents of all classes and backgrounds. Sheila's desire to stay at home with her daughter is no different from all the other working moms who long to have more time to spend with their young children. Her longing for a job flexible enough to allow her to care for her child is shared by most working parents today. Her sense of regret over taking off those career-building years in order to be with her daughter mimics all the stay-at-home mothers who worry that they will never be able to recoup their lost time in the labor market.[4] And the fact that Sheila feels committed to staying at home with her terminally ill mother puts her in the same position as the millions of (mainly) women who care for their aging parents—many of whom suffer serious economic hardship because of it.[5] What makes Sheila's case distinct is solely that these realities landed her in the welfare office.

No matter what the edicts of welfare reform might mean to Sheila in the coming years, and no matter what we might think of the paths she chose at the multiple crossroads of her early adulthood, the difficulties she has faced speak to much larger social problems. To the extent that the Personal Responsibility Act is our collective cultural response, it is clear that this law has done little to address the underlying causes of the strains Sheila has experienced and the choices she was forced to make. . . .

The "Success" of Welfare Reform

Most welfare mothers share the core values of most Americans. They share a concern with contemporary problems in work and family life and a commitment to finding solutions—including the overhaul of the welfare system. The trouble is, welfare reform was founded on the assumption that welfare mothers do not share American values and are, in fact, personally responsible for *undermining* our nation's moral principles. The policies and procedures instituted by welfare reform have thus been aimed at "fixing" these women. . . .

Shared Values, Symbolic Boundaries, and the Politics of Exclusion

In responding to welfare reform, the welfare mothers I met often offered a perfect mirror of the complex mix of higher values, genuine concerns, exclusionary judgments, and cultural distortions that informed the Personal Responsibility Act. One mother, Denise, captured nearly all these elements in her response, offering the full range of the more prominent patterns I encountered and mimicking the words of welfare mothers you have heard throughout the book. A black woman with two daughters, at the time I met her Denise was recently employed at Mailboxes-R-Us for $6.50 an hour and was making ends meet with the help of welfare reform's (time-limited) income supplement, transportation vouchers, and childcare subsidy. This is what she had to say when I asked her for her overall assessment of reform:

When I was younger, years ago, anybody could get on welfare. And I think that's what's good about welfare reform. People have to show some sort of initiative. Before, the welfare office didn't pressure you to find a job, but now they do. And I think that's a good system. They've really helped me out a lot.

Plus, I think people are sick of having to pay their tax money. They say, "Look, I am out here working, and I don't make that much money, and I have kids of my own. I'm tired of having to take care of your babies." People are getting upset and it's rightly so. I think it's rightly so.

And lots of people abuse the system. You see it every day. A lot of people that you run into and a lot of people that live in your neighborhood—I mean a lot of peo-

ple do hair and get paid in cash. And I hear about these people who had children just to get a welfare check, just because they didn't want to go out and work. I've seen women that's on welfare, they're looking good and their children look poorly. I see that happening.

Some of them are lazy and don't want to work. I think that some just want to stay home with their kids. But then they should have thought about that before they had the children.

At this point in her argument, Denise had hit upon nearly all the concerns of hardworking Americans who conscientiously pay their taxes, raise their children, and struggle to make it all work. She had also hit upon nearly all the well-worn stereotypes of poor mothers—implicitly labeling them as welfare cheats, lazy couch potatoes, promiscuous breeders, and lousy parents. But Denise wasn't finished.

I think some people on welfare are being greedy—taking away from people that are homeless, people that really need the help. I mean there are truly people out there living at the Salvation Army. I hear tell that there are people who can't get in those shelters because they're so full. And I think that's the sad part about it. Those women that don't really need welfare shouldn't be taking money away from the homeless.

But there are gonna be problems. Like, there are women that want to go out there and get a job, but who's gonna watch their kids? And there are people who will still need that little extra help to pay the bills. So that's a glitch in the system. And some of these women are already pregnant, and they're already poor, and they really do need the help. I think that we have to weigh things and maybe investigate a bit more. There are a lot of people that are disabled and need welfare; there are women who have been abused. Some of those people that are in a lot of trouble, you know, their kids are gonna be the ones you see on TV, shooting up the schools and everything.[6]

I know a lot of people say that this welfare reform is a good thing—and it is really gonna help a lot of people. But in the end things are probably gonna get worse. There's gonna be more crime 'cause people can't get on welfare and they're not gonna have any money and they're gonna go out and rob people, and kill people. And it happens, it happens. So that's a problem with the system.

This same sort of ambivalence is evident in Americans' response to welfare reform. Although most are positive about reform, the majority of Americans also say that they are "very" concerned about poverty. Most additionally believe that the national standards for poverty are set too low, stating that a family of four with an income of less than $20,000 is, in fact, "poor," even if the federal government does not label them as such. More significantly, a majority of Americans are in favor of further aid to the poor—including the expansion of job opportunities, tax credits, medical coverage, subsidies for childcare and housing, and the provision of better schools. Still, Americans worry about the government's ability to appropriately and effectively provide that aid, and many don't want to have to pay higher taxes to subsidize the poor.

Denise is also much like most Americans in that the central moral categories she uses to frame her response are work and family values, independence and commitment to others, self-sufficiency and concern for the common good. Women should take the "initiative," they should work, they should not rely on the help of others, they should support their own children, they should think twice before they give birth to children they cannot afford to raise. At the same time, people should not be "greedy," they should care for those who are more vulnerable than themselves, and they should consider the impact of their actions on the nation as a whole. All this makes perfect sense, and all this resonates perfectly with our nation's values. The trouble is that managing these commitments is hard enough if you have a spouse, a house in the suburbs, two cars in the garage, good health insurance, reliable childcare, a willingness to make compromises, a great deal of determination, empathy, and energy, and a household income of $60,000. The more items on this list that you lack, the tougher it becomes to live up to this demanding system of values. Denise, like most Americans, implicitly understands these "glitches." Yet her reasoning becomes a bit cloudy at this point—in large measure, I would argue, because of the loophole provided by the final significant element in her response to welfare reform.

It is hard to miss that Denise's support for the Personal Responsibility Act is predicated on the construction of a moral distinction between herself and all those "other" bad welfare mothers who fail to live up to social standards. Denise is making use of what Michèle Lamont has called "symbolic boundaries" to develop an implicit hierarchy of social worth. Like most people who use this strategy, she is not simply engaging in a mean-spirited attack on others or a self-interested attempt to highlight her own virtues. These symbolic boundaries also allow her to positively affirm shared values and specify the proper way to live one's life.[7]

Yet, given that many observers consider Denise herself a member of the deviant group she describes, the fact that she and other welfare mothers persist in this technique is curious. It testifies not just to the power and ubiquity of boundary making as a social strategy, it also speaks to the power and ubiquity of the demonization of poor single mothers. When welfare mothers distinguish themselves from those other "bad" women, they are calling on widely disseminated negative images of welfare mothers. These images seem to match all those strangers, those loud neighbors, those people who appear to spend their lives hanging out on street corners. The lives of the women they actually know, on the other hand, seem much more complex, their actions more understandable, their futures more redeemable.

The demonization of welfare mothers and the dichotomy between "us" and "them" can thus provide a dividing line that allows Denise and other Americans to say, if some welfare mothers can't make it, it's not because the problems they encounter in trying to manage work and family and still keep their heads above water are that bad or that widespread; it's because they didn't try hard enough or weren't good enough. Symbolic boundaries thus become *exclusionary* boundaries—simultaneously offering a means to affirm shared values and a means to think of "outsiders" in terms of individual blame. The obvious problem, in Denise's case, is that her own logic might ultimately leave her as one of the "accused." In broader terms, this exclusionary process means that all those Americans who are suffering from childcare woes, second shifts, inadequate health insurance, precarious jobs, unmanageable debt, and unstable communities are left to feel that their problems are *personal* problems for which no public solutions can be found. . . .

Winners and Losers

The extent to which the facts about the declining welfare rolls are read as a success ultimately depends on one's primary goals. If the goal of reform was solely to trim the rolls, then it has surely succeeded. If the goal was to place more single mothers in jobs regardless of wages, that goal has been met. If we sought to ensure that more welfare mothers would face a double shift of paid work and childcare, placing them on an "equal" footing with their middle-class counterparts, then some celebrations are in order. If the aim was to ensure that poor men are prosecuted for failure to pay child support, then welfare reform has been relatively effective. If the goal was to make low-income single mothers more likely to seek out the help of men, no matter what the costs, there is some (inconclusive) evidence that this strategy may be working.[8] If the goal was to decrease poverty overall, there is no indication that anything but the cycle of the economy has had an impact. Beyond this, the answers are more complicated.

Thinking about losers, one can start with the families who have left welfare. One-half are sometimes without enough money to buy food. One-third have to cut the size of meals. Almost half find themselves unable to pay their rent or utility bills. Many more families are turning to locally funded services, food banks, churches, and other charities for aid. Many of those charities are already overburdened. In some locales, homeless shelters and housing assistance programs are closing their doors to new customers, food banks are running out of food, and other charities are being forced to tighten their eligibility requirements.[9]

Among the former welfare families who are now living with little or no measurable income, will those charities be enough? At ground level, Nancy, the supervisor in Arbordale's welfare office, told me more than once that she was deeply concerned about these families, particularly the children. Melissa, the supervisor in Sunbelt City, on the other hand, repeatedly responded to my questions regarding the fate of former welfare recipients with the simple statement, "They have other resources." Melissa was referring not only to all those (overloaded) charities, but also to all the boyfriends and family members who could help in paying the bills, and to all those unreported or underreported side jobs (doing hair, cleaning houses, caring for other people's children, selling sex or drugs).[10] Between these two welfare supervisors, both of whom have spent many years working with poor mothers, who is right? And what about Denise, who both agreed with Melissa that many welfare mothers didn't *really* need the help, and who predicted that welfare reform would result in frightening hardship, including a rise in crime?

Consider the "other resources" available to the women I have introduced in this chapter. In the case of Sheila, the Sunbelt mother who was caring for her seven-year-old daughter and her terminally ill mother, the three of them might be able to survive somehow on her mom's disability check (about $550 per month) with the help of food stamps and local charities. If worse came to worst, she might be able to find some work on the graveyard shift so that she wouldn't have to leave her mom and daughter alone during the day (but she would be faced with leaving them alone at night in that very dangerous housing project).

Most welfare mothers *do* have other resources. Yet many of those resources are only temporary, and many are, at best, inadequate. Most will likely add greater instability and uncertainty to the lives of these families. And nearly all these resources have their own price tags—practical, emotional, moral, and social. . . .

The real winners in the story of welfare reform are all the restaurant, hotel, retail, and food service chains, and all the corporations, manufacturers, and small business owners across America who employ low-wage workers. These owners (and their stockholders) benefit not just from the availability of millions of poor women desperate to find work and willing to accept the lowest wages and the worst working conditions, they benefit not just from the additional availability of all those now more-desperate poor men, they also benefit because all this desperation creates more profitable labor market conditions overall. Welfare reform helps to convince all low-wage workers that they can be easily displaced by former welfare recipients and therefore makes them less likely to complain, change jobs, join unions, or demand higher wages. The logic of reform also means that low-wage employers can rest assured, for the moment at least, that no one will be calling into question the fact that their policies are less than family friendly and their workers are unable to support their children on the wages they take home.[11]

On a superficial level, the "end of welfare" appears to hold in place the symbolic messages that work is better than welfare and marriage is better than single parenthood. But by no stretch of the imagination could one argue that welfare reform brings with it anything resembling the triumph of "family values." And the practical reality of most low-wage employment no more offers "independence" and self-sufficiency to former welfare recipients than it does to all the middle-class teenagers who spend their summers working in fast-food restaurants and retail chains.

NOTES

1. U.S. Congress (1996, PL104–193, Title I, Section 401).

2. Terry and Manlove (1999); see also Luker (1996) and Waller (1999).

3. Luker (1996), Waller (1999), and Ventura et al. (2000).

4. See, for instance, Hays (1996), Hochschild (1989, 1997).

5. See Arno et al. (1999) and Harvard School of Public Health (2000) on the number of women caring for disabled or aged family members.

6. Denise is referring to then-prominent news stories on the Columbine school shooting and the other school shootings that followed.

7. On symbolic boundaries, see Lamont (1992, 2000).

8. See Sorenson and Zibman (2000); Cherlin and Fomby (2002).

9. See Loprest (1999), Boushev and Gunderson (2001), Sherman et al. (1998), National Campaign for Jobs and Income Support (2001A, 2001B). A study of major U.S. cities found that from 2000 to 2001, requests for food had increased by 23 percent and requests for emergency housing were up by 13 percent (U.S. Conference of Mayors 2001).

10. See Edin and Lein (1997).

11. See, for instance, Newman (1988, 1999), Piven (1999), Blau (1999), Edin and Lein (1997), Ehrenreich (2001).

REFERENCES

Arno, Peter, Carol Levine, and Margaret Memmott. 1999. "The Economic Value of Informal Caregiving." *Health Affairs* 18: 182–188.

Boushev, Heather and Bethney Gunderson. 2001. *When Work Just Isn't Enough: Measuring Hardships Faced by Families after Moving from Welfare to Work.* Washington, DC: Economic Policy Institute.

Cherlin, Andrew J. and Paula Fomby. 2002. *A Closer Look at Changes in Children's Living Arrangements.* Welfare, Children, and Families: A Three-City Study, Working Paper 02–01. Baltimore, MD: Johns Hopkins University.

Edin, Kathryn and Laura Lein. 1997. *Making Ends Meet: How Single Mothers Survive Welfare and Low-Wage Work.* New York: Russell Sage Foundation.

Ehrenreich, Barbara. 2001. *Nickel and Dimed: On (Not) Getting By in America.* New York: Metropolitan Books.

Harvard School of Public Health. 2000. *Caregiving by Women: A Disproportionately Large Load."* Project on Global Working Families. Cambridge, MA: President and Fellows of Harvard College.

Hays, Sharon. 1996. *The Cultural Contradictions of Motherhood.* New Haven, CT: Yale University Press.

Hochschild, Arlie Russell with Anne Machung. 1989. *The Second Shift: Working Parents and the Revolution at Home.* New York: Viking.

Hochschild, Arlie Russell. 1997. *The Time Bind: When Work Becomes Home and Home Becomes Work.* New York: Metropolitan Books.

Lamont, Michèle. 1992. *Money, Morals, and Manners.* Chicago: University of Chicago Press.

Lamont, Michèle. 2000. *The Dignity of Working Men: Morality and the Boundaries of Race, Class, and Immigration.* New York: Russell Sage Foundation.

Loprest, Pamela. 1999. *Families Who Left Welfare: Who Are They and How Are They Doing?* Washington, DC: Urban Institute.

Luker, Kristin. 1996. *Dubious Conceptions: The Politics of Teenage Pregnancy.* Cambridge, MA: Harvard University Press.

National Campaign for Jobs and Income Support. 2001A. *A Recession Like No Other: New Analysis Finds Safety Net in Tatters as Economic Slump Deepens.* Washington, DC: National Campaign for Jobs and Income Support.

National Campaign for Jobs and Income Support. 2001B. *Leaving Welfare, Left Behind:*

Employment Status, Income, and Well-Being of Former TANF Recipients. Washington, DC: National Campaign for Jobs and Income Support.

Newman, Katherine S. 1988. *Falling from Grace.* New York: Free Press.

Newman, Katherine S. 1999. *No Shame in My Game: The Working Poor in the Inner City.* New York: Vintage Books.

Piven, Frances Fox. 1999. "Welfare and Work," pp. 83–99 in *Whose Welfare?* edited by Gwendolyn Mink. Ithaca, NY: Cornell University Press.

Sherman, Arloc, Cheryl Amey, Barbara Duffield, Nancy Ebb, and Deborah Weinstein. 1998. *Welfare to What? Early Findings on Family Hardship and Well-Being.* National Coalition for the Homeless. Washington, DC: Children's Defense Fund.

Sorensen, Elaine and Chava Zibman. 2000. *Child Support Offers Some Protection Against Poverty.* Assessing the New Federalism, Series B, No. B–10. Washington, DC: Urban Institute.

Terry, Elizabeth and Jennifer Manlove. 1999. *Trends in Sexual Activity and Contraceptive Use Among Teens.* Washington, DC: Child Trends.

U.S. Conference of Mayors. 2001. *A Status Report on Hunger and Homelessness in America's Cities:* A 27-City Survey. Washington, DC: Conference of Mayors.

U.S. Congress. 1996. *Personal Responsibility and Work Opportunity Reconciliation Act of 1996.* Public Law 104–193, H.R. 3734.

Ventura, Stephanie and Christine A. Bachrach. 2000. *Nonmarital Childbearing in the United States, 1940–99.* U.S. Department of Health and Human Services, National Vital Statistics Reports 48 (16). Washington, DC: U.S. Government Printing Office.

Waller, Maureen R. 1999. "Meanings and Motives in New Family Stories: The Separation of Reproduction and Marriage Among Low-Income Black and White Parents," pp. 182–218 in *The Cultural Territories of Race: Black and White Boundaries,* edited by Michèle Lamont. Chicago: University of Chicago Press.

21

Incarceration, Unemployment, and Inequality

BRUCE WESTERN

In the later 1990s, two remarkable conditions influenced the employment opportunities of young, unskilled men in the United States. First, the unemployment rate fell to its lowest level in 30 years— around 4.5 percent by the summer of 1998. Second, the incarceration rate rose to its highest level in U.S. history. In 1998 1.78 million men were detained in American prisons and jails.

In removing so many from the labor force, U.S. incarceration policy has had significant but largely overlooked effects on unemployment. In the short run, it has lowered conventional measures of unemployment by concealing joblessness among a large group of able-bodied, working-age men. In the long run, it may raise unemployment rates by curtailing the job prospects of exconvicts and will certainly deepen economic inequality, because its effects are increasingly detrimental to young, black, unskilled men, whose incarceration rates are the highest of all and whose market power is weak. In this article I explore both short- and long-run effects.

The Penal System as a Labor Market Institution

In industrial relations and welfare state development, the United States stands apart from other major western nations. Its employment system is far more market-driven: rates of unionization and unemployment insurance coverage are lower than in most other countries in the Organisation for Economic Cooperation and Development (OECD), and social welfare spending accounts for only about 15 percent of gross domestic product (GDP), compared to about a quarter of GDP in the large European countries.

In recent years, the highly regulated European labor market has been burdened with persistent unemployment and apparently stagnant rates of economic growth, whereas the unregulated U.S. labor market has seen unemployment steadily falling in a booming economy. These trends have been used to buttress the argument that unregulated labor markets yield stronger economic performance than highly regulated markets.

Bruce Western, "Incarceration, Unemployment, and Inequality," *Focus* 21 (Spring 2001), pp. 32–36.

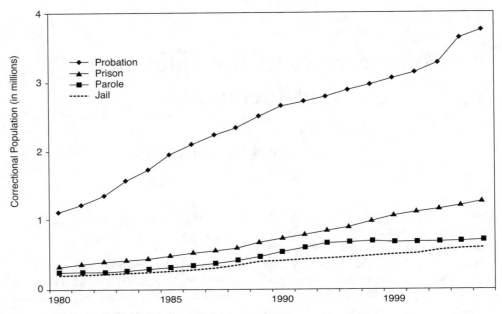

Figure 21.1   Adult Correctional Populations, 1980–99.
Source: Bureau of Justice Statistics http://www.ojp.usdoj.gov/bjs/glance/corr2.txt.

But the argument is too narrowly framed. Labor markets are embedded in a wide array of social arrangements that extend beyond the welfare state or industrial relations. The weakness of social protection mechanisms does not alone explain the superior U.S. employment record. In the United States, criminal justice policy constitutes a significant state intervention, providing a sizeable, nonmarket reallocation of labor that has significant effects on employment trends.

The magnitude of this intervention is reflected in incarceration and budget figures. Rates of incarceration began to increase in the early 1970s, but the most rapid growth took place in the 1980s and 1990s (see Figure 21.1). Between 1980 and 1999, the number of people in prisons and jails in the United States grew from half a million to almost two million. . . .

Incarceration is spread unevenly across the adult population. Men make up more than 90 percent of all inmates. In the mid-1990s, about two-thirds of those inmates were under 35, and about half had not completed high school. The dramatic expansion of the prison population most seriously affected young African Americans. In 1930, blacks accounted for 22 percent of all those in prison. In 1992, over half the prison population was black. By 1995, one out of three black male youths was under some form of state supervision and nearly 7 percent of all black males were incarcerated.

The U.S. incarceration rate—the number incarcerated on a single day per 100,000 of the adult population—is very much greater than incarceration rates in other industrialized democracies. In 1992–93, for instance, the overall U.S. rate was 5–10 times greater than the rate for other OECD countries;

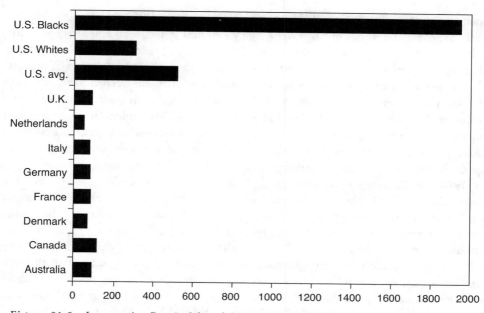

Figure 21.2   Incarceration Rate in Selected OECD Countries, 1992–93.

Source: B. Western and K. Beckett, "How Unregulated Is the U.S. Labor Market? The Penal System as a Labor Market Institution," *American Journal of Sociology* 104, no. 4 (1999): 130–60, Table 2.

among American blacks, the incarceration rate was 20 times greater (Figure 21.2). These high rates correspond to large absolute numbers. The entire Western European prison population is measured in hundreds of thousands, the prison and jail population in the United States in millions. This disparity does not reflect higher crime rates in the United States. The evidence, indeed, suggests that U.S. crime rates are only slightly above the average among industrialized countries. Thus U.S. incarceration rates appear to result from more aggressive prosecutorial practices, tougher sentencing standards, and intensified criminalization of drug-related activity.

The Short-Run Effect of Incarceration

The performance of national labor markets is commonly summarized by the unem-ployment rate—the percentage of unemployed individuals among the civilian labor force. This definition excludes from its calculations those in the military and those in prison and jail, as well as the "discouraged," those no longer looking for work and therefore out of the labor force. A broader concept tries to tap the idleness or economic dependence of a group by extending the definition of "unemployed" to include those incarcerated.

In the short run, incarceration keeps those with a high risk of unemployment out of the labor market. National surveys of prisons and jails from the early 1990s indicate that, on average, more than a third of male inmates were unemployed at the time they were sent to prison. If, for example, we count among the unemployed those inmates who were not working when incarcerated, the adjusted unemployment rate for 1995 was 6.2 percent, versus the conventional rate of 5.6 percent.

If we pursue the calculation further, including all inmates among the unemployed, the adjusted U.S. unemployment rate for 1995 rises to 7.5 percent, an increase of 1.9 percentage points over the conventional rate.[1] According to this adjusted measure, U.S. rates of labor inactivity never fell below 7 percent throughout the 1980s. In the economically buoyant period of the mid-1990s, the rate of inactivity was about 8 percent, higher than any conventional unemployment rate since the recession of the early 1980s.

In Europe, the short-run effect of incarceration is tiny, because incarceration rates are so low. In all European countries, unemployed males outnumber imprisoned males by very large ratios—between 20:1 and 50:1 (in the United States the ratio is 3:1). Including prison inmates in the jobless count, therefore, changes the unemployment rate for most European countries by only a few tenths of a percentage point, a striking contrast with the large U.S. difference.

By the conventional measure, the United States enjoyed consistently lower unemployment than Europe after the mid-1980s. But adjusted figures that count the incarcerated population as unemployed suggest that the U.S. labor market performed worse, not better, than Europe for most of the period between 1976 and 1994.

The Long-Run Effect of Incarceration

The long-run effects of incarceration highlight the employment experiences of convicts after they are released. Ex-convicts must reintegrate themselves into mainstream society, surmounting the psychological, social, and financial consequences of imprisonment. In this process, the ability to find stable, legal employment is crucial, yet job prospects for ex-convicts are poorer than the prospects of applicants with no criminal record. Incarceration erodes the value of vocational skills, and the increasingly violent and overcrowded state of prisons and jails produces attitudes and practices that may enhance survival in the prison but are not compatible with success in the conventional job market. Job prospects may be even worse in the current context, because resources for educational and vocational training in prisons have declined. Such experiences are better observed through survey data than through aggregate labor market statistics; I drew upon the National Longitudinal Survey of Youth (NLSY), which surveys a national sample of Americans aged 14 to 21 in 1979, to follow workers as they moved from prison to the labor market. I examined employment as a function of youth incarceration, jail time, and work experience, controlling also for personal and regional characteristics such as the extent of juvenile contact with the criminal justice system and the local unemployment rate. I included employment status both before and after incarceration, because the same characteristics that place men at risk of unemployment or low wages also raise their chances of criminal conviction.

The regression analysis indicates that youth who spent time in prison worked less four years later than youth who had no prison time. Incarceration, on average, reduced employment by about 5 percentage points, or three weeks a year. The effect is particularly large for black youth, whose employment was reduced by about 9 percentage points (5 weeks) by juvenile jail time. The effect of jail time on adult employment was greater than the effect of dropping out of high school or living in a high-unemployment area. Moreover, these effects did not decay over time. Even after 15 years, men incarcerated as juveniles worked between 5 and 10 percentage points less than their counterparts who never went to prison. The effects of adult incarceration, although large in the short run (5–10 weeks a year), were less persistent, and largely disappeared within four to five years of release.

With nearly two million men now in prison, these effects are not small. The penal system, when viewed as a labor market institution, appears to significantly undermine the productivity and employment chances of the male workforce.

The Penal System and Racial Inequality in Employment

A large and growing proportion of young black men has had experience with the penal system; can we estimate the likely effect on their future prospects and on black-white economic inequality?

The short-run effects of incarceration are very much worse for black than for white men. As the prison and jail population grew throughout the 1980s, the labor market effects of incarceration for black men becomes much larger if all those incarcerated are counted among the unemployed. In 1990–94, the adjusted unemployment rate is only one percentage point higher for white men, but it is seven percentage points higher for black men. During the 1990s almost one in five African American men, on average, was without a job.

Standard labor force data report a persistent gap in joblessness between black and white men that dates at least from the late 1960s.[2] Employment-population ratios calculated from these data show that employment inequality grew most sharply for young high school dropouts.[3] By including the incarcerated in calculating these ratios, we gain a more accurate picture, because marginalized groups at the fringes of the labor market have especially high incarceration rates.

If we include men in prison or jail, employment among black high school dropouts aged 20–35 declines from 46 to 29.3 percent in 1996. Furthermore, the adjusted employment ratios for black high school dropouts show steady decline over time, whereas conventional ratios show black employment as stable or even rising slightly.

The long-run effects are also serious. The incarceration of youth disrupts transitions from school to a career and hinders the acquisition of work experience. Ex-prisoners find it difficult to access jobs in the primary sector that offer opportunities for training, pay schedules that rise strongly with experience and age, and other characteristics of stable employment.[4] Instead, many ex-inmates find themselves stuck in low-wage job trajectories, confined to casual or illegitimate employment in the secondary labor market.

These kinds of disruptions materially affect earnings. In general, black ex-convicts earn about 10 percent less per hour than comparable men who were never incarcerated, after adjusting for such factors as work experience, schooling, youth delinquency, and drug use. They also have generally flat earnings profiles. My estimates suggest that, by 1998, the disproportionate incarceration of black men and the low-wage job trajectory of ex-inmates, taken together, had raised black-white earnings inequality by about 15 percent. . . .

By the end of the twentieth century, the prison experience was routinely shaping the working lives of young, less-educated, minority men. Because their incarceration rates are so high, labor market and earnings statistics as conventionally measured may significantly understate the extent of racial inequality in employment. The evidence suggests that the U.S. prison system may be exercising a systematic influence on large-scale patterns of economic inequality.

NOTES

1. The unemployed are usually defined as those without paid employment who are actively seeking work in the month before the survey.

2. F. Wilson, M. Tienda, and L. Wu, "Race and Unemployment: Labor Market Experiences of Black and White Men, 1968–1988," *Work and Occupations* 22, no. 3 (1995): 245–70.

3. J. Bound and R. Freeman, "What Went Wrong? The Erosion of Relative Earnings and Employment among Young Black Men in the 1980s," *Quarterly Journal of Economics* 107 (1992): 201–32.

4. M. Duneier, *Sidewalk* (New York: Farrar, Strauss, and Giroux, 1999), R. Sampson and J. Laub, *Crime in the Making: Pathways and Turning Points Through Life* (Cambridge, MA: Harvard University Press, 1993), J. Waldfogel, "The Effect of Criminal Conviction on Income and the Trust 'Reposed in the Workmen'," *Journal of Human Resources* 29 (1994): 62–81, and "Does Conviction Have a Persistent Effect on Income and Employment?" *International Review of Law and Economics* 14 (1994): 103–19.

22

Racial Formation in the United States

From the 1960s to the 1990s

MICHAEL OMI
HOWARD WINANT

In 1982–83, Susie Guillory Phipps unsuccessfully sued the Louisiana Bureau of Vital Records to change her racial classification from black to white. The descendant of an 18th-century white planter and a black slave, Phipps was designated "black" in her birth certificate in accordance with a 1970 state law which declared anyone with at least 1/32nd "Negro blood" to be black.

The Phipps case raised intriguing questions about the concept of race, its meaning in contemporary society, and its use (and abuse) in public policy. Assistant Attorney General Ron Davis defended the law by pointing out that some type of racial classification was necessary to comply with federal record-keeping requirements and to facilitate programs for the prevention of genetic diseases. Phipps's attorney, Brian Begue, argued that the assignment of racial categories on birth certificates was unconstitutional and that the 1/32nd designation was inaccurate. He called on a retired Tulane University professor who cited research indicating that most Louisiana whites have at least 1/20th "Negro" ancestry.

In the end, Phipps lost. The court upheld the state's right to classify and quantify racial identity.[1]

Phipps's problematic racial identity, and her effort to resolve it through state action, is in many ways a parable of America's unsolved racial dilemma. It illustrates the difficulties of defining race and assigning individuals or groups to racial categories. It shows how the racial legacies of the past—slavery and bigotry—continue to shape the present. It reveals both the deep involvement of the state in the organization and interpretation of race, and the inadequacy of state institutions to carry out these functions. It demonstrates how deeply Americans both as individuals and as a civilization are shaped, and indeed haunted, by race.

Having lived her whole life thinking that she was white, Phipps suddenly discovers that by legal definition she is not. In U.S. society, such an event is indeed catastrophic. But if she is not white, of what race is she? The *state* claims that she is black, based on its rules of classification, and another state agency, the court, upholds this judgment.

Michael Omi and Howard Winant, *Racial Formations in the United States*, pp. 53–61, 180–181. Copyright © 1986 by Routledge and copyright © 1994 by Michael Omi and Howard Winant.

But despite these classificatory standards which have imposed an either-or logic on racial identity, Phipps will not in fact "change color." Unlike what would have happened during slavery times if one's claim to whiteness was successfully challenged, we can assume that despite the outcome of her legal challenge, Phipps will remain in most of the social relationships she had occupied before the trial. Her socialization, her familial and friendship networks, her cultural orientation, will not change. She will simply have to wrestle with her newly acquired "hybridized" condition. She will have to confront the "Other" within.

The designation of racial categories and the determination of racial identity is no simple task. For centuries, this question has precipitated intense debates and conflicts, particularly in the U.S.—disputes over natural and legal rights, over the distribution of resources, and indeed, over who shall live and who shall die.

A crucial dimension of the Phipps case is that it illustrates the inadequacy of claims that race is a mere matter of variations in human physiognomy, that it is simply a matter of skin color. But if race cannot be understood in this manner, how *can* it be understood? We cannot fully hope to address this topic—no less than the meaning of race, its role in society, and the forces which shape it—in one chapter, nor indeed in one book. Our goal in this chapter, however, is far from modest: we wish to offer at least the outlines of a theory of race and racism.

What Is Race?

There is a continuous temptation to think of race as an *essence,* as something fixed, concrete, and objective. And there is also an opposite temptation: to imagine race as a mere *illusion,* a purely ideological construct which some ideal non-racist social order would eliminate. It is necessary to challenge both these positions, to disrupt and reframe the rigid and bipolar manner in which they are posed and debated, and to transcend the presumably irreconcilable relationship between them.

The effort must be made to understand race as an unstable and "decentered" complex of social meanings constantly being transformed by political struggle. With this in mind, let us propose a definition: *race is a concept which signifies and symbolizes social conflicts and interests by referring to different types of human bodies.* Although the concept of race invokes biologically based human characteristics (so-called "phenotypes"), selection of these particular human features for purposes of racial signification is always and necessarily a social and historical process. In contrast to the other major distinction of this type, that of gender, there is no biological basis for distinguishing among human groups along the lines of race. Indeed, the categories employed to differentiate among human groups along racial lines reveal themselves, upon serious examination, to be at best imprecise, and at worst completely arbitrary.

If the concept of race is so nebulous, can we not dispense with it? Can we not "do without" race, at least in the "enlightened" present? This question has been posed often, and with greater frequency in recent years. An affirmative answer would of course present obvious practical difficulties: it is rather difficult to jettison widely held beliefs, beliefs which moreover are central to everyone's identity and understanding of the social world. So the attempt to banish the concept as an archaism is at best counterintuitive. But a deeper difficulty, we believe, is inherent in the very formulation of this schema, in its way of posing race as a *problem,* a misconception left over from the past, and suitable now only for the dustbin of history.

A more effective starting point is the recognition that despite its uncertainties and contradictions, the concept of race continues to play a fundamental role in structuring and representing the social world. The task for theory is to explain this situation. It is to avoid both the utopian framework which sees race as an illusion we can somehow "get beyond," and also the essentialist formulation which sees race as something objective and fixed, a biological datum. Thus we should think of race as an element of social structure rather than as an irregularity within it; we should see race as a dimension of human representation rather than an illusion. These perspectives inform the theoretical approach we call racial formation.

Racial Formation

We define *racial formation* as the sociohistorical process by which racial categories are created, inhabited, transformed, and destroyed. Our attempt to elaborate a theory of racial formation will proceed in two steps. First, we argue that racial formation is a process of historically situated *projects* in which human bodies and social structures are represented and organized. Next we link racial formation to the evolution of hegemony, the way in which society is organized and ruled. Such an approach, we believe, can facilitate understanding of a whole range of contemporary controversies and dilemmas involving race, including the nature of racism, the relationship of race to other forms of differences, inequalities, and oppression such as sexism and nationalism, and the dilemmas of racial identity today.

From a racial formation perspective, race is a matter of both social structure and cultural representation. Too often, the attempt is made to understand race simply or primarily in terms of only one of these two analytical dimensions.[2] For example, efforts to explain racial inequality as a purely social structural phenomenon are unable to account for the origins, patterning, and transformation of racial difference.

Conversely, many examinations of racial difference—understood as a matter of cultural attributes *à la* ethnicity theory, or as a society-wide signification system, *à la* some poststructuralist accounts—cannot comprehend such structural phenomena as racial stratification in the labor market or patterns of residential segregation.

An alternative approach is to think of racial formation processes as occurring through a linkage between structure and representation. Racial *projects* do the ideological "work" of making these links. *A racial project is simultaneously an interpretation, representation, or explanation of racial dynamics, and an effort to reorganize and redistribute resources along particular racial lines.* Racial projects connect what race *means* in a particular discursive practice and the ways in which both social structures and everyday experiences are racially *organized,* based upon that meaning. Let us consider this proposition, first in terms of large-scale or macro-level social processes, and then in terms of other dimensions of the racial formation process.

Racial Formation as a Macro-Level Social Process

To *interpret the meaning of race is to frame it social structurally.* Consider for example, this statement by Charles Murray on welfare reform:

My proposal for dealing with the racial issue in social welfare is to repeal every bit of legislation and reverse every court decision that in any way requires, recommends, or awards differential treatment according to race, and thereby put us back onto the track that we left in 1965. We may argue about the appropriate limits of government intervention in trying to enforce the ideal, but at least it should be possible to identify the ideal: Race is not a morally admissible reason for treating one person differently from another. Period.[3]

Here there is a partial but significant analysis of the meaning of race: it is not a morally valid basis upon which to treat people "differently from one another." We may notice someone's race, but we cannot act upon that awareness. We must act in a "color-blind" fashion. This analysis of the meaning of race is immediately linked to a specific conception of the role of race in the social structure: it can play no part in government action, save in "the enforcement of the ideal." No state policy can legitimately require, recommend, or award different status according to race. This example can be classified as a particular type of racial project in the present-day U.S.—a "neoconservative" one.

Conversely, *to recognize the racial dimension in social structure is to interpret the meaning of race.* Consider the following statement by the late Supreme Court Justice Thurgood Marshall on minority "set-aside" programs:

A profound difference separates governmental actions that themselves are racist, and governmental actions that seek to remedy the effects of prior racism or to prevent neutral government activity from perpetuating the effects of such racism.[4]

Here the focus is on the racial dimensions of *social structure*—in this case of state activity and policy. The argument is that state actions in the past and present have treated people in very different ways according to their race, and thus the government cannot retreat from its policy responsibilities in this area. It cannot suddenly declare itself "color-blind" without in fact perpetuating the same type of differential, racist treatment. Thus, race continues to signify difference and structure inequality. Here, racialized social structure is immediately linked to an interpretation of the meaning of race. This example too can be classified as a particular type of racial project in the present-day U.S.—a "liberal" one. . . .

These two examples of contemporary racial projects are drawn from mainstream political debate; they may be characterized as center-right and center-left expressions of contemporary racial politics. We can, however, expand the discussion of racial formation processes far beyond these familiar examples. In fact, we can identify racial projects in several other analytical dimensions: first, the political spectrum can be broadened to include radical projects, on both the left and right, as well as along other political axes. Second, analysis of racial projects can take place not only at the macro-level of racial policy-making, state activity, and collective action, but also at the micro-level of everyday experience. . . .

The Political Spectrum of Racial Formation

We have encountered examples of a neoconservative racial project, in which the significance of race is denied, leading to a "color-blind" racial politics and "hands off" policy orientation; and of a "liberal" racial project, in which the significance of race is affirmed, leading to an egalitarian and "activist" state policy. But these by no means exhaust the political possibilities. Other racial projects can be readily identified on the contemporary U.S. scene. For example, "far right" projects, which uphold biologistic and racist views of difference, explicitly argue for white supremacist policies. "New right" projects overtly claim to hold "colorblind" views, but covertly manipulate racial fears in order to achieve political gains. On the left, "radical democratic" projects invoke notions of racial "difference" in combination with egalitarian politics and policy.

Further variations can also be noted. For example, "nationalist" projects, both conservative and radical, stress the incompatibility of racially defined group identity with the legacy of white supremacy, and therefore advocate a social structural solution of separation, either complete or partial. Nationalist currents represent a profound legacy of the centuries of racial absolutism that initially defined the meaning of race in the U.S. Nationalist concerns continue to influence racial debate in the form of Afrocentrism and other expressions of identity politics.

Taking the range of politically organized racial projects as a whole, we can "map" the current pattern of racial formation at the level of the public sphere, the "macro-level" in which public debate and mobilization takes place. But important as this is, the terrain on which racial formation occurs is broader yet.

Racial Formation as Everyday Experience

At the micro-social level, racial projects also link signification and structure, not so much as efforts to shape policy or define large-scale meaning, but as the applications of "common sense." To see racial projects operating at the level of everyday life, we have only to examine the many ways in which, often unconsciously, we "notice" race.

One of the first things we notice about people when we meet them (along with their sex) is their race. We utilize race to provide clues about *who* a person is. This fact is made painfully obvious when we encounter someone whom we cannot conveniently racially categorize—someone who is, for example, racially "mixed" or of an ethnic/racial group we are not familiar with. Such an encounter becomes a source of discomfort and momentarily a crisis of racial meaning.

Our ability to interpret racial meanings depends on preconceived notions of a racialized social structure. Comments such as, "Funny, you don't look black," betray an underlying image of what black should be. We expect people to act out their apparent racial identities; indeed we become disoriented when they do not. The black banker harassed by police while walking in casual clothes through his own well-off neighborhood, the Latino or white kid rapping in perfect Afro patois, the unending *faux pas* committed by whites who assume that the non-whites they encounter are servants or tradespeople, the belief that non-white colleagues are less qualified persons hired to fulfill affirmative action guidelines, indeed the whole gamut of racial stereotypes—that "white men can't jump," that Asians can't dance, etc., etc.—all testify to the way a racialized social structure shapes racial experience and conditions meaning. Analysis of such stereotypes reveals the always present, already active link between our view of the social structure—its demography, its laws, its customs, its threats—and our conception of what race means.

Conversely, our ongoing interpretation of our experience in racial terms shapes our relations to the institutions and organizations through which we are imbedded in social structure. Thus we expect differences in skin color, or other racially coded characteristics, to explain social differences. Temperament, sexuality, intelligence, athletic ability, aesthetic preferences, and so on are presumed to be fixed and discernible from the palpable mark of race. Such diverse questions as our confidence and trust in others (for example, clerks or salespeople, media figures, neighbors), our sexual preferences and romantic images, our tastes in music, films, dance, or sports, and our very ways of talking, walking, eating, and dreaming become racially coded simply because we live in a society where racial awareness is so pervasive. Thus in ways too comprehensive even to monitor consciously, and despite periodic calls—neoconservative and otherwise—for us to ignore race and adopt "color-blind" racial attitudes, skin color "differences" continue to rationalize distinct treatment of racially identified individuals and groups.

To summarize the argument: the theory of racial formation suggests that society is suffused with racial projects, large and small, to which all are subjected. This racial "subjection" is quintessentially ideological. Everybody learns some combination, some version, of the rules of racial classification, and of her own racial identity, often without obvious teaching or conscious inculcation. Thus are we inserted in a comprehensively racialized social structure. Race becomes "common sense"—a way of comprehending, explaining, and acting in the world. A vast web of racial projects mediates between the discursive or representational means in which race is identified and signified on the one hand, and the institutional and organizational forms in which it is routinized and standardized on the other. These projects are the heart of the racial formation process.

Under such circumstances, it is not possible to represent race discursively without simultaneously locating it, explicitly or implicitly, in a social structural (and historical) context. Nor is it possible to organize, maintain, or transform social structures without simultaneously engaging, once more either explicitly or implicitly, in racial signification. Racial formation, therefore, is a kind of synthesis, an outcome, of the interaction of racial projects on a society-wide level. These projects are, of course, vastly different in scope and effect. They include large-scale public action, state activities, and interpretations of racial conditions in artistic, journalistic, or academic fora, as well as the seemingly infinite number of racial judgments and practices we carry out at the level of individual experience. . . .

NOTES

1. *San Francisco Chronicle,* 14 September 1982, 19 May 1983.

2. Michael Omi and Howard Winant, "On the Theoretical Status of the Concept of Race" in Warren Crichlow and Cameron McCarthy, eds., *Race, Identity, and Representation in Education* (New York: Routledge, 1993).

3. Charles Murray, *Losing Ground: American Social Policy, 1950–1980* (New York: Basic Books, 1984), p. 223.

4. Justice Thurgood Marshall, dissenting in *City of Richmond v. J. A. Croson Co.,* 488 U.S. 469 (1989).

23

Immigration, Intermarriage, and the Challenges of Measuring Racial/Ethnic Identities

MARY C. WATERS

The new race question in the 2000 census addresses major demographic changes in American society and poses many challenges for researchers and policymakers. In this article, I review 2 major demographic trends that create difficulties for those trying to measure and classify the population by race and ethnicity—immigration and intermarriage. I then review the lessons researchers have learned from examining the census ancestry question. I propose that the variability, complexity, and indeterminacy of the census ancestry question, which has allowed multiple responses since it was first asked in 1980, may be a model for what we might expect with the race and Hispanic-origin questions in the 2000 census and beyond.

Immigration

We are in the midst of a large wave of immigration to the United States that is transforming the ethnic and racial composition of the population. Since the 1965 Immigration Law, which removed the national-ori-

gin quotas that had limited much legal immigration to those originating in Europe, immigration to the United States has been high and mostly from non-European sources. By 1998, 10% of the population (26.3 million) were foreign born, and another 10% (28.1 million) were the children of immigrants—the second generation. The foreign-born share of the population has doubled since 1970, when it was only 5% of the nation's population.[1] By the 1990s, 17% of immigrants to the United States came from Europe or Canada, 30% from Asia, and almost half from Latin America. The United States has changed from a society that before the mid-20th century was largely Black and White to one with a large number of groups we define as "racial" or "ethnic." In addition, heterogeneity within each of the ethnic and racial categories has increased. The future composition of the population will reflect how these new immigrants and their children identify themselves and how much they marry across ethnic and racial lines.

Mary C. Waters, "Immigration, Intermarriage, and the Challenges of Measuring Racial/Ethnic Identities," *American Journal of Public Health* (2000) 90, pp. 1735–1737.

In 1997, 61% of Asians, 38% of Hispanics, 8% of Whites, 6% of Blacks, and 6% of American Indians were foreign born.[2] One of the tasks immigrants face in assimilating in America is learning how to classify themselves in the American racial classification scheme.[3] Many immigrants from Latin America and the Caribbean come from multiracial societies in which different categories that fall somewhere between White and Black are more socially recognized than in the United States. Indeed, until the recent change in the Office of Management and Budget (OMB) guidelines allowing multiple identities, these immigrants had to exchange their Latin American conception of race for the American "one-drop rule," which classified people as Black if they had any Black ancestors at all. These immigrants may now feel more free to identify all of their racial backgrounds in the census and on other forms.

Intermarriage

Rates of intermarriage have been growing since 1960 for all groups, even those defined as "racial" groups. While the proportion of non-Hispanic Whites marrying non-Whites or Hispanics is still small, the rate of increase in recent decades has been dramatic. According to Harrison and Bennett, "in 1960 there were about 150000 interracial couples in the United States. This number grew rapidly to more than 1.0 million in 1990. When marriages with Hispanics are added the intergroup marriages totaled about 1.6 million in 1990.[4] While over 93% of Whites and of Blacks marry within their own groups, 70% of Asians and of Hispanics and only 33% of American Indians do. Although Black–White intermarriages are still the least prevalent,

among younger people there is evidence of dramatic change. Richard Alba reports that "10% of 25 to 34 year old black men have intermarried, most with white women."[5]

By 1997, 4% of married couples were in intergroup marriages as defined by OMB (Office of Management and Budget) race and Hispanic categories. Among Whites, the foreign born and native born have similar intermarriage rates. Among Asians and Hispanics, the native born have higher intermarriage rates, but among Blacks, the foreign born have higher intermarriage rates.[6] Thus, continued high immigration will have different effects on the intermarriage rates for different racial and ethnic groups. This will ultimately affect the numbers in each of these groups who might choose to check more than 1 race.

Assimilation in the Past

While the major race and ethnic groups in the United States stay relatively stable in the short run, there is enormous uncertainty in measurement at the boundaries of the groups and at the individual level. This uncertainty is due to a variety of causes—both substantive in terms of the socially constructed and volatile nature of ethnicity itself and technical in terms of the measurement error that is present in any attempt to measure social phenomena.

Groups we think of as "ethnic groups" were seen in earlier times as "racial groups." In the 19th century, the Irish were seen as a "race" apart from other European groups. They were stereotyped for their criminality, lack of education, and poor family values, and they were often portrayed as apes in cartoons of the time and referred to as "niggers turned inside out."[7] If those debating immigration restrictions in the early part of the 20th century had made population projections to predict the "race suicide" they felt new immigrants were causing, they would have projected the numbers of Southern and Central Europeans and Irish and shown how these growing groups would have made White Protestants a minority by some date in the far-off future. Such predictions would have failed to factor in the decline in the relevance of the boundaries separating European groups from one another. These groups have reached equality with White Protestants in education, income, and residential distribution. These social and cultural changes have interacted with ethnic intermarriage to produce an ethnic fluidity that would have been unthinkable then.

Ethnic identity is thus increasingly a matter of choice for Whites in the United States. An American of Italian, Irish, and Scottish ancestry, for example, can "choose" to identify with 1 or more of these ethnic ancestries and discard or "forget" others.[8,9] Current "racial" population projections do not take into account the possibility that today's "racial" groups will become tomorrow's "ethnic groups," with all of the uncertainty in measurement and identity that entails.

Ancestry Data

Research on how individuals of mixed European ethnic ancestries report their identities to the census can provide some clues as to how individuals of mixed race might choose an identity. The ancestry question on the 1980, 1990, and 2000 censuses was a fill-in-the-blank question that asked, "What is this person's ancestry or ethnic origin?" Under the blank line, a number of possible responses were given as examples. In 1980, up to 3 write-in responses were coded; in 1990, up to 2 were coded. The instructions said, "Persons who have more than one origin and cannot identify with a single group may report two ancestry groups.". . .

Analyses show that, regarding the ancestry question, intermarried parents filling out the census form simplify their children's ancestries. In situations where one parent reports one single White ethnic origin (X) and the other parent reports another (Y), a substantial percentage of the children (around 40%) are not described as the logical combination of parental ancestries (XY); instead, only one parent's origin is reported.[11] These inconsistencies between the ethnicity parents report for themselves and what they report for their children lead to estimates that are from 14% to 17% less than what would be expected if parents gave their children their exact ancestries.

Life-course changes have been documented as well. As people get older, they report fewer ancestries. When the complexity of ethnic-origin responses are tabulated by age, a sharp simplification is observed in the late teens and early 20s, when young people leave home and establish their own households, compared with younger ages. There is also evidence that when some people marry, they change their ancestry to match that of their spouses.[10,11] For instance, if a woman who was Italian and Polish married an Italian man, it is likely that she would drop the Polish ancestry and that both spouses would report that they were Italian. Lieberson and Waters suggest that standard demographic studies of intermarriage that ask whether ethnicity affects choice of marriage partner might actually be measuring the opposite—whether choice of marriage partner affects choice of ethnic identity.[10,12] . . .

Implications for
Multiple-Race Reporting

What are the implications of these findings for multiracial reporting? One is that the categories provided on the census form and the instructions given to respondents can have a large effect on people's answers to the census. Another is that parents report more detail on their children's ancestries than do the children themselves as they age and especially after they leave home. To the extent that the movement to include multiracial categories on the census form is led by parents who are concerned about having to choose a race for their children, there may not be much of an issue if the children themselves merely simplify their identity to 1 race when they leave home.

The pool of potential multiple-race respondents is quite high. In the 1990 census, 5% of the US population reported an ancestry that differed from their primary race or Hispanic identification. By race, 4% of Whites and 5% of Blacks report multiple ancestries. More than 25% of those reporting their race as American Indian report a non-American Indian ancestry, and about 10% of Asian and Hispanic respondents report a non-Asian or non-Hispanic ancestry, respectively.[13] These people are all "potential multiracials"—people who choose 1 race in the census but feel strongly enough about their other ancestries that they report them on another question. . . .

So far in the debate about multiple-race reporting, political attention has focused on Black–White interracials and on the implications of an interracial category for the long-run political and social fortunes of African Americans. This reflects the enormous importance of the Black–White color line in American society and the distinctive

legacy of slavery. Yet the Asian, American Indian, and Hispanic populations are much more likely to be strongly affected because of their much higher rates of intermarriage and their much smaller numbers overall.

American Indians may be a model for what we might expect with other groups as intermixing and the reporting of intermixing grow. Much of the growth in the self-identified American Indian population in recent decades has been due to "potential" American Indians, previously self-identified as White, claiming American Indian racial identity. To receive certain government benefits, such as treatment at the Indian health service, Indians have had to "prove" their identity—either through blood quantum certification or tribal enrollment in a federally recognized tribe. Self-identification as an Indian is not enough. This is an extreme model of what might happen in the future if the rates of intermarriage become very high and identity choices become unstable across racial groups and if the government continues to allocate some resources to individuals because of their racial and ethnic identities.

Comparison of those people who self-identify racially as American Indian and those who self-identify as American Indian by ancestry shows that racially identified American Indians are poorer, more concentrated on reservations, and more likely to report only 1 identity.[14] Any study of changing income patterns among American Indians must be mindful of the fact that changes in socioeconomic status could be due to new, more affluent people identifying as Indian. The addition of a multiracial category will affect not only the size of groups but also their measurable characteristics. Increasingly, changes in the health status of particular racial and ethnic groups could be due to changes in the composition of those identifying with the groups.

It is tempting to conclude that the subjective nature of identity, the difficulty of accurately measuring it, and the increasing variability in individual responses mean that we should no longer use race and ethnicity to classify the population. Yet that would be the wrong lesson to draw from the more subjective ancestry data. As difficult as they may be to use (and the race data will become increasingly more difficult to use and interpret), the ancestry data from 1980 and 1990 have yielded a great deal of important and useful conclusions about our society. Ancestry data have been used to document how well we as a society have reduced inequality and social distance among European-origin groups. Our goal for the future should be to continue to collect data on race and Hispanic origin, however messy and complicated, until we can document the same amount of progress and equality for all Americans. Until that day, we need these data to monitor our progress and to protect people whose skin color and culture put them at risk in our society.

REFERENCES

1. Borjas G. *Heaven's Door: Immigration Policy and the American Economy.* Princeton, NJ: Princeton University Press; 1999.

2. Council of Economic Advisors. *Changing America: Indicators of Social and Economic Well-Being by Race and Hispanic Origin.* Washington, DC: President's Initiative on Race; 1998.

3. Waters MC. *Black Identities: West Indian Immigrant Dreams and American Realities.* Cambridge, Mass: Harvard University Press; 1999.

4. Harrison R, Bennett C. Racial and ethnic diversity. In: Farley R. ed. *State of the Union: America in the 1990's. Vol 2: Social Trends.* New York, NY: Russell Sage Foundation Press; 1995:165.

5. Alba R. Assimilation's quiet tide. *The Public Interest.* 1995;119(Spring):3–18.

6. Smith JP, Edmonston B. *The New Americans: Economic, Demographic and Fiscal Effects of Immigration.* Washington, DC: National Academy Press: 1997.

7. Ignatiev N. *How the Irish Became White.* New York, NY: Routledge; 1995.

8. Alba RD. *Ethnic Identity: The Transformation of White America.* New Haven, Conn: Yale University Press; 1990.

9. Waters MC. *Ethnic Options: Choosing Identities in America.* Berkeley: University of California Press; 1990.

10. Lieberson S, Waters MC. The ethnic responses of Whites: what causes their instability, simplification and inconsistency? *Soc Forces.* 1993;72:421–450.

11. Lieberson S, Waters MC. *From Many Strands: Ethnic and Racial Groups in Contemporary America.* New York, NY: Russell Sage Foundation Press; 1988.

12. Lieberson S, Waters MC. Ethnic groups in flux: the changing ethnic responses of American Whites. *Ann Am Acad Political Soc Sci.* 1986; 487:79–91.

13. Edmonston B, Goldstein J, Lott T. *Spotlight on Heterogeneity: The Federal Standards for Racial and Ethnic Classification.* Washington, DC: National Academy Press; 1996:32.

14. Snipp M. *American Indians: First of This Land.* New York, NY: Russell Sage Foundation Press; 1989.

24

The New Second Generation

Segmented Assimilation and Its Variants

ALEJANDRO PORTES

MIN ZHOU

My name is Herb
and I'm not poor;
I'm the Herbie that you're looking for,
like Pepsi,
a new generation
of Haitian determination—
I'm the Herbie that you're looking for.

A beat tapped with bare hands, a few dance steps, and the Haitian kid was rapping. His song, titled "Straight Out of Haiti," was being performed at Edison High, a school that sits astride Little Haiti and Liberty City, the largest black area of Miami. The lyrics captured well the distinct outlook of his immigrant community. The panorama of Little Haiti contrasts sharply with the bleak inner city. In Miami's Little Haiti, the storefronts leap out at the passersby. Bright blues, reds, and oranges vibrate to Haitian merengue blaring from sidewalk speakers.[1] Yet, behind the gay Caribbean exteriors, a struggle goes on that will define the future of this community. As we will see later on, it involves the second generation—children like Herbie—subject to conflicting pressure from parents and peers and to pervasive outside discrimination.

Growing up in an immigrant family has always been difficult, as individuals are torn by conflicting social and cultural demands while they face the challenge of entry into an unfamiliar and frequently hostile world. And yet the difficulties are not always the same. The process of growing up American oscillates between smooth

Alejandro Portes and Min Zhou, "The New Second Generation: Segmented Assimilation and Its Variants," *The Annals of the American Academy of Political and Social Science* 530 (November, 1993), pp. 75–77, 81–92, 96. Copyright © 1993 by Sage Publications, Inc. Reprinted by permission of Sage Publications, Inc.

acceptance and traumatic confrontation depending on the characteristics that immigrants and their children bring along and the social context that receives them. In this article, we explore some of these factors and their bearing on the process of social adaptation of the immigrant second generation. We propose a conceptual framework for understanding this process and illustrate it with selected ethnographic material and survey data from a recent survey of children of immigrants.

Research on the new immigration—that which arose after the passage of the 1965 Immigration Act—has been focused almost exclusively on the first generation, that is, on adult men and women coming to the United States in search of work or to escape political persecution. Little noticed until recently is the fact that the foreign-born inflow has been rapidly evolving from single adult individuals to entire family groups, including infant children and those born to immigrants in the United States. By 1980, 10 percent of dependent children in households counted by the census were second-generation immigrants.[2] In the late 1980s, another study put the number of students in kindergarten through twelfth grade in American schools who spoke a language other than English at home at 3 to 5 million.[3]

The great deal of research and theorizing on post–1965 immigration offers only tentative guidance on the prospects and paths of adaptation of the second generation because the outlook of this group can be very different from that of their immigrant parents. For example, it is generally accepted among immigration theorists that entry-level menial jobs are performed without hesitation by newly arrived immigrants but are commonly shunned by their U.S.-reared offspring. This disjuncture gives rise to a race between the social and economic progress of first-generation immigrants and the material conditions and career prospects that their American children grow to expect.[4]

Nor does the existing literature on second-generation adaptation, based as it is on the experience of descendants of pre-World War I immigrants, offer much guidance for the understanding of contemporary events. The last sociological study of children of immigrants was Irving Child's *Italian or American? The Second Generation in Conflict,* published fifty years ago.[5] Conditions at the time were quite different from those confronting settled immigrant groups today. Two such differences deserve special mention. First, descendants of European immigrants who confronted the dilemmas of conflicting cultures were uniformly white. Even if of a somewhat darker hue than the natives, their skin color reduced a major barrier to entry into the American mainstream. For this reason, the process of assimilation depended largely on individual decisions to leave the immigrant culture behind and embrace American ways. Such an advantage obviously does not exist for the black, Asian, and mestizo children of today's immigrants.

Second, the structure of economic opportunities has also changed. Fifty years ago, the United States was the premier industrial power in the world, and its diversified industrial labor requirements offered to the second generation the opportunity to move up gradually through better-paid occupations while remaining part of the working class. Such opportunities have increasingly disappeared in recent years following a rapid process of national deindustrialization and global industrial restructuring. This process has left entrants to the American labor force confronting a widening gap between the minimally paid menial jobs that immigrants commonly accept and the high-tech and professional occupations requiring college degrees that native elites occupy.[6] The gradual disappearance of intermediate opportunities also bears directly on the race between first-generation economic progress and second-generation expectations, noted previously. . . .

Assimilation as a Problem

The Haitian immigrant community of Miami is composed of some 75,000 legal and clandestine immigrants, many of whom sold everything they owned in order to buy passage to America. First-generation Haitians are strongly oriented toward preserving a strong national identity, which they associate both with community solidarity and with social networks promoting individual success.[7] In trying to instill national pride and an achievement orientation in their children, they clash, however, with the youngsters' everyday experiences in school. Little Haiti is adjacent to Liberty City, the main black inner-city area of Miami, and Haitian adolescents attend predominantly inner-city schools. Native-born youths stereotype Haitians as too docile and too subservient to whites and they make fun of French and Creole and of the Haitians' accent. As a result, second-generation Haitian children find themselves torn between conflicting ideas and values: to remain Haitian they would have to face social ostracism and continuing attacks in school; to become American— black American in this case—they would have to forgo their parents' dreams of making it in America on the basis of ethnic solidarity and preservation of traditional values.[8]

An adversarial stance toward the white mainstream is common among inner-city minority youths who, while attacking the newcomers' ways, instill in them a consciousness of American-style discrimination. A common message is the devaluation of education as a vehicle for advancement of all black youths, a message that directly contradicts the immigrant parents' expectations. Academically outstanding Haitian American students, "Herbie" among them, have consciously attempted to retain their ethnic identity by cloaking it in black American cultural forms, such as rap music. Many others, however, have followed the path of least effort and become thoroughly assimilated. Assimilation in this instance is not into mainstream culture but into the values and norms of the inner city. In the process, the resources of solidarity and mutual support within the immigrant community are dissipated.

An emerging paradox in the study of today's second generation is the peculiar forms that assimilation has adopted for its members. As the Haitian example illustrates, adopting the outlooks and cultural ways of the native-born does not represent, as in the past, the first step toward social and economic mobility but may lead to the exact opposite. At the other end, immigrant youths who remain firmly ensconced in their respective ethnic communities may, by virtue of this fact, have a better chance for educational and economic mobility through use of the material and social capital that their communities make available.[9]

This situation stands the cultural blueprint for advancement of immigrant groups in American society on its head. As presented in innumerable academic and journalistic writings, the expectation is that the foreign-born and their offspring will first acculturate and then seek entry and acceptance among the native-born as a prerequisite for their social and economic advancement. Otherwise, they remain confined to the ranks of the ethnic lower and lower-middle classes.[10] This portrayal of the requirements for mobility, so deeply embedded in the national consciousness, stands contradicted today by a growing number of empirical experiences.

A closer look at these experiences indicates, however, that the expected consequences of assimilation have not entirely reversed signs, but that the process has become segmented. In other words, the question is into what sector of American society a particular immigrant group assimilates. Instead of a relatively uniform mainstream whose mores and prejudices dictate a common path of integration, we observe today several distinct forms of adaptation. One of them replicates the time-honored portrayal of growing acculturation and parallel integration into the white middle-class; a second leads straight in the opposite direction to permanent poverty and assimilation into the underclass; still a third associates rapid economic advancement with deliberate preservation of the immigrant community's values and tight solidarity. This pattern of segmented assimilation immediately raises the question of what makes some immigrant groups become susceptible to the downward route and what resources allow others to avoid this course. In the ultimate analysis, the same general process helps explain both outcomes. We advance next our hypotheses as to how this process takes place and how the contrasting outcomes of assimilation can be explained. This explanation is then illustrated with recent empirical material in the final section.

Vulnerability and Resources

Along with individual and family variables, the context that immigrants find upon arrival in their new country plays a decisive role in the course that their offspring's lives will follow. This context includes such broad variables as political relations between sending and receiving countries and the state of the economy in the latter and such specific ones as the size and structure of preexisting coethnic communities. The concept of modes of incorporation provides a useful theoretical tool to understand this diversity. As developed in prior publications, modes of incorporation consist of the complex formed by the policies of the host government; the values and prejudices of the receiving society; and the characteristics of the coethnic community. These factors can be arranged in a tree of contextual situations, illustrated by Figure 24.1. This figure provides a first approximation to our problem.[11]

To explain second-generation outcomes and their segmented character, however, we need to go into greater detail into the meaning of these various modes of incorporation from the standpoint of immigrant youths. There are three features of the social contexts encountered by today's newcomers that create vulnerability to downward assimilation. The first is color, the second is location, and the third is the absence of mobility ladders. As noted previously, the majority of contemporary immigrants are nonwhite. Although this feature may appear at first glance as an individual characteristic, in reality it is a trait belonging to the host society. Prejudice is not intrinsic to a particular skin color or racial type, and, indeed, many immigrants never experienced it in their native lands. It is by virtue of moving into a new social environment, marked by

212

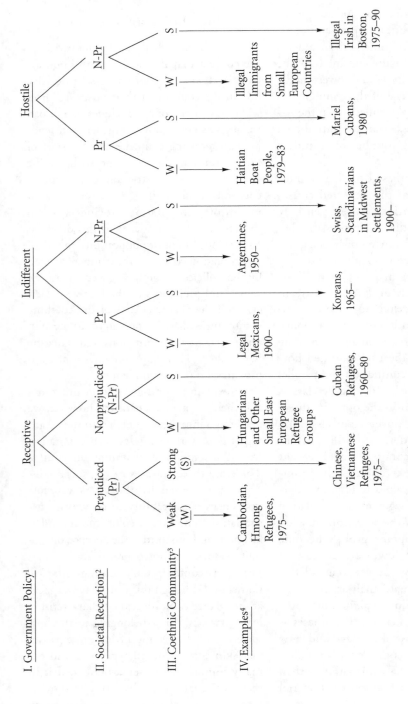

Figure 24.1 Models of Incorporation: A Typology

Source: Adapted from Alejandro Portes and Rubén G. Rumbaut, *Immigrant America: A Portrait* (Berkeley: University of California Press, 1990), p. 91. Copyright © 1990 by the Regents of the University of California.

1. Receptive policy is defined as legal entry with resettlement assistance, indifferent as legal entry without resettlement assistance, hostile as active opposition to a group's entry or permanence in the country; 2. Prejudiced reception is defined as that accorded to nonphenotypically white groups; nonprejudiced is that accorded to European and European-origin whites; 3. Weak coethnic communities are either small in numbers or composed primarily of manual workers; strong communities feature sizable numerical concentrations and a diversified occupational structure including entrepreneurs and professionals; 4. Examples include immigrant groups arriving from the start of the century to the present. Dates of migration are approximate. Groups reflect broadly but not perfectly the characteristics of each ideal type.

different values and prejudices, that physical features become redefined as a handicap.

The concentration of immigrant households in cities and particularly in central cities, as documented previously, gives rise to a second source of vulnerability because it puts new arrivals in close contact with concentrations of native-born minorities. This leads to the identification of the condition of both groups—immigrants and the native poor—as the same in the eyes of the majority. More important, it exposes second-generation children to the adversarial subculture developed by marginalized native youths to cope with their own difficult situation.[12] This process of socialization may take place even when first-generation parents are moving ahead economically and, hence, their children have no objective reasons for embracing a counter-cultural message. If successful, the process can effectively block parental plans for intergenerational mobility.

The third contextual source of vulnerability has to do with changes in the host economy that have led to the evaporation of occupational ladders for intergenerational mobility. As noted previously, new immigrants may form the backbone of what remains of labor-intensive manufacturing in the cities as well as in their growing personal services sector, but these are niches that seldom offer channels for upward mobility. The new hourglass economy, created by economic restructuring, means that children of immigrants must cross a narrow bottleneck to occupations requiring advanced training if their careers are to keep pace with their U.S.-acquired aspirations. This race against a narrowing middle demands that immigrant parents accumulate sufficient resources to allow their children to effect the passage and to simultaneously prove to them the viability of aspirations for

upward mobility. Otherwise, assimilation may not be into mainstream values and expectations but into the adversarial stance of impoverished groups confined to the bottom of the new economic hourglass.

The picture is painted in such stark terms here for the sake of clarity, although in reality things have not yet become so polarized. Middle-level occupations requiring relatively modest educational achievements have not completely vanished. By 1980, skilled blue-collar jobs—classified by the U.S. census as "precision production, craft, and repair occupations"—had declined by 1.1 percent relative to a decade earlier but still represented 13 percent of the experienced civilian labor force, or 13.6 million workers. Mostly clerical administrative support occupations added another 16.9 percent, or 17.5 million jobs. In 1980, occupations requiring a college degree had increased by 6 percent in comparison with 1970, but they still employed less than a fifth—18.2 percent—of the American labor force.[13] Even in the largest cities, occupations requiring only a high school diploma were common by the late 1980s. In New York City, for example, persons with 12 years or less of schooling held just over one half of the jobs in 1987. Clerical, service, and skilled blue-collar jobs not requiring a college degree represented 46 percent.[14] Despite these figures, there is little doubt that the trend toward occupational segmentation has increasingly reduced opportunities for incremental upward mobility through well-paid blue-collar positions. The trend forces immigrants today to bridge in only one generation the gap between entry-level jobs and professional positions that earlier groups took two or three generations to travel.

Different modes of incorporation also make available, however, three types of resources to confront the challenges of contemporary assimilation. First, certain groups, notably political refugees, are eligible for a variety of government programs including educational loans for their children. The Cuban Loan Program, implemented by the Kennedy administration in connection with its plan to resettle Cuban refugees away from South Florida, gave many impoverished first- and second-generation Cuban youths a chance to attend college. The high proportion of professionals and executives among Cuban American workers today, a figure on a par with that for native white workers, can be traced, at least in part, to the success of that program.[15] Passage of the 1980 Refugee Act gave to subsequent groups of refugees, in particular Southeast Asians and Eastern Europeans, access to a similarly generous benefits package.[16]

Second, certain foreign groups have been exempted from the traditional prejudice endured by most immigrants, thereby facilitating a smoother process of adaptation. Some political refugees, such as the early waves of exiles from Castro's Cuba, Hungarians and Czechs escaping the invasions of their respective countries, and Soviet Jews escaping religious persecution, provide examples. In other cases, it is the cultural and phenotypical affinity of newcomers to ample segments of the host population that ensures a welcome reception. The Irish coming to Boston during the 1980s are a case in point. Although many were illegal aliens, they came into an environment where generations of Irish Americans had established a secure foothold. Public sympathy effectively neutralized governmental hostility in this case, culminating in a change of the immigration law directly benefiting the newcomers.[17]

Third, and most important, are the resources made available through networks in the coethnic community. Immigrants who join well-established and diversified ethnic groups have access from the start to a range of moral and material resources well beyond those available through official assistance programs. Educational help for second-generation youths may include not only access to college grants and loans but also the existence of a private school system geared to the immigrant community's values. Attendance at these private ethnic schools insulates children from contact with native minority youths, while reinforcing the authority of parental views and plans.

In addition, the economic diversification of several immigrant communities creates niches of opportunity that members of the second generation can occupy, often without a need for an advanced education. Small-business apprenticeships, access to skilled building trades, and well-paid jobs in local government bureaucracies are some of the ethnic niches documented in the recent literature.[18] In 1987, average sales per firm of the smaller Chinese, East Indian, Korean, and Cuban enterprises exceeded $100,000 per year and they jointly employed over 200,000 workers. These figures omit medium-sized and large ethnic firms, whose sales and work forces are much larger.[19] Fieldwork in these communities indicates that up to half of recently arrived immigrants are employed by coethnic firms and that self-employment offers a prime avenue for mobility to second-generation youths.[20] Such community-mediated opportunities provide a solution to the race between material resources and second-generation aspirations not available through competition in the open labor market. Through creation of a capitalism of their own, some immigrant groups have thus been able to circumvent outside discrimination and the threat of vanishing mobility ladders.

In contrast to these favorable conditions are those foreign minorities who either lack a community already in place or whose co-ethnics are too poor to render assistance. The condition of Haitians in South Florida, cited earlier, provides an illustration of one of the most handicapped modes of incorporation encountered by contemporary immigrants, combining official hostility and widespread social prejudice with the absence of a strong receiving community.[21] From the standpoint of second-generation outcomes, the existence of a large but downtrodden coethnic community may be even less desirable than no community at all. This is because newly arrived youths enter into ready contact with the reactive subculture developed by earlier generations. Its influence is all the more powerful because it comes from individuals of the same national origin, "people like us" who can more effectively define the proper stance and attitudes of the newcomers. To the extent that they do so, the first-generation model of upward mobility through school achievement and attainment of professional occupations will be blocked.

Three Examples

Mexicans and Mexican Americans

Field High School (the name is fictitious) is located in a small coastal community of central California whose economy has long been tied to agricultural production and immigrant farm labor. About 57 percent of the student population is of Mexican descent. An intensive ethnographic study of the class of 1985 at Field High began with school records that showed that the majority of U.S.-born Spanish-surname students who had entered the school in 1981 had dropped out by their senior year. However, only 35 percent of the Spanish-surname students who had been originally classified by the school as limited English proficient (LEP) had dropped out. The figure was even lower than the corresponding one for native white students, 40 percent. LEP status is commonly assigned to recently arrived Mexican immigrants.[22]

Intensive ethnographic fieldwork at the school identified several distinct categories in which the Mexican-origin population could be classified. Recent Mexican immigrants were at one extreme. They dressed differently and unstylishly. They claimed an identity as Mexican and considered Mexico their permanent home. The most academically successful of this group were those most proficient in Spanish, reflecting their prior levels of education in Mexico. Almost all were described by teachers and staff as courteous, serious about their schoolwork, respectful, and eager to please as well as naive and unsophisticated. They were commonly classified as LEP.

The next category comprised Mexican-oriented students. They spoke Spanish at home and were generally classified as fluent English proficient (FEP). They had strong bicultural ties with both Mexico and the United States, reflecting the fact that most were born in Mexico but had lived in the United States for more than five years. They were proud of their Mexican heritage but saw themselves as different from the first group, the recién llegados (recently arrived), as well as from the native-born Chicanos and Cholos, who were derided as people who had lost their Mexican roots. Students from this group were active in soccer and the Sociedad Bilingue and in celebrations of May 5th, the anniversary of the Mexican defeat of French occupying forces. Virtually all of the Mexican-descent students who graduated in the top 10 percent of their class in 1981 were identified as members of this group.

Chicanos were by far the largest Mexican-descent group at Field High. They were mostly U.S.-born second- and third-generation students whose primary loyalty was to their in-group, seen as locked in conflict with white society. Chicanos referred derisively to successful Mexican students as "schoolboys" and "schoolgirls" or as "wannabes." According to M. G. Matute-Bianchi,

> To be a Chicano meant in practice to hang out by the science wing . . . *not* eating lunch in the quad where all the "gringos" and "schoolboys" hang out . . . cutting classes by faking a call slip so you can be with your friends at the 7–11 . . . sitting in the back of classes and not participating . . . *not* carrying your books to class . . . *not* taking the difficult classes . . . doing the minimum to get by.[23]

Chicanos merge imperceptibly into the last category, the Cholos, who were commonly seen as "low riders" and gang members. They were also native-born Mexican Americans, easily identifiable by their deliberate manner of dress, walk, speech, and other cultural symbols. Chicanos and Cholos were generally regarded by teachers as "irresponsible," "disrespectful," "mistrusting," "sullen," "apathetic," and "less motivated," and their poor school performance was attributed to these traits.[24] According to Matute-Bianchi, Chicanos and Cholos were faced with what they saw as a forced-choice dilemma between doing well in school or being a Chicano. To act white was regarded as disloyalty to one's group.

The situation of these last two groups exemplifies losing the race between first-generation achievements and later generations' expectations. Seeing their parents and grandparents confined to humble menial jobs and increasingly aware of discrimination against them by the white mainstream, U.S.-born children of earlier Mexican immigrants readily join a reactive subculture as a means of protecting their sense of self-worth. Participation in this subculture then leads to serious barriers to their chances of upward mobility because school achievement is defined as antithetical to ethnic solidarity. Like Haitian students at Edison High, newly arrived Mexican students are at risk of being socialized into the same reactive stance, with the aggravating factor that it is other Mexicans, not native-born strangers, who convey the message. The principal protection of *mexicanos* against this type of assimilation lies in their strong identification with home-country language and values, which brings them closer to their parents' cultural stance.

Punjabi Sikhs in California

Valleyside (a fictitious name) is a northern California community where the primary economic activity is orchard farming. Farm laborers in this area come often from India; they are mainly rural Sikhs from the Punjab. By the early 1980s, second-generation Punjabi students already accounted for 11 percent of the student body at Valleyside High. Their parents were no longer only farm laborers, since about a third had become orchard owners themselves and another third worked in factories in the nearby San Francisco area. An ethnographic study of Valleyside High School in 1980–82 revealed a very difficult process of assimilation for Punjabi Sikh students. According to its author, M. A. Gibson, Valleyside is "redneck country," and white residents are extremely hostile to immigrants who look different and speak a different language: "Punjabi teenagers are told they stink . . . told to go back to India . . . physically abused by majority students who spit at them, refuse to sit by them in class or in buses, throw food at them or worse."[25]

Despite these attacks and some evidence of discrimination by school staff, Punjabi students performed better academically than majority Anglo students. About 90 percent of the immigrant youths completed high school, compared to 70–75 percent of native whites. Punjabi boys surpassed the average grade point average, were more likely to take advanced science and math classes, and expressed aspirations for careers in science and engineering. Girls, on the other hand, tended to enroll in business classes, but they paid less attention to immediate career plans, reflecting parental wishes that they should marry first. This gender difference is indicative of the continuing strong influence exercised by the immigrant community over its second generation. According to Gibson, Punjabi parents pressured their children against too much contact with white peers who may "dishonor" the immigrants' families, and defined "becoming Americanized" as forgetting one's roots and adopting the most disparaged traits of the majority, such as leaving home at age 18, making decisions without parental consent, dating, and dancing. At the same time, parents urged children to abide by school rules, ignore racist remarks and avoid fights, and learn useful skills, including full proficiency in English.[26]

The overall success of this strategy of selective assimilation to American society is remarkable because Punjabi immigrants were generally poor on their arrival in the United States and confronted widespread discrimination from whites without the benefit of either governmental assistance or a well-established coethnic community. In terms of our typology of vulnerability and resources, the Punjabi Sikh second generation was very much at risk except for two crucial factors. First, immigrant parents did not settle in the inner city or in close proximity to any native-born minority whose offspring could provide an alternative model of adaptation to white-majority discrimination. In particular, the absence of a downtrodden Indian American community composed of children of previous immigrants allowed first-generation parents to influence decisively the outlook of their offspring, including their ways of fighting white prejudice. There was no equivalent of a Cholo-like reactive subculture to offer an alternative blueprint of the stance that "people like us" should take.

Second, Punjabi immigrants managed to make considerable economic progress, as attested by the number who had become farm owners, while maintaining a tightly knit ethnic community. The material and social capital created by this first-generation community compensated for the absence of an older coethnic group and had decisive effects on second-generation outlooks. Punjabi teenagers were shown that their parents' ways paid off economically, and this fact, plus their community's cohesiveness, endowed them with a source of pride to counteract outside discrimination. Through this strategy of selective assimilation, Punjabi Sikhs appeared to be winning the race against the inevitable acculturation of their children to American-style aspirations.

Caribbean Youths in South Florida

Miami is arguably the American city that has been most thoroughly transformed by post–1960 immigration. The Cuban Revolution had much to do with this transformation, as it sent the entire Cuban upper class out of the country, followed by thousands of refugees of more modest backgrounds. Over time, Cubans created a highly diversified and prosperous ethnic community that provided resources for the adaptation process of its second generation. Reflecting this situation are average Cuban family incomes that, by 1989, approximated those of the native-born population; the existence in 1987 of more than 30,000 Cuban-owned small businesses that formed the core of the Miami ethnic enclave; and the parallel rise of a private school system oriented toward the values and political outlook of this community.[27] In terms of the typology of vulnerability and resources, well-sheltered Cuban American teenagers lack any extensive exposure to outside discrimination, they have little contact with youths from disadvantaged minorities, and the development of an enclave creates economic opportunities beyond the narrowing industrial and tourist sectors on which most other immigrant groups in the area depend. Across town, Haitian American teenagers face exactly the opposite set of conditions, as has been shown.

Among the other immigrant groups that form Miami's ethnic mosaic, two deserve mention because they represent intermediate situations between those of the Cubans and Haitians. One comprises Nicaraguans escaping the Sandinista regime during the 1980s. They were not as welcomed in the United States as were the Cuban exiles, nor were they able to develop a large and diversified community. Yet they shared with Cubans their language and culture, as well as a militant anti-Communist discourse. This common political outlook led the Cuban American community to extend its resources

in support of their Nicaraguan brethren, smoothing their process of adaptation.[28] For second-generation Nicaraguans, this means that the preexisting ethnic community that provides a model for their own assimilation is not a downtrodden group but rather one that has managed to establish a firm and positive presence in the city's economy and politics.

The second group comprises West Indians coming from Jamaica, Trinidad, and other English-speaking Caribbean republics. They generally arrive in Miami as legal immigrants, and many bring along professional and business credentials as well as the advantage of fluency in English. These individual advantages are discounted, however, by a context of reception in which these mostly black immigrants are put in the same category as native-born blacks and discriminated against accordingly. The recency of West Indian migration and its small size have prevented the development of a diversified ethnic community in South Florida. Hence new arrivals experience the full force of white discrimination without the protection of a large coethnic group and with constant exposure to the situation and attitudes of the inner-city population. Despite considerable individual resources, these disadvantages put the West Indian second generation at risk of bypassing white or even native black middle-class models to assimilate into the culture of the underclass. . . .

Conclusion

Fifty years ago, the dilemma of Italian American youngsters studied by Irving Child consisted of assimilating into the American mainstream, sacrificing in the process their parents' cultural heritage in contrast to taking refuge in the ethnic community from the challenges of the outside world. In the contemporary context of segmented assimilation, the options have become less clear. Children of nonwhite immigrants may not even have the opportunity of gaining access to middle-class white society, no matter how acculturated they become. Joining those native circles to which they do have access may prove a ticket to permanent subordination and disadvantage. Remaining securely ensconced in their coethnic community, under these circumstances, may be not a symptom of escapism but the best strategy for capitalizing on otherwise unavailable material and moral resources. As the experiences of Punjabi Sikh and Cuban American students suggest, a strategy of paced, selective assimilation may prove the best course for immigrant minorities. But the extent to which this strategy is possible also depends on the history of each group and its specific profile of vulnerabilities and resources. The present analysis represents a preliminary step toward understanding these realities.

NOTES

1. Alejandro Portes and Alex Stepick, *City on the Edge: The Transformation of Miami* (Berkeley: University of California Press, 1993), chap. 8.

2. Defined as native-born children with at least one foreign-born parent or children born abroad who came to the United States before age 12.

3. Joan N. First and John W. Carrera, *New Voices: Immigrant Students in U.S. Public Schools* (Boston: National Coalition of Advocates for Students, 1988).

4. Michael Piore, *Birds of Passage* (New York: Cambridge University Press, 1979); Herbert Gans, "Second-Generation Decline: Scenarios for the Economic and Ethnic Futures of the Post–1965 American Immigrants," *Ethnic and Racial Studies* 15:173–92 (Apr. 1992).

5. Irving L. Child, *Italian or American? The Second Generation in Conflict* (New Haven, CT: Yale University Press, 1943).

6. See, for example, Saskia Sassen, "Changing Composition and Labor Market Location of Hispanic Immigrants in New York City, 1960–1980," in *Hispanics in the U.S. Economy,* ed. George J. Borjas and Marta Tienda (New York: Academic Press, 1985), pp. 299–322.

7. See Alex Stepick, "Haitian Refugees in the U.S." (Report no. 52, Minority Rights Group, London, 1982); Alex Stepick and Alejandro Portes, "Flight into Despair: A Profile of Recent Haitian Refugees in South Florida," *International Migration Review,* 20:329–50 (Summer 1986).

8. This account is based on fieldwork in Miami conducted in preparation for a survey of immigrant youths in public schools.

9. On the issue of social capital, see James S. Coleman, "Social Capital in the Creation of Human Capital," *American Journal of Sociology,* supplement, 94:S95–121 (1988); Alejandro Portes and Min Zhou, "Gaining the Upper Hand: Economic Mobility among Immigrant and Domestic Minorities," *Ethnic and Racial Studies,* 15:491–522 (Oct. 1992). On ethnic entrepreneurship, see Ivan H. Light, *Ethnic Enterprise in America: Business and Welfare among Chinese, Japanese, and Blacks* (Berkeley: University of California Press, 1972); Kenneth Wilson and W. Allen Martin, "Ethnic Enclaves: A Comparison of the Cuban and Black Economies in Miami," *American Journal of Sociology,* 88:135–60 (1982).

10. See W. Lloyd Warner and Leo Srole, *The Social Systems of American Ethnic Groups* (New Haven, CT: Yale University Press, 1945); Thomas Sowell, *Ethnic America: A History* (New York: Basic Books, 1981).

11. See Alejandro Portes and Rubén G. Rumbaut, *Immigrant America: A Portrait* (Berkeley: University of California Press, 1990), chap. 3.

12. See Mercer L. Sullivan, *"Getting Paid": Youth, Crime, and Work in the Inner City* (Ithaca, NY: Cornell University Press, 1989), chaps. 1, 5.

13. U.S. Department of Commerce, Bureau of the Census, *Census of Population and Housing, 1980: Public Use Microdata Samples A (MRDF)*

(Washington, DC: Department of Commerce, 1983).

14. Thomas Bailey and Roger Waldinger, "Primary, Secondary, and Enclave Labor Markets: A Training System Approach," *American Sociological Review,* 56:432–45 (1991).

15. Professionals and executives represented 25.9 percent of Cuban-origin males aged 16 years and over in 1989; the figure for the total adult male population was 26 percent. See Jesus M. García and Patricia A. Montgomery, *The Hispanic Population of the United States: March 1990,* Current Population Reports, ser. P–20, no. 449 (Washington, DC: Department of Commerce, 1991).

16. Portes and Rumbaut, *Immigrant America,* pp. 23–25; Robert L. Bach et al., "The Economic Adjustment of Southeast Asian Refugees in the United States," in *World Refugee Survey, 1983* (Geneva: United Nations High Commission for Refugees, 1984), pp. 51–55.

17. The 1990 Immigration Act contains tailor-made provisions to facilitate the legalization of Irish immigrants. Those taking advantage of the provisions are popularly dubbed "Kennedy Irish" in honor of the Massachusetts Senator who coauthored the act. On the 1990 act, see Michael Fix and Jeffrey S. Passel, "The Door Remains Open: Recent Immigration to the United States and a Preliminary Analysis of the Immigration Act of 1990" (Working paper, Urban Institute and RAND Corporation, 1991). On the Irish in Boston, see Karen Tumulty, "When Irish Eyes Are Hiding. . .," *Los Angeles Times,* 29 Jan. 1989.

18. Bailey and Waldinger, "Primary, Secondary, and Enclave Labor Markets"; Min Zhou, *New York's Chinatown: The Socioeconomic Potential of an Urban Enclave* (Philadelphia: Temple University Press, 1992); Wilson and Martin, "Ethnic Enclaves"; Suzanne Model, "The Ethnic Economy: Cubans and Chinese Reconsidered" (Manuscript, University of Massachusetts at Amherst, 1990).

19. U.S. Department of Commerce, Bureau of the Census, *Survey of Minority-Owned Business*

Enterprises, 1987, MB–2 and MB–3 (Washington, DC: Department of Commerce, 1991).

20. Alejandro Portes and Alex Stepick, "Unwelcome Immigrants: The Labor Market Experiences of 1980 (Mariel) Cuban and Haitian Refugees in South Florida," *American Sociological Review,* 50:493–514 (Aug. 1985); Zhou, *New York's Chinatown;* Luis E. Guarnizo, "One Country in Two: Dominican-Owned Firms in New York and the Dominican Republic" (Ph.D. diss. Johns Hopkins University, 1992); Bailey and Waldinger, "Primary, Secondary, and Enclave Labor Markets."

21. Stepick, "Haitian Refugees in the U.S."; Jake C. Miller, *The Plight of Haitian Refugees* (New York: Praeger, 1984).

22. M. G. Matute-Bianchi, "Ethnic Identities and Patterns of School Success and Failure among Mexican-Descent and Japanese-American Students in a California High School," *American Journal of Education,* 95:233–55 (Nov. 1986). This study is summarized in Rubén G. Rumbaut, "Immigrant Students in California Public Schools: A Summary of Current Knowledge" (Report no. 11, Center for Research on Effective Schooling for Disadvantaged Children, Johns Hopkins University, Aug. 1990).

23. Matute-Bianchi, "Ethnic Identities and Patterns," p. 253.

24. Rumbaut, "Immigrant Students," p. 25.

25. M. A. Gibson, *Accommodation without Assimilation: Sikh Immigrants in an American High School* (Ithaca, NY: Cornell University Press, 1989), p. 268.

26. Gibson, *Accommodation without Assimilation.* The study is summarized in Rumbaut, "Immigrant Students," pp. 22–23.

27. García and Montgomery, Hispanic Population; U.S. Department of Commerce, Bureau of the Census, *Survey of Minority-Owned Business Enterprises,* MB–2.

28. Portes and Stepick, *City on the Edge,* chap. 7.

25

Black Identities

West Indian Immigrant Dreams and American Realities

MARY C. WATERS

A key proposition of the new models of immigrant incorporation studies how the social capital immigrants bring with them, and the racial and ethnic definitions of nonwhite immigrants as minorities, combine to create a situation where becoming American in terms of culture and identity and achieving economic success are decoupled. Some immigrants and their children do better economically by maintaining a strong ethnic identity and culture and by resisting American cultural and identity influences. In fact, many authors now suggest that remaining immigrant-or-ethnic-identified eases economic and social incorporation into the United States. These new assumptions turn models of identity change on their head—now those who resist becoming American do well and those who lose their immigrant ethnic distinctiveness become downwardly mobile. West Indians, it turns out, fit this model very well because when West Indians lose their distinctiveness as immigrants or ethnics they become not just Americans, but black Americans.

Given the ongoing prejudice and discrimination in American society, this represents downward mobility for the immigrants and their children. . . .

The main argument of this chapter is that black immigrants from the Caribbean come to the United States with a particular identity/culture/worldview that reflects their unique history and experiences. This culture and identity are different from the immigrant identity and culture of previous waves of European immigrants because of the unique history of the origin countries and because of the changed contexts of reception the immigrants face in the United States. This culture and identity are also different from the culture and identity of African Americans.

At first, two main aspects of the culture of West Indians help them to be successful in America. First, because they are immigrants they have a different attitude toward employment, work, and American society than native-born Americans. Employers value this highly. Their background characteristics,

---

including human capital and social net-work ties, ease their entry into the U.S. labor force. Middle-class immigrants come with qualifications and training that are needed in the U.S. economy (nurses, for example). Because English is their native language, they are able to transfer their for-eign qualifications (teaching credentials, nursing degrees) into American credentials. In addition, working-class immigrants have extensive networks of contacts that facili-tate their entry into low-level jobs.

Second, the immigrants' unique under-standing and expectations of race relations allow them to interact with American racial structures in a successful way. Specifically, their low anticipation of sour race relations allows them to have better interpersonal in-teractions with white Americans than many native African Americans. Because they come from a society with a majority of blacks and with many blacks in high posi-tions, the immigrants have high ambitions and expectations. Yet their experience with blocked economic mobility due to race and their strong racial identities lead them to challenge blocked mobility in a very mili-tant fashion when they encounter it. This combination of high ambitions, friendly re-lations with whites on an interpersonal level, and strong militance in encountering any perceived discrimination leads to some better outcomes in the labor market for West Indians than for black Americans.

Ultimately, however, the structural reali-ties of American race relations begin to swamp the culture of the West Indians. Per-sistent and obvious racial discrimination undermines the openness toward whites the immigrants have when they first arrive. Low wages and poor working conditions are no longer attractive to the children of the immigrants, who use American, not

Caribbean, yardsticks to measure how good a job is. Racial discrimination in housing channels the immigrants into neighbor-hoods with inadequate city services and high crime rates. Inadequate public schools undermine their hopes for their children's future. Over time the distinct elements of West Indian culture the immigrants are most proud of—a willingness to work hard, a lack of attention to racialism, a high value on education, and strong interests in saving for the future—are undermined by the real-ities of life in the United States.

These changes are particularly concen-trated among the working-class and poor immigrants. Middle-class immigrants are able to pass along aspects of their culture and worldview to their children, but the majority of the working-class immigrants are not. Race as a master status in the United States soon overwhelms the identi-ties of the immigrants and their children, and they are seen as black Americans. Many of the children of the immigrants develop "oppositional identities" to deal with that status. These identities stress that doing well in school is "acting white." The cul-tural behaviors associated with these oppo-sitional identities further erode the life chances of the children of the West Indian immigrants.

While many white conservatives blame the culture of African Americans for their failures in the economy, the experiences of the West Indians show that even "good cul-ture" is no match for racial discrimination. Over the course of one generation the structural realities of American race rela-tions and the American economy under-mine the cultures of the West Indian immigrants and create responses among the immigrants, and especially their children, that resemble the cultural responses of

African Americans to long histories of exclusion and discrimination. . . .

The key factor brought to fresh light by the West Indian immigrants' experiences is the role of continuing racial inequality—the institutional failures in our inner cities to provide jobs, education, and public safety—in sustaining a cultural response of disinvestment in the face of discrimination rather than increased striving. A lifetime of interpersonal attacks based on race can lead to bitterness and anger on the part of an individual. A community of people coping with economic marginality and a lack of any avenues of institutional support for individual mobility leads to a culture of opposition. That culture might serve individuals well for those times when it protects them from the sting of racism and discrimination, but ultimately as a long-term political response to discrimination and exclusion it serves to prevent people from taking advantage of the new opportunities that do arise. Those opportunities are reserved by whites in power for immigrants who make them feel less uncomfortable about relations between the races and especially about taking orders from white supervisors or customers.

One of the African-American teachers [interviewed in this study] eloquently describes how even one act of cruelty or disdain by a white person can have long-standing effects on a young black person and on the whole cycle of black-white race relations:

I have had this happen to me so let me relate this incident. I have been going or coming from a building and held the door for some old white person and had them walk right past me, as if I am supposed to hold the door for them. Not one word, a thank-you, or an acknowledgment of your presence was made. A seventeen-year-old,

when he has something like that happen to him, the next time he is going to slam that door in the old lady's face, because I had that tendency myself. I had the hostility build up in me. The next time it happens I won't do that because I am older, but when I was seventeen it might not have made any difference to me that this was a different old lady. I would have flashed back to that previous incident and said I am not holding that door for you. Now that old lady who may have been a perfectly fine individual, who got this door slammed in her face by this young black person, her attitude is "boy, all those people are really vicious people." Her not understanding how it all came to pass. That on a large scale is what is happening in our country today. That's why our young people are very aggressive and very, very hostile when they are put in a situation of black-white confrontation. They say to themselves, "I am not going to let you treat me the way you treated my grandparents, or the way I have read or seen in books or movies that they were treated." I would rather for you to hate me than to disrespect me, is the attitude I think is coming out from our black youth today. (Black American male teacher, age 41)

The policy implications of this study lie in the ways in which the economic and cultural disinvestment in American cities erodes the social capital of immigrant families. The families need recognition of their inherent strengths and the supports necessary to maintain their ambitions. The erosion of the optimism and ambition of the first generation that I saw in their children could be stopped if job opportunities were more plentiful, inner-city schools were nurturing and safe environments that provided good educations, and neighborhoods were safer. Decent jobs, effective schools, and safe streets are not immigrant- or race-based policies. They are universal policies that would benefit all urban residents. Indeed, the strengths these immigrant families have may be in part due to their immigrant status, but the problems they face are much more likely to be due to their class status and their urban residence. Policies that benefit immigrants would equally benefit Americans.

But, in addition, the experience of these immigrants tells us that we must recognize the continuing significance of interpersonal racism in creating psychological tensions and cultural adaptations in the black community. The cycle of attack and disrespect from whites, anger and withdrawal from blacks, and disengagement and blaming behaviors by whites must be broken by changing whites' behaviors. This involves policies that specifically address racial discrimination. The immigrants' tales of blatant housing and job discrimination directly point to needed vigilance in protecting all blacks in the United States from unequal treatment in the private sector. The more difficult problem is dealing with the everyday subtle forms of prejudice and discrimination that also plague foreign-born and American-born blacks. We cannot pass laws forbidding white women from clutching their handbags when black teenagers walk past them. We cannot require old white women to thank young black men who show them courteous behavior. Those kinds of behaviors can only change when whites no longer automatically fear blacks and when whites begin to perceive the humanity and diversity of the black people they encounter.

26

The Declining Significance of Race
Blacks and Changing American Institutions

WILLIAM JULIUS WILSON

Race relations in America have undergone fundamental changes in recent years, so much so that now the life chances of individual blacks have more to do with their economic class position than with their day-to-day encounters with whites. In earlier years the systematic efforts of whites to suppress blacks were obvious to even the most insensitive observer. Blacks were denied access to valued and scarce resources through various ingenious schemes of racial exploitation, discrimination, and segregation, schemes that were reinforced by elaborate ideologies of racism. But the situation has changed. However determinative such practices were for the previous efforts of the black population to achieve racial equality, and however significant they were in the creation of poverty-stricken ghettoes and a vast underclass of black proletarians—that massive population at the very bottom of the social class ladder plagued by poor education and low-paying, unstable jobs—they do not provide a meaningful explanation of the life chances of black Americans today. The traditional patterns of interaction between blacks and whites, particularly in the labor market, have been fundamentally altered.

In the antebellum period, and in the latter half of the nineteenth century through the first half of the twentieth century, the continuous and explicit efforts of whites to construct racial barriers profoundly affected the lives of black Americans. Racial oppression was deliberate, overt, and is easily documented, ranging from slavery to segregation, from the endeavors of the white economic elite to exploit black labor to the actions of the white masses to eliminate or neutralize black competition, particularly economic competition.[1] As the nation has entered the latter half of the twentieth century, however, many of the traditional barriers have crumbled under the weight of the political, social, and economic changes of the civil rights era. A new set of obstacles has emerged from basic structural shifts in the economy. These obstacles are therefore impersonal but may prove to be even more formidable for certain segments of the black population. Specifically, whereas the previous barriers were usually designed to control and restrict the entire black population, the new barriers create hardships essentially for the black underclass; whereas the old barriers were based explicitly on racial motivations derived from intergroup contact, the new barriers have racial significance only in their consequences, not in their origins. In short, whereas the old barriers bore the pervasive features of racial oppression, the new barriers indicate an important and emerging form of class subordination.

It would be shortsighted to view the traditional forms of racial segregation and discrimination as having essentially disappeared in contemporary America; the presence of blacks is still firmly resisted in various institutions and social arrangements, for example, residential areas and private social clubs. However, in the economic sphere, class has become more important than race in determining black access to privilege and power. It is clearly evident in this connection that many talented and educated blacks are now entering positions of prestige and influence at a rate comparable to or, in some situations, exceeding that of whites with equivalent qualifications. It is equally clear that the black underclass is in a hopeless state of economic stagnation, falling further and further behind the rest of society. . . .

Three Stages of American Race Relations

My basic thesis is that American society has experienced three major stages of black-white contact and that each stage embodies a different form of racial stratification structured by the particular arrangement of both the economy and the polity. Stage one coincides with antebellum slavery and the early postbellum era and may be designated the period of *plantation economy and racial-caste oppres-*

sion. Stage two begins in the last quarter of the nineteenth century and ends at roughly the New Deal era and may be identified as the period of *industrial expansion, class conflict, and racial oppression.* Finally, stage three is associated with the modern, industrial, post–World War II era, which really began to crystallize during the 1960s and 1970s, and may be characterized as the period of *progressive transition from racial inequalities to class inequalities.* For the sake of brevity I shall identify the different periods respectively as the preindustrial, industrial, and modern industrial stages of American race relations.

Although this abbreviated designation of the periods of American race relations seems to relate racial change to fundamental economic changes rather directly, it bears repeating that the different stages of race relations are structured by the unique arrangements and interactions of the economy and the polity. Although I stress the economic basis of structured racial inequality in the preindustrial and industrial periods of race relations, I also attempt to show how the polity more or less interacted with the economy either to reinforce patterns of racial stratification or to mediate various forms of racial conflict. Moreover, for the modern industrial period, I try to show how race relations have been shaped as much by important economic changes as by important political changes. Indeed, it would not be possible to understand fully the subtle and manifest changes in race relations in the modern industrial period without recognizing the dual and often reciprocal influence of structural changes in the economy and political changes in the state. Thus, my central argument is that different systems of production and/or different arrangements of the polity have imposed different constraints on the way in which racial groups have interacted in the United States, constraints that have structured the relations between racial groups and that have produced dissimilar contexts not only for the manifestation of racial antagonisms but also for racial group access to rewards and privileges.

In contrast to the modern industrial period in which fundamental economic and political changes have made economic class affiliation more important than race in determining Negro prospects for occupational advancement, the preindustrial and industrial periods of black-white relations have one central feature in common, namely, overt efforts of whites to solidify economic racial domination (ranging from the manipulation of black labor to the neutralization or elimination of black economic competition) through various forms of juridical, political, and social discrimination. Since racial problems during these two periods were principally related to group struggles over economic resources, they readily lend themselves to the economic class theories of racial antagonisms that associate racial antipathy with class conflict. A brief consideration of these theories, followed by a discussion of their basic weaknesses, will help to raise a number of theoretical issues that will be useful for analyzing the dynamics of racial conflict in the preindustrial and industrial stages of American race relations. However, in a later section of this chapter I shall attempt to explain why these theories are not very relevant to the modern industrial stage of American race relations.

Economic Class Theories

Students of race relations have paid considerable attention to the economic basis of racial antagonism in recent years, particularly to the theme that racial problems in historical situations are related to the more general problems of economic class conflict. A common assumption of this theme is that racial conflict is merely a special manifestation of class conflict. Accordingly, ideologies of racism, racial prejudices, institutionalized discrimination, segregation, and other factors that reinforce or embody racial stratification are seen as simply part of a superstructure determined and shaped by the particular arrangement of the class structure.[2] However, given this basic assumption, which continues to be the most representative and widely used economic class argument,[3] proponents have advanced two major and somewhat divergent explanations of how class conflicts actually shape and determine racial relations—the orthodox Marxist theory of capitalist exploitation,[4] and the *split labor-market theory* of working-class antagonisms.[5]

The orthodox Marxist theory, which is the most popular variant of the Marxists' explanations of race,[6] postulates that because the ultimate goal of the capitalist class is to maximize profits, efforts will be made to suppress workers' demands for increased wages and to weaken their bargaining power by promoting divisions within their ranks. The divisions occur along racial lines to the extent that the capitalist class is able to isolate the lower-priced black labor force by not only supporting job, housing, and educational discrimination against blacks, but also by developing or encouraging racial prejudices and ideologies of racial subjugation such as racism. The net effect of such a policy is to insure a marginal working class of blacks and to establish a relatively more privileged position for the established white labor force. Since discrimination guarantees a situation where the average wage rate of the black labor force is less than the average wage rate of the established white labor force, the probability of labor solidarity against the capitalist class is diminished.

At the same time, orthodox Marxists argue, the members of the capitalist class benefit not only because they have created a reserved army of labor that is not united against them and the appropriation of surplus from the black labor force is greater than the exploitation rate of the white labor force,[7] but also because they can counteract ambitious claims of the white labor force for higher wages either by threatening to increase the average wage rate of black workers or by replacing segments of the white labor force with segments of the black labor force in special situations such as strikes. The weaker the national labor force, the more likely it is that it will be replaced by lower-paid black labor especially during organized strikes demanding wage increases and improved working conditions. In short, orthodox Marxists argue that racial antagonism is designed to be a "mask for privilege" that effectively conceals the efforts of the ruling class to exploit subordinate minority groups and divide the working class.

In interesting contrast to the orthodox Marxist approach, the split labor-market theory posits the view that rather than attempting to protect a segment of the laboring class, business "supports a liberal or *laissez faire* ideology that would permit all workers to compete freely in an open market. Such open competition would displace higher paid labor. Only under duress does business yield to a labor aristocracy [i.e., a privileged position for white workers]."[8]

The central hypothesis of the split labor-market theory is that racial antagonism first develops in a labor market split along racial lines. The term "antagonism" includes all aspects of intergroup conflict, from beliefs and ideologies (e.g., racism), to overt behavior (e.g., discrimination), to institutions (e.g., segregationist laws). A split labor market occurs when the price of labor for the same work differs for at least two groups, or would differ if they performed the same work. The price of labor "refers to labor's total cost to the employer, including not only wages, but the cost of recruitment, transportation, room and board, education, health care (if the employer must bear these), and the cost of labor unrest."[9]

There are three distinct classes in a split labor market: (1) business or employers; (2) higher-paid labor; and (3) cheaper labor. Conflict develops between these three classes because of different interests. The main goal of business or employers is to maintain as cheap a labor force as possible in order to compete effectively with other businesses and to maximize economic returns. Employers will often import laborers from other areas if local labor costs are too high or if there is a labor shortage. Whenever a labor shortage exists, higher-paid labor is in a good bargaining position. Accordingly, if business is able to attract cheaper labor to the market place, the interests of higher-paid labor are threatened. They may lose some of the privileges they enjoy, they may lose their bargaining power, and they may even lose their jobs. Moreover, the presence of cheaper labor in a particular job market may not only represent actual competition but potential competition as well. An "insignificant trickle" could be seen as the beginning of a major immigration. If the labor market is split along ethnic lines, for example, if higher-paid labor is white and lower-paid labor is black, class antagonisms are transformed into racial antagonisms. Thus, "while much rhetoric of ethnic antagonism concentrates on ethnicity and race, it really in large measure (though probably not entirely) expresses this class conflict."[10]

In some cases members of the lower-paid laboring class, either from within the territorial boundaries of a given country or from another country, are drawn into or motivated to enter a labor market because they feel they can improve their standard of living. As Edna Bonacich points out, "the poorer the economy of the recruits, the less the inducement needed for them to enter the new labor market."[11] In other cases, individuals are forced into a new labor-market situation, such as the involuntary migration of blacks into a condition of slavery in the United States. In this connection, the greater the employer's control over lower-priced labor, the more threatening is lower-paid labor to higher-paid labor.

However, if more expensive labor is strong enough, that is, if it possesses the power resources to preserve its economic interests, it can prevent being replaced or undercut by cheaper labor. On the one hand it can exclude lower-paid labor from a given territory. "Exclusion movements clearly serve the interests of higher paid labor. Its standards are protected, while the capitalist class is deprived of cheaper labor."[12] On the other hand, if it is not possible for higher-paid labor to rely on exclusion (cheaper labor may be indigenous to the territory or may have been imported early in business-labor relations when higher-paid labor could not prevent the move) then it will institutionalize a system of ethnic stratification which could (1) monopolize skilled positions, thereby ensuring the effectiveness of strike action; (2) prevent cheaper labor from developing the skills necessary to compete with higher-paid labor (for example, by imposing barriers to equal access to education); and (3) deny cheaper labor the political resources that

would enable them to undercut higher-paid labor through, say, governmental regulations. "In other words, the solution to the devastating potential of weak, cheap labor is, paradoxically, to weaken them further, until it is no longer in business' immediate interest to use them as replacement."[13] Thus, whereas orthodox Marxist arguments associate the development and institutionalization of racial stratification with the motivations and activities of the capitalist class, the split labor-market theory traces racial stratification directly to the powerful, higher-paid working class.

Implicit in both of these economic class theories is a power-conflict thesis associating the regulation of labor or wages with properties (ownership of land or capital, monopolization of skilled positions) that determine the scope and degree of a group's ability to influence behavior in the labor market. Furthermore, both theories clearly demonstrate the need to focus on the different ways and situations in which various segments of the dominant racial group perceive and respond to the subordinate racial group. However, as I examine the historical stages of race relations in the United States, I find that the patterns of black/white interaction do not consistently and sometimes do not conveniently conform to the propositions outlined in these explanations of racial antagonism. In some cases, the orthodox Marxian explanation seems more appropriate; in other instances, the split labor-market theory seems more appropriate; and in still others, neither theory can, in isolation, adequately explain black-white conflict.

If we restrict our attention for the moment to the struggle over economic resources, then the general pattern that seems to have characterized race relations in the United States during the preindustrial and industrial stages was that the economic elite segments of the white population have been principally responsible for those forms of racial inequality that entail the exploitation of labor (as in slavery), whereas whites in the lower strata have been largely responsible for those forms of imposed racial stratification that are designed to eliminate economic competition (as in job segregation). Moreover, in some situations, the capitalist class and white workers form an alliance to keep blacks suppressed. Accordingly, restrictive arguments to the effect that racial stratification was the work of the capitalist class or was due to the "victory" of higher-paid white labor obscure the dynamics of complex and variable patterns of black-white interaction.

However, if we ignore the more categorical assertions that attribute responsibility for racial stratification to a particular class and focus seriously on the analyses of interracial contact in the labor market, then I will be able to demonstrate that, depending on the historical situation, each of the economic class theories provides arguments that help to illuminate race relations during the preindustrial and industrial periods of black-white contact. By the same token, I hope to explain why these theories have little application to the third, and present, stage of modern industrial race relations. My basic argument is that the meaningful application of the arguments in each theory for any given historical period depends considerably on knowledge of the constraints imposed by the particular systems of production and by the particular laws and policies of the state during that period, constraints that shape the structural relations between racial and class groups and which thereby produce different patterns of intergroup interaction. . . .

The Influence of the System of Production

The term "system of production" not only refers to the technological basis of economic processes or, in Karl Marx's terms, the "forces of production," but it also implies the "social relations of production," that is, "the interaction (for example, through employment and property arrangement) into which men enter at a given level of the development of the forces of production."[14] As I previously indicated, different systems of production impose constraints on racial group interaction. In the remainder of this section I should like to provide a firmer analytical basis for this distinction as it applies specifically to the three stages of American race relations, incorporating in my discussion relevant theoretical points raised in the foregoing sections of this chapter.

It has repeatedly been the case that a non-manufacturing or plantation economy with a simple division of labor and a small aristocracy that dominates the economic and political life of a society has characteristically generated a paternalistic rather than a competitive form of race relations, and the antebellum South was no exception.[15] Paternalistic racial patterns reveal close symbiotic relationships marked by dominance and subservience, great social distance and little physical distance, and clearly symbolized rituals of racial etiquette. The southern white aristocracy created a split labor market along racial lines by enslaving blacks to perform tasks at a cheaper cost than free laborers of the dominant group. This preindustrial form of race relations was not based on the actions of dominant-group laborers, who, as we shall see, were relatively powerless to effect significant change in race relations during this period, but on the structure of the relations established by the aristocracy. Let me briefly amplify this point.

In the southern plantation economy, public power was overwhelmingly concentrated in the hands of the white aristocracy. This power was not only reflected in the control of economic resources and in the development of a juridical system that expressed the class interests of the aristocracy, but also in the way the aristocracy was able to impose its viewpoint on the larger society.[16] This is not to suggest that these aspects of public power have not been disproportionately controlled by the economic elite in modern industrialized Western societies; rather it indicates that the hegemony of the southern ruling elite was much greater in degree, not in kind, than in these societies. The southern elite's hegemony was embodied in an economy that required little horizontal or vertical mobility. Further, because of the absence of those gradations of labor power associated with complex divisions of labor, white workers in the antebellum and early postbellum South had little opportunity to challenge the control of the aristocracy. Because white laborers lacked power resources in the southern plantation economy, their influence on the form and quality of racial stratification was minimal throughout the antebellum and early postbellum periods. Racial stratification therefore primarily reflected the relationships established between blacks and the white aristocracy, relationships which were not characterized by competition for scarce resources but by the exploitation of black labor.[17] Social distance tended to be clearly symbolized by rituals of racial etiquette: gestures and behavior reflecting dominance and subservience. Consequently, any effort to impose a system of public segregation was superfluous. Furthermore, since the social gap between the aristocracy and black slaves

was wide and stable, ideologies of racism played less of a role in the subordination of blacks than they subsequently did in the more competitive systems of race relations following the Civil War. In short, the relationship represented intergroup paternalism because it allowed for "close symbiosis and even intimacy, without any threat to status inequalities."[18] This was in sharp contrast to the more competitive forms of race relations that accompanied the development of industrial capitalism in the late nineteenth century and first few decades of the twentieth century (the industrial period of American race relations), wherein the complex division of labor and opportunities for greater mobility not only produced interaction, competition, and labor-market conflict between blacks and the white working class, but also provided the latter with superior resources (relative to those they possessed under the plantation economy) to exert greater influence on the form and content of racial stratification.

The importance of the system of production in understanding race relations is seen in a comparison of Brazil and the southern United States during the post-slavery periods. In the United States, the southern economy experienced a fairly rapid rate of expansion during the late nineteenth century, thereby creating various middle level skilled and unskilled positions that working-class whites attempted to monopolize for themselves. The efforts of white workers to eliminate black competition in the South generated an elaborate system of Jim Crow segregation that was reinforced by an ideology of biological racism. The white working class was aided not only by its numerical size, but also by its increasing accumulation of political resources that accompanied changes in its relation to the means of production.

As white workers gradually translated their increasing labor power into political power, blacks experienced greater restrictions in their efforts to achieve a satisfactory economic, political, and social life. In Brazil, on the other hand, the large Negro and mulatto population was not thrust into competition with the much smaller white population over access to higher-status positions because, as Marvin Harris notes, "there was little opportunity for any member of the lower class to move upward in the social hierarchy."[19] No economic class group or racial group had much to gain by instituting a rigid system of racial segregation or cultivating an ideology of racial inferiority. Racial distinctions were insignificant to the landed aristocracy, who constituted a numerically small upper class in what was basically a sharply differentiated two-class society originally shaped during slavery. The mulattoes, Negroes, and poor whites were all in the same impoverished lower-ranking position. "The general economic stagnation which has been characteristic of lowland Latin America since the abolition of slavery," observes Marvin Harris, "tends to reinforce the pattern of pacific relationships among the various racial groups in the lower ranking levels of the social hierarchy. Not only were the poor whites out-numbered by the mulattoes and Negroes, but there was little of a significant material nature to struggle over in view of the generally static condition of the economy."[20] Accordingly, in Brazil, segregation, discrimination, and racist ideologies failed to crystallize in the first several decades following the end of slavery. More recently, however, industrialization has pushed Brazil toward a competitive type of race relations, particularly the southern region (for example, São Paulo) which has experienced rapid industrialization and has blacks in economic competition with many lower-status white immigrants.[21]

Whereas the racial antagonism in the United States during the period of industrial race relations (such as the Jim Crow segregation movement in the South and the race riots in northern cities) tended to be either directly or indirectly related to labor-market conflicts, racial antagonism in the period of modern industrial relations tends to originate outside the economic order and to have little connection with labor-market strife. Basic changes in the system of production have produced a segmented labor structure in which blacks are either isolated in the relatively non-unionized, low-paying, basically undesirable jobs of the noncorporate sector, or occupy the higher-paying corporate and government industry positions in which job competition is either controlled by powerful unions or is restricted to the highly trained and educated, regardless of race. If there is a basis for labor-market conflict in the modern industrial period, it is most probably related to the affirmative action programs originating from the civil rights legislation of the 1960s. However, since affirmative action programs are designed to improve job opportunities for the talented and educated, their major impact has been in the higher-paying jobs of the expanding government sector and the corporate sector. The sharp increase of the more privileged blacks in these industries has been facilitated by the combination of affirmative action and rapid industry growth. Indeed despite the effectiveness of affirmative action programs the very expansion of these sectors of the economy has kept racial friction over higher-paying corporate and government jobs to a minimum.

Unlike the occupational success achieved by the more talented and educated blacks, those in the black underclass find themselves locked in the low-paying and dead-end jobs of the noncorporate industries, jobs which are not in high demand and which therefore do not generate racial competition or strife among the national black and white labor force. Many of these jobs go unfilled, and employers often have to turn to cheap labor from Mexico and Puerto Rico. As Nathan Glazer has pointed out, "Expectations have changed, and fewer blacks and whites today will accept a life at menial labor with no hope for advancement, as their fathers and older brothers did and as European immigrants did."[22]

Thus in the modern industrial era neither the corporate nor government sectors nor the noncorporate low-wage sector provide the basis for the kind of interracial competition and conflict that has traditionally plagued the labor market in the United States. This, then, is the basis for my earlier contention that the economic class theories which associate labor-market conflicts with racial antagonism have little application to the present period of modern industrial race relations.

The Polity and American Race Relations

If the patterned ways in which racial groups have interacted historically have been shaped in major measure by different systems of production, they have also been undeniably influenced by the changing policies and laws of the state. For analytical purposes, it would be a mistake to treat the influences of the polity and the economy as if they were separate and unrelated. The legal and political systems in the antebellum South were effectively used as instruments of the slaveholding elite to strengthen and legitimate the institution of slavery. But as industrialization altered the economic class structure in the postbellum South, the organizing power and political consciousness of the white lower class increased and its members were able to gain enough control of the political and juridical systems to legalize a new system of racial domination (Jim Crow segregation) that clearly reflected their class interests.

In effect, throughout the preindustrial period of race relations and the greater portion of the industrial period the role of the polity was to legitimate, reinforce, and regulate patterns of racial inequality. However, it would be unwarranted to assume that the relationship between the economic and political aspects of race necessarily implies that the latter is simply a derivative phenomenon based on the more fundamental processes of the former. The increasing intervention, since the mid-twentieth century, of state and federal government agencies in resolving or mediating racial conflicts has convincingly demonstrated the political system's autonomy in handling contemporary racial problems. Instead of merely formalizing existing racial alignments as in previous periods, the political system has, since the initial state and municipal legislation of the 1940s, increasingly created changes leading to the erosion of traditional racial alignments; in other words, instead of reinforcing racial barriers created during the preindustrial and industrial periods, the political system in recent years has tended to promote racial equality.

Thus, in the previous periods the polity was quite clearly an instrument of the white population in suppressing blacks. The government's racial practices varied, as I indicated above, depending on which segment of the white population was able to assert its class interests. However, in the past two decades the interests of the black population have been significantly reflected in the racial policies of the government, and this change is one of the clearest indications that the racial balance of power has been significantly altered. Since the early 1940s the black population has steadily gained political resources and, with the help of sympathetic white allies, has shown an increasing tendency to utilize these resources in promoting or protecting its group interests.

By the mid-twentieth century the black vote had proved to be a major vehicle for political pressure. The black vote not only influenced the outcome of national elections but many congressional, state, and municipal elections as well. Fear of the Negro vote produced enactment of public accommodation and fair employment practices laws in northern and western municipalities and states prior to the passage of federal civil rights legislation in 1964. This political resurgence for black Americans increased their sense of power, raised their expectations, and provided the foundation for the proliferation of demands which shaped the black revolt during the 1960s. But there were other factors that helped to buttress Negro demands and contributed to the developing sense of power and rising expectations, namely, a growing, politically active black middle class following World War II and the emergence of the newly independent African states.

The growth of the black middle class was concurrent with the growth of the black urban population. It was in the urban areas, with their expanding occupational opportunities, that a small but significant number of blacks were able to upgrade their occupations, increase their income, and improve their standard of living. The middle-class segment of an oppressed minority is most likely to participate in a drive for social justice that is disciplined and sustained. In the early phases of the civil rights movement, the black middle class channeled its energies through organizations such as the National Association for the Advancement of Colored People, which emphasized developing political resources and successful litigation through the courts. These developments were paralleled by the attack against traditional racial alignments in other parts of the world. The emerging newly independent African states led the assault. In America, the so-called "leader of the free world," the manifestation of racial tension and violence has been a constant source of embarrassment to national government officials. This sensitivity to world opinion made the national government more vulnerable to pressures of black protest at the very time when blacks had the greatest propensity to protest.

The development of black political resources that made the government more sensitive to Negro demands, the motivation and morale of the growing black middle class that resulted in the political drive for racial equality, and the emergence of the newly independent African states that increased the federal government's vulnerability to civil rights pressures all combined to create a new sense of power among black Americans and to raise their expectations as they prepared to enter the explosive decade of the 1960s. The national government was also aware of this developing sense of power and responded to the pressures of black protest in the 1960s with an unprecedented series of legislative enactments to protect black civil rights.

The problem for blacks today, in terms of government practices, is no longer one of legalized racial inequality. Rather the problem for blacks, especially the black underclass, is that the government is not organized to deal with the new barriers imposed by structural changes in the economy. With the passage of equal employment legislation and the authorization of affirmative action programs the government has helped clear the path for more privileged blacks, who have the requisite education and training, to enter the mainstream of American occupations. However, such government programs do not confront the impersonal economic barriers confronting members of the black underclass, who have been effectively screened out of the corporate and government industries. And the very attempts of the government to eliminate traditional racial barriers through such programs as affirmative action have had the unintentional effect of contributing to the growing economic class divisions within the black community.

Class Stratification and Changing Black Experiences

The problems of black Americans have always been compounded because of their low position in both the economic order (the average economic class position of blacks as a group) and the social order (the social prestige or honor accorded individual blacks because of their ascribed racial status). It is of course true that the low economic position of blacks has helped to shape the categorical social definitions attached to blacks as a racial group, but it is also true that the more blacks become segmented in terms of economic class position, the more their concerns about the social significance of race will vary.

In the preindustrial period of American race relations there was of course very little variation in the economic class position of blacks. The system of racial-caste oppression relegated virtually all blacks to the bottom of the economic class hierarchy. Moreover, the social definitions of racial differences were heavily influenced by the ideology of racism and the doctrine of paternalism, both of which clearly assigned a subordinate status for blacks vis-à-vis whites. Occasionally, a few individual free blacks would emerge and accumulate some wealth or property, but they were the overwhelming exception. Thus the uniformly low economic class position of blacks reinforced and, in the eyes of most whites, substantiated the social definitions that asserted Negroes were culturally and biogenetically inferior to whites. The uniformly low economic class position of blacks also removed the basis for any meaningful distinction between race issues and class issues within the black community.

The development of a black middle class accompanied the change from a preindustrial to an industrial system of production. Still, despite the fact that some blacks were able to upgrade their occupation and increase their education and income, there were severe limits on the areas in which blacks could in fact advance. Throughout most of the industrial period of race relations, the growth of the black middle class occurred because of the expansion of institutions created to serve the needs of a growing urbanized black population. The black doctor, lawyer, teacher, minister, businessman, mortician, excluded from the white community, was able to create a niche in the segregated black community. Although the income levels and life-styles of the black professionals were noticeably and sometimes conspicuously different from those of the black masses, the two groups had one basic thing in common, a racial status contemptuously regarded by most whites in society. If E. Franklin Frazier's analysis of the black bourgeoisie is correct, the black professionals throughout the industrial period of American race relations tended to react to their low position in the social order by an ostentatious display of material possessions and a conspicuous effort to disassociate themselves from the black masses.[23]

Still, as long as the members of the black middle class were stigmatized by their racial status; as long as they were denied the social recognition accorded their white counterparts; more concretely, as long as they remained restricted in where they could live, work, socialize, and be educated, race would continue to be a far more salient and important issue in shaping their sense of group position than their economic class position. Indeed, it was the black middle class that provided the leadership and generated the momentum for the civil rights movement during the mid-twentieth century. The influence and interests of this class were clearly reflected in the way the race issues were defined and articulated. Thus, the concept of "freedom" quite clearly implied, in the early stages of the movement, the right to swim in certain swimming pools, to eat in certain restaurants, to attend certain movie theaters, and to have the same voting privileges as whites. These basic concerns were reflected in the 1964 Civil Rights Bill which helped to create the illusion that, when the needs of the black middle class were met, so were the needs of the entire black community.

However, although the civil rights movement initially failed to address the basic needs of the members of the black lower class, it did increase their awareness of racial oppression, heighten their expectations about improving race relations, and increase their impatience with existing racial arrangements. These feelings were dramatically manifested in a series of violent ghetto outbursts that rocked the nation throughout the late 1960s. These outbreaks constituted the most mas-

sive and sustained expression of lower-class black dissatisfaction in the nation's history. They also forced the political system to recognize the problems of human survival and de facto segregation in the nation's ghettoes—problems pertaining to unemployment and underemployment, inferior ghetto schools, and deteriorated housing.

However, in the period of modern industrial race relations, it would be difficult indeed to comprehend the plight of inner-city blacks by exclusively focusing on racial discrimination. For in a very real sense, the current problems of lower-class blacks are substantially related to fundamental structural changes in the economy. A history of discrimination and oppression created a huge black underclass, and the technological and economic revolutions have combined to insure it a permanent status.

As the black middle class rides on the wave of political and social changes, benefiting from the growth of employment opportunities in the growing corporate and government sectors of the economy, the black underclass falls behind the larger society in every conceivable respect. The economic and political systems in the United States have demonstrated remarkable flexibility in allowing talented blacks to fill positions of prestige and influence at the same time that these systems have shown persistent rigidity in handling the problems of lower-class blacks. As a result, for the first time in American history class issues can meaningfully compete with race issues in the way blacks develop or maintain a sense of group position.[24]

Conclusion

The foregoing sections of this chapter present an outline and a general analytical basis for the arguments that will be systematically explored [elsewhere].[25] I have tried to show that race relations in American society have been historically characterized by three major stages and that each stage is represented by a unique form of racial interaction which is shaped by the particular arrangement of the economy and the polity. My central argument is that different systems of production and/or different policies of the state have imposed different constraints on the way in which racial groups interact—constraints that have structured the relations between racial groups and produced dissimilar contexts not only for the manifestation of racial antagonisms but also for racial-group access to rewards and privileges. I emphasized in this connection that in the preindustrial and industrial periods of American race relations the systems of production primarily shaped the patterns of racial stratification and the role of the polity was to legitimate, reinforce, or regulate these patterns. In the modern industrial period, however, both the system of production and the polity assume major importance in creating new patterns of race relations and in altering the context of racial strife. Whereas the preindustrial and industrial stages were principally related to group struggles over economic resources as different segments of the white population overtly sought to create and solidify economic racial domination (ranging from the exploitation of black labor in the preindustrial period to the elimination of black competition for jobs in the industrial period) through various forms of political, juridical, and social discrimination; in the modern industrial period fundamental economic and political changes have made economic class posi-

tion more important than race in determining black chances for occupational mobility. Finally, I have outlined the importance of racial norms or belief systems, especially as they relate to the general problem of race and class conflict in the preindustrial and industrial periods.

My argument that race relations in America have moved from economic racial oppression to a form of class subordination for the less-privileged blacks is not meant to suggest that racial conflicts have disappeared or have even been substantially reduced. On the contrary, the basis of such conflicts have shifted from the economic sector to the sociopolitical order and therefore do not play as great a role in determining the life chances of individual black Americans as in the previous periods of overt economic racial oppression.

NOTES

1. See William J. Wilson, *Power, Racism and Privilege: Race Relations in Theoretical and Sociohistorical Perspectives* (New York: The Free Press, 1973).

2. In Marxist terminology, the "superstructure" refers to the arrangements of beliefs, norms, ideologies, and noneconomic institutions.

3. However, not all theorists who emphasize the importance of economic class in explanations of race relations simply relegate problems of race to the superstructure. The Marxist scholars Michael Burawoy and Eugene Genovese recognize the reciprocal influence between the economic class structure and aspects of the superstructure (belief systems, political systems, etc.), a position which I also share and which is developed more fully in subsequent sections of this chapter. See Eugene D. Genovese, *Roll, Jordan, Roll: The World the Slaves Made* (New York: Pantheon, 1974); idem, *In Red and Black: Marxian Explorations in Southern and Afro-American History* (New York: Vintage Press, 1971); and Michael Burawoy, "Race, Class, and

Colonialism," *Social and Economic Studies* 23 (1974): 521–50.

4. Oliver C. Cox, *Caste, Class and Race: A Study in Social Dynamics* (Garden City, New York: Doubleday, 1948); Paul A. Baran and Paul M. Sweezy, *Monopoly Capital: An Essay on the American Economic and Social Order* (Harmondsworth: Penguin, 1966); Michael Reich, "The Economics of Racism," in *Problems in Political Economy,* ed. David M. Gordon (Lexington, Mass.: Heath, 1971); and M. Nikolinakos, "Notes on an Economic Theory of Racism," *Race: A Journal of Race and Group Relations* 14 (1973): 365–81.

5. Edna Bonacich, "A Theory of Ethnic Antagonism: The Split Labor Market," *American Sociological Review* 37 (October 1972): 547–59; idem, "Abolition, the Extension of Slavery and the Position of Free Blacks: A Study of Split Labor Markets in the United States," *American Journal of Sociology* 81 (1975): 601–28.

6. For examples of alternative and less orthodox Marxist explanations of race, see Eugene D. Genovese, *The Political Economy of Slavery: Studies in the Economy and Society of the Slave South* (New York: Pantheon, 1966); idem, *The World the Slaveholders Made: Two Essays in Interpretation* (New York: Pantheon, 1969); idem, *In Red and Black;* idem, *Roll, Jordan, Roll;* and Burawoy, "Race, Class, and Colonialism."

7. "Exploitation," in Marxian terminology, refers to the difference between the wages workers receive and the value of the goods they produce. The size of this difference, therefore, determines the degree of exploitation.

8. Bonacich, "A Theory of Ethnic Antagonism," p. 557.

9. Ibid., p. 549.

10. Ibid., p. 553.

11. Ibid., p. 549.

12. Ibid., p. 555.

13. Ibid., p. 556.

14. Neil J. Smelser, *Karl Marx on Society and Social Change* (Chicago: University of Chicago Press, 1974), p. xiv. According to Smelser, Marx used the notions "forces of production" and "social relations of production" as constituting the "mode of production." However, in Marx's writings the mode of production is often discussed as equivalent only to the "forces of production." To avoid confusion, I have chosen the term "system of production" which denotes the interrelation of the forces of production and the mode of production.

15. Pierre L. van den Berghe, *Race and Racism: A Comparative Perspective* (New York: John Wiley and Sons, 1967), p. 26.

16. See, for example, Genovese, *Roll, Jordan, Roll.*

17. An exception to this pattern occurred in the cities of the antebellum South, where nonslaveholding whites played a major role in the development of urban segregation. However, since an overwhelming majority of the population resided in rural areas, race relations in the antebellum southern cities were hardly representative of the region.

18. van den Berghe, *Race and Racism,* p. 27.

19. Marvin Harris, *Patterns of Race in the Americas* (New York: Walker, 1964), p. 96.

20. Ibid., p. 96.

21. van den Berghe, *Race and Racism,* p. 28.

22. Nathan Glazer, "Blacks and Ethnic Groups: The Difference, and the Political Difference It Makes," in *Key Issues in the Afro-American Experience,* ed. Nathan I. Huggins, Martin Kilson, and Daniel M. Fox (New York: Harcourt Brace Jovanovich, 1971), 2: 209.

23. E. Franklin Frazier, *Black Bourgeoisie* (New York: The Free Press, 1957). See also Nathan Hare, *Black Anglo-Saxons* (New York: Collier, 1965).

24. The theoretical implications of this development for ethnic groups in general are discussed by Milton Gordon under the concept "ethclass." See Milton M. Gordon, *Assimilation in American Life* (New York: Oxford University Press, 1964).

25. See William Julius Wilson, *The Declining Significance of Race: Blacks and Changing American Institutions* (Chicago and London: University of Chicago Press, 1978).

27

The Continuing Significance of Race
Antiblack Discrimination in Public Places

JOE R. FEAGIN

Racial discrimination as a continuing and major problem for middle-class blacks has been downplayed as analysts have turned to the various problems of the "underclass." For example, Wilson (1978, pp. 110–1) has argued that the growth of the black middle class since the 1960s is the result of improving economic conditions and of government civil rights laws, which virtually eliminated overt discrimination in the workplace and public accommodations. According to Wilson, the major problem of the 1964 Civil Rights Act is its failure to meet the problems of the black underclass (Wilson 1987, pp. 146–7).

Here I treat these assertions as problematic. Do middle-class black Americans still face hostile treatment in public accommodations and other public places? If so, what form does this discrimination take? Who are the perpetrators of this discrimination? What is the impact of the discrimination on its middle-class victims? How do middle-class blacks cope with such discrimination?

Discrimination can be defined in social-contextual terms as "actions or practices carried out by members of dominant racial or ethnic groups that have a differential and negative impact on members of subordinate racial and ethnic groups" (Feagin and Eckberg 1980, pp. 1–2). This differential treatment ranges from the blatant to the subtle (Feagin and Feagin 1986). Here I focus primarily on blatant discrimination by white Americans targeting middle-class blacks. . . .

To examine discrimination, I draw primarily on 37 in-depth interviews from a larger study of 135 middle-class black Americans in Boston, Buffalo, Baltimore, Washington, D.C., Detroit, Houston, Dallas, Austin, San Antonio, Marshall, Las Vegas, and Los Angeles. The interviewing was done in 1988–1990; black interviewers were used. . . .

Responses to Discrimination: Public Accommodations

Two Fundamental Strategies: Verbal Confrontation and Withdrawal

In the following account, a black news director at a major television station shows the interwoven character of discriminatory

Joe R. Feagin, "The Continuing Significance of Race: Antiblack Discrimination in Public Places," *American Sociological Review* 56 (February, 1991), pp. 101–103, 105–106, 108–112, 114–116.

action and black response. The discrimination took the form of poor restaurant service, and the responses included both suggested withdrawal and verbal counterattack.

He [her boyfriend] was waiting to be seated. . . . He said, "You go to the bathroom and I'll get the table. . . ." He was standing there when I came back; he continued to stand there. The restaurant was almost empty. There were waiters, waitresses, and no one seated. And when I got back to him, he was ready to leave, and said, "Let's go." I said, "What happened to our table?" He wasn't seated. So I said, "No, we're not leaving, please." And he said, "No, I'm leaving." So we went outside, and we talked about it. And what I said to him was, you have to be aware of the possibilities that this is not the first time that this has happened at this restaurant or at other restaurants, but this is the first time it has happened to a black news director here or someone who could make an issue of it, or someone who is prepared to make an issue of it.

So we went back inside after I talked him into it and, to make a long story short, I had the manager come. I made most of the people who were there (while conducting myself professionally the whole time) aware that I was incensed at being treated this way. . . . I said, "Why do you think we weren't seated?" And the manager said, "Well, I don't really know." And I said, "Guess." He said, "Well I don't know, because you're black?" I said, "Bingo. Now isn't it funny that you didn't guess that I didn't have any money (and I opened up my purse) and I said, "because I certainly have money. And isn't it odd that you didn't guess that it's because I couldn't pay for it because I've got two American

Express cards and a Master Card right here. I think it's just funny that you would have assumed that it's because I'm black.". . . And then I took out my card and gave it to him and said, "If this happens again, or if I hear of this happening again, I will bring the full wrath of an entire news department down on this restaurant." And he just kind of looked at me. "Not [just] because I am personally offended. I am. But because you have no right to do what you did, and as a people we have lived a long time with having our rights abridged. . . ." There were probably three or four sets of diners in the restaurant and maybe five waiters/waitresses. They watched him standing there waiting to be seated. His reaction to it was that he wanted to leave. I understood why he would have reacted that way, because he felt that he was in no condition to be civil. He was ready to take the place apart and . . . sometimes it's appropriate to behave that way. We hadn't gone the first step before going on to the next step. He didn't feel that he could comfortably and calmly take the first step, and I did. So I just asked him to please get back in the restaurant with me, and then you don't have to say a word, and let me handle it from there. It took some convincing, but I had to appeal to his sense of this is not just you, this is not just for you. We are finally in a position as black people where there are some of us who can genuinely get their attention. And if they don't want to do this because it's right for them to do it, then they'd better do it because they're afraid to do otherwise. If it's fear, then fine, instill the fear.

This example provides insight into the character of modern discrimination. The discrimination was not the "No Negroes" exclusion of the recent past, but rejection in the form of poor service by restaurant personnel. The black response indicates the change in black-white interaction since the 1950s and 1960s, for discrimination is handled with vigorous confrontation rather than deference. It is possible that the white personnel defined the couple as "poor blacks" because of their jeans, although the jeans were fashionable and white patrons wear jeans. In comments not quoted here the news director rejects such an explanation. She forcefully articulates a theory of rights—a response that signals the critical impact of civil rights laws on the thinking of middle-class blacks. The news director articulates the American dream: she has worked hard, earned the money and credit cards, developed the appropriate middle-class behavior, and thus has under the law a *right* to be served. There is defensiveness in her actions too, for she feels a need to legitimate her status by showing her purse and credit cards. One important factor that enabled her to take such assertive action was her power to bring a TV news team to the restaurant. This power marks a change from a few decades ago when very few black Americans had the social or economic resources to fight back successfully.

This example underscores the complexity of the interaction in such situations, with two levels of negotiation evident. The negotiation between the respondent and her boyfriend on withdrawal vs. confrontation highlights the process of negotiating responses to discrimination and the difficulty in crafting such responses. Not only is there a process of dickering with whites within the discriminatory scene but also a negotiation between the blacks involved. . . .

The confrontation response is generally so costly in terms of time and energy that acquiescence or withdrawal are common options. An example of the exit response was provided by a utility company executive in an east coast city:

I can remember one time my husband had picked up our son . . . from camp; and he'd stopped at a little store in the neighborhood near the camp. It was hot, and he was going to buy him a snowball. And the proprietor of the store—this was a very old, white neighborhood, and it was just a little sundry store. But the proprietor said he had the little window where people could come up and order things. Well, my husband and son had gone into the store. And he told them, "Well, I can't give it to you here, but if you go outside to the window, I'll give it to you." And there were other [white] people in the store who'd been served [inside]. So, they just left and didn't buy anything.

Here the act seems a throwback to the South of the 1950s, where blacks were required to use the back or side of a store. This differential treatment in an older white neighborhood is also suggestive of the territorial character of racial relations in many cities. The black response to degradation here was not to confront the white person or to acquiesce abjectly, but rather to reject the poor service and leave. . . .

Careful Situation Assessments

We have seen in the previous incidents some tendency for blacks to assess discriminatory incidents before they act. . . .

The complex process of evaluation and response is described by a college dean, who commented generally on hotel and restaurant discrimination encountered as he travels across the United States:

When you're in a restaurant and . . . you notice that blacks get seated near the kitchen. You notice that if it's a hotel, your room is near the elevator, or your room is always way down in a corner somewhere. You find that you are getting the undesirable rooms. And you come there early in the day and you don't see very many cars on the lot and they'll tell you that this is all we've got. Or you get the room that's got a bad television set. You know that you're being discriminated against. And of course you have to act accordingly. You have to tell them, "Okay, the room is fine, [but] this television set has got to go. Bring me another television set." So in my personal experience, I simply cannot sit and let them get away with it [discrimination] and not let them know that I know that that's what they are doing. . . .

When I face discrimination, first I take a long look at myself and try to determine whether or not I am seeing what I think I'm seeing in 1989, and if it's something that I have an option [about]. In other words, if I'm at a store making a purchase, I'll simply walk away from it. If it's at a restaurant where I'm not getting good service, I first of all let the people know that I'm not getting good service, then I [may] walk away from it. But the thing that I have to do is to let people know that I know that I'm being singled out for a separate treatment. And then I might react in any number of ways—depending on where I am and how badly I want whatever it is that I'm there for.

This commentary adds another dimension to our understanding of public discrimination, its cumulative aspect. Blacks confront not just isolated incidents—such as a bad room in a luxury hotel once every few years—but a lifelong series of such incidents. Here again the omnipresence of careful assessments is underscored. The dean's interview highlights a major difficulty in being black—one must be constantly prepared to assess accurately and then decide on the appropriate response. This long-look approach may indicate that some middle-class blacks are so sensitive to white charges of hypersensitivity and paranoia that they err in the opposite direction and fail to see discrimination when it occurs. In addition, as one black graduate student at a leading white university in the Southeast put it: "I think that sometimes timely and appropriate responses to racially motivated acts and comments are lost due to the processing of the input." The "long look" can result in missed opportunities to respond to discrimination. . . .

Responses to Discrimination: The Street

Reacting to White Strangers

As we move away from public accommodations settings to the usually less protected street sites, racial hostility can become more fleeting and severer, and thus black responses are often restricted. The most serious form of street discrimination is violence. Often the reasonable black response to street discrimination is withdrawal, resigned acceptance, or a quick verbal retort. The difficulty of responding to violence is seen in this report by a man working for a media surveying firm in a southern industrial city:

I was parked in front of this guy's house. . . . This guy puts his hands on the window and says, "Get out of the car, nigger.". . . So, I got out, and I thought, "Oh, this is what's going to happen here." And I'm talking fast. And they're, "What are you doing here?" And I'm, "This is who I am. I work with these people. This is the man we want to put in the survey." And I pointed to the house. And the guy said, "Well you have an out-of-state license tag, right?" "Yea." And he said, "If something happened to you, your people at home wouldn't know for a long time, would they?". . . I said, "Look, I deal with a company that deals with television. [If] something happens to me, it's going to be a national thing. . . . So, they grab me by the lapel of my coat, and put me in front of my car. They put the blade on my zipper. And now I'm thinking about this guy that's in the truck [behind me], because now I'm thinking that I'm going to have to run somewhere. Where am I going to run? Go to the police? [laughs] So, after a while they bash up my headlight. And I drove [away].

Stigmatized and physically attacked solely because of his color, this man faced verbal hostility and threats of death with courage. Cautiously drawing on his middle-class resources, he told the attackers his death would bring television crews to the town. This resource utilization is similar to that of the news director in the restaurant incident. Beyond this verbal threat his response had to be one of caution. For most whites threatened on the street, the police are a sought-after source of protection, but for black men this is often not the case.

At the other end of the street continuum is nonverbal harassment such as the "hate stare.". . . A middle-class student with dark skin reported that on her way to university classes she had stopped at a bakery in a white residential area where very few blacks live or shop. A white couple in front of the store stared intently and hatefully at her as she crossed the sidewalk and entered and left the bakery. She reported that she had experienced this hate stare many times. The incident angered her for some days thereafter, in part because she had been unable to respond more actively to it. . . .

It seems likely that for middle-class blacks the street is the site of recurring encounters with various types of white malevolence. A vivid example of the cumulative character and impact of this discrimination was given by another black student at a white university, who recounted his experiences walking home at night from a campus job to his apartment in a predominantly white residential area:

So, even if you wanted to, it's difficult just to live a life where you don't come into conflict with others. Because every day you walk the streets, it's not even like once a week, once a month. It's every day you walk the streets. Every day that you live as a black person you're reminded how you're perceived in society. You walk the streets at night; white people cross the streets. I've seen white couples and individuals dart in front of cars to not be on the same side of the street. Just the other day, I was walking down the street, and this white female with a child, I saw her pass a young white male about 20 yards ahead. When she saw me, she quickly dragged the child and herself across the busy street. What is so funny is that this area has had an unknown white rapist in the area for about four years. [When I pass] white men tighten their grip on their women. I've seen people turn around and seem like they're going to take blows from me. The police constantly make circles around me as I walk home, you know, for blocks. I'll walk, and they'll turn a block. And they'll come around me just to make sure, to find out where I'm going. So, every day you realize [you're black]. Even though you're not doing anything wrong; you're just existing. You're just a person. But you're a black person perceived in an unblack world. (This quote includes a clarification sentence from a follow-up interview.)

Unable to "see" his middle-class symbols of college dress and books, white couples (as well as individuals) have crossed the street in front of cars to avoid walking near this modest-build black student, in a predominantly white neighborhood. Couples moving into defensive postures are doubtless reacting to the stigma of "black maleness." The student perceives such avoidance as racist, however, not because he is paranoid, but because he has previously encountered numerous examples of whites taking such defensive measures. . . .

Conclusion

I have examined the sites of discrimination, the types of discriminatory acts, and the responses of the victims and have found the color stigma still to be very important in the public lives of affluent black Americans. The sites of racial discrimination range from relatively protected home sites, to less protected workplace and educational sites, to the even less protected public places. The 1964 Civil Rights Act guarantees that black Americans are "entitled to the full and equal enjoyment of the goods, services, facilities, privileges, advantages, and accommodations" in public accommodations. Yet the interviews indicate that deprivation of

full enjoyment of public facilities is not a relic of the past; deprivation and discrimination in public accommodations persist. Middle-class black Americans remain vulnerable targets in public places. . . .

Particular instances of discrimination may seem minor to outside white observers when considered in isolation. But when blatant acts of avoidance, verbal harassment, and physical attack combine with subtle and covert slights, and these accumulate over months, years, and lifetimes, the impact on a black person is far more than the sum of the individual instances. . . .

The cumulative impact of racial discrimination accounts for the special way that blacks have of looking at and evaluating interracial incidents. One respondent, a clerical employee at an adoption agency, described the "second eye" she uses:

I think that it causes you to have to look at things from two different perspectives. You have to decide whether things that are done or slights that are made are made because you are black or they are made because the person is just rude, or unconcerned and uncaring. So it's kind of a situation where you're always kind of looking to see with a second eye or a second antenna just what's going on.

The language of "second eye" suggests that blacks look at white-black interaction through a lens colored by personal and group experience with cross-institutional and cross-generational discrimination.

Blacks must be constantly aware of the repertoire of possible responses to chronic and burdensome discrimination. One older respondent spoke of having to put on her "shield" just before she leaves the house each morning. When quizzed, she said that for more than six decades, as she leaves her home, she has tried to be prepared for insults and discrimination in public places, even if nothing happens that day. This extraordinary burden of discrimination was eloquently described by the female professor who resented having to worry about life-threatening incidents that her "very close white friends . . . simply don't have to worry about." Another respondent was articulate on this point:

> . . . if you can think of the mind as having one hundred ergs of energy, and the average man uses fifty percent of his energy dealing with the everyday problems of the world—just general kinds of things—then he has fifty percent more to do creative kinds of things that he wants to do. Now that's a white person. Now a black person also has one hundred ergs; he uses fifty percent the same way a white man does, dealing with what the white man has [to deal with], so he has fifty percent left. But he uses twenty-five percent fighting being black, [with] all the problems being black and what it means. Which means he really only has twenty-five percent to do what the white man has fifty percent to do, and he's expected to do just as much as the white

man with that twenty-five percent. . . . So, that's kind of what happens. You just don't have as much energy left to do as much as you know you really could if you were free, [if] your mind were free.

The individual cost of coping with racial discrimination is great, and, as he says, you cannot accomplish as much as you could if you retained the energy wasted on discrimination. This is perhaps the most tragic cost of persisting discrimination in the United States. In spite of decades of civil rights legislation, black Americans have yet to attain the full promise of the American dream.

REFERENCES

Feagin, Joe R. and Douglas Eckberg. 1980. "Prejudice and Discrimination." *Annual Review of Sociology* 6:1–20.

Feagin, Joe R. and Clairece Booher Feagin. 1986. *Discrimination American Style* (rev. ed). Melbourne, FL: Krieger Publishing Co.

Wilson, William J. 1978. *The Declining Significance of Race.* Chicago: University of Chicago Press.

_____. 1987. *The Truly Disadvantaged: The Inner City, the Underclass, and Public Policy.* Chicago: University of Chicago Press.

28

Are Emily and Greg More Employable Than Lakisha and Jamal?

A Field Experiment on Labor Market Discrimination

MARIANNE BERTRAND
SENDHIL MULLAINATHAN

Every measure of economic success reveals significant racial inequality in the U.S. labor market. Compared to Whites, African-Americans are twice as likely to be unemployed and earn nearly 25 percent less when they are employed (Council of Economic Advisers, 1998). This inequality has sparked a debate as to whether employers treat members of different races differentially. When faced with observably similar African-American and White applicants, do they favor the White one? Some argue yes, citing either employer prejudice or employer perception that race signals lower productivity. Others argue that differential treatment by race is a relic of the past, eliminated by some combination of employer enlightenment, affirmative action programs and the profit-maximization motive. In fact, many in this latter camp even feel that stringent enforcement of affirmative action programs has produced an environment of reverse discrimination. They would argue that faced with identical candidates, employ-

ers might favor the African-American one. Data limitations make it difficult to empirically test these views. Since researchers possess far less data than employers do, White and African-American workers that appear similar to researchers may look very different to employers. So any racial difference in labor market outcomes could just as easily be attributed to differences that are observable to employers but unobservable to researchers.

To circumvent this difficulty, we conduct a field experiment that builds on the correspondence testing methodology that has been primarily used in the past to study minority outcomes in the United Kingdom. We send resumes in response to help-wanted ads in Chicago and Boston newspapers and measure callback for interview for each sent resume. We experimentally manipulate perception of race via the name of the fictitious job applicant. We randomly assign very White-sounding names (such as Emily Walsh or Greg Baker) to half the resumes

Marianne Bertrand and Sendhil Mullainathan. "Are Emily and Greg More Employable Than Lakisha and Jamal? A Field Experiment on Labor Market Discrimination." *The American Economic Review* (September, 2004), pp. 991–992, 1006–1007, 1009–1013.

and very African-American-sounding names (such as Lakisha Washington or Jamal Jones) to the other half. Because we are also interested in how credentials affect the racial gap in callback, we experimentally vary the quality of the resumes used in response to a given ad. Higher-quality applicants have on average a little more labor market experience and fewer holes in their employment history; they are also more likely to have an e-mail address, have completed some certification degree, possess foreign language skills, or have been awarded some honors. In practice, we typically send four resumes in response to each ad: two higher-quality and two lower-quality ones. We randomly assign to one of the higher- and one of the lower-quality resumes an African-American-sounding name. In total, we respond to over 1,300 employment ads in the sales, administrative support, clerical, and customer services job categories and send nearly 5,000 resumes. The ads we respond to cover a large spectrum of job quality, from cashier work at retail establishments and clerical work in a mail room, to office and sales management positions.

We find large racial differences in callback rates. Applicants with White names need to send about 10 resumes to get one callback whereas applicants with African-American names need to send about 15 resumes. This 50-percent gap in callback is statistically significant. A White name yields as many more callbacks as an additional eight years of experience on a resume. Since applicants' names are randomly assigned, this gap can only be attributed to the name manipulation.

Race also affects the reward to having a better resume. Whites with higher-quality resumes receive nearly 30-percent more callbacks than Whites with lower-quality re-

sumes. On the other hand, having a higher-quality resume has a smaller effect for African-Americans. In other words, the gap between Whites and African-Americans widens with resume quality. While one may have expected improved credentials to alleviate employers' fear that African-American applicants are deficient in some unobservable skills, this is not the case in our data.

The experiment also reveals several other aspects of the differential treatment by race. First, since we randomly assign applicants' postal addresses to the resumes, we can study the effect of neighborhood of residence on the likelihood of callback. We find that living in a wealthier (or more educated or Whiter) neighborhood increases callback rates. But, interestingly, African-Americans are not helped more than Whites by living in a "better" neighborhood. Second, the racial gap we measure in different industries does not appear correlated to Census-based measures of the racial gap in wages. The same is true for the racial gap we measure in different occupations. In fact, we find that the racial gaps in callback are statistically indistinguishable across all the occupation and industry categories covered in the experiment. Federal contractors, who are thought to be more severely constrained by affirmative action laws, do not treat the African-American resumes more preferentially; neither do larger employers or employers who explicitly state that they are "Equal Opportunity Employers." In Chicago, we find a slightly smaller racial gap when employers are located in more African-American neighborhoods.[1] . . .

Interpretation

Three main sets of questions arise when interpreting the results above. First, does a higher callback rate for White applicants imply that employers are discriminating against African-Americans? Second, does our design only isolate the effect of race or is the name manipulation conveying some other factors than race? Third, how do our results relate to different models of racial discrimination?

Interpreting Callback Rates

Our results indicate that for two identical individuals engaging in an identical job search, the one with an African-American name would receive fewer interviews. Does differential treatment within our experiment imply that employers are discriminating against African-Americans (whether it is rational, prejudice-based, or other form of discrimination)? In other words, could the lower callback rate we record for African-American resumes *within our experiment* be consistent with a racially neutral review of the *entire pool* of resumes the surveyed employers receive?

In a racially neutral review process, employers would rank order resumes based on their quality and call back all applicants that are above a certain threshold. Because names are randomized, the White and African-American resumes we send should rank similarly on average. So, irrespective of the skill and racial composition of the applicant pool, a race-blind selection rule would generate equal treatment of Whites and African-Americans. So our results must imply that employers use race as a factor when reviewing resumes, which matches the legal definition of discrimination.

But even rules where employers are not trying to interview as few African-American applicants as possible may generate observed differential treatment in our experiment. One such hiring rule would be employers trying to interview a target level of African-American candidates. For example, perhaps the average firm in our experiment aims to produce an interview pool that matches the population base rate. This rule could produce the observed differential treatment if the average firm receives a higher proportion of African-American resumes than the population base rate because African-Americans disproportionately apply to the jobs and industries in our sample.

Some of our other findings may be consistent with such a rule. For example, the fact that "Equal Opportunity Employers" or federal contractors do not appear to discriminate any less may reflect the fact that such employers receive more applications from African-Americans. On the other hand, other key findings run counter to this rule. As we discuss above, we find no systematic difference in the racial gap in callback across occupational or industry categories, despite the large variation in the fraction of African-Americans looking for work in those categories. African-Americans are underrepresented in managerial occupations, for example. If employers matched base rates in the population, the few African-Americans who apply to these jobs should receive a higher callback rate than Whites. Yet, we find that the racial gap in managerial occupations is the same as in all the other job categories. This rule also runs counter to our findings on returns to skill. Suppose firms are struggling to find White applicants but overwhelmed with African-American ones. Then they should be less sensitive to the quality of White applicants (as they are trying to fill in their hiring quota for Whites) and much more sensitive to the quality of Black applicants (when they have so many to pick from). Thus, it is unlikely that the differential treatment we observe is generated by hiring rules such as these.

Potential Confounds

While the names we have used in this experiment strongly signal racial origin, they may also signal some other personal trait. More specifically, one might be concerned that employers are inferring social background from the personal name. When employers read a name like "Tyrone" or "Latoya," they may assume that the person comes from a disadvantaged background. In the extreme form of this social background interpretation, employers do not care at all about race but are discriminating only against the social background conveyed by the names we have chosen.

While plausible, we feel that some of our earlier results are hard to reconcile with this interpretation. For example, we found that while employers value "better" addresses, African-Americans are not helped more than Whites by living in Whiter or more educated neighborhoods. If the African-American names we have chosen mainly signal negative social background, one might have expected the estimated name gap to be lower for better addresses. Also, if the names mainly signal social background, one might have expected the name gap to be higher for jobs that rely more on soft skills or require more interpersonal interactions. We found no such evidence.

There is one final potential confound to our results. Perhaps what appears as a bias against African-Americans is actually the result of *reverse discrimination*. If qualified African-Americans are thought to be in high demand, then employers with average quality jobs might feel that an equally talented African-American would never accept an offer from them and thereby never call her or him in for an interview. Such an argument might also explain why African-Americans do not receive as strong a return as Whites to better resumes, since higher qualification only strengthens this argument. But this interpretation would suggest that among the better jobs, we ought to see evidence of reverse discrimination, or at least a smaller racial gap. However, we do not find any such evidence. The racial gap does not vary across jobs with different skill requirements, nor does it vary across occupation categories. Even among the better jobs in our sample, we find that employers significantly favor applicants with White names.

Relation to Existing Theories

What do these results imply for existing models of discrimination? Economic theories of discrimination can be classified into two main categories: taste-based and statistical discrimination models. Both sets of models can obviously "explain" our average racial gap in callbacks. But can these models explain our other findings? More specifically, we discuss the relevance of these models with a focus on two of the facts that have been uncovered in this paper: (i) the lower returns to credentials for African-Americans; (ii) the relative uniformity of the race gap across occupations, job requirements and, to a lesser extent, employer characteristics and industries.

Taste-based models (Gary S. Becker, 1961) differ in whose prejudiced "tastes" they emphasize: customers, coworkers, or employers. Customer and co-worker discrimination models seem at odds with the lack of significant variation of the racial gap by occupation and industry categories, as the amount of customer contact and the fraction of White employees vary quite a lot across these categories. We do not find a larger racial gap among jobs that explicitly require "communication skills" and jobs for which we expect either customer or coworker contacts to be higher (retail sales for example).

Because we do not know what drives employer tastes, employer discrimination models could be consistent with the lack of occupation and industry variation. Employer discrimination also matches the finding that employers located in more African-American neighborhoods appear to discriminate somewhat less. However, employer discrimination models would struggle to explain why African-Americans get relatively lower returns to their credentials. Indeed, the cost of indulging the discrimination taste should increase as the minority applicants' credentials increase.

Statistical discrimination models are the prominent alternative to the taste-based models in the economics literature. In one class of statistical discrimination models, employers use (observable) race to proxy for *unobservable* skills (e.g., Edmund S. Phelps, 1972; Kenneth J. Arrow, 1973). This class of models struggle to explain the credentials effect as well. Indeed, the added credentials should lead to a larger update for African-Americans and hence greater returns to skills for that group.

A second class of statistical discrimination models "emphasize the precision of the information that employers have about individual productivity" (Altonji and Blank, 1999). Specifically, in these models, employers believe that the same observable signal is more precise for Whites than for African-Americans (Dennis J. Aigner and Glenn G. Cain, 1977; Shelly J. Lundberg and Richard Startz, 1983; Bradford Cornell and Ivo Welch, 1996). Under such models,

African-Americans receive lower returns to observable skills because employers place less weight on these skills. However, how reasonable is this interpretation for our experiment? First, it is important to note that we are using the same set of resume characteristics for both racial groups. So the lower precision of information for African-Americans cannot be that, for example, an employer does not know what a high school degree from a very African-American neighborhood means (as in Aigner and Cain, 1977). Second, many of the credentials on the resumes are in fact externally and easily verifiable, such as a certification for a specific software.

An alternative version of these models would rely on bias in the observable signal rather than differential variance or noise of these signals by race. Perhaps the skills of African-Americans are discounted because affirmative action makes it easier for African-Americans to get these skills. While this is plausible for credentials such as an employee-of-the-month honor, it is unclear why this would apply to more verifiable and harder skills. It is equally unclear why work experience would be less rewarded since our study suggests that getting a job is more, not less, difficult for African-Americans.

The uniformity of the racial gap across occupations is also troubling for a statistical discrimination interpretation. Numerous factors that should affect the level of statistical discrimination, such as the importance of unobservable skills, the observability of qualifications, the precision of observable skills and the ease of performance measurement, may vary quite a lot across occupations.

This discussion suggests that perhaps other models may do a better job at explaining our findings. One simple alternative model is lexicographic search by employers. Employers receive so many resumes that they may use quick heuristics in reading these resumes. One such heuristic could be to simply read no further when they see an African-American name. Thus they may never see the skills of African-American candidates and this could explain why these skills are not rewarded. This might also to some extent explain the uniformity of the race gap since the screening process (i.e., looking through a large set of resumes) may be quite similar across the variety of jobs we study.

Conclusion

This paper suggests that African-Americans face differential treatment when searching for jobs and this may still be a factor in why they do poorly in the labor market. Job applicants with African-American names get far fewer callbacks for each resume they send out. Equally importantly, applicants with African-American names find it hard to overcome this hurdle in callbacks by improving their observable skills or credentials.

Taken at face value, our results on differential returns to skill have possibly important policy implications. They suggest that training programs alone may not be enough to alleviate the racial gap in labor market outcomes. For training to work, some general-equilibrium force outside the context of our experiment would have to be at play. In fact, if African-Americans recognize how employers reward their skills, they may rationally be less willing than Whites to even participate in these programs.

NOTE

1. For further details on this experiment, see Bertrand and Mullainathan (2004).

REFERENCES

Aigner, Dennis J. and Cain, Glenn G. "Statistical Theories of Discrimination in Labor Markets." *Industrial and Labor Relations Review,* January 1977, *30*(1), pp. 175–87.

Altonji, Joseph G. and Blank, Rebecca M. "Race and Gender in the Labor Market," in Orley Ashenfelter and David Card, eds., *Handbook of labor economics,* Vol. 30. Amsterdam: North-Holland, 1999, pp. 3143–259.

Arrow, Kenneth, J. "The Theory of Discrimination," in Orley Ashenfelter and Albert Rees, eds., *Discrimination in labor markets.* Princeton, NJ: Princeton University Press, 1973, pp. 3–33.

Becker, Gary S. *The economics of discrimination,* 2nd Ed. Chicago: University of Chicago Press, 1961.

Bertrand, Marianne and Sendhil Mullainathan. "Are Emily and Greg More Employable Than Lakisha and Jamal? A Field Experiment on Labor Market Discrimination." *American Economic Review* 94 (September 2004): 991–1013.

Cornell, Bradford and Welch, Ivo. "Culture, Information, and Screening Discrimination." *Journal of Political Economy,* June 1996, *104*(3), pp. 542–71.

Council of Economic Advisers. *Changing America: Indicators of social and economic well-being by race and Hispanic origin.* September 1998, http://w3.access.gpo.gov/eop/ca/pdfs/ca.pdf.

Lundberg, Shelly J. and Starz, Richard. "Private Discrimination and Social Intervention in Competitive Labor Market." *American Economic Review,* June 1983, *73*(3), pp. 340–47.

Phelps, Edmund S. "The Statistical Theory of Racism and Sexism." *American Economic Review,* September 1972, *62*(4), pp. 659–61.

29

Stereotype Threat and African-American Student Achievement

CLAUDE STEELE

Over the past four decades African-American college students have been more in the spotlight than any other American students. This is because they aren't just college students; they are a cutting edge in America's effort to integrate itself in the nearly forty years since the passage of the Civil Rights Act. These students have borne much of the burden for our national experiment in racial integration. And to a significant degree the success of the experiment will be determined by their success.

Nonetheless, throughout the 1990s the national college dropout rate for African Americans has been 20 to 25 percent higher than that for whites. Among those who finish college, the grade point average of Black students is two-thirds of a grade below that of whites. . . .

Virtually all aspects of underperformance—lower standardized test scores, lower college grades, lower graduation rates—persist among students from the African-American middle class. This situation forces on us an uncomfortable recognition: that beyond class, something racial is depressing the academic performance of these students.

Some time ago two of my colleagues, Joshua Aronson and Steven Spencer, and I tried to see the world from the standpoint of African-American students, concerning ourselves less with features of theirs that might explain their troubles than with features of the world they see. A story I was told recently depicts some of these. The storyteller was worried about his friend, a normally energetic Black student who had broken up with his longtime girlfriend and had since learned that she, a Hispanic, was now dating a white student. This hit him hard. Not long after hearing about his girlfriend, he sat through an hour's discussion of *The Bell Curve* in his psychology class, during which the possible genetic inferiority of his race was openly considered. Then he overheard students at lunch arguing that affirmative action allowed in too many underqualified Blacks. By his own account, this young man had experienced very little

Claude Steele. "Stereotype Threat and African-American Student Achievement," *Young, Gifted, and Black: Promoting High Achievement Among African-American Students,* Theresa Perry, Claude Steele, and Asa Hilliard III, pp. 109-116, 120-123, 172-174, 176-177. Copyright © 2003 by Theresa Perry, Claude Steele, and Asa Hilliard III.

of what he thought of as racial discrimination on campus. Still, these were features of his world. Could they have a bearing on his academic life?

My colleagues and I have called such features "stereotype threat"—the threat of being viewed through the lens of a negative stereotype, or the fear of doing something that would inadvertently confirm that stereotype. Everyone experiences stereotype threat. We are all members of some group about which negative stereotypes exist, from white males and Methodists to women and the elderly. And in a situation where one of those stereotypes applies—a man talking to women about pay equity, for example, or an aging faculty member trying to remember a number sequence in the middle of a lecture—we know that we may be judged by it.

Like the young man in the story, we can feel mistrustful and apprehensive in such situations. For him, as for African-American students generally, negative stereotypes apply in many situations, even personal ones. Why was that old roommate unfriendly to him? Did that young white woman who has been so nice to him in class not return his phone call because she's afraid he'll ask her for a date? Is it because of his race or something else about him? He cannot know the answers, but neither can his rational self fully dismiss the questions. Together they raise a deeper question: Will his race be a boundary to his experience, to his emotions, to his relationships?. . .

Measuring Stereotype Threat

Can stereotype threat be shown to affect academic performance? And if so, who would be most affected—stronger or weaker students? Which has a greater influence on

academic success among Black college students—the degree of threat or the level of preparation with which they enter college?

As we confronted these questions in the course of our research, we came in for some surprises. We began with what we took to be the hardest question: Could something as abstract as stereotype threat really affect something as irrepressible as intelligence? Ours is an individualistic culture; forward movement is seen to come from within. Against this cultural faith one needs evidence to argue that something as "sociological" as stereotype threat can repress something as "individualistic" as intelligence.

To acquire such evidence, Joshua Aronson and I (following a procedure developed with Steven Spencer) designed an experiment to test whether the stereotype threat that Black students might experience when taking a difficult standardized test could depress their performance on the test to a statistically reliable degree. We brought white and Black Stanford students into the laboratory and gave them, one at a time, a very difficult thirty-minute section of a Graduate Record Exam subject test in English literature. Most of these students were sophomores, which meant that the test—designed for graduating seniors—was particularly hard for them—precisely the feature, we reasoned, that would make this simple testing situation different for our Black participants than for our white participants, despite the fact that all the participants were of equal ability levels measured by all available criteria. (The difficulty of the test guaranteed that both Black and white students would find the test frustrating. And it is in these situations that members of ability-stereotyped groups are most likely to experience the extra burden of stereotype threat. First, the experience of frustration with the test gives credibility to the limitation alleged in the stereotype. For this reason, frustration can be especially stinging and disruptive for test-takers to whom the stereotype is relevant. Second, it is on a demanding test that one can least afford to be bothered by the thoughts that likely accompany stereotype threat.)

A significant part of the negative stereotype about African Americans concerns intellectual ability. Thus, in the stereotype threat conditions of the experiments in this series, we merely mentioned to participants that the test was a measure of verbal ability. This was enough, we felt, to make the negative stereotype about African Americans' abilities relevant to their performance on the test, and thus to put them at risk of confirming, or being seen to confirm, the negative stereotype about their abilities. If the pressure imposed by the relevance of a negative stereotype about one's group is enough to impair an important intellectual performance, then Black participants should perform worse than whites in the "diagnostic" condition of this experiment but not in the "nondiagnostic" condition. As figure 29.1 depicts, this is precisely what happened: Blacks performed a full standard deviation lower than whites under the stereotype threat of the test being "diagnostic" of their intellectual ability, even though we had statistically matched the two groups in ability level. Something other than ability was involved; we believed it was stereotype threat.

But maybe the Black students performed less well than the white students because they were less motivated, or because their skills were somehow less applicable to the advanced material of this test. We needed some way to determine if it was indeed

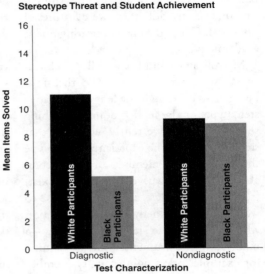

Stereotype Threat and Student Achievement

Figure 29.1 White and Black Participants' Score (Controlled for SAT) on a Difficult English Test as a Function of Characterization of the Test

stereotype threat that depressed the Black students' scores. We reasoned that if stereotype threat had impaired their performance on the test, then reducing this threat would allow their performance to improve. We presented the same test as a laboratory task that was used to study how certain problems are generally solved. We stressed that the task did not measure a person's level of intellectual ability. A simple instruction, yes, but it profoundly changed the meaning of the situation. In one stroke "spotlight anxiety," as the psychologist William Cross once called it, was turned off—and the Black students' performance on the test rose to match that of equally qualified whites (see figure 29.1). In the nonstereotype threat conditions, we presented the same test as an instrument for studying problem solving that was "nondiagnostic" of individual differences in ability—thus making the racial stereotype irrelevant to their performance.

Aronson and I decided that what we needed next was direct evidence of the subjective state we call stereotype threat. To seek this, we looked into whether simply sitting down to take a difficult test of ability was enough to make Black students mindful of their race and stereotypes about it. This may seem unlikely. White students I have taught over the years have sometimes said that they have hardly any sense of even having a race. But Blacks have many experiences with the majority "other group" that make their race salient to them.

We again brought Black and white students in to take a difficult verbal test. But just before the test began, we gave them a long list of words, each of which had two letters missing. They were told to complete the words on this list as fast as they could. We knew from a preliminary survey that twelve of the eighty words we had selected could be completed in such a way as to relate to the stereotype about Blacks' intellectual ability. The fragment "—ce," for example, could become "race." If simply taking a difficult test of ability was enough to make Black students mindful of stereotypes about their race, these students should complete more fragments with stereotype-related words. That is just what happened. When Black students were told that the test would measure ability, they completed the fragments with significantly more stereotype-related words than when they were told that it was not a measure of ability. Whites made few stereotype-related completions in either case. . . .

How Stereotype Threat Affects People Differently

Is everyone equally threatened and disrupted by a stereotype? One might expect, for example, that it would affect the weakest students most. But in all our research the most achievement-oriented students, who were also the most skilled, motivated, and confident, were the most impaired by stereotype threat. This fact had been under our noses all along—in our data and even in our theory. A person has to care about a domain in order to be disturbed by the prospect of being stereotyped in it. That is the whole idea of disidentification—protecting against stereotype threat by ceasing to care about the domain in which the stereotype applies. Our earlier experiments had selected Black students who identified with verbal skills and women who identified with math. But when we tested participants who identified less with these domains, what had been under our noses hit us in the face. None of them showed any effect of stereotype threat whatsoever.

These weakly identified students did not perform well on the test: once they discovered its difficulty, they stopped trying very hard and got a low score. But their performance did not differ depending on whether they felt they were at risk of being judged stereotypically.

This finding, I believe, tells us two important things. The first is that the poorer college performance of Black students may have another source in addition to the one—lack of good preparation and, perhaps, of identification with school achievement—that is commonly understood. This additional source—the threat of being negatively stereotyped in the environment—has not been well understood. The distinction has important policy implications: different kinds of students may require different pedagogies of improvement.

The second thing is poignant: what exposes students to the pressure of stereotype threat is not weaker academic identity and skills but stronger academic identity and skills. They may have long seen themselves as good students—better than most. But led into the domain by their strengths, they pay an extra tax on their investment—vigilant worry that their future will be compromised by society's perception and treatment of their group.

This tax has a long tradition in the Black community. The Jackie Robinson story is a central narrative of Black life, literature, and journalism. *Ebony Magazine* has run a page for fifty years featuring people who have broken down one or another racial barrier. Surely the academic vanguard among Black college students today knows this tradition—and knows, therefore, that the thing to do, as my father told me, is to buckle down, pay whatever tax is required, and disprove the damn stereotype.

That, however, seems to be precisely what these students are trying to do. In some of our experiments we administered the test of ability by computer, so that we could see how long participants spent looking at different parts of the test questions. Black students taking the test under stereotype threat seemed to be trying too hard rather than not hard enough. They reread the questions, reread the multiple choices, rechecked their answers, more than when they were not under stereotype threat. The threat made them inefficient on a test that, like most standardized tests, is set up so that thinking long often means thinking wrong, especially on difficult items like the ones we used. . . .

In the old song about the "steel-drivin' man," John Henry races the new steam-driven drill to see who can dig a hole faster. When the race is over, John Henry has prevailed by digging the deeper hole—only to drop dead. The social psychologist Sherman James uses the term "John Henryism" to describe a psychological syndrome that he

found to be associated with hypertension in several samples of North Carolina Blacks: holding too rigidly to the faith that discrimination and disadvantage can be overcome with hard work and persistence. Certainly this is the right attitude. But taken to extremes, it can backfire. A deterioration of performance under stereotype threat by the skilled, confident Black students in our experiments may be rooted in John Henryism.

This last point can be disheartening. Our research, however, offers an interesting suggestion about what can be done to overcome stereotype threat and its detrimental effects. The success of Black students may depend less on expectations and motivation—things that are thought to drive academic performance—than on trust that stereotypes about their group will not have a limiting effect in their school world.

Putting this idea to the test, Joseph Brown and I asked, How can the usual detrimental effect of stereotype threat on the standardized-test performance of these students be reduced? By strengthening students' expectations and confidence, or by strengthening their trust that they are not at risk of being judged on the basis of stereotypes? In the ensuing experiment we strengthened or weakened participants' confidence in their verbal skills, by arranging for them to have either an impressive success or an impressive failure on a test of verbal skills, just before they took the same difficult verbal test we had used in our earlier research. When the second test was presented as a test of ability, the boosting or weakening of confidence in their verbal skills had no effect on performance: Black participants performed less well than equally skilled white participants. What does this say about the commonsense idea that black students' academic problems are rooted in lack of self-confidence?

What did raise the level of black students' performance to that of equally qualified whites was reducing stereotype threat—in this case by explicitly presenting the test as racially fair. When this was done, Blacks performed at the same high level as whites even if their self-confidence had been weakened by a prior failure.

These results suggest something that I think has not been made clear elsewhere: when strong Black students sit down to take a difficult standardized test, the extra apprehension they feel in comparison with whites is less about their own ability than it is about having to perform on a test and in a situation that may be primed to treat them stereotypically. We discovered the extent of this apprehension when we tried to develop procedures that would make our Black participants see the test as "race-fair." It wasn't easy. African-Americans have endured so much bad press about test scores for so long that, in our experience, they are instinctively wary about the tests' fairness. We were able to convince them that our test was race-fair only when we implied that the research generating the test had been done by Blacks. When they felt trust, they performed well regardless of whether we had weakened their self-confidence beforehand. And when they didn't feel trust, no amount of bolstering of self-confidence helped.

REFERENCES

Aronson, J. 1997. *The Effects of Conceptions of Ability on Task Valuation.* Unpublished manuscript, New York University.

_____. 1999. *The Effects of Conceiving Ability as Fixed or Improvable on Responses to Stereotype Threat.* Unpublished manuscript, New York University.

Brown, J. L., and C. M. Steele. 2001. *Performance Expectations Are Not a Necessary Mediator of Stereotype Threat in African American Verbal Test Performance.* Unpublished manuscript, Stanford University.

Cross, W. E., Jr. 1991. *Shades of Black: Diversity in African-American Identity.* Philadelphia: Temple University Press.

Spencer, S. J., E. Iserman, P. G. Davies, and D. M. Quinn. 2001. *Suppression of Doubts, Anxiety, and Stereotypes as a Mediator of the Effect of Stereotype Threat on Women's Math Performance.* Unpublished manuscript, University of Waterloo.

Spencer, S. J., C. M. Steele, and D. M. Quinn. 1999. "Stereotype Threat and Women's Math Performance." *Journal of Experimental Social Psychology* 35: 4–28.

Steele, C. M. 1975. "Name-Calling and Compliance." *Journal of Personality and Social Psychology* 31: 361–69.

_____. 1992. "Race and the Schooling of Black Americans." *Atlantic Monthly* 269: 68–78.

_____. 1997. "A Threat in the Air: How Stereotypes Shape Intellectual Identity and Performance." *American Psychologist* 52: 613–29.

_____. 1999. "Thin Ice: Stereotype Threat and Black College Students." *Atlantic Monthly* 248: 44–54.

Steele, C. M., and J. Aronson. 1995. "Stereotype Threat and the Intellectual Test Performance of African Americans." *Journal of Personality and Social Psychology* 69: 797–811.

Steele, C. M., S. J. Spencer, and J. Aronson. 2002. "Contending with Group Image: The Psychology of Stereotype and Social Identity Threat." In *Advances in Experimental Social Psychology,* vol. 34, ed. M. Zanna. Academic Press.

Steele, C. M., S. J. Spencer, P. G. Davies, K. Harber, and R. E. Nisbett. 2001. *African American College Achievement: A "Wise" Intervention.* Unpublished manuscript, Stanford University.

Steele, S. 1990. *The Content of Our Character: A New Vision of Race in America.* New York: St. Martin's.

30

Black Wealth/White Wealth

A New Perspective on Racial Inequality

MELVIN L. OLIVER
THOMAS M. SHAPIRO

Each year two highly publicized news reports capture the attention and imagination of Americans. One lists the year's highest income earners. Predictably, they include glamorous and highly publicized entertainment, sport, and business personalities. For the past decade that list has included many African Americans: musical artists such as Michael Jackson, entertainers such as Bill Cosby and Oprah Winfrey, and sports figures such as Michael Jordan and Magic Johnson. During the recent past as many as half of the "top ten" in this highly exclusive rank have been African Americans.

Another highly publicized list, by contrast, documents the nation's wealthiest Americans. The famous *Forbes* magazine profile of the nation's wealthiest 400 focuses not on income, but on wealth.[1] This list includes those people whose assets—or command over monetary resources—place them at the top of the American economic hierarchy. Even though this group is often ten times larger than the top earners list, it contains few if any African Americans. An examination of these two lists creates two very different perceptions of the well-being of America's black community on the eve of the twenty-first century. The large number of blacks on the top income list generates an optimistic view of how black Americans have progressed economically in American society. The near absence of blacks in the *Forbes* listing, by contrast, presents a much more pessimistic outlook on blacks' economic progress.

This chapter develops a perspective on racial inequality that is based on the analysis of private wealth. Just as a change in focus from income to wealth in the discussion above provides a different perspective on racial inequality, our analysis reveals deep patterns of racial imbalance not visible when viewed only through the lens of income. This analysis provides a new perspective on racial inequality by exploring how material assets are created, expanded, and preserved.

The basis of our analysis is the analytical distinction between wealth and other traditional measures of economic status, of how people are "making it" in America (for ex-

Melvin L. Oliver and Thomas M. Shapiro, *Black Wealth/White Wealth: A New Perspective on Racial Inequality*, pp. 1–10, 12. Copyright © 1997 by Routledge, Inc./Taylor & Francis, Inc. Reproduced by permission of Routledge, Inc./Taylor & Francis, Inc., http://www.routledge-ny.com. The excerpts included here are not presented in the same order as they appear in the original.

ample, income, occupation, and education). Wealth is a particularly important indicator of individual and family access to life chances. Income refers to a flow of money over time, like a rate per hour, week, or year; wealth is a stock of assets owned at a particular time. Wealth is what people own, while income is what people receive for work, retirement, or social welfare. Wealth signifies the command over financial resources that a family has accumulated over its lifetime along with those resources that have been inherited across generations. Such resources, when combined with income, can create the opportunity to secure the "good life" in whatever form is needed—education, business, training, justice, health, comfort, and so on. Wealth is a special form of money not used to purchase milk and shoes and other life necessities. More often it is used to create opportunities, secure a desired stature and standard of living, or pass class status along to one's children. In this sense the command over resources that wealth entails is more encompassing than is income or education, and closer in meaning and theoretical significance to our traditional notions of economic well-being and access to life chances.

More important, wealth taps not only contemporary resources but material assets that have historic origins. Private wealth thus captures inequality that is the product of the past, often passed down from generation to generation. Given this attribute, in attempting to understand the economic status of blacks, a focus on wealth helps us avoid the either-or view of a march toward progress or a trail of despair. Conceptualizing racial inequality through wealth revolutionizes our conception of its nature and magnitude, and of whether it is declining or increasing. While most recent analyses have concluded that contemporary class-based

factors are most important in understanding the sources of continuing racial inequality, our focus on wealth sheds light on both the historical and the contemporary impacts not only of class but of race. . . .

The argument for class, most eloquently and influentially stated by William Julius Wilson in his 1978 book *The Declining Significance of Race,* suggests that the racial barriers of the past are less important than present-day social class attributes in determining the economic life chances of black Americans. Education, in particular, is the key attribute in whether blacks will achieve economic success relative to white Americans. Discrimination and racism, while still actively practiced in many spheres, have marginally less effect on black Americans' economic attainment than whether or not blacks have the skills and education necessary to fit in a changing economy. In this view, race assumes importance only as the lingering product of an oppressive past. As Wilson observes, this time in his *The Truly Disadvantaged,* racism and its most harmful injuries occurred in the past, and they are today experienced mainly by those on the bottom of the economic ladder, as "the accumulation of disadvantages . . . passed from generation to generation."[2]

We believe that a focus on wealth reveals a crucial dimension of the seeming paradox of continued racial inequality in American society. Looking at wealth helps solve the riddle of seeming black progress alongside economic deterioration. Black wealth has grown, for example, at the same time that it has fallen further behind that of whites. Wealth reveals an array of insights into black and white inequality that challenge our conception of racial and social justice in America.

The empirical heart of our analysis resides in an examination of differentials in black and white wealth holdings. This focus paints a vastly different empirical picture of social inequality than commonly emerges from analyses based on traditional inequality indicators. The burden of our claim is to demonstrate not simply the taken-for-granted assumption that wealth reveals "more" inequality—income multiplied x times is not the correct equation. More importantly we show that wealth uncovers a qualitatively different pattern of inequality on crucial fronts. Thus the goal of this work is to provide an analysis of racial differences in wealth holding that reveals dynamics of racial inequality otherwise concealed by income, occupational attainment, or education. It is our argument that wealth reveals a particular network of social relations and a set of social circumstances that convey a unique constellation of meanings pertinent to race in America. This perspective significantly adds to our understanding of public policy issues related to racial inequality; at the same time it aids us in developing better policies for the future. In stating our case, we do not discount the important information that the traditional indicators provide, but we argue that by adding to the latter an analysis of wealth a more thorough, comprehensive and powerful explanation of social inequality can be elaborated. . . .

Economists argue that racial differences in wealth are a consequence of disparate class and human capital credentials (age, education, experience, skills), propensities to save, and consumption patterns. A sociology of wealth seeks to properly situate the social context in which wealth generation occurs. Thus the sociology of wealth accounts for racial differences in wealth holding by demonstrating the unique and diverse social circumstances that blacks and

whites face. One result is that blacks and whites also face different structures of investment opportunity, which have been affected historically and contemporaneously by both race and class. We develop three concepts to provide a sociologically grounded approach to understanding racial differentials in wealth accumulation. These concepts highlight the ways in which this opportunity structure has disadvantaged blacks and helped contribute to massive wealth inequalities between the races.

Our first concept, "racialization of state policy," refers to how state policy has impaired the ability of many black Americans to accumulate wealth—and discouraged them from doing so—from the beginning of slavery throughout American history. From the first codified decision to enslave African Americans to the local ordinances that barred blacks from certain occupations to the welfare state policies of today that discourage wealth accumulation, the state has erected major barriers to black economic self-sufficiency. In particular, state policy has structured the context within which it has been possible to acquire land, build community, and generate wealth. Historically, policies and actions of the United States government have promoted homesteading, land acquisition, home ownership, retirement, pensions, education, and asset accumulation for some sectors of the population and not for others. Poor people—blacks in particular—generally have been excluded from participation in these state-sponsored opportunities. In this way, the distinctive relationship between whites and blacks has been woven into the fabric of state actions. The modern welfare state has racialized citizenship, social organization, and economic status while consigning blacks to a relentlessly impoverished and subordinate position within it.

Our second focus, on the "economic detour," helps us understand the relatively low level of entrepreneurship among and the small scale of the businesses owned by black Americans. While blacks have historically sought out opportunities for self-employment, they have traditionally faced an environment, especially from the postbellum period to the middle of the twentieth century, in which they were restricted by law from participation in business in the open market. Explicit state and local policies restricted the rights of blacks as free economic agents. These policies had a devastating impact on the ability of blacks to build and maintain successful enterprises. While blacks were limited to a restricted African American market to which others (for example, whites and other ethnics) also had easy access, they were unable to tap the more lucrative and expansive mainstream white markets. Blacks thus had fewer opportunities to develop successful businesses. When businesses were developed that competed in size and scope with white businesses, intimidation and ultimately, in some cases, violence were used to curtail their expansion or get rid of them altogether. The lack of important assets and indigenous community development has thus played a crucial role in limiting the wealth-accumulating ability of African Americans.

The third concept we develop is synthetic in nature. The notion embodied in the "sedimentation of racial inequality" is that in central ways the cumulative effects of the past have seemingly cemented blacks to the bottom of society's economic hierarchy. A history of low wages, poor schooling, and segregation affected not one or two generations of blacks but practically all

African Americans well into the middle of the twentieth century. Our argument is that the best indicator of the sedimentation of racial inequality is wealth. Wealth is one indicator of material disparity that captures the historical legacy of low wages, personal and organizational discrimination, and institutionalized racism. The low levels of wealth accumulation evidenced by current generations of black Americans best represent the economic status of blacks in the American social structure.

To argue that blacks form the sediment of the American stratificational order is to recognize the extent to which they began at the bottom of the hierarchy during slavery, and the cumulative and reinforcing effects of Jim Crow and de facto segregation through the mid-twentieth century. Generation after generation of blacks remained anchored to the lowest economic status in American society. The effect of this inherited poverty and economic scarcity for the accumulation of wealth has been to "sediment" inequality into the social structure. The sedimentation of inequality occurred because the investment opportunity that blacks faced worked against their quest for material self-sufficiency. In contrast, whites in general, but well-off whites in particular, were able to amass assets and use their secure financial status to pass their wealth from generation to generation. What is often not acknowledged is that the same social system that fosters the accumulation of private wealth for many whites denies it to blacks, thus forging an intimate connection between white wealth accumulation and black poverty. Just as blacks have had "cumulative disadvantages," many whites have had "cumulative advantages." Since wealth builds over a lifetime and is then passed along to kin, it is, from our perspective, an essential indicator of black economic well-being. By focusing on wealth we discover how a black's socioeconomic status results from a socially layered accumulation of disadvantages passed on from generation to generation. In this sense we uncover a racial wealth tax.

Our empirical analysis enables us to raise and answer several key questions about wealth: How has wealth been distributed in American society over the twentieth century? What changes in the distribution of wealth occurred during the 1980s? And finally, what are the implications of these changes for black-white inequality?

During the eighties the rich got much richer, and the poor and middle classes fell further behind. Why? The Reagan tax cuts provided greater discretionary income for middle- and upper-class taxpayers. One asset whose value grew dramatically during the eighties was real estate, an asset that is central to the wealth portfolio of the average American. Home ownership makes up the largest part of wealth held by the middle class, whereas the upper class more commonly hold a greater degree of their wealth in financial assets. Owning a house is the hallmark of the American Dream, but it is becoming harder and harder for average Americans to afford their own home and fewer are able to do so.

In part because of the dramatic rise in home values, the wealthiest generation of elderly people in America's history is in the process of passing along its wealth. Between 1987 and 2011 the baby boom generation stands to inherit approximately $7 trillion. Of course, all will not benefit equally, if at all. One-third of the worth of all estates will be divided by the richest 1 percent, each legatee receiving an average inheritance of $6 million. Much of this wealth will be in the form of property, which, as the philosopher Robert Nozick is quoted as saying in a 1990 *New York Times* piece, "sticks out as a special kind of unearned benefit that produces unequal opportunities."[3] Kevin, a seventy-five-year-old retired homeowner interviewed for this study, captures the dilemma of unearned inheritance:

> You heard that saying about the guy with a rich father? The kid goes through life thinking that he hit a triple. But really he was born on third base. He didn't hit no triple at all, but he'll go around telling everyone he banged the fucking ball and it was a triple. He was born there!

Inherited wealth is a very special kind of money imbued with the shadows of race. Racial difference in inheritance is a key feature of our story. For the most part, blacks will not partake in divvying up the baby boom bounty. America's racist legacy is shutting them out. The grandparents and parents of blacks under the age of forty toiled under segregation, where education and access to decent jobs and wages were severely restricted. Racialized state policy and the economic detour constrained their ability to enter the post–World War II housing market. Segregation created an extreme situation in which earlier generations were unable to build up much, if any, wealth. The average black family headed by a person over the age of sixty-five has no net financial assets to pass down to its children. Until the late 1960s there were few older African Americans with the ability to save much at all, much less invest. And no savings and no inheritance meant no wealth.

The most consistent and strongest common theme to emerge in interviews conducted with white and black families was that family assets expand choices, horizons, and opportunities for children while lack of assets limit opportunities. Because parents want to give their children whatever advantages they can, we wondered about the ability of the average American household to expend assets on their children. We found that the lack of private assets intrudes on the dreams that many Americans have for their children. Extreme resource deficiency characterizes several groups. It may surprise some to learn that 62 percent of households headed by single parents are without savings or other financial assets, or that two of every five households without a high school degree lack a financial nest egg. Nearly one-third of all households—and 61 percent of all black households—are without financial resources. These statistics lead to our focus on the most resource-deficient households in our study—African Americans.

We argue that, materially, whites and blacks constitute two nations. One of the analytic centerpieces of this work tells a tale of two middle classes, one white and one black. Most significant, the claim made by blacks to middle-class status depends on income and not assets. In contrast, a wealth pillar supports the white middle class in its drive for middle-class opportunities and a middle-class standard of living. Middle-class blacks, for example, earn seventy cents for every dollar earned by middle-class whites but they possess only fifteen cents for every dollar of wealth held by middle-class whites. For the most part, the economic foundation of the black middle class lacks one of the pillars that provide stability and security to middle-class whites—assets. The black middle class position is precarious and fragile with insubstantial wealth resources. This analysis means it is entirely premature to celebrate the rise of the black middle class. The glass is both half empty and half full, because the wealth data reveal the paradoxical situation in which blacks' wealth has grown while at the same time falling further behind that of whites.

The social distribution of wealth discloses a fresh and formidable dimension of racial inequality. Blacks' achievement at any given level not only requires that greater effort be expended on fewer opportunities but also bestows substantially diminished rewards. Examining blacks and whites who share similar socioeconomic characteristics brings to light persistent and vast wealth discrepancies. Take education as one prime example: the most equality we found was among the college educated, but even here at the pinnacle of achievement whites control four times as much wealth as blacks with the same degrees. This predicament manifests a disturbing break in the link between achievement and results that is essential for democracy and social equality.

The central question of this study is, Why do the wealth portfolios of blacks and whites vary so drastically? The answer is not simply that blacks have inferior remunerable human capital endowments—substandard education, jobs, and skills, for example—or do not display the characteristics most associated with higher income and wealth. We are able to demonstrate that even when blacks and whites display similar characteristics—for example, are on a par educationally and occupationally—a potent difference of $43,143 in home equity and financial assets still remains. Likewise, giving the average black household the same attributes as the average white household leaves a $25,794 racial gap in financial assets alone.

The extent of discrimination in institutions and social policy provides a persuasive index of bias that undergirds the drastic differences between blacks and whites. We show that skewed access to mortgage and housing markets and the racial valuing of neighborhoods on the basis of segregated markets result in enormous racial wealth disparity. Banks turn down qualified blacks much more often for home loans than they do similarly qualified whites. Blacks who do qualify, moreover, pay higher interest rates on home mortgages than whites. Residential segregation persists into the 1990s, and we found that the great rise in housing values is color-coded.[4] Why should the mean value of the average white home appreciate at a dramatically higher rate than the average black home? Home ownership is without question the single most important means of accumulating assets. The lower values of black homes adversely affect the ability of blacks to utilize their residences as collateral for obtaining personal, business, or educational loans. We estimate that institutional biases in the residential arena have cost the current generation of blacks about $82 billion. Passing inequality along from one generation to the next casts another racially stratified shadow on the making of American inequality. Institutional discrimination in housing and lending markets extends into the future the effects of historical discrimination within other institutions.

Placing these findings in the larger context of public policy discussions about racial and social justice adds new dimensions to these discussions. A focus on wealth changes our thinking about racial inequality. The more one learns about wealth differences, the more mistaken current policies appear. To take these findings seriously, as we do, means not shirking the responsibility of seeking alternative policy

ideas with which to address issues of inequality. We might even need to think about social justice in new ways. In some key respects our analysis of disparities in wealth between blacks and whites forms an agenda for the future, the key principle of which is to link opportunity structures to policies promoting asset formation that begin to close the racial wealth gap.

Closing the racial gap means that we have to target policies at two levels. First, we need policies that directly address the situation of African Americans. Such policies are necessary to speak to the historically generated disadvantages and the current racially based policies that have limited the ability of blacks, as a group, to accumulate wealth resources.

Second, we need policies that directly promote asset opportunities for those on the bottom of the social structure, both black and white, who are locked out of the wealth accumulation process. More generally, our analysis clearly suggests the need for massive redistributional policies in order to reforge the links between achievement, reward, social equality, and democracy. These policies must take aim at the gross inequality generated by those at the very top of the wealth distribution. Policies of this type are the most difficult ones on which to gain consensus but the most important in creating a more just society.

This chapter's underlying goal is to establish a way to view racial inequality that will serve as a guide in securing racial equality in the twenty-first century. Racial equality is not an absolute or idealized state of affairs, because it cannot be perfectly attained. Yet the fact that it can never be perfectly attained in the real world is a wholly insufficient excuse for dismissing it as utopian or impossible. What is important are the bearings by which a nation chooses to orient its character. We can choose to let racial inequality fester and risk heightened conflict and violence. Americans can also make a different choice, a commitment to equality and to closing the gap as much as possible.

NOTES

1. Harold Senecker, 1993, "The *Forbes* 400: The Richest People in America," *Forbes,* 18 October, pp. 110–113.

2. William J. Wilson, 1987, *The Truly Disadvantaged,* Chicago: University of Chicago Press.

3. Nick Ravo, 1990, "A Windfall Nears in Inheritances from the Richest Generation," *New York Times,* 22 July E4.

4. Reynolds Farley and William H. Frey, 1994, "Changes in the Segregation of Whites from Blacks During the 1980s: Small Steps Toward a More Integrated Society," *American Sociological Review* 59: 23–45. Douglas S. Massey and Nancy A. Denton, 1993, *American Apartheid: Segregation and the Making of the Underclass,* Cambridge: Harvard University Press.

31

The Possibility of
a New Racial Hierarchy in the
Twenty-First-Century United States

HERBERT J. GANS

Over the last decade, a number of social scientists writing on race and ethnicity have suggested that the country may be moving toward a new racial structure (Alba 1990; Sanjek 1994; Gitlin 1995). If current trends persist, today's multiracial hierarchy could be replaced by what I think of as a dual or bimodal one consisting of "nonblack" and "black" population categories, with a third, "residual," category for the groups that do not, or do not yet, fit into the basic dualism.[1]

More important, this hierarchy may be based not just on color or other visible bodily features, but also on a distinction between undeserving and deserving, or stigmatized and respectable, races.[2] The hierarchy is new only insofar as the old white-nonwhite dichotomy may be replaced by a nonblack-black one, but it is hardly new for blacks, who are likely to remain at the bottom once again. I fear this hierarchy could develop even if more blacks achieve educational mobility, obtain professional and managerial jobs, and gain access to middle-class incomes, wealth, and other "perks." Still, the hierarchy could also end, particularly if the black distribution of income and wealth resembles that of the then dominant races, and if interracial marriage eliminates many of the visible bodily features by which Americans now define race. . . .

The Dual Racial Hierarchy

Before what is now described, somewhat incorrectly, as the post–1965 immigration, the United States was structured as a predominantly Caucasian, or white, society, with a limited number of numerically and otherwise inferior races, who were typically called Negroes, Orientals, and American Indians—or blacks, yellows, and reds to go with the pinkish-skinned people called

---

whites. There was also a smattering of groups involving a huge number of people who were still described by their national or geographic origins rather than language, including Filipinos, Mexicans and Puerto Ricans, Cubans, etc.[3]

After 1965, when many other Central and Latin American countries began to send migrants, the Spanish-speaking groups were all recategorized by language and called Hispanics. Newcomers from Southeast Asia were classified by continental origin and called Asians, which meant that the later Indian, Pakistani, and Sri Lankan newcomers had to be distinguished regionally, and called South Asians.

At the end of the twentieth century, the country continues to be dominated by whites. Nevertheless, both the immigrants who started to arrive after the end of World War II and the political, cultural, and racial changes that took place in the wake of their arrival have further invalidated many old racial divisions and labels. They have also set into motion what may turn out to be significant transformations in at least part of the basic racial hierarchy.

These transformations are still in an early phase but one of the first has been the elevation of a significant, and mostly affluent, part of the Asian and Asian-American population into a "model minority" that also bids to eradicate many of the boundaries between it and whites. Upward socioeconomic mobility and increasing intermarriage with whites may even end up in eliminating the boundary that now constructs them as a separate race. Thus, one possible future trend may lead to all but poor Asians and Asian-Americans being perceived and even treated so much like whites that currently visible bodily differences will no longer be judged negatively or

even noticed, except when and where Asians or Asian-Americans threaten white interests (e.g., Newman 1993). The same treatment as quasi whites may spread to other successfully mobile and intermarrying immigrants and their descendants, for example Filipinos and white Hispanics.[4]

What these minorities have in common now with Asians, and might have in common even more in the future, is that they are all nonblack, although not as many are currently as affluent as Asians. Nonetheless, by the middle of the twenty-first century, as whites could perhaps become, or will worry about becoming, a numerical minority in the country, they might cast about for political and cultural allies.[5] Their search for allies, which may not even be conscious or deliberate, could hasten the emergence of a new, non-black racial category, whatever it is named, in which skin color, or in the case of "Hispanics," racially constructed ethnic differences, will be ignored, even if whites would probably remain the dominant subcategory.

The lower part of the emerging dual hierarchy will likely consist of people classified as blacks, including African-Americans, as well as Caribbean and other blacks, dark-skinned or black Hispanics, Native Americans, and anyone else who is dark skinned enough and/or possessed of visible bodily features and behavior patterns, actual or imagined, that remind nonblacks of blacks. Many of these people will also be poor, and if whites and other nonblacks continue to blame America's troubles on a low-status scapegoat, the new black category will be characterized as an undeserving race.

In effect, class will presumably play nearly as much of a role in the boundary changes as race, but with some important exceptions. For example, if a significant number of very poor whites remain as the twenty-first-century equivalent of today's "white trash," they will probably be viewed as less undeserving than equally poor blacks simply because they are whites.[6]

Furthermore, the limits of class are indicated, at least for today, by the continued stigmatization of affluent and otherwise high-status blacks, who suffer some of the same indignities as poor blacks (Feagin and Sykes 1994).[7] So, of course, do moderate- and middle-income members of the working class, who constitute the majority of blacks in America even if whites do not know it. The high visibility of "black" or Negroid physical features renders class position invisible to whites, so that even affluent blacks are suspected of criminal or pathological behavior that is actually found only among a minority of very poor blacks.

Despite continuing white hatreds and fears of blacks that continue almost 150 years after the Civil War, racial classification systems involving others have been more flexible. When the first Irish immigrants came to New York, they were so poor that they were perceived by Anglo-Saxon whites as the black Irish and often treated like blacks. Even so, it did not take the Irish long to separate themselves from blacks, and more important, to be so separated by the city's Anglo-Saxons. A generation later, the Irish were whites (Roediger 1991; Ignatiev 1995).

Perhaps their new whiteness was reinforced by the arrival of the next set of newcomers: people from Eastern and Southern Europe who were often described as members of "swarthy races." Even though the word *race* was used the way we today use *ethnicity*, the newcomers were clearly not white in the Anglo-Saxon sense, and Southern Italians were sometimes called "guineas" because of their dark skin. Nonetheless, over

time, they too became white, thanks in part to their acculturation, their integration into the mainstream economy, and after World War II, their entry into the middle class. Perhaps the disappearance of their swarthiness was also reinforced by the arrival in the cities of a new wave of Southern blacks during and after World War II.

A less typical racial transformation occurred about that time in Mississippi, where whites began to treat the Chinese merchants who provided stores for poor blacks as near whites. As Loewen (1988) tells the story, increased affluence and acculturation were again relevant factors. Although whites neither socialized nor intermarried with the Chinese, they accorded them greater social deference and political respect than when they had first arrived. They turned the Chinese into what I previously called a residual category, and in the process created an early version of the nonblack-black duality that may appear in the United States in the next century.

As the Mississippi example suggests, changes in racial classification schemes need not require racial or class equality, for as long as scarce resources or positions remain, justifications for discrimination also remain and physical features that are invisible in some social settings can still become visible in others. Glass ceilings supply the best example, because they seem to change more slowly than some other hierarchical boundaries. Even ceilings for Jews, non-Irish Catholics, and others long classified as whites are still lower than those for WASPs in the upper reaches of the class and prestige structures.

I should note that the racial hierarchy I have sketched here, together with the qualifications that follow, are described both from the perspective of the (overtly) detached social scientist, and also from the perspective of the populations that end up as dominant in the structure. A longer paper would analyze how very differently the people who are fitted into the lower or residual parts of the hierarchy see it.[8]

Qualifications to the Dual Hierarchy

Even if the country would someday replace its current set of racial classifications, the result would not be a simple dual structure, and this model needs to be qualified in at least three ways.

Residuals

The first qualification is the near certainty of a residual or middle category that includes groups placed in a waiting position by the dominant population until it becomes clear whether they will be allowed to become non-black, face the seemingly permanent inferiority that goes with being black, or become long-term residuals.

If such a structure were to develop in the near future, those likely to be placed in a residual category would include the less affluent members of today's Asian, Hispanic and Filipino, Central and South American Indian, and mixed Indian-Latino populations. The future of the dark-skinned members of the South Asian newcomers is harder to predict. Indeed, their treatment will become an important test of how whites deal with the race-class nexus when the people involved are very dark skinned but are not Negroid—and when their class position is so high that in 1990 it outranked that of all other immigrants (Rumbaut 1997, table 1.4).[9]

Who is classified as residual will, like all other categorizations, be shaped by both class and race. To borrow Milton Gordon's (1964) useful but too rarely used notion of "ethclass," what may be developing are "race-classes," with lower-class members of otherwise racially acceptable groups and higher-class members of racially inferior ones being placed in the residual category.

It is also possible for two or more residual categories to emerge, one for nonwhite and Hispanic populations of lower- and working-class position, and another for nonwhites and Hispanics of higher-class position, with the latter more likely to be eligible eventually to join whites in the nonblack portion of a dual hierarchy. Yet other variations are conceivable, however, for white America has not yet given any clues about how it will treat middle-class Latinos of various skin colors and other bodily features. Perhaps today's ad hoc solution, to treat nonblack Hispanics as a quasi-racial ethnic group that is neither white nor black, may survive for another generation or more, particularly if enough Hispanics remain poor or are falsely accused of rejecting linguistic Americanization.

Being placed in a residual classification means more than location in a middle analytic category; it is also a socially enforced, even if covert, category, and it will be accompanied by all the social, political, and emotional uncertainties that go with being placed in a holding pattern and all the pains these create (Marris 1996). True, residuals may not know they are waiting, but then the second-generation white ethnic "marginal men" identified by Stonequist (1937) did not know they were waiting for eventual acculturation and assimilation.

Multiracials

A second qualification to the dual model is created by the emergence of biracials or multiracials that result from the rising intermarriage rates among Asian, Hispanic, and black and white immigrants as well as black and white native-born Americans.[10] Interracial marriages increased from 1 percent of all marriages in 1960 to 3 percent in 1990 (Harrison and Bennett 1995, 165).[11] They are expected to increase much faster in the future, particularly Asian-white ones, since even now, about a third of all Asian marriages, and more than half of all Japanese ones, are intermarriages.[12] If Hispanic-white marriages were also counted, they would exceed all the rest in current number and expected growth, but these are usually treated as ethnic rather than racial intermarriages.

Another set of recruits for a residual position includes the light-skinned blacks, once called mulattos, who today dominate the African-American upper class, some of whom may be sufficiently elite and light-skinned to be viewed as nonblack. Even now, the most prominent among the light-skinned black-white biracials, including business and civic leaders, celebrities and entertainers, are already treated as honorary whites, although many refuse this option and take special pride in their blackness and become "race leaders."[13]

Meanwhile, "multiracial" is in the process of slowly becoming a public racial category, and someday it could become an official one codified by the U.S. Census.[14] At this writing, however, many people of mixed race are not ready to define themselves publicly as such, and those who can choose which racial origin to use are sometimes flexible on instrumental grounds, or may choose different racial origins on different occasions.[15] How people of various racial mixtures construct themselves in the longer run is impossible to tell, since issues of their identification and treatment by others, their own identity, and the social, occupational, financial, and political benefits and costs involved cannot be predicted either.

As far as the country's long-term future racial structure is concerned, however, what matters most is how whites will eventually view and treat multiracial people. This will be affected by the variations in class and visible physical features among multiracial people—for example, how closely they resemble whites or other deserving races. Another question is the future of the traditional identification of race with "blood," which counts all nonwhites in halves, quarters, or even eighths, depending on how many and which ancestors intermarried with whom.[16] If the late twentieth-century belief in the power of genes continues, blood might simply be replaced by genes someday.

Mixed race is a particularly complex category, for several reasons. In any racial intermarriage with more than one offspring, each sibling is likely to look somewhat different racially from the others, ranging from darker to lighter or more and less nonwhite. Thus, one black-white sibling could be viewed as black and another as nonblack—even before they decide how they view themselves. What happens in subsequent generations is virtually unimaginable, since even if mixed-race individuals marry others of the same mixture, their children will not resemble their grandparents and some may barely resemble their parents. Eventually, a rising number will be treated as, and will think of themselves as, white or nonblack, but this is possible only when people of multiracial origin can no longer bear children who resemble a black ancestor.

Empirical evidence about the effects of racial intermarriage from countries where it has taken place for a long time is unfortunately not very relevant. The closest case, the Caribbean islands, are for the most part, tiny. They are also former plantation societies, with a small number of white and light-skinned elites, and a large number of nonwhites—and a differential conception of white and nonwhite from island to island.[17] Caribbean nonwhites appear to intermarry fairly freely but skin color does count and the darkest-skinned peoples are invariably lowest in socioeconomic class and status (Mintz 1989; Rodriguez 1989).

The only large country, Brazil, also began as a plantation society, and it differs from the United States particularly in that the Brazilian state eschewed racial legislation. As a result, Brazil never passed Jim Crow laws, but as of this writing (January 1998) it has not passed civil rights legislation either. Racial stratification, as well as discrimination and segregation, has persisted nonetheless, but it has been maintained through the class system. Drastic class inequalities, including a high rate of illiteracy among the poor, have enabled whites to virtually monopolize the higher class and status positions.

The absence of state involvement has given Brazil an undeserved reputation as a society that encourages intermarriage but ignores racial differences, a reputation the state has publicized as "racial democracy." The reality is not very different from that of the United States, however, for while there has been more intermarriage, it appears to have taken place mainly among blacks and black-white biracials, who together make up about half the country's population. Moreover, biracials gain little socioeconomic advantage from their lighter skins, even as the darkest-skinned blacks are kept at the bottom, forced into slums and prisons as in the United States.[18]

In effect, the Brazilian experience would suggest an empirical precedent for my hypothesis that blacks will remain a separate, and discriminated-against, population in the United States of the future. Indeed, in just about every society in which blacks first arrived as slaves, they are still at the bottom, and the political, socioeconomic, and cultural mechanisms to keep them there remain in place. Although blacks obtain higher incomes and prestige than Asians or white Hispanics in a number of American communities, the descendants of nonblack immigrants are, with some notable exceptions, still able to overtake most blacks in the long run.

Since parts of the United States were also a plantation society in which the slaves were black, the leftovers of the racial stratification pattern will likely continue here as well. Thus, children of black-white intermarriages who turn out to be dark skinned are classified as blacks, even if the United States is on the whole kinder to light-skinned biracials than Brazil.

The future of Asian-white biracials remains more unpredictable, in part because no empirical data exist that can be used to shore up guesses about them. The same observation applies to the endless number of other multiracial combinations that will be created when the children of multiracial parents intermarry with yet other multiracials. There will be few limits to new variations in bodily features, though which will be visible or noticed, and which of the latter will be stigmatized or celebrated as exotic cannot be guessed now.[19] Most likely, however, the larger the number of multiracials and of multiracial variations, the more difficult it will be for nonblacks to define and enforce racial boundaries, or to figure out which of the many darker-skinned varieties of multiracials had black ancestors. In that case, an eventual end to racial discrimination is possible.

If future racial self-identification patterns will also resemble today's ethnic ones, the racial equivalent of today's voluntary white ethnicity and its associated lack of ethnic loyalty may mean that many future triracial, quadriracial, and other multiracial people may eventually know little, and care even less, about the various racial mixtures they have inherited. It is even conceivable that this change will extend to black multiracials, and should race become voluntary for them as well, the possibility of an end to racial discrimination will be increased. Unfortunately, at the moment such extrapolations are far closer to utopian thinking than to sociological speculation.

Regional Variations

A third qualification to the dual model is that the portrait I have drawn is national, but given the regional variations in old racial groups and new immigrant populations, it fits no single U.S. region. Moreover, some parts of the country are now still so devoid of new immigrants, with the exception of the handful who come to establish "ethnic" restaurants, that the present racial hierarchies, categories, and attitudes, many of them based on stereotypes imported from elsewhere, could survive unchanged for quite a while in such areas. Furthermore, some areas that have experienced heavy immigration from Asia and Latin America are currently seeing an outmigration of whites, especially lower-income ones (Frey 1996). Thus, even current patterns in the racial makeup of U.S. regions could change fairly quickly.

In addition, regional differences remain in the demography of the lowest strata. The racial hierarchy of the Deep South will probably continue to bear many direct marks of slavery, although the de facto black experience elsewhere in the country has so far not been totally different. Moreover, in some regions, Latin American and other poor non-black immigrants have already been able to jump over the poor black population economically and socially, partly because whites, including institutions such as banks, are less hostile—or less necessary—to them than they are to blacks.

In the Southwest, Mexicans and other Hispanics remain at the socioeconomic bottom, although in California, they may be joined by the Hmong, Laotians, and other very poor Asians. And Native Americans still occupy the lowest socioeconomic stratum in the handful of mostly rural parts of the country where they now live, although tribes with gambling casinos may be able to effect some changes in that pattern.

Even though some of the new immigrants can by now be found just about everywhere in America, the Los Angeles and New York City areas not only remain the major immigrant arrival centers but also contain the most diverse populations. As a result, a number of the issues discussed in this paper will be played out there, even as they are barely noticeable in the many smaller American cities that may have attracted only a handful of the newcomers. Since these two cities are also the country's prime creators of popular culture, however, their distinctive racial and ethnic characteristics will probably be diffused in subtle ways through the country as a whole. . . .

Conclusion

Since no one can even guess much less model the many causal factors that will influence the future, the observations above are not intended to be read as a prediction but as an exercise in speculative analysis. The weakness of such an analysis is its empirical reliance on the extrapolation of too many current trends and the assumed persistence of too many current phenomena. The analysis becomes a justifiable exercise, however, because it aims only to speculate about what future "scenarios" are possible, and what variables might shape these.

Obviously, the observations about such a hierarchy are not meant to suggest that it is desirable. Indeed, I wrote the paper with the hope that if such a future threatens to become real, it can be prevented.

NOTES

I am grateful for comments on earlier drafts of this paper from Margaret Chin, Jennifer Lee, an anonymous reviewer—and from my fellow authors in the volume *The Cultural Territories of Race: Black and White Boundaries,* edited by Michèle Lamont (Chicago and New York: University of Chicago Press and Russell Sage Foundation, 1999).

1. These categories are constructions, but they also contain populations experiencing all the pleasures and pains of being located in a hierarchy. And although I am often discussing constructions, I will forgo the practice of putting all racial, national, and related names and labels between quotes, except for unusual racial stereotypes.

2. The two races may not be called that openly, but ambiguous pejoratives have long been part of the American vocabulary, for example *underclass* now, and *pauper* a century earlier (Gans 1995). Since races are social constructions, their names will depend in large part on who does the naming—and whose names become dominant in the public vocabulary.

3. Puerto Ricans are still often described as immigrants, even though they have been American citizens for a long time and their move from the island to the mainland is a form of interstate mo-

bility. Racial, class, and linguistic considerations have undoubtedly influenced this labeling.

The same dominant-race thinking led Irving Kristol and other neoconservatives to argue in the 1960s that blacks were similar enough to the white European immigrants to be able to adopt and act on immigrant values. They also assumed that blacks would then assimilate like immigrants, ignoring such facts as that blacks had originally come as slaves, not immigrants; had been here several centuries; and had not yet been allowed by whites to assimilate. Thirty years later, many whites ignore the same facts to propose the newest immigrants as role models for blacks.

4. Much less is said about black Hispanics, including Puerto Ricans, who suffer virtually all of the discriminatory and other injustices imposed on African-Americans.

5. Some highly placed whites are already worrying, for example in a *Time* cover story by William Henry III (1990), but then similar whites worried a century earlier what the then arriving Catholic and Jewish newcomers would do to *their* country. The current worries are as meaningless as the old ones, since they are based on extrapolations of current patterns of immigration, not to mention current constructions of (nonwhite) race and (Hispanic) ethnicity.

6. Hacker (1996) notes, for example, that the term "white trash" is no longer in common use. Indeed, for reasons worth studying, the more popular term of the moment is "trailer trash," which nonetheless seems to be applied solely to poor whites.

7. In this respect, the United States differs from many other countries in the Western hemisphere, where blacks who have managed to become affluent are treated, within limits, as whites.

8. Not only might they perceive it more angrily than I am here doing, but they might be angrier about it than about the present hierarchy, simply because it is new but no great improvement. One result could be their constructions of new racial identities for themselves that depart drastically from the ones future nonblacks consider reasonable.

9. Being far fewer than Asians in number, South Asians are nationally not very visible now.

Moreover, for religious and other reasons, South Asian immigrants have so far often been able to discourage their children from intermarrying.

10. My observations on multiracial constructions and people have benefited from many conversations with Valli Rajah.

11. Between 1970 and 1994, the number of people in interracial marriages grew from 676,000 to more than three million (Fletcher 1997). In 1990, biracial children made up 4 percent of all children, increasing from half a million in 1970 to about two million that year. The largest number were Asian-white children, followed by Native American-white and African American-white ones (Harrison and Bennett 1995).

12. Some observers currently estimate that 70 percent of all Japanese and Japanese-Americans are intermarried, mostly with whites. Since they came to the United States as families long before 1965, this estimate may supply a clue about what will happen to second-, third-, and later-generation descendants of other Asian-American populations.

13. Presumably class position will affect how other descendants of old Southern mulatto and creole populations (Dominguez 1986) will be classified.

14. In the political debates over the racial categories to be used in the Year 2000 Census, vocal multiracials preferred to be counted as and with various people of color. African-Americans and other officially recognized racial groups also indicated their opposition to a multiracial category, being reluctant to reduce the power of their numbers or the federal benefits that now go to racial minorities (e.g., Holmes 1996).

15. Kohne (1996) reports that light-skinned biracial Columbia University students who identify as whites also apply for scholarships as blacks. But then, four decades earlier, I met Italian-Americans in Boston's West End who took Irish names in order to obtain jobs in Irish-dominated city hall.

16. The practice of quantifying racial bloods has a long history in Europe and the United States, thanks to both eugenics and slavery. Perhaps it will disappear when enough people have to start counting three or more races. However, people also still use blood fractions when they marry across religions, so that the notion of racial, ethnic, or religious "blood" is by no means obsolete.

17. They are also different, for "one and the same person may be considered white in the Dominican Republic or Puerto Rico . . . 'colored' in Jamaica, Martinique, or Curacao . . . [and] a 'Negro' in Georgia" (Hoetink 1967, xii).

18. This account is based mainly on the data summarized in Fiola 1990 and Skidmore 1992, the classic analysis of the Brazilian racial system in Skidmore 1993, Adamo's 1983 case study of race and class in Rio de Janeiro, and the sociopolitical analyses by Marx (1995, 1996). I am indebted to Anthony Marx for guiding me into the literature on Brazil, although there is still precious little social research, especially with current data, in English.

19. No one has so far paid much attention to who is constructed as exotic and why, except the multiracial people, mostly women, to whom it is applied. Some of them benefit because they are sought by industries that hire workers with exotic facial features; but women without these occupational interests resent such labeling because it turns them into sexual objects.

Industries that employ workers with exotic features, facial and otherwise, such as the fashion and entertainment industries, play an interesting, and probably unduly influential, role in the country's public racial construction.

REFERENCES

Adamo, Samuel C. 1983. "The Broken Promise: Race, Health and Justice in Rio de Janeiro, 1890–1940." Ph.D. diss., University of New Mexico.

Alba, Richard D. 1990. *Ethnic Identity.* New Haven: Yale University Press.

Dominguez, Virginia R. 1986. *White by Definition.* New Brunswick: Rutgers University Press.

Feagin, Joe R., and Michael P. Sykes. 1994. *Living with Racism.* Boston: Beacon.

Fiola, Jan. 1990. "Race Relations in Brazil: A Reassessment of the 'Racial Democracy' Thesis." Occasional Papers Series no. 34. University of

Massachusetts Latin American Studies Program, Amherst.

Fletcher, Michael A. 1997. "More Than a Black-White Issue." *Washington Post National Weekly Edition,* May 26, 34.

Frey, William H. 1996. "Immigration, Domestic Migration and Demographic Balkanization in America." *Population and Development Review* 22:741–63.

Gans, Herbert J. 1995. *The War Against the Poor.* New York: Basic.

Gitlin, Todd. 1995. *The Twilight of Common Dreams.* New York: Metropolitan.

Gordon, Milton M. 1964. *Assimilation in American Life.* New York: Oxford University Press.

Hacker, Andrew. 1996. Foreword to *The Coming Race War?* by Richard Delgado. New York: New York University Press.

Harrison, Roderick J., and Claudette Bennett. 1995. "Racial and Ethnic Diversity." In *State of the Union: America in the 1990s,* vol. 2, *Social Trends,* edited by Reynolds Farley. New York: Russell Sage Foundation.

Henry, William, III. 1990. "Beyond the Melting Pot." *Time,* April 9, 29–32.

Hoetink, Harry. 1967. *The Two Variants in Caribbean Race Relations.* London: Oxford University Press.

Holmes, Steven. 1996. "Census Tests New Category to Identify Racial Groups." *New York Times,* December 4, A25.

Ignatiev, Noel. 1995. *How the Irish Became White.* New York: Routledge.

Kohne, Natasha G. 1996. "The Experience of Mixed-Race Women: Challenging Racial Boundaries." Unpublished senior thesis, Department of Sociology, Columbia University, New York.

Loewen, James W. 1988. *The Mississippi Chinese.* 2d ed. Prospect Heights, Ill.: Waveland.

Marris, Peter. 1996. *The Politics of Uncertainty.* New York: Routledge.

Marx, Anthony W. 1995. "Contested Citizenship: The Dynamics of Racial Identity and Social Movements." *International Review of History* 40, supplement 3: 159–83.

———. 1996. "Race-Making and the Nation-State." *World Politics,* January, 180–208.

Mintz, Sidney W. 1989. *Caribbean Transformations.* New York: Columbia University Press.

Newman, Katherine. 1993. *Declining Fortunes.* New York: Basic.

Rodriguez, Clara E. 1989. *Puerto Ricans: Born in the U.S.A.* Boston: Unwin Hyman.

Roediger, David R. 1991. *Wages of Whiteness.* London: Verso.

Rumbaut, Ruben G. 1997. "Ties that Bind: Immigration and Immigrant Families in the United States." In *Immigration and the Family,* edited by Alan Booth, Ann C. Crouter, and Nancy Landale. Mahwah, N.J.: Erlbaum.

Sanjek, Roger. 1994. "Intermarriage and the Future of the Races in the United States." In *Race,* edited by Steven Gregory and Roger Sanjek. New Brunswick: Rutgers University Press.

Skidmore, Thomas L. 1992. "Fact and Myth: Discovering a Racial Problem in Brazil." Working paper 173. Helen Kellogg Institute for International Studies, University of Notre Dame.

———. 1993. *Black into White.* Durham: Duke University Press.

Stonequist, Everett V. 1937. *The Marginal Man.* New York: Scribner's.

32

The Social Construction of Gender

JUDITH LORBER

Talking about gender for most people is the equivalent of fish talking about water. Gender is so much the routine ground of everyday activities that questioning its taken-for-granted assumptions and presuppositions is like thinking about whether the sun will come up. Gender is so pervasive that in our society we assume it is bred into our genes. Most people find it hard to believe that gender is constantly created and re-created out of human interaction, out of social life, and is the texture and order of that social life. Yet gender, like culture, is a human production that depends on everyone constantly "doing gender" (West and Zimmerman 1987).

And everyone "does gender" without thinking about it. Today, on the subway, I saw a well-dressed man with a year-old child in a stroller. Yesterday, on a bus, I saw a man with a tiny baby in a carrier on his chest. Seeing men taking care of small children in public is increasingly common—at least in New York City. But both men were quite obviously stared at—and smiled at, approvingly. Everyone was doing gender—the men who were changing the role of fa-thers and the other passengers, who were applauding them silently. But there was more gendering going on that probably fewer people noticed. The baby was wear-ing a white crocheted cap and white clothes. You couldn't tell if it was a boy or a girl. The child in the stroller was wearing a dark blue T-shirt and dark print pants. As they started to leave the train, the father put a Yankee baseball cap on the child's head. Ah, a boy, I thought. Then I noticed the gleam of tiny earrings in the child's ears, and as they got off, I saw the little flowered sneakers and lace-trimmed socks. Not a boy after all. Gender done.

Gender is such a familiar part of daily life that it usually takes a deliberate disruption of our expectations of how women and men are supposed to act to pay attention to how it is produced. Gender signs and sig-nals are so ubiquitous that we usually fail to note them—unless they are missing or am-biguous. Then we are uncomfortable until we have successfully placed the other per-son in a gender status; otherwise, we feel socially dislocated. In our society, in addi-tion to man and woman, the status can be

Judith Lorber, "Night to His Day: The Social Construction of Gender," *Paradoxes of Gender*, 13–17, 22, 25–27, 32–35, 305–306. Copyright © 1994 by Yale University Press.

transvestite (a person who dresses in opposite-gender clothes) and *transsexual* (a person who has had sex-change surgery). Transvestites and transsexuals carefully construct their gender status by dressing, speaking, walking, gesturing in the ways prescribed for women or men—whichever they want to be taken for—and so does any "normal" person.

For the individual, gender construction starts with assignment to a sex category on the basis of what the genitalia look like at birth. Then babies are dressed or adorned in a way that displays the category because parents don't want to be constantly asked whether their baby is a girl or a boy. A sex category becomes a gender status through naming, dress, and the use of other gender markers. Once a child's gender is evident, others treat those in one gender differently from those in the other, and the children respond to the different treatment by feeling different and behaving differently. As soon as they can talk, they start to refer to themselves as members of their gender. Sex doesn't come into play again until puberty, but by that time, sexual feelings and desires and practices have been shaped by gendered norms and expectations. Adolescent boys and girls approach and avoid each other in an elaborately scripted and gendered mating dance. Parenting is gendered, with different expectations for mothers and for fathers, and people of different genders work at different kinds of jobs. The work adults do as mothers and fathers and as low-level workers and high-level bosses, shapes women's and men's life experiences, and these experiences produce different feelings, consciousness, relationships, skills—ways of being that we call feminine or masculine. All of these processes constitute the social construction of gender.

Gendered roles change—today fathers are taking care of little children, girls and boys are wearing unisex clothing and getting the same education, women and men are working at the same jobs. Although many traditional social groups are quite strict about maintaining gender differences, in other social groups they seem to be blurring. Then why the one-year-old's earrings? Why is it still so important to mark a child as a girl or a boy, to make sure she is not taken for a boy or he for a girl? What would happen if they were? They would, quite literally, have changed places in their social world.

To explain why gendering is done from birth, constantly and by everyone, we have to look not only at the way individuals experience gender but at gender as a social institution. As a social institution, gender is one of the major ways that human beings organize their lives. Human society depends on a predictable division of labor, a designated allocation of scarce goods, assigned responsibility for children and others who cannot care for themselves, common values and their systematic transmission to new members, legitimate leadership, music, art, stories, games, and other symbolic productions. One way of choosing people for the different tasks of society is on the basis of their talents, motivations, and competence—their demonstrated achievements. The other way is on the basis of gender, race, ethnicity—ascribed membership in a category of people. Although societies vary in the extent to which they use one or the other of these ways of allocating people to work and to carry out other responsibilities, every society uses gender and age grades. Every society classifies people as "girl and boy children," "girls and boys ready to be married," and "fully adult women and men," constructs similarities among them and differences between them, and assigns them to different roles and responsibilities. Personality characteristics, feelings, motivations, and ambitions flow from these different life experiences so that the members of these different groups become different kinds of people. The process of gendering and its outcome are legitimated by religion, law, science, and the society's entire set of values. . . .

Western society's values legitimate gendering by claiming that it all comes from physiology—female and male procreative differences. But gender and sex are not equivalent, and gender as a social construction does not flow automatically from genitalia and reproductive organs, the main physiological differences of females and males. In the construction of ascribed social statuses, physiological differences such as sex, stage of development, color of skin, and size are crude markers. They are not the source of the social statuses of gender, age grade, and race. Social statuses are carefully constructed through prescribed processes of teaching, learning, emulation, and enforcement. Whatever genes, hormones, and biological evolution contribute to human social institutions is materially as well as qualitatively transformed by social practices. . . .

For Individuals, Gender Means Sameness

Although the possible combinations of genitalia, body shapes, clothing, mannerisms, sexuality, and roles could produce infinite varieties in human beings, the social institution of gender depends on the production and maintenance of a limited number of gender statuses and of making the members of these statuses similar to each other. Individuals are born sexed but not gendered, and they have to be taught to be masculine or feminine. As Simone de Beauvoir said: "One is not born, but rather becomes, a woman. . . ; it is civilization as a whole that produces this creature . . . which is described as feminine." (1952, 267).

Children learn to walk, talk, and gesture the way their social group says girls and boys should. Ray Birdwhistell, in his analysis of body motion as human communication, calls these learned gender displays *tertiary* sex characteristics and argues that they are needed to distinguish genders because humans are a weakly dimorphic species—their only sex markers are genitalia (1970, 39–46). Clothing, paradoxically, often hides the sex but displays the gender.

In early childhood, humans develop gendered personality structures and sexual orientations through their interactions with parents of the same and opposite gender. As adolescents, they conduct their sexual behavior according to gendered scripts. Schools, parents, peers, and the mass media guide young people into gendered work and family roles. As adults, they take on a gendered social status in their society's stratification system. Gender is thus both ascribed and achieved (West and Zimmerman 1987). . . .

For human beings there is no essential femaleness or maleness, femininity or masculinity, womanhood or manhood, but once gender is ascribed, the social order constructs and holds individuals to strongly gendered norms and expectations. Individuals may vary on many of the components of gender and may shift genders temporarily or permanently, but they must fit into the limited number of gender statuses their society recognizes. In the process, they re-create their society's version of women and men: "If we do gender appropriately, we simultaneously sustain, reproduce, and render legitimate the institutional arrangements. . . . If we fail to do gender appropriately, we as individuals—not the institutional arrangements—may be called to account (for our character, motives, and predispositions)" (West and Zimmerman 1987, 146).

The gendered practices of everyday life reproduce a society's view of how women and men should act (Bourdieu [1980] 1990). Gendered social arrangements are justified by religion and cultural productions and backed by law, but the most powerful means of sustaining the moral hegemony of the dominant gender ideology is that the process is made invisible; any possible alternatives are virtually unthinkable (Foucault 1972; Gramsci 1971).

For Society, Gender Means Difference

The pervasiveness of gender as a way of structuring social life demands that gender statuses be clearly differentiated. Varied talents, sexual preferences, identities, personalities, interests, and ways of interacting fragment the individual's bodily and social experiences. Nonetheless, these are organized in Western cultures into two and only two socially and legally recognized gender statuses, "man" and "woman."[1] In the social construction of gender, it does not matter what men and women actually do; it does not even matter if they do exactly the same thing. The social institution of gender insists only that what they do is *perceived* as different.

If men and women are doing the same tasks, they are usually spatially segregated to maintain gender separation, and often the tasks are given different job titles as well, such as executive secretary and administrative assistant (Reskin 1988). If the differences between women and men begin to blur, society's "sameness taboo" goes into action (G. Rubin 1975, 178). At a rock and roll dance at West Point in 1976, the year women were admitted to the prestigious military academy for the first time, the school's administrators "were reportedly perturbed by the sight of mirror-image couples dancing in short hair and dress gray trousers," and a rule was established that women cadets could dance at these events only if they wore skirts (Barkalow and Raab 1990, 53). Women recruits in the U.S. Marine Corps are required to wear makeup—at a minimum, lipstick and eye shadow—and they have to take classes in makeup, hair care, poise, and etiquette. This feminization is part of a deliberate policy of making them clearly distinguishable from men Marines. Christine Williams quotes a twenty-five-year-old woman drill instructor as saying: "A lot of the recruits who come here don't wear makeup; they're tomboyish or athletic. A lot of them have the preconceived idea that going into the military means they can still be a tomboy. They don't realize that you are a *Woman* Marine" (1989, 76–77).

If gender differences were genetic, physiological, or hormonal, gender bending and gender ambiguity would occur only in hermaphrodites, who are born with chromosomes and genitalia that are not clearly female or male. Since gender differences are socially constructed, all men and all women can enact the behavior of the other, because they know the other's social script: "'Man' and 'woman' are at once empty and overflowing categories. Empty because they have no ultimate, transcendental meaning.

Overflowing because even when they appear to be fixed, they still contain within them alternative, denied, or suppressed definitions." (J. W. Scott 1988, 49). . . .

Gender as Process, Stratification, and Structure

As a social institution, gender is a process of creating distinguishable social statuses for the assignment of rights and responsibilities. As part of a stratification system that ranks these statuses unequally, gender is a major building block in the social structures built on these unequal statuses.

As a *process,* gender creates the social differences that define "woman" and "man." In social interaction throughout their lives, individuals learn what is expected, see what is expected, act and react in expected ways, and thus simultaneously construct and maintain the gender order: "The very injunction to be a given gender takes place through discursive routes: to be a good mother, to be a heterosexually desirable object, to be a fit worker, in sum, to signify a multiplicity of guarantees in response to a variety of different demands all at once" (J. Butler 1990, 145). Members of a social group neither make up gender as they go along nor exactly replicate in rote fashion what was done before. In almost every encounter, human beings produce gender, behaving in the ways they learned were appropriate for their gender status, or resisting or rebelling against these norms. Resistance and rebellion have altered gender norms, but so far they have rarely eroded the statuses.

Gendered patterns of interaction acquire additional layers of gendered sexuality, parenting, and work behaviors in childhood, adolescence, and adulthood. Gendered norms and expectations are enforced through informal sanctions of gender-inappropriate behavior by peers and by formal punishment or threat of punishment by those in authority should behavior deviate too far from socially imposed standards for women and men.

Everyday gendered interactions build gender into the family, the work process, and other organizations and institutions, which in turn reinforce gender expectations for individuals.[2] Because gender is a process, there is room not only for modification and variation by individuals and small groups but also for institutionalized change (J. W. Scott 1988, 7).

As part of a *stratification* system, gender ranks men above women of the same race and class. Women and men could be different but equal. In practice, the process of creating difference depends to a great extent on differential evaluation. As Nancy Jay (1981) says: "That which is defined, separated out, isolated from all else is A and pure. Not-A is necessarily impure, a random catchall, to which nothing is external except A and the principle of order that separates it from Not-A" (45). From the individual's point of view, whichever gender is A, the other is Not-A; gender boundaries tell the individual who is like him or her, and all the rest are unlike. From society's point of view, however, one gender is usually the touchstone, the normal, the dominant, and the other is different, deviant, and subordinate. In Western society, "man" is A, "wo-man" is Not-A. (Consider what a society would be like where woman was A and man Not-A.)

The further dichotomization by race and class constructs the gradations of a heterogeneous society's stratification scheme. Thus, in the United States, white is A,

African American is Not-A; middle class is A, working class is Not-A, and "African-American women occupy a position whereby the inferior half of a series of these dichotomies converge" (P. H. Collins 1990, 70). The dominant categories are the hegemonic ideals, taken so for granted as the way things should be that white is not ordinarily thought of as a race, middle class as a class, or men as a gender. The characteristics of these categories define the Other as that which lacks the valuable qualities the dominants exhibit.

In a gender-stratified society, what men do is usually valued more highly than what women do because men do it, even when their activities are very similar or the same. In different regions of southern India, for example, harvesting rice is men's work, shared work, or women's work: "Wherever a task is done by women it is considered easy, and where it is done by [men] it is considered difficult" (Mencher 1988, 104). A gathering and hunting society's survival usually depends on the nuts, grubs, and small animals brought in by the women's foraging trips, but when the men's hunt is successful, it is the occasion for a celebration. Conversely, because they are the superior group, white men do not have to do the "dirty work," such as housework; the most inferior group does it, usually poor women of color (Palmer 1989). . . .

Societies vary in the extent of the inequality in social status of their women and men members, but where there is inequality, the status "woman" (and its attendant behavior and role allocations) is usually held in lesser esteem than the status "man." Since gender is also intertwined with a society's other constructed statuses of differential evaluation—race, religion, occupation, class, country of origin, and so on—men

and women members of the favored groups command more power, more prestige, and more property than the members of the disfavored groups. Within many social groups, however, men are advantaged over women. The more economic resources, such as education and job opportunities, are available to a group, the more they tend to be monopolized by men. In poorer groups that have few resources (such as working-class African Americans in the United States), women and men are more nearly equal, and the women may even outstrip the men in education and occupational status (Almquist 1987).

As a *structure,* gender divides work in the home and in economic production, legitimates those in authority, and organizes sexuality and emotional life (Connell 1987, 91–142). As primary parents, women significantly influence children's psychological development and emotional attachments, in the process reproducing gender. Emergent sexuality is shaped by heterosexual, homosexual, bisexual, and sadomasochistic patterns that are gendered—different for girls and boys, and for women and men—so that sexual statuses reflect gender statuses.

When gender is a major component of structured inequality, the devalued genders have less power, prestige, and economic rewards than the valued genders. In countries that discourage gender discrimination, many major roles are still gendered; women still do most of the domestic labor and child rearing, even while doing full-time paid work; women and men are segregated on the job and each does work considered "appropriate"; women's work is usually paid less than men's work. Men dominate the positions of authority and leadership in government, the military, and the law; cultural productions, religions, and sports reflect men's interests.

In societies that create the greatest gender difference, such as Saudi Arabia, women are kept out of sight behind walls or veils, have no civil rights, and often create a cultural and emotional world of their own (Bernard 1981). But even in societies with less rigid gender boundaries, women and men spend much of their time with people of their own gender because of the way work and family are organized. This spatial separation of women and men reinforces gendered differentness, identity, and ways of thinking and behaving (Coser 1986).

Gender inequality—the devaluation of "women" and the social domination of "men"—has social functions and a social history. It is not the result of sex, procreation, physiology, anatomy, hormones, or genetic predispositions. It is produced and maintained by identifiable social processes and built into the general social structure and individual identities deliberately and purposefully. The social order as we know it in Western societies is organized around racial ethnic, class, and gender inequality. I contend, therefore, that the continuing purpose of gender as a modern social institution is to construct women as a group to be the subordinates of men as a group. The life of everyone placed in the status "woman" is "night to his day—that has forever been the fantasy. Black to his white. Shut out of his system's space, she is the repressed that ensures the system's functioning" (Cixous and Clément [1975] 1986, 67).

NOTES

1. Other societies recognize more than two categories, but usually no more than three or four (Jacobs and Roberts 1989).

2. On the "logic of practice," or how the experience of gender is embedded in the norms of everyday interaction and the structure of formal organizations, see Acker 1990; Bourdieu [1980] 1990; Connell 1987; Smith 1987.

BIBLIOGRAPHY

Acker, Joan. 1990. "Hierarchies, Jobs, and Bodies: A Theory of Gendered Organizations." *Gender and Society* 4: 139–58.

Almquist, Elizabeth M. 1987. "Labor Market Gendered Inequality in Minority Groups." *Gender and Society* 1:400–14.

Barkalow, Carol, with Andrea Raab. 1990. *In the Men's House.* New York, NY: Poseidon Press.

Bernard, Jessie. 1981. *The Female World.* New York, NY: Free Press.

Birdwhistell, Ray L. 1970. *Kinesics and Context: Essays on Body Motion Communication.* Philadelphia: University of Pennsylvania Press.

Bourdieu, Pierre. [1980] 1990. *The Logic of Practice.* Stanford, California: Stanford University Press.

Butler, Judith. 1990. *Gender Trouble: Feminism and the Subversion of Identity.* New York and London: Routledge.

Cixous, Hélène and Catherine Clément. [1975] 1986. *The Newly Born Woman,* translated by Betsy Wing. Minneapolis: University of Minnesota Press.

Collins, Patricia Hill. 1990. *Black Feminist Thought: Knowledge, Consciousness, and the Politics of Empowerment.* Boston: Unwin Hyman.

Connell, R. W. 1987. *Gender and Power: Society, the Person, and Sexual Politics.* Stanford, California: Stanford University Press.

Coser, Rose Laub. 1986. "Cognitive Structure and the Use of Social Space." *Sociological Forum* 1:1–26.

De Beauvoir, Simone. 1953. *The Second Sex,* translated by H. M. Parshley. New York, NY: Knopf.

Foucault, Michel. 1972. *The Archeology of Knowledge and the Discourse on Language,* translated by A. M. Sheridan Smith. New York, NY: Pantheon.

Gramsci, Antonio. 1971. *Selections from the Prison Notebooks,* translated and edited by

Quintin Hoare and Geoffrey Nowell Smith. New York, NY: International Publishers.

Jacobs, Sue-Ellen and Christine Roberts. 1989. "Sex, Sexuality, Gender, and Gender Variance." In *Gender Anthropology,* edited by Sandra Morgen. Washington, DC: American Anthropological Association.

Jay, Nancy. 1981. "Gender and Dichotomy." *Feminist Studies* 7: 38–56.

Mencher, Joan. 1988. "Women's Work and Poverty: Women's Contribution to Household Maintenance in South India. In *A Home Divided: Women and Income in the Third World,* edited by Daisy Dwyer and Judith Bruce. Stanford, CA: Stanford University Press.

Palmer, Phyllis. 1989. *Domesticity and Dirt: Housewives and Domestic Servants in the United States, 1920–1945.* Philadelphia: Temple University Press.

Reskin, Barbara F. 1988. "Bringing the Men Back In: Sex Differentiation and the Devaluation of Women's Work." *Gender and Society* 2:58–81.

Rubin, Gayle. 1975. "The Traffic in Women: Notes on the Political Economy of Sex." In *Toward an Anthropology of Women,* edited by Rayna R. Reiter. New York, NY: Monthly Review Press.

Scott, Joan Wallach. 1988. *Gender and the Politics of History.* New York, NY: Columbia University Press.

Smith, Dorothy. 1987. *The Everyday World as Problematic: A Feminist Sociology.* Toronto: University of Toronto Press.

West, Candace and Don Zimmerman. 1987. "Doing Gender." *Gender and Society* 1:125–51.

Williams, Christine L. 1989. *Gender Differences at Work: Women and Men in Nontraditional Occupations.* Berkeley, CA: University of California Press.

33

The Time Bind

When Work Becomes Home and Home Becomes Work

ARLIE RUSSELL HOCHSCHILD

The Waving Window

It is 6:45 A.M. on a fine June day in the midwestern town of Spotted Deer. At a childcare center in the basement of the Baptist church, Diane Caselli, a childcare worker in blue jeans and loose shirt, methodically turns over small upended chairs that rest on a Lilliputian breakfast table. She sets out small bowls, spoons, napkins, and a pitcher of milk around a commanding box of Cheerios. The room is cheerful, clean, half-asleep. Diane moves slowly past neatly shelved puzzles and toys, a hat rack hung with floppy, donated dress-up hats and droopy pocketbooks, a tub filled with bits of colored paper. Paintings of swerving trains and tipsy houses are taped to the wall.

At seven, a tall, awkward-looking man peers hesitantly into the room, then ventures a few steps forward looking for Diane. His son Timmy tromps in behind him. Diane walks over, takes Timmy's hand, and leads him to the breakfast table, where she seats him and helps him pour cereal and

milk into his bowl. Timmy's dad, meanwhile, hurries toward the door.

One wall of the room has four large windows that overlook a sidewalk. In front of the second window is a set of small wooden steps children climb to wave good-bye to their departing parents. It's called "the waving window." Timmy dashes from the breakfast table, climbs up the wooden steps, and waits.

His dad, an engineer, briskly strides past the first window toward his red Volvo parked down the street. He stops for a moment in front of the waving window, tilts his head, eyebrows lifted clownishly, then walks on without a backward glance. Timmy returns to his cereal, sighs, and declares excitedly, "My Dad sawed me wave!". . .

At 7:40 A.M., four-year-old Cassie sidles in, her hair half-combed, a blanket in one hand, a fudge bar in the other. "I'm late," her mother explains to Diane. "Cassie wanted the fudge bar so bad, I gave it to her," she adds apologetically—though Diane has said nothing. Gwen Bell is a

Arlie Russell Hochschild, *The Time Bind: When Work Becomes Home and Home Becomes Work,* pp. 3–5, 11–14. Copyright © 1997 by Arlie Russell Hochschild. Arlie Russell Hochschild, "Time in the Balance," *The Nation,* May 26, 1997, pp. 11–12.

284

sturdy young woman, with short-cropped dark hair. Lightly made up and minimally adorned with gold stud earrings, she is neatly dressed in khaki slacks and jacket. Some Amerco mothers don business suits as soldiers don armor while a few wear floral dresses suggesting festivity and leisure. But Cassie's mother is dressed in a neutral way, as if she were just getting the job of self-presentation done.

"Pleeese, can't you take me with you?" Cassie pleads.

"You know I can't take you to work," Gwen replies in a tone that suggests she's heard this request before. Cassie's shoulders droop in defeat. She's given it a try, but now she's resigned to her mother's imminent departure, and she's agreed, it seems, not to make too much fuss about it. Aware of her mother's unease about her long day at childcare, however, she's struck a hard bargain. Every so often she gets a morning fudge bar. This is their deal, and Cassie keeps her mother to it. As Gwen Bell later explained to me, she continually feels that she owes Cassie more time than she actually gives her. She has a time-debt to her daughter. If many busy parents settle such debts on evenings or weekends when their children eagerly "collect" promised time, Cassie insists on a morning down payment, a fudge bar that makes her mother uneasy but saves her the trouble and embarrassment of a tantrum. Like other parents at the center, Gwen sometimes finds herself indulging her child with treats or softened rules in exchange for missed time together. Diane speaks quietly to Cassie, trying to persuade her to stop sulking and join the others.

The center works on "child time." Its rhythms are child-paced, flexible, mainly slow. Teachers patiently oversee the laborious task of tying a shoelace, a prolonged sit on the potty, the scrambled telling of a tall tale. In this and other ways it is an excellent childcare center, one of a dozen islands of child time I was to discover in my three summers of field research at Amerco, a Fortune 500 company headquartered in Spotted Deer.[1] Scattered throughout the town, such islands—a playground, a pediatrician's waiting room, the back of a family van—stand out against the faster paced, more bureaucratically segmented blocks of adult work time. . . .

At the Spotted Deer Childcare Center, the group of young breakfasters gradually expands, early arrivals watching the entertainment provided by yet more newcomers. Sally enters sucking her thumb. Billy's mother carries him in even though he's already five. Jonathan's mother forgets to wave, and soon after, Jonathan kicks the breakfast table from below, causing milk to spill and children to yell. Marie ushers him away to dictate a note to his mother explaining that it hurts his feelings when she doesn't wave.

Cassie still stands at the front door holding her fudge bar like a flag, the emblem of a truce in a battle over time. Every now and then, she licks one of its drippy sides while Diane, uncertain about what to do, looks on disapprovingly. The cereal eaters watch from their table, fascinated and envious. Gwen Bell turns to leave, waving goodbye to Cassie, car keys in hand. By our prior arrangement, I am her shadow for this day, and I follow her out the door and into the world of Amerco.

Arriving at her office, as always, exactly at 7:50 A.M., Gwen finds on her desk a cup of coffee in her personal mug, milk no sugar (exactly as she likes it), prepared by a coworker who has managed to get in ahead of her. The remaining half of a birthday cake has been left on a table in the hall outside her office by a dieting coworker who wants someone else to eat it before she does. Gwen prepares materials for her first meeting (having e-mailed messages to the other participants from home the previous night), which will inaugurate her official 8 A.M. to 5:45 P.M. workday. As she does so, she nibbles at a sliver of the cake while she proofreads a memo that must be Xeroxed and handed out at a second meeting scheduled for 9 A.M.

As the assistant to the head of the Public Relations Office, Gwen has to handle Amerco's responses to any press reports that may appear about the company. This time the impending media attention is positive, and her first meeting has been called to discuss how to make the most of it. As the members of the publicity team straggle into her office and exchange friendly greetings, she sighs. She's ready.

Gwen loves her job at Amerco, and she is very good at it. Whatever the daily pressures, she also feels remarkably at home there. Her boss, a man who she says reminds her of the best aspects of her father, helps her deal with work problems and strongly supports her desire to rise in the company. In many ways, her "Amerco dad" has been better to her than her own father, who, when she was small, abruptly walked out on her mother and her. She feels lucky to have such a caring boss, and working for him has reinforced her desire to give her all to work—insofar as she can. She and her husband need her salary, she tells me, since his job, though more lucrative than hers, is less steady.

Gradually, over the last three years Gwen's workday has grown longer. She used to work a straight eight-hour day.

Now it is regularly eight and a half to nine hours, not counting the work that often spills over into life at home. Gwen is not happy about this. She feels Cassie's ten-hour day at Spotted Deer is too long, but at the same time she is not putting energy into curbing her expanding workday. What she does do is complain about it, joke about it, compare stories with friends at work. Hers are not the boastful "war stories" of the older men at Amerco who proudly proclaim their ten-hour workdays and biweekly company travel schedules. Rather, Gwen's stories are more like situation comedies: stories about forgetting to shop and coming home to a refrigerator containing little more than wilted lettuce and a jar of olives, stories told in a spirit of hopeless amusement. Gwen is reasonably well informed about Amerco's flextime and reduced-hours policies, which are available to white-collar employees like her. But she has not talked with her boss about cutting back her hours, nor have her joking coworkers, and her boss hasn't raised the possibility himself. There is just so much to get done at the office.

At 5:45 P.M. on the dot, Gwen arrives back at Spotted Deer. Cassie is waiting eagerly by the door, her coat over her arm, a crumpled picture she has drawn in her hand. Gwen gives Cassie a long, affectionate hug. By the time Gwen and Cassie roll into the driveway of their two-story white frame house, surrounded by a border of unruly shrubs, it is 6:25 P.M. John Bell is already there, having shopped, taken the messages off the phone machine, set the table, and heated the oven. This is one of two days a week he leaves home and returns earlier than his wife. He has eaten an ample lunch, knowing that they usually have a late, light dinner, but this evening he's hungrier than he means to be. He plays with Cassie while Gwen makes dinner.

To protect the dinner "hour"—8:00 to 8:30—Gwen checks that the phone machine is on, and we hear a series of abbreviated rings several times during dinner. John says grace, and we all hold hands. It is time, it seems, to let go and relax. Right after dinner, though, it's Cassie's bath time. Cassie both loves and protests her nightly bath. Gwen has come to expect Cassie to dawdle as she undresses or searches for a favorite bath toy, trying to make a minivacation of it. Gwen lets Cassie linger, scans through her phone messages, and sets them aside.

At 9 P.M., the bath over, Gwen and Cassie have "quality time" or "QT," as John affectionately calls it. This they see as their small castle of time protected from the demands of the outside world. Half an hour later, at 9:30 P.M., Gwen tucks Cassie into bed.

Later, as Gwen and John show me around their home, John points out in passing an expensive electric saw and drill set he bought two years earlier with the thought of building a tree house for Cassie, a bigger hutch for her rabbit Max, and a guest room for visiting friends. "I have the tools," John confides. "I just don't have the time to use them." Once, those tools must have represented the promise of future projects. Now they seemed to be there in place of the projects. Along with the tools, perhaps John has tried to purchase the illusion of leisure they seemed to imply. Later, as I interviewed other working parents at Amerco, I discovered similar items banished to attics and garages. Timmy's father had bought a boat he hadn't sailed all year. Jarod and Tylor's parents had a camper truck they had hardly driven. Others had cameras, skis, guitars, encyclopedia sets,

even the equipment to harvest maple syrup, all bought with wages that took time to earn.

John's tools seemed to hold out the promise of another self, a self he would be "if only I had time." His tools had become for him what Cassie's fudge bar was for her—a magical substitute for time, a talisman.

There were, in a sense, two Bell households: the rushed family they actually were and the relaxed family they imagined they could be if only they had time. Gwen and Bill complained that they were in a time bind: they wanted more time for life at home than they had. It wasn't that they wanted more small segments of "quality time" added into their over-busy days. They wanted a quality life, and Gwen, at least, worked for a family-friendly company whose policies seemed to hold out hope for just that. So what was preventing them from getting it?

Time in the Balance

We've gotten ourselves into a time bind. Feeling that we are always late, having no free time, trying to adapt as best we can to the confines of our time prisons—these are all symptoms of what has become a national way of life. There are several reasons for this. Over the past two decades, global competition and inflation have lowered the buying power of the male wage. In response, many women have gone to work in order to maintain the family income. But the legacy of patriarchy has given cultural shape to this economic story. As women have joined men at work, they have absorbed the views of an older, male-oriented work world—its views of "an honest day's work"—at a much faster rate than men have absorbed their share of domestic work and culture. One reason women have changed more than men is that the world of "male" work seems more honorable and valuable than the "female" world of home and children.

There is another factor too—we are increasingly anxious about our "culture of care." Where do we turn when we are down and out? This is a question we ask, understandably, even when we are up and in. With recent welfare "reform," the government is cutting off aid to women and the poor. With the growth of the benefit-less contingency labor force, many corporations are doing the same thing to middle-class men. Meanwhile, modern families have grown more ambiguous: It's a little less clear than it once was who's supposed to take care of whom, how much and for how long. So we've grown more anxious. Given our tradition of individualism, many of us feel alone in this anxiety, and insofar as work is our rock, we cling to it.

In this context, the idea of cutting back the workday is an idea that seems to have died, gone to heaven and become an angel of an idea. We dream about it, but it's something we'd never really expect to do. No matter how a movement for work-family balance is structured, in the long run, no such balance will ever take hold if the social conditions that would make it possible— men who are willing to share parenting and housework, supportive communities, and policy-makers and elected officials who are prepared to demand family-friendly reforms—remain out of reach. . . .

As my study of Amerco has shown, however, even when the jobs of working parents are secure, pay a sufficient wage and provide family-friendly programs, many working parents are still reluctant to spend more time at home. American fathers spend less time at home than mothers do, expand their work hours when children are small and, if Amerco is any indication, are reluctant to take paternity leaves. We know from previous research that many men have found a haven at work. This isn't news. The news is that growing numbers of working women are leery of spending more time at home as well. They feel guilty and stressed out by long hours at work, but they feel ambivalent about cutting back on those hours.

Women fear losing their place at work; having such a place has become a source of security, pride and a powerful sense of being valued. As a survey conducted by Bright Horizons (a Boston-based company that runs on-site daycare centers in twenty-three states) indicates, women are just as likely to feel appreciated as men at the workplace; as likely as men to feel underappreciated at home; and even more likely than men to have friends at work. To cut back on work hours means risking loosening ties to a world that, tension-filled as it is, offers insurance against even greater tension and uncertainty at home. For a substantial number of time-bound working parents, the stripped-down home and the community-denuded neighborhood are simply losing out to the pull of the workplace.

Many women are thus joining men in a flight from the "inner city" of home to the "suburbs" of the workplace. In doing so, they have absorbed the views of an older, male-oriented work world about what a "real career" and "full commitment to the job" really mean. Women now make up nearly half the labor force. The vast majority of them need and want to be there. There is definitely no going back. But women have entered the workplace on "male" terms. It would be less problematic for women to adopt a male model of work—to finally enjoy privileges formerly reserved for men—if the male model of work were one of balance. But it is not.

All this is unsettling news, in part because the children of working parents are being left to adjust to or resist the time bind—and all of its attendant consequences—more or less on their own. It is unsettling because while children remain precious to their parents, the "market value" of the world in which they are growing up has declined drastically. One need not compare their childhoods with a perfect childhood in a mythical past to conclude that our society needs to face up to a serious problem.

NOTE

1. To protect the privacy of the people in this chapter, I have given the company a fictional name and declined to specify what its workers produce or where they live. I've also altered the names, occupations, and defining details of the personal lives of individuals. I have, however, tried to document as accurately as possible their experiences of life at home and at work and to capture the essence of the culture that infuses both worlds.

34

The Opt-Out Revolution

LISA BELKIN

The scene in this cozy Atlanta living room would—at first glance—warm an early feminist's heart. Gathered by the fireplace one recent evening, sipping wine and nibbling cheese, are the members of a book club, each of them a beneficiary of all that feminists of 30-odd years ago held dear.

The eight women in the room have each earned a degree from Princeton, which was a citadel of everything male until the first co-educated class entered in 1969. And after Princeton, the women of this book club went on to do other things that women once were not expected to do. They received law degrees from Harvard and Columbia. They chose husbands who could keep up with them, not simply support them. They waited to have children because work was too exciting. They put on power suits and marched off to take on the world.

Yes, if an early feminist could peer into this scene, she would feel triumphant about the future. Until, of course, any one of these polished and purposeful women opened her mouth.

"I don't want to be on the fast track leading to a partnership at a prestigious law firm," says Katherine Brokaw, who left that track in order to stay home with her three children. "Some people define that as success. I don't."

"I don't want to be famous; I don't want to conquer the world; I don't want that kind of life," says Sarah McArthur Amsbary, who was a theater artist and teacher and earned her master's degree in English, then stepped out of the work force when her daughter was born. "Maternity provides an escape hatch that paternity does not. Having a baby provides a graceful and convenient exit."

Wander into any Starbucks in any Starbucks kind of neighborhood in the hours after the commuters are gone. See all those mothers drinking coffee and watching over toddlers at play? If you look past the Lycra gym clothes and the Internet-access cell phones, the scene could be the '50s, but for the fact that the coffee is more expensive and the mothers have M.B.A.s. . . .

Arguably, the barriers of 40 years ago are down. Fifty percent of the undergraduate class of 2003 at Yale was female; this year's graduating class at Berkeley Law School

Lisa Belkin. "The Opt-Out Revolution," *The New York Times Magazine* (October 26, 2003, Section 6), pp. 42, 44–46, 85–86.

was 63 percent women; Harvard was 46 percent; Columbia was 51. Nearly 47 percent of medical students are women, as are 50 percent of undergraduate business majors (though, interestingly, about 30 percent of M.B.A. candidates). They are recruited by top firms in all fields. They start strong out of the gate.

And then, suddenly, they stop. Despite all those women graduating from law school, they comprise only 16 percent of partners in law firms. Although men and women enter corporate training programs in equal numbers, just 16 percent of corporate officers are women, and only eight companies in the Fortune 500 have female C.E.O.s. Of 435 members of the House of Representatives, 62 are women; there are 14 women in the 100-member Senate.

Measured against the way things once were, this is certainly progress. But measured against the way things were expected to be, this is a revolution stalled. During the '90s, the talk was about the glass ceiling, about women who were turned away at the threshold of power simply because they were women. The talk of this new decade is less about the obstacles faced by women than it is about the obstacles faced by mothers. As Joan C. Williams, director of the Program on WorkLife Law at American University, wrote in the *Harvard Women's Law Journal* last spring, "Many women never get near" that glass ceiling, because "they are stopped long before by the maternal wall."

Look, for example, at the Stanford class of '81. Fifty-seven percent of mothers in that class spent at least a year at home caring for their infant children in the first decade after graduation. One out of four have stayed home three or more years. Look at Harvard Business School. A survey of

women from the classes of 1981, 1985 and 1991 found that only 38 percent were working full time. Look at professional women in surveys across the board. Between one-quarter and one-third are out of the work force, depending on the study and the profession. Look at the United States Census, which shows that the number of children being cared for by stay-at-home moms has increased nearly 13 percent in less than a decade. At the same time, the percentage of new mothers who go back to work fell from 59 percent in 1998 to 55 percent in 2000.

Look, too, at the mothers who have not left completely but have scaled down or redefined their roles in the crucial career-building years (25 to 44). Two-thirds of those mothers work fewer than 40 hours a week—in other words, part time. Only 5 percent work 50 or more hours weekly. Women leave the workplace to strike out on their own at equally telling rates; the number of businesses owned or co-owned by women jumped 11 percent since 1997, nearly twice the rate of businesses in general.

Look at how all these numbers compare with those of men. Of white men with M.B.A.'s, 95 percent are working full time, but for white women with M.B.A.'s, that number drops to 67 percent. (Interestingly, the numbers for African-American women are closer to those for white men than to those for white women.)

And look at the women of this Atlanta book club. A roomful of Princeton women each trained as well as any man. Of the 10 members, half are not working at all; one is in business with her husband; one works part time; two freelance; and the only one with a full-time job has no children.

Social scientists—most of them women— have made a specialty in recent years of

studying why all this is so. Joan Williams
("Unbending Gender"), Sylvia Ann Hewlett
("Creating a Life"), Arlie Russell Hochschild
(who coined the phrase "the second shift")
and Felice N. Schwartz (who made popular
the phrase "the mommy track"), to name
just a few, have done important work about
how the workplace has failed women.

But to talk to the women of the book
club—or to the women of a San Francisco
mothers' group with whom I also spent
time, or the dozens of other women I interviewed, or the countless women I have
come to know during the four years I have
reported on the intersection of life and
work—is to sense that something more is
happening here. It's not just that the workplace has failed women. It is also that
women are rejecting the workplace. . . .

As these women look up at the "top,"
they are increasingly deciding that they
don't want to do what it takes to get there.
Women today have the equal right to make
the same bargain that men have made for
centuries—to take time from their family
in pursuit of success. Instead, women are
redefining success. And in doing so, they
are redefining work.

Time was when a woman's definition of
success was said to be her apple-pie recipe.
Or her husband's promotion. Or her well-
turned-out children. Next, being successful
required becoming a man. Remember those
awful padded-shoulder suits and floppy
ties? Success was about the male definition
of money and power.

There is nothing wrong with money or
power. But they come at a high price. And
lately when women talk about success
they use words like satisfaction, balance
and sanity.

That's why a recent survey by the research firm Catalyst found that 26 percent

of women at the cusp of the most senior
levels of management don't want the promotion. And it's why *Fortune* magazine
found that of the 108 women who have appeared on its list of the top 50 most powerful women over the years, at least 20 have
chosen to leave their high-powered jobs,
most voluntarily, for lives that are less intense and more fulfilling.

It's why President Bush's adviser Karen
Hughes left the White House, saying her
family was homesick and wanted to go
back to Austin. It's why Brenda C. Barnes,
who was the president and C.E.O. of Pepsi-
Cola North America, left that job to move
back to Illinois with her family. And it's
why Wendy Chamberlin, who was ambas-
sador to Pakistan, resigned, because security
concerns meant she never saw her two
young daughters.

Why don't women run the world?

Maybe it's because they don't want to.

Attitudes cluster in place and time. This
is particularly true of a college campus,
where one-quarter of the student population turns over every year. Undergraduates
tend to think that the school they find is
the one that always was, with no knowledge
of the worldview of those even a few short
years before. Looked at that way, the
women of the Atlanta book club are a
panoramic snapshot of change.

Sally Sears, the oldest of the group, entered Princeton in the fall of 1971. Women
had been fully admitted two years earlier,
and the school was still very much a boys
club. Sears had gone to a small public
school in Alabama and entered college
"very conscious of being a representative of
women and a representative of the South."
As she describes it the air was electric with
feminism. "Margaret Mead came to talk
one night, and I was stunned by how pene-

trating her questions were about what it was like to be the first women," she says. "I thought, my God, she's thinking of us as Samoans."

Upon graduation in 1975, Sears felt both entitled and obligated to make good. "The clear message was, 'You've been given the key to a kingdom that used to be denied to people like you,'" she says. "It never occurred to me that my choices would be proscribed. I could have anything I wanted."

What she wanted, at first, was to be "a confirmed single person, childless, a world traveler." She spent a couple of years running *The Childersburg Star*, a small Alabama newspaper owned by her family, and then, in 1978, she took a job on the air at a television station in Birmingham. That led to a job in Memphis, followed by a year-long trip around the world, then another TV job in Dallas. By 1984 she was on the air in Atlanta, where she became a local celebrity and where she met Richard Belcher, a fellow reporter and now a local anchor. They were married in 1988, when Sears was 35.

Three years later, their son, Will, was born. Soldiers of feminism take only the shortest of maternity leaves, and as soon as Sears recovered from her C-section she was back at work. The O.J. Simpson trial was the first real test of what she calls "work plus love plus a child," because both she and her husband were sent out to California for the duration. "I got my mom and dad to bring Will out, and we all camped out at the New Otani Hotel for a few weeks," she says. "I was determined not to blink.". . .

Sears took nine years to quit. And she did so with great regret. "I would have hung in there, except the days kept getting longer and longer," she explains. "My five-day 50-hour week was becoming a 60-hour

week." As news reports could be transmitted farther and farther from the "mother ship," she found herself an hour or two from home when the nightly news was done. "Will was growing up, and I was driving home from a fire," she says. "I knew there would always be wrecks and fires, but there wouldn't always be his childhood."

First she tried to reduce her schedule. "The station would not give me a part-time contract," she says. "They said it was all or nothing." So in August 2000, she walked away from her six-figure income and became a homeroom mom at her son's school.

"It was wrenching for me to leave Channel 2," she says. "I miss being the lioness in the newsroom—to walk through and have the interns say, 'There she goes.' It kills me that I'm not contributing to my 401(k) anymore. I do feel somehow that I let the cause down.". . .

Sarah McArthur Amsbary of the Atlanta group leads a much-examined life. Back in college, she says, she gave no thought to melding life and work, but now, "I think about it almost constantly."

And what she has concluded, after all this thinking, is that the exodus of professional women from the workplace isn't really about motherhood at all. It is really about work. "There's a misconception that it's mostly a pull toward motherhood and her precious baby that drives a woman to quit her job, or apparently, her entire career," she says. "Not that the precious baby doesn't magnetize many of us. Mine certainly did. As often as not, though, a woman would have loved to maintain some version of a career, but that job wasn't cutting it anymore. Among women I know, quitting is driven as much from the job-dissatisfaction side as from the pull-to-motherhood side."

She compares all this to a romance gone sour. "Timing one's quitting to coincide with a baby is like timing a breakup to coincide with graduation," she says. "It's just a whole lot easier than breaking up in the middle of senior year."

That is the gift biology gives women, she says. It provides pauses, in the form of pregnancy and childbirth, that men do not have. And as the workplace becomes more stressful and all-consuming, the exit door is more attractive. "Women get to look around every few years and say, 'Is this still what I want to be doing?'" she says. "Maybe they have higher standards for job satisfaction because there is always the option of being their child's primary caregiver. When a man gets that dissatisfied with his job, he has to stick it out."

This, I would argue, is why the workplace needs women. Not just because they are 50 percent of the talent pool, but for the very fact that they are more willing to leave than men. That, in turn, makes employers work harder to keep them. It is why the accounting firm Deloitte & Touche has more than doubled the number of employees on flexible work schedules over the past decade and more than quintupled the number of female partners and directors (to 567, from 97) in the same period. It is why

I.B.M. employees can request up to 156 weeks of job-protected family time off. It is why Hamot Medical Center in Erie, Pa., hired a husband and wife to fill one neonatology job, with a shared salary and shared health insurance, then let them decide who stays home and who comes to the hospital on any given day. It is why, everywhere you look, workers are doing their work in untraditional ways.

Women started this conversation about life and work—a conversation that is slowly coming to include men. Sanity, balance and a new definition of success, it seems, just might be contagious. And instead of women being forced to act like men, men are being freed to act like women. Because women are willing to leave, men are more willing to leave, too—the number of married men who are full-time caregivers to their children has increased 18 percent. Because women are willing to leave, 46 percent of the employees taking parental leave at Ernst & Young last year were men.

Looked at that way, this is not the failure of a revolution, but the start of a new one. It is about a door opened but a crack by women that could usher in a new environment for us all.

Why don't women run the world?

"In a way," Amsbary says, "we really do."

35

The Time Divide
Work, Family, and Gender Inequality

JERRY A. JACOBS
KATHLEEN GERSON

As families diversify and workers face new challenges, people feel increasingly torn between their public and private worlds. Whether they are working more or less, workers confront new pressures and dilemmas as they attempt to cope with the conflicts that inevitably arise between family and work. These conflicts are real and growing. Yet it remains unclear whether they stem from workers' preferences to spend more time at work or, alternatively, from a growing gap between what workers prefer and what they feel they must do.

Some have argued that the emergence of time binds reflects a widespread cultural shift in which workers increasingly look to work as an escape from the complexities of contemporary family life. From this perspective, workers' preferences are at the heart of changes at work and at home. Arlie Hochschild's study of Amerco, a fictionally named American company, shows in illuminating and powerful detail how some workers cope with complexities at home by spending more time at work (Hochschild 1997). The average employee at Amerco,

however, works nearly one day per week more than the average American worker. This makes Amerco a great place to study the coping strategies of overworked parents, but it is not an ideal vantage point from which to generalize about overall trends in labor force behavior and cultural changes in America. Nearly all the vignettes presented by Hochschild describe workers who put in fifty or more hours per week, from the sixty-hour-per-week executive to the "over-time hound" assembly-line worker. This is an important and growing segment of the labor force, but it does not represent the average worker.

To reach broad conclusions about general cultural, structural, and individual change, we need a broader look at workers in a range of work settings. How are workers' experiences embedded in larger social and economic forces, and how do workers' options and perceptions vary with their circumstances?. . .

Changes in family structure have transformed the lives of workers in several ways. As men have faced stagnant wages and women have become increasingly committed to work outside the home, most households

---

Jerry A. Jacobs and Kathleen Gerson. *The Time Divide: Work, Family, and Gender Inequality,* pp. 60–65, 67–69, 71–73, 76–77, 223. Copyright © 2004 by the President and Fellows of Harvard College.

now rely on women's earnings. These economic transformations have fueled women's need and desire for secure, well-paying jobs and left dual-earner and single-parent households to cope without an unpaid worker at home. Women are thus likely to prefer good jobs with reasonable hours, and fathers who share breadwinning responsibilities with an employed partner also need flexible hours and some measure of control at work.

These profound changes in the private lives of women and men are thus generating changes in worker preferences that may not fit with the supply of jobs. While people face new needs for balance and flexibility in their working lives, employers have good reasons to offer jobs with either long or short workweeks. This forces workers to choose between time and income—a difficult decision that clashes with the exigencies of the new family economy.

Ideal versus Actual Working Hours

If changes in the shape and character of the labor force are clashing with economic forces that influence the structure of jobs, workers are indeed likely to feel caught in the conflict. This clash between job demands and private needs can take several forms. Many may feel compelled to work more than they would wish, while others are likely to wish to work more than they are able. As workers' circumstances vary, so do the kinds of time binds workers experience. Yet so many now face family time squeezes that those who desire to put in less time at work are likely to outnumber those who wish to work more.

The 1997 Changing Workforce survey (Bond, Galinsky, and Swanberg 1998) provides a wide array of information about workers' actual and preferred commitments to work, family, and personal pursuits, which makes it possible to examine the contours and causes of actual and ideal working time. This survey is distinctive in terms of the range of questions asked regarding workers' values and preferences and in its focus on the links, tensions, and conflicts between work and family. People were asked how many hours per week they usually worked at their principal job and also at any additional jobs they held. They were also asked: "Ideally, how many hours, in total, would you like to work each week?" Thus, because people were asked about their ideal as well as their actual working hours, we can examine whether their overall level of work reflects their desires. We can also ascertain whether variation in preferences across groups of workers corresponds to variations in actual work levels.

Comparing people's actual and ideal hours also makes it possible to measure the difference between a worker's usual time on all jobs and his or her ideal working time. Table 35.1, which compares ideal hours to total hours worked for employed women and men, demonstrates that most American workers experience a significant gap between how much they work and how much they would like to work. One fifth said that their actual and ideal hours correspond precisely; but fully three in five felt that their usual workweek was longer than their ideal hours, and an additional one in five preferred to work more than they currently do. (The unemployed should be added to this group of underworked Americans, but the Changing Workforce survey only includes the currently employed.)

The vast majority of those who preferred fewer working hours wished to work at

Table 35.1   Comparison of Total Hours Worked and Ideal Hours, by Gender

	Men	*Women*
Total hours usually worked (all jobs)	47.3	41.4
Ideal hours	37.5	32.1
Difference (actual – ideal)	9.8	9.3
Percent wanting to work less	60.2	60.1
Percent ideal equals actual	20.5	21.4
Percent wanting to work more	19.3	18.5
Percent wanting to work at least 5 hours less	58.4	58.6
Percent wanting to work at least 10 hours less	47.4	48.8
Percent wanting to work at least 20 hours less	28.3	27.9

Source: National Study of the Changing Workforce, 1997.

Note: All percentages are of total male and female samples, respectively. Thus, 60.2% of men reported wanting to work less; 58.4% of the total wanted to work at least 5 hours less. In other words, the great majority (58.4% over 60.2%) of those men who reported wanting to work less reported at least a 5-hour gap between their actual and ideal working hours.

least 5 hours less per week. Nearly half (over 47 percent of both men and women) wished to work 10 hours less per week, and over one quarter wanted to work at least 20 hours less.

While women work an average of about 6 fewer hours per week than men, the difference between their actual and ideal hours is quite similar. Women and men wished to work less by approximately the same amount. Men preferred to work 9.8 fewer hours, compared to 9.3 fewer hours for women (a difference that is not statistically significant). If both groups were able to realize their wishes, the gender gap in hours worked—which, at about 6 hours per week, is not large—would probably not change significantly.

Whether or not contemporary Americans are actually working more than earlier generations, the majority seem to *feel* overworked—at least compared to their ideals. Excessively long workweeks certainly do not emerge as ideal or an aspiration. But neither are short workweeks desirable to those who wish to work more. . . .

Occupational Position

Professional, managerial, and technical workers are most likely to feel overworked (Table 35.2). Women in these positions would prefer to work 13 hours less than they do, while women in other occupations want to work about 7 fewer hours. Male professionals want to work just under 12 hours less, while their counterparts in other occupational categories wish to work about 9 hours less. And while professionals and managers tend to put in longer workweeks than others, their *ideal* work schedules are not longer. Men who are professionals and managers wish to work about the same amount of time as other male workers. Women professionals and managers prefer to work about 2 hours less per week but actually work 4 hours more than women in other occupations.

Occupational position is a key factor in shaping the needs and desires of both men and women. Despite the persistent view that female professionals are less committed to work than their male counterparts,

Table 35.2   Total Hours Worked and Ideal Hours, by Occupation, Marital Status, and Gender

	Men			Women		
	Total Hours	*Ideal Hours*	*Difference*	*Total Hours*	*Ideal Hours*	*Difference*
Occupation						
Managerial, professional, and technical	48.9	37.3	11.6	43.9	30.9	13.0
Other	46.4	37.7	8.7	39.6	33.0	6.6
Marital Status						
Married (or living with partner)	48.2	37.8	10.4	40.9	30.8	10.1
Not currently married	45.7	37.1	8.6	42.0	33.8	8.2
Married, employed spouse	48.1	38.2	9.9	41.4	30.4	11.0
Married, nonemployed spouse	48.3	37.3	11.0	38.5	32.8	5.7
Children						
With children under six	49.3	38.9	10.4	39.4	30.0	9.4
Without children under six	46.8	37.3	9.5	41.8	32.5	9.3

Source: National Study of the Changing Workforce, 1997.

workers of both sexes appear to be looking for a reasonable balance between paid work and other pursuits. Those who put in long hours, regardless of gender, would like to cut back, while those who face shortened workweeks would like to work more. The most highly educated and well remunerated professionals and managers face the greatest demands to put in many hours at work. Rather than insulating one from overwork, well-paid jobs that offer advancement may actually increase the pressures to work more as well as the penalties for working less.

It could be argued that since those with the highest levels of education and income are working as much as, if not more than, other employees, these choices simply reflect a reasonable preference to enhance financial and career opportunities through hard work. Yet affluent workers, no less than other workers, face economic and other workplace constraints. Our analysis supports the widespread conviction and case histories presented elsewhere that exceptionally long workweeks are routinely required for career advancement, but not necessarily

desired by those who experience them (see, for example, Epstein et al. 1999).. . .

Marriage, Children, and Gender

The life course has grown increasingly fluid and unpredictable, and age may simply be too crude a measure to reveal the dynamics between personal circumstances and work constraints. Regardless of the age at which people choose to marry or have children, family commitments are almost certain to increase the need for domestic time. Marriage and parenthood should thus influence the gap between ideal and actual working time.

Gender also shapes the pressures and dilemmas of private life; marriage and especially parenthood are likely to affect women and men in different ways. Although men's participation in domestic work has increased in recent decades, women continue to bear a greater share of the load, especially when children arrive. And amid the growing strength of mothers' work commitments, fathers continue to face pressures to provide primary economic support for their families (see, for example, Gerson 1993). This means that, while both men and women are likely to feel torn between family and work, they are also likely to feel this conflict in different degrees and to respond in different ways.

Despite the growing convergence between women's and men's work commitments, they continue to face different pressures as parents. And though women and men express roughly equal desires to work fewer hours, a more complicated relationship emerges between gender and family situation in Table 35.2. First, married and single workers of both sexes differ in their ideal working hours. Married women work almost 1 hour less per week than women who are not married, but they would like to work 3 hours less. The gap between actual and ideal working time is thus 2 hours greater for married than for single women. Ideally, married women would prefer to work 10 hours less per week, while single women would prefer to work 8 hours less per week.

In contrast, married men work more than single men, by about 2.5 hours per week. Married and single men wish, however, to work about the same amount of time.[1] Married men thus experience a larger gap between actual and ideal hours (10 hours per week) than do single men (8 hours per week). For both women and men, married life adds to the feeling of being squeezed for time, but they have somewhat different reasons for feeling this way. Married men feel torn because they are spending more time on the job than single men. Married women are prone to cut back slightly in their working time, but would like to cut back more.

Within marriage, differences emerge among women living in different family situations, although they are not as large as might be expected. Women with employed husbands work about 3 hours per week less

than those few whose husbands do not work, but this small difference is not statistically significant. Women in dual-earner marriages want to work 30 hours per week instead of the 41 hours they actually work, creating a sizable gap of 11 hours per week. For those with husbands who are not employed, the gap is 6 hours (and, again, the difference between the two is not statistically significant).

Women with preschool children show a similar pattern. These women work 39 hours per week on average, but would prefer to work 30 hours per week, for a gap of 9 hours per week. For women without children under six, there is also a 9 hour per week differential, which is statistically indistinguishable from the gap for those with preschool children. Having preschool children and employed husbands thus shapes women's desired and actual working time, but does not create a dramatic change in the gap between the two.

Marriage and parenthood also influence men's actual and ideal working time but, as in the case of women, in only modest ways. Surprisingly, men whose wives are employed do not differ from those with non-employed partners in either actual or ideal working time. Having preschool children does increase the total number of hours worked per week for men, but it also increases their desired working time. The fathers of young children are thus likely to conclude that their family's financial needs require them to put in more time at work. And since actual working time increases by more than desired time, a higher proportion of these men want to work less.

To some extent, the modest gap in women's actual and ideal working time reflects the fact that they have already made strategic adjustments to avoid work-family conflict. After all, their average working hours are lower than men's at the outset. The larger pattern nevertheless suggests that family circumstances are as important as gender and that both mothers *and* fathers with young children want more time away from work than do other groups. Marriage clearly creates a context that pulls both women and men toward personal commitments outside of work. Yet we find little support for the oft-stated argument that married women with young children are the primary group wishing to work less. In fact, about half of married men and women across a range of family situations express such a desire. While some have argued that the arrival of children increases the number of hours that both mothers and fathers spend at the workplace, we find that women with small children cut back on their time at paid work, but to a smaller extent than in previous generations. The larger message in these findings is that all parents, whether they are mothers or fathers, need job arrangements that enable them to strike a balance between the economic and caretaking work that parenthood entails. . . .

Divided Options, Shared Aspirations

Although much of the debate concerning overwork in America has focused on the time women and men are spending at the workplace, we have looked closely in this chapter at how contemporary workers *feel* about their time at work. The concept of overwork depends as much on ideals as on actual working time, and we have found a notable gap between what workers do and what they would prefer. Most workers experience a significant time divide between their circumstances and their aspirations.

Yet this does not mean that all, or even most, workers feel overworked. Workers disagree considerably about whether they would like to work more or less. This disagreement makes it clear that the perception of overwork is not a general problem, but is nevertheless an important one to those whose jobs require that they put in very long workweeks and those whose family responsibilities are at their height. Far from using work to avoid family time, these workers would prefer more balance in their lives, with more time for private and family pursuits.

The problems of overworked Americans should also not blind us to the difficulties faced by those workers who cannot find sufficient employment to meet their own or their families' needs. As we have seen, many of those with relatively short workweeks would actually prefer to work more. Essentially, the gap between ideals and realities, rather than overwork *per se,* is the core problem for contemporary workers. Among women and men alike, most aspire to a balance that neither the overworked nor the underworked can achieve.

NOTE

1. The difference between single and married men in their ideal working hours is not statistically significant.

REFERENCES

Bond, James T., Ellen Galinsky, and Jennifer E. Swanberg. 1998. *The 1997 National Study of the Changing Workforce.* New York, NY: Families and Work Institute.

Epstein, Cynthia Fuchs, Carroll Seron, Bonnie Oglensky, and Robert Sauté. 1999. *The Part-Time Paradox: Time Norms, Professional Lives, Family, and Gender.* New York: Routledge.

Hochschild, Arlie. 1997. *The Time Bind: When Work Becomes Home and Home Becomes Work.* New York, NY: Metropolitan Books.

‖ 36 ‖

Orchestrating Impartiality
The Impact of "Blind" Auditions
on Female Musicians

CLAUDIA GOLDIN
CECILIA ROUSE

Sex-biased hiring has been alleged for many occupations but is extremely difficult to prove. The empirical literature on discrimination, deriving from the seminal contributions of Gary Becker (1971) and Kenneth Arrow (1973), has focused mainly on disparities in earnings between groups (e.g., males and females), given differences in observable productivity-altering characteristics. With the exception of various audit studies (e.g., Genevieve Kenney and Douglas A. Wissoker, 1994; David Neumark et al., 1996) and others, few researchers have been able to address directly the issue of bias in hiring practices. A change in the way symphony orchestras recruit musicians provides an unusual way to test for sex-biased hiring.

Until recently, the great symphony orchestras in the United States consisted of members who were largely handpicked by the music director. Although virtually all had auditioned for the position, most of the contenders would have been the (male) students of a select group of teachers. In an attempt to overcome this seeming bias in the hiring of musicians, most major U.S. orchestras changed their audition policies in the 1970s and 1980s, making them more open and routinized. Openings became widely advertised in the union papers, and many positions attracted more than 100 applicants where fewer than 20 would have been considered before. Audition committees were restructured to consist of members of the orchestra, not just the conductor and section principal. The audition procedure became democratized at a time when many other institutions in America did as well.

But democratization did not guarantee impartiality, because favorites could still be identified by sight and through resumes. Another set of procedures was adopted to ensure, or at least give the impression of, impartiality. These procedures involve hiding the identity of the player from the jury. Although they take several forms, we use the terms "blind" and "screen" to describe the group. The question we pose is whether

---

Claudia Goldin and Cecilia Rouse. "Orchestrating Impartiality: The Impact of 'Blind' Auditions on Female Musicians," *American Economic Review* 90 (2000), 715–726, 734–738, 740–741.

the hiring process became more impartial through the use of blind auditions. Because we are able to identify sex, but no other characteristics, for a large sample, we focus on the impact of the screen on the employment of women.

Screens were not adopted by all orchestras at once. Among the major orchestras, one still does not have any blind round to their audition procedure (Cleveland) and one adopted the screen in 1952 for the preliminary round (Boston Symphony Orchestra), decades before the others. Most other orchestras shifted to blind preliminaries from the early 1970s to the late 1980s. The variation in screen adoption at various rounds in the audition process allows us to assess its use as a treatment.

The change in audition procedures with the adoption of the screen allows us to test whether bias exists in its absence. In both our study and studies using audits, the issue is whether sex (or race or ethnicity), apart from objective criteria (e.g., the sound of a musical performance, the content of a resume), is considered in the hiring process. Why sex might make a difference is another matter. . . .

Sex Composition of Orchestras

Symphony orchestras consist of about 100 musicians and, although the number has varied between 90 and 105, it is rarely lower or higher. The positions, moreover, are nearly identical between orchestras and over time. As opposed to firms, symphony orchestras do not vary much in size and have virtually identical numbers and types of jobs. Thus we can easily look at the proportion of women in an orchestra without being concerned about changes in the composition of occupations and the number of workers. An increase in the number of women from, say, 1 to 10 cannot arise because the number of harpists (a female-dominated instrument) has greatly expanded. It must be because the proportion female within many groups has increased.

Among the five highest-ranked orchestras in the nation (known as the "Big Five")—the Boston Symphony Orchestra (BSO), the Chicago Symphony Orchestra, the Cleveland Symphony Orchestra, the New York Philharmonic (NYPhil), and the Philadelphia Orchestra—none contained more than 12 percent women until about 1980.[1] As can be seen in Figure 36.1A, each of the five lines (giving the proportion female) greatly increases after some point. For the NYPhil, the line steeply ascends in the early 1970s. For the BSO, the turning point appears to be a bit earlier. The percentage female in the NYPhil is currently 35 percent, the highest among all 11 orchestras in our sample after being the lowest (generally at zero) for decades. Thus the increase of women in the nation's finest orchestras has been extraordinary. The increase is even more remarkable because, as we discuss below, turnover in these orchestras is exceedingly low. The proportion of new players who were women must have been, and indeed was, exceedingly high.

Similar trends can be discerned for four other orchestras—the Los Angeles Symphony Orchestra (LA), the San Francisco Philharmonic (SF), the Detroit Symphony Orchestra, and the Pittsburgh Symphony Orchestra (PSO)—given in Figure 36.1B.[2] The upward trend in the proportion female is also obvious in Figure 36.1B, although initial levels are higher than in Figure 36.1A. There is somewhat more choppiness to the graph, particularly during the 1940s.

Figure 36.1 Proportion Female in Nine Orchestras, 1940 to 1990s. A: The "Big Five"; B: Four Others
Source: Roster sample. See text.

Although we have tried to eliminate all substitute, temporary, and guest musicians, especially during World War II and the Korean War, this was not always possible.

The only way to increase the proportion women is to hire more female musicians and turnover during most periods was low.

The number of new hires is graphed in Figure 36.2 for five orchestras. Because "new hires" is a volatile construct, we use a centered five-year moving average. In most years after the late 1950s, the top-ranked orchestras in the group (Chicago and NYPhil) hired about four musicians a year,

Figure 36.2   Number of New Hires in Five Orchestras, 1950 to 1990s
Source: Roster Sample. See text.

whereas the other three hired about six. Prior to 1960 the numbers are extremely high for LA and the PSO, because, it has been claimed, their music directors exercised their power to terminate, at will, the employment of musicians. Also of interest is that the number of new hires trends down, even excluding years prior to 1960. The important points to take from Figure 36.2 are that the number of new hires was small after 1960 and that it declined over time.

The proportion female among the new hires must have been sizable to increase the proportion female in the orchestras. Figure 36.3 shows the trend in the share of women among new hires for four of the "Big Five" (Figure 36.3A) and four other orchestras (Figure 36.3B).[3] In both groups the female share of new hires rose over time, at a somewhat steeper rate for the more prestigious orchestras. Since the early 1980s the share female among new hires has been about 35 percent for the BSO and Chicago, and

about 50 percent for the NYPhil, whereas before 1970 less than 10 percent of new hires were women.

Even though the fraction of new hires who are female rises at somewhat different times across the orchestras, there is a discernible increase for the group as a whole from the late 1970s to early 1980s, a time when the labor force participation of women increased generally and when their participation in various professions greatly expanded. The question, therefore, is whether the screen mattered in a direct manner or whether the increase was the result of a host of other factors, including the appearance of impartiality or an increased pool of female contestants coming out of music schools. Because the majority of new hires are in their late twenties and early thirties, the question is whether the most selective music schools were producing considerably more female students in the early 1970s. We currently have information by instrument for only the Juilliard School

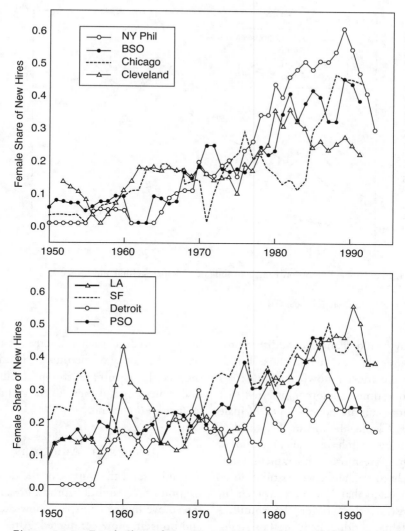

Figure 36.3   Female Share of New Hires in Eight Orchestras, 1950 to 1990s.
A: Four of the "Big Five"; B: Four Others

Source: Roster sample. See text.

Note: A five-year centered moving average is used. New hires are musicians who were not with the orchestra the previous year, who remain for at least one additional year and who were not substitute musicians in the current year.

of Music. With the exception of the brass section, the data, given in Figure 36.4, do not reveal any sharp breaks in the fraction of all graduates who are female. Thus, it is not immediately obvious that an expansion in the supply of qualified female musicians explains the marked increase in female symphony orchestra members; it could, therefore, be because of changes in the hiring procedures of orchestras.

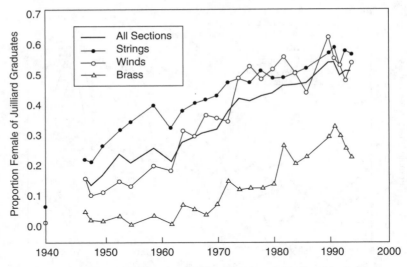

Figure 36.4   Proportion Female of Juilliard Graduates, Total and by Section: 1947 to 1995.

Source: Juilliard Music School files

But why would changes in audition procedures alter the sex mix of those hired? Many of the most renowned conductors have, at one time or another, asserted that female musicians are not the equal of male musicians. Claims abound in the world of music that "women have smaller techniques than men," "are more temperamental and more likely to demand special attention or treatment," and that "the more women [in an orchestra], the poorer the sound."[4] Zubin Mehta, conductor of the Los Angeles Symphony from 1964 to 1978 and of the New York Philharmonic from 1978 to 1990, is credited with saying, "I just don't think women should be in an orchestra."[5] Many European orchestras had, and some continue to have, stated policies not to hire women. The Vienna Philharmonic has only recently admitted its first female member (a harpist). Female musicians, it can be convincingly argued, have historically faced considerable discrimination. Thus a blind hiring procedure, such as a screen that conceals the identity of the musician auditioning, could eliminate the possibility of discrimination and increase the number of women in orchestras.

Orchestral Auditions

To understand the impact of the democratization of the audition procedure and the screen, we must first explain how orchestra auditions are now conducted. After determining that an audition must be held to fill an opening, the orchestra advertises that it will hold an audition. Each audition attracts musicians from across the country and, often, from around the world. Musicians interested in auditioning are required to submit a resume and often a tape of compulsory music (recorded according to specific guidelines) to be judged by members of the orchestra. In some orchestras this prescreening is dispositive; in others the musician has the right to audition live in the preliminary round, even if the audition committee rejects the candidate on the basis of the tape. All candidates are given, in advance, most of the music they are expected to perform at the live audition.

Live auditions today generally consist of three rounds: preliminary, semifinal, and final. But there is considerable variation. Although all orchestras now have a preliminary round, some have two final rounds and in many there was no semifinal round until the 1980s. The preliminary is generally considered a screening round to eliminate unqualified candidates. As a result, the committee is free to advance as many, or as few, as they wish. Candidates advanced from the semifinal round are generally considered "acceptable for hire" by the audition committee (which does not include the music director, a.k.a. conductor, until the finals). Again, this means that the committee can advance as many as it wishes. The final round generally results in a hire, but sometimes does not.

In blind auditions (or audition rounds) a screen is used to hide the identity of the player from the committee. The screens we have seen are either large pieces of heavy (but sound-porous) cloth, sometimes suspended from the ceiling of the symphony hall, or look like large room dividers. Some orchestras also roll out a carpet leading to center stage to muffle footsteps that could betray the sex of the candidate. Each candidate for a blind audition is given a number, and the jury rates the candidate's performance next to the number on a sheet of paper. Only the personnel manager knows the mapping from number to name and from name to other personal information. The names of the candidates are not revealed to the juries until after the last blind round.

Almost all preliminary rounds are now blind. The semifinal round, added as the number of applicants grew, may be blind. Finals are rarely blind and almost always involve the attendance and input of the music director. Although the music director still wields considerable power, the self-governance that swept orchestras in the 1970s has served to contain the conductor's authoritarianism. The music director can ignore the audition committee's advice, but does so at greater peril. Once an applicant is chosen to be a member of an orchestra, lifetime tenure is awarded after a brief probationary period. The basis for termination is limited and rarely used. The positions we are analyzing are choice jobs in the musical world. In 1995 the *minimum starting* base salary for musicians at the BSO was $1,400 per week (for a 52-week year), not including recording contracts, soloist fees, overtime and extra service payments, bonuses, and per diem payments for tours and Tanglewood. . . .

The audition procedures of the 11 orchestras in the roster sample are summarized in Table 36.1.[6] Although audition procedures are now part of union contracts, that was not the case in the more distant past and the procedures were not apparently recorded in any surviving documents. We gathered information on these procedures from various sources, including union contracts, interviews with personnel managers, archival documents on auditions, and a mail survey we conducted of orchestral musicians concerning the procedures employed during the audition that won them their current position.

An obvious question to ask is whether the adoption of the screen is endogenous. Of particular concern is that more meritocratic orchestras adopted blind auditions

Table 36.1　Orchestra Audition Procedure Summary Table

Orchestra	Preliminaries	Semifinals	Finals
A	Blind since 1973	Blind (varies) since 1973	Not Blind
B	Blind since at least 1967	Use of screen varies	Blind 1967–1969; since winter 1994
C	Blind since at least 1979 (definitely after 1972)	Not blind: 1991–present Blind: 1984–1987	Not blind
D	Blind since 1986	Blind since 1986; varies until 1993	1st part blind since 1993; 2nd part not blind
E	Use of screen varies until 1981	Use of screen varies	Not blind
F	Blind since at least 1972	Blind since at least 1972	Blind since at least 1972
G	Blind since 1986	Use of screen varies	Not blind
H	Blind since 1970	Not blind	Not blind
I	Blind since 1979	Blind since 1979	Blind since fall 1983
J	Blind since 1952	Blind since 1952	Not blind
K	Not blind	Not blind	Not blind

Notes: The eleven orchestras (A through K) are those in the roster sample described in the text. A subset of eight form the audition sample (also described in the text). All orchestras in the sample are major big-city U.S. symphony orchestras and include the "Big Five."

Sources: Orchestra union contracts (from orchestra personnel managers and libraries), personal conversations with orchestra personnel managers, and our mail survey of current orchestra members who were hired during the probable period of screen adoption.

earlier, producing the spurious result that the screen increased the likelihood that women were hired.[7] We estimate a probit model of screen adoption by year, conditional on an orchestra's not previously having adopted the screen (an orchestra exits the exercise once it adopts the screen). Two time-varying covariates are included to assess commonly held notions about screen adoption: the proportion female (lagged) in the orchestra, and a measure of tenure (lagged) of then-current orchestra members. Tenure is included because personnel managers maintain the screen was advocated more by younger players.

As the proportion female in an orchestra increases, so does the likelihood of screen adoption in the preliminary round, as can be seen in columns (1) and (2) in Table 36.2, although the effects are very small and far from statistically significant. We estimate a similar effect when we assess the role of female presence on the adoption of blind finals [see column (3)]. The impact of current tenure, measured by the proportion with less than six years with the orchestra, is—contrary to general belief—negative and the results do not change controlling for whether the orchestra is one of the "Big Five." In all, it appears that orchestra sex composition had little influence on screen adoption, although the stability of the personnel may have increased its likelihood.

Table 36.2   Estimated Probit Models for the Use of a Screen

| | Preliminaries blind | | Finals blind |
	(1)	(2)	(3)
(Proportion female)$_{t-1}$	2.744	3.120	0.490
	(3.265)	(3.271)	(1.163)
	[0.006]	[0.004]	[0.011]
(Proportion of orchestra personnel with <6 years tenure)$_{t-1}$	−26.46	−28.13	−9.467
	(7.314)	(8.459)	(2.787)
	[−0.058]	[−0.039]	[−0.207]
"Big Five" orchestra		0.367	
		(0.452)	
		[0.001]	
pseudo R^2	0.178	0.193	0.050
Number of observations	294	294	434

Notes: The dependent variable is 1 if the orchestra adopts a screen, 0 otherwise. Huber standard errors (with orchestra random effects) are in parentheses. All specifications include a constant. Changes in probabilities are in brackets. "Proportion female" refers to the entire orchestra. "Tenure" refers to years of employment in the current orchestra. "Big Five" includes Boston, Chicago, Cleveland, New York Philharmonic, and Philadelphia. The data begin in 1947 and an orchestra exits the exercise once it adopts the screen. The unit of observation is an orchestra-year.

Source: Eleven-orchestra roster sample. See text.

The Role of Blind Auditions on the Audition and Hiring Process

A. Data and Methods

Audition Records.   We use the actual audition records of eight major symphony orchestras obtained from orchestra personnel managers and the orchestra archives. The records are highly confidential and occasionally contain remarks (including those of the conductor) about musicians currently with the orchestra. To preserve the full confidentiality of the records, we have not revealed the names of the orchestras in our sample.

Although availability differs, taken together we obtained information on auditions dating from the late 1950s through 1995. Typically, the records are lists of the names of individuals who attended the auditions, with notation near the names of those advanced to the next round. For the

preliminary round, this would indicate advancement to either the semifinal or final round. Another list would contain the names of the semifinalists or finalists with an indication of who won the audition. From these records, we recorded the instrument and position (e.g., section, principal, substitute) for which the audition was held. We also know whether the individual had an "automatic" placement in a semifinal or final round. Automatic placement occurs when a musician is already known to be above some quality cutoff and is invited to compete in a semifinal or final round. We also recorded whether the individual was advanced to the next round of the current audition.

We rely on the first name of the musicians to determine sex. For most names establishing sex was straightforward. Sexing the Japanese and Korean names was equally straightforward, at least for our Japanese and Korean consultants. For more difficult cases, we checked the names in three baby books (Connie Lockhard Ellefson, 1990; Alfred J. Kolatch, 1990; Bruce Lansky, 1995). If the name was listed as male- or female-only, we considered the sex known. The gender-neutral names (e.g., Chris, Leslie, and Pat) and some Chinese names (for which sex is indeterminate in the absence of Chinese characters) remained ambiguous. Using these procedures, we were able to determine the sex of 96 percent of our audition sample.

In constructing our analysis sample, we exclude incomplete auditions, those in which there were no women (or only women) competing, rounds from which no one was advanced, and the second final round, if one exists, for which the candidates played with the orchestra. In addition, we generally consider each round of the audition separately. These sample restrictions exclude 294 rounds (199 contained no women) and 1,539 individuals. Our final analysis sample has 7,065 individuals and 588 audition rounds (from 309 separate auditions) resulting in 14,121 person-rounds and an average of 2.0 rounds per musician. . . .

Roster Data. Our second source of information comes from the final results of the audition process, the orchestra personnel rosters. We collected these data from the personnel page of concert programs, one each year for eleven major symphony orchestras. These records are in the public domain and thus we have used the orchestra names in the graphs containing those data alone. As opposed to the auditionees, we were able to confirm the sex of the players with the orchestra personnel managers and archivists. We considered a musician to be

new to the orchestra in question if he or she had not previously been a regular member of that orchestra (i.e., we did not count returning members as new). We excluded, when possible, temporary and substitute musicians, as well as harpists and pianists. Our final sample for 1970 to 1996 has 1,128 new orchestra members. . . .

B. The Effect of the Screen on the Hiring of Women

Using the Audition Sample. We turn now to the effect of the screen on the actual hire and estimate the likelihood an individual is hired out of the initial audition pool.[8] Whereas the use of the screen for each audition round was, more or less, an unambiguous concept, that for the entire process is not and we must define a blind audition. The definition we have chosen is that a blind audition contains all rounds that use the screen. In using this definition, we compare auditions that are completely blind with those that do not use the screen at all or use it for the early rounds only. We divide the sample into auditions that have a semifinal round and those that do not, because the earlier analysis suggested they might differ (Goldin and Rouse 2000).

The impact of completely blind auditions on the likelihood of a woman's being hired is given in Table 36.3, for which all results include individual fixed effects.[9] The impact of the screen is positive and large in magnitude, but only when there is no semifinal round. Women are about 5 percentage points more likely to be hired than are men in a completely blind audition, although the effect is not statistically significant. The effect is nil, however, when there is a semifinal round. The impact for all rounds [columns (5) and (6)] is about 1 percentage point, although the standard errors are

Table 36.3 Linear Probability Estimates of the Effect of Blind Auditions on the Likelihood of Being Hired with Individual Fixed Effects

	Without semifinals		With semifinals		All	
	(1)	(2)	(3)	(4)	(5)	(6)
Completely blind audition	−0.024 (0.028)	0.047 (0.041)	0.001 (0.009)	0.006 (0.011)	0.001 (0.008)	0.005 (0.009)
Completely blind audition × female	0.051 (0.046)	0.036 (0.048)	0.001 (0.016)	−0.004 (0.016)	0.011 (0.013)	0.006 (0.013)
Year effects?	No	Yes	No	Yes	No	Yes
Other covariates?	No	Yes	No	Yes	No	Yes
R²	0.855	0.868	0.692	0.707	0.678	0.691
Number of observations	4,108	4,108	5,883	5,883	9,991	9,991

Notes: The unit of observation is a person-round. The dependent variable is 1 if the individual is advanced (or hired) from the final round and 0 if not. Standard errors are in parentheses. All specifications include individual fixed effects, whether the sex is missing, and an interaction for sex being missing and a completely blind audition. "Other covariates" are the size of the audition, the proportion female at the audition, the number of individuals advanced (hired), whether a "Big Five" orchestra, the number of previous auditions, and whether the individual had an automatic semifinal or final.

Source: Eight-orchestra audition sample. See text.

large and thus the effect is not statistically significant. Given that the probability of winning an audition is less than 3 percent, we would need more data than we currently have to estimate a statistically significant effect, and even a 1-percentage-point increase is large, as we later demonstrate.

Using the Roster Data. The roster data afford us another way to evaluate the effect of the screen on the sex composition of orchestras. Using the rosters we know the sex of new hires each year for 11 orchestras, and we also have information (see Table 36.1) on the year the screen was adopted by each orchestra. We treat the orchestra position as the unit of observation and ask whether the screen affects the sex of the individual who fills the position. We model the likelihood that a female is hired in a

particular year as a function of whether the orchestra's audition procedure involved a screen, again relying on the variation over time within a particular orchestra. Thus, in all specifications, we include orchestra fixed effects and an orchestra-specific time trend.

The roster data extend further back in time than do the audition data and could conceivably begin with the orchestra's founding, although there is no obvious reason to include many years when none used the screen. We report, in Table 36.4, the effects of the screen on the hiring of women from 1970 to 1996 using a probit model. The screen is first defined to include any blind auditions [column (1)]. In column (2) we estimate separate effects for orchestras using blind preliminary (and semifinal) rounds but not blind finals and those with completely blind auditions.

Table 36.4   Probit Estimates of the Effect of Blind Auditions on the Sex of New Members: 1970 to 1996

	Any blind auditions	*Only blind preliminaries and/or semifinals vs. completely blind auditions*
	(1)	*(2)*
Any blind auditions	0.238 (0.183) [0.075]	
Only blind preliminaries and/or semifinals		0.232 (0.184) [0.074]
Completely blind auditions		0.361 (0.438) [0.127]
Section:		
Woodwinds	−0.187 (0.114) [−0.058]	−0.188 (0.114) [−0.058]
Brass	−1.239 (0.157) [−0.284]	−1.237 (0.157) [−0.284]
Percussion	−1.162 (0.305) [−0.235]	−1.164 (0.305) [−0.235]
p-value of test: only blind preliminaries and/or semifinals = completely blind		0.756
pseudo R^2	0.106	0.106
Number of observations	1,128	1,128

Notes: The dependent variable is 1 if the individual is female and 0 if male. Standard errors are in parentheses. All specifications include orchestra fixed effects and orchestra-specific time trends. Changes in probabilities are in brackets; see text for an explanation of how they are calculated. New members are those who enter the orchestra for the first time. Returning members are not considered new. The omitted section is strings.

Source: Eleven-orchestra roster sample. See text.

To interpret the probit coefficient, we first predict a base probability, under the assumption that each orchestra does not use a screen. We then predict a new probability assuming the orchestra uses a screen. The mean difference in the probabilities is given in brackets.

The coefficient on blind in column (1) is positive, although not significant at any usual level of confidence. The estimates in column (2) are positive and equally large in magnitude to those in column (1). Further,

these estimates show that the existence of any blind round makes a difference and that a completely blind process has a somewhat larger effect (albeit with a large standard error). According to the point estimates in column (1) of Table 36.4, blind auditions increase the likelihood a female will be hired by 7.5 percentage points. The magnitude of the effect must be judged relative to the overall average and, for the period under consideration, it was about 30 percent. Thus blind auditions increased the likelihood a female would be hired by 25 percent. . . .[10]

Conclusion

The question is whether hard evidence can support an impact of discrimination on hiring. Our analysis of the audition and roster data indicates that it can, although we mention various caveats before we summarize the reasons. Even though our sample size is large, we identify the coefficients of interest from a much smaller sample. Some of our coefficients of interest, therefore, do not pass standard tests of statistical significance and there is, in addition, one persistent result that goes in the opposite direction. The weight of the evidence, however, is what we find most persuasive and what we have emphasized. . . .

As in research in economics and other fields on double-blind refereeing (see, e.g., Blank, 1991), the impact of a blind procedure is toward impartiality and the costs to the journal (here to the orchestra) are relatively small. We conclude that the adoption of the screen and blind auditions served to help female musicians in their quest for orchestral positions.

NOTES

1. The data referred to, and used in Figures 36.1 to 36.3, are from orchestral rosters, described in more detail below.

2. Our roster sample also includes the Metropolitan Opera Orchestra and the St. Louis Symphony.

3. A centered five-year moving average is also used for this variable.

4. Seltzer (1989), p. 215.

5. Seltzer (1989), p. 215.

6. We identify the orchestras by letter, rather than by name, to preserve confidentiality of the audition sample.

7. Note, however, it is unlikely that the orchestras that sought to hire more women chose to adopt the screen earlier since the best way to increase the number of women in the orchestra is to have not-blind auditions (so that one could be sure to hire more women).

8. The original article (Goldin and Rouse 2000) includes much additional analysis examining the effect of the screen on the likelihood of being advanced through each stage of the audition process.—EDS

9. There are four auditions in which the committee could not choose between two players and therefore asked each to play with the orchestra. We consider both to be winners. The results are not sensitive to this classification. For this analysis we exclude auditions with no women, all women, or no winner; these exclusions do not change the results.

10. In Table 36.3 we are identified off of individuals who competed in auditions that were completely blind *and* those that were not completely blind (that is, *any* one round could not be blind). The unit of observation is the person-round and there are 92 fulfilling this criterion for auditions without a semifinal [columns (1) and (2)]; on average these persons competed in 3.6 auditions in this sample. There are 625 person-rounds fulfilling this criterion that included a semifinal [columns (3) and (4)] and on average these persons competed in 3.5 auditions in this sample. Finally, there are 911 person-rounds fulfilling this criterion across all auditions [columns (5) and (6)] and on average these persons competed in 3.5 auditions in this sample. The sample off of which we are identified is larger for all auditions than for the sum of the other two because some individuals auditioned both with and without a semifinal round.

REFERENCES

Arrow, Kenneth. "The Theory of Discrimination," in Orley Ashenfelter and Albert Rees, eds., *Discrimination in labor markets.* Princeton, NJ: Princeton University Press, 1973, pp. 3–33.

Becker, Gary. *The economics of discrimination,* 2nd Ed. Chicago: University of Chicago Press, 1971 [orig. pub. 1957].

Blank, Rebecca. "The Effects of Double-Blind versus Single-Blind Refereeing: Experimental Evidence from the *American Economic Review.*" *American Economic Review,* December 1991, *81*(5), pp. 1041–67.

Ellefson, Connie Lockhard. *The melting pot book of baby names,* 2nd Ed. Cincinnati, OH: Better Way Books, 1990.

Goldin, Claudia and Cecilia Rouse. 2000. "Orchestrating Impartiality: The Impact of "Blind" Auditions on Female Musicians." *American Economic Review* 90 (September): 715–741.

Kenney, Genevieve and Wissoker, Douglas A. "An Analysis of the Correlates of Discrimina-tion Facing Young Hispanic Job-Seekers." *American Economic Review,* June 1994, *84*(3), pp. 674–83.

Kolatch, Alfred J. *The Jonathan David dictionary of first names.* New York: Perigee Books, 1990.

Lansky, Bruce. *35,000+ baby names.* New York: Meadowbrook Press, 1995.

Neumark, David (with Bank, Roy and Van Nort, Kyle D.). "Sex Discrimination in Restaurant Hiring: An Audit Study." *Quarterly Journal of Economics,* August 1996, *111*(3), pp. 915–41.

Seltzer, George. *Music matters: The performer and the American Federation of Musicians.* Metuchen, NJ: Scarecrow Press, 1989.

37

Labor Markets as Queues

A Structural Approach to Changing Occupational Sex Composition

BARBARA F. RESKIN

The historic persistence of sex segregation (Gross 1968; Beller 1984) made women's dramatic gains during the 1970s in such diverse male occupations as pharmacy, bank management, bartending, and typesetting noteworthy. Why did women disproportionately enter these and a few other male occupations when they made only modest progress in most and lost ground in a few? To answer this question, Patricia Roos and I conducted a two-part study: multivariate analyses of the changing sex composition in all detailed census occupations and in-depth case studies of 14 occupations in which women's representation increased at least twice as much as it had in the labor force as a whole (see Table 37.1). This chapter draws on those case studies: bank managers (Bird 1990), bartenders (Detman 1990), systems analysts (Donato 1990a), public relations specialists (Donato 1990b), pharmacists (Phipps 1990a), insurance adjusters/examiners (Phipps 1990b), typesetters/compositors (Roos 1990), insurance salespersons (Thomas 1990), real estate salespersons (Thomas and Reskin 1990), bakers (Steiger and Reskin 1990), book editors (Reskin and Roos 1990), print and broadcast reporters, and accountants.[1] Although the case studies revealed that widely different factors precipitated these occupations' feminization, the process of change can be encompassed in a single perspective—queuing. This chapter begins by outlining the queuing approach. It then shows how the determinants of occupational feminization conformed to queuing processes. Finally, it argues that the queue model as I have developed it offers a structural approach to understanding change in job composition.

Queuing: an Overview

Simply stated, a queuing perspective views labor markets as composed of labor queues and job queues that reflect, respectively, employers' ranking of possible workers and workers' ranking of jobs.[2] The idea of the *labor* queue originated in Lester Thurow's

Barbara F. Reskin, "Labor Markets as Queues: A Structural Approach to Changing Occupational Sex Composition," in *Micro-Macro Linkages in Sociology,* edited by Joan Huber, pp. 170–186, 188–192. Copyright © 1991 by Sage Publications, Inc.

Table 37.1   Percent Females in Feminizing Occupations, 1970, 1980, 1988

Occupation	1970 %	1980 %	1988 %	1970–1988 Increase %
Financial managers	19.4	31.4	42.4	23.0
Accountants/auditors	24.6	38.1	49.6	25.0
Operation/systems analysts	11.1	27.7	39.6	28.5
Pharmacists	12.1	24.0	31.9	19.8
Public relations specialists	26.6	48.8	59.1	32.5
Editors and reporters	41.6	49.3	n.a.	n.a.
Insurance sales	12.9	25.4	29.7	16.8
Real estate sales	31.2	45.2	48.5	17.3
Insurance adjusters/examiners	29.6	60.2	72.2	42.6
Bartenders	21.2	44.3	49.6	28.4
Bakers	25.4	40.7	47.8	22.4
Bus Drivers	28.3	45.8	48.5	20.2
Typesetters/compositors	16.8	55.7	73.9	57.1
Labor force	38.0	42.6	45.0	7.0

(1969) work on race differences in unemployment and was elaborated by Hodge (1973) and Lieberson (1980). Rotella's (1977) analysis of the feminization of clerical work, Lieberson's (1980) study of racial and ethnic inequality, and Strober's (1984) theory of sex segregation implicitly invoked *job* as well as *labor* queues. The queuing perspective presented here views occupational composition as resulting from the simultaneous operation of job and labor queues (also see Reskin and Roos 1990). Employers hire workers from as high in the labor queue as possible, and workers accept the best jobs available to them, so the most desirable jobs go to the most preferred workers, less attractive jobs go to workers lower in the labor queue, and the most lowly workers end up jobless or in jobs others have rejected.

Three structural properties characterize both job and labor queues: (a) the ordering of their elements, (b) whether or not their elements overlap, and (c) their shape. By *elements,* I mean the constituent units—groups of potential workers or jobs. Thus

the *ordering of elements* simply indicates in what order workers rank possible jobs and employers rank prospective workers. I pass over how workers order jobs in the labor queue as something both sociologists and workers understand. In ordering the labor queue, employers consider potential productivity and cost.[3] However, the indirect effect of workers' sex on employers' estimations of the former and its direct influence on how employers rank workers result in labor queues that encompass and often act as *gender queues.*

The absolute and relative numbers of elements in a queue determine its *shape.* Thus the number of prospective workers in each subgroup in a labor market sets the shape of the labor queue, and the number of jobs at each level in the job queue fixes its shape. Panels A and B of Figure 37.1 show how the shape of labor and job queues can vary while their order remains constant. This variation influences each group's probable access to occupations of varying desirability. (Put differently, it shows how a queue's shape influences each

Panel A. Hypothetical labor queues ordered by race for predominantly white and predominantly black labor markets, respectively

Panel B. Hypothetical job queues ordered by nonmanual-manual work for predominantly nonmanual and predominantly manual occupational structures, respectively

Figure 37.1   Illustration of Variation in the Shape of Labor and Job Queues

occupation's chance of recruiting workers from particular groups.) For example, in a society with relatively few workers in the preferred group (A2) and few desirable jobs (B2), preferred groups will monopolize better or worse jobs than persons from their group normally command. In consequence, when good jobs sharply outnumber highly ranked workers as in panels A2 and B1, employers must fill the better jobs with workers from lower in the labor queue than they usually hire. In contrast, when the *job queue* is bottom heavy, only the highest-ranked workers get desirable jobs, and workers moderately high in the labor queue are forced to settle for less. As Lieberson (1980, p. 297) has shown, both the *absolute* and the *relative* sizes of each group in the labor queue affect lower-ranked workers' chances of getting desirable jobs. The larger

a subordinate group relative to the size of the preferred group, the more costly it is for employers to deny its members good jobs (Hodge 1973).

Whether or not *elements overlap* denotes the strength of rankers' preferences for one element over another. Among some employers, group membership is the overriding consideration in ordering the labor queue, and rankers favor persons from the group they prefer, regardless of qualifications. For other labor queues, employers are indifferent to group membership except to break ties between otherwise equally qualified prospects. Figure 37.2 illustrates variation in the intensity of raters' preferences with respect to workers' race in three hypothetical labor queues. The space between the races in panel A depicts the ranking for employers who invariably hire the lowest-ranked white

Panel A. Racial group membership is an overriding consideration to rankers. Employers hire applicants as qualified as possible, but hire unqualified whites before hiring highly qualified blacks.

Blacks	Blacks	Blacks		Whites	Whites	Whites
Low	Moderate	High		Low	Moderate	High

Level of Qualification

Panel B. Racial group membership is a minor consideration to rankers. Employers hire the most qualified applicants, but within levels of qualification, give white applicants an edge over equally qualified blacks.

Blacks	Whites	Blacks		Whites	Blacks	Whites
Low	Low	Moderate		Moderate	High	High

Level of Qualification

Panel C. Racial group membership is an intermediate consideration to rankers. Employers will prefer a more qualified white over a less qualified black, but will hire very qualified blacks over unqualified whites.

Blacks	Blacks	Whites		Blacks	Whites	Whites
Low	Moderate	Low		High	Moderate	High

Level of Qualification

Figure 37.2   Illustration of Variation in the Intensity of Raters' Preferences with Respect to Race

worker over the best black worker; the overlapping groups in panel B depict the situation in which raters' aversion to blacks is slight. Panel C illustrates an intermediate situation in which employers prefer white workers over equally qualified blacks but will set aside racial biases to hire very talented blacks over mediocre whites. Where preferences are weak, substantial job-level integration exists. In contrast, when preferences are overriding, all members of the favored group precede all members of the disfavored group in the labor queue, and the labor market is totally segmented.

Workers' job preferences also vary in intensity. Some workers may categorically prefer any job in a high-ranked occupation to working in a lower occupation (expressed, for example, in rejecting manual jobs in favor of non-manual work). Alternatively, they may be more attuned to specific job characteristics than their overall rank, occasionally eschewing jobs in occupations usually reserved for the preferred group and appropriating more desirable jobs within lower-ranked occupations that usually go to less preferred groups. Strong preferences mean that workers invariably prefer one type of job (e.g., professional or nonmanual work) over another.

Changes in any of these structural features of queues—employers' rankings of workers or workers' ranking of jobs, the intensity of either groups' preferences, and the relative distributions of workers or jobs—can transform occupations' composition.

Queuing Models as Structural Approaches to Occupational Composition

Queuing emphasizes how employers rank groups of potential workers as well as how workers rank jobs. Because rankings simply boil down to preferences, is *queuing* not simply a fancy way to say that workers' and employers' preferences affect their labor market decisions? What does the queuing perspective add to the neoclassical economic approach to occupational segregation?

The neoclassical economic approach assumes (a) that workers' labor market decisions represent attempts to maximize their lifetime earnings, (b) that differences in the sexes' distributions across jobs stem primarily from women's family responsibilities, (c) that employers act to maximize revenues, and (d) that, in the short run, discriminatory "tastes" sometimes divert employers from their economic best interests, but, in the long run, competitive disadvantages that accrue from indulging economically irrational tastes lead discrimination to decline over time (Becker 1957). Thus traditional economic analysis treats sex segregation as the *aggregate* outcome of the mostly rational choices of *individual* workers and employers.

A queuing approach to changing occupational sex composition differs in several ways. First, queuing emphasizes the *collec-*

tive nature of sex segregation that results from *socially structured rankings* by *groups in conflict*. In contrast to the neoclassical perspective, queuing highlights the roles played by power and conflict between groups with contradictory interests in shaping occupations' composition. As I show below, the queuing perspective elucidates the role of group power in determining occupational access.

Second, it takes seriously the effects of noneconomic factors on workers' rankings of occupations and employers' rankings of prospective workers. It reminds us that working conditions, autonomy, social standing, career opportunities, and sex composition influence how workers appraise jobs and that employers' prejudices, stereotypes, and desire to preserve their own and other men's advantages influence how they rank workers.

Third, the queuing perspective assumes that the sexes rank most occupations similarly, so it predicts women's influx into accessible male occupations in view of their superior rewards. In explaining occupational feminization, it directs our attention to changes in employers' need for women and to declining barriers to women's access to traditionally male jobs. In other words, the queuing perspective redirects us from characteristics of female workers to structural properties of labor markets that in turn are shaped by the preferences of employers and male workers.

Power and Coalitions in Ordering the Labor Queue

In examining how conflict affects occupations' composition, we must bear in mind three points: First, three groups with competing interests have a stake in which sex predominates in an occupation—employers (who are overwhelmingly male), male workers, and female workers. Second, the greater social and economic power of employers and of men give them a substantial advantage in the struggle over what sex heads the queue for desirable occupations. Third, the outcome of the struggle over what sex dominates an occupation—occupations' sex compositions—represents a de facto coalition between competing groups.

Employers. Given their orientation toward minimizing costs and maximizing labor docility, employers should prefer female workers for all jobs. That so few have done so reminds us that other considerations affect male employers' labor decisions. Foremost among these is the personal stake of both male employers and male workers in excluding women from male-labeled jobs to preserve sex differentiation and hence male privilege in all spheres. Because sex differentiation both legitimates and facilitates unequal treatment, physically segregating the sexes at work and assigning them different tasks preserves male dominance by legitimating unequal wages, insulating men from female competition, supporting men's dominance in other public realms and the home, and shoring up myths of essential sex differences and male superiority (Reskin 1988). As Cockburn (1988, p. 41) put it, "Behind occupational segregation is gender differentiation, and behind that is male power."

Other considerations inclining employers to preserve good jobs for men include (a) the ability of male workers—and sometimes customers—to penalize employers for hiring women for "men's" jobs (Bergmann and Darity 1981; Strober 1988); (b) organizational inertia that makes following standard practices the course of least resis-

tance; (c) custom—in other words, jobs' sex labels—combined with the uncertainties attendant on radically altering employment practices (Cohn 1985; Strom 1987; Figart and Bergmann 1989, p. 36); (d) gender solidarity with male workers;[4] and (e) forestalling later threats to their own jobs. As long as employers can operate profitably, preserving male jobs can be a fairly cheap amenity, especially if their competitors also practice male preference (Stolzenberg 1982; Strober 1988). Thus, in reserving male-dominated jobs for men, employers at once appease male workers, who could make hiring women costly; simplify organizational decisions; and shore up the gender hierarchy from which they benefit.

Male Workers. Male workers' disadvantaged economic position vis-à-vis employers and their advantaged sex status divide their interests. They stand to gain in the long run from acting collectively with *all* workers, but, in the short run, men are vulnerable to job and wage competition from women who must settle for lower wages. Equal job opportunities for women can also cost men domestic benefits they derive from sex inequality in the workplace and can threaten the gender hierarchy from which working men benefit (Hartmann 1976; Reskin 1988). Thus, for the most part, male workers do better in the short run by monopolizing male jobs than by welcoming female coworkers with whom they could collectively fight for better pay. Only when large numbers of women already have their foot in the door, or when labor shortages or outside agencies have imposed integration, are male workers freed to pursue their class interests collectively with female workers (Hirsch 1986; Milkman 1987; Cobble forthcoming). Under such conditions, male unions have tried to organize women and advocated equal pay.

Coalitions Between Employers and Male Workers. Male workers' monopoly of most occupations stems from the de facto coalition between male employers and male workers. Although I use the term *coalition* figuratively, employers' power to hire workers and assign them jobs means that ordinarily male workers can resist women's entry only with their male bosses' active contrivance (Baker 1964; Hartmann 1976; Cockburn 1988). The result of this coalition between male workers and employers is also seen in feminizing occupations in women's confinement to the least desirable jobs, thereby providing male workers a refuge from integration in still-male jobs (Cockburn 1988). For example, when outside pressure forced a large publishing firm to promote women to jobs as editorial assistants, it created a new, higher rank into which it promoted male former editorial assistants (Osterman 1979).

Despite the forces that preserve sex segregation, it broke down in the occupations we studied when male employers or male workers withdrew from their coalition. Employers never violated a coalition by directly substituting women for men, but they set aside customary practices, their own sex biases, and concern with the reactions of male workers when their firms' survival depended on cutting labor costs or averting unionization. In the occupations we studied, increased competition and the concomitant need to cut costs as well as vulnerability to work disruptions by unions precipitated this action. For example, industry-wide demand for increased profits during the high-inflation 1970s prompted insurance companies to cut costs by stan-

dardizing the work of insurance adjusters and examiners. Heightened competition for customers following deregulation forced banks to provide more customer services while trying to increase productivity and keep the lid on wages. In typesetting and composing, the International Typographical Union's frequent recourse to strikes spurred newspaper publishers to develop a printing technology that the union could not control, and then they hired women for the newly clericalized typesetting and composing jobs. It is important, however, that, in occupations that became less attractive to men for reasons not tied to employers' actions (book editing, real estate sales, retail pharmacy, and bartending), employers did not counter by improving male jobs. Employers' economic interests prevailed, and they replaced men with cheaper women.

In sum, the case studies suggested that employers put women ahead of men in labor queues *only* when labor costs became a pressing concern or when action by women or government regulators raised the cost of male preference.[5] Faced with economic exigencies, employers' willingness to donate profits to support white male privilege went by the wayside, and they struck a bargain with women workers.

Coalitions Between Male Employers and Female Workers. Why women should enter into de facto coalitions with male employers is no mystery. Disadvantaged relative to both male workers and male employers, women stand to gain from cooperating with either group. Employers are more likely to accept a coalition with women when their numbers are large. Cobble's (forthcoming) comparison of women's efforts early in this century to preserve the right to serve drinks with their efforts to tend bar illustrates the importance of numbers. Women waitresses' moderate representation within union locals gave them the clout to block proposed restrictions against their serving alcoholic drinks. In contrast, women's small numbers doomed their efforts to tend bar until they could invoke the Civil Rights Act. In the 1970s, women capitalized on their numbers in the book publishing, newspaper, broadcasting, and banking industries to challenge their exclusion from male jobs or their confinement in low-status posts. Large numbers mean that women can better spot their concentration in the least desirable jobs and more effectively protest it. Thus women's increased share in labor queues for male occupations contributed to their gains both by increasing the odds that employers would get down to women in the hiring queue and by making them more powerful adversaries.

Resistance by Male Workers. Male workers' stake in monopolizing the best jobs encourages them to oppose employers' efforts to integrate women. To this end, they may try to reduce women's productivity by denying them training and information or withhold their own labor (Doeringer and Piore 1971; Bergmann and Darity 1981).[6] Whether men win the battle depends on their power base. For example, early in the Industrial Revolution, before strong unions existed, employers could easily feminize jobs (Kessler-Harris 1982, p. 266; Cohn 1985; Milkman 1987; Cockburn 1988). However, once unions were well established, they could preserve their domains. They did so in bartending, baking, and typesetting and composing as well as many other occupations throughout most of the century.

Obviously, men did not ultimately prevent women's entry in the occupations we studied. In most of those occupations, by abandoning jobs, male workers gave employers the go-ahead to hire women. Sometimes men do not see women as a threat. For instance, although men fought women's integration into clerical jobs in the British railroads (Cohn 1985), they did not resist women's movement in similar jobs in the United States because integration occurred slowly, and Pullman reserved the best jobs for men (Hirsch 1986, p. 33). In rapidly growing occupations, men did not resist women's entry because growth ensured that good jobs were plentiful, and within-occupation segregation assured men's access to the best jobs.

Thus the case studies of accounting and systems analysis revealed no systematic efforts to exclude women. Male incumbents in high-turnover occupations like book editing, bartending, and residential real estate sales had no stake in what happened in the long run. High turnover also means workers were too poorly organized to resist integration. Finally, in reorganizing work, employers had an effective tool in phasing out men. By changing the work process to incorporate female-labeled tasks, employers could disguise the fact that they were filling what had been men's jobs with women (Davies 1975, p. 282; Rotella 1977, pp. 162, 165) and recast them as women's work. For instance, after transforming the work of adjusters, industry trade journals construed the ideal insurance adjuster as a woman.[7]

However, men did effectively resist women's employment in the most desirable specialties within desegregating occupations, such as production baking, commercial real estate, and industrial pharmacy—partly by informal pressures that discouraged women's entry. I suspect, however, that women's continued exclusion depended more on employer discrimination in job assignment and promotion practices than on male workers' actions.

Conclusions

In summary, the queuing model proposed here holds that (a) employers rank prospective workers in terms of their potential productivity as well as their personal characteristics, but that they are also influenced by current employees and others who can impose costs for hiring or failing to hire women; (b) shortages—whether from job growth or from a job's inability to attract enough customary workers—prompt employers to hire workers from lower in the labor queue; (c) male workers affect women's access to jobs through their ability to preempt jobs, their power to enforce their monopoly over desirable jobs, and their ability, in abandoning jobs, to bestow them on workers lower in the labor queue; and (d) women's search for better jobs leads them to individually and collectively challenge their exclusion from men's jobs and to move into male lines of work that become open. The case study data support these predictions. I caution readers that our selection of case studies of occupations in which women's gains were exceptionally large limits the generalizability of these findings. However, most occupations included specialties or work settings that had feminized at varying rates, so the case studies provide variation on the dependent variable. Nonetheless, the bases for women's movement into occupations not marked by rapid feminization may have differed. Patricia Roos and I addressed this question in statistical analyses of all 503 detailed occupations (Reskin and Roos 1985).

The case studies support two empirical generalizations both of which are consistent with the operation of queuing processes. First, in most of the occupations we studied, after they had become less attractive to men, employers hired disproportionate numbers of women. Second, within these nominally desegregating occupations, women tended to be relegated to female enclaves, while men retained the most desirable jobs.[8] These findings confirm Bielby and Baron's (1986) contention that greater balance in the sex composition of *occupations* does not necessarily imply decreased segregation of *jobs* and also establish the fallacy of inferring declines in sex segregation from occupational-level data. Yet social analysts cannot ignore such data, because policy makers and the media use them to assess change, and, as W. I. Thomas said, situations men define as real are real in their consequences. Exaggerated conclusions about women's progress in male occupations support claims that governmental agencies no longer need to intervene in the workplace to ensure equal treatment. Thus it is incumbent on researchers to determine whether or not the trends that superficial comparisons imply are genuine.

NOTES

I am grateful to Ross Boylan, Lowell L. Hargens, Heidi Hartmann, and Patricia A. Roos for their comments on earlier drafts of this chapter and to James N. Baron and Ronnie Steinberg for helpful discussions of the issues it addresses. The larger study that gave rise to the ideas in this chapter is a collaborative project with Patricia A. Roos. The case studies on which this chapter is based appear in our book, *Job Queues, Gender Queues: Explaining Women's Inroads into Male Occupations* (1990).

1. I conducted the last two unpublished studies. Unless otherwise noted, assertions about

these occupations are based on the case studies whose full citations are in the references. For a description of the case study method, see Reskin and Roos (1990).

2. This analysis takes for granted the existence of multiple labor markets, each composed of a labor queue of potential workers and a job queue of available jobs.

3. Incumbent workers can affect the ordering of the labor queue, for example, through seniority rules that restrict employers' hiring prerogatives.

4. This should be especially common among bosses who share a similar background with male workers, previously held the jobs in question, and currently work with or remain friendly with their former coworkers. Two examples are blue-collar supervisors or sales managers.

5. Unless it is backed by threats from regulatory agencies, pressure from women rarely suffices to persuade employers to assign women to male jobs, partly because it elicits opposition from male workers.

6. Employers can rarely forestall resistance by feminizing entire work teams. Seniority rules may prevent their replacing men, they may doubt whether enough qualified women are available, and they may be unable to train women because male unions control training or because training is too long and expensive.

7. Kessler-Harris (1986) and Strober and Arnold (1987) also recounted how banks exploited sex stereotypes to justify hiring women for banking jobs as well as to exclude them from the same jobs.

8. For further evidence on this point, see Chapter 3 in Reskin and Roos (1990).

REFERENCES

Baker, Ross. 1964. "Entry of Women into Federal Job World—At a Price." *Smithsonian* 8:82–91.

Becker, Gary. 1957. *The Economics of Discrimination.* Chicago: University of Chicago Press.

Beller, Andrea. 1984. "Trends in Occupational Segregation by Sex, 1960–1981." Pp. 11–26 in *Sex Segregation in the Workplace: Trends, Ex-* *planations, Remedies,* edited by B. Reskin. Washington, DC: National Academy Press.

Bergmann, Barbara R., and William Darity. 1981. "Social Relations, Productivity, and Employer Discrimination." *Monthly Labor Review* 104:47–49.

Bielby, William T., and James N. Baron. 1986. "Men and Women at Work: Sex Segregation and Statistical Discrimination." *American Journal of Sociology* 91:759–99.

Bird, Chloe. 1990. "High Finance, Small Change: Women's Increased Representation in Bank Management." Pp. 145–66 in B. F. Reskin and P. A. Roos, *Job Queues, Gender Queues: Explaining Women's Inroads into Male Occupations,* Philadelphia: Temple University Press.

Cobble, Dorothy Sue. Forthcoming. "'Drawing the Line': The Construction of a Gendered Workforce in the Food Service Industry." In *Work Engendered,* edited by Ava Baron. Ithaca: Cornell University Press.

Cockburn, Cynthia. 1988. "The Gendering of Jobs: Workplace Relations and the Reproduction of Sex Segregation." Pp. 29–42 in *Gender Segregation at Work,* edited by S. Walby. Milton Keynes, England; New York: Open University Press.

Cohn, Samuel. 1985. *The Process of Occupational Sex-Typing: The Feminization of Clerical Labor in Great Britain.* Philadelphia: Temple University Press.

Davies, Margery W. 1975. "Women's Place Is at the Typewriter: The Feminization of the Clerical Labor Force." Pp. 279–96 in *Labor Market Segmentation,* edited by R. Edwards, M. Reich, and D. Gordon. Lexington, MA: D. C. Heath.

Detman, Linda. 1990. "Women Behind Bars: The Feminization of Bartending." Pp. 241–56 in B. F. Reskin and P. A. Roos, *Job Queues, Gender Queues: Explaining Women's Inroads into Male Occupations.* Philadelphia: Temple University Press.

Doeringer, Peter B., and Michael J. Piore. 1971. *Internal Labor Markets and Manpower Analysis.* Lexington, MA: D. C. Heath.

Donato, Katharine M. 1990a. "Programming for Change? The Growing Demand for Women Systems Analysts." Pp. 167–82 in B. F. Reskin and P. A. Roos, *Job Queues, Gender Queues: Explaining Women's Inroads into Male Occupations.* Philadelphia: Temple University Press.

———. 1990b. "Keepers of the Corporate Image: Women in Public Relations." Pp. 129–44 in B. F. Reskin and P. A. Roos, *Job Queues, Gender Queues: Explaining Women's Inroads into Male Occupations.* Philadelphia: Temple University Press.

Figart, Deborah M., and Barbara Bergmann. 1989. "Facilitating Women's Occupational Integration." Paper prepared for the U.S. Department of Labor, Commission on Workforce Quality and Labor Market Efficiency, American University.

Gross, Edward. 1968. *"Plus ça Change. . . .* The Sexual Segregation of Occupations over Time." *Social Problems* 16:198–208.

Hartmann, Heidi I. 1976. "Capitalism, Patriarchy, and Segregation by Sex." *Signs* 1: 137–70.

Hirsch, Susan E. 1986. "Rethinking the Sexual Division of Labor: Pullman Repair Shops, 1900–1969." *Radical History Review* 3:26–48.

Hodge, Robert W. 1973. "Toward a Theory of Racial Differences in Employment." *Social Forces* 52:16–31.

Kessler-Harris, Alice. 1982. *Out to Work.* New York: Oxford University Press.

———. 1986. "Women's History Goes to Trial: EEOC vs. Sears, Roebuck and Co." *Signs* 1:767–79.

Lieberson, Stanley. 1980. *A Piece of the Pie.* Berkeley: University of California Press.

Milkman, Ruth. 1987. *Gender at Work.* Urbana: University of Illinois Press.

Osterman, Paul. 1979. "Sex Discrimination in Professional Employment: A Case Study." *Industrial and Labor Relations Review* 32: 451–64.

Phipps, Polly A. 1990a. "Occupational and Industrial Change: Prescription for Feminization." Pp. 111–28 in B. F. Reskin and P. A. Roos, *Job Queues, Gender Queues: Explaining Women's Inroads into Male Occupations.* Philadelphia: Temple University Press.

———. 1990b. "Occupational Resegregation: A Case Study of Insurance Adjusters and Examiners." Pp. 224–40 in B. F. Reskin and P. A. Roos, *Job Queues, Gender Queues: Explaining Women's Inroads into Male Occupations.* Philadelphia: Temple University Press.

Reskin, Barbara F. 1988. "Bringing the Men Back In: Sex Differentiation and the Devaluation of Women's Work." *Gender & Society* 2:58–81.

Reskin, Barbara F., and Patricia A. Roos. 1985. "Collaborative Research on the Determinants of Changes in Occupations' Sex Composition Between 1970 and 1980." National Science Foundation Grant no. 85-NSF-SES–85–12452. Manuscript.

———. 1990. *Job Queues, Gender Queues: Explaining Women's Inroads into Male Occupations.* Philadelphia: Temple University Press.

Roos, Patricia A. 1990. "Hot Metal to Electronic Composition: Gender, Technology, and Social Change." Pp. 275–98 in B. F. Reskin and P. A. Roos, *Job Queues, Gender Queues: Explaining Women's Inroads into Male Occupations.* Philadelphia: Temple University Press.

Rotella, Elyce. 1977. *From Home to Office: U.S. Women at Work, 1870–1930.* Ann Arbor: UMI Research Press.

Steiger, Thomas, and Barbara F. Reskin. 1990. "Baking and Baking off: Deskilling and the Changing Sex Make Up of Bakers." Pp. 257–74 in B. F. Reskin and P. A. Roos, *Job Queues, Gender Queues: Explaining Women's Inroads into Male Occupations.* Philadelphia: Temple University Press.

Stolzenberg, Ross. 1982. "Industrial Profits and the Propensity to Employ Women Workers." Paper presented at the Workshop on Job Segregation by Sex, Committee on Women's Employment and Related Social Issues, National Research Council, Washington, DC.

Strober, Myra. 1984. "Toward a General Theory of Occupational Sex Segregation." Pp. 144–56 in *Sex Segregation in the Workplace: Trends, Explanations, Remedies,* edited by B. Reskin. Washington, DC: National Academy Press.

_____. 1988. "The Processes of Occupational Segregation: Relative Attractiveness and Patriarchy." Paper presented at the meetings of the American Educational Research Association, New Orleans.

Strober, Myra, and Carolyn Arnold. 1987. "The Dynamics of Occupational Segregation Among Bank Tellers." Pp. 107–48 in *Gender in the Workplace,* edited by C. Brown and J. Pechman. Washington, DC: Brookings Institution.

Strom, Sharon Hartman. 1987. "'Machines Instead of Clerks': Technology and the Feminization of Bookkeeping, 1910–1950." Pp. 63–97 in *Computer Chips and Paper Clips.* Vol. 2, edited by H. Hartmann. Washington, DC: National Academy Press.

Thomas, Barbara J. 1990. "Women's Gains in Insurance Sales: Increased Supply, Uncertain Demand." Pp. 183–204 in B. F. Reskin and P. A. Roos, *Job Queues, Gender Queues: Explaining Women's Inroads into Male Occupations.* Philadelphia: Temple University Press.

Thomas, Barbara J., and Barbara F. Reskin. 1990. "A Woman's Place Is Selling Homes: Women's Movement into Real Estate Sales." Pp. 205–24 in B. F. Reskin and P. A. Roos, *Job Queues, Gender Queues: Explaining Women's Inroads into Male Occupations.* Philadelphia: Temple University Press.

Thurow, Lester. 1969. *Poverty and Discrimination.* Washington, DC: Brookings Institution.

_____. 1972. "Education and Economic Equality." *The Public Interest* 28:66–81.

38

Egalitarianism and Gender Inequality

MARIA CHARLES

DAVID B. GRUSKY

The rise of egalitarian values and associated egalitarian institutional reforms is a distinctive feature of modernity and postmodernity. This development, which dates at least to the Enlightenment, intensified throughout the twentieth century as formal legal rights were extended to previously excluded groups (e.g., women), wide-reaching institutional reforms were implemented to equalize life chances (e.g., bureaucratic personnel policies), and anti-egalitarian doctrines (e.g., racism) were challenged. These processes of equalization, dramatic though they are, obviously do not exhaust the story of modernity and postmodernity. As is well known, this story is replete with counterpoints at which the forces for egalitarianism have been resisted, sometimes violently (as with recurrences of eugenics and fascism) and sometimes in quieter but still profound ways (as in the persistence of residential segregation).

This chapter is about one of those quieter anti-egalitarian forces currently playing out in the domain of gender stratification. At first blush, the forces for equalization may appear to be straightforwardly triumphing in this domain, as evidenced by (a) the rapid diffusion of egalitarian views on gender roles, (b) the withering away of the long-standing gender gap in college attendance and graduation, and (c) the steady increase in rates of female labor force participation (see Figure 38.1). These developments, although spectacular and unprecedented, have nonetheless been coupled with equally spectacular forms of resistance to equalization, especially within the workplace. Most notably, women and men continue to work in very different occupations, with women crowding into a relatively small number of historically female occupations (e.g., teacher, secretary, nurse). If one sought, for example, to undo all sex segregation by reallocating women to less segregated occupations, a full 52 percent of the employed women in the United States would have to be shifted out of their current occupational categories (Jacobs 2003). This extreme sex segregation is typical of what prevails throughout the advanced industrial world. Because sex segregation is so

---

This is a commissioned chapter that draws heavily on material in a previous publication (Maria Charles and David B. Grusky, *Occupational Ghettos: The Worldwide Segregation of Women and Men.* Copyright © 2004 by the Board of Trustees of the Leland Stanford Junior University.)

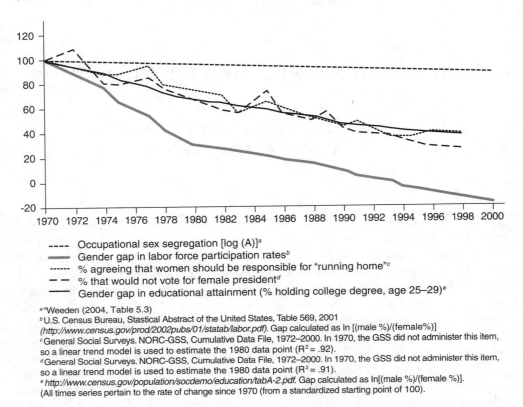

    ----   Occupational sex segregation [log (A)][a]
    ——   Gender gap in labor force participation rates[b]
    ······ % agreeing that women should be responsible for "running home"[c]
    – –   % that would not vote for female president[d]
    ——   Gender gap in educational attainment (% holding college degree, age 25–29)[e]

[a] "Weeden (2004, Table 5.3)
[b] U.S. Census Bureau, Stastical Abstract of the United States, Table 569, 2001
(http://www.census.gov/prod/2002pubs/01/statab/labor.pdf). Gap calculated as ln [(male %)/(female%)]
[c] General Social Surveys. NORC-GSS, Cumulative Data File, 1972–2000. In 1970, the GSS did not administer this item,
so a linear trend model is used to estimate the 1980 data point (R² = .92).
[d] General Social Surveys. NORC-GSS, Cumulative Data File, 1972–2000. In 1970, the GSS did not administer this item,
so a linear trend model is used to estimate the 1980 data point (R² = .91).
[e] http://www.census.gov/population/socdemo/education/tabA-2.pdf. Gap calculated as ln[(male %)/(female %)].
(All times series pertain to the rate of change since 1970 (from a standardized starting point of 100).

Figure 38.1   Parameters of Gender Stratification, 1970–2000

extreme, and because it colors the life chances and life experiences of so many women and men, we characterize the contemporary occupational structure as "hypersegregated" (see Massey and Denton 1993 for a related usage).

Why is the occupational structure so resistant to egalitarian forces? It could be argued that fundamental institutional change is inevitably prolonged and that full integration will ultimately be achieved through ongoing reform efforts (Jackson 1998). Although we cannot rule out the possibility of full integration in the distant future, we would stress that this outcome is by no means inevitable under prevailing policies, practices, and commitments. That is, rather than viewing sex segregation as a residual that is destined to wither away under contemporary egalitarian pressures, it is best regarded as an organic feature of modern economies that is ideologically consistent with egalitarianism, at least as the latter is understood and practiced today. In this sense, there is a deep structure to sex segregation that makes it a viable long-term feature of modern economies, even as pressures for equalization mount in other domains of the social stratification system.

The foregoing interpretation is consistent with the relatively slow pace of integrative change, the failure of conventional egalitarian policy to reduce occupational segregation, and the long-term persistence of pockets of especially extreme segregation ("occupational ghettos"). We briefly review each of these pieces of supporting evidence in the following paragraphs.

Slow Pace of Change

The clearest evidence of resistance to egalitarian pressures emerges in comparing the rate of desegregative change with corresponding rates of change elsewhere in the gender stratification system. As indicated in Figure 38.1, the moderate declines in occupational sex segregation over the past thirty years stand in stark contrast to the more precipitous changes in (a) attitudes toward gender roles, (b) rates of female labor force participation, and (c) the gender gap in educational investments. These differences in the pacing of change suggest that the segregation regime has been shielded from the equalizing forces that have played out more dramatically in other domains.

The Failure of Egalitarianism

It is also instructive to ask whether countries that have committed most explicitly to family-friendly policies, antidiscrimination legislation, and other forms of egalitarianism have made substantial headway in reducing sex segregation. If they have, such progress suggests that conventional egalitarian commitments, at least when carried out to their logical extremes, can serve to more quickly root out residual segregative processes. The available evidence is largely disappointing on this front. For example, Sweden is well known for its egalitarian and family-friendly policies, yet it remains deeply sex segregated to the present day. Conversely, countries that are commonly viewed as bastions of conservative gender practice, such as Japan and Italy, are *not* any more segregated than less conservative countries.

Unevenness of Change

There is, to be sure, clear and substantial evidence of desegregation in many sectors of the occupational structure, yet any careful observer of this process has to be struck by its unevenness and by the persistence, in particular, of many female occupational ghettos (e.g., secretary, nursery school teacher). Moreover, when male-dominated occupations embark on what appears to be integrative trajectories, the influx of women often continues well past the point of gender parity and ultimately creates a new female-dominated ghetto (e.g., Reskin and Roos 1990). These results suggest that sex segregation, far from being a holdover, is actively advanced by dynamics that are part and parcel of modern industrialism.

We therefore present the following puzzle: Why has sex segregation proven resistant to egalitarian pressures even as other forms of gender inequality have given way? Although we return to this puzzle repeatedly, it is important to recognize that it is but one part of a larger complex of perplexing findings that scholars of segregation have recently reported. The following two puzzles might, in particular, be cited: (a) the common view that male power and privilege allows men to dominate the best occupations fails to accord with the typical pattern of contemporary sex segregation; and (b) the highest levels of segregation are often found in socially and culturally progressive countries (such as Sweden) rather than in their more traditional counterparts (such as Japan). Taken together, these findings seem to suggest a topsy-turvy world in which males do not straightforwardly dominate the best jobs, family-friendly policies have a perverse segregating effect, and contemporary gender regimes continue to have a highly segregated "1950s feel" even in the twenty-first century.

We argue here that these empirical puzzles have emerged in the literature because stratification scholars tend to treat sex segregation in unidimensional terms and accordingly fail to appreciate that a complex amalgam of processes underlies gender inequality and renders some forms of segregation more entrenched than others. Although the tendency to represent segregation unidimensionally is widespread, it emerges especially clearly in classical theorizing about long-term trends in inequality. For example, structural-functional theorists typically treat all forms of "ascription," including sex segregation, as a generic residue destined to wither away either because discriminatory practices are inefficient or because bureaucratic forms of social organization have diffused widely and served to undermine discriminatory practices (e.g., Parsons 1970). In similar fashion, neoinstitutionalists assume that egalitarian practices and organizational forms will gradually diffuse and generate across-the-board reductions in segregation, although the main impetus for such diffusion is not so much the intrinsic efficiency of universalistic practices as the characteristically modern commitment to cultural *stories* about their efficiency (e.g., Meyer 2001). Finally, some early feminist scholars (e.g., Huber 1988) conceptualized occupational sex segregation as one of the main outcomes of "patriarchal" forms of social organization, again implying that the fate of sex segregation is simply a function of the larger fate of patriarchal social relations

that "create solidarity and interdependence among men and enable them to dominate women" (Hartmann 1981, p. 14). This approach typically treats both patriarchy and inequality in monolithic terms and thus draws scholars into weaving stories about the extent of segregation rather than its many dimensions and their different responsiveness to egalitarian forces.

These various theories share the prejudice that the explanandum of interest (segregation) may be represented in unidimensional terms, but they differ in their claims about the extent or pacing of change in this explanandum. If segregation is seen as persistent or ubiquitous, then reference is made to the strength and durability of patriarchal norms, institutions, or values (Chafetz 1988; Hartmann 1981; Ridgeway 1997; Williams 2000). If segregation is seen as relatively weak or declining in strength, this is attributed to (a) the gradual displacement of traditional gender roles and ideologies with universalistic values, (b) the diffusion of bureaucratic forms of organization, or (c) the discrimination-eroding discipline of the competitive market (Goode 1963; Ramirez 1987). These discrepant interpretations are typically evaluated by applying scalar measures of segregation that likewise presume unidimensionality (such as the index of dissimilarity). There is accordingly a close correspondence between classical unidimensional theorizing and the methodologies that have until now been adopted to describe and compare sex segregation.

We argue, then, that various puzzles have emerged in the literature because conventional theories and methods blind us to the multidimensional structure of segregation. By advancing a two-dimensional conceptualization of sex segregation and a matching methodological approach, we seek to solve

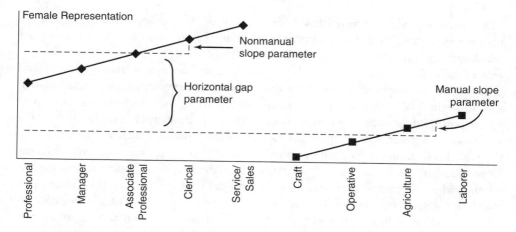

Note: In our models, the major occupational categories are coded in terms of a socioeconomic scale, thus allowing the intercategory distances to vary freely. For the purpose of simplifying the presentation, we have assumed here that intercategory distances are the same.

Figure 38.2   Anatomy of a Hypothetical Sex-Segregation Regime

the puzzles and build an alternative understanding of the development of segregation regimes.

A New Multidimensional Model

It is useful to begin by asking whether the underlying structure of sex segregation is consistent with unidimensional accounts of segregation. In many such accounts, it is simply presumed that the best occupations will be dominated by men, either because women have disproportionate domestic responsibilities that reduce their incentive to invest in demanding careers (e.g., Becker 1991), or because employers practice discrimination through "glass ceiling" personnel policies and other forms of male-biased queuing in the labor market (e.g., Reskin and Roos 1990).

This conventional account falls short because it fails to appreciate the distinction between vertical and horizontal forms of segregation and, in particular, the interac-

tion between these two forms (see Blackburn, Jarman, and Brooks 2000; Semyonov and Jones 1999). The model in Figure 38.2, which underlies all our analysis, builds explicitly on this distinction: the "nonmanual slope parameter" governs the extent to which men dominate the most desirable classes in the nonmanual sector; the "manual slope parameter" governs the extent to which men dominate the most desirable classes in the manual sector; and the "horizontal gap parameter" governs the extent to which men are disproportionately allocated into the manual sector rather than the nonmanual one.

The horizontal axis of this figure arrays the nine major occupational categories defined by the International Labour Office (ILO) on an approximate socioeconomic scale ranging from high (professional) to low (agricultural). Following convention, the first five categories in this list may be characterized as nonmanual, and the second four may be characterized as manual.

The vertical axis of this figure, labeled "female representation," indicates the extent to which women or men are overrepresented in each of these nine categories. In the interior of the figure, the slopes of the two lines reveal the strength of vertical segregation, with a steep positive slope indicating that men are much advantaged in the competition for desirable occupations, a moderate positive slope indicating that men are only weakly advantaged in this competition, and a negative slope (which is logically possible but empirically unlikely) indicating that women are advantaged. The extent of horizontal segregation (the "horizontal gap parameter") is given by the vertical distance between the manual and nonmanual lines.[1] The foregoing three-parameter specification, which serves to summarize the aggregate structure of segregation, allows us to resolve long-standing empirical puzzles in the field that arose because most scholars have defaulted to a unidimensional view.

The two vertical slope parameters in Figure 38.2 are partly consistent with a unidimensional queuing formulation (whereby men secure better occupations than women), but our specification may be understood as a revision of this formulation because queuing theory does not allow for a "horizontal gap" expressing the tendency of women to be disproportionately allocated to the nonmanual sector (even though nonmanual occupations are, on average, more desirable than manual ones). Moreover, we allow the vertical principle to be stronger in some regions of the labor market (i.e., the manual sector) than in others, and we also allow the vertical principle to be stronger at the aggregate level than at the level of detailed occupations (which are not represented in Figure 38.2). Although queuing theory thus motivates some aspects of our parameterization, it cannot provide a complete account of segregation (see Reskin and Roos 1990; Strober 1984).

The deficiencies of queuing theory and other unidimensional formulations arise in large part because the cultural underpinnings of segregation are fundamentally two-dimensional. Under the parameterization of Figure 38.2, it is assumed that (a) the cultural tenet of male primacy undergirds vertical segregation, and (b) the complementary cultural tenet of gender essentialism undergirds horizontal segregation. The tenet of male primacy represents men as more status-worthy than women and better suited for positions of authority and domination, and the tenet of gender essentialism represents women as more competent than men in personal service, nurturance, and social interaction. In the modern context, these two cultural tenets tend to coexist with one another, thus giving segregation systems a hybrid character. We review these two tenets below.

Essentialism

Why do women crowd into the nonmanual sector and men crowd into the manual sector? In addressing this question, one has to be struck by the strong correspondence between (a) the traits that are regarded as distinctively male or female (gender essentialism) and (b) the task requirements of manual and nonmanual labor. Although prevailing characterizations of male and female traits are complex and multifaceted, a core feature of such characterizations is that women are presumed to excel in personal service, nurturance, and interpersonal interaction, and men are presumed to excel in interaction with things (rather than people) and in strenuous or physical labor. These stereotypes about natural male and female characteristics are disseminated and perpetuated through popular culture and media, through social interaction in which significant others (parents, peers, teachers) implicitly or explicitly support such interpretations, and through micro-level cognitive processes in which individuals pursue and remember evidence consistent with their preexisting stereotypes and ignore, discount, or forget evidence that undermines those stereotypes (Fiske 1998; Reskin 2000). The main claim we wish to advance is that horizontal segregation is maintained and reproduced in large part because nonmanual occupations embody characteristics (such as service orientation) regarded as prototypically female, while manual occupations embody characteristics (such as strenuousness and physicality) regarded as prototypically male (see, e.g., Crompton 2001; Lorber 1993; Milkman and Townsley 1994; Tilly 1998). This linkage is converted into durable horizontal segregation because (a) employers internalize these essentialist presumptions and allocate occupations to men and women in accord with them (i.e., essentialist discrimination), and (b) workers internalize the same essentialist presumptions and aspire to occupations that satisfy them (i.e., essentialist preferences). It follows that horizontal segregation has both demand-side and supply-side sources.

Male Primacy

Why are men disproportionately allocated to the best-paid and most desirable occupations in both the nonmanual and manual sectors? In accounting for such vertical segregation, we again understand the main forces at work as being cultural in form, but now the relevant cultural principle is the long-standing belief that men are more status-worthy than women and accordingly better suited for positions of high pay or authority. Despite the rise of universalistic ideals, there persist deeply rooted and widely shared cultural beliefs that men are better suited than women for all forms of labor outside the family, and that men are, in particular, better suited than women for labor involving the exercise of authority and power (Deaux and Kite 1987; Ridgeway 1997). We argue, then, that vertical segregation is maintained and reproduced in part because it is consistent with the cultural value of male primacy. The main proximate mechanisms by which beliefs in male primacy are translated into vertical segregation are (a) the recognition among men that, because they are regarded as primary breadwinners, they should make substantial investments in human capital (i.e., supply-side sources), and (b) the recognition among employers that, because men are regarded as primary breadwinners, their commitment to the labor force will be greater and hence there is a greater payoff to investing in them rather than in women (who may exhibit intermittency). Moreover, employers reward men with better jobs not just because they assume that men have a greater commitment to the labor force, but also because they regard men as intrinsically more competent. Because such assumptions about intrinsic competency are internalized by everyone, male workers will also come to believe that they are more competent at high-status tasks than females and hence more likely to succeed in those tasks, thereby motivating them to make the requisite investments in human capital. The premise of male primacy, like that of gender essentialism, is therefore expressed in supply-side as well as demand-side processes.

The Dynamics of Gender Segregation

This two-dimensional understanding of segregation casts light on the processes by which the spread of egalitarian commitments will affect the structure of gender inequality. Within the cultural domain, the diffusion of egalitarianism is an extremely important development, one that will likely continue apace unless some unforeseen catastrophic event has a recalibrating effect. Although the future of egalitarianism appears bright, one should consider the limits of the particular version of egalitarianism that has taken hold and that continues to diffuse. Among the many competing egalitarian visions, it is clear that "liberal egalitarian" strands remain dominant, implying that our collective commitment to gender equality mainly takes the form of developing procedural guarantees of equal opportunity. This commitment to liberal egalitarianism is quite compatible with the essentialist presumption that men and women have fundamentally different tastes, skills, and abilities (see Charles and Grusky 2004). That is, the liberal egalitarian vision of women and men as autonomous agents entitled to equal rights, opportunities, and treatment allows for the persistence of fundamentally gendered outlooks and identities. For a liberal egalitarian, it is enough to defend the right of women to fairly compete for any occupation to which they aspire, without in any way questioning how those aspirations were formed or why they may differ from the aspirations of men. It follows that liberal egalitarians embrace an "equal but different" conceptualization of gender and social justice.

Insofar as this version of egalitarianism continues to diffuse, the push toward complete equality may be slowed. This suppressive effect occurs through proximate mechanisms on both the supply and demand sides. On the supply side, we cannot expect liberal egalitarians to pay much attention to individual aspirations and self-assessments, meaning that the persistence of gender differences in these outlooks and identities will not be scrutinized or challenged to the extent that they would be under more radical egalitarian commitments. On the demand side, the liberal egalitarian commitment delegitimates all forms of pure discrimination, but it does not as directly challenge statistical discrimination that rests on essentialist presumptions. In a world in which women have disproportionately "invested" in nurturance and service, essentialist presumptions about gender differences in capabilities have ample room to flourish, and employers may well reason that gender provides a good signal of capabilities in nurturing and service. The main argument we would make, then, is that liberal variants of egalitarianism serve principally to undermine the presumption of male primacy rather than gender essentialism; and, consequently, horizontal forms of segregation may prove to be quite resistant to egalitarianism.

Is the Argument Supported?

This argument can be addressed with the international data archive described in Table 38.1. We apply a cross-nationally harmonized classification of sixty-four detailed occupational categories to census segregation data from ten industrial market economies. The data are organized in the form of a three-dimensional, 1,280-cell matrix with sixty-four occupations, two sexes, and ten countries. For most of our

Table 38.1   Data and Sample Characteristics

Country	Census Year	Sample Size
Belgium	1991	3,418,512
France	1990	900,255
West Germany	1993	128,912
Italy	1991	21,071,282
Portugal	1991	4,037,130
Sweden	1990	4,059,813
Switzerland	1990	3,076,445
United Kingdom	1991	2,405,091
United States	1990	1,152,885
Japan	1990	12,220,974

analyses, we examine segregation principally in terms of nine major classes, each of which is an aggregation of a subset of the sixty-four detailed occupations in the full array. We report results based on "self-weighted" data in which the actual sample size in each country is preserved. Because large-sample countries (such as Italy and Japan) have much leverage on our estimates, we have reestimated many of our models after standardizing sample sizes to an arbitrary constant (N = 10,000), but such standardized results have proved to be much the same as self-weighted results and therefore will not be reported here.

We have measured horizontal inequality at the aggregate level by distinguishing the five nonmanual categories (managerial, professional, associate professional, clerical, service/sales) from the four manual categories (agriculture, craft, operative, laborer). We measure vertical inequality with the internationally standardized socioeconomic index (SEI) published by Ganzeboom and Treiman (1996). This index, which is constructed as a weighted average of the educational attainment and income of occupational incumbents, is highly correlated with an international occupational prestige index. We apply two variants of this scale in our analy-

ses: (a) the aggregate variant (V1) assigns average SEI values to each of the nine major categories, and (b) the detailed variant (V2) assigns SEI values to each of the sixty-four detailed occupations. The aggregate variant of this scale is used to examine the extent to which aggregate segregation is vertically organized, whereas the detailed variant is used to examine the extent to which detailed segregation is vertically organized.

The key question that arises is whether the between-category component may be explained in vertical terms. In its purest form, a queuing model implies that men are disproportionately allocated to the most desirable major occupations, thus suggesting the following specification:

$$m_{ijk} = \alpha_k \beta_{ik} \gamma_{jk} e^{\varepsilon(Z_i V1_j)},$$

where i, j, and k index gender, occupation, and country respectively, α_k is the grand mean in the kth country, β_{ik} is the country-specific marginal effect for the ith gender, γ_{jk} is the country-specific marginal effect for the jth occupation, ε refers to the effect of socioeconomic status on female representation (at the aggregate level), Z_i is an indicator variable for gender (i.e., $Z_1 = 0$ and $Z_2 = 1$), and $V1_j$ refers to the aggregate version of our socioeconomic scale. We have identified this model by imposing standard constraints on the parameters.

The test statistic for this model, L^2 = 16,081,116 with 629 df, implies that only 2.5 percent of the total association at the aggregate level can be explained in vertical terms. Moreover, our estimate of ε under this model is .008, meaning that female representation increases by a factor of 1.008 for each unit increase in socioeconomic status. This estimate, which indicates that women are (slightly) overrepresented in high-status occupations, is of course inconsistent with simple queuing perspectives (see Blackburn, Brooks, and Jarman 2001; Charles and Grusky 1995; Roos 1985). Although such a result is counterintuitive, it is consistent with the long-standing argument that socioeconomic scores overstate the desirability of routine nonmanual occupations and hence create the (misleading) appearance of female advantage (e.g., Acker 1980; England 1979). We have no quarrels with this long-standing account, but it may not be complete. The queuing model fails, as we see it, not only because socioeconomic scales are flawed or because the vertical dynamic is weak but also because this dynamic is obscured in the absence of controls for horizontal segregation. The structure of segregation is in this sense fundamentally multidimensional.

We can test this argument by examining whether the vertical coefficient reverses sign and strengthens in the context of a multidimensional model. When vertical and horizontal effects are simultaneously fit, the following model is generated:

$$m_{ijk}=\alpha_k\beta_{ik}\gamma_{jk}e^{\varepsilon(Z_iV1_j)+\omega(Z_iH_j)},$$

where H_j is the horizontal term (i.e., $H_j = 1$ if j is a manual occupation and $H_j = 0$ otherwise), ω is the effect of horizontal status

on female representation, and the remaining terms are defined as before. The explained association under this specification increases dramatically from 2.5 to 80.4 percent, and the vertical coefficient further assumes the expected negative sign and becomes quite strong (-.050). The horizontal coefficient is likewise very strong: The estimate of ω, −1.96, implies that female representation is 7.10 times greater in a nonmanual occupation than a corresponding manual occupation of the same socioeconomic status. This effect, which is equivalent to that associated with a downward shift in status of nearly forty points, is surely strong enough to suggest that scholars of gender stratification should move beyond their long-standing focus on vertical inequality and begin attending to horizontal forms of stratification.

We might also allow the strength of the vertical effect to differ across sectors. This model may be represented as follows:

$$m_{ijk}=\alpha_k\beta_{ik}\gamma_{jk}e^{\psi(Z_iN_jV1_j)+\varepsilon(Z_iM_jV1_j)+\omega(Z_iH_j)},$$

where N_j is an indicator variable for nonmanual occupations (i.e., $N_j = 1$ if j is a nonmanual occupation and $N_j = 0$ otherwise), M_j is an indicator variable for manual occupations (i.e., $M_j = H_j$), and ψ and ε express the strength of vertical segregation within the nonmanual and manual sectors respectively.[2] With this specification, the explained association increases modestly (from 80.4 to 85.3 percent), and the vertical effect is revealed to be slightly weaker in the nonmanual sector (-.040) than in the manual sector (-.047). The modern segregation regime thus takes on the three-parameter form represented in Figure 38.2: The horizontal gap parameter captures the dramatic overrepresentation of women in the nonmanual sector, and the two slope parame-

ters capture the tendency for men to dominate the best occupations within the manual and nonmanual sectors.

It follows that our three-parameter specification effectively exhausts the structure of
segregation at the aggregate level. Is disaggregate segregation equally amenable to a
parsimonious account? Although we shall
not attempt any elaborate modeling here,
we can at least test the simple claim that
segregation across detailed categories assumes a simple vertical form. This hypothesis can be tested with the following model:

$$m_{ijk} = \alpha_k \beta_{ik} \gamma_{jk} e^{\varepsilon(Z_i V2_j) + \rho_c(Z_i)},$$

where ρ refers to the scale values for major
occupational categories (indexed by c), and
$V2_j$ refers to the detailed variant of our socioeconomic scale. This model explains a
mere 3.3 percent of the total disaggregate
association; and the vertical coefficient, estimated at -.034, is only 68 percent as
strong as the corresponding vertical coefficient (-.050) at the aggregate level (under
the model of equation 2). We can conclude
that the forces of patriarchy do not operate
all that efficiently in allocating men to the
most desirable occupations within each
major category. It is possible, of course, that
the vertical coefficient is suppressed because
various types of essentialist effects (such as a
nurturing effect or service effect) have been
improperly omitted from our model. It is
surely worth exploring this possibility in future research. Without explicit evidence of
such bias, our provisional conclusion is
nonetheless that disaggregate segregation
does not have a clear vertical character to it,
again calling conventional queuing models
into question.

We next ask whether our three-parameter
specification suffices to describe the structure
of aggregate segregation in *all* advanced in-

dustrial countries. We have estimated single-
country models analogous to the foregoing
pooled models and reported the relevant parameters and fit statistics in Table 38.2. The
main conclusions that emerge are: (a) a simple unidimensional model explains only a
small minority of the aggregate association
in each country (see panel A); (b) the vertical segregation coefficient from this unidimensional model assumes the same positive
(and counterintuitive) sign in each country;
(c) our alternative multidimensional specification explains more than 70 percent of the
aggregate association in each country (see
panel D); (d) the vertical segregation coefficients from this model become strong and
negative in each country; (e) the horizontal
segregation effect is likewise strong in most
countries (except Italy and Portugal) and
may therefore be regarded as an important,
if neglected, source of contemporary hyper-
segregation; and (f) the nonmanual slope
coefficient is weaker than the corresponding
manual coefficient in all but two countries
(the United States and Japan).

We can now turn to the question of why
countries with a comparatively deep commitment to egalitarianism, such as France,
West Germany, Sweden, the United Kingdom, and the United States, have remained
quite sex segregated. As shown in Panel C
of Table 38.2, the average value of the horizontal segregation parameter for these five
"egalitarian" countries is -3.20, whereas the
corresponding average for the five less egalitarian countries in our sample is -2.07.
There is accordingly no evidence that egalitarianism reduces the horizontal variant of
segregation. To the contrary, it would appear to increase such segregation, an effect
that may arise because egalitarianism has
drawn women into the labor force at precisely the time when the nonmanual sector

Table 38.2   Single-Country Models of Vertical and Horizontal Sex Segregation

Model	Aggregate Segregation Explained (%)	Segregation Coefficient Vertical	Segregation Coefficient Horizontal
A. Vertical Effect			
Belgium	3.66	0.01	
France	2.40	0.01	
West Germany	1.54	0.01	
Italy	12.78	0.01	
Portugal	0.52	0.00	
Sweden	1.02	0.01	
Switzerland	0.68	0.01	
United Kingdom	0.71	0.01	
United States	9.15	0.02	
Japan	0.61	0.00	
B. Horizontal Effect			
Belgium	43.48		−1.10
France	40.41		−1.40
West Germany	42.34		−1.32
Italy	59.55		−0.83
Portugal	18.36		−0.49
Sweden	41.64		−1.53
Switzerland	42.01		−1.49
United Kingdom	39.34		−1.39
United States	55.44		−1.54
Japan	20.82		−0.65
C. Vertical and Horizontal Effect (Additive)			
Belgium	75.08	−.053	−2.37
France	79.64	−.086	−3.45
West Germany	84.82	−.077	−3.14
Italy	75.73	−.027	−1.38
Portugal	39.02	−.034	−1.19
Sweden	79.95	−0.80	−3.40
Switzerland	82.43	−.080	−3.23
United Kingdom	83.03	−0.84	−3.34
United States	75.02	−.049	−2.69
Japan	77.63	−.075	−2.16

D. Vertical and Horizontal Effect (Ineractive)

Model	Aggregate Segregation Explained (%)	Vertical Nonmanual	Vertical Manual	Horizontal
Belgium	85.84	−.039	−.085	−2.89
France	87.99	−.066	−.110	−4.09
West Germany	92.11	−0.62	−.090	−3.61
Italy	83.84	−.017	−.046	−1.56
Portugal	71.93	−.004	−.089	−1.42
Sweden	87.84	−.065	−.114	−4.13
Switzerland	88.37	−.068	−.101	−3.86
United Kingdom	87.42	−.071	−.077	−3.80
United States	75.64	−.045	−.027	−2.86
Japan	77.94	−.078	−.013	−2.11

Table 38.3   Frequencies for Gender Egalitarianism Variable

Country	Value
Belgium	51.52
France	58.95
West Germany	58.46
Italy	47.66
Portugal	54.27
Sweden	87.93
Switzerland	54.70
United Kingdom	58.62
United States	71.06
Japan	25.71

is expanding (see Charles and Grusky 2004 for details).

This counterintuitive result can be formalized by developing an explicit measure of gender egalitarianism and then asking how it varies with horizontal segregation. We may define "gender egalitarianism" as a commitment to gender-based equality of opportunity and operationalize it as the percentage of respondents in each country disagreeing with the statement that "men have greater rights to jobs during periods of high unemployment." This survey item, which comes out of the 1990 World Values Survey (WVS), signals whether respondents accept the assumption of male economic dominance or reject it in favor of the norms of universalism and equal opportunity (see Table 38.3 for country-level values). If we then regress the coefficients for horizontal segregation (Panel C) on our measure of egalitarianism, we secure a coefficient of -.026. This coefficient implies that a 40 point increase in egalitarianism, a difference roughly equal to that between Italy and Sweden, raises horizontal segregation by a factor of 2.83. The "Swedish puzzle" is solved, therefore, by recognizing that the logic of egalitarian policy is not inconsistent with the persistence and even the growth of horizontal forms of segregation.

We of course appreciate that many other macro-level variables may well affect the extent of vertical and horizontal segregation. For example, we have argued elsewhere that service-sector expansion and economic rationalization are important structural forces affecting modern segregation, forces that can again perversely work to increase rather than reduce horizontal segregation (Charles and Grusky 2004). Although the effects of service-sector expansion and rationalization rest on complicated mechanisms that cannot be reviewed here, they are consistent with our larger argument that sex segregation cannot necessarily be expected to straightforwardly decline.

Conclusion

The preceding discussion suggests that the future of gender inequality rests on a struggle between egalitarian and essentialist forces that is not quite as one-sided as modernization theorists have sometimes claimed (see, e.g., Jackson 1998; Parsons 1970). If gender segregation is especially durable, it is partly because it has a deep essentialist undergirding. The "first revolution" in gender inequality, which has generated important reductions in segregation over the past thirty years, has been driven in large part by declines in vertical inequality (see Weeden 2004). Will there be a "second revolution" that leads to an analogous decline in horizontal segregation? In answering this question, conventional functionalist and neoinstitutionalist accounts fall short because they fail to recognize that horizontal segregation proceeds from an essentialist ideology that can persist—even thrive—in the context of liberal egalitarian norms of equal opportunity.

In the contemporary context, men and women are presumed to have rather different tastes and aptitudes, and liberal egalitarianism works merely to ensure that such differences, however they might be generated, can then be pursued or expressed in a fair (gender-neutral) contest. The assumption that men and women have fundamentally different tastes and capacities is reinforced in various social settings, not just in families (with their gender-specific socialization practices) and work organizations (with their discriminatory hiring practices) but in other institutional contexts as well. By way of (trivial) example, consider the practice among American fast-food restaurants of providing gender-specific toys to children, a practice of interest only because it is widely diffused and evidently unobjectionable to all but a small minority of "gender progressives." If these same restaurants distributed toys on the basis of racial or class standing, the practice would be deemed absurd at best and racist or classist at worst. This example suggests that, at least in the United States, it is less legitimate to interpret racial or class-based inequalities in essentialist terms than to interpret gender segregation and inequality in these terms.

In the long run, it is of course possible that a yet deeper form of egalitarianism will emerge and delegitimate (a) the tendency of males and females to develop different tastes, aspirations, and market capacities, and (b) the tendency of employers to make judgments about productivity through essentialist lenses. There are indeed many signs that just such a form of egalitarianism is developing. Most notably, conventional sociological understandings of the roles of socialization, social exchange, and power differentials in generating preferences have diffused widely in contemporary industrial societies, suggesting that preferences and choices formerly regarded as sacrosanct are increasingly treated as outcomes of unequal and unfair social processes. This deeper form of egalitarianism is reflected in attempts by some parents to minimize gender bias in the socialization of their children, at least in the early years of childrearing before the unremitting influence of societywide essentialism typically undermines their efforts. It is surely plausible that this deeper form of egalitarianism will ultimately take hold (see Ramirez 1987, p. 270).

For our part, we would merely stress that prevailing forms of egalitarianism do not fully delegitimate essentialist processes and that a true "second revolution," one that establishes this new and broader definition of equality, will therefore be needed to eliminate essentialist segregation. There should be no illusions about how formidable the remaining barriers are. Far from being some "inevitable destiny" (Jackson 1998, p. 271), the second revolution will face many obstacles, not the least of which is an entrenched tradition of classical liberalism that celebrates individual choice and thus supports and sustains those forms of inequality that can be represented as consistent with it.

NOTES

1. If the two vertical segregation lines are parallel, the distance between them is of course constant. However, insofar as the slopes of these lines are allowed to differ, the size of the horizontal parameter will depend on the implicit zero point of the vertical scale.

2. Under this specification, the two vertical parameters no longer generate parallel lines, meaning that the estimated size of the horizontal parameter depends on the implied zero point of the socioeconomic scale. We have fixed the zero point of this scale at 37 (which is the midpoint between the score for the lowest nonmanual cate-

gory [40] and the highest manual category [34]). The two vertical segregation lines are furthest from one another at this point (assuming that the nonmanual slope is weaker than the manual one).

REFERENCES

Acker, Joan R. 1980. "Women and Stratification: A Review of Recent Literature." *Contemporary Sociology* 9: 25–39.

Becker, Gary S. 1991. *A Treatise on the Family*. Cambridge, MA: Harvard University Press.

Blackburn, Robert M., Jennifer Jarman, and Bradley Brooks. 2000. "The Puzzle of Gender Segregation and Inequality: A Cross-National Analysis." *European Sociological Review* 16: 119–135.

_____. 2001. "Occupational Stratification: The Vertical Dimension of Occupational Segregation." *Work, Employment, and Society* 15: 5111–5138.

Chafetz, Janet Saltzman. 1988. "The Gender Division of Labor and the Reproduction of Female Disadvantage: Toward an Integrated Theory." *Journal of Family Issues* 9: 108–131.

Charles, Maria, and David B. Grusky. 1995. "Models for Describing the Underlying Structure of Sex Segregation." *American Journal of Sociology* 100: 931–971.

_____. 2004. *Occupational Ghettos: The Worldwide Segregation of Women and Men*. Stanford, CA: Stanford University Press.

Crompton, Rosemary. 2001. "The Gendered Restructuring of the Middle Classes." In Janeen Baxter and Mark Western, eds., *Reconfigurations of Class and Gender*, pp. 29–54. Stanford, CA: Stanford University Press.

Deaux, Kay, and Mary Kite. 1987. "Thinking about Gender." In B. Hess and M. Ferree, eds., *Analyzing Gender: A Handbook of Social Science Research*, pp. 92–117. Newbury Park, CA: Sage.

England, Paula. 1979. "Women and Occupational Prestige: A Case of Vacuous Sex Equality." *Signs* 5: 252–265.

Fiske, Susan T. 1998. "Stereotyping, Prejudice, and Discrimination." In D. T. Gilbert, S.T. Fiske, and G. Lindzey, eds., *Handbook of Social Psychology*, pp. 357–411. New York: McGraw-Hill.

Ganzeboom, Harry B. G., and Donald J. Treiman. 1996. "Internationally Comparable Measures of Occupational Status for the 1988 International Standard Classification of Occupations." *Social Science Research* 25: 201–239.

Goode, William J. 1963. *World Revolution and Family Patterns*. New York: Free Press.

Hartmann, Heidi I. 1981. "The Unhappy Marriage of Marxism and Feminism: Towards a More Progressive Union." In Lydia Sargent, ed., *Women and Revolution: A Discussion of the Unhappy Marriage of Marxism and Feminism*, pp. 1–41. Boston: South End Press.

Huber, Joan. 1988. "A Theory of Family, Economy, and Gender." *Journal of Family Issues* 9: 9–26.

Jackson, Robert Max. 1998. *Destined for Equality: The Inevitable Rise of Women's Status*. Cambridge, MA: Harvard University Press.

Jacobs, Jerry. 2003. "Detours on the Road to Equality: Women, Work, and Higher Education." *Contexts* 2: 32–41.

Lorber, Judith. 1993. *Paradoxes of Gender*. New Haven, CT: Yale University Press.

Massey, Douglas S., and Nancy A. Denton. 1993. *American Apartheid: Segregation and the Making of the Underclass*. Cambridge, MA: Harvard University Press.

Meyer, John W. 2001. "The Evolution of Modern Stratification Systems." In David B. Grusky, ed., *Social Stratification: Class, Race, and Gender in Sociological Perspective*, 2d ed., pp. 881–90. Boulder, CO: Westview Press.

Milkman, Ruth, and Eleanor Townsley. 1994. "Gender and the Economy." In Neil J. Smelser and Richard Swedberg, eds., *The Handbook of Economic Sociology*, pp. 600–619. Princeton, NJ: Princeton University Press.

Parsons, Talcott. 1970. "Equality and Inequality in Modern Society, or Social Stratification Revisited." In Edward O. Laumann, ed., *Social Stratification: Research and Theory for the 1970s*, pp. 14–72. Indianapolis: Bobbs-Merrill.

Ramirez, Francisco O. 1987. "Global Changes, World Myths, and the Demise of Cultural Gender: Implications for the United States."

In Terry Boswell and Albert Bergesen, eds., *America's Changing Role in the World System*, pp. 257–73. New York: Praeger.

Reskin, Barbara F. 2000. "The Proximate Causes of Employment Discrimination." *Contemporary Sociology* 29: 319–328.

Reskin, Barbara F., and Patricia A. Roos. 1990. *Job Queues, Gender Queues: Explaining Women's Inroads into Male Occupations*. Philadelphia: Temple University Press.

Ridgeway, Cecilia L. 1997. "Interaction and the Conservation of Gender Inequality: Considering Employment." *American Sociological Review* 62: 218–235.

Roos, Patricia A. 1985. *Gender and Work: A Comparative Analysis of Industrial Societies*. New York: State University of New York Press.

Semyonov, Moshe, and Frank L. Jones. 1999. "Dimensions of Gender Occupational Differentiation in Segregation and Inequality: A Cross-National Analysis." *Social Indicators Research* 46: 225–247.

Strober, Myra H. 1984. "Toward a General Theory of Occupational Sex Segregation: The Case of Public School Teaching." In Barbara F. Reskin, ed., *Sex Segregation in the Workplace*. Washington, DC: National Academy Press.

Tilly, Charles. 1998. *Durable Inequality*. Berkeley: University of California Press.

Weeden, Kim A. 2004. "Profiles of Change: Sex Segregation in the United States." In Maria Charles and David B. Grusky, *Occupational Ghettos: The Worldwide Segregation of Women and Men*. Stanford, CA: Stanford University Press.

Williams, Joan. 2000. *Unbending Gender: Why Family and Work Conflict and What to Do About It*. New York: Oxford University Press.

39

The Within-Job Gender Wage Gap

TROND PETERSEN
LAURIE A. MORGAN

There are three types of discrimination that can produce wage differences between men and women. (1) Women are differentially allocated to occupations and establishments that pay lower wages. This may involve discrimination partly through differential access to occupations and establishments—that is, the matching process at the point of hire—and partly through subsequent promotions. We call this process *allocative discrimination*. (2) Occupations held primarily by women are paid lower wages than those held primarily by men, although skill requirements and other wage relevant factors are the same. This process, which we call *valuative discrimination,* is addressed by comparable worth initiatives. (3) Women receive lower wages than men within a given occupation and establishment. We call this process *within-job wage discrimination*. Allocative and valuative discrimination involve the segregation of men and women into different occupations, establishments, or both, and may

occur without within-job wage discrimination. Thus, although it may be the case that where men and women share the same jobs they receive the same pay, they simply do not share the same jobs all that often. One conjecture currently accepted by many researchers is that wage differences are less an issue of within-job wage discrimination and more a matter of allocative and valuative processes. That is, the segregation of women into lower paying occupations, establishments, or both, and lower pay in occupations held primarily by women are more important than pay differences within the same job in explaining the gender wage gap. Treiman and Hartmann (1981, 92–93) write, "Although the committee recognizes that instances of unequal pay for the same work have not been entirely eliminated, we believe that they are probably not now the major source of differences in earnings."

This conjecture is drawn primarily from a large literature that focuses on pay differences

---

This is a commissioned chapter that draws heavily on material in a previous publication (Trond Petersen and Laurie A. Morgan, "Separate and Unequal: Occupation-Establishment Sex Segregation and the Gender Wage Gap," *American Journal of Sociology* 101 [September 1995], pp. 329–61. Copyright © 1995 by the University of Chicago Press).

across and within occupations. One pattern of findings is that the wage gap between men and women becomes smaller as occupational controls become finer, suggesting that a large proportion of the wage gap is explained by occupational distribution (Treiman and Hartmann 1981; Reskin and Roos 1990). For example, Treiman and Hartmann (1981, 33–39) explained 10 to 20 percent of the raw gap using 222 occupational categories and 35 to 40 percent using 479 categories. These studies usually draw on data from the Census or national probability samples that allow no analysis of practices in specific establishments. Additional evidence suggests that, within occupations, the distribution of women across firms or establishments also accounts for some portion of the wage gap. For example, Blau (1977) found that in 11 clerical occupations, differences in men's and women's wages were larger between than within establishments.

Yet the prevailing conjecture remains a conjecture. It has not been shown that men and women receive equal pay within given occupations in given establishments. What has been shown is that sex segregation is extensive and pervasive (Bielby and Baron 1984; Petersen and Morgan 1995), but not the extent to which sex segregation accounts for the wage gap or that, when sex segregation is absent, the sexes receive more or less equal treatment. To confirm such a claim, one needs data on wages of men and women in the same detailed occupational group or position within the same establishment. Such data are not widely available except for isolated establishments.

This article reports a large-scale empirical investigation of wage differences between men and women within the same detailed occupational position within the same estab-

lishment. We use establishment-level data from a wide variety of industries. In each establishment, individual-level wage data for a large array of detailed occupational groups were collected, providing more accurate wage as well as occupational data than probably any other surveys available, except in some case studies of single establishments (e.g., Hartmann 1987). We focus first on production and clerical employees in 16 U.S. industries in the 1974 to 1983 period, primarily 1974 to 1978, analyzing data on 787,577 employees, 705 industry-specific occupations, 6,057 establishments, and 71,214 occupation-establishment pairs. Second, we focus on seven professional and three administrative occupations across a broad range of industries in 1981, analyzing data on about 740,000 employees distributed across 2,162 establishments and 16,433 occupation-establishment pairs.

We make no attempt to settle the important conceptual issues that go along with the empirical patterns we address, namely the sources of observed patterns, neither from the demand side—that is, discriminatory behavior by employers—or the supply side—that is, behaviors by employees and prospective employees (see England 1992, chap. 2). Nevertheless, our results have implications for the kinds of theoretical issues that are most in need of being addressed and for the type of data that need to be collected and analyzed.

Data

We use two large-scale data sets. The first data set comes from 16 Industry Wage Surveys (IWS) conducted by the U.S. Bureau of Labor Statistics (BLS) in the period 1974 to 1983 (see, e.g., U.S. Department of Labor 1976), corresponding to industry codes at three and more digits as defined in the *Standard Industrial Classification Manual* (see U.S. Executive Office of the President 1987). Eleven industries were surveyed in 1974 to 1978, whereas 5 were surveyed in 1980 to 1983. The populations for the surveys and the sampling from the populations are described in several U.S. Department of Labor publications (see Petersen and Morgan 1995, table 1). Of the 16, 11 are manufacturing industries, and 5 are service industries.

In each industry, the BLS drew a sample of several hundred establishments, often covering a large proportion of the establishments in the industry. For each establishment, information was obtained from establishment records both on establishment characteristics and on a large number of the production and/or clerical workers in the establishment. Within each industry, only a selection of occupations were surveyed—on average 42 occupations per industry. The occupations were selected by the BLS in order to provide a wide representation of production or clerical occupations in an industry. The individual-level data provide information on each individual in the relevant occupation and establishment. Excluded from the data collection were professional and managerial employees. Because these occupations may have exhibited wider variations in wages, even at the occupation-establishment level, there may have been less occupation-establishment level variation in wages here than in samples including professionals and managers.

For each employee surveyed, information was obtained on sex, occupation (an industry-specific code), method of wage payment (incentive- or time-rated), and hourly earnings. No information was collected on race, age, experience, or educa-

tion. The occupational classification is unusually detailed, corresponding in many cases to nine digits in the *Dictionary of Occupational Titles* (see U.S. Department of Labor 1977). In other cases, the titles are specific to the BLS data, based on industry-specific codes, but are usually as detailed as the nine-digit titles in the *Dictionary of Occupational Titles*.

Wage data are straight-time hourly wages in 13 industries and full-time weekly earnings in the other three, excluding premium pay for overtime and work on weekends, holidays, and late shifts. Thus, we do not conflate pay earned on regular hours with pay earned on overtime and irregular hours, making the wage data less prone to bias than virtually any other study used for assessing wage discrimination. Men work more overtime hours than women, due either to preference for or better access to overtime hours, and overtime hours are usually paid at a higher rate. Non-production bonuses, such as year-end bonuses, are also excluded, whereas incentive pay is included.

The second data set we use is the National Survey of Professional, Administrative, Technical, and Clerical (PATC) employees in 1981, also conducted by the BLS (U.S. Department of Labor 1981). The sampling and data collection design for this survey is similar to that in the IWS data. We use the data on weekly pay for full-time employees in seven professional and three administrative occupations.

Methods

We report all statistics separately for each of the 16 industries in the IWS data.[1] The raw (average) wages, either hourly or full-time weekly earnings, for women and men in an industry are given by $\overline{w}_f$ and $\overline{w}_m$, and the raw proportional wage between women and men is $w_{r,r} = \overline{w}_f / \overline{w}_m$. The average wages for women and men in occupation o are $\overline{w}_{o,f}$ and $\overline{w}_{o,m}$, and the proportional wage is $w_{o,r} = \overline{w}_{o,f} / \overline{w}_{o,m}$. The average wages for women and men in establishment e are $\overline{w}_{e,f}$ and $\overline{w}_{e,m}$, and the proportional wage is $w_{e,r} = \overline{w}_{e,f} / \overline{w}_{e,m}$. The average wages for women and men in occupation-establishment pair oe are $\overline{w}_{oe,f}$ and $\overline{w}_{oe,m}$, and the proportional wage is $w_{oe,r} = \overline{w}_{oe,f} / \overline{w}_{oe,m}$. These computations can only be done for units that are integrated by sex. We multiply each proportional wage by 100 in order to get the average female wage as percent of average male wage at the relevant level. This percentage is referred to as the relative wage in what follows.

We make three computations with relative wages. Each computation answers the following question: suppose sex segregation—by occupation, establishment, or occupation-establishment—were abolished, what then would the remaining relative wage be? These computations are defined in the appendix.

At the occupation level, we report the average of the relative wage across all sex-integrated occupations. We do the same at the establishment level. At the occupation-establishment level, we likewise report the average of the relative wage ($w_{oe,r} \times 100$) across all sex-integrated occupation-establishment units (oe). The female wage gap at each of these levels is then given as 100 minus the average of the relative wage at each level. This equals the percent by which women are paid less than men.

The remaining wage gap at the occupation-establishment level can reasonably be interpreted as an estimate of the upper bound on the amount of within-job wage discrimination, the gap one would observe in the absence of occupation-establishment sex segregation. It is an upper bound because the remaining gap at that level could have been caused by other factors, such as differences in experience and human capital between men and women in a given category. The difference between the raw wage gap and the wage gap at the occupation-establishment level can thus be interpreted as being attributable to occupation-establishment sex segregation. This part of course need not be caused by discrimination alone.

Results

Table 39.1 gives first in column 2 the raw relative wage and then in columns 3 to 5 the relative wages controlling for occupation, for establishment, and for occupation-establishment, computed from equations (1) to (4) in the appendix. Column 1 shows the percentage female in each industry. Column 2 shows that the average of the industry-specific raw relative wages between men and women was 81 percent. Thus the average of the industry-specific female wage gaps was 19 percent, where the wage gap is the percentage by which women earned less than men, computed as 100 minus the relative wage.

Column 3 shows that the female wage gap is reduced to an average, across the 16 industries, of 8 percent when we control for occupation, using equation (2). Column 4 shows that the female wage gap is reduced, across the 16 industries, to an average of 15 percent when we control for establishment, using equation (3). Column 5 shows that the female wage gap is reduced to about 0 to 4 percent when we control for the occupation-establishment pair, using equation (4). The average of the industry-specific female

Table 39.1   Women's Wages Relative to Men's With and Without Occupation, Establishment, and Occupation-Establishment Controls

Industry	%F	Women's Wages as a Percentage of Men's				Percent of Raw Wage Gap Explained by:		
		Raw	Occ	Est	Occ-Est	Occ	Est	Occ-Est
	1	2	3	4	5	6	7	8
Men's and Boys' Shirts	92.5	84.0	92.7	83.1	98.0	54.5	−5.4	87.5
Hospitals	84.8	105.3	95.8	103.7	101.0	178.7	30.7	81.3
Banking*	82.8	64.7	97.3	65.5	98.1	92.4	2.3	94.6
Life Insurance*	75.9	61.5	98.0	61.4	98.9	94.8	−0.3	97.1
Wool Textiles	55.4	87.3	93.8	91.7	98.6	51.3	34.8	89.0
Cotton Man-Made Fiber Textiles	54.6	89.2	96.5	90.5	99.7	67.5	11.8	97.2
Miscellaneous Plastics Products	51.9	77.5	87.4	80.6	97.8	44.1	14.0	90.2
Hotels and Motels	51.5	87.0	91.9	89.1	99.7	37.9	16.4	97.7
Computer and Data Processing*	44.5	67.5	98.4	81.4	98.9	95.1	42.8	96.6
Wood Household Furniture	35.9	85.4	91.3	90.4	95.7	40.3	34.2	70.5
Textile Dyeing and Finishing	19.8	82.7	92.2	90.2	99.0	55.0	43.4	94.2
Machinery	15.5	74.3	88.8	89.0	99.6	56.4	57.2	98.4
Nonferrous Foundries	9.4	81.3	84.1	84.4	97.5	15.1	16.7	86.7
Paints and Varnishes	5.6	85.1	92.6	91.8	96.6	50.2	44.8	77.1
Industrial Chemicals	2.5	83.2	93.2	90.1	97.1	59.6	41.2	82.8
Fabricated Structural Steel	0.6	80.7	86.0	81.5	96.9	27.4	4.1	83.9
Average Across Industries**	42.7	81.0	92.5	85.3	98.3	63.8	24.3	89.1

Note: Column 1, %F, gives the percent female in the industry. Column 2 gives the raw relative wage, from equation (1) in the Appendix. Columns 3–5 give the average of the within occupation–within establishment and within occupation-establishment relative wages, computed from equations (2)–(4). Columns 6–8 give the percent of the raw wage gap, defined as 100 minus the number in column 2, that can be attributed to occupation, establishment, and occupation-establishment segregation, computed from equations (5)–(7).

*This is based on weekly wages for full-time employees.

**Each column gives the unweighted average across industries of the percentages in the respective column.

wage gaps is 1.7 percent, after controlling for the occupation-establishment pair.

These results are striking. Controlling for occupation or establishment alone reduces the wage gap somewhat, but not drastically.

However, controlling for the occupation-establishment pair reduces the wage gap to a point of virtually no difference between men and women. The remaining female wage gap is on average 1.7 percent across the 16 industries, even without controlling for any individual-level characteristics such as education, age, seniority, and race. Occupation-establishment segregation accounts better for wage differences between men and women than any other set of variables studied in the literature on wage differences.[2]

Columns 6 to 8 give a decomposition of the raw wage gap, calculated as 100 minus the relative wage from column 2, into the percentage that is due to occupation, to establishment, and to occupation-establishment segregation, when each dimension is considered alone. These results are based on equations (5) to (7) in the appendix. Column 6 shows that occupational sex segregation alone accounts for about 64 percent of the wage gap, somewhat more than other studies have shown (e.g., Treiman and Hartmann 1981; Reskin and Roos 1990). Column 7 shows that establishment sex segregation alone accounts for about 24 percent of the wage gap. This is a new result. To date, occupational segregation has been the primary focus of gender wage gap studies. Column 8 shows that occupation-establishment sex segregation alone accounts for a large percentage of the wage gap, ranging from a low of 70.5 percent to a high of 98.4 percent. In 14 of 16 industries, more than 80 percent of the wage gap is explained by occupation-establishment segregation, and among seven of those more than 90 percent is explained, whereas in two industries only 70 percent and 77 percent of the gap is explained.

Again, we have the striking result that the interaction of occupation and establishment segregation not only explains dramatically more of the wage gap than either establishment or occupational segregation alone, it also explains most of the wage differences between men and women. Had men and women been equally distributed on occupation-establishment pairs, on the average 89 percent of the wage gap would have disappeared, assuming that other forms of discrimination would not have emerged.

One point requires discussion here. The female wage gap for the workers in our sample is about 20 percent. This is substantially less than the about 40 percent gap for all full-time workers during the period of the surveys (e.g., Goldin 1990, 61). There are several reasons for this discrepancy. One is that prior studies look at median or average annual earnings for full-time employees. It is probable that men on the average work more hours per year than women and that they also work more overtime hours. Therefore, differences between men and women are likely overstated. Another reason for this difference is that the occupations covered here comprise a relatively narrow range of the overall spectrum. In particular, professional and managerial occupations are excluded from the sample. The excluded occupations are expected to be on average higher paid than those included and to be occupied primarily by men. As a result, we have, when computing the raw wage gap of 19 percent, some degree of de facto control for occupation.

The latter results were based on data mostly for blue-collar, clerical, and some technical employees. It might be suspected that the wage gap among professional, administrative, and managerial employees is greater. However, when we turn our attention to analysis of wage differences among these employees using PATC data, the results are similar to those in the IWS data. The wage gap in the PATC data is just 3.1 percent among men and women in the same position (occupation and rank) and the same establishment.

Conclusion and Discussion

The findings of this article are simple to summarize. First, wage differences within given occupation-establishment pairs were relatively small: on average 1.7 percent among blue-collar and clerical as well as some technical employees, and on average 3.1 percent in seven professional and three administrative occupations, ranging from 1 percent in the lower to 5 percent in the higher ranks in an occupation. Thus, occupation-establishment segregation, not within-job wage discrimination was the driving force for observed wage differences.[3] Second, establishment segregation, was important for wage differences between men and women, although not as important as occupational segregation, a result we could compute only for the blue-collar, clerical, and some technical employees in the IWS data.

The first finding is important. It shows that occupation-establishment segregation accounted for more of the gender wage gap than any other variable or set of variables currently used in studying the gender wage gap. Occupational segregation alone tends to account for about 40 percent of the wage gap, and human capital and other variables also account for about 40 percent (e.g., Treiman and Hartmann 1981, chap. 2). But no set of variables, either individual or structural, accounts for as much as 89 percent, as occupation-establishment segregation did here in the case of blue-collar, clerical, and some technical employees in the IWS data.

This first finding establishes the conjecture already made in the literature, but not yet documented: wage differences are to a larger extent generated by occupation-establishment segregation than by within-job wage discrimination. Along with the first, the second finding shows the need to study establishment as well as occupational segregation.

The implications of the findings are straightforward. In terms of policy, allocative and valuative processes should be given the most attention, and within-job wage discrimination, which is covered by the Equal Pay Act of 1963 and which has been the implicit or explicit focus of much discussion and research, should receive less. Future research on differential wage attainment between men and women should be refocused as follows. The emphasis should be less on within-job wage discrimination and more on three prior processes: (1) the entry of employees into occupations and establishments, that is, the differential access of men and women to positions during the initial hiring or matching process, an allocative mechanism that is not easy to research; (2) career advancement within establishments, that is, the differential rates of promotion for men and women, also an allocative mechanism, but one which is more easily studied (Spilerman 1986); and (3) how jobs occupied primarily by women tend to be paid less than those occupied by men—the comparable worth issue, or what we refer to as valuative discrimination, also a line of research well under way (see England 1992).

Two issues arise in the identification of allocative processes as responsible for the gender wage gap. The first is whether segregation patterns are due primarily to discrimination or to differences in productive capacities. The meaning of our results for theory and policy depends on which mechanism operated here. This cannot be settled with our data and is obviously a task for future research. It requires information about productive capacities and would require an analysis of the matching between these and particular jobs.

The second issue concerns the role of supply-side sources of differential attainment between men and women. Of particular interest are the constraints put on women's career attainment from family obligations and household choices. Although these constraints may result most proximally from a traditional household division of labor, not directly from discriminatory behaviors by employers, household decisions are made in light of labor market opportunities, so the two are interdependent. The role of supply-side behaviors and their interrelationship with employer behaviors in generating the observed occupation-establishment segregation is in need of research.

Appendix

The *raw* relative wage between women and men is given as

$$w_{(r,r)} = \frac{\overline{w}_f}{\overline{w}_m} \times 100. \tag{1}$$

The relative wage controlling for occupation obtains as

$$w_{(o,r)} = \frac{1}{N_{o(I)}} [\Sigma_{o=1}^{N_{o(I)}} (w_{o,r})] \times 100. \tag{2}$$

Here, $N_{o(I)}$ is the number of occupations in which both men and women are present.

The establishment-level relative wage obtains as

$$w_{(e,r)} = \frac{1}{N_{e(I)}} [\Sigma_{e=1}^{N_{e(I)}} (w_{e,r})] \times 100. \tag{3}$$

Here, $N_{e(I)}$ is the number of establishments where both men and women are present.

The occupation-establishment-level relative wage obtains as

$$w_{(oe,r)} = \frac{1}{N_{oe(I)}} [\Sigma_{oe=1}^{N_{oe(I)}} (w_{oe,r})] \times 100. \tag{4}$$

Here, $N_{oe(I)}$ is the number of occupation-establishment pairs in which both men and women are present.

The raw wage gap obtains as 100 minus the number in (1). The percentage of the raw wage gap due to occupational segregation alone is given by

$$\%w_{(o,r)} = \frac{w_{(o,r)} - w_{(r,r)}}{100 - w_{(r,r)}} \times 100. \tag{5}$$

The percentage of the raw wage gap due to establishment segregation alone is given by

$$\%w_{(e,r)} = \frac{w_{(e,r)} - w_{(r,r)}}{100 - w_{(r,r)}} \times 100. \tag{6}$$

The percentage of the raw wage gap due to occupation-establishment segregation alone is given by

$$\%w_{(oe,r)} = \frac{w_{(oe,r)} - w_{(r,r)}}{100 - w_{(r,r)}} \times 100. \tag{7}$$

NOTES

The article is a version of Petersen and Morgan (1995) that was excerpted and partially rewritten for this volume by Petersen and Morgan with the help of David Grusky.

1. Unfortunately, we cannot compare wages across industries, because the industry data come from different years and hence reflect inflation as well as general wage increases.

2. Although Groshen (1991) and Tomaskovic-Devey (1993) report similar results on wage differences, neither author reported the wage gap at the occupation-establishment level.

3. Similar results are shown in Petersen et al. (1997) for Norway in 1984 and 1990.

REFERENCES

Bielby, William T., and James N. Baron. 1984. "A Woman's Place Is with Other Women: Sex Segregation Within Organizations." Pages 27–55 in *Sex Segregation in the Workplace: Trends, Explanations, Remedies,* edited by Barbara F. Reskin. Washington, D.C.: National Academy Press.

Blau, Francine D. 1977. *Equal Pay in the Office.* Lexington, MA: Lexington Books.

England, Paula. 1992. *Comparable Worth: Theories and Evidence.* Hawthorne, NY: Aldine de Gruyter.

Goldin, Claudia. 1990. *Understanding the Gender Gap: An Economic History of American Women.* New York: Oxford University Press.

Groshen, Erica L. 1991. "The Structure of the Female/Male Wage Differential: Is It Who You Are, What You Do, or Where You Work?" *Journal of Human Resources* 26(3):457–72.

Hartmann, Heidi I. 1987. "Internal Labor Markets and Gender: A Case Study of Promotion." Pages 59–92 in *Gender in the Workplace,* edited by Clair Brown and Joseph Pechman. Washington, D.C.: Brookings Institution.

Petersen, Trond, and Laurie A. Morgan. 1995. "Separate and Unequal: Occupation-Establishment Sex Segregation and the Gender Wage Gap." *American Journal of Sociology* 101(2): 329–61.

Petersen, Trond, Vemund Snartland, Lars-Erik Becken, and Karen Modesta Olsen. 1997. "Within-Job Wage Discrimination and the Gender Wage Gap, The Case of Norway." *European Sociological Review* 13(2):199–215.

Reskin, Barbara F., and Patricia Roos (Eds.). 1990. *Job Queues, Gender Queues: Explaining Women's Inroads into Male Occupations.* Philadelphia: Temple University Press.

Spilerman, Seymour. 1986. "Organizational Rules and the Features of Work Careers." *Research in Social Stratification and Mobility* 5:41–102.

Tomaskovic-Devey, Donald. 1993. *Gender and Race Inequality at Work: The Sources and Consequences of Job Segregation.* Ithaca, NY: ILR Press.

Treiman, Donald J., and Heidi I. Hartmann (Eds.). 1981. *Women, Work, and Wages: Equal Pay for Jobs of Equal Value.* Washington, D.C.: National Academy Press.

U.S. Department of Labor. 1976. *Industry Wage Survey: Miscellaneous Plastics, September 1974.* Bureau of Labor Statistics, Bulletin 1914. Washington, D.C.: U.S. Government Printing Office.

———. 1977. *Dictionary of Occupational Titles.* 4th ed. Bureau of Employment Security. Washington, D.C.: U.S. Government Printing Office.

———. 1981. *National Survey of Professional, Administrative, Technical, and Clerical Pay, March 1981.* Bureau of Labor Statistics, Bulletin 2108. Washington, D.C.: U.S. Government Printing Office.

U.S. Executive Office of the President. 1987. *Standard Industrial Classification Manual.* 1987. Office of Management and Budget. Washington, D.C.: U.S. Government Printing Office.

40

Devaluation and the Pay of Comparable Male and Female Occupations

PAULA ENGLAND

The terms *comparable worth* and *pay equity* refer to a form of sex discrimination that went virtually unrecognized until the 1980s. Evidence abounds that jobs filled mostly by women have pay levels lower than they would be if the jobs were filled mostly by men. This is seen as sex discrimination by advocates of the principle of comparable worth, which posits that jobs that are equally demanding and onerous and of equal value to society should be paid equally. The theory positing that employers assign lower wages to some jobs because they are filled largely with women has come to be called the devaluation perspective. Petersen and Saporta (2004) have referred to this type of discrimination as "valuative discrimination."

At first glance, the issue of comparable worth sounds like the more familiar issue of "equal pay for equal work," which refers to men and women in the same job with the same seniority, performing the same work equally well, but being paid differently. Petersen and Saporta (2004) have called this "within job discrimination," and it has been illegal in the United States since the 1963 Equal Pay Act and Title VII of the 1964 Civil Rights Act. However, comparable worth is distinct because it refers to comparisons between the pay in different jobs that entail at least some distinct tasks. Comparable worth advocates compare jobs that are largely male with those that are largely female (which I will sometimes, for brevity, refer to as "male" and "female" jobs) and, in some cases, claim that the difference between the pay of the two jobs results from gender bias in wage setting rather than from other job characteristics. Needless to say, this approach creates a thorny issue in distinguishing when two distinct jobs are comparable in the sense that we would expect them to pay the same in the absence of sex discrimination.

The wage discrimination at issue in a comparable worth scenario is also distinct from discrimination in hiring, initial job placement, and promotion, all of which Petersen and Saporta (2004) refer to as "allocative discrimination." Such discrimination is a viola-

This is a commissioned chapter that draws heavily on material in previous publications (Paula England, *Comparable Worth: Theories and Evidence*. Copyright © 1992 by Aldine Press; Paula England, Joan M. Hermsen, David A. Cotter, "The Devaluation of Women's Work: A Comment on Tam," *American Journal of Sociology* 105 [2000], pp. 1741–1751).

tion of Title VII of the Civil Rights Act of 1964. Hiring discrimination against women seeking to enter traditionally male jobs is one (although not the only) reason for occupational sex segregation. There are supply-side processes at work as well, such as those that lead women and men to major in different fields in college. Without segregation of jobs, female jobs could not be given a discriminatory pay level. But engaging in discrimination on the basis of sex in setting the pay levels assigned to male and female jobs is analytically distinct from engaging in hiring discrimination on the basis of sex. Moreover, valuative discrimination may exist whether or not the segregation came from allocative discrimination or from supply-side forces.

Some examples may help the reader to visualize the sorts of comparisons at issue in comparable worth. In 1975, nurses in Denver, Colorado, sued the city claiming that their jobs paid less than male jobs such as tree trimmer and sign painter. It would be hard to argue that the latter two jobs require as much skill or are as demanding as nursing. Women workers for the city of San Jose, California, discovered that secretaries were generally earning less than workers in male jobs that required no more than an eighth grade education, including, for example, men who washed cars for the city. Eventually, women in San Jose succeeded in getting the city to do a job evaluation study. The results showed, to choose some examples, that nurses earned $9,120 less annually than fire truck mechanics and that legal secretaries made $7,288 less annually than equipment mechanics. In 1985, the California School Employees Association complained that school librarians and teaching assistants (female jobs) were paid less than custodians and groundskeepers (male jobs). In recent years, the city of Philadelphia, Pennsylvania,

was paying practical nurses (mostly women) less than gardeners (mostly men). These are not atypical examples. In addition, one is hard-pressed to come up with a single example of a male job paying less than a female job that reasonable people would find comparable in skill, effort, and difficulty of working conditions. Nor are these differences in pay a result of men averaging more years of seniority than women, since in the above comparisons (from England 1992: 2), a constant level of experience was assumed.

U.S. courts have ruled that, under most conditions, this type of valuative discrimination and lack of comparable worth is not a violation of U.S. law (Nelson and Bridges 1999; England 1992: Chapter 5). Studies on data from a single employer like those reviewed here are not seen as evidence of illegal discrimination in wage setting. At present there is no legal remedy for this kind of discrimination unless there is a "smoking-gun" statement by employers that the reason they paid one job less than another was simply because it was filled with women. Statistical evidence of consistently biased pay levels is not enough. However, occasionally, some of the job evaluation studies have led private and city or state government entities to revise their pay scales to equalize salaries in jobs deemed comparable.

Economists propose two explanations for the lower pay of occupations with a high percent of female workers. The first is the theory of compensating differentials, which posits that the full pay of a job consists of both pecuniary (wage) and nonpecuniary compensation (the utility experienced from doing the work itself). Jobs with more comfortable, less hazardous working conditions can be filled with workers easily at lower wages, ceteris paribus. If women care more about nonpecuniary rewards (such as avoiding physical danger or having mother-friendly work conditions such as flexible hours or on-site child care centers) than men, and men focus more on maximizing earnings, then women will trade off earnings for amenities by choosing safer, more mother-friendly jobs. Most tests have failed to find that greater nonpecuniary amenities explain much of the lower pay of women's jobs (England 1992; Glass 1990; Glass and Camarigg 1992; Jacobs and Steinberg 1990; Kilbourne et al. 1994). The idea that women might choose lower-paying jobs for other compensations seems on first glance consistent with the finding that mothers earn less than nonmothers, even after controlling for part-time work status, experience, and seniority (Budig and England 2001; Lundberg and Rose 2000; Waldfogel 1997). But neither Glass (1990) nor Glass and Camarigg (1992) found women's jobs to have more mother-friendly characteristics than men's jobs. Similarly, Budig and England (2001) could not find any job characteristics (except part-time status) that reduced the motherhood wage penalty. Nonmothers were about as concentrated in female jobs as mothers. Thus, oddly enough, in the United States, segregation by sex does not seem to stem from women choosing or being consigned to more mother-friendly jobs. The "motherhood penalty" explains only some of the sex gap in pay, and this portion is largely unrelated to the effect of occupational sex segregation on the sex gap in pay. Thus, although the general theory of compensating differentials may have some merit, it cannot explain most of the lower pay of female jobs.

A second explanation offered by economists for the lower pay in female jobs is crowding. Bergmann (1986) argues that women's jobs pay less because they are crowded. According to this view, women seeking to enter male occupations face sex discrimination in hiring (the allocative discrimination discussed above), leading to a supply of applicants for traditionally female jobs larger than it would be in the absence of hiring discrimination as women denied entrance to male jobs crowd the female jobs. The excess supply lowers wages in female jobs. Although this is plausible, it is very difficult to test directly.

Sociologists have proposed the devaluation thesis, which posits that gender bias leads to valuing (and thus paying) female jobs less than comparably skilled male jobs (England et al. 2000; Steinberg 2001). According to these sociologists, it doesn't matter if segregation arises from allocative discrimination (in hiring and job placement) or not; employers engage in valuative discrimination once the segregation has occurred. Of course, the same evidence offered for this view would also be consistent with crowding. However, sociologists believe it is unlikely that hiring is the only place where bias occurs; it occurs in wage-setting between jobs as well.

Evidence that the sex composition of an occupation or job affects its wage level supports the devaluation theory. Such effects of sex composition, after statistically controlling for the other factors already discussed, have led some researchers to conclude that employers set lower wages (relative to job demands) when jobs are filled largely by women. One type of study takes the U.S. Census Bureau's detailed occupational categories as units of analysis. The measures include the percent female of those in the occupation, average or median male wage, median female wage, average education of incumbents, and a myriad of measures of skill demands from the *Dictionary of Occupational Titles*. These studies examine the effect of occupational percent female on average male and female wages (separately for men and women) after adding all the educational, skill, and working condition demands as control variables whose effects are adjusted out statistically. These studies find that both men and women earn less when in a more female occupation (England 1992; England et al. 2001). That is, in a regression predicting median wage, percent female of the occupation is significant and negative. (See Filer 1989 for a contrary finding.)

Other studies use individuals as units of analysis, and find that individuals in more female occupations earn less, after similar statistical controls to those described above (England et al. 2000; see Tam 1997, 2000 for a contrary view). Other studies take person/years as units of analysis, and percent female in occupations as contextual variables. The studies with person/years as units employ person-fixed effects to remove omitted variable bias; that is, they use persons as their own control and generally show that the same person earns more when moving to a more male-dominated occupation or earns less when moving to a more female-dominated occupation (Kilbourne et al. 1994; MacPherson and Hirsch 1995).

Other studies use jobs from a single employer as cases and show that female jobs pay less than male jobs when a job evaluation (of skill demands and working conditions) finds these jobs comparable (reviewed in England 1992).

All of these studies suggest that jobs pay either men or women less if they are filled mostly by women. The low pay of the largely female jobs cannot be entirely explained by how much skill the job requires or how onerous the working conditions are, because measures of these factors are controlled in the regression analyses that find a significant negative effect of the percent female in the occupation or job. These studies convince many sociologists that employers' evaluation of jobs is gendered—and that devaluation infects the wage levels of female jobs. Sociologists posit that this devaluation is perpetuated through cultural, institutional, and market mechanisms. Although the evidence of devaluation is quite strong, there is little direct evidence of the mechanisms through which it occurs.

I close with a somewhat speculative description of the process by which the devaluation of female jobs has probably occurred. At certain points in the life of organizations, particularly when they are first formed, or undergo significant restructuring, the relative wages of various jobs are somewhat up for grabs, although not unaffected by market forces. At these points, gender bias infects the decisions managers or consultants make about the wage levels for various jobs. In part, this results from a cognitive distortion in underestimating the relative contribution to profits or other organization goals of the work done in female jobs. In part, this bias on the part of organizational decision makers results from generalizing to women's jobs the relatively low status accorded women as persons by our culture. Later, bureaucratic inertia takes over, setting the wage consequences of these cultural biases in stone; the relative wage levels of jobs within an organization often remain quite constant for decades. Relative wage scales get institutionalized. If any attempt is made to change relative wage levels in a way favorable to female occupations, individual or collective action by male workers may increase the wages in male-dominated jobs over those of female-dominated jobs again. Market processes then reproduce all these effects. That is, if most employers have at some point inscribed these biases into their wage structures, this affects the "going wage" in predominantly female and male occupations that other new organizations must pay to hire workers of typical quality into the occupation. These market forces dictate that even an organization not beset by these cognitive and cultural biases will be forced to pay a higher wage to recruit in male occupations than comparable female occupations. Although they could choose to pay more than they need to in female occupations—more than the market or average wage—few profit-minded employers will do so. In these ways, gender bias is perpetuated over time. Absent significant collective action or new legislation that requires comparable worth in pay scales, the devaluing social and inertial forces described above may keep the pay penalty for working in female jobs in force indefinitely.

REFERENCES CITED

Bergmann, Barbara. 1986. *The Economic Emergence of Women*. New York: Basic Books.

Budig, Michelle J., and Paula England. 2001. "The Wage Penalty for Motherhood." *American Sociological Review* 66: 204–225.

England, Paula. 1992. *Comparable Worth: Theories and Evidence*. New York: Aldine.

England, Paula, Jennifer Thompson, and Carolyn Aman. 2001. "The Sex Gap in Pay and Comparable Worth: An Update." Pp. 551–556 in Ivar Berg and Arne Kalleberg, eds., *Sourcebook on Labor Markets: Evolving Structures and Processes*. New York: Plenum.

England, Paula, Joan M. Hermsen, and David A. Cotter. 2000. "The Devaluation of Women's Work: A Comment on Tam." *American Journal of Sociology* 105: 1741–1751.

Filer, Randall K. 1989. "Occupational Segregation, Compensating Differentials and Comparable Worth." Pp. 153–170 in Michael, Robert T., Heidi I. Hartmann, and Brigid O. Farrell, eds., *Pay Equity: Empirical Inquiries*. Washington, DC: National Academy Press.

Glass, Jennifer. 1990. "The Impact of Occupational Segregation on Working Conditions." *Social Forces* 68: 779–796.

Glass, Jennifer, and Valerie Camarigg. 1992. "Gender, Parenthood, and Job-Family Compatibility." *American Journal of Sociology* 98: 131–151.

Jacobs, Jerry, and Ronnie Steinberg. 1990. "Compensating Differentials and the Male-Female Wage Gap: Evidence from the New York State Comparable Worth Study." *Social Forces* 69: 439–468.

Kilbourne, Barbara S., Paula England, George Farkas, Kurt Beron, and Dorothea Weir. 1994. "Returns to Skill, Compensating Differentials, and Gender Bias: Effects of Occupational Characteristics on the Wages of White Women and Men." *American Journal of Sociology* 100: 689–719.

Lundberg, Shelley, and Elaina Rose. 2000. "Parenthood and the Earnings of Married Men and Women." *Labour Economics* 7:689–710.

MacPherson, D. A., and B. T. Hirsch. 1995. "Wages and Gender Composition: Why Do Women's Jobs Pay Less?" *Journal of Labor Economics* 13: 426–471.

Nelson, Robert, and William Bridges. 1999. *Legalizing Gender Inequality*. New York: Cambridge University Press.

Petersen, Trond, and Ishak Saporta. 2004. "The Opportunity Structure for Discrimination." *American Journal of Sociology* 109: 852–901.

Steinberg, Ronnie. J. 2001. "Comparable Worth in Gender Studies." Pp. 2293–2397 in N. J. Smelser and P. B. Baltes, eds., *International Encyclopedia of the Social and Behavioral Sciences*, vol. 4. London: Elsevier.

Tam, Tony. 1997. "Sex Segregation and Occupational Gender Inequality in the United States: Devaluation or Specialized Training?" *American Journal of Sociology* 102: 1652–1692.

Tam, Tony. 2000. "Occupational Wage Inequality and Devaluation: A Cautionary Tale of Measurement Error." *American Journal of Sociology* 105: 1752–1760.

Waldfogel, Jane. 1997. "The Effect of Children on Women's Wages." *American Sociological Review* 62: 209–217.

41

The Nanny Chain

ARLIE RUSSELL HOCHSCHILD

Vicky Diaz, a 34-year-old mother of five, was a college-educated schoolteacher and travel agent in the Philippines before migrating to the United States to work as a housekeeper for a wealthy Beverly Hills family and as a nanny for their two-year-old son. Her children, Vicky explained to Rhacel Parrenas,

> were saddened by my departure. Even until now my children are trying to convince me to go home. The children were not angry when I left because they were still very young when I left them. My husband could not get angry either because he knew that was the only way I could seriously help him raise our children, so that our children could be sent to school. I send them money every month.

In her book *Servants of Globalization,* Parrenas, an affiliate of the Center for Working Families at the University of California, Berkeley, tells an important and disquieting story of what she calls the "globalization of mothering." The Beverly Hills family pays "Vicky" (which is the pseudonym Parrenas gave her) $400 a week, and Vicky, in turn, pays her own family's live-in domestic worker back in the Philippines $40 a week. Living like this is not easy on Vicky and her family. "Even though it's paid well, you are sinking in the amount of your work. Even while you are ironing the clothes, they can still call you to the kitchen to wash the plates. It . . . [is] also very depressing. The only thing you can do is give all your love to [the two-year-old American child]. In my absence from my children, the most I could do with my situation is give all my love to that child."

Vicky is part of what we could call a *global care chain*: a series of personal links between people across the globe based on the paid or unpaid work of caring. A typical global care chain might work something like this: An older daughter from a poor family in a third world country cares for her siblings (the first link in the chain) while her mother works as a nanny caring for the children of a nanny migrating to a first world country (the second link), who, in turn, cares for the child of a family in a rich country (the final link). Each kind of chain expresses an invisible human *ecology of care,* one care worker depending on another and

Arlie Russell Hochschild, "The Nanny Chain," *The American Prospect* (Volume 11, January 3, 2000), pp. 1–4.

so on. A global care chain might start in a poor country and end in a rich one, or it might link rural and urban areas within the same poor country. More complex versions start in one poor country and extend to another slightly less poor country and then link to a rich country.

Global care chains may be proliferating. According to 1994 estimates by the International Organization for Migration, 120 million people migrated—legally or illegally—from one country to another. That's 2 percent of the world's population. How many migrants leave loved ones behind to care for other people's children or elderly parents, we don't know. But we do know that more than half of legal migrants to the United States are women, mostly between ages 25 and 34. And migration experts tell us that the proportion of women among migrants is likely to rise. All of this suggests that the trend toward global care chains will continue. . . .

If it is true that attention, solicitude, and love itself can be "displaced" from one child (let's say Vicky Diaz's son Alfredo, back in the Philippines) onto another child (let's say Tommy, the son of her employers in Beverly Hills), then the important observation to make here is that this displacement is often upward in wealth and power. This, in turn, raises the question of the equitable distribution of care. It makes us wonder, is there—in the realm of love—an analogue to what Marx calls "surplus value," something skimmed off from the poor for the benefit of the rich?

Seen as a thing in itself, Vicky's love for the Beverly Hills toddler is unique, individual, private. But might there not be elements in this love that are borrowed, so to speak, from somewhere and someone else? Is time spent with the first world child in

some sense "taken" from a child further down the care chain? Is the Beverly Hills child getting "surplus" love, the way immigrant farm workers give us surplus labor? Are first world countries such as the United States importing maternal love as they have imported copper, zinc, gold, and other ores from third world countries in the past?

This is a startling idea and an unwelcome one, both for Vicky Diaz, who needs the money from a first world job, and for her well-meaning employers, who want someone to give loving care to their child. Each link in the chain feels she is doing the right thing for good reasons—and who is to say she is not?

But there are clearly hidden costs here, costs that tend to get passed down along the chain. One nanny reported such a cost when she described (to Rhacel Parrenas) a return visit to the Philippines: "When I saw my children, I thought, 'Oh children do grow up even without their mother.' I left my youngest when she was only five years old. She was already nine when I saw her again but she still wanted for me to carry her [weeps]. That hurt me because it showed me that my children missed out on a lot."

Sometimes the toll it takes on the domestic worker is overwhelming and suggests that the nanny has not displaced her love onto an employer's child but rather has continued to long intensely for her own child. As one woman told Parrenas, "The first two years I felt like I was going crazy. . . . I would catch myself gazing at nothing, thinking about my child. Every moment, every second of the day, I felt like I was thinking about my baby. My youngest, you have to understand, I left when he was only two months old. . . . You know, whenever I receive a letter from my children, I cannot sleep. I cry. It's good that my job is more demanding at night."

Despite the anguish these separations clearly cause, Filipina women continue to leave for jobs abroad. Since the early 1990s, 55 percent of migrants out of the Philippines have been women; next to electronic manufacturing, their remittances make up the major source of foreign currency in the Philippines. The rate of female emigration has continued to increase and includes college-educated teachers, businesswomen, and secretaries. . . .

The End of the Chain

Just as global capitalism helps create a third world supply of mothering, it creates a first world demand for it. The past half-century has witnessed a huge rise in the number of women in paid work—from 15 percent of mothers of children aged 6 and under in 1950 to 65 percent today. Indeed, American women now make up 45 percent of the American labor force. Three-quarters of mothers of children 18 and under now work, as do 65 percent of mothers of children 6 and under. In addition, a recent report by the International Labor Organization reveals that the average number of hours of work per week has been rising in this country.

Earlier generations of American working women would rely on grandmothers and other female kin to help look after their children; now the grandmothers and aunts are themselves busy doing paid work outside the home. Statistics show that over the past 30 years a decreasing number of families have relied on relatives to care for their children—and hence are compelled to look for nonfamily care. At the first world end of care chains, working parents are grateful to find a good nanny or child care provider, and they are generally able to pay far more than the nanny could earn in her native country. This is not just a child care problem. Many American families are now relying on immigrant or out-of-home care for their *elderly* relatives. As a Los Angeles elder-care worker, an immigrant, told Parrenas, "Domestics here are able to make a living from the elderly that families abandon." But this often means that nannies cannot take care of their own ailing parents and therefore produce an elder-care version of a child care chain—caring for first world elderly persons while a paid worker cares for their aged mother back in the Philippines.

My own research for two books, *The Second Shift* and *The Time Bind,* sheds some light on the first world end of the chain. Many women have joined the law, academia, medicine, business—but such professions are still organized for men who are free of family responsibilities. The successful career, at least for those who are broadly middle class or above, is still largely built on some key traditional components: doing professional work, competing with fellow professionals, getting credit for work, building a reputation while you're young, hoarding scarce time, and minimizing family obligations by finding someone else to deal with domestic chores. In the past, the professional was a man and the "someone else to deal with [chores]" was a wife. The wife oversaw the family, which—in pre-industrial times, anyway—was supposed to absorb the human vicissitudes of birth, sickness, and death that the workplace discarded. Today, men take on much more of the child care and housework at home, but they still base their identity on demanding careers in the context of which children are beloved impediments; hence, men resist sharing care equally at home. So when parents don't have enough "caring time" between them, they feel forced to look for that care further down the global chain.

The ultimate beneficiaries of these various care changes might actually be large multinational companies, usually based in the United States. In my research on a Fortune 500 manufacturing company I call Amerco, I discovered a disproportionate number of women employed in the human side of the company: public relations, marketing, human resources. In all sectors of the company, women often helped others sort out problems—both personal and professional—at work. It was often the welcoming voice and "soft touch" of women workers that made Amerco seem like a family to other workers. In other words, it appears that these working mothers displace some of their emotional labor from their children to their employer, which holds itself out to the worker as a "family." So, the care in the chain may begin with that which a rural third world mother gives (as a nanny) the urban child she cares for, and it may end with the care a working mother gives her employees as the vice president of publicity at your company.

42

The Experience of Social Mobility

JOHN H. GOLDTHORPE (IN COLLABORATION WITH CATRIONA LLEWELLYN AND CLIVE PAYNE)

Our principal aim in this chapter is to investigate how far a correspondence exists between the analyses of social mobility in modern Britain that we have earlier presented, on the basis of our 1972 and 1974 inquiries (Goldthorpe 1987), and the actual experience of mobility, or immobility, among those individuals who have been the subjects of these inquiries. . . .

While recognizing the need to give some place in our analyses to our respondents' own awareness and understanding of their mobility, we were, however, faced in this respect with a major problem of data collection. In basing our follow-up study on a number of relatively small subsamples, drawn from respondents to our 1972 investigation, our aim was to obtain more detailed information than it was feasible to collect and process from a sample of over 10,000. . . .

We decided to try as far as possible to link the collection of life-histories, focused on our respondents' mobility experience, to our basic survey approach, and proceeded in fact in the following manner. Each respondent to our follow-up inquiry was asked at the end of his interview if he would be willing to help us further in our research by writing for us what we referred to as a set of 'life-history notes'. . . .

The questions that we wished respondents to consider were posed in everyday language, in an entirely open-ended form and, we hoped, in such a way as to give a respondent every encouragement to 'tell his own story'. To judge at least from the sets of notes that we received, the questions were in general found meaningful and indeed stimulating.

However, the chief problem that we anticipated with the procedure we followed, and which did in fact arise, was that of persuading respondents actually to produce notes. Only a small minority refused at the outset to undertake the task; but despite two, or in some cases three, reminders, a majority even of those who had agreed in principle to write notes still failed to do so. In the end, usable notes were secured from 247 men, representing 38 per cent of the 652 respondents to our 1974 study or 27

John H. Goldthorpe (in collaboration with Catriona Llewellyn and Clive Payne), *Social Mobility and Class Structure in Modern Britain, 2nd edition*, pp. 217–220, 230–237, 246, 367. Copyright © 1995 by Clarendon Press.

per cent of the total number of 926 men who were selected for re-interview from our 1972 respondents.

What we succeeded in obtaining was thus a body of material which, while substantial in itself and apparently highly illuminating of the mobility experience of those who had supplied it, related none the less to the experience of only a minority of the men in our subsamples, and which had in consequence to be viewed with, to say the least, extreme caution so far as its representativeness was concerned. . . .

As well as asking respondents to comment on the major differences of which they were aware between their own and their fathers' work and way of life, we also asked them what they saw as the reasons for such differences; and, following our questions concerning the pattern of their working lives, we asked further about the part they believed luck had played in shaping this pattern as compared with other more determinate factors, such as their individual qualities or family backgrounds. On the basis of the material prompted by these questions, our aim was to form some idea of the main 'mobility ideologies' that prevailed among our respondents, in the sense of the cognitive and evaluative notions through which they themselves sought to 'make sense' of their mobility experience.

The resulting analyses condition on the same class scheme that was earlier developed for the objective analyses (see Table 42.1). We may most usefully begin with respondents intergenerationally stable in Classes VI and VII, among whom we have observed a widespread awareness of upward mobility in terms of pay and conditions of employment and of living standards generally.

To a large extent, it would appear, these men regarded the explanation of this kind of mobility experience as being self-evident: to describe its nature—participation in a collective economic advance—was in effect to imply its cause, and the majority were content to leave their accounts in this form. There was, however, one clear variation, found chiefly in the case of men who as well as referring to higher levels of consumption also specifically cited improvements in working life, and this was to emphasize the role of trade unionism and the growing strength and expectations of the working class.

> I feel the trade unions must be given a lot of the credit [for] the working man's steady progress—not that I agree with all the unions say and do. Basically the idea of unions is good, it's the officers who sometimes get misguided. I'm sure without the unions the workers of this country would be being exploited far more than they are at present by what is still a capitalist society. (foundry annealer; electrical assembler—crank-shaft grinder)

> The power has moved from the employer to the employee, with much stronger unions who are not afraid to use their power. . . . The children who now leave school are better educated and would not stand for the conditions my father lived under. (compositor; apprentice printer—compositor)

> Whereas . . . at work [my father] was supervised for most of his working life, I rarely see a foreman or chargehand. This is solely because nowadays we have brought management to realise that workers given responsibility to manage their own job do a better and more exact job because they are not watched. There is also the different approach to

Table 42.1 The Class Schema

Full version	Collapsed versions		
	Seven-class	Five-class	Three-class
I Higher-grade professionals, administrators, and officials; managers in large industrial establishments; large proprietors	I + II Service class: professionals, administrators and managers; higher-grade technicians; supervisors of non-manual workers	I–III White-collar workers	Non-manual workers
II Lower-grade professionals, administrators, and officials; higher-grade technicians; managers in small industrial establishments; supervisors of non-manual employees			
IIIa Routine non-manual employees, higher grade (administration and commerce)	III Routine non-manual workers: routine non-manual employees in administration and commerce; sales personnel; other rank-and-file service workers		
IIIb Routine non-manual employees, lower grade (sales and services)			
IVa Small proprietors, artisans, etc., with employees	IVa + b Petty bourgeoisie: small proprietors and artisans, etc., with and without employees	IVa + b Petty bourgeoisie	
IVb Small proprietors, artisans, etc., without employees			
IVc Farmers and smallholders; other self-employed workers in primary production	IVc Farmers and smallholders and other self-employed workers in primary production	IVc + VIIb Farm workers	Farm workers
V Lower-grade technicians; supervisors of manual workers	V + VI Skilled workers: lower-grade technicians; supervisors of manual workers; skilled manual workers	V + VI Skilled workers	Manual workers
VI Skilled manual workers			
VIIa Semi- and unskilled manual workers (not in agriculture, etc.)	VIIa Non-skilled workers: semi- and unskilled manual workers (not in agriculture, etc.)	VIIa Non-skilled workers	
VIIb Agricultural and other workers in primary production	VIIb Agricultural labourers: agricultural and other workers in primary production		

work—my father was brought up to believe he was lucky to be working, while I and my generation believe we have the right to work . . . (wagon repairer; wagon repairer—steel-mill hand)

In this view, then, the social advancement experienced by wage-workers is represented as being in some part the result of their own efforts, rather than simply the more or less automatic outcome of a period of economic growth. None the less, it is important to note that the process is still envisaged as a collective one, involving the working class as a whole or, at all events, sizeable sections of it.

In contrast with this, we may remark first of all that in those instances where our stable intermediate-class respondents expressed an awareness of improved living standards, relative to those of their fathers, no reference to trade unionism occurred, and that long-term historical factors, such as 'increased commercial activity' or 'the growth of technology', were more often invoked. Secondly, though, as might be expected, the more important contrast is with the explanations that were provided for their mobility experience by those men whom we ourselves categorized as having been upwardly mobile in class terms. For in their case, of course, the experience that typically required explanation was one of intergenerational advancement not only in living standards but also in position within the occupational hierarchy. Correspondingly, then, the accounts offered by these men tend to take on a more elaborate form. While the importance of secular trends of social change is again perceived, indeed emphasized, the changes in question are ones relevant to advancement of an individual rather than a collective kind: the dominant theme is not that of the growth of

incomes or consumption, but rather that of the growth of *opportunity*. For our upwardly mobile respondents, the differences between themselves and their fathers are primarily attributable to the 'chances' which they had and which their fathers were denied. Among those men who had followed direct mobility routes, the reference was almost exclusively to the expansion of educational and training opportunities of one type or another; but among those whose mobility had been indirect, a wider view was sometimes found in which the expansion of higher-level employment opportunities was also stressed.

The main reason for the differences [between my father and myself] is, I believe, education, in the broadest sense of the word. I left school with 'O' levels and then obtained further qualifications via day-release, which enabled me to start my career further up the proverbial ladder, whereas my father had to start as an apprentice at the very bottom. (vehicles inspector; plastics technologist—sales manager)

Without doubt, the main reason [for my higher-level work and living standards] is that I have had the opportunity to go to a Grammar School and carry on with further education after I left school with the aid of local authority grants and courses, etc. Also . . . my father, never having had the opportunity, always was behind me to see that I did not waste [it]. (sheet-steel worker; clerk in solicitor's office—legal executive)

My father grew up in the 'good old days' with a lack of educational facilities and a family need to get out and earn some money. The opportunities in the years 1914 (when he started work) onwards were very few and far between for anyone to progress to better things. Fortunately, when I started work, in 1953, there was opportunity for part-time day release and evening studies at the local technical college, and it was entirely up to the individual to exploit the education system. (garage foreman; draughtsman—development engineer)

I think the main reason for the difference [between my father's occupational level and my own] is that I started work during a period of reasonable economic activity . . . the chances for good jobs existed, and I 'stuck at it' through a poorly paid training period. (paper-mill labourer; engineering apprentice—contracts manager)

The main variation on this theme of widening opportunity, or more often in fact a complement to it (as the above extracts also illustrate), was some reference to individual, or perhaps family, attributes which were seen as crucial to the educational or occupational success that the respondent had actually obtained: in other words, one could say, attributes which had enabled him to *take advantage* of the opportunities that existed. However, this aspect of the mobility ideology prevalent among our upwardly mobile men is one that can be fully brought out only when we turn next to consider specifically the ways in which our respondents understood their experience of mobility in work-life perspective, and in particular the role of luck.

To begin again here with our grouping of men stable in Classes VI and VII, their typical experience was one chiefly of immobility in working life, in the sense that they saw progress, if at all, only in their level of pay and not in the type of work they performed. One might then have expected these men to

have inclined to the view that, so far at least as individual advancement was concerned, luck had been against them—that they had 'never had a chance'. However, if such a view did prevail, it was far more often implied than directly expressed. The assessments of the role of luck that were offered showed in fact a good deal of diversity, but with a majority tending to discount or to minimize its importance. In part, this resulted from luck being sometimes taken to mean simply *good* luck; but further, and more significantly for our purposes, it was evident that our working-class respondents did not, in the main, see the essentially non-progressive character of their working lives—any more than their rising living standards—as something requiring specific explanation, whether in terms of luck or otherwise. Rather, they accepted it as a more or less given, insurmountable feature of their social situation—which then in turn served to delimit their conceptions of what the role of luck in their lives *might be*, regardless of whether in the end they adjudged this important or not.

Thus, for example, where men regarded luck as being relatively unimportant, this was predominantly for one or other of two reasons. Either it was on the grounds that being working class in itself more or less precluded the possibility that (good) luck might enter into their lives, at least in any way that would transform their situation; or, more frequently, it was on the grounds that their present situation, fairly obviously, owed little or nothing to any good fortune—no one had ever done *them* any favours—and that to achieve and to maintain what they had, they were forced to rely on their own efforts and abilities.

I don't believe luck has played any part in my working life. If one is lower working-class, it's almost impossible to be anything else. (Electricity Board labourer; news-stand assistant—process worker)

I don't think a working-class family such as mine has any luck, they merely exist through life. (dock labourer; lift attendant—bus conductor)

[My working life has been] a series of jobs that were just different from each other—no major crises or important turning points. The way I see it, luck has nothing to do with it. You have to make your own way as best you can. (drill operator; butcher's apprentice—machine moulder)

There has been no luck in my life. All I've ever had or got, I've had to work for or do without. It's just as simple as that. (office cleaner; milk roundsman—bus driver)

Ireland or parts of Wales. (painter and decorator; filing clerk—painter and decorator)

I always consider that I've been lucky up to yet. I regard one of life's most important things as good health—which I've had. When one has good health, then they can work for any goal they may seek. (building labourer; messenger boy—diesel-engine tester)

I think luck has been important in my life as I have never been badly hurt down the pit. (excavator driver; colliery surface worker—colliery face worker)

[I have had] bad luck due to health reasons, causing lost working days . . . [A] major crisis [came in 1974 with the] three-day working week due to the power strike, followed by hospitalisation. (clicker [shoe manufacturing]; milk roundsman—shoe machinist)

Similarly, where these working-class respondents felt that luck *had* been important in their lives, its role was again generally seen in relation to the maintenance of their position as wage-workers—as opposed, that is, not to their advancement, but rather to their becoming unemployed, sick, or disabled. The role of good luck in working life was to help in some way to prevent their employment from being disrupted; that of bad luck was to bring this about or make it more likely.

Everything relating to my present way of life depends on my being consistently at work . . . I consider myself lucky to have been based in the South East of England . . . where there doesn't appear to be the same uncertainty about future prospects for work etc. [as in] the 'depressed areas' of Scotland, Northern

Moving on now to men in our upwardly mobile groupings, we may note first of all that they too, like our stable working-class respondents and indeed more strongly, favoured the view that luck had played no major part in the course of their working lives. While, as we have seen, these men were often prepared to acknowledge, implicitly at least, their good fortune in having had wider opportunities than their fathers, in accounting for the work-life advancement of which they were so overwhelmingly aware, they clearly wished to represent this as being primarily their own achievement. But there is of course no real contradiction here, and once more we can readily understand the outlook prevalent among a grouping of our respondents by relating it to those features of their situation which had greatest subjective salience for them.

So far as their working lives were concerned, the dominant reality for these upwardly mobile men is that of the careers that they had 'made for themselves' in their present professional, administrative, and managerial occupations and, of course, in securing access to the service class in the first place. In their lifetimes the opportunities for such mobility may have increased but these opportunities had none the less to be seized: more specifically, examinations had to be passed, qualifications gained, promotions won, new posts 'held down', and so on. The existence of opportunities in itself obviously provides no guarantee that any particular individual will succeed. Thus, viewed in this perspective, it can in no way be surprising that these men should be disinclined to accord luck any very prominent part in their advancement, and that they should rather place the emphasis on their own endeavours and on the personal qualities, plus perhaps the family support, which had enabled them to sustain their ambition over often lengthy periods. It is furthermore of interest to find that where luck did figure in the accounts they gave of the realization of their mobility, its role was, just as with our working-class respondents, defined essentially in terms of their dominant reality. That is to say, the instances of luck that were cited—good luck more often than bad—were very largely references to career contingencies, largely in fact ones illustrating in various ways the advantage of 'being in the right place at the right time'.

I can't really think luck has played a big part in my working life. I worked very hard to ensure that I had the experience and knowledge necessary to meet the requirements of each position I have held . . . I gave up all my spare time—evenings and week-ends for four years—to study for my accountancy qualifications, and have spent a lot of time since then reading and studying to keep up to date . . . I have steadily advanced, I believe, through ability. (Rescue Superintendent, A.R.P.; junior clerk—Divisional Administrative Manager, large brewing company)

Having chosen my intended career fairly early, luck did not enter into the picture at all. Ability to work and ability to relax have been the most important factors . . . One of our family ideas is that if you want something, you must work for it. (foreman fitter; army apprentice—Captain, R.E.M.E.)

I am a firm believer that you make your own 'luck' in life, by accepting, if need be, the slightest half-chance to improve your career or life-style . . . When the Sales Manager in my last employment asked me to become a Technical Representative, instead of Assistant Production Manager . . . this completely altered my career . . . At the time, I had no experience or training [in sales] and I accepted the challenge to better myself—obviously not luck. (vehicles inspector; plastics technologist—sales manager)

I have always believed that the major turning point in my working life was the untimely and sad death of an elderly colleague . . . I was invited to take his position but obviously as a complete novice . . . Since acceding to that position I have never looked back . . . [But] I am able to state that with [this] definite exception . . . I have achieved my present position through hard work, long hours and possibly having a personality that happens to fit this particularly erratic occupation. (foreman in plastics factory; order clerk—senior contracts administrator, aircraft manufacturing company)

Finally, we gain some further indication that it is the experience of career advance that basically conditions the mobility ideology of our upwardly mobile men, if we turn, by way of comparison, to the life-history notes of those groupings of respondents whom we have thus far largely neglected in this section. On the one hand, we may observe that men intergenerationally stable in Class I, who, like our upwardly mobile respondents, show a general awareness of work-life advance, also show the same strong tendency to reject the idea of luck as having been of key importance in their progress. These men mostly recognize, implicitly if not explicitly, a continuity between their fathers' class position and life-style and their own; but they appear in fact little more likely than upwardly mobile men to attribute their work-life attainments to the good fortune of their birth or to any advantages that may have accrued to them from their family background. Rather, it is evident that the experience that is subjectively crucial for them is again that of making a career—of overcoming the successive obstacles or challenges of professional qualification or bureaucratic 'pyramid climbing'; and, in turn, the accounts that they offer of their advancement are again ones in which the emphasis is heavily on effort and ability, together perhaps with some references to how they had 'made the most' of any lucky 'breaks' that had happened to come their way.

On the other hand, we may also draw usefully, if rather selectively, on the life-history notes provided by men who were either intergenerationally stable in intermediate-class positions or downwardly mobile from Class I. Although these respondents displayed a good deal of variation in how they saw the pattern of their working lives, they followed for the most part those in other groupings in playing down the role of luck—either, that is, from the typical working-class or the typical service-class standpoint as we have represented these, depending on whether their awareness was primarily of work-life immobility or of career advance. However, within these groupings there were also to be found some few cases in which work-life experience was in fact largely accounted for in terms of luck, and what is, we believe, of some significance is that these were almost all ones where the 'course' for mobility, so to speak, had *not* taken the form of a series of career stages. Rather, the cases in question were ones of men who had either succeeded in establishing themselves, like their fathers, within our Class IV—that is, in self-employed and minor entrepreneurial positions; or who had been downwardly mobile from Class I origins chiefly as the result of entrepreneurial failure. What is implied in these respondents' accounts is the relatively insignificant role of individual striving in the face of the quite decisive influence that may be exerted by 'chance' events.

> Luck was the main factor in my business becoming a success. For the first month of trying to work a round up [for a mobile shop] I was only having a moderate success. But luck came along in the form of an ex-employer. Apparently I had started my round up on the territory of a bread van driver who was employed by the same bread firm that I used to work for. On hearing of this, my old boss, the manager of the bakery, came to see me, and in a sort of compromise he offered me all his customers

in the area I was working, on condition I sold their bread and cakes. It was like a dream come true and my business has never looked back. (grocer; shop assistant—mobile-shop proprietor)

[The crisis in my working life] was a heart attack at the age of 45. [I also had] bad luck in business due to other people's greed: i.e. manufacturers cashing in on shops and businesses by opening shops themselves in their factories and getting away with rates etc. . . . Previous to my illness [my goal] was to provide for the future. Since then it has been hopeless. Success in work now is a faraway dream. (works manager; apprentice packer—haberdasher)

One is thus led to the suggestion that, in present-day society at least, it is not private enterprise that provides the prime social context for a mobility ideology of a distinctively 'meritocratic' kind, but rather higher-level salaried employment: in other words, not the 'free' market itself but rather bureaucracy, public and private.

Perhaps the most significant conclusion to emerge from the discussion of this section is then that our respondents' attempts to account for their mobility experience tend to take on a quite different character depending on whether they view their mobility in intergenerational or in work-life perspective. Where men are seeking to explain differences of which they are aware between their own and their father's social position, they readily 'appeal to history', so to speak, and recognize the importance of secular trends of change in society at large— economic growth, the progress of the working class, the expansion of mobility opportunities—in which they have been caught up but to which, as individuals, they

can have contributed only negligibly if at all. Where, in contrast, they are concerned with accounting for their present positions as the outcome of their own working lives, they are far more likely to take individual responsibility in some degree—that is to say, for the way in which they have conducted themselves *within* the actual conditions that they have encountered: for example, in the case of those who have followed their fathers as wage-workers, by responding to the 'money for effort' bargain, which, even while shifting in their favour, remains central to their work situation; or, in the case of those who achieved professional, administrative or managerial occupations, by taking advantage of the growth of educational and training facilities and of career openings.

Thus, when sociologists seek, as we have earlier done, to link the mobility rates and patterns that they have observed to the forms, and changes in the forms, of the occupational and class structures, it would seem important that they should keep in mind that the individuals who 'live through' the mobility in question may well complement a recognition of the macro-social factors involved with interpretations in which their own agency is given a central part. And, we may add, it would also appear desirable that those sociologists who have construed the mobility process in terms of occupational attainment and who have then accorded luck a substantial part in this process should reflect on the distinct possibility that the majority of the individuals whom they have studied might be in serious disagreement with them.

BIBLIOGRAPHY

Goldthorpe, John H. 1987. *Social Mobility and Class Structure in Modern Britain*. Oxford: Clarendon Press.

43

No Degree, and No Way Back
to the Middle

TIMOTHY EGAN

Over the course of his adult life, Jeff Martinelli has married three women and buried one of them, a cancer victim. He had a son and has watched him raise a child of his own. Through it all, one thing was constant: a factory job that was his ticket to the middle class.

It was not until that job disappeared, and he tried to find something—anything—to keep him close to the security of his former life that Martinelli came to an abrupt realization about the fate of a workingman with no college degree in twenty-first-century America.

He has skills developed operating heavy machinery, laboring over a stew of molten bauxite at Kaiser Aluminum, once one of the best jobs in Spokane, Washington, a city of 200,000. His health is fine. He has no shortage of ambition. But the world has changed for people like him.

"For a guy like me, with no college, it's become pretty bleak out there," said Martinelli, who is fifty years old and deals with life's curves with a resigned shrug.

His son Caleb already knows what it is like out there. Since high school, Caleb has had six jobs, none very promising. Now twenty-eight, he may never reach the middle class, he said. But for his father and others of a generation that could count on a comfortable life without a degree, the fall out of the middle class has come as a shock. They had been frozen in another age, a time when Kaiser factory workers could buy new cars, take decent vacations, and enjoy full health care benefits.

They have seen factory gates close and not reopen. They have taken retraining classes for jobs that pay half their old wages. And as they hustle around for work, they have been constantly reminded of the one thing that stands out on their résumés: the education that ended with a high school diploma.

It is not just that the American economy has shed six million manufacturing jobs over the last three decades; it is that the market value of those put out of work, people like Jeff Martinelli, has declined considerably over their lifetimes, opening a gap that has left millions of blue-collar workers at the margins of the middle class.

And the changes go beyond the factory floor. Mark McClellan worked his way up from the Kaiser furnaces to management. He did it by taking extra shifts and learning everything he could about the aluminum business.

Still, in 2001, when Kaiser closed, McClellan discovered that the job market did not value his factory skills nearly as much as it did four years of college. He had the experience, built over a lifetime, but no degree. And for that, he said, he was marked.

He still lives in a grand house in one of the nicest parts of town, and he drives a big white Jeep. But they are a facade.

"I may look middle class," said McClellan, who is forty-five, with a square, honest face and a barrel chest. "But I'm not. My boat is sinking fast."

By the time these two Kaiser men were forced out of work, a man in his fifties with a college degree could expect to earn 81 percent more than a man of the same age with just a high school diploma. When they started work, the gap was only 52 percent. Other studies show different numbers, but the same trend—a big disparity that opened over their lifetimes.

Martinelli refuses to feel sorry for himself. He has a job in pest control now, killing ants and spiders at people's homes, making barely half the money he made at the Kaiser smelter, where a worker with his experience would make about $60,000 a year in wages and benefits.

"At least I have a job," he said. "Some of the guys I worked with have still not found anything. A couple of guys lost their houses."

Martinelli and other former factory workers say that, over time, they have come to fear that the fall out of the middle class could be permanent. Their new lives—the frustrating job interviews, the bills that arrive with red warning letters on the out-

side—are consequences of a decision made at age eighteen.

The management veteran McClellan was a doctor's son, just out of high school, when he decided he did not need to go much farther than the big factory at the edge of town. He thought about going to college. But when he got on at Kaiser, he felt he had arrived.

His father, a general practitioner, now dead, gave him his blessing, even encouraged him in the choice, McClellan said.

At the time, the decision to skip college was not that unusual, even for a child of the middle class. Despite McClellan's lack of skills or education beyond the twelfth grade, there was good reason to believe that the aluminum factory could get him into middle-class security quicker than a bachelor's degree could, he said.

By twenty-two, he was a group foreman. By twenty-eight, a supervisor. By thirty-two, he was in management. Before his fortieth birthday, McClellan hit his earnings peak, making $100,000 with bonuses.

Friends of his, people with college degrees, were not earning close to that, he said.

"I had a house with a swimming pool, new cars," he said. "My wife never had to work. I was right in the middle of middle-class America and I knew it and I loved it."

If anything, the union man, Martinelli, appreciated the middle-class life even more, because of the distance he had traveled to get there. He remembers his stomach growling at night as a child, the humiliation of welfare, hauling groceries home through the snow on a little cart because the family had no car.

"I was ashamed," he said.

He was a C student without much of a future, just out of high school, when he got his break: the job on the Kaiser factory floor. In-side, it was long shifts around hot furnaces. Outside, he was a prince of Spokane.

College students worked inside the fac-tory in the summer, and some never went back to school.

"You knew people leaving here for col-lege would sometimes get better jobs, but you had a good job, so it was fine," said Mike Lacy, a close friend of Martinelli and a coworker at Kaiser.

The job lasted just short of thirty years. Kaiser, debt-ridden after a series of failed management initiatives and a long strike, closed the plant in 2001 and sold the fac-tory carcass for salvage.

McClellan has yet to find work, living off his dwindling savings and investments from his years at Kaiser, though he contin-ues with plans to open his own car wash. He pays $900 a month for a basic health insurance policy—vital to keep his wife, Vicky, who has a rare brain disease, alive. He pays an additional $500 a month for her medications. He is both husband and nurse.

"Am I scared just a little bit?" he said. "Yeah, I am."

He has vowed that his son David will never do the kind of second-guessing that he does. Even at sixteen, David knows what he wants to do: go to college and study medicine. He said his father, whom he has seen struggle to balance the tasks of home nurse with trying to pay the bills, had grown heroic in his eyes.

He said he would not make the same choice his father did twenty-seven years earlier. "There's nothing like the Kaiser plant around here anymore," he said.

McClellan agrees. He is firm in one con-clusion, having risen from the factory floor only to be knocked down: "There is no working up anymore."

44

Trends in Class Mobility

The Post-War European Experience

ROBERT ERIKSON

JOHN H. GOLDTHORPE

Introduction

The issue of trends in class mobility in industrial societies is one characterised by a wide-ranging dissensus which, unfortunately, extends to matters of fact as well as of interpretation. We do not suppose that in this paper we will be able to resolve all the disagreements that are apparent. We do, however, believe that we can address the issue on the basis of comparative mobility data of a distinctively higher quality than those previously utilised, and that the results we report have significant consequences—positive or negative—for most of the rival positions that have been taken up.[1]

From the 1960s onwards, perhaps the dominant view on mobility trends has been that derived from what we will refer to as the 'liberal theory' of industrialism, as developed by various American authors (Kerr *et al.*, 1960, 1973; Kerr, 1969, 1983; Dunlop *et al.*, 1975; cf. also Parsons, 1960: chs. 3 and 4; 1967: chs. 4 and 15; 1971). This theory is a functionalist one which aims at establishing the distinctive properties of industrial societies in terms of the essential prerequisites for, or necessary consequences of, the technical and economic rationality that is seen as their defining characteristic. What is implied so far as social mobility is concerned may be put in the form of the following three-part proposition.

In industrial societies, in comparison with preindustrial ones

(i) absolute rates of social mobility are generally high, and moreover upward mobility—i.e. from less to more advantaged positions—predominates over downward mobility;

(ii) relative rates of mobility—or, that is, mobility opportunities—are more equal, in the sense that individuals of differing social origins compete on more equal terms to attain (or to avoid) particular destinations; and

(iii) both the level of absolute rates of mobility and the degree of equality in relative rates tend to increase over time.

This chapter, originally prepared for the European Research Conference ("European Society or European Societies," Gausdal, Norway, 1991), relies on material also used in a subsequent publication (Robert Erikson and John H. Goldthorpe, *The Constant Flux: A Study of Class Mobility in Industrial Societies*. Copyright © 1992 by Oxford University Press. Used by permission of Oxford University Press).

To explain *why* these contrasts between mobility in pre-industrial and industrial society should arise, a number of arguments are deployed which have, moreover, been elaborated and extended in the specialist literature by authors generally sympathetic to the liberal position (see esp. Blau and Duncan, 1967: ch. 12; Treiman, 1970). While all the arguments in question take on a functionalist form, one may usefully distinguish between those relating to three different kinds of effect—*structural, processual* and *compositional.*

First, it is held that within industrial society the dynamism of a rationally developed technology calls for continuous, and often rapid, change in the structure of the social division of labour, which also tends to become increasingly differentiated. High rates of mobility thus follow as from generation to generation, and in the course of individual lifetimes, the redistribution of the active population is required: that is, among economic sectors— first, from agriculture to manufacturing and then from manufacturing to services—and, in turn, among industries and among a growing diversity of occupations. Furthermore, the overall tendency is for advancing technology to *upgrade* levels of employment. Although some skills are rendered obsolete, new ones are created and the *net* effect is a reduction in the number of merely labouring and routine occupations and a rising demand for technically and professionally qualified personnel. At the same time, both the increasing scale of production, dictated by economic rationality, and the expansion of the services sector of the economy promote the growth of large bureaucratic organisations in which managerial and administrative positions also multiply. Industrial societies become increasingly 'mid-dleclass' or at least 'middle-mass' societies. Consequently, upward mobility is more likely than downward in both intergenerational and worklife perspective. Under industrialism, the chances of 'success' are steadily improved for all.

Secondly, it is further claimed that as well as thus reshaping the objective structure of opportunity, industrialism transforms the processes through which particular individuals are allocated to different positions within the division of labour. Most fundamentally, rational procedures of social selection require a shift away from *ascription* and towards *achievement* as the leading criterion: what counts is increasingly what individuals can do, and not who they are. Moreover, the growing demand for highly qualified personnel promotes the expansion of education and training, and also the reform of educational institutions so as to increase their accessibility to individuals of all social backgrounds. Human resources cannot be wasted; talent must be fully exploited wherever it is to be found. Thus, as within a society of widening educational provision 'meritocratic' selection comes to predominate, the association between individuals' social origins and their eventual destinations tends steadily to weaken and the society takes on a more 'open' character. And at the same time various other features of industrialism also serve to reduce the influence of social origins on individuals' future lives. For example, urbanisation and greater geographical mobility loosen ties of kinship and community; mass communications spread information, enlarge horizons and raise aspirations; and a greater equality of condition—that is, in incomes and living standards—means that the resources necessary for the realisation of ambition are more widely available.

Thirdly, it is argued that the foregoing effects interact with each other, in that the emphasis on achievement as the basis for social selection will be strongest within the expanding sectors of the economy—that is, the more technologically advanced manufacturing industries and services—and within the increasingly dominant form of large-scale bureaucratic organisation. Conversely, ascriptive tendencies will persist chiefly within declining sectors and organisational forms—for example, within agriculture or small-scale, family-based business enterprise. In other words, compositional effects on mobility occur in that, once a society begins to industrialise, the proportion of its population that is subject to the new 'mobility regime' characteristic of industrialism not only increases as that regime imposes itself, but further as those areas and modes of economic activity that are most resistant to it become in any event ever more marginal.

One reason that may then be suggested for the degree of dominance exerted by the liberal position is the coherent way in which the underlying theory has been developed. Another is the manifest failure of the main attempt made directly to controvert it. That is, the revision and extension of the Marxist theory of proletarianisation (cf. Braverman, 1974; Carchedi, 1977; Wright and Singelmann, 1982; Crompton and Jones, 1984) which sought to show the necessity for the systematic 'degrading', rather than upgrading, of labour under the exigencies of late capitalism—with the consequence of large-scale *downward* mobility of a collective kind. This undertaking lacked from the start any secure empirical foundation, and the accumulation of results incompatible with the new theory resulted in its eventual abandonment even by those who had been among its most resourceful supporters (see e.g., Singelmann and Tienda, 1985; Wright and Martin, 1987). However, various other positions can still be identified that to a greater or lesser extent come into conflict with the liberal view and that continue to merit serious attention.

First of all, it should be noted that the theory of mobility in industrial society advanced by Lipset and Zetterberg (1956, 1959) and sometimes simply assimilated to the liberal theory (see e.g., Kerr, 1983: 53) does in fact differ from it in crucial respects. For example, Lipset and Zetterberg do not seek to argue that mobility steadily *increases* with industrial development: indeed, they remark that *among* industrial societies no association is apparent between mobility rates and rates of economic growth. What they propose (1959: 13) is, rather, some kind of 'threshold' effect: 'our tentative interpretation is that the social mobility of societies becomes relatively high once their industrialization, and hence their economic expansion, reaches a certain level'. And although Lipset and Zetterberg's claim that (absolute) mobility rates in industrial societies become *uniformly* high would now be generally regarded as empirically untenable, their suggestion that a historic upward shift in such rates tends to occur at some—perhaps quite early—stage in the industrialisation process has not been similarly disconfirmed. Again, it is not part of Lipset and Zetterberg's case that the high mobility that they see as characteristic of industrial societies is the result of a tendency towards greater openness. Rather, they place the emphasis firmly on the effects of structural change, and in turn they are at pains to point out (1959: 27) that 'the fact that one country contains a greater percentage of mobile individuals than another does *not* mean that that country approximates a model of equal opportunity more closely'.

Secondly, a yet more radical challenge to the liberal view may be derived from the pioneering work of Sorokin (1927/1959). Taking a synoptic view, as much dependent on historical and ethnographic evidence as on contemporary social research, Sorokin was led to the conclusion that in modern western societies mobility was at a relatively high level, and he was further ready to acknowledge the possibility that, from the eighteenth century onwards, mobility rates had in general shown a tendency to rise. However, he was at the same time much concerned to reject the idea that what was here manifested was in effect 'the end of history' and the start of a 'perpetual and "eternal" increase of vertical mobility'. Rather, Sorokin argued, the present situation represented no more than a specific historical phase; in some societies in some periods mobility increased, while in other periods it declined. Overall, no 'definite perpetual trend' was to be seen towards either greater or less mobility, but only 'trendless fluctuation'. Those who were impressed by the distinctiveness of the modern era knew too little about historical societies and their diversity: 'What has been happening is only an alternation—the waves of greater mobility superseded by the cycles of greater immobility—and that is all' (1959: 152–4).

It might from the foregoing appear that Sorokin's position was merely negative. But, in fact, underlying his denial of developmental trends in mobility and his preference for a cyclical view, at least the elements of a theory can be discerned. In arguing against the supposition that rates of mobility in the modern period are quite unprecedented, one of the points Sorokin most stresses is that while certain barriers to mo-

bility have been largely re-moved—for example, juridical and religious ones—it is important to recognise that other barriers have become more severe or have been newly introduced: for example, those represented by systems of educational selection and occupational qualification (1959: 153–4, 169–79). This, moreover, is what must always be expected: the forms of social stratification which provide the context for mobility are themselves structures expressing differential power and advantage, and thus possess important self-maintaining properties. Those who hold privileged positions will not readily cede them and, in the nature of the case, can draw on superior resources in their defence. Indeed, Sorokin remarks that if he *had* to believe in the existence of a permanent trend in mobility, it would be in a declining one, since social strata are often observed to become more 'closed' over time as the cumulative result of those in superior positions using their power and advantage to restrict entry from below (1959: 158–60). However, this propensity for closure—which we may understand as being *endogenous* to all forms of stratification—is not the only influence on mobility rates. A further point that Sorokin several times makes (see e.g. 1959: 141–152, 466–72) is that in periods of both political and economic upheaval—associated, say, with revolution or war or with rapid commercial, industrial and technological change—marked surges in mobility are typically produced as the social structure as a whole, including the previously existing distribution of power and advantage, is disrupted. In other words, increased mobility here results from the impact of factors that are *exogenous* to the stratification order.

Thirdly and finally, one may note a more recently developed position which, however, has evident affinities with that of Sorokin. Featherman, Jones and Hauser (1975) aim at presenting a reformulation of Lipset and Zetterberg's hypothesis that across industrial societies rates of social mobility display a basic similarity. This hypothesis cannot stand if expressed in terms of absolute rates but, they argue, becomes far more plausible if applied, rather, to relative rates. When mobility is considered at the 'phenotypical' level of absolute rates cross-national similarity can scarcely be expected. This is because these rates are greatly influenced by the structural context of mobility and, in turn, by effects deriving from a range of economic, technological and demographic circumstances which are known to vary widely and which, so far as particular individuals and families are concerned, must be regarded as 'exogenously determined'. When, however, mobility is considered *net of* all such effects, or that is, at the 'genotypical' level of relative rates, the likelihood of cross-national similarity being found is much greater. For at this level only those factors are involved that bear on the relative chances of individuals of differing social origin achieving or avoiding, in competition with each other, particular destination positions among those that are structurally given. And there is reason to suppose that in modern societies the conditions under which such 'endogenous mobility regimes' operate—for example, the degree of differentiation in occupational hierarchies and in job rewards and requirements—may not be subject to substantial variation.

For present purposes, then, the chief significance of the FJH hypothesis lies in the rather comprehensive challenge that it poses to the claims of liberal theorists. On the one hand, so far as absolute mobility rates are concerned, it implies a basic scepticism, essentially akin to that of Sorokin, about the possibility of *any* long-term, developmentally-driven trend; while, on the other hand, it stands directly opposed to the proposition that under industrialism a steady increase occurs in the equality of mobility chances. Although some initial developmental effect in this direction early in the industrialisation process might be compatible with the hypothesis, any continuing change in relative mobility rates is clearly precluded (cf. Grusky and Hauser, 1984: 20). Once societies can be deemed to have become industrial, their mobility regimes should stabilise in some approximation to the common pattern that the FJH hypothesis proposes, and should not thereafter reveal any specific or persistent tendencies, whether towards convergence on greater openness or otherwise. No forces are recognised inherent in the functional dynamics of industrialism that work systematically to expand mobility opportunities.

The divergent arguments concerning mobility trends that we have reviewed in this section will then provide the context within which we present our empirical analyses of data for European nations. First, though, we must say something about what we take to be the particular relevance to evaluating these arguments of the European experience over the post-war years.

The Relevance of the European Experience

It is not difficult to detect within the liberal theory of industrialism a degree of American or, more accurately perhaps, of Anglo-American ethnocentricity. Historically, the origins of modern industrial society are traced back to late eighteenth- and early nineteenth-century England; and other western nations, including the USA, are then seen as having successively followed England's lead in breaking free of the constraints of a traditional social order and entering the industrial world.[2] Contemporaneously, it is the USA rather than England that is recognised as the vanguard nation; and with industrialisation now on the global agenda, the major differences between industrial and pre-industrial, or modern and traditional, society are seen as best revealed through explicit or implicit USA–Third World comparisons. Within these perspectives, therefore, the experience of industrialisation of the mainland European nations is viewed in only a rather restrictive way. It tends either to be taken for granted, as fitting unproblematically into the trajectories defined by the two paradigm cases, or alternatively as providing interesting instances of 'deviations', over which, however, the logic of industrialism has eventually to prevail.[3]

This schematic background to the liberal theory must be regarded as excessively simplified, and possibly misleading, in at least two respects. On the one hand, while England did indeed industrialise early, the supposition that other western nations then followed along the same path, being differentiated only by the degree of their 'retardation', is one that has no sound historiographic basis. What is chiefly significant about the process of industrialisation in England is that—in part *because* of England's priority, but for other reasons too—it took on a quite distinctive character which subsequent cases could scarcely reflect (cf. Kemp, 1978: ch. 1 esp.). Rather than having simply followed in England's wake, other European nations do in fact display in their recent economic histories a great diversity of developmental paths; and it is, furthermore, important to recognise

that later industrialisation and economic retardation should not always be equated—as, for example, the French case can well illustrate (cf. O'Brien and Keyder, 1978).

On the other hand, it would also be mistaken to suppose that by the end of the nineteenth century the industrialisation of Europe was essentially completed. This would be to neglect the great economic and social importance that agriculture and also artisanal and other 'pre-industrial' forms of production continued to have throughout the nineteenth, and for well into the twentieth, century—and in many of the more advanced European nations as well as in those on the 'periphery'. It was in fact, as Bell has remarked (1980: 233), only in the period *after the second world war* that Europe as a whole became an industrial society. Indeed, various interpretations of the 'long boom' of this period have seen it as reflecting aspects of this culmination—for example, as being driven by the final phase of the supply of surplus rural labour (Kindleberger, 1967) or as marking the ultimate overcoming of the dualism of traditional and modern sectors within European economies (Lutz, 1984).[4]

The fact, then, that we here concentrate on the experience of European nations by no means implies that we will be treating questions of mobility trends within an unduly limited context. To the contrary, we have the advantage that while these nations can supply us with high quality data (far better, for example, than those usually available from Third World nations), they do also display a remarkably wide range of variation in their levels and patterns of industrial development—and even if we consider only that time-span to which our mobility data have some reference: that is, from the 1970s back to the first two decades of the century, in which the oldest respondents within our national samples were born. (For details of the surveys utilised, see Appendix Table 1). . . .

It will from the foregoing have become evident that, in seeking to exploit the historical richness of our European data, we are prepared to make a large assumption: namely, that valid inferences about the presence or absence of mobility trends can be drawn from the data of single inquiries. What we are in effect proposing is that age-groups distinguished within our samples from the 1970s can be treated as successive birth-cohorts, and that the mobility experience of their members can then be taken as indicative of whether or not change over time has occurred in mobility rates and patterns. In such an approach certain well-known difficulties arise, above all in treating intergenerational mobility, and in the conclusion of this section we should therefore give these some attention.

To begin with, we must recognise that we are not in fact dealing with true birth cohorts within the nations we consider but only with what might better be called 'quasi-cohorts': that is, with the survivors of true cohorts, following on losses due to mortality and emigration, to whom immigrants will then be added. In such cases as those of the FRG, Ireland and Poland, the numbers here involved will obviously be substantial. This, however, is a situation that we can do little to remedy; we can only trust that no serious distortions will be introduced into our data of a kind that might affect our conclusions regarding trends.[5]

Further, there is the so-called 'identification problem'. If for the members of a national sample one compares their present class position (i.e. at time of inquiry) with their class of origin (i.e. father's class), the mobility experience of the individuals within successive 'quasi-cohorts' will be likely to reflect several different effects: not only those of the historical period through which they have lived but also those of their age and of their cohort membership *per se*. Thus, the problem is that of how we can assess 'period' effects—which are those relevant to questions of mobility trends—separately from effects of the other kinds. No clear-cut solution is, or can be, available (cf. Glenn, 1977), since birth-cohorts and age-groups are inescapably 'embedded' in historical time. However, several considerations would lead us to believe that in pursuing our present purposes we need not in fact be at so great a disadvantage in this respect as might initially appear.

First, it would seem empirically defensible to regard men of around 30–35 years of age as having reached a stage of 'occupational maturity', beyond which further major changes in their class positions become relatively unlikely (Goldthorpe, 1980, 1987: ch. 3; cf. also Blossfeld, 1986). Thus, we may take results for cohorts of this age or older as giving a reasonably reliable indication of the 'completed' pattern of the collective class mobility of their members.

Secondly, for all of our European nations except one, the Federal Republic of Germany, we have information on individuals' experience of mobility from their class of origin to their class of *first* employment. For this transition, therefore, age effects at least will obviously be much reduced, since attention is focused on a fairly well defined life-cycle stage. We would not wish to regard data on this transition as a very satisfactory basis for cross-national comparisons of intergenerational mobility, on grounds that we discuss elsewhere (Erikson and Goldthorpe,

1992: ch. 8). None the less, we are thus provided with the possibility of checking whether or not the conclusions that we reach on trends, or their absence, in mobility from class of origin to present class are consistent with ones that pertain to mobility rates of a more age-specific kind.[6]

Thirdly, it is important for us to emphasise that in the analyses that follow our concern will be not so much with the actual empirical description of mobility trends as with the evaluation of particular claims about such trends. What, therefore, we can always consider is whether, if we were to suppose some confounding of effects in our results, these would be of a kind that would tend unduly to favour or disfavour a given position. Thus, for example, in the case of the liberal claim that within industrial nations mobility and openness tend steadily to increase, it is difficult to see why any confounding of period effects by age effects should produce unfairly *negative* results: that is to say, it would appear unlikely that an actual increase in openness and mobility among the more recent cohorts within our national samples would be concealed by the fact that these cohorts are made up of young persons. If anything, one might expect the contrary, since younger persons will have benefited more widely from the expansion of educational provision which, according to the liberal theory, is one of the major sources of greater mobility and equality of opportunity. Likewise, there would seem no reason why age effects should obscure any trends within our data for the mobility rates of different nations to converge—as would be expected under the liberal theory as differences between nations' levels of industrial development are reduced. For if, as the theory maintains, the determinants and processes of mobility become increasingly

standardised through the logic of industrialism, then convergence in mobility rates should, presumably, be *more* apparent among the younger than the older age groups in our samples (for an elaboration of this point, see Erikson, Goldthorpe and Portocarero, 1983: 307–10 and Figure 1).

As Glenn has observed (1977: 17), cohort analysis should never be a mechanical exercise, uninformed by theory and by additional 'external' evidence; and this point obviously applies *a fortiori* in the case of analyses, such as those we shall present, which rest only on 'quasi-cohorts'. But since we do have some knowledge about both the historical setting of the mobility that we consider and its life-course phasing, and since we are addressing a number of more or less specific and theoretically grounded hypotheses rather than proceeding quite empirically, our strategy is, we believe, one capable of producing results that can be interpreted in a reasonably reliable and consequential way. It is to these results that we now turn.

Absolute Rates

In seeking to assess the arguments that we have earlier reviewed, we start with evidence on intergenerational class mobility in the form of absolute rates: that is, rates based on differing versions of our class schema (see Table 42.1, page 363) and expressed in simple percentage terms. So as to avoid marked age effects in considering the transition from class of origin to present class, we restrict our attention to men in our national samples who were over age 30 at the time of inquiry (i.e. at some point in the early or mid-1970s; cf. Appendix Table 1). These men, we suppose, would be approaching, or would have attained, a stage

Figure 44.1   Total Mobility Rates for Men in the Nine Nations by Birth Year

of relative occupational maturity. The maximum age-limit that we apply here—and in all subsequent analyses—is 64.[7]

First of all, we consider *total* mobility rates. That is, the percentage of all men in our national samples found in cells off the main diagonal of the intergenerational mobility table based on the sevenfold version of the class schema; or, in other words, the percentage of all men whose 'present', or destination, class was different to their class of origin—the latter being indexed by the respondent's *father's* class at the time of the respondent's early adolescence.[8] In Figure 44.1 we seek to plot the course followed by the total mobility rate in each of our nine European nations on the basis of moving weighted averages of this rate for men *in successive birth years,* using a method of graduation that has been developed by Hoem and Linneman (1987).[9]

From inspection of Figure 44.1, the general impression gained must be one of support for the contention that absolute mobility rates display merely trendless change. It would, at all events, be difficult to ally the data here presented with the idea of mobility increasing steadily as industrialism advances. No regular tendency is apparent for the mobility of older respondents—of men born, say, in the first two decades of the century—to be exceeded by that of respondents who were born some twenty years later, and who would have reached occupational maturity during the long boom of the post-war years. And we may add that no essentially different picture emerges if, using the same technique, we plot total mobility rates from class of origin to class of *first* employment.[10] It would thus seem improbable that the failure of the graphs of Figure 44.1 to move upwards to the right, as would be expected from the liberal theory, can be explained simply in terms of the confounding of period by age effects.

The one possible pattern that might be discerned in Figure 44.1 is some tendency for total mobility rates to converge—even if not while steadily rising. That is to say, some narrowing down could be claimed in the cross-national range of mobility levels as between those displayed by the oldest and the youngest cohorts in our samples. For the former, as can be seen, the range of total mobility rates is from around 40 to over 70 per cent, while for the latter it is from 50 to under 70 per cent—and, one might add, would be some ten percentage points narrower still if the one case of Scotland were to be discounted.

However, it is important to note how this convergence comes about. It is in fact to a large extent the result of an increase in total mobility in two nations, Ireland and Poland, in which the rate among older cohorts, at around the 40 per cent mark, was substantially lower than in other nations. Ireland and Poland are—together with Hungary—those nations in our sample in which, as we have earlier indicated, industrialisation was most delayed. An alternative interpretation of Figure 44.1 would therefore be that instead of revealing a general tendency towards convergence in mobility rates, it rather supports a hypothesis of the kind suggested by Lipset and Zetterberg: that is, of a specific upturn in mobility occurring at a stage relatively early in the industrialisation process when the first major impact of structural change is felt.

That Hungary would then appear as deviant, in showing a high total mobility rate even among the oldest men considered, need not be found surprising. This could be seen as the result of the quite exceptional amount of mobility imposed upon the Hungarian agricultural workforce through direct political intervention, and which is thus reflected across the experience of all age-groups alike. In the period immediately following the second world war, the land reforms of the provisional government created over half-a-million new peasant proprietors; but then, under the subsequent state socialist regime, agriculture was within a decade almost entirely collectivised through the establishment of co-operatives or state farms (Kulcsár, 1984: 78–84, 96–100; Brus, 1986a, 1986b). Thus, respondents to our 1973 survey who were the sons of agricultural proprietors—over a quarter of the total—held different class positions to their fathers more or less of necessity, and even in fact where they continued to work the same land.[11]

These findings on total mobility do, we believe, carry significant implications, to which we shall wish to return. It is, however, of further interest here to try to obtain a somewhat more detailed picture of tendencies in absolute rates by considering also intergenerational *outflow* rates. Unfortunately, the relative smallness of the sizes of certain of our national samples means that we cannot reliably base our examination of such rates on the seven-class version of our schema but must, for the most part, resort to the three-class version (cf. Table 42.1, page 363) which distinguishes simply between non-manual, manual and farm classes.[12]

Figures 44.2 to 44.6, which are produced via the same procedures as Figure 44.1, show the course followed in each of our nations by five different outflow rates calculated from 3 x 3 intergenerational mobility tables (again for men aged 30–64). As is indicated, the rates in question are those for

Figure 44.2   Outflow Rates from Farm Origins to Farm Destinations for Men in Nine Nations by Birth Year

intergenerational immobility within the farm class, for mobility from farm origins to manual and to nonmanual destinations, and for mobility from manual origins to nonmanual destinations and *vice versa*. Of the other transitions possible within the 3 x 3 tables, those from manual and nonmanual origins to farm positions were generally followed by too few individuals to allow any reliable rates to be established; and the fact that the numbers involved here are more or less negligible means in turn that trends in the remaining rates—that is, rates of immobility within the manual and nonmanual classes—need scarcely be plotted separately, since they will be essentially the complements of those already examined of mobility between these two classes.

Figure 44.2 displays the changing proportions of men across birth-cohorts in our nine nations who were of farm origins and who were themselves found in farm work. A broad tendency is apparent for such intergenerational immobility to decline, which might be expected in consequence of the general contraction of agricultural employment. The decline in the cases of Ireland and Poland from farm immobility rates of upwards of 70 per cent in the oldest cohorts is of particular interest in view of the interpretation we have suggested of the increases in total mobility in these nations revealed in Figure 44.1. By resorting to the raw data, we can in fact show that changes within the farm sector here played a crucial part. Thus, the contribution of this sector to the total *im*mobility rate (i.e. the proportion of all cases in the mobility table found in cells on the main diagonal) fell in the Irish case from 69 per cent for men born before 1925 to only 27 per cent for those born after 1940, while in the Polish case the corresponding decline was from 77 to 35 per cent.

In two other nations, France and Hungary, the decline in farm immobility is also more or less continuous over the period to which our data refer. However, the cases of England, Scotland and Northern Ireland and likewise that of the FRG would suggest that, once the decline of agriculture has reached a certain point, rates of farm immobility tend to level out or to become rather variable. And Sweden appears quite distinctive in that farm immobility is shown at a low level—never more than 25 per cent—throughout the decades in which agricultural employment was falling. Here, though, we do have evidence to suggest some distortion in our results. Our corresponding plot for the transition to class of first employment indicates a strong decline in farm immobility; but, on account perhaps of the very rapidity of agricultural contraction in the post-war years, it would seem that many men also left the farm workforce at a quite late age, thus obscuring the downward trend when the transition to present class is considered.

Finally, it may be observed that in Figure 44.2, as in Figure 44.1, any impression of converging rates is created essentially by the rather dramatic Irish and Polish graphs. If these are disregarded, the cross-national range in rates of farm immobility merely fluctuates, being, for example, no narrower—at around 15 to 50 per cent—for men born from the mid-1930s onwards than it was for men born around 1920.

Figures 44.3 and 44.4 then display the course of outflow rates from farm origins to manual and nonmanual destinations respectively. Figure 44.3 would suggest that

in those cases where declining trends in intergenerational immobility in farming were revealed in Figure 44.2, their counterpart has been increased outflows from farm origins into manual wage-earning positions in industry. France, Hungary, Ireland and Poland all show such increases of a continuous kind. In the remaining nations, however, trends are less readily discerned. In the cases of the FRG and Sweden, increasing proportions of men in the cohorts born up to about 1930 moved from farm origins into manual work—following what might perhaps be taken as a characteristic tendency of the drive to 'mature' industrialism. But in later cohorts this tendency is clearly not sustained, although for Sweden there is probably some underestimation of the rate in question as the converse of the distortion noted in regard to farm immobility. For England, Northern Ireland and Scotland, the graphs undulate in no readily interpretable way. Turning to the outflow rates from farm origins to nonmanual destinations presented in Figure 44.4, we find that trendless change is here still more manifest. The most remarkable feature of the graphs displayed is indeed their flatness, apart from the early rise from a near-zero level in the Irish case.[13]

The remaining point to be observed from Figures 44.3 and 44.4 together is that we find little indication at all of national mobility rates converging. Over the period covered, the cross-national range for farm-to-manual outflows shifts upwards, but with little narrowing, from around 10 to 55 per cent to 30 to 70 per cent; while the rates for farm-to-non-manual outflows are notable for being almost entirely confined within a range of 10 to 25 per cent.

The last two Figures in the series, 44.5 and 44.6, show changes in rates of inter-

Figure 44.3 Outflow Rates from Farm Origins to Manual Destinations for Men
in Nine Nations by Birth Year

Figure 44.4 Outflow Rates from Farm Origins to Non-manual Destinations for Men
in Nine Nations by Birth Year

generational mobility between the broad manual and non-manual classes that we distinguish. From inspection of the graphs, it would once again seem difficult to avoid the conclusion that no clear trends emerge. Although some impression may perhaps be given that, overall, mobility from manual origins to nonmanual destinations has decreased while that in the reverse direction has increased, it is in fact only in the Polish case that monotonic trends in these directions can be found. In general, fluctuating rates are displayed, and the graphs for different nations frequently cross. Moreover, as earlier remarked, the negligible volume of outflows from both manual and non-manual origins to farm destinations means that the plots of Figures 44.5 and 44.6 can be taken as essentially the obverses of those relating to *im*mobility within our manual and nonmanual classes; so in the case of these rates too an absence of trends may be claimed.

Finally, Figures 44.5 and 44.6 again fail to provide evidence of cross-national convergence in mobility rates. Over the period covered, the cross-national range for rates of mobility from manual origins to non-manual destinations narrows only slightly as it falls from around 30 to 55 per cent for the oldest cohorts down to 20 to 40 per cent for the youngest; and the range for mobility in the reverse direction shows no narrowing at all in moving from 20 to 45 up to 30 to 55 per cent.[14]

It is the results contained in these last two figures—and also in Figure 44.4—that may occasion most surprise among those presented so far. It would be generally accepted that nonmanual work tends to grow and manual work to contract as industrial societies reach the more advanced stages of their development—regardless of whether this is seen as contributing to a net degrading or upgrading of the employment structure overall. And thus, within the context of the three-class version of our schema, increasing mobility into nonmanual destinations from farm and manual origins alike should be 'structurally' favoured. Yet, in our data, no consistent indication of such tendencies is to be found, even within the more advanced nations or among the younger cohorts.

However, it must in this connection be noted that our nonmanual class is very widely defined. It includes some groupings, such as routine nonmanual employees in administration, commerce and services, which have grown primarily through the greater workforce participation of women; and others, such as small proprietors and other self-employed workers, which, over the period that our data cover, were typically in decline. If, then, we wish to consider mobility flows into the nonmanual groupings that have most clearly expanded among the male workforce, which are in fact mostly at the higher levels of the white-collar range, we need to draw on data from mobility tables of a more elaborated kind. Although, as we have explained, we cannot go over entirely to the seven-class version of our schema, we can, for present purposes, make a useful compromise: we can construct mobility tables that apply the seven-class version to destinations while retaining the three-class version for origins.

In Figures 44.7 and 44.8 we show the course followed by two outflow rates derived from such 3 x 7 tables: that is, outflow rates from farm and from manual origins respectively into Class I+II of the seven-class version—the service class of primarily professional, higher technical, administrative and managerial employees. In

387

Figure 44.5 Outflow Rates from Manual Origins to Non-manual Destinations for Men in Nine Nations by Birth Year

Figure 44.6 Outflow Rates from Non-Manual Origins to Manual Destinations for Men in Nine Nations by Birth Year

other words, we here focus on subsets of the rates presented in Figures 44.4 and 44.5 where the mobility in question is into types of employment that *have* been in general expansion. Furthermore, we can also in this way examine changes in mobility flows which, in the light of the hierarchical divisions that we make within our class schema (cf. Appendix Table 2), could be regarded as representing mobility *upwards* from less to more advantaged class positions.[15]

A preliminary point to be noted about Figures 44.7 and 44.8 is that, because the rates we are here concerned with are generally lower and less differentiated than those presented in previous figures, we have doubled the vertical scale, thus of course 'enlarging' the changes that are depicted. Even so, they do not appear as highly dramatic.

In Figure 44.7, some increase in mobility from farm origins into the service class is shown among younger cohorts in several nations—that is, in England, the FRG and Sweden and, more weakly, in Ireland. But in the remainder any increase that can be detected occurs among older cohorts, and the trend then fades out—so that cross-national differences in rates in fact *widen*. In Figure 44.8, rates of mobility from manual origins into the service class likewise display an increase in England and Sweden which is at least held, and in the FRG they turn sharply upwards among the youngest cohorts. But again, too, the other nations differ, with the most common tendency being for rates first to rise but then at some later point to decline. It is of interest to note that this tendency is most marked in Figure 44.8, and also appears in Figure 44.7, in the graphs for our two eastern European nations. Upward mobility into the service class among Hungarian and Polish men born in the early 1920s—who would

reach occupational maturity in the period of post-war 'socialist reconstruction'—rose to a level that later cohorts quite fail to match.

Where, among younger cohorts, the graphs of Figures 44.7 and 44.8 level out or turn down, we cannot preclude the possibility that this is in some part the result of age effects—so that in fact, as the men in these cohorts become older, a larger proportion will enter into service-class positions. However, what we would doubt is that such effects are likely to an extent that would make the graphs seriously misleading. There are good empirical grounds for supposing—and the liberal theory would certainly predict—that the younger the men in our samples, the more probable it is that they will achieve upward mobility through education, so that this mobility will be apparent at a relatively early stage in their working lives. And in this connection, it is then further relevant to emphasise that the graphs corresponding to those of Figures 44.7 and 44.8 which depict mobility to class of first employment similarly fail to reveal consistently rising trends. It emerges rather that even if one considers only men born from the 1920s onwards, a steady increase in mobility into the service class from farm and manual origins alike is found in just one nation—namely, Sweden.

What, we believe, should be emphasised here is that although the service class does show a general tendency to expand within modern societies, it does not do so at a steady pace simply in response to the exigencies of industrial development. Periods of relatively rapid growth and of stasis will alternate under the influence of other factors, not least political ones, thus producing rises and falls in rates of upward mobility into this class of a kind which the Hungar-

Figure 44.7   Outflow Rates from Farm Origins to Service Class Destinations for Men in Nine Nations by Birth Year

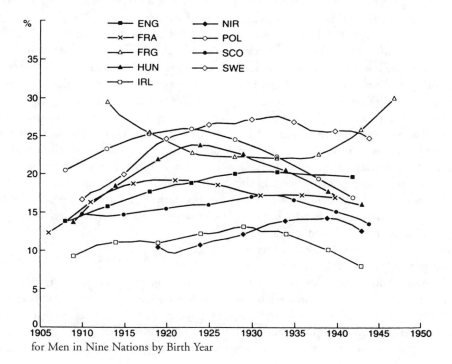

for Men in Nine Nations by Birth Year

ian and Polish cases do no more perhaps than exemplify at their most striking.[16]

How, then, can we best sum up the foregoing findings in regard to trends in absolute rates? To begin with, we can say that our investigation of outflow rates points to certain trends which seem likely to have occurred in most, if not all, of the nations we consider at *some* stage of their industrial development:

(i) a decline in intergenerational immobility within the farm sector;
(ii) an increase in mobility from farm origins into manual employment in industry; and
(iii) some upturn in mobility from farm and manual origins into service-class positions.

To this extent, therefore, we might stop short of an extreme antinomianism of the kind that Sorokin could be taken to represent, and recognise that industrialism does carry typical implications for the direction of several broad mobility flows—as indeed Carlsson (1963) argued some time ago in a critique of Sorokin's position.

However, we must then also say that the trends that we are able to identify have rarely appeared as continuous over the period to which our data refer; that from nation to nation their phasing within the developmental process evidently differs; and moreover that changes in all other rates that we have examined would appear to be essentially directionless. In turn, therefore, we can produce little evidence that within our European nations mobility rates overall are moving steadily towards some relatively well defined 'industrial' pattern in the way that the liberal theory would suggest—and certainly not towards one that is charac-terised by steadily rising mobility. The outflow rates that we have considered show no clear tendency to converge; and, whatever course they may follow, they are not associated with any consistent upward trend in total mobility rates. In the light of the evidence presented, and in particular of that of Figure 44.1, it could not be claimed that men in our national samples whose working lives began, say, after the second world war have generally lived in more mobile societies than those who first entered employment in the 1920s.

The one possible qualification that might here be made is suggested by our findings for Ireland and Poland. These could be taken as meeting the expectation that an upward shift in the level of total mobility will occur in the course of industrialisation where a rapid decline in agricultural employment or, more specifically perhaps, the break-up of a predominantly peasant economy goes together with a rising demand for industrial labour. But even if, as Lipset and Zetterberg would hold, a shift of this kind can be regarded as a general characteristic of the emergence of industrial societies, at least two further points would still, on our evidence, need to be made. First, the upturn in mobility has to be seen as being of a delimited, once-and-for-all kind; and secondly, it still leaves ample room for subsequent variation in absolute mobility rates and patterns as nations proceed to the further stages of their development.[17]

Relative Rates

We move on now to consider trends in intergenerational class mobility from the standpoint of relative rates, which we shall treat in terms of odds ratios. That is, ratios which show the relative odds of individuals in two different classes of origin being found in one rather than another of two different classes of destination; or, alternatively, one could say, which show the degree of *net* association that exists between the classes of origin and of destination involved. Two further points concerning such ratios may here be noted.

First, the total set of odds ratios that can be calculated within a mobility table may be taken as representing the 'endogenous mobility regime' or 'pattern of social fluidity' that the table embodies. And since odds ratios are 'margin insensitive' measures, it is then possible for this underlying regime or pattern to remain unaltered as between two or more mobility tables even though their marginal distributions differ and, thus, all absolute rates that can be derived from them. Further, we might add, it would be possible for relative rates as expressed by odds ratios to differ from table to table in some systematic way without this being readily apparent from an inspection of absolute rates.

Secondly, odds ratios are the elements of loglinear models; and, thus, where these ratios are taken as the measure of relative mobility rates, hypotheses about the latter can be presented and formally tested through the application of such models. This is the approach that we shall here follow.

In examining relative rates, we shall attempt, in the same way as we did with absolute rates, to make inferences about the extent of changes over time from the mobility experience of successive birth-cohorts within our national samples. However, instead of here working with yearly cohorts, we distinguish four ten-year birth-cohorts, which can then be regarded, given the closeness of the dates of the inquiries from which the samples derive, as having more or less comparable locations within the broad sweep of recent European economic history.

The first—that is, the earliest—of these cohorts comprises men aged 55 to 64, who were thus mostly born in the first two decades of the century, and who entered employment before or during the inter-war depression years. The second is of men aged 45 to 54, the majority of whom were born in the 1920s and entered employment in the later 1930s or the war years. The third is that of men aged 35 to 44, who were born between the late 1920s and the early 1940s, and whose working lives have fallen very largely within the post-war period. And finally the fourth cohort is that of men aged 25 to 34, who were born from the end of the 1930s onwards and who mostly entered employment while the long boom was in train. This last cohort is clearly made up of respondents who could not be generally assumed to have reached a stage of occupational maturity, and this we must recall where it might be relevant to the interpretation of our results.

When we thus divide our national samples into cohorts, we again have a potential problem of unduly low cell counts in the mobility tables for each cohort. To obviate this, we base our analyses throughout on the five-class version of our schema (cf. Table 42.1, page 363).

As regards relative rates, there is, as we have noted, an obvious opposition between the expectations that follow from the liberal theory and those that may be derived from the FJH hypothesis. According to the former, a tendency should be found in the course of the development of industrial societies for relative rates to become more equal—or, one could say, for all odds ratios to move closer to the value of 1, which signifies the complete independence of class origins and destinations or 'perfect mobility'. According to the latter, relative rates will be basically the same across all societies that have market economies and (at least) nuclear family systems, whatever stage their level of industrial development may have reached; and thus, when examined over time within particular industrial societies, relative rates should reveal little change at all.

We may then start off from an attempt at evaluating these rival positions, and, to this end, we introduce a rather simple log-linear model which is, however, able to provide a direct representation of expectations under the FJH hypothesis, at least if this is taken *stricto sensu*. This model, which we have earlier labelled the 'constant social fluidity' (CnSF) model (Goldthorpe, 1980, 1987: ch.3; Erikson, Goldthorpe and Portocarero, 1983) may, for present purposes, be written as

$$\log F_{ijk} = \mu + \lambda_i^O + \lambda_j^D + \lambda_k^C \qquad (1)$$
$$+ \lambda_{ik}^{OC} + \lambda_{jk}^{DC} + \lambda_{ij}^{OD}$$

where F_{ijk} is the expected frequency in cell ijk of a three-way table comprising class of origin (O), class of destination (D) and cohort (C) and, on the right-hand side of the equation, μ is a scale factor, λ_i^O, λ_j^D and λ_k^C represent the 'main' effects of the distribution of individuals over origins, destinations and cohorts respectively, and the remaining terms represent the effects for the three possible two-way associations in the table.

Thus, the model entails a number of substantive propositions, most of which are unproblematic: for example, that an association exists between class of origin and class of destination; and that further associations exist between class of origin and cohort and

between class of destination and cohort—in other words, men in different cohorts have different origin and destination distributions. It is, however, a further proposition that is critical. Since no *three-way* association is provided for in the model (the λ_{ijk}^{ODC} term does not appear), it is also entailed that the level of association between class of origin and of destination is *constant across cohorts* or, one could alternatively say, that over the mobility tables for successive cohorts all corresponding relative rates, as measured by odds ratios, are identical.

We can then consider our nine nations separately, and in each case fit the above CnSF model to a three-way table which comprises the five classes of origin, five classes of destination and four cohorts that we propose to distinguish. The results of so doing are presented in Table 44.1.

In this table we also report the results of applying a model that represents the hypothesis of the (conditional) independence of class origins and destinations; that is, the CnSF model minus the λ_{ij}^{OD} term. We do not expect this independence model to fit the data—and, as can be seen, in no case does it—but it serves as a useful baseline, by reference to which we can assess, through the rG^2 statistic in the fourth column of the table, how much of the total association between class of origin and class of destination the CnSF model is able to account for.[18]

Also in addition to the more usual 'goodness of fit' statistics, we give in the last column of Table 44.1 values for the statistic G^2(S). This we introduce here to attempt to deal with a difficulty arising from the large variation in the sizes of our national samples. In consequence of this variation, our national mobility tables differ quite widely in their capacity to show up as statistically significant relatively small deviations from

TABLE 1
Results of Fitting the CnSF Model to Intergenerational Class Mobility for Four Birth-Cohorts

Model*	G^2	df	p	$rG^{2\dagger}$	$\Delta^{\ddagger}$	$G^2(S)$ (1,746)
ENG						
(N = 8,343)						
OC DC (con. ind.)	1,695.0	64	0.00	—	16.1	405
OC DC OD (CnSF)	53.1	48	0.28	96.9	2.6	49
FRA						
(N = 16,431)						
OC DC	6,370.6	64	0.00	—	24.7	734
OC DC OD	96.7	48	0.00	98.5	2.0	53
FRG						
(N = 3,570)						
OC DC	1,092.0	64	0.00	—	21.2	567
OC DC OD	81.9	48	0.00	92.5	4.4	65
HUN						
(N = 10,319)						
OC DC	2,386.0	64	0.00	—	19.2	457
OC DC OD	69.9	48	0.02	97.1	2.4	52
IRL						
(N = 1,746)						
OC DC	902.3	64	0.00	—	29.2	902
OC DC OD	60.2	48	0.11	93.3	5.2	60
NIR						
(N = 1,808)						
OC DC	780.6	64	0.00	—	25.5	756
OC DC OD	44.5	48	>0.50	94.3	5.0	45
POL						
(N = 27,993)						
OC DC	7,357.7	64	0.00	—	19.6	519
OC DC OD	66.7	48	0.04	99.1	1.4	49
SCO						
(N = 3,985)						
OC DC	1,146.6	64	0.00	—	18.1	538
OC DC OD	66.3	48	0.04	94.2	4.4	56
SWE						
(N = 1,882)						
OC DC	403.9	64	0.00	—	17.3	379
OC DC OD	45.2	48	>0.50	88.8	5.1	45

Notes:
    * O = origin class; D = destination class; C = cohort.
    † rG^2 shows the percentage reduction in the G^2 for a model taken as baseline (here the conditional independence model) that is achieved by a more complex model (here the CnSF model). For further discussion of this statistic, see n. 18.
    ‡ Δ is the dissimilarity index, showing the percentage of all cases in the table analysed that are misclassified—that is, allocated to the wrong cell—by a particular model.

models that we fit to them. It is as if we were looking at slides through microscopes of greatly differing power: we have the possibility of seeing far more detail in some cases than in others. Thus, there is the evident danger that we do not evaluate a model in an evenhanded way from nation to nation. We could, for example, be led to reject a model in the Polish case on account of deviations which, were they present also in the case of, say, Ireland, we would simply not observe. Thus, we evidently need some measure of goodness of fit that is standardised by sample size. One possibility would be to take G^2/N. However, we prefer, as a more refined measure, Schwartz's suggestion of $G2(S)$ which is given by $((G^2 - df)/N) \times K + df$, where K is the sample size which is to be taken as standard.[19] We will follow the conservative practice of setting K equal to the size of the *smallest* of the national samples with which we are concerned—and thus, in Table 44.1, at 1746. To help remind the reader of the hypothetical nature of $G^2(S)$—that it is the ^{2} value that we would expect from a sample of size K, all other things being equal—we report it only to the nearest integer.

What, then, can we learn from the content of Table 44.1? It would in fact appear that the CnSF model performs fairly well. It is true that the p values reported indicate that in only four of the nine nations—England, Ireland, Northern Ireland and Sweden—would one retain this model, taken as the null hypothesis, according to the conventional 0.05 criterion. However, it is also evident that much of the variation in the G^2 and p values returned is attributable to differences in sample size. When one examines the $G^2(S)$ values in the final column of the table, one finds that these are in fact contained within a rather narrow range,

and moreover that in no case do they exceed the 65 mark, thus implying, with df = 48, p values of above 0.05. In other words, if we were restricted throughout to sample sizes of 1746, such as that we have for Ireland, we would find it difficult to reject the CnSF model for any nation—although the FRG would have to be regarded as a borderline case.

What could therefore be claimed on the basis of the foregoing is that while significant deviations from the CnSF model do have to be recognised in some at least of our nations, such deviations would not appear to be at all substantial. In this connection, it is of further relevance to note that in all cases but one the CnSF model accounts for more than 90 per cent of the total association existing between class of origin and of destination—the exception being Sweden, where the independence model fits least badly; and again, that within the different national mobility tables the CnSF model leads to the misclassification of, at most, only a little over 5 per cent of all cases.[20] . . .

Conclusions

We have sought in this chapter to use data from European nations in order to evaluate various arguments concerning mobility trends within industrial societies. The major outcome, it might be said, has been a negative one: that is, considerable doubt has been thrown on claims associated with what we have called the liberal theory of industrialism. We have found no evidence of general and abiding trends towards either higher levels of total mobility or of social fluidity within the nations we have considered; nor evidence that mobility rates, whether absolute or relative, are changing in any other consistent direction; nor again evidence that such rates show a tendency over time to become cross-nationally more similar. The most that could be said on the side of arguments proposing some linkage between industrial development and increased and more standardised mobility rates would be that structural changes—most importantly, the decline in agriculture—appear likely to generate upturns in total, and also perhaps in certain outflow rates over periods of limited duration and of very variable phasing.

Such results are all the more damaging to the liberal theory since, as we earlier emphasised, Europe over the middle decades of the twentieth century, and above all in the postwar era, provides a context in which the theory should have every chance of showing its force. Furthermore, we may reiterate the point that any distortions in our findings that derive from our reliance on (quasi-) cohort analysis, and in particular from the confounding of age and period effects, are unlikely to be ones that tell unfairly against liberal claims: if anything, the contrary should be supposed.

We would therefore believe that the attempt to represent changes in mobility rates in modern societies as displaying regular developmental patterns, driven by a functional logic of industrialism, is one that faces serious empirical difficulties; and, in turn, we would argue that the need must be recognised to search for ways in which these changes might be more satisfactorily understood. In this connection, there is then one further outcome of the analyses of the present chapter which should, in our judgment, be seen as having major significance: namely, that while it appears that liberal expectations of directional tendencies in absolute and relative mobility rates

are in both respects largely unfounded, *the nature of the contrary evidence is quite different from one case to the other: with absolute rates it is evidence of trendless, though often quite wide, fluctuation, but with relative rates it is evidence of considerable stability.* What is thus suggested is that in attempts to go beyond the liberal theory, the treatment of absolute and of relative rates is likely to set quite different kinds of problem and of analytical task.

As regards absolute rates, liberal expectations most obviously fail, we would suggest, because changes in structural influences on mobility do not themselves have the regularity that liberal theorists have been wont to suppose. Analyses of economic growth advanced in the 1950s and 1960s by authors such as Clark (1957), Rostow (1960) and Kuznets (1966) were taken as demonstrating clear sequences of change in the sectoral and occupational, and hence in the class, composition of labour forces. However, it would by now be widely accepted that, whatever theoretical insights the work of these authors may provide, it does *not* allow one to think, at a historical level, in terms of a well-defined series of developmental stages through which the structure of the labour forces of different nations will pass in turn as industrialisation proceeds. While certain very general tendencies of change may in this respect be identified, considerable variation still prevails from case to case in relation to the speed with which change occurs and the extent to which different aspects of change are separated in time or overlap (Singelmann, 1978; Gagliani, 1985).

The European experience of industrialisation, which has provided the setting for our analyses in this paper, itself well illustrates the variety of paths that the development of labour forces may follow; and it does, moreover, bring out the diversity of the causal factors at work here—by no means all of which can be plausibly seen as part of some englobing developmental process. Thus, the historical formation of national class structures has to be seen as reflecting not only early or late industrialisation but, in addition, important influences stemming, on the one hand, from the international political economy and, on the other, from the various strategies pursued by national governments in response to both external and internal pressures. To take but one example here, the contraction of agriculture—which we have found to play a major part in the pattern of change in absolute class mobility rates—cannot be understood, as it has occurred in particular cases, simply in terms of the shifting marginal productivity of sectors and differences in the elasticities of demand for their products that the theory of economic growth would emphasise. As the agrarian histories of our nations can amply show (see, e.g., Priebe, 1976), the pace and timing of agricultural contraction also—and often far more decisively—reflects whether nations were at the centre or on the periphery of international trading relations; in a position of economic dominance or dependence; and, further, the policies that their governments adopted towards agriculture both in regard to its social organisation and its protection against or exposure to market forces.[21]

Once, therefore, the variability and complexity of the determination of the structural contexts of mobility is appreciated, the extent to which the movement of absolute rates over time appears as merely trendless can no longer be found especially surprising. If changes in such rates do largely express the shifting conjunctures of a diversity of exoge-nous effects, then 'trendlessness' as suggested by Sorokin is indeed what must be expected. It is noteworthy that it is essentially an argument on these lines that has been pursued by the several European economic and social historians who have sought to join in the sociological debate. In rejecting 'the idea of a sustained growth in social mobility during industrialization', these authors have emphasised the 'multitude of factors' which affect mobility levels; and, in place of developmental stages, they have sought rather to establish empirically a number of different 'eras' or 'phases' of both rising *and falling* mobility within the period in which European industrialisation has occurred (see esp. Kaelble, 1984: 490; also Kaelble, 1981; Mendels, 1976; Kocka, 1980).

Thus, we would maintain, the crucial issue that arises so far as absolute rates of mobility are concerned is that of whether, or how far the course of change they follow is in fact a phenomenon open to explanation in macrosociological terms. Investigators who have been impressed by the degree of temporal variation in absolute, as compared with relative, rates have gone on to conclude that the dynamism of the former must lie primarily in structural effects, and in turn they have urged that these should not be treated as merely a 'nuisance factor' but should become themselves the focus of inquiry (e.g. Hauser *et al.,* 1975; Grusky and Hauser, 1984; Goldthorpe, 1985). However, while this argument has an evident logic, it does leave quite undecided the question of just what *kind* of understanding of structural effects—and thence of change in absolute rates—it might be possible to achieve. In so far as generalisations about such effects can be made, will they prove to be of any great explanatory value when applied to particular instances? Or may one be in this respect forced back willy-nilly to a reliance largely on specific historical descriptions—as a position such as that of Sorokin would in effect imply? Or again are there perhaps intermediate possibilities?

Turning now to relative rates, we meet with a very different situation. In this case, the liberal theory is undermined because, instead of the anticipated trend of change, in the direction of greater equality, we find evidence of an essential stability. Although shifts in relative rates can in some cases be detected (see Erikson and Goldthorpe 1992: 90–101), these are not only ones which go in various directions but, more importantly, ones which, as against those observed in absolute rates, are of very limited magnitude—so that one might wish to speak more of 'oscillation' than of fluctuation. In other words, the liberal theory would here appear to fail because the logic of industrialism has not in fact automatically generated the changes within processes of social selection which were expected of it, and through which a steady increase in fluidity and openness would be promoted.

It is in this connection of interest to note that of late exponents of the liberal theory appear to have modified their position in regard to relative rates quite significantly. Thus, for example, Treiman initially sought to provide the hypothesis of a trend towards greater openness with a rationale largely in terms of the functional exigencies of industrialism (1970: 218). However, in a recent paper (with Yip), he puts much stronger emphasis on the part that is played in creating greater openness and equality of opportunity by the more proximate factor of greater *equality of condition*—that is, by a greater equality in the economic, cultural and social resources that families possess. And while it is still maintained that this in-

crease in equality of condition itself ultimately derives from the development of industrialism, it is at the same time accepted that 'industrialization and inequality do not move in perfect concert' and, further, that *other* factors, especially political ones—for example, whether a nation has a socialist regime—may also affect the degree of inequality that exists (Treiman and Yip, 1989: 376–7). That is to say, it would here seem to be recognised that even in cases where a trend towards greater fluidity may be empirically established, this cannot be regarded as simply a matter of developmental necessity but must rather be explained as the contingent outcome of quite complex patterns of social action (cf. also Ganzeboom, Luijkx and Treiman, 1989; Simkus *et al.,* 1990). And conversely, this revised, and evidently much weaker, position is then of course able to accommodate the alternative possibility that, in particular instances, no trend of this kind is observed—because countervailing forces have in fact proved too strong.

The stability in relative rates that we have shown gains in significance, we may add, not only because the period that our data cover comprised decades of unprecedented economic growth but also because it was, of course, one of major political upheavals, in which, in the train of war and revolution, national frontiers were redrawn and massive shifts of population occurred.[22] The fact that the relative rates underlying the mobility experience of cohorts within our national samples should then reveal so little change—whether directional or otherwise—becomes all the more remarkable. While we have not been able to support the claim of a sustained developmental trend, we have, it appears, found indications of something of no less sociological interest: that is, of a constancy in social process prevailing within our several nations over decades that would in general have to be characterised in terms of the transformation and turbulence that they witnessed.

Furthermore, this finding is, as we have indicated, one which may be related to a larger sociological argument, namely, that represented by the FJH hypothesis. We have presented analyses which indicate that *some* variation in fluidity patterns does in fact occur among nations—indeed, more than within nations over time—and also that this variation shows no tendency to diminish (see Erikson and Goldthorpe 1992: 90–101). Thus, expectations of convergence are not met. However, neither would cross-national variation appear to be increasing; and, more importantly, as we have elsewhere sought to show (Erikson and Goldthorpe 1987, 1992: ch. 5), it could not be reckoned as sufficiently wide to rule out the possibility that the 'basic'

similarity in relative rates that the FJH hypothesis claims is the major source of the temporal stability that we have observed; or, that is, the possibility that *constancy* above all reflects *commonality.*

In other words, in so far as the degree of similarity proposed by the FJH hypothesis is established, we may think of temporal shifts in fluidity within nations as being no more than oscillations occurring around the standard pattern that the hypothesis implies or, at all events, as being restricted in their frequency and extent by whatever set of effects it is that generates this pattern. And in this regard, then, the ultimate task becomes that of understanding these effects; or, that is, of seeking to explain not variance, to which, as Lieberson (1987) has observed, analytical strategies within macrosociology have thus far been chiefly oriented, but rather a *lack* of variance—for which, unfortunately, appropriate strategies remain largely to be devised.

Appendix Table 1   National Inquiries Used as Data Sources

	Inquiry	Date	References for survey details
England & Wales (ENG)	Oxford National Occupational Mobility Inquiry	1972	Goldthorpe (1980)
France (FRA)	INSEE Enquête Formation-Qualification Professionelle	1970	Pohl, Thélot and Jousset (1974)
Federal Republic of Germany (FRG)	ZUMA Superfile	1976–1978	Erikson *et al.* (1988)
Hungary (HUN)	Social Mobility and Occupational Change in Hungary	1973	Andorka and Zagórski (1980)
Irish Republic (IRL)	Determinants of Occupational Mobility	1973–1974	O'Muircheartaigh and Wiggins (1977)
Northern Ireland (NIR)	Determinants of Occupational Mobility	1973–1974	O'Muircheartaigh and Wiggins (1977)
Poland (POL)	Change in the Socio-Occupational Structure	1972	Zagórski (1977–8)
Scotland (SCO)	Scottish Mobility Study	1974–1975	Payne (1987)
Sweden (SWE)	Level of Living Survey	1974	Andersson (1987)

APPENDIX TABLE 2
The Class Schema

Full version		Collapsed versions		
		Seven-class*	Five-class	Three-class
I	Higher-grade professionals, administrators, and officials; managers in large industrial establishments; large proprietors	I+II Service class: professionals, administrators and managers; higher-grade technicians; supervisors of non-manual workers		
II	Lower-grade professionals, administrators, and officials; higher-grade technicians; managers in small industrial establishments; supervisors of non-manual employees		I–III White-collar workers	
IIIa	Routine non-manual employees, higher grade (administration and commerce)	III Routine non-manual workers: routine non-manual employees in administration and commerce; sales personnel; other rank-and-file service workers		Non-manual workers
IIIb	Routine non-manual employees, lower grade (sales and services)			
IVa	Small proprietors, artisans, etc., with employees	IVa+b Petty bourgeoisie: small proprietors and artisans, etc., with and without employees	IVa+b Petty bourgeoisie	
IVb	Small proprietors, artisans, etc., without employees			
IVc	Farmers and smallholders; other self-employed workers in primary production	IVc Farmers: farmers and smallholders and other self-employed workers in primary production	IVc+VIIb Farm workers	Farm workers
V	Lower-grade technicians; supervisors of manual workers	V+VI Skilled workers: lower-grade technicians; supervisors of manual workers; skilled manual workers	V+VI Skilled workers	Manual workers
VI	Skilled manual workers			
VIIa	Semi- and unskilled manual workers (not in agriculture, etc.)	VIIa Non-skilled workers: semi- and unskilled manual workers (not in agriculture, etc.)	VIIa Non-skilled workers	
VIIb	Agricultural and other workers in primary production	VIIb Agricultural labourers: agricultural and other workers in primary production		

NOTES

1. This paper is based on chapter 3 of Robert Erikson and John H. Goldthorpe, *The Constant Flux: A Study of Class Mobility in Industrial Societies,* The Clarendon Press, Oxford, 1992. The research on which this book reports was carried out under the auspices of the CASMIN-Projekt, based at the Institüt für Sozialwissenschaften of the University of Mannheim and funded by grants from the Stiftung Volkswagenwerk, Hanover. Readers are referred to the above work (chapter 2 esp.) for full details of the comparative methodology followed in research.

2. The influence here of the 'stages-of-growth' model of Rostow (1960: see esp. Chart 1) would seem to be of particular importance and also, perhaps—though the evidence is indirect—the interpretation of European industrial development provided by Landes (1957, 1965, 1972), which places major emphasis upon the rate and pattern of diffusion of techniques of production from Britain to the more 'backward' economies of the European mainland.

3. Thus, for example, in Kerr *et al.* (1960) discussion of France and Italy is largely concerned with the impediments to industrial development that result from the persisting importance of 'family-dominated enterprises' with 'patrimonial management' (see e.g. pp. 80, 141–2; and cf. Landes, 1957); and discussion of Germany, with difficulties of social rigidity and authoritarianism, following from the promotion of industrialisation by a dynastic elite (e.g. pp. 54–5, 150–1).

4. It is of interest that Bell should refer to the situation on which he comments as one 'that has gone relatively unexamined'. This statement may well be true for American theorists of industrialism, but it can scarcely hold in the case of European economic and social historians. See, for

example, the discussion of issues central to the 'reperiodisation' of the development of industrial society in Europe that are found in Wrigley (1972) and Mayer (1981).

5. So far as emigration is concerned, a detailed review of the possible and likely effects on mobility rates and propensities is provided in Hout (1989), with special reference to the Irish case.

6. For our present purposes, it is the confounding of period by age effects that is most likely to create problems. To the extent that cohort effects are present in the data, this may be regarded as valid evidence against the occurrence of secular trends.

7. This is in fact the highest maximum age that we could apply across all nine of our national samples.

8. The wording of the questions from which this information was derived varied somewhat from one national inquiry to another but not, we believe, in ways likely to have any significant effects on the comparability of data. In this and all similar instances full details of question wording, construction of variables, etc. are to be found in the documentation to the CASMIN International Social Mobility Superfile (Erikson *et al.,* 1988).

9. We are greatly endebted to Jan Hoem for his most generous help in this aspect of our work.

10. These plots are not shown but in what follows it may be assumed that where no reference is made to rates of mobility from class origins to class of first employment, our findings in this respect would not lead us seriously to qualify those we have obtained for rates from class origins to present class.

11. The results that we report here for Hungary do of course depend on our treating workers on agricultural co-operatives or state farms as having a different class position (VIIb) from that of peasant proprietors (IVc). Some analysts of mobility in Hungary have not made this distinction; but we would argue the desirability of so doing, wherever it is practically feasible. It was, after all, precisely the aim both of the immediate post-war land reform and of the subsequent collectivisation programme to *change* agrarian class relations. In the Polish case, it should be noted,

the attempt to collectivise agriculture that the regime launched at the end of the 1940s met with fierce peasant opposition and was finally abandoned in 1956 (cf. Lewis, 1973).

12. Although, then, we are here forced back to the obviously rather crude three-class basis of much earlier comparative research, we must stress that we still do achieve a much higher standard of data comparability. As a result of our systematic recoding of the original unit-record data (see Erikson and Goldthorpe, 1992: ch. 2), we have a reasonable assurance that the categories of 'non-manual', 'manual' and 'farm' are being applied in a consistent manner from nation to nation, rather than providing comparability of a merely nominal kind.

13. It may be noted that in Figure 44.4 the left tail of the curve for Sweden has been deleted. This is on account of its unreliability, as determined by a test developed by Hoem (see Erikson and Goldthorpe, 1992: ch. 3, Annex). For the same reason, we have also deleted the left tail of the curve for Northern Ireland in Figure 44.8.

14. These results are of direct relevance to the Lipset-Zetterberg hypothesis of cross-national similarity in absolute rates, since this was in fact formulated in terms of outflow rates from non-manual to manual positions and *vice versa.* We do not take up this issue here (but see further Erikson and Goldthorpe, 1992: ch. 6).

15. Following the hierarchical levels that we propose, a further upward flow—that our 3 x 7 tables do not enable us to distinguish—would be represented by men entering Class I + II positions from Class III origins.

16. Thus, for example, in the English case the more or less continuous rise in upward mobility into the service class across the cohorts we distinguish can be related to a corresponding steady expansion of this class from a time somewhere between 1931 and 1951 (there was no 1941 Census)—following, however, on several decades in which it grew scarcely at all (see Goldthorpe, 1980, 1987: ch. 2 esp.). As regards socialist societies, it may further be noted that evidence of a 'parabolic' curve for upward mobility, similar to that we record in Hungary and Poland, is also found for post-war Czechoslovakia in data from a survey conducted in

1984 (personal communication from Marek Bo-guszak and cf. Boguszak, 1990).

17. It would, moreover, be mistaken simply to equate a peasant economy—or society—with a 'traditional' one. Thus, while one may with justi-fication speak of a peasant economy existing in substantial areas of Ireland at least up to the 1940s, many of its key institutional features—most importantly, perhaps, non-partible inheri-tance—were relatively new (cf. Hannan, 1979). The Irish peasant community, as classically de-picted by Arensberg and Kimball (1940, 1968), has in fact to be seen as the historical product of economic and social conditions in Ireland follow-ing the Great Famine of 1846–9 and then of the land reform legislation introduced between 1870 and the First World War.

18. It is important that rG^2, referred to by Goodman (1972) as the 'coefficient of multiple determination', should be interpreted within the particular context of loglinear modelling, rather than being taken as the equivalent of the perhaps more familiar R^2 of regression analysis. As Schwartz has pointed out (1985), the fact that R^2s are typically much lower than rG^2s reflects the fact that in regression the units of analysis are usually individuals while in loglinear modelling they are the cells of cross-tabulations and the scores are the numbers of individuals in a cell. Such aggregate data must then be expected to reveal stronger reg-ularities than individual-level data. Schwartz's summary (1985: 2–3) is apt: rG^2 'measures how adequately a model accounts for the observed *as-sociations* among a pre-specified set of variables while R^2 and Eta^2 measure the amount of *varia-tion* in one variable that can be accounted for by its (linear) association with specified independent variables'. The point may be added that the sub-stantive meaning of rG^2 will of course depend on the model that is chosen as baseline.

19. This suggestion was made to us by Joseph E. Schwartz in a personal communication, for which we are duly grateful.

20. We may add that results from equivalent analyses of data referring to mobility from class of origin to class of first employment are essentially similar. In only one case, that of Ireland, would the CnSF model be rejected on the basis of the

$G^2(S)$ statistic; and again only in the Swedish case does the model not account for at least 90 per cent of the total origin-destination association, while at most only a little over 5 per cent of all cases are misclassified. It should, however, be re-called that we cannot undertake an analysis of the kind in question for the FRG, owing to lack of information on first employment.

21. Moreover, while we would believe that 'de-mand side' factors are generally of major impor-tance in promoting structural change, 'supply side' ones may also have to be taken into ac-count—for example, the effects of demographic change, including in- and out-migration, and of changes in the workforce participation rates of women and of different age-groups. And in these respects too political intervention may obviously play a crucial role.

22. Most importantly, in the aftermath of World War II the FRG was created out of the division of the Third Reich, and Poland's fron-tiers were moved some 150–200 miles to the west—both changes being accompanied by large population movements. In addition, one may note the truncation of Hungary in 1920 (with the loss of almost 70 per cent of its area and 60 per cent of its population); and the partition of Ireland in 1920–2, following the War of Inde-pendence and the Civil War, so as to create the Irish Free State (which became the Irish Repub-lic in 1949) and the six counties of Northern Ireland, a constituent element of the United Kingdom with, up to 1973, its own parliament and executive.

BIBLIOGRAPHY

Andersson, L. (1987): 'Appendix A: Sampling and Data Collection' in R. Erikson and R. Åberg eds., *Welfare in Transition: A Survey of Living Conditions in Sweden 1968–1981*. Ox-ford: Clarendon Press.

Andorka, R. and K. Zagórski (1980): *Socio-Occu-pational Mobility in Hungary and Poland*. War-saw: Polish Academy of Sciences.

Arensberg, C.M. and S.T. Kimball (1940, 2nd ed. 1968): *Family and Community in Ireland*. Cambridge, Mass.: Harvard University Press.

Bell, D. (1980): 'Liberalism in the Post-Industrial Society' in *Sociological Journeys*. London: Heinemann.

Blau, P.M. and O.D. Duncan (1967): *The American Occupational Structure*. New York: Wiley.

Blossfeld, H.-P. (1986): 'Career Opportunities in the Federal Republic of Germany'. *European Sociological Review* 2.

Boguszak, M. (1990): 'Transition to Socialism and Intergenerational Class Mobility: The Model of Core Social Fluidity Applied to Czechoslovakia' in M. Haller ed., *Class Structure in Europe*. Armonk, N.Y.: Sharpe.

Boyle, J.F. (1976): 'Analysis of the Irish Occupational Index'. Department of Social Studies, The Queen's University, Belfast.

Braverman, H. (1974): *Labor and Monopoly Capitalism*. New York: Monthly Review Press.

Brus, W. (1986a): 'Postwar Reconstruction and Socio-Economic Transformation' in M.C. Kaser and E.A. Radice eds., *The Economic History of Eastern Europe, 1919–1975*, vol. 2. Oxford: Clarendon Press.

Brus, W. (1986b): '1950 to 1953: The Peak of Stalinism' in M.C. Kaser ed., *The Economic History of Eastern Europe, 1919–1975*, vol. 3. Oxford: Clarendon Press.

Carchedi, G. (1977): *On the Economic Identification of Classes*. London: Routledge.

Carlsson, G. (1963): 'Sorokin's Theory of Social Mobility' in P.J. Allen ed., *Pitirim A. Sorokin in Review*. Durham, N.C.: Duke University Press.

Clark, C. (3rd ed., 1957): *The Conditions of Economic Progress*. London: Macmillan.

Crompton, R. and G. Jones (1984): *White-Collar Proletariat: Deskilling and Gender in Clerical Work*. London: Macmillan.

Duncan, O.D. (1961): 'A Socioeconomic Index for All Occupations' in A.J. Reiss ed., *Occupations and Social Status*. New York: Free Press.

Dunlop, J.T., F.H. Harbison, C. Kerr and C.A. Myers (1975): *Industrialism and Industrial Man Reconsidered*. Princeton: Inter-University Study of Human Resources in National Development.

Erikson, R. and J.H. Goldthorpe (1987): 'Commonality and Variation in Social Fluidity in Industrial Nations. Part I: A Model for Evaluating the "FJH Hypothesis"; Part II: The Model of Core Social Fluidity Applied'. *European Sociological Review* 3.

Erikson, R. and J.H. Goldthorpe (1992): *The Constant Flux: A Study of Class Mobility in Industrial Societies*. Oxford: Clarendon Press.

Erikson, R., J.H. Goldthorpe and L. Portocarero (1983): 'Intergenerational Class Mobility and the Convergence Thesis'. *British Journal of Sociology* 34.

Erikson, R., J.H. Goldthorpe, W. König, P. Lüttinger and W. Müller (1988): 'CASMIN International Mobility Superfile: Documentation'. Mannheim: Institut für Sozialwissenschaften, University of Mannheim.

Featherman, D.L., F.L. Jones and R.M. Hauser (1975): 'Assumptions of Social Mobility Research in the US: The Case of Occupational Status'. *Social Science Research* 4.

Gagliani, G. (1985): 'Long-Term Changes in the Occupational Structure'. *European Sociological Review* 1.

Ganzeboom, H., R. Luijkx and D.J. Treiman (1989): 'Intergenerational Class Mobility in Comparative Perspective'. *Research in Social Stratification and Mobility* 8.

Glenn, N.D. (1977): *Cohort Analysis*. Beverly Hills: Sage.

Goldthorpe, J.H. (with Catriona Llewellyn and Clive Payne) (1980, 2nd ed. 1987): *Social Mobility and Class Structure in Modern Britain*. Oxford: Clarendon Press.

Goldthorpe, J.H. (1985): 'On Economic Development and Social Mobility'. *British Journal of Sociology* 36.

Goldthorpe, J.H. and K. Hope (1974): *The Social Grading of Occupations: A New Approach and Scale*. Oxford: Clarendon Press.

Goodman, L.A. (1972): 'A General Model for the Analysis of Surveys'. *American Journal of Sociology* 77.

Grusky, D.B. and R.M. Hauser (1984): 'Comparative Social Mobility Revisited: Models of Convergence and Divergence in 16 Countries'. *American Sociological Review* 49.

Hannan, D.F. (1979): *Displacement and Development: Class, Kinship and Social Change in Irish Rural Communities*. Dublin: The Economic and Social Research Institute.

Hauser, R.M., P.J. Dickinson, H.P. Travis and J.M. Koffel (1975): 'Temporal Change in Occupational Mobility: Evidence for Men in the United States'. *American Sociological Review* 40.

Hoem, J.M. and P. Linneman (1987): 'The Tails in Moving Average Graduation'. Stockholm: Research Reports in Demography 37, University of Stockholm.

Hout, M. (1989): *Following in Father's Footsteps: Social Mobility in Ireland.* Cambridge, Mass.: Harvard University Press.

Kaelble, H. (1981): *Historical Research on Social Mobility.* London: Croom Helm.

Kaelble, H. (1984): 'Eras of Social Mobility in 19th and 20th Century Europe'. *Journal of Social History* 17.

Kemp, T. (1978): *Historical Patterns of Industrialization.* London: Longman.

Kerr, C. (1969): *Marshall, Marx and Modern Times.* Cambridge: Cambridge University Press.

Kerr, C. (1983): *The Future of Industrial Societies.* Cambridge, Mass.: Harvard University Press.

Kerr, C., J.T. Dunlop, F.H. Harbison and C.A. Myers (1960, 2nd ed. 1973): *Industrialism and Industrial Man.* Cambridge, Mass.: Harvard University Press.

Kindleberger, C.P. (1967): *Europe's Postwar Growth: The Role of Labor Supply.* Cambridge, Mass.: Harvard University Press.

Kocka, J. (1980): 'The Study of Social Mobility and the Formation of the Working Class in the 19th Century'. *Le mouvement social* 111.

Kulcsár, K. (1984): *Contemporary Hungarian Society.* Budapest: Corvina.

Kuznets, S. (1966): *Modern Economic Growth.* New Haven: Yale University Press.

Landes, D.S. (1957): 'Observations on France: Economy, Society and Politics'. *World Politics,* April.

Landes, D.S. (1965, 2nd ed. 1972): *The Unbound Prometheus: Technological Change and Industrial Development in Western Europe from 1750 to the Present.* Cambridge: Cambridge University Press.

Lewis, P. (1973): 'The Peasantry' in D. Lane and G. Kolankiewicz eds., *Social Groups in Polish Society.* London: Macmillan.

Lieberson, S. (1985, 2nd ed. 1987): *Making It Count.* Berkeley, University of California Press.

de Lillo, A. and A. Schizzerotto (1985): *La valutazione sociale delle occupazioni.* Bologna: II Mulino.

Lipset, S.M. and H.L. Zetterberg (1956): 'A Theory of Social Mobility'. *Transactions of the Third World Congress of Sociology,* vol. 3. London: International Sociological Association.

Lipset, S.M. and H.L. Zetterberg (1959): 'Social Mobility in Industrial Societies' in S.M. Lipset and R. Bendix, *Social Mobility in Industrial Society.* Berkeley: University of California Press.

Lutz, B. (1984): *Der kurze Traum immerwährender Prosperität.* Frankfurt: Campus.

Mayer, A.J. (1981): *The Persistence of the Old Regime: Europe to the Great War.* New York: Pantheon.

Mendels, F.F. (1976): 'Social Mobility and Phases of Industrialisation'. *Journal of Interdisciplinary History* 7.

Naoi, A. (1979): 'Shokugyoteki Chiishakudo no Kosei' (The Construction of the Occupational Status Scale) in K. Tominaga ed., *Nihon no Kaiso Kozo* (The Stratification Structure in Japan). Tokyo: Todai Shuppan Kai.

O'Brien, P. and C. Keyder (1978): *Economic Growth in Britain and France, 1780–1914.* London: Allen and Unwin.

O'Muircheartaigh, C.A. and R.D. Wiggins (1977): 'Sample Design and Evaluation for an Occupational Mobility Study'. *Economic and Social Review* 8.

Parsons, T. (1960): *Structure and Process in Modern Societies.* Glencoe: Free Press.

Parsons, T. (1967): *Sociological Theory and Modern Society.* New York: Free Press.

Parsons, T. (1971): *The System of Modern Societies.* Englewood Cliffs: Prentice-Hall.

Payne, G. (1987): *Employment and Opportunity.* London: Macmillan.

Pohl, R., C. Thélot and M-F. Jousset (1974): *L'Enquête Formation-Qualification Professionelle de 1970.* Paris: INSEE.

Priebe, H. (1976): 'The Changing Role of Agriculture, 1920–1970' in C.M. Cipolla ed., *Fontana Economic History of Europe,* vol. 5 (ii). London: Fontana.

Rostow, W.W. (1960): *The Stages of Economic Growth: A Non-Communist Manifesto*. Cambridge: Cambridge University Press.

Schwartz, J.E. (1985): 'Goodman's Coefficient of Multiple Determination: Why it is *Not* Analogous to R². Stockholm: Swedish Institute for Social Research.

Simkus, A.A., R. Andorka, J. Jackson, K-B. Yip and D.J. Treiman (1990): 'Changes in Social Mobility in Two Societies in the Crux of Transition: A Hungarian-Irish Comparison, 1943–1973'. *Research in Social Stratification and Mobility* 9.

Singelmann, J. (1978): *From Agriculture to Services: The Transformation of Industrial Employment*. Beverly Hills: Sage.

Singelmann, J. and M. Tienda (1985): 'The Process of Occupational Change in a Service Society: The Case of the United States, 1960–1980' in B. Roberts, R. Finnegan and D. Gallie, eds., *New Approaches to Economic Life*. Manchester: Manchester University Press.

Sorokin, P.A. (1927, 2nd ed. 1959): *Social and Cultural Mobility*. Glencoe: Free Press.

Treiman, D.J. (1970): 'Industrialisation and Social Stratification' in E.O. Laumann ed., *Social Stratification: Research and Theory for the 1970s*. Indianapolis: Bobbs Merrill.

Treiman, D.J. (1977): *Occupational Prestige in Comparative Perspective*. New York: Academic Press.

Treiman, D.J. and K-B. Yip (1989): 'Educational and Occupational Attainment in 21 Countries' in M.L. Kohn ed., *Cross-National Research in Sociology*. Newbury Park: Sage.

Wegener, B. (1988): *Kritik des Prestiges*. Opladen: Westdeutscher Verlag.

Wright, E.O. and J. Singelmann (1982): 'Proletarianization in the Changing American Class Structure'. *American Journal of Sociology* 88.

Wright, E.O. and B. Martin (1987): 'The Transformation of the American Class Structure, 1960–1980'. *American Journal of Sociology* 93.

Wrigley, E.A. (1972): 'The Process of Modernization and the Industrial Revolution in England'. *Journal of Interdisciplinary History* 3.

Zagórski, K. (1977–8): 'Transformations of Social Structure and Social Mobility in Poland'. *International Journal of Sociology* 7.

45

Social Mobility in Europe

RICHARD BREEN

I discuss here the findings of a project that looks at social mobility in 11 European countries over a period of almost 30 years (see Breen 2004 for details). I want to summarize some of the main results and discuss how they relate to previous research in this area; and I also want to make some comments about the consequences of this research and of these findings for the study of social mobility. But I will begin by briefly explaining what the project is all about.

class); III (routine non-manual class); IVab (petty bourgeoisie with and without employees); IVc (farmers); V + VI (skilled manual workers, technicians and supervisors of manual workers); VIIa (unskilled manual workers not in agriculture) and VIIb (farm workers). One consequence of choosing this categorization is that it allows our results to be compared with those of *The Constant Flux* (Erikson and Goldthorpe 1993), where the same categories were used.

Data

The data used in the project comprise 117 mobility surveys covering the period 1970 to 2000. The sources of the data are shown in Table 45.1. The number of tables per country ranges from two in Israel and Italy to 35 in the Netherlands.

In general the age range of the respondents in our mobility tables is 25 to 64, and we coded social class according to the seven-class 'CASMIN' scheme (see Table 45.2). This identifies classes I + II (the service

Methodological Issues

As Table 45.1 showed, the 11 countries contribute rather different numbers of mobility tables to our cross-national analyses. Sweden, for example, has a table for every year from 1976 to 1999, whereas Poland and Ireland have only three tables each, covering the years between the early 1970s and 1994. The amount of information we possess regarding change over time, and the reliability of the conclusions based on this information, will vary between countries. If we have

---

Table 45.1   Sources of Data

Country	# tables	Sources of data	Years for which data are included
Germany	22	Zumabus	1976–77 1979(2) 1980 1982
		Allbus	1980 1982 1984 1986 1988 1990–92 1994 1996 1998
		Politik in der BRD	1978 1980
		Wohlfahrtssurvey	1978
		German socio-economic panel	1986 1999
France	4	Formation-qualification professionnelle Insee surveys	1970 1977 1985 1993
Italy	2	National survey on social mobility	1985
		Italian household longitudinal survey	1997
Ireland	3	Survey of the determinants of occupational status and mobility	1973
		Survey of income distribution and poverty	1987
		Living in Ireland survey	1994
Great Britain	15	General household survey	1973 1975–76 1979–1984 1987–1992
Sweden	24	Annual surveys of living conditions (ULF)	1976–1999
Norway	3	Colbjørnsen et al. 1987	1982
		Moen et al. 1996	1994
		Level of Living Survey	1995
Poland	3	Zagorski 1976	1972
		Slomczynski 1989	1988
		Treiman/ Szelényi	1994
Hungary	4	Social mobility and life history survey	1973 1983 1992
		Way of Life and Time Use Survey (Hungarian Central Statistical Office)	2000
Israel	2	Matras and Weintraub, 1977	1974
		Kraus and Toren 1992	1991
Netherlands	35	Parliamentiary Election Study	1970 1971 1977 1981 1982 1986 1994 1998
		Political Action Survey I	1974 1979
		Justice of Income Survey	1976
		CBS Life Situation Survey	1977 1986
		National Labour Market Survey	1982
		National Prestige and Mobility Survey	1982 1985 1988 1990 1992 1994 1996
		Strategic Labour Market Survey	1998
		Cultural Changes [ISSP]	1987
		Justice of Income Survey	1987
		Primary and Social Relationships	1987
		Social and Cultural Trends	1990
		Justice of Income Survey [ISJP]	1991
		Family Survey I, 1992–93	1992
		Households in the Netherlands pilot	1994
		Households in the Netherlands	1995
		Social Inequality in the Netherlands	1996
		National Crime Study	1996
		Social and Economic Attitudes	1998
		Netherlands Family Survey II	1998
		Use of Information Technology	1999

Table 45.2   The Goldthorpe Class Schema

Goldthorpe Class	Description	Employment relations	CASMIN version
I	Higher-grade professionals, administrators and officials; managers in large industrial establishments; large proprietors	Employer or service relationship	I + II Service class
II	Lower-grade professionals, administrators and officials; higher-grade technicians; managers in small industrial establishments; supervisors of non-manual employees	Service relationship	
IIIa	Routine non-manual employees, higher-grade (administration and commerce)	Intermediate	III Routine non-manual
IIIb	Routine non-manual employees, lower-grade (sales and services)	Labour contract	
IVa	Small proprietors, artisans, etc., with employees	Employer	IVab Non-farm petty-bourgeoisie
IVb	Small proprietors, artisans, etc., without employees	Self-employed	
IVc	Farmers and smallholders; other self-employed workers in primary production	Employer or self-employed	IVc Farmers and other self-employed workers in primary production
V	Lower-grade technicians; supervisors of manual workers	Intermediate	V + VI Technicians, supervisors and skilled manual workers
VI	Skilled manual workers	Labour contract	
VIIa	Semi- and unskilled manual workers (not in agriculture, etc.)	Labour contract	VIIa Semi- and unskilled manual workers (not in agriculture)
VIIb	Semi- and unskilled manual workers in agriculture	Labour contract	VIIb Semi- and unskilled manual workers in agriculture

a small number of observations, any one of them may be very influential in determining whether or not the data display a trend (as we shall see) and this will inevitably lead to uncertainty in the conclusions we draw. All else equal we must, as a consequence, attach more credence to results about temporal trends drawn from countries with a larger number of observations (Sweden, the Netherlands, Great Britain and Germany).

Furthermore, the data that we use are never free of error, and differences in data quality may easily be mistaken for substantive differences. We have used the best quality data available from each of our 11 countries, but we still need to be aware of the potential for differential reliability and validity to induce spurious cross-national variation and temporal change. As far as the differences between countries are concerned, the fieldwork for the surveys we use was in all cases carried out according to internationally accepted procedures and the subsequent coding of the variables—notably class origins and destinations—followed a common, and widely implemented procedure. Nevertheless, while adherence to such norms is some reassurance that the data attain high standards of quality, the surveys in the various countries were carried out independently of each other, and so we should be cautious about what we infer from them concerning cross-national differences. As far as change within countries is concerned, we can have more faith in our findings when the various surveys have been administered in a consistent fashion. In three cases the data always come from the same survey series: these are France (the FQP—Formation-Qualification Professionnelle—surveys), Britain (the General Household Survey) and Sweden (the ULF series). In a further five countries the data sets come from highly comparable sources: these are Ireland (where the three surveys were all carried out by the same fieldwork organization), Hungary (where the four surveys were all fielded by the Hungarian Central Statistical Office), Italy (where a number of the same academics were involved in the design and execution of the two surveys), Germany and Israel. But in the remaining three cases—Norway, Poland and the Netherlands—the data come from various sources within each

country and thus the possibility that variations in data quality might be mistaken for temporal change is greatest here. We believe that more reliance can be placed on estimates of trends *within* countries than measures of differences *between* them: thus our discussion, later in this chapter, of which countries are more or less open in their mobility regime, should be interpreted with some caution. Finally, while the data that we have are probably adequate for presenting a picture of broad trends and differences, we would have less confidence in the extent to which they allow the specifics of the pattern of social fluidity to be compared across either time or countries. This consideration has then dictated our choice of models. Rather than seeking to develop detailed models of the fluidity regime we prefer instead to fit rather general models and to assess their adequacy using several measures (including the conventional chi-squared goodness of fit test and the index of dissimilarity).

Absolute Mobility and Class Structure

In contemporary studies of social mobility a key distinction is drawn between observed patterns of social mobility, sometimes referred to as 'absolute mobility', and social fluidity (or 'relative mobility'). Absolute mobility is concerned with patterns and rates of mobility, where mobility is understood simply as movement between class origins (the social class in which someone was brought up) and class destinations (the class they occupy at the time of the survey). Social fluidity concerns the relationship between class origins and current class position: specifically it is based on the comparison, between people of different

Table 45.3a   Aggregate Class Structures (All Men) in the 11 Countries by Decade

	1970s	1980s	1990s
I + II	23.1	28.6	30.8
III	8.7	9.0	10.1
IVa + b	7.9	8.6	10.4
IVc	8.6	5.7	4.0
V + VI	27.7	27.6	27.1
VIIa	20.6	18.3	15.7
VIIb	3.5	2.3	2.0

Note: Each country is weighted equally in computation of aggregate class structure.

Table 45.3b   Aggregate Class Structures (Women in the Labour Force) in the 10 Countries by Decade

	1970s	1980s	1990s
I + II	22.1	30.5	34.6
III	32.8	32.3	35.1
IVa + b	6.5	6.0	6.1
IVc	8.6	4.4	2.3
V + VI	6.1	6.3	7.1
VIIa	21.1	18.6	13.7
VIIb	2.8	1.7	1.2

Note: Each country is weighted equally in computation of aggregate class structure.

class origins, of their chances of being found in one destination class rather than another. If these chances were the same regardless of origins then the mobility table would display perfect mobility: the class in which a respondent was found would not depend on (would be independent of) the class in which she or he was brought up. Social fluidity is often interpreted as an index of equality in the chances of access to more or less advantageous social positions between people coming from different social origins (in other words, as an index of societal openness),[1] and contemporary research on social mobility accordingly pays much more attention to social fluidity than to absolute mobility. I will follow that precedent here and so will make only a few comments about absolute mobility.

In fact, our results concerning absolute mobility can be summarised quite easily. There has been a marked convergence in the class structures of European countries and in their patterns of absolute mobility, and these things are true for both men and women.

A. Convergence in class structures has been driven by some internationally consistent trends, such as the growth in the service class, I + II, and the decline in manual work, particularly of the unskilled kind. Among women, increased rates of labour force participation have been associated with a reduction in international variation as more and more of them enter occupations in the white collar classes, I + II and III. But the single biggest cause of this convergence has been the declining significance of the farm classes, IVc and VIIb, in those countries (such as Poland, Ireland, and Hungary) where a large farm sector persisted until the last quarter of the 20th century.

B. This trend towards convergence in class structures has occurred together with decreasing variation between countries in their rates of overall mobility, of vertical, of upward and of downward mobility—and, again, this is evident among both sexes, as Tables 44.4 and 44.5 show. But, further, the distribution of people in the mobility tables of the different countries has also grown more similar. If we calculate the index of dissimilarity (Δ) from comparisons, between all pairs of countries, of their entire mobility tables, we find that the average Δ (the average difference between countries) falls from 43 per cent in the 1970s, to 33 in the 1980s and 30 in the 1990s, among women, with the comparable figures for men being 39, 30 and 30 per cent. And the variance around these means has also declined: from 163.2 to 62.6 to 41.6 among women and from 137.5 to 62.9 to 56.1 among men. Although European countries continue to show differences in their absolute mobility flows, these have become smaller.

Absolute mobility concerns the observed rates and patterns of flows between origin and destination classes and, in mobility analysis, is treated as the consequence of social fluidity (the relative chances of people from each origin being found in each destination class) operating within fixed origin and destination distributions. A model in which origins and destinations are independent, given the observed distributions of these two in each country and at each point in time, correctly classifies over 80 per cent of cases, while a model which also assumes a common level and pattern of social fluidity correctly classifies around 95 per cent of cases. It is evident, therefore, that changes over time, and differences between countries, in absolute mobility are driven by variation in the origin and destination distributions rather than in social fluidity.

Can such variation be said to follow a pattern? We believe that the answer, in very broad terms, is yes. We might imagine societies following a developmental path that incorporates two major transitions: from an agricultural to an industrial society, and from an industrial to a post-industrial society. The consequences, for the class structure, of the former transition are a decline in the proportions in classes IVc and VIIb and a growth in the remaining classes, especially (among men) the manual working classes V + VI and VIIa. The transition to a post-industrial society sees the decline of V + VI and VIIa and the growth of I + II and III. Everywhere the decline in agriculture is either more or less complete (Britain, Germany, Sweden, Israel, the Netherlands) or well underway while, in eight of our 11 countries (Ireland, Poland and Hungary being the exceptions), between the 1970s and 1990s, the class structure saw a steady fall in the proportion of men in classes V + VI and VIIa and a consistent increase in the proportion in I + II and III. Among women the pattern was exactly the same. These differences mean that some countries display a post-industrial class structure with a heavy concentration of people in classes I + II and III: this is particularly true of the male class structure in Britain and the Netherlands

Table 45.4   Percentage Mobile by Country in Each Decade (All Men)

Total Mobility

	Germany	France	Italy	Ireland	Great Britain	Sweden	Norway	Poland	Hungary	Israel	N'lands	Mean	Variance
1970s	61.6	66.6	—	56.7	63.0	70.8	—	59.4	77.5	74.4	66.3	66.3	48.0
1980s	62.1	67.5	69.5	61.3	61.8	71.4	71.9	61.0	74.9	—	67.7	66.9	25.8
1990s	60.3	67.0	72.1	66.1	60.8	71.0	68.1	67.4	71.6	74.3	65.7	67.7	19.9

Vertical Mobility

	Germany	France	Italy	Ireland	Great Britain	Sweden	Norway	Poland	Hungary	Israel	N'lands	Mean	Variance
1970s	44.1	43.8	—	39.9	50.7	54.0	—	40.9	53.0	43.7	50.6	46.7	28.5
1980s	45.8	45.9	40.8	42.6	50.8	54.7	55.2	42.9	55.8	—	54.1	48.9	34.6
1990s	46.3	46.3	46.3	45.5	50.7	55.2	52.1	45.9	53.7	50.4	54.0	49.7	13.9

Upward Mobility

	Germany	France	Italy	Ireland	Great Britain	Sweden	Norway	Poland	Hungary	Israel	N'lands	Mean	Variance
1970s	31.7	25.9	—	21.6	32.8	35.1	—	22.1	26.9	20.1	36.1	28.0	37.1
1980s	33.6	29.1	29.0	27.9	33.1	35.3	39.3	24.8	34.7	—	38.9	32.6	22.9
1990s	33.3	29.9	35.9	31.4	31.7	36.6	34.2	26.3	35.9	35.0	37.7	33.4	11.4

Downward Mobility

	Germany	France	Italy	Ireland	Great Britain	Sweden	Norway	Poland	Hungary	Israel	N'lands	Mean	Variance
1970s	12.4	17.9	—	18.4	17.9	19.0	—	18.8	26.2	23.5	14.5	18.7	17.3
1980s	12.2	16.8	11.8	14.7	17.7	19.4	15.9	18.0	21.1	—	15.2	16.3	8.7
1990s	13.0	16.4	10.4	14.1	19.0	18.6	17.9	19.6	17.8	15.4	16.3	16.2	8.0

Table 45.5 Percentage Mobile by Country in Each Decade (Women in the Labour Force)

Total Mobility

	Germany	France	Italy	Great Britain	Sweden	Norway	Poland	Hungary	Israel	N'lands	Mean	Variance
1970s	74.0	71.4	—	78.8	73.1	—	50.8	81.0	76.5	74.0	72.5	86.4
1980s	75.6	77.6	74.3	76.3	73.6	76.2	66.3	79.5	—	73.9	74.8	13.7
1990s	72.6	77.2	75.0	73.9	73.2	77.4	76.2	76.5	82.2	72.3	75.7	8.8

Vertical Mobility

	Germany	France	Italy	Great Britain	Sweden	Norway	Poland	Hungary	Israel	N'lands	Mean	Variance
1970s	48.6	41.7	—	52.1	55.4	—	34.0	54.1	44.9	51.4	47.8	52.2
1980s	48.8	45.7	51.0	52.6	56.4	54.1	48.5	58.2	—	51.4	51.9	15.7
1990s	47.3	46.0	47.9	53.2	57.9	53.0	50.3	55.7	53.5	53.6	51.8	14.8

Upward Mobility

	Germany	France	Italy	Great Britain	Sweden	Norway	Poland	Hungary	Israel	N'lands	Mean	Variance
1970s	25.8	27.8	—	27.5	23.9	—	19.5	23.3	26.0	30.9	25.6	11.7
1980s	29.6	32.9	38.5	29.0	27.5	34.4	31.7	38.8	—	33.6	32.9	15.7
1990s	32.2	33.2	36.7	30.6	33.5	37.1	34.1	42.0	39.0	34.8	35.3	11.6

Downward Mobility

	Germany	France	Italy	Great Britain	Sweden	Norway	Poland	Hungary	Israel	N'lands	Mean	Variance
1970s	22.8	13.9	—	24.6	31.5	—	14.4	30.8	19.0	20.5	22.2	44.2
1980s	19.2	12.8	12.5	23.7	28.9	19.8	16.8	19.4	—	17.8	19.0	26.0
1990s	15.2	12.8	11.3	22.5	24.4	15.9	16.2	13.7	14.5	18.8	16.5	17.6

and it is true of the female class structure in several countries. But the important thing, from the point of view of the study of absolute mobility, is the recent rapidity of the transition out of agriculture. Similarly, we saw in our comparative analysis that the shift towards a concentration of women in the white-collar classes has been more rapid in countries such as Hungary and Poland where the class distribution in the 1970s differed most from this. The result has been the growing similarity in destination distributions that we have already remarked upon. But because countries embarked on this developmental path long before the first of our surveys was fielded, there is also decreasing variation in class origins. The mean value of the Δ between class origins for each pair of countries fell from 33 per cent in the 1970s to 23 in the 1980s and 24 in the 1990s.[2] Absolute mobility flows converged because their main determinants did.

This convergence chiefly occurred between the 1970s and 1980s and whether the trend will persist, or even strengthen, is, of course, difficult to say. Clearly, if the working classes continue to decline in those countries where the decline has begun, and if this extends from VIIa to V + VI, then further convergence will be inevitable as men, like women, come to be heavily concentrated in classes I + II and III. Recent historical experience of the location of industrial production would suggest that we can expect further convergence; in any event, it seems unlikely that any of these countries will display a growth in classes V + VI and VIIa, while some at least will experience a decline. As for the countries in which these classes have not yet begun to decline (Ireland, Poland and Hungary), the outlook seems less certain. In Ireland the growth of classes I + II and III has outstripped that of V + VI and VIIa over this period, but this is not true of the male class structure in Poland and Hungary. On the other hand, among women in Poland and Hungary there has been a steady growth in classes I + II and III and an increase, then a decline, in V + VI and VIIa, suggesting that the second transition may be under way. Much here depends on the nature of economic development. Foreign direct investment in manufacturing, as in the Irish case, is one mechanism by which the size of the working class may be sustained and the rate of convergence consequently slowed.

Social Fluidity

In our comparative analysis we found that trends in social fluidity are very similar among men and women, showing a widespread tendency towards greater fluidity. Britain is the sole clear exception to this: here there has been little or not change. In other cases—notably Germany—there is no statistically significant change, though the trend, at least for men, is towards a weaker association between origins and destinations. Elsewhere—in France, Ireland, Sweden, Poland, Hungary and the Netherlands—there is a statistically significant increase in fluidity, though the small number of observations for Ireland (three), Poland (three), and Hungary (four), and the lack of a consistent pattern of change in these countries, must leave some room for uncertainty. But in contrast to absolute mobility we see no evidence of convergence among countries in their social fluidity. Figures 45.1 (for men) and 45.2 (for women) show these within-country trends in the form of the annual β coefficients from an LmSF model[3] with common local association among all the yearly tables of a given country.

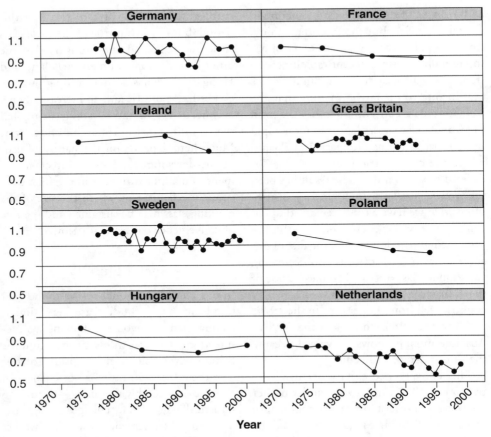

Figure 45.1   Annual LmSF (or Unidiff) Coefficients by Country (All Men)

Figure 45.3 (for men) and Figure 45.4 (for women) show the LmSF β parameters from a model, applied to decade data from each country, which assumes common local association in each table, varying only by β. The value for Britain in the 1980s is set to unity. Among men, Figure 45.3 shows that, in the 1970s, levels of social fluidity were lowest in Germany, France, Italy, Ireland, Hungary and the Netherlands and highest in Britain, Sweden, Norway, Poland and Israel. Fluidity increased in France, Sweden and the Netherlands and possibly in Ireland, Hungary and Poland too. The in-

creases in the Netherlands and Hungary were particularly marked. These different trends have left several countries—Sweden, Norway, Poland, Hungary and the Netherlands—with, as far as we can tell, rather similar rates of fluidity, followed by Britain (where the absence of change has led to a shift in its relative position), Ireland, France, Italy and Germany, which remains the country with the strongest association between class origins and class destinations. At the other extreme, Israel is consistently more open than any other country. Overall, however, we can find no convincing evi-

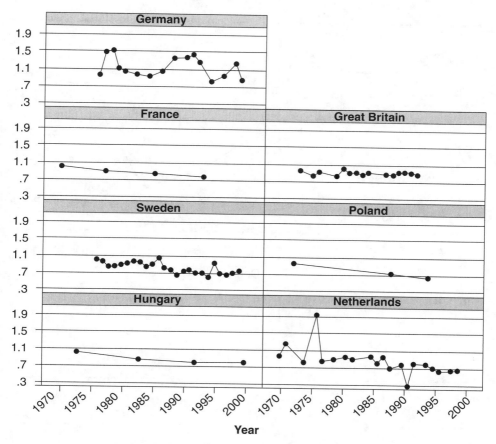

Figure 45.2   Annual LmSF (or Unidiff) Coefficients by Country (Women in the Workforce)

dence of convergence in fluidity regimes: for example, the within decade variance of the βs shown in Figure 45.3 is largest for the 1980s and the Δ for CnSF across countries in each decade is larger for the 1990s than for the 1980s.

The picture among women (Figure 45.4) is very similar. Once again, the points for the 1970s are above those for the 1980s which are above those for the 1990s, indicating a general tendency for fluidity to increase, with Britain being an exception. The average β falls from 1.28 in the 1970s to 1.14 in the 1980s and 1.05 in the 1990s.

France and Germany are the least fluid societies; Britain, Sweden Poland and, by the 1990s, the Netherlands are the most fluid. Hungary presents a different picture for women than men, the former showing much lower fluidity, compared with other countries, than the latter. In Israel the values are 0.84 in the 1970s and 0.71 in the 1990s. Taken together with the results for men this is evidence of the exceptionally fluid nature of Israeli society.

Overall, the results from our 11 countries point to a clear conclusion: there is a widespread tendency for social fluidity to

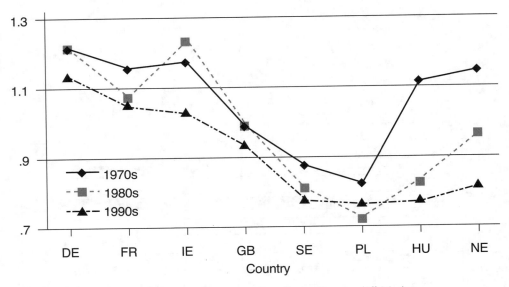

Figure 45.3   LmSF (or Unidiff) Coefficients per Decade, per Country (All Men)

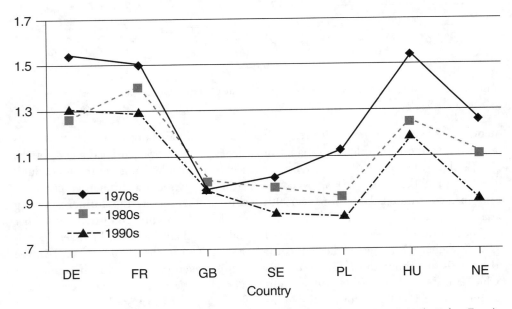

Figure 45.4   LmSF (or Unidiff) Coefficients per Decade, per Country (Women in the Labor Force)

increase, even though this might not be a statistically significant trend in every case. Among men, fluidity is greater at the end of the period than at the start in every country except Britain and Israel (where the values remain the same). Furthermore, of the 20 decade to decade changes in fluidity reported in Breen (2004), we find that in 16 of them fluidity increased and it declined in three—in Ireland and Britain between the 1970s and 1980s and in Norway between the 1980s and 1990s. There is just one further notable case in which fluidity fell (but which is obscured by the use of aggregated decade data) and that is Hungary where fluidity declined significantly between the 1992 and 2000 observations. Although there are some cases (such as Sweden) where we cannot be unequivocal about an increase in fluidity, we can say with confidence that nowhere (with the possible exception of post-Communist Hungary) is there any evidence of a trend in the opposite direction. For women the picture is very similar. Of 18 decade to decade changes, two of them show a decline in fluidity (Germany between the 1980s and 1990s, Britain between the 1970s and 1980s) while 14 show an increase.

Previous Research

These results differ quite substantially from those of the previous major comparative study of social mobility, namely *The Constant Flux,* in which Erikson and Goldthorpe (1993) argue strongly in favour of the so-called FJH hypothesis of a basic similarity in social fluidity in all industrial societies 'with a market economy and a nuclear family system' (Featherman, Jones and Hauser 1975: 340) and they also claim (1992: 367) that 'relative rates possess a high degree of temporal stability'. Indeed, our results are somewhat closer to those of the slightly earlier comparative study by Ganzeboom, Luijkx and Treiman (1989). They used 149 mobility tables for men drawn from 35 countries spanning the period 1947–86. They claim that they show that 'although . . . there is a basic similarity in mobility *patterns* . . . at the same time there are substantial cross-national and cross-temporal differences in the *extent* of mobility.' Furthermore, 'a smaller but significant part of the variance in mobility regimes can be explained by the trend towards increasing openness over time' (Ganzeboom, Luijkx and Treiman 1989: 47). However, although our results and GLT's results are rather similar, it should be noted that the latter have been heavily criticised, notably by Wong (1994: 138), who re-analyses their data and finds that 'the model of temporal invariance cannot be rejected for a majority of countries . . . Hungary and Sweden are the only countries giving irrefutable evidence of temporal variation'.

Why do we find evidence for change and cross-national difference when Erikson and Goldthorpe did not? As far as temporal change is concerned, because Erikson and Goldthorpe have only one mobility table per country, their claim that there is little systematic temporal variation in patterns of social fluidity within countries is based on analyses in which age groups are taken to represent different birth cohorts. But as Breen and Jonsson (2003) have pointed out, this approach confounds lifecycle and cohort effects and makes no allowance for either selective mortality or recall errors. In an assessment of the reliability of measures of class origin and class destination in mobility tables, Breen and Jonsson (1997) found that reliability was lower for origin information from older age groups, implying that the common practice of using age groups to draw conclusions about cohort change over time in mobility regimes may be unsound. More simply, one cannot properly make inferences about change from cross-sectional data.

An important reason why we observe a trend towards increasing social fluidity and Erikson and Goldthorpe do not is that our data, by and large, refer to later-born cohorts. Although our analyses, like those of the overwhelming majority of mobility studies, are based on period data, there is, I believe, good reason to suppose that social fluidity is driven by cohort, rather than period, effects.

Erikson and Goldthorpe's data represents cohorts born between, approximately, 1900 and 1945, whereas our data extends this to cohorts born around 1970. This means that our data contain a larger share of people who benefited from what has been called the Golden Age of Welfare Capitalism—in other words, the long post-war economic boom and the generally more egalitarian educational and social welfare policies that followed in its wake. Work that I have done with Janne Jonsson on Sweden clearly shows that here the major reduction in class inequalities in educational attainment took place among cohorts of people born between 1910 and 1950 and that since then there has been no further equalization. But this means that, as we compare period data for the 1970s, 1980s and 1990s, we gradually lose the older, less fluid cohorts, who are replaced by younger, more fluid cohorts. In the case of Sweden such a process will continue until the second decade of the 21st century, after which we expect to see no further increase in period social fluidity. But it seems likely that the specific cohorts which benefited from the Golden Age will

have differed between countries, so leading to variation between them in the fluidity they display in particular periods.

Whereas we argue that countries display considerable variation in social fluidity, Erikson and Goldthorpe argue the contrary. But in their own analyses (Erikson and Goldthorpe 1992: 381) the logarithm of each odds ratio in their mobility table from Czechoslovakia (which is the country in which they find the greatest fluidity) is two-thirds as strong as in Scotland (the country with the least fluidity). So, for example, given an odds ratio of 3 in Czechoslovakia, the comparable odds ratio would be 5.3 in Scotland. On this basis it is difficult to argue for commonality in the strength of social fluidity, and, indeed, these results are quite similar to ours: in our data the logarithm of the odds ratios in Israel are around half those in Germany. So, an odds ratio of 3 in Israel would be an odds ratio of 7 in Germany. Given this, one might ask why Erikson and Goldthorpe, like many others, conclude that there is little variation in fluidity. The reason is the following. All comparative mobility studies find that the difference in the goodness of fit between a model in which social fluidity is common across all countries (the model of Common Social Fluidity or CnSF) and a model in which fluidity can differ between them is small, relative to the difference between the CnSF model and one in which origins and destinations are independent. It is certainly true that the model of variation in fluidity is a significantly better fit to the data than CnSF, but this incremental improvement to any goodness of fit measure is small. For example, when we analyzed our data according to decade, a very small index of dissimilarity was returned by a model that allowed for no temporal or cross-national variation in social fluidity (3.95 per cent for men and 3.81 for women) and allowing for such variation only improved Δ by, at most, two percentage points. This compares with a Δ of around 15 per cent in models in which origins and destinations are independent. Much the same picture emerged when we used annual data, and arguments like this usually lead to the conclusion that most social fluidity is common and invariant over time. Sometimes the same point is made using the deviance, rather than Δ, as the yardstick, and here the result is even more extreme. For example, 90 per cent of the deviance returned by the model of independence disappears when we add common (among countries and over decades) social fluidity, and a model allowing fluidity to change over time and differ between countries improves it only by a further seven per cent. Taken together, the decompositions of the deviance and of Δ would seem to indicate that more than 85 per cent of social fluidity is common over nations and time.

This then seems to conflict with our finding of large variation between countries in their odds ratios. The problem with using arguments based on Δ or the deviance to support the argument that social fluidity is largely invariant is that variation in fluidity is assessed using measures of the consequences of fluidity for the whole mobility regime (i.e. for absolute mobility), and, as we have seen, these consequences are unanimously agreed to be quite minor. An analogy may help to make the point. In a linear regression, $Y = a + bX$; X (analogous to social fluidity) may display a lot of variation, but it will have little impact on Y (analogous to overall mobility) if the coefficient, b, is close to zero. But simply because b is small we could not then claim that

there was little variation in X. Measures such as the change in Δ or in G^2 might be said to capture the strength of effect of fluidity on overall mobility, but they do not measure the variation in fluidity itself, and it is therefore mistaken to conclude, on this basis, that social fluidity is common and invariant. It is empirically the case that, between countries or over time, large variations in social fluidity can be found which nevertheless have little impact on the overall mobility regime. To illustrate this: if we take the fluidity pattern from the 1997 Italian men's table in our data and insert it into the 1991 Israeli men's table, while preserving the Israeli marginal distributions, the Δ between the real and the constructed Israeli tables is 6 per cent.[4] When we consider that the Israeli and Italian mobility regimes are close to the extremes of the range of fluidity found in our data this suggests that 6 per cent represents the maximum impact of differences in fluidity on the distribution of individuals in the mobility table. The conclusion to be drawn from these apparently contradictory measures of the variation in fluidity is not that it is common or invariant, but, rather, that even quite substantial differences in fluidity have little impact on the distribution of cases over the mobility table—i.e. on observed, absolute mobility flows.

Explanation

Thus far I have said nothing about how we might explain patterns of social mobility or social fluidity, aside from some rather vague remarks about the impact of policies pursued during the Golden Age of Welfare Capitalism. In broad terms, explanations of variations in social fluidity are usually pitched at a macro-sociological level: that is, fluidity is assumed to be related to other, societal level measures. The very influential 'liberal theory of industrialism', for example, argues that fluidity will increase with economic development. In our case, the stage of economic development of our countries varies rather little, but, even so, we could find no evident link between their ranking in fluidity terms and their GDP per capita. Nor did we find any support for Erikson and Goldthorpe's argument that fluidity is related to income inequality: there is no significant association between a country's fluidity and its Gini coefficient. Overall we could discern no tendencies towards either convergence or divergence in fluidity, and thus the hypothesis that, as nations have come to follow different policy trajectories—particularly in economic policy—so we might see growing differences between them in fluidity, receives no support. There is some indication, however, that fluidity is greater in state socialist (Poland and Hungary) and social democratic (Norway and Sweden) countries, and the argument for such a political explanation receives additional support from the finding of declining fluidity in Hungary during the 1990s. But, on the other hand, we observe very high fluidity in Israel and data from the General Social Survey (made available to us by Mike Hout) shows that fluidity is high in the United States. This leads to the conclusion that direct political intervention of the kinds associated with state-socialist and social democratic societies may be one means by which a society can reach relatively high rates of fluidity, but it is not the only one.

One major difficulty in devising theories to explain variation in mobility or fluidity is that mobility tables, especially period-based tables, reflect a large number of underlying processes—artefactual, contingent and substantive. For one thing, this aggre-gation of processes renders it difficult to explain variations in fluidity; for another, it may also be the case that some of the commonality that has often been observed in comparisons of social fluidity derives from the mixing together in the mobility tables of processes that, when investigated separately, might show greater and more systematic societal and temporal differences.

While it is reasonable to suppose that fluidity in a nation is shaped by government policy, the education system, the workings of the labour market and suchlike, it is also the case that what we observe in a mobility table may also reflect purely artefactual sources of variation arising from differences in the way that the data themselves represent the underlying phenomenon of interest. Furthermore, what we might call contingent factors, which are usually omitted from any theoretical discussion of social fluidity, may play an important role in shaping what we observe. Walter Müller and Reinhard Pollak (see Breen 2004) attribute the high fluidity they find among Germans born in the 1920s to the massive migration from the eastern part of Germany that occurred following the Second World War. The measured class origins of this cohort are thus their pre-migration origins, which had very little relevance in shaping their subsequent mobility patterns: the physical detaching of a large share of the cohort from their true origins led to higher measured social fluidity. The same argument may explain the high level of fluidity in Israel, a country in which a very large share of the population is comprised of immigrants.

Conclusions

The experience of this project should lead us to question the balance that mobility research has struck between social fluidity and absolute mobility. The emphasis has lain heavily on the former but, insofar as we are concerned with the mobility regime, this now seems inappropriate. This is by no means to deny that social fluidity tells us important things about the prevailing degree of inequality in the chances of attaining one class position rather than another, and may be indicative of other characteristics of society. Nevertheless, although one would not want to say that fluidity can never make a difference (since we can easily construct examples in which extreme patterns of fluidity will be highly consequential for the distribution of cases in a mobility table), within the advanced industrial and post-industrial societies, the range of fluidity that we observe is relatively inconsequential in determining variation in mobility flows and in the life chances of individuals and families as these are captured in measures of class position. Many previous authors (such as Grusky and Hauser 1984; Goldthorpe 1985) have called for more attention to be paid to structural change, but, as Erikson and Goldthorpe (1992: 104, 189) suggest, it is not clear how such change should be explained nor, indeed, whether it might not better be approached as a matter of historical description rather than sociological explanation. But while this might be a valid concern if we conceive of class structures as macro-sociological phenomena, it may be less so, and may leave open the possibility of sociological explanation, if we were to turn our attention to the detailed evolution of businesses and firms and of the jobs that constitute classes.

Furthermore, it now seems to me that a period perspective on social mobility may not be the most appropriate if, as I have suggested, social fluidity in driven by factors related to cohorts, rather than periods. The cohort perspective on social mobility has not been entirely neglected, but it has certainly played a very secondary role to the usual period view. Under the cohort approach, change in the association between origins and destinations is believed to occur in specific cohorts, while, from a period point of view, this association is considered to change among all cohorts at similar historical points in time. The importance, for social change, of the replacement of older by younger cohorts has been stressed by several sociologists. In the specific field of mobility research, Erikson and Goldthorpe (1992), for example, argue that equality of condition is essential for equality of opportunity, and that changes in the latter will then predominantly take effect during a person's upbringing and schooling. As a result, the overall level of inequality of opportunity in society will change mainly through cohort replacement, with younger cohorts experiencing a different degree of inequality of educational attainment than older. It has long been education that is the major channel of social mobility: if this is so, then social fluidity should respond to changes in the level of class inequality in educational attainment, which, because educational inequality is itself a characteristic of cohorts, implies a cohort explanation of change in fluidity.

Though rarely spelled out, there is a tension between the cohort interpretation of change in social fluidity and the belief that period effects drive variation in the origin-destination association over the lifecycle through labour market changes that simultaneously affect different birth cohorts. We believe that there are strong arguments for adopting a cohort rather than, or in addition to, a period perspective. It is widely agreed that changes in an individual's social class position are relatively rare after the age of about 35 (Goldthorpe 1980: 51–2, 69–71; Erikson and Goldthorpe 1992: 72). Such stability implies that, except in unusual circumstances in which this stability is disrupted, period effects will be a less important source of change in fluidity when compared with cohort replacement and within-cohort change that occurs during the early years in the labour force.

NOTES

1. The terms association and social fluidity can be used interchangeably: greater social fluidity implies lower origin–destination association. In the log-linear modeling context in which this paper is situated this association is captured by odds ratios.

2. These figures are for men. For women the figures are 36, 24 and 24 per cent. The slight differences arise because our samples of women include only those in the labour force and we have no data for women in Ireland.

3. LmSF means 'log-multiplicative social fluidity' (by analogy with CnSF—'common social fluidity'). We use LmSF to refer to the unidiff (Erikson and Goldthorpe 1992) or log-multiplicative layer effect model (Xie 1992) when the local association is modeled in a completely unspecified way (as it is in CnSF).

4. We use the observed Italian fluidity pattern, and thus the magnitude of the difference that we

report does not depend on the adequacy of any particular model of fluidity.

REFERENCES

Breen, Richard (ed.). 2004. *Social Mobility in Europe.* Oxford: Oxford University Press.

Erikson, Robert and John H. Goldthorpe. 1992. *The Constant Flux: A Study of Class Mobility in Industrial Societies.* Oxford: Oxford University Press.

Featherman, David L., F. L. Jones, and Robert M. Hauser. 1975. "Assumptions of Mobility Research in the United States: The Case of Occupational Status." *Social Science Research* 4: 329–60.

Ganzeboom, Harry B. G., Ruud Luijkx, and Donald J. Treiman. 1989. "Intergenerational Class Mobility in Comparative Perspective." *Research in Social Stratification and Mobility* 8: 3–84.

Goldthorpe, John H. 1980. *Social Mobility and Class Structure in Modern Britain.* Oxford: Clarendon Press.

Goldthorpe, John H. 1985. "On Economic Development and Social Mobility." *British Journal of Sociology* 36: 549–573.

Grusky, David B. and Robert M. Hauser. 1984. "Comparative Social Mobility Revisited: Models of Convergence and Divergence in 16 Countries." *American Sociological Review* 49: 19–38.

Wong, Raymond S. 1994. "Postwar Mobility Trends in Advanced Industrial Societies." *Research in Social Stratification and Mobility* 13: 121–44.

46

Are Lifetime Incomes Growing More Unequal?

Looking at New Evidence on Family Income Mobility

KATHARINE BRADBURY

JANE KATZ

The United States has always taken great pride in its reputation as a land of opportunity, a place where people have a chance to move up instead of being trapped where they start. But is this really the case? Can families who start at the bottom move up, or are most of them mired at the lower end of the income scale? Is the only way to reach the top to start there? These questions go to the heart of our identity as a nation as well as to our social and economic health.

Whether we still deserve our reputation has been called into question in light of the fact that over the last thirty years, Americans' household incomes have become increasingly unequal (see Figure 46.1). In the early 1970s, the change was small; but by the late 1970s, the growing disparity between rich and poor was clearly evident. The difference grew even larger in the 1980s and continued to increase into the 1990s. In 1969, the richest one-fifth of households had about 10 times as much income, on average, as the poorest households; by 1998, the figure was almost 14 times. This increasing disparity was a significant reversal of the U.S. experience between 1950 and 1970, when rapid economic growth occurred along with a decrease in the difference between the incomes of the rich and poor. Moreover, the pattern stands virtually undisputed among researchers. No matter what data are used, whether looking at individuals or families, incomes in the United States have become increasingly unequal over the past quarter-century.

Should We Care?

Is growing inequality a significant problem? Should the government support policies to do anything about it? These are bigger questions that provoke far greater debate.

Katherine Bradbury and Jane Katz, "Are Lifetime Incomes Growing More Unequal?," *Regional Review* (Q4, 2002), pp. 3–5.

Mean real income for each quintile of U.S. Households

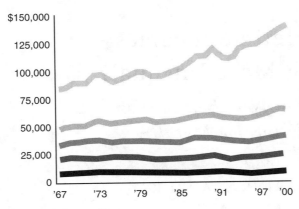

Source: U.S. Census Bureau

Figure 46.1   A Dramatic Rise in Inequality

That debate centers on whether the increased inequality of year-by-year incomes tells us anything about the distribution of success and opportunity over longer time periods.

To see why, imagine two economies. Both show the pattern of increasing inequality noted above, but they differ in how that inequality falls on individual families over time.

In the first economy, the range of incomes is wide every year simply due to luck. Some people might have unexpected medical problems and lose paid time at work, while others win the lottery. Or perhaps one part of the country has unusually bad weather causing local crops to fail, while another enjoys ideal growing conditions for local produce. In any case, this random luck causes a number of families to experience unusually low or high incomes that year. Next year, other people or regions will have the good and bad luck and receive high or low incomes; the rest return to the *status quo*. Although incomes may be quite unequal in any given year, families in this economy will experience a fair amount of mobility year to year as their incomes bounce up and down along with the good and bad luck. Even if inequality is increasing over time, families at the bottom still have a shot at the middle and top each year as their luck changes. Over the long haul, the good and bad years for any particular family tend to cancel out, and all families have roughly equal lifetime incomes.

The second economy also has a wide spread of incomes; however, rather than being distributed randomly every year, the differences in incomes are persistent. Families at the top stay at the top, those in the middle stay in the middle, and those at the bottom stay at the bottom. That is, families experience no mobility relative to other families. This might occur because society enforces a class or caste system or because certain families or groups are discriminated against. Or it might be that individuals differ along some key dimensions that help to determine their family income—talent, willingness to work hard, access to a high-quality education or a good job—and those differences tend to persist. In this economy, if inequality is increasing over time, families at the top will enjoy both large and growing advantages over those at the bottom, and those at the bottom will be increasingly worse off and have no prospect of moving up.

This exercise suggests that how much attention inequality deserves from voters and policymakers depends, in part, upon whether inequality reflects short-run difficulties that families will get through or longer-term hardships that trap some at the

Table 46.1   Income Mobility: 1969–79 Decade

Where Families Started in 1969, By Quintile	Where Families Ended Up in 1979, By Quintile				
	Poorest	Second	Third	Fourth	Richest
Poorest	49.4	24.5	13.8	9.1	3.3
Second	23.2	27.8	25.2	16.2	7.7
Third	10.2	23.4	24.8	23.0	18.7
Fourth	9.9	15.0	24.1	27.4	23.7
Richest	5.0	9.0	13.2	23.7	49.1
Percentages sum to 100 across rows					

Note: Data are from the Panel Study of Income Dynamics (PSID). Income is in constant 2000 dollars and is adjusted using the PSID measure of needs, which takes into account family size and composition. One-person families (persons living alone or with nonrelatives) are included. Families in which there are no adults below retirement age are excluded.

Source: Katharine Bradbury and Jane Katz, "Women's Labor Market Involvement and Family Income Mobility When Marriages End," *New England Economic Review* Q4 2002, Appendix Table A1 (which also includes the mobility table for the 1980s).

bottom. And that determination depends, in turn, upon how much mobility—year-to-year shifts in position along the income scale—is also occurring. If increasing inequality, such as that experienced in the United States since the early 1970s, is not accompanied by increasing mobility, the short-run dispersion in incomes will tend to accumulate and lifetime incomes will grow increasingly unequal. Some argue that a growing gap between the top and bottom is not a problem so long as everyone's income is rising in real terms. But to the extent that we judge our well-being by comparison with others, then the widening inequality of lifetime incomes may indeed threaten our standing as a "land of opportunity."

Has Mobility Increased?

To answer this question, we need to know how individual families' incomes change over time; the Panel Study of Income Dynamics collects such information. Using their data on working-age households, we find no evidence of an increase in family income mobility since the 1970s. Consistent with earlier studies, we find that mobility held more or less constant from the 1970s to the 1980s. Based on newly available data from the 1990s, we estimate that mobility *decreased* slightly in the 1990s.

Looking at the 1970s, the movement of families up and down the income ladder seems unlikely to have been produced by chance. If we rank families from poorest to richest and divide them into five equal-sized groups (quintiles), we find that about half of all families in the poorest quintile at the beginning of the decade were still in the poorest quintile 10 years later; only about one-quarter of these families made it past the bottom two quintiles (see Table 46.1). Rich families also tended to stay put—about half of families that started in the top quintile ended there.

Mobility patterns during the 1980s appear very similar to the 1970s. About 33

Trends in Mobility — Percent of All Families

Source: Authors' calculations from data collected by
the Panel Study of Income Dynamics

Figure 46.2   Trends in Mobility

percent of all families moved up one quintile or more between 1969 and 1979; during the 1980s, the figure is 32 percent (see
Figure 46.2). Downward mobility was
about the same in both decades. Although
mobility would need to *increase* over time
to offset the impact of increasing inequal-

ity on lifetime incomes, our calculations suggest that mobility was about
the same.

In the 1990s, however, mobility
declined noticeably. About 53 percent
of families that began the decade in
the poorest quintile were still there
ten years later (see Table 46.2), several
percentage points higher than before.
Families in the richest quintile were
also more likely to remain there than
previously.

Overall, about 40 percent of families ended the 1990s where they
began, as compared with 36 and 37
percent in the 1970s and 1980s, respectively (see Figure 46.2). While
some hoped that increased mobility had
offset the increased inequality in the 1980s
and 1990s, these data provide no evidence
of such an offsetting role. Rather, we find a
slight decrease in mobility, which suggests
that the lifetime incomes of rich and poor
families have indeed grown more unequal.

Table 46.2   Income Mobility: 1988–98 Decade

Where Families Started in 1988, By Quintile	*Where Families Ended Up in 1998, By Quintile*				
	Poorest	Second	Third	Fourth	Richest
Poorest	53.3	23.6	12.4	6.4	4.3
Second	25.7	36.3	22.6	11.0	4.3
Third	10.9	20.7	28.3	27.5	12.6
Fourth	6.5	12.9	23.7	31.1	25.8
Richest	3.0	5.7	14.9	23.2	53.2
Percentages sum to 100 across rows					

Note: Data are from the Panel Study of Income Dynamics (PSID). Income is in constant 2000 dollars and is adjusted
using the PSID measure of needs, which takes into account family size and composition. One-person families (persons living alone or with nonrelatives) are included. Families in which there are no adults below retirement age are
excluded.

Source: Katharine Bradbury and Jane Katz, "Women's Labor Market Involvement and Family Income Mobility When
Marriages End," *New England Economic Review* Q4 2002, Appendix Table A1 (which also includes the mobility table
for the 1980s).

Shrinking Opportunity?

These findings suggest that those who are concerned about the future for families at the lower rungs of the income ladder may have cause to worry. Compared to 30 years ago, families at the bottom are poorer relative to families at the top and also a bit more stuck there. Mobility alone has not and is not likely to counteract the hardships caused by increasing inequality. Instead, we might want to look more seriously at policies to even up and improve the possibilities for those at the bottom in order to maintain our standing as a land of opportunity.

47

The Process of Stratification

PETER M. BLAU AND OTIS DUDLEY DUNCAN, WITH THE COLLABORATION OF ANDREA TYREE

Stratification systems may be characterized in various ways. Surely one of the most important has to do with the processes by which individuals become located, or locate themselves, in positions in the hierarchy comprising the system. At one extreme we can imagine that the circumstances of a person's birth—including the person's sex and the perfectly predictable sequence of age levels through which he is destined to pass—suffice to assign him unequivocally to a ranked status in a hierarchical system. At the opposite extreme his prospective adult status would be wholly problematic and contingent at the time of birth. Such status would become entirely determinate only as adulthood was reached, and solely as a consequence of his own actions taken freely— that is, in the absence of any constraint deriving from the circumstances of his birth or rearing. Such a pure achievement system is, of course, hypothetical, in much the same way that motion without friction is a purely hypothetical possibility in the physical world. Whenever the stratification system of any moderately large and complex society is described, it is seen to involve both ascriptive and achievement principles.

In a liberal democratic society we think of the more basic principle as being that of achievement. Some ascriptive features of the system may be regarded as vestiges of an earlier epoch, to be extirpated as rapidly as possible. Public policy may emphasize measures designed to enhance or to equalize opportunity—hopefully, to overcome ascriptive obstacles to the full exercise of the achievement principle.

The question of how far a society may realistically aspire to go in this direction is hotly debated, not only in the ideological arena but in the academic forum as well. Our contribution, if any, to the debate will consist largely in submitting measurements and estimates of the strength of ascriptive forces and of the scope of opportunities in a large contemporary society. The problem of the relative importance of the two principles in a given system is ultimately a quantitative one. We have pushed our ingenuity to its limit in seeking to contrive relevant quantifications.

The governing conceptual scheme in the analysis is quite a commonplace one. We think of the individual's life cycle as a sequence in time that can be described, however partially and crudely, by a set of classificatory or quantitative measurements taken at successive stages. Ideally we should like to have under observation a cohort of births, following the individuals who make up the cohort as they pass through life. As a practical matter we resorted to retrospective questions put to a representative sample of several adjacent cohorts so as to ascertain those facts about their life histories that we assumed were both relevant to our problem and accessible by this means of observation.

Given this scheme, the questions we are continually raising in one form or another are: how and to what degree do the circumstances of birth condition subsequent status? and, how does status attained (whether by ascription or achievement) at one stage of the life cycle affect the prospects for a subsequent stage? The questions are neither idle nor idiosyncratic ones. Current policy discussion and action come to a focus in a vaguely explicated notion of the "inheritance of poverty." Thus a spokesman for the Social Security Administration writes:

It would be one thing if poverty hit at random and no one group were singled out. It is another thing to realize that some seem destined to poverty almost from birth—by their color or by the economic status or occupation of their parents.[1]

Another officially sanctioned concept is that of the "dropout," the person who fails to graduate from high school. Here the emphasis is not so much on circumstances operative at birth but on the presumed effect of early achievement on subsequent opportunities. Thus the "dropout" is seen as facing "a lifetime of uncertain employment,"[2] probable assignment to jobs of inferior status, reduced earning power, and vulnerability to various forms of social pathology.

In this study we do not have measurements on all the factors implicit in a full-blown conception of the "cycle of poverty" nor all those variables conceivably responding unfavorably to the achievement of "dropout" status. . . . This limitation, however, is not merely an analytical convenience. We think of the selected quantitative variables as being sufficient to describe the major outlines of status changes in the life cycle of a cohort. Thus a study of the relationships among these variables leads to a formulation of a basic model of the process of stratification.

A Basic Model

To begin with, we examine only five variables. For expository convenience, when it is necessary to resort to symbols, we shall designate them by arbitrary letters but try to remind the reader from time to time of what the letters stand for. These variables are:

V: Father's educational attainment
X: Father's occupational status
U: Respondent's educational attainment
W: Status of respondent's first job
Y: Status of respondent's occupation in 1962

Each of the three occupational statuses is scaled by the [socioeconomic] index described [elsewhere],[3] ranging from 0 to 96. The two education variables are scored on the following arbitrary scale of values ("rungs" on the "educational ladder") corresponding to specified numbers of years of formal schooling completed:

0: No school
1: Elementary, one to four years
2: Elementary, five to seven years
3: Elementary, eight years
4: High school, one to three years
5: High school, four years
6: College, one to three years
7: College, four years
8: College, five years or more (i.e., one or more years of postgraduate study)

Actually, this scoring system hardly differs from a simple linear transformation, or "coding," of the exact number of years of school completed. In retrospect, for reasons given [elsewhere],[4] we feel that the score implies too great a distance between intervals at the lower end of the scale; but the resultant distortion is minor in view of the very small proportions scored 0 or 1.

A basic assumption in our interpretation of regression statistics—though not in their calculation as such—has to do with the causal or temporal ordering of these variables. In terms of the father's career we should naturally assume precedence of V (education) with respect to X (occupation when his son was 16 years old). We are not concerned with the father's career, however, but only with his statuses that comprised a configuration of background circumstances or origin conditions for the cohorts of sons who were respondents in the Occupational Changes in a Generation (OCG) study. Hence we generally make no assumption as to the priority of V with respect to X; in effect, we assume the measurements on these variables to be contemporaneous from the son's viewpoint. The respondent's education, U, is supposed to follow in time—and

thus to be susceptible to causal influence from—the two measures of father's status. Because we ascertained X as of respondent's age 16, it is true that some respondents may have completed school before the age to which X pertains. Such cases were doubtlessly a small minority and in only a minor proportion of them could the father (or other family head) have changed status radically in the two or three years before the respondent reached 16.

The next step in the sequence is more problematic. We assume that W (first job status) follows U (education). The assumption conforms to the wording of the questionnaire, which stipulated "the first full-time job you had after you left school." In the years since the OCG study was designed we have been made aware of a fact that should have been considered more carefully in the design. Many students leave school more or less definitively, only to return, perhaps to a different school, some years later, whereupon they often finish a degree program.[5] The OCG questionnaire contained information relevant to this problem, namely the item on age at first job. Through an oversight no tabulations of this item were made for the present study. Tables prepared for another study[6] using the OCG data, however, suggest that approximately one-eighth of the respondents report a combination of age at first job and education that would be very improbable unless (a) they violated instructions by reporting a part-time or school-vacation job as the first job, or (b) they did, in fact, interrupt their schooling to enter regular employment. (These "inconsistent" responses include men giving 19 as their age at first job and college graduation or more as their education; 17 or 18 with some college or more; 14, 15, or 16 with high-school graduation or more; and under 14 with some high school or more.) When the two variables are studied in combination with occupation of first job, a very clear effect is evident. Men with a given amount of education beginning their first jobs early held lower occupational statuses than those beginning at a normal or advanced age for the specified amount of education.

Despite the strong probability that the U-W sequence is reversed for an appreciable minority of respondents, we have hardly any alternative to the assumption made here. If the bulk of the men who interrupted schooling to take their first jobs were among those ultimately securing relatively advanced education, then our variable W is downwardly biased, no doubt, as a measure of their occupational status immediately after they finally left school for good. In this sense, the correlations between U and W and between W and Y are probably attenuated. Thus, if we had really measured "job after completing education" instead of "first job," the former would in all likelihood have loomed somewhat larger as a variable intervening between education and 1962 occupational status. We do not wish to argue that our respondents erred in their reports on first job. We are inclined to conclude that their reports were realistic enough, and that it was our assumption about the meaning of the responses that proved to be fallible.

The fundamental difficulty here is conceptual. If we insist on *any* uniform sequence of the events involved in accomplishing the transition to independent adult status, we do violence to reality. Completion of schooling, departure from the parental home, entry into the labor market, and contracting of a first marriage are crucial steps in this transition, which all normally

occur within a few short years. Yet they occur at no fixed ages nor in any fixed order. As soon as we aggregate individual data for analytical purposes we are forced into the use of simplifying assumptions. Our assumption here is, in effect, that "first job" has a uniform significance for all men in terms of its temporal relationship to educational preparation and subsequent work experience. If this assumption is not strictly correct, we doubt that it could be improved by substituting any other *single* measure of initial occupational status. (In designing the OCG questionnaire, the alternative of "job at the time of first marriage" was entertained briefly but dropped for the reason, among others, that unmarried men would be excluded thereby.)

One other problem with the U-W transition should be mentioned. Among the younger men in the study, 20 to 24 years old, are many who have yet to finish their schooling or to take up their first jobs or both—not to mention the men in this age group missed by the survey on account of their military service.[7] Unfortunately, an early decision on tabulation plans resulted in the inclusion of the 20 to 24 group with the older men in aggregate tables for men 20 to 64 years old. We have ascertained that this results in only minor distortions by comparing a variety of data for men 20 to 64 and for those 25 to 64 years of age. Once over the U-W hurdle, we see no serious objection to our assumption that both U and W precede Y, except in regard to some fraction of the very young men just mentioned.

In summary, then, we take the somewhat idealized assumption of temporal order to represent an order of priority in a causal or processual sequence, which may be stated diagrammatically as follows:

Table 47.1   Simple Correlations for Five Status Variables

	Variable				
Variable	Y	W	U	X	V
Y: 1962 occ. status	—	.541	.596	.406	.322
W: First-job status		—	.538	.417	.332
U: Education			—	.438	.453
X: Father's occ. status				—	.516
V: Father's education					—

$$(V\!,\!X) - (U) - (W) - (Y).$$

In proposing this sequence we do not overlook the possibility of what Carlsson calls "delayed effects,"[8] meaning that an early variable may affect a later one not only via intervening variables but also directly (or perhaps through variables not measured in the study).

In translating this conceptual framework into quantitative estimates the first task is to establish the pattern of associations between the variables in the sequence. This is accomplished with the correlation coefficient. Table 47.1 supplies the correlation matrix on which much of the subsequent analysis is based. In discussing causal interpretations of these correlations, we shall have to be clear about the distinction between two points of view. On the one hand, the simple correlation—given our assumption as to direction of causation—measures the gross magnitude of the effect of the antecedent upon the consequent variable. Thus, if $r_{YW} = .541$, we can say that an increment of one standard deviation in first job status produces (whether directly or indirectly) an increment of just over half of one standard deviation in 1962 occupational status. From another point of view we are more concerned with net effects. If both first job and 1962 status have a common antecedent cause—say, father's occupation—we may

want to state what part of the effect of W on Y consists in a transmission of the prior influence of X. Or, thinking of X as the initial cause, we may focus on the extent to which its influence on Y is transmitted by way of its prior influence on W.

We may, then, devote a few remarks to the pattern of gross effects before presenting the apparatus that yields estimates of net direct and indirect effects. Since we do not require a causal ordering of father's education with respect to his occupation, we may be content simply to note that $r_{XV} = .516$ is somewhat lower than the corresponding correlation, $r_{YU} = .596$, observed for the respondents themselves. The difference suggests a heightening of the effect of education on occupational status between the fathers' and the sons' generations. Before stressing this interpretation, however, we must remember that the measurements of V and X do not pertain to some actual cohort of men, here designated "fathers." Each "father" is represented in the data in proportion to the number of his sons who were 20 to 64 years old in March 1962.

The first recorded status of the son himself is education (U). We note that r_{UV} is just slightly greater than r_{UX}. Apparently both measures on the father represent factors that may influence the son's education.

In terms of gross effects there is a clear ordering of influences on first job. Thus

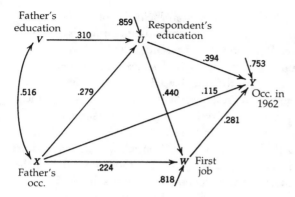

Figure 47.1   Path Coefficients in Basic Model of the Process of Stratification

$r_{WU} > r_{WX} > r_{WV}$. Education is most strongly correlated with first job, followed by father's occupation, and then by father's education.

Occupational status in 1962 (Y) apparently is influenced more strongly by education than by first job; but our earlier discussion of the first-job measure suggests we should not overemphasize the difference between r_{YW} and r_{YU}. Each, however, is substantially greater than r_{YX}, which in turn is rather more impressive than r_{YV}.

Figure 47.1 is a graphic representation of the system of relationships among the five variables that we propose as our basic model. The numbers entered on the diagram, with the exception of r_{XV}, are path coefficients, the estimation of which will be explained shortly. First we must become familiar with the conventions followed in constructing this kind of diagram. The link between V and X is shown as a curved line with an arrowhead at both ends. This is to distinguish it from the other lines, which are taken to be paths of influence. In the case of V and X we may suspect an influence running from the former to the latter. But if the diagram is logical for the respon-

dent's generation, we should have to assume that for the fathers, likewise, education and occupation are correlated not only because one affects the other but also because common causes lie behind both, which we have not measured. The bidirectional arrow merely serves to sum up all sources of correlation between V and X and to indicate that the explanation thereof is not part of the problem at hand.

The straight lines running from one measured variable to another represent *direct* (or net) influences. The symbol for the path coefficient, such as P_{YW}, carries a double subscript. The first subscript is the variable at the head of the path, or the effect; the second is the causal variable. (This resembles the convention for regression coefficients, where the first subscript refers to the "dependent" variable, the second to the "independent" variable.)

Finally, we see lines with no source indicated carrying arrows to each of the effect variables. These represent the residual paths, standing for all other influences on the variable in question, including causes not recognized or measured, errors of measurement, and departures of the true relationships from additivity and linearity, properties that are assumed throughout the analysis.

An important feature of this kind of causal scheme is that variables recognized as effects of certain antecedent factors may, in turn, serve as causes for subsequent variables. For example, U is caused by V and X, but it in turn influences W and Y. The algebraic representation of the scheme is a system of equations, rather than the single equation more often employed in multiple regression analysis. This feature permits a flexible conceptualization of the *modus operandi* of the causal network. Note that Y is shown here as being influenced directly by W, U, and X, but not by V (an assumption that will be justified shortly). But this does not imply that V has no influence on Y. V affects U, which does affect Y both directly and indirectly (via W). Moreover, V is correlated with X, and thus shares in the gross effect of X on Y, which is partly direct and partly indirect. Hence the gross effect of V on Y, previously described in terms of the correlation r_{YV}, is here interpreted as being entirely indirect, in consequence of V's effect on intervening variables and its correlation with another cause of Y.

Path Coefficients

Whether a path diagram, or the causal scheme it represents, is adequate depends on both theoretical and empirical considerations. At a minimum, before constructing the diagram we must know, or be willing to assume, a causal ordering of the observed variables (hence the lengthy discussion of this matter earlier in this chapter). This information is external or *a priori* with respect to the data, which merely describe associations or correlations. Moreover, the causal scheme must be complete, in the sense that all causes are accounted for. Here, as in most problems involving analysis of observational data, we achieve a formal completeness of the scheme by representing unmeasured causes as a residual factor, presumed to be uncorrelated with the remaining factors lying behind the variable in question. If any factor is known or presumed to operate in some other way it must be represented in the diagram in accordance with its causal role, even though it is not measured. Sometimes it is possible to deduce interesting im-

plications from the inclusion of such a variable and to secure useful estimates of certain paths in the absence of measurements on it, but this is not always so. A partial exception to the rule that all causes must be explicitly represented in the diagram is the unmeasured variable that can be assumed to operate strictly as an intervening variable. Its inclusion would enrich our understanding of a causal system without invalidating the causal scheme that omits it. Sociologists have only recently begun to appreciate how stringent are the logical requirements that must be met if discussion of causal processes is to go beyond mere impressionism and vague verbal formulations.[9] We are a long way from being able to make causal inferences with confidence, and schemes of the kind presented here had best be regarded as crude first approximations to adequate causal models.

On the empirical side, a minimum test of the adequacy of a causal diagram is whether it satisfactorily accounts for the observed correlations among the measured variables. In making such a test we employ the fundamental theorem in path analysis, which shows how to obtain the correlation between any two variables in the system, given the path coefficients and correlations entered on the diagram.[10] Without stating this theorem in general form we may illustrate its application here. For example,

$$r_{YX} = p_{YX} + p_{YU} r_{UX} + p_{YW} r_{WX}$$

and

$$r_{WX} = p_{WX} + p_{WU} r_{UX}.$$

We make use of each path leading to a given variable (such as Y in the first example) and the correlations of each of its causes with all other variables in the system. The latter correlations, in turn, may be analyzed; for example, r_{WX}, which appeared as such in the first equation, is broken down into two parts in the second. A complete expansion along these lines is required to trace out all the indirect connections between variables; thus,

$$r_{YX} = p_{YX} + p_{YU}p_{UX} + p_{YU}p_{UV}r_{VX} + p_{YW}p_{WX}$$

$$+ p_{YW}p_{WU}p_{UX} + p_{YW}p_{WU}p_{UV}r_{VX}$$

Now, if the path coefficients are properly estimated, and if there is no inconsistency in the diagram, the correlations calculated by a formula like the foregoing must equal the observed correlations. Let us compare the values computed from such a formula with the corresponding observed correlations:

$$r_{WV} = p_{WX}r_{XV} + p_{WU}r_{UV}$$

$$= (.224)(.516) + (.440)(.453)$$

$$= .116 + .199 = .315$$

which compares with the observed value of .332; and

$$r_{YV} = p_{YU}r_{UV} + p_{YX}r_{XV} + p_{YW}r_{WV}$$

$$= (.394)(.453) + (.115)(.516) + (.281)(.315)$$

$$= .326$$

(using here the calculated rather than the observed value of r_{WV}), which resembles the actual value, .322. Other such comparisons—for r_{YX}, for example—reveal, at most, trivial discrepancies (no larger than .001).

We arrive, by this roundabout journey, at the problem of getting numerical values for the path coefficients in the first place. This involves using equations of the foregoing type inversely. We have illustrated how to obtain correlations if the path coefficients are known, but in the typical empirical problem we know the correlations (or at least some of them) and have to estimate the paths. For a diagram of the type of Figure 47.1 the solution involves equations of the same form as those of linear multiple regression, except that we work with a recursive system of regression equations[11] rather than a single regression equation.

Table 47.2 records the results of the regression calculations. It can be seen that some alternative combinations of independent variables were studied. It turned out that the net regressions of both W and Y on V were so small as to be negligible. Hence V could be disregarded as a direct influence on these variables without loss of information. The net regression of Y on X was likewise small but, as it appears, not entirely negligible. Curiously, this net regression is of the same order of magnitude as the proportion of occupational inheritance in this population—about 10 percent, as discussed [elsewhere].[12] We might speculate that the direct effect of the father's occupation on the occupational status of a mature man consists of this modest amount of strict occupational inheritance. The remainder of the effect of X on Y is indirect, inasmuch as X has previously influenced U and W, the son's education and the occupational level at which he got his start. For reasons noted [elsewhere][13] we do not assume that the full impact of the tendency to take up the father's occupation is registered in the choice of first job.

With the formal properties of the model in mind we may turn to some general problems

Table 47.2   Partial Regression Coefficients in Standard Form (Beta Coefficients) and Coefficients of Determination, for Specified Combinations of Variables

Dependent Variables[a]	Independent Variables[a]				Coefficient of Determination (R^2)
	W	U	X	V	
U[b]	—	—	.279	.310	.26
W	—	.433	.214	.026	.33
W[b]	—	.440	.224	—	.33
Y	.282	.397	.120	-.014	.43
Y[b]	.281	.394	.115	—	.43
Y	.311	.428	—	—	.42

[a] V: Father's education
  X: Father's occ. status
  U: Respondent's education
  W: First-job status
  Y: 1962 occ. status
[b] Beta coefficients in these sets taken as estimates of path coefficients for Figure 47.1

confronting this kind of interpretation of our results. One of the first impressions gained from Figure 47.1 is that the largest path coefficients in the diagram are those for residual factors, that is, variables not measured. The residual path is merely a convenient representation of the extent to which measured causes in the system fail to account for the variation in the effect variables. (The residual is obtained from the coefficient of determination; if $R^2_{Y(WUX)}$ is the squared multiple correlation of Y on the three independent variables, then the residual for Y is $\sqrt{1 - R^2_{Y(WUX)}}$.) Sociologists are often disappointed in the size of the residual, assuming that this is a measure of their success in "explaining" the phenomenon under study. They seldom reflect on what it would mean to live in a society where nearly perfect explanation of the dependent variable could be secured by studying causal variables like father's occupation or respondent's education. In such a society it would indeed be true that some are "destined to poverty almost from birth . . . by the economic status or occupation of their par-

ents" (in the words of the reference cited in endnote 1). Others, of course, would be "destined" to affluence or to modest circumstances. By no effort of their own could they materially alter the course of destiny, nor could any stroke of fortune, good or ill, lead to an outcome not already in the cards.

Thinking of the residual as an index of the adequacy of an explanation gives rise to a serious misconception. It is thought that a high multiple correlation is presumptive evidence that an explanation is correct or nearly so, whereas a low percentage of determination means that a causal interpretation is almost certainly wrong. The fact is that the size of the residual (or, if one prefers, the proportion of variation "explained") is *no* guide whatever to the validity of a causal interpretation. The best-known cases of "spurious correlation"—a correlation leading to an egregiously wrong interpretation—are those in which the coefficient of determination is quite high.

The relevant question about the residual is not really its size at all, but whether the unobserved factors it stands for are properly represented as being uncorrelated with the measured antecedent variables. We shall entertain [elsewhere][14] some conjectures about unmeasured variables that clearly are not uncorrelated with the causes depicted in Figure 47.1. It turns out that these require us to acknowledge certain possible modifications of the diagram, whereas other features of it remain more or less intact. A delicate question in this regard is that of the burden of proof. It is all too easy to make a formidable list of unmeasured variables that someone has alleged to be crucial to the process under study. But the mere existence of such variables is already acknowledged by the very presence of the residual. It would seem to be part of the task of the critic to *show*, if only hypothetically, but *specifically*, how the modification of the causal scheme to include a new variable would disrupt or alter the relationships in the original diagram. His argument to this effect could then be examined for plausibility and his evidence, if any, studied in terms of the empirical possibilities it suggests.

Our supposition is that the scheme in Figure 47.1 is most easily subject to modification by introducing additional measures of the same kind as those used here. If indexes relating to socioeconomic background other than V and X are inserted we will almost certainly estimate differently the direct effects of these particular variables. If occupational statuses of the respondent intervening between W and Y were known we should have to modify more or less radically the right-hand portion of the diagram. Yet we should argue that such modifications may amount to an enrichment or extension of the basic model rather than an invalidation of it. The same may be said of other variables that function as intervening causes. In theory, it should

be possible to specify these in some detail, and a major part of the research worker's task is properly defined as an attempt at such specification. In the course of such work, to be sure, there is always the possibility of a discovery that would require a fundamental reformulation, making the present model obsolete. Discarding the model would be a cost gladly paid for the prize of such a discovery.

Postponing the confrontation with an altered model, the one at hand is not lacking in interest. An instructive exercise is to compare the magnitudes of gross and net relationships. Here we make use of the fact that the correlation coefficient and the path coefficient have the same dimensionality. The correlation $r_{YX} = .405$ (Table 47.1) means that a unit change (one standard deviation) in X produces a change of 0.4 unit in Y, in gross terms. The path coefficient, $P_{YX} = .115$ (Figure 47.1), tells us that about one-fourth of this gross effect is a result of the direct influence of X on Y. (We speculated above on the role of occupational inheritance in this connection.) The remainder ($.405 - .115 = .29$) is indirect, via U and W. The sum of all indirect effects, therefore, is given by the difference between the simple correlation and the path coefficient connecting two variables. We note that the indirect effects on Y are generally substantial, relative to the direct. Even the variable temporally closest (we assume) to Y has "indirect effects"—actually, common antecedent causes—nearly as large as the direct. Thus $r_{YW} = .541$ and $p_{YW} = .281$, so that the aggregate of "indirect effects" is .26, which in this case are common determinants of Y and W that spuriously inflate the correlation between them.

To ascertain the indirect effects along a given chain of causation we must multiply the path coefficients along the chain. The procedure is to locate on the diagram the dependent variable of interest, and then trace back along the paths linking it to its immediate and remote causes. In such a tracing we may reverse direction once but only once, following the rule "first back, then forward." Any bidirectional correlation may be traced in either direction. If the diagram contains more than one such correlation, however, only one may be used in a given compound path. In tracing the indirect connections no variable may be intersected more than once in one compound path. Having traced all such possible compound paths, we obtain the entirety of indirect effects as their sum.

Let us consider the example of effects of education on first job, U on W. The gross or total effect is $r_{WU} = .538$. The direct path is $p_{WU} = .440$. There are two indirect connections or compound paths: from W back to X then forward to U; and from W back to X, then back to V, and then forward to U. Hence we have:

$$r_{WU} = \underbrace{p_{WU}}_{} + \underbrace{p_{WX}p_{UX} + p_{WX}r_{XV}p_{UV}}_{}$$

(gross) (direct)   *(indirect)*

or, numerically,

$$.538 = .440 + (.224)(.279) + (.224)(.516)(.310)$$

$$= .440 + .062 + .036$$

$$= .440 + .098.$$

In this case all the indirect effect of U on W derives from the fact that both U and W have X (plus V) as a common cause. In other instances, when more than one common cause is involved and these causes are them-

selves interrelated, the complexity is too great to permit a succinct verbal summary.

A final stipulation about the scheme had best be stated, though it is implicit in all the previous discussion. The form of the model itself, but most particularly the numerical estimates accompanying it, are submitted as valid only for the population under study. No claim is made that an equally cogent account of the process of stratification in another society could be rendered in terms of this scheme. For other populations, or even for subpopulations within the United States, the magnitudes would almost certainly be different, although we have some basis for supposing them to have been fairly constant over the last few decades in this country. The technique of path analysis is not a method for discovering causal laws but a procedure for giving a quantitative interpretation to the manifestations of a known or assumed causal system as it operates in a particular population. When the same interpretive structure is appropriate for two or more populations there is something to be learned by comparing their respective path coefficients and correlation patterns. We have not yet reached the stage at which such comparative study of stratification systems is feasible. . . .

The Concept of a Vicious Circle

Although the concept of a "cycle of poverty" has a quasi-official sanction in U.S. public policy discussion, it is difficult to locate a systematic explication of the concept. As clear a formulation as any that may be found in academic writing is perhaps the following:[15]

Occupational and social status are to an important extent self-perpetuating. They are associated with many factors which make it difficult for individuals to modify their status. Position in the social structure is usually associated with a certain level of income, education, family structure, community reputation, and so forth. These become part of a vicious circle in which each factor acts on the other in such a way as to preserve the social structure in its present form, as well as the individual family's position in that structure. . . . The cumulation of disadvantages (or of advantages) affects the individual's entry into the labor market as well as his later opportunities for social mobility.

The suspicion arises that the authors in preparing this summary statement were partly captured by their own rhetoric. Only a few pages earlier they had observed that the "widespread variation of educational attainment within classes suggests that one's family background plays an enabling and motivating rather than a determining role."[16] But is an "enabling and motivating role" logically adequate to the function of maintaining a "vicious circle"? In focusing closely on the precise wording of the earlier quotation we are not interested in splitting hairs or in generating a polemic. It merely serves as a convenient point of departure for raising the questions of what is specifically meant by "vicious circle," what are the operational criteria for this concept, and what are the limits of its usefulness.

To begin with, there is the question of fact—or, rather, of how the quantitative facts are to be evaluated. How "difficult" is it, in actuality, "for individuals to modify their status" (presumably reference is to the status of the family of orientation)? We have found that the father-son correlation for occupational status is of the order of .4.

(Assuming attenuation by errors of measurement, this should perhaps be revised slightly upward.) Approaching the measurement problem in an entirely different way, we find that the amount of intergenerational mobility between census major occupation groups is no less than seven-eighths, as much as would occur if there were no statistical association between the two statuses whatsoever, or five-sixths as much as the difference between the "minimum" mobility involved in the intergenerational shift in occupation distributions and the amount required for "perfect" mobility.[17] Evidently a very considerable amount of "status modification" or occupational mobility does occur. (There is nothing in the data exhibited by Lipset and Bendix to indicate the contrary.) If the existing amount of modification of status is insufficient in terms of some functional or normative criterion implicitly employed, the precise criterion should be made explicit: *How much mobility must occur to contradict the diagnosis of a "vicious circle"?*

Next, take the postulate that occupational status (of origin) is "associated with many factors" and that "each factor acts on the other" so as "to preserve . . . the individual family's position." Here the exposition virtually cries out for an explicit *quantitative* causal model; if not one of the type set forth in the first section of this chapter, then some other model that also takes into account the way in which several variables combine their effects. Taking our own earlier model, for want of a better alternative, as representative of the situation, what do we learn about the "associated factors"? Family "position" is, indeed, "associated with . . . education," and education in turn makes a sizable difference in early and subsequent occupational achievement. Yet of the total or gross effect of education (U) on Y, occupational status in 1962 (r_{YU} = .596), only a minor part consists in a transmission of the prior influence of "family position," at least as this is indicated by measured variables V (father's education) and X (father's occupation). . . . A relevant calculation concerns the compound paths through V and X linking Y to U. Using data for men 20 to 64 years old with nonfarm background, we find:

$$p_{YX}p_{UX} = .025$$

$$p_{YX}r_{XV}p_{UV} = .014$$

$$p_{YX}p_{WX}p_{UX} = .014$$

$$p_{YW}p_{WX}r_{XV}p_{UV} = .008$$

$$\overline{\qquad\qquad\qquad\qquad}$$

$$Sum = .061$$

This is the *entire* part of the effect of education that has to do with "perpetuating" the "family's position." By contrast, the direct effect is p_{YU} = .407 and the effect via W (exclusive of prior influence of father's education and occupation on respondent's first job) is $p_{YW}p_{WU}$ = .128, for a total of .535. Far from serving in the main as a factor perpetuating initial status, education operates *primarily* to induce variation in occupational status that is independent of initial status. The simple reason is that the large residual factor for U is an indirect cause of Y. But by definition it is quite uncorrelated with X and V. This is not to gainsay the equally cogent point that the degree of "perpetuation" (as measured by r_{YX}) that does occur is mediated in large part by education. . . .

Our model also indicates where the "vicious circle" interpretation is vulnerable. In the passage on the vicious circle quoted there seems to be an assumption that because of the substantial intercorrelations between a number of background factors, each of which has a significant relationship to subsequent achievement, the total effect of origin on achievement is materially enhanced. Here, in other words, the concept of "cumulation" appears to refer to the intercorrelations of a collection of independent variables. But the effect of such intercorrelations is quite opposite to what the writers appear to suppose. They are not alone in arguing from a fallacious assumption that was caustically analyzed by Karl Pearson half a century ago.[18] The crucial point is that if the several determinants are indeed substantially intercorrelated with each other, then their combined effect will consist largely in redundancy, not in "cumulation." This circumstance does not relieve us from the necessity of trying to understand better *how* the effects come about (a point also illustrated in a less fortunate way in Pearson's work). It does imply that a refined estimate of how much effect results from a combination of "associated factors" will not differ greatly from a fairly crude estimate based on the two or three most important ones.

NOTES

1. Mollie Orshansky, "Children of the Poor," *Social Security Bulletin,* 26(July 1963).

2. Forrest A. Bogan, "Employment of High School Graduates and Dropouts in 1964," *Special Labor Force Report,* No. 54 (U.S. Bureau of Labor Statistics, June 1965), p. 643.

3. Peter M. Blau and Otis Dudley Duncan, *The American Occupational Structure,* New York: The Free Press, 1967, ch. 4.

4. *Ibid.*

5. Bruce K. Eckland, "College Dropouts Who Came Back," *Harvard Educational Review,* 34(1964), 402–420.

6. Beverly Duncan, *Family Factors and School Dropout: 1920–1960,* U.S. Office of Education, Cooperative Research Project No. 2258, Ann Arbor: Univ. of Michigan, 1965.

7. Blau and Duncan, *op. cit.,* Appendix C.

8. Gösta Carlsson, *Social Mobility and Class Structure,* Lund: CWK Gleerup, 1958, p. 124.

9. H. M. Blalock, Jr., *Causal Inferences in Non-experimental Research,* Chapel Hill: Univ. of North Carolina Press, 1964.

10. Sewall Wright, "Path Coefficients and Path Regressions," *Biometrics,* 16(1960), 189–202; Otis Dudley Duncan, "Path Analysis," *American Journal of Sociology,* 72(1966), 1–16.

11. Blalock, *op. cit.,* pp. 54 ff.

12. Blau and Duncan, *op. cit.,* ch. 4.

13. *Ibid.,* ch. 3.

14. *Ibid.,* ch. 5.

15. Seymour M. Lipset and Reinhard Bendix, *Social Mobility in Industrial Society,* Berkeley: Univ. of California Press, 1959, pp. 198–199.

16. *Ibid.,* p. 190.

17. U.S. Bureau of the Census, "Lifetime Occupational Mobility of Adult Males: March 1962," *Current Population Reports,* Series P–23, No. 11 (May 12, 1964), Table B.

18. Karl Pearson, "On Certain Errors with Regard to Multiple Correlation Occasionally Made by Those Who Have Not Adequately Studied This Subject," *Biometrika,* 10(1914), 181–187.

48

Family Background and Income in Adulthood, 1961–1999

DAVID J. HARDING, CHRISTOPHER JENCKS, LEONARD M. LOPOO, AND SUSAN E. MAYER

Most Americans endorse the ideal of equal opportunity, and many interpret this ideal as requiring that children from different backgrounds have an equal chance of achieving economic success. Most Americans also recognize that children whose parents have "all the advantages" are more likely to prosper than children whose parents lack these advantages. Understanding this relationship has therefore become a prominent goal of social research, especially since the 1960s. This chapter investigates how the relationship between American family income during adulthood and family background during childhood changed from 1961 to 1999.

Our approach to measuring trends in intergenerational inheritance differs from earlier studies. Almost all earlier studies have focused on the determinants of individuals' occupational rank or earnings. We focus instead on an individual's total family income. This change allows us to assess the impact of family background on the eco-nomic status of individuals who are not working. It also allows us to take account of the fact that individuals' economic status often depends more on how they fare in the "marriage market" than on how they fare in the labor market.

The changing importance of marriage for one's family income is clear when we examine changes in the correlation between a mature adult's own earnings in a given year and his or her total family income in the same year. Among men the correlation[1] between earnings and total family income fell from 0.87 in 1968 to 0.75 in 1996.[2] Among women, the correlation rose from 0.18 in 1968 to 0.39 in 1996. Earnings are still a much better proxy for living standards among men than among women. But since family background influences an individual's chance of having a well-paid spouse, ignoring this fact is likely to bias trend estimates of how background affects economic status among both men and women.

This is a commissioned chapter that draws heavily on material in a previous publication (David J. Harding, Christopher Jencks, Leonard M. Lopoo, and Susan E. Mayer, "The Changing Effect of Family Background on the Incomes of American Adults," in *Unequal Chances: Family Background and Economic Success*, Samuel Bowles, Herbert Gintis, and Melissa Osborne, eds. Copyright © 2005 by Russell Sage Foundation).

How Family Background Affects Adult Family Income

Figure 48.1 shows some of the pathways by which family background can influence children's eventual income in adulthood.[3] It contains several concepts that require brief discussion.

Genetic Advantages

A growing body of evidence suggests that genetic differences can influence an individual's earnings. Studies based on comparisons of monozygotic (MZ) twins and dizygotic (DZ) twins (Ashenfelter and Rouse 1998; Taubman 1976) suggest that genes are likely to play a significant role in explaining the intergenerational inheritance of economic advantages.[4] However, because estimates based on twin studies require a number of questionable assumptions (Björklund, Jäntti, and Solon 2005; Goldberger 1978), the exact magnitude of the importance of genes is difficult to measure. Björklund and Chadwick's (2002) study of the earnings of fathers and sons in Sweden also suggests that genes play a role.

However, the fact that genetic resemblance helps explain economic resemblance between parents and children does not mean that this source of economic resemblance operates independently of the environment. Suppose, for example, that myopia has a genetic component. Most affluent societies ensure that myopic children get glasses. As a result, myopic children can usually see almost as well as other children. In poor societies where glasses are not available to everyone, the genes that contribute to myopia have a larger impact. People's genes also influence the environments they choose for themselves. Consider two sisters, one of whom finds reading easy and one of whom finds it difficult. The sister who finds reading easier is likely to enjoy reading more and do more of it. As a result, she is likely to score higher on vocabulary and reading tests, get higher grades, stay in school longer, and earn more when she enters the labor force.

Human Capital

Economists use the term "human capital" to describe the skills, knowledge, and character traits that influence a worker's potential earnings. If employers value the same attributes for several generations, parents with above-average human capital are likely to have children with above-average human capital. To begin with, parents with traits that employers value tend to have above-average earnings, so they can invest more in their children's nutrition, health care, and education. Such parents also tend to live in political jurisdictions where the government invests a lot in children.

Although economists use the term "human capital" to describe characteristics that pay off in the labor market, one can easily broaden the concept to include characteristics that pay off in the marriage market. As we shall see, family background explains slightly more of the variation in daughters' family incomes than in sons' family incomes. This difference suggests that family background may exert even more influence on a daughter's success in the marriage market than on a son's success in the labor market.

Taste for Market Goods

Families vary dramatically in the number of hours that their adult members spend doing paid labor. Family members also vary in the extent to which they maximize their hourly wages. Some always take the best-paid

444

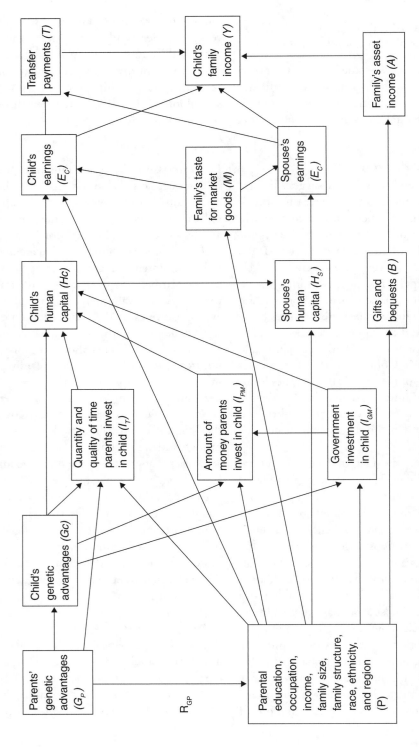

Figure 48.1   Some Possible Links Between Respondents' Adult Incomes and Their Family Background

job they can find, and others settle for less money to get shorter hours, more congenial colleagues, more interesting work, or other nonmonetary advantages. Family background appears to influence how much people work (Altonji and Dunn 2000), and it probably also influences the weight that individuals assign to earnings relative to goals like short hours and interesting work. If these associations change over time, the association between adult income and family background is also likely to change.

Gifts and Bequests

Dividends, interest, and rent accounted for 7 percent of all income received by individuals between the ages of 25 and 64 in 1999.[5] Estimates suggest that income from assets accounts for between 1 and 5 percent of all money income among thirty- to fifty-nine year olds (Gale and Scholz 1994; Wolff 2002). We do not know how this figure has changed over time, but the age at which adults inherit their parents' assets is rising, so the relative importance of inherited assets could be falling for those under the age of sixty.

Two Sources of Change over Time

Figure 48.1 suggests that the effects of family background on incomes can change for two quite different reasons. First, the effects of various family background characteristics on children's characteristics, such as years of schooling, cognitive ability, or taste for market goods, can change. Second, the effects of children's characteristics on their eventual adult income can change. Children's education illustrates both of these possibilities.

The association between parents' socioeconomic advantages and the number of years of school that their children complete declined between World War I and the early 1970s (Hauser and Featherman 1976). As a result, educational disparities among adults from different kinds of families kept shrinking throughout the twentieth century. This trend should have reduced the impact of family background on children's eventual family income. However, the economic value of an extra year of schooling also changed. The effect of an extra year of school on men's annual earnings fell between 1940 and 1975. This change accentuated the declining impact of family background on children's educational attainment, making it doubly difficult for economically advantaged parents to pass along their advantages by keeping their children in school. But after 1975 the labor market returns to schooling rose.

The payoff to schooling also rose in the marriage market. If we compare the most educated third of all mothers to the least educated third, about 93 percent of the most educated and 87 percent of the least educated were living with a husband in both 1940 and 1960. By 1990 the proportions were 84 percent for the most educated and 70 percent for the least educated.[6] The marriage gap between the most and least educated mothers had thus risen from 6 to 14 percentage points. The net result was that although family background had less impact on how much schooling young people got in the last third of the century than earlier in the century, the value of each year of school rose during the last decades of the century.

Mature adults seldom go back to school, so the association between educational attainment and family background when a birth cohort reaches sixty is about the same as when it was thirty. The association does change as more recent birth cohorts replace earlier ones, but this takes a long time. In principle, we can hold changes of this kind constant by tracking the same birth cohort over time. When we do this, almost all the remaining changes in the association between adult family income and family background are attributable to changes in the way employment, marriage, and earnings are distributed among individuals with different background characteristics.

Whereas cohort replacement is slow, the economic value of respondents' characteristics can change relatively rapidly. When job opportunities improved for black workers in the wake of the civil rights movement, for example, young blacks benefited the most, but older blacks also gained. Likewise, when the wage gap between high school and college graduates widened in the 1980s, the change was largest among younger workers but it also affected mature workers. Changes in the marriage market can also change the value of personal characteristics quite rapidly. When divorce rates rise, all women are more likely to experience sudden reductions in family income, but the change is likely to be largest among those with disadvantaged parents, because their divorce rates are likely to rise the most.

Data

We concentrate on trends among men and women between the ages of thirty and fifty-nine, whom we refer to as "mature adults." We use two sources of data, the Occupational Changes in a Generation (OCG) surveys and the General Social Survey (GSS). The OCG surveys were conducted in 1962 and 1973. They both asked men (but not women) about their family background. Our first sample of mature OCG

men was born between 1902 and 1932. Our second sample was born between 1913 and 1943. The GSS is a smaller survey that has been conducted either annually or biennially since 1972. The GSS asks both men and women about their family income and family background. We analyze the surveys conducted between 1972 and 2000, so our samples of mature adults were born between 1912 and 1970.

Our primary dependent variable is family income in the year preceding the survey. Although there is some variation across data sources in how our variables are measured, one can think of adult family income as the sum of all sources of income for the respondent and his or her spouse (if married).[7] Variation in income due to survey year, gender, and age has been removed, and we analyze the effect of parental characteristics on the natural logarithm of this adjusted income. We measure family background using seven characteristics of the family in which the respondent grew up, including the family head's occupational ranking (measured by an updated version of Duncan's socioeconomic index, which is based on occupations' educational requirements and economic rewards; see Hauser and Warren 1997), the family head's education in years, the number of siblings, and whether the respondent is black, Hispanic, grew up in the South, and/or grew up in a family with both parents.

Changes in Inequality of Family Background

Suppose that a 10 percent income difference between parents was always associated with a 4 percent income difference between their children. The income gap between children raised by rich and poor parents would then depend on the income gap separating rich and poor parents. If inequality between rich and poor parents falls, as it did during the first two-thirds of the twentieth century, and if all else remains equal, the subsequent income gap between their children will also fall. If inequality between rich and poor parents rises, as it did in the last third of the twentieth century, and if all else remains equal, the income gap between their children will also widen. The same logic holds for other parental advantages, like educational attainment and occupational position.

The degree to which the distribution of background characteristics changed over time varies according to which family background characteristics we examine. Inequality in parental occupation rose by about 15 percent between 1962 and 1999. Inequality in parental years of schooling rose slightly between 1962 and 1973 and declined slightly thereafter, so educational inequality among parents was about the same in 1999 as in 1962. Disparities in the size of children's families declined by about 10 percent between the early 1960s and the 1990s.

Of the four remaining measures of background characteristics—intact family, black, Hispanic, and Southern origins, the only one that changes appreciably is Hispanic. The GSS shows substantial growth in the English-speaking Hispanic population between the 1970s and 1990s. Because Hispanics have relatively low family incomes, the fact that more adults had Hispanic parents implies an increase in the overall level of inequality among parents.

Changes in the Intergenerational Inheritance of Advantage

We turn now to changes in the relationship between mature adults' income and their family background (as measured by the seven background characteristics). We measure this relationship with the multiple correlations between income and family background characteristics, which we denote as R_{pc}.[8] When R_{pc} falls, we can infer that intergenerational changes in rank (what sociologists call "exchange mobility") have become larger or more frequent. When R_{pc} rises, intergenerational changes in rank have become either smaller or less frequent.

Table 48.1 shows multiple correlations between respondents' adult family income and their background characteristics. Among OCG men we see a dramatic decline in R_{pc} between 1961 and 1972. This decline recurs for all age groups. The diagonal arrows track birth cohorts as they age. Here again we see declines between 1961 and 1972. The GSS tells a very different story about changes in R_{pc} after 1972. The multiple correlations for men in different age groups show no consistent trend between the 1970s and the 1990s. When we track the same cohort of men over time, the multiple correlations almost always rise as a cohort ages. This is in sharp contrast to what we saw between 1961 and 1972.

The GSS also provides data on post-1972 trends among women. Table 48.1 shows that although R_{pc} was essentially stable among GSS men, it declined by about one-seventh among GSS women. Whereas R_{pc} was substantially higher among women than men in the 1970s, this gender difference had largely disappeared by the 1990s. This pattern of differences is consistent with the hypothesis that family background influences success in the marriage market somewhat more than it influences success in the labor market, although other explanations are also possible.

Table 48.1   Multiple Correlations of Family Income with Seven Family Background Measures in OCG and GSS, by Age, Sex, and Decade

	OCG Men		GSS Men			GSS Women		
Respondents' Age	1961	1972[a]	1970s	1980s	1990s	1970s	1980s	1990s
30 to 39	.399	.309	.330	.289	.306	.399	.361	.374
40 to 49	.397	.305	.355	.362	.352	.437	.388	.361
50 to 59	.414	.323	.327	.410	.360	.440	.429	.350
Weighted Mean For All 30 to 59 year olds	.403	.312	.337	.342	.335	.423	.385	.364[b]
Approximate Sampling Error of Multiple R[c]	(.008)	(.006)	(.014)	(.017)	(.015)	(.012)	(.015)	(.014)
Sample Size	12,829	23,824	2,382	3,040	3,817	2,761	3,703	4,657

Note: The seven measures of family background are race, ethnicity, Southern origins, living with both parents at age 16, number of siblings, parental education, and parental occupation (see text for details)

[a] The decline between 1961 and 1972 is significant at the .01 level for all age groups.

[b] The average decline between the 1970s and the 1990s is significant at the .01 level.

[c] Approximated using $[(1-R^2)/(N-8)]^5$.

For those who find it hard to decide whether the correlations in Table 48.1 are "large" or "small," Table 48.2 displays the association between family background and income in adulthood in a more intuitively understandable form. Table 48.2 shows the proportion of respondents in the top and bottom quartiles of family background who ended up in each of the four income quartiles as adults. We focus on the probability that those born into the top or bottom quartile were in the top or bottom income quartile as mature adults.

Consistent with the results in Table 48.1, the proportion of men who remained in the bottom or top quartiles declined between 1961 and 1972 and stayed the same afterward.

Among women the story is more complicated. Among GSS women, R_{pc} fell between the 1970s and the 1990s, so we expected a parallel decline in the proportions of GSS women who stayed in both the top and bottom quartiles. Table 48.2 confirms this pre-diction for women born into the top quartile: their chances of having slipped into a lower quartile were clearly higher in the 1990s than in the 1970s. However, there was little change in the percentage of women born into the bottom quartile who had risen into a higher quartile, although those women who did move up moved further in the 1990s than in the 1970s.

Specific Background Characteristics

Previously we examined the relationship between adult income and family background by combining the seven background measures. Now we separate these characteristics to see which ones became more and less important. Column 1 of Table 48.3 shows the bivariate relationship of logged family income in 1961 to each of the seven family background characteristics. Column 2 shows the change in this coefficient between 1961 and 1972. Almost

Table 48.2   Percent of 30- to 59-Year-Old Sons and Daughters in Each Quartile of Family Income
By Quartile of Family Background and Year in OCG and GSS

Parents' Quartile and Survey	Family Income Quartile					
	Bottom	Second	Third	Top	Total	Sample Size
Sons from bottom quartile						
OCG: 1961	46.2	27.7	16.7	9.5	100	2,537
OCG: 1972	40.7	29.8	21.2	8.4	100	6,454
GSS: 1970s	40.3	29.6	19.8	10.2	100	595
GSS: 1980s	39.4	30.0	21.2	9.4	100	840
GSS: 1990s	40.6	25.8	21.1	12.6	100	954
Trend: 1961 to 1990s[a]	−5.3	−1.7	5.7	1.4		
Sons from top quartile						
OCG-I	9.5	20.9	32.1	37.6	100	2,678
OCG-II	11.8	24.0	29.2	35.0	100	4,899
GSS: 1970s	11.6	20.5	30.2	37.8	100	596
GSS: 1980s	12.3	19.7	28.8	39.2	100	728
GSS: 1990s	11.6	21.4	29.0	38.0	100	954
Trend: 1961 to 1990s[a]	2.4	3.9	−4.1	−2.3		
Daughters from bottom quartile						
GSS: 1970s	44.4	26.2	19.6	9.9	100	690
GSS: 1980s	44.5	25.5	18.8	11.2	100	1,070
GSS: 1990s	43.7	25.9	18.8	11.6	100	1,164
Trend: 1970s to 1990s	−0.6	−0.4	−0.8	1.7		
Daughters from top quartile						
GSS: 1970s	10.1	19.1	27.1	42.8	100	691
GSS: 1980s	12.1	19.3	29.7	38.9	100	878
GSS: 1990s	11.7	23.5	27.1	37.7	100	1,164
Trend: 1970s to 1990s	1.5	4.4	0.0	−5.2		

Parents are assigned to quartiles of parental advantages using the same seven measures as in Table 48.1, with each advantage weighted by its coefficient in the equation predicting log family income. Family incomes are assigned to quartiles after eliminating variation due to age, gender, and survey year.

[a] Sum of within-survey changes: (OCG II − OCG I) + (GSS 1990s − GSS 1970s).

all the coefficients decline significantly between 1961 and 1972. However, when we examine each coefficient controlling for the other six, only the changes in the effects of parental occupation, black race, and Southern origins remain statistically significant (results not shown).

The decline in the effect of parental occupation is partly attributable to the steady decline in the proportion of respondents whose fathers were farmers. Among respon-dents not raised on farms, the main reason for decline was that respondents from the top tenth of the occupational distribution enjoyed less of an economic advantage in 1972 than in 1961 (results not shown). The declining effect of Southern origins probably reflects the narrowing of the income gap between the South and the North. The declining effect of race reflects a decline in the educational gap between blacks and whites, movement of blacks

450

Table 48.3 Bivariat Regression Coefficients of Seven Family Background Measures When Predicting Log Family Income at Ages 30 to 59 Among OCG Men and GSS Men and Women

Background Measure	OCG Men		GSS Men		GSS Women		GSS Women Minus Men	
	Coefficient for 1961	Change From 1961 to 1972	Coefficient For 1971	Change From 1971 to 1999	Coefficient For 1971	Change From 1971 to 1999	Coefficient For 1971	Change From 1971 to 1999
Father's Occupation								
B	**.257**	**-.089**	**.131**	.037	**.207**	-.010	**.076**	-.047
(S.E.)	(.007)	(.009)	(.017)	(.026)	(.017)	(.028)	(.024)	(.038)
Parent's Education								
B	**.053**	**-.012**	**.037**	**.015**	**.057**	-.010	**.020**	**-.025**
(S.E.)	(.002)	(.002)	(.004)	(.006)	(.004)	(.007)	(.006)	(.009)
Number of Siblings								
B	**-.058**	**-.011**	**-.043**	**-.029**	**-.067**	.007	**-.024**	**.036**
(S.E.)	(.002)	(.003)	(.006)	(.010)	(.006)	(.010)	(.008)	(.014)
Intact Family								
B	**.164**	.033	**.090**	**.205**	**.262**	.081	**.172**	-.124
(S.E.)	(.018)	(.024)	(.039)	(.062)	(.039)	(.062)	(.055)	(.088)
Black								
B	**-.824**	**.359**	**-.415**	-.065	**-.770**	**.179**	**-.355**	.244
(S.E.)	(.023)	(.031)	(.051)	(.081)	(.051)	(.079)	(.072)	(.133)
Hispanic								
B	**-.405**	.082	**-.573**	**.443**	**-.482**	.168	.091	-.275
(S.E.)	(.047)	(.055)	(.095)	(.147)	(.095)	(.144)	(.134)	(.206)
Southern Regions								
B	**-.424**	**.191**	**-.260**	.093	**-.367**	**.226**	**-.107**	.133
(S.E.)	(.015)	(.019)	(.035)	(.057)	(.036)	(.060)	(.050)	(.083)
Unweighted Sample	32,242		9,268		11,107			

*Coefficients in boldface are significant at the .05 level

from the South to the North, and some re-duction in discrimination.

The remainder of Table 48.3 shows the bivariate results from GSS. Column 3 shows the estimated coefficients of family background measures for men in 1971, and column 4 shows the estimated change in the bivariate coefficients for men between 1971 and 1999. The bivariate relationships of men's family income to their parents' ed-ucation, number of siblings, and whether they grew up in an intact family become significantly stronger over time. The bivari-ate effect of parental occupation also grows slightly stronger, but the change is not sig-nificant. The bivariate effect of being His-panic grows weaker over time.

Columns 5 and 7 show that in 1971 al-most every family background measure had more impact on women than on men. Columns 6 and 8 show that most of the co-efficients for men and women converged be-tween 1971 and 1999. The effects of parental education, race, and Southern origins all weakened significantly for women and were very close to those for men by the late 1990s. The adverse effect of coming from a large family was significantly larger for women than men in 1971, but this difference had also disappeared by the late 1990s. The mul-tivariate GSS results (not shown) are broadly similar to the bivariate results except that the coefficients are smaller.

Summary

Intergenerational Inheritance

The relationship between a mature man's family income in adulthood and his family background fell during the 1960s and then remained stable from the 1970s through the 1990s. But men's incomes began grow-ing more unequal in the 1970s, so the in-come gap between men raised by advan-taged rather than disadvantaged parents widened between the 1970s and the 1990s.

We have no data on trends among women during the 1960s. In the early 1970s inter-generational correlations were higher among daughters than among sons, and daughters' family incomes were also more unequal. The economic cost of having grown up in a dis-advantaged family was therefore consider-ably larger for daughters than for sons. But whereas the association between a mature man's family income and his parents' so-cioeconomic position was almost constant between the 1970s and the 1990s, this asso-ciation fell among women. As a result, the economic cost of growing up in a disad-vantaged family was roughly constant for women, although it remained larger for women than for men.

Race, Ethnicity, and Region

Disparities in adult family income between blacks and whites, between Hispanics and Anglos, and between those raised in the South and North narrowed between 1961 and 1999.

Parental Education

The effect of parental education on men's family income fell during the 1960s but rose again over the next three decades. Parental education mattered more for ma-ture women's family income than for men's in the 1970s, but this difference had disap-peared by the late 1990s.

Parental Occupation

When we rank occupations in terms of their educational requirements and eco-nomic rewards, the effect of differences be-tween fathers' occupations on their mature sons' family incomes declined during the

1960s. The effect of a father's occupation shows no clear trend after that for either men or women, but it is consistently larger for women than for men, partly because women's family incomes are more unequal than men's.

Taken together these findings suggest that there were significant changes in equality of opportunity in the United States between 1961 and 1999. For men, equality of opportunity increased during the 1960s but changed little thereafter. Among women there was less equality of opportunity in the early 1970s than among men, but equality of opportunity among women increased during the 1970s. By the late 1990s, the importance of family background for a woman's economic prospects (relative to other women) was similar to its importance for a man's economic prospects (relative to other men). In addition, the importance of race, ethnicity, and region declined between 1961 and 1999. Nevertheless, as we begin the twenty-first century, there are still sizable inequalities of opportunity in the United States. Gender and family background, including race, ethnicity, and region, remain strong predictors of economic well-being in adulthood.

NOTES

1.In this chapter we often measure the relationship between two attributes with a "correlation," which ranges from zero (no relationship) to one (perfect relationship) and which can be thought of as assessing the degree to which two characteristics are associated in the data. A "multiple correlation" can be thought of as a correlation between one attribute and a set of attributes considered together.

2. Men and women without earnings are included and assigned earnings of zero.

3. Figure 48.1 is not a complete causal model. It omits many links that are well established in the research literature, such as the reciprocal ef-

fects of spouses' earnings on one another, to highlight the links that we think are most likely to have changed.

4. Monozygotic (MZ) twins have all their genes in common, and dizygotic (DZ) twins share roughly half their genes.

5. Estimate based on data from U.S. Bureau of the Census (2000, pp. 55 and D–4). Our estimates of family income do not include the implicit return on home equity.

6. These estimates are from tabulations by Andrew Clarkwest using the Integrated Public Use Microsamples from the decennial census.

7. See Harding et al. (2005) for further details on the data and methodology.

8. The square of the multiple correlation is the percentage of the income variance explained by parental characteristics.

REFERENCES

Altonji, Joseph, and Thomas Dunn. 2000. "An Intergenerational Model of Wages, Hours, and Earnings." *Journal of Human Resources* 35(2): 221–258.

Ashenfelter, Orley, and Cecelia Rouse. 1998. "Income, Schooling, and Ability: Evidence from a New Sample of Identical Twins." *Quarterly Journal of Economics* 113: 317–323.

Björklund, Anders, and Laura Chadwick. 2002. "Intergenerational Income Mobility in Permanent and Separated Families." Swedish Institute for Social Research, Stockholm University.

Björklund, Anders, Markus Jäntti, and Gary Solon. 2005. "Influences of Nature and Nurture of Earnings: A Report on a Study of Various Sibling Types in Sweden," in Samuel Bowles, Herbert Gintis, and Melissa Osborne, eds., *Unequal Chances: Family Background and Economic Success*. Princeton, NJ: Princeton University Press and Russell Sage.

Gale, William G., and John Karl Scholz. 1994. "Intergenerational Transfers and the Accumulation of Wealth." *Journal of Economic Perspectives* 8(4): 145–160.

Goldberger, Arthur. 1978. "The Genetic Determination of Income: Comment." *American Economic Review* 68(5): 960–969.

Harding, David J., Christopher Jencks, Leonard M. Lopoo, and Susan E. Mayer. 2005. "The Changing Effect of Family Background on the Incomes of American Adults." In Samuel Bowles, Herbert Gintis, and Melissa Osborne, eds., *Unequal Chances: Family Background and Economic Success*. Princeton, NJ: Princeton University Press and Russell Sage.

Hauser, Robert, and David Featherman. 1976. "Equality of Schooling: Trends and Prospects." *Sociology of Education* 49(2): 99–120.

Hauser, Robert, and John Robert Warren. 1997. "Socioeconomic Indexes for Occupations: A Review, Update, and Critique." *Sociological Methodology* 27: 177–298.

Taubman, Paul. 1976. "The Determinants of Earnings: Genetics, Family, and Other Environments; A Study of Male Twins." *American Economic Review* 66(5): 858–870.

U.S. Bureau of the Census. 2000. "Money Income in the United States, 1999." *Current Population Reports*. Washington, DC: Government Printing Office.

Wolff, Edward. 2002. "Inheritances and Wealth Inequality, 1989–1998." *American Economic Review* 92(2): 260–264.

49

The Educational and
Early Occupational Attainment Process

WILLIAM H. SEWELL, ARCHIBALD O. HALLER,
AND ALEJANDRO PORTES

Blau and Duncan (1967:165–172) have recently presented a path model of the occupational attainment process of the American adult male population. This basic model begins with two variables describing the early stratification position of each person; these are his father's educational and occupational attainment statuses. It then moves to two behavioral variables; these are the educational level the individual has completed and the prestige level of his first job. The dependent variable is the person's occupational prestige position in 1962. That the model is not without power is attested by the fact that it accounts for about 26 percent of the variance in educational attainment, 33 percent of the variance in first job, and 42 percent of the variance in 1962 level of occupational attainment. Various additions to the basic model are presented in the volume, but none is clearly shown to make much of an improvement in it. These include nativity, migration, farm origin, subgroup position, marriage, and assortative mating. Without detracting from the excellence of the Blau and Duncan analysis, we may make several observations.

1) Because the dependent behaviors are occupational prestige attainments—attainment levels in a stratification system—it is appropriate to single out variables indicating father's stratification position as the most relevant social structural inputs. It is unfortunate that practical considerations prevented the inclusion of psychological inputs in their model, especially considering the repeated references to one such—mental ability—in the literature on differential occupational attainment (Lipset and Bendix, 1959:203–226; Sewell and Armer, 1966). More recently, this gap has been partially filled (Duncan, 1968).

2) Also omitted are social psychological factors which mediate the influence of the input variables on attainment. This, too, is unfortunate in view not only of the speculative theory but also the concrete research in social psychology, which suggests the importance of such intervening variables as reference groups (Merton, 1957:281–386), significant others (Gerth and Mills, 1953:84–91), self-concept (Super, 1957:80–100), behavior expectations (Gross et al., 1958), levels of educational and oc-

William H. Sewell, Archibald O. Haller, and Alejandro Portes, "The Educational and Early Occupational Attainment Process," *American Sociological Review* 34 (February 1969), pp. 82–92.

cupational aspiration (Haller and Miller, 1963; Kuvlesky and Ohlendorf, 1967; Ohlendorf et al., 1967), and experiences of success or failure in school (Parsons, 1959; Brookover et al., 1965).

It remains to be seen whether the addition of such psychological and social psychological variables is worthwhile, although there are reasons for believing that at least some of them may be. First, an explanation of a behavior system requires a plausible causal argument, not just a set of path coefficients among temporally ordered variables. As indicated in Duncan's (1969) recent work, the introduction of social psychological mediating variables offers this possibility, but it does not guarantee it. As it stands, the Blau-Duncan model fails to indicate why any connection at all would be expected between the input variables, father's education and occupation, and the three subsequent factors: respondent's education, respondent's first job, and respondent's 1962 occupation. Granting differences among social psychological positions, they all agree that one's cognitions and motivations (including, among others, knowledge, self-concept, and aspirations) are developed in structured situations (including the expectations of others), and that one's actions (attainments in this case) are a result of the cognitive and motivational orientations one brings to the action situation, as well as the factors in the new situation itself. Second, if valid, a social psychological model will suggest new points at which the causal system may be entered in order to change the attainment behaviors of persons, an issue not addressed by the Blau and Duncan volume. Variables such as the expectations of significant others offer other possibilities for manipulating the outcomes, including educational attainments. Third, in addition to the above advantages,

a social psychological model of educational and occupational attainment might add to the explanation of variance in the dependent variables.

The Problem

The present report extends the attempts of the writers (Sewell and Armer, 1966; Sewell and Orenstein, 1965; Sewell and Shah, 1967; Sewell, 1964; Haller and Sewell, 1967; Portes et al., 1968; Haller, 1966; Haller and Miller, 1963; Miller and Haller, 1964; Sewell et al., 1957) to apply social psychological concepts to the explanation of variation in levels of educational and occupational attainment. We assume (1) that certain social structural and psychological factors—initial stratification position and mental ability, specifically—affect both the sets of significant others' influences bearing on the youth, and the youth's own observations of his ability; (2) that the influence of significant others, and possibly his estimates of his ability, affect the youth's levels of educational and occupational aspiration; (3) that the levels of aspiration affect subsequent levels of educational attainment; (4) that education in turn affects levels of occupational attainment. In the present analysis we assume that all effects are linear; also, that the social psychological variables perform only mediating functions.

More specifically, we present theory and data regarding what we believe to be a logically consistent social psychological model. This provides a plausible causal argument to link stratification and mental ability inputs through a set of social psychological and behavioral mechanisms to educational and occupational attainments. One compelling feature of the model is that some of the inputs may be manipulated through

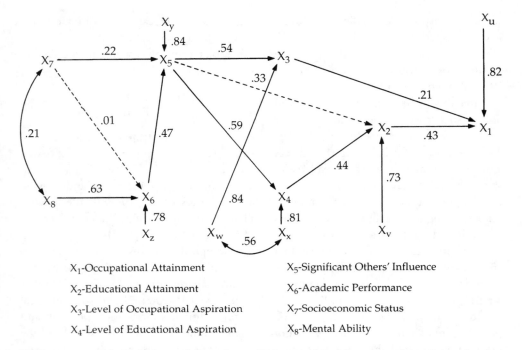

X₁-Occupational Attainment   X₅-Significant Others' Influence

X₂-Educational Attainment   X₆-Academic Performance

X₃-Level of Occupational Aspiration X₇-Socioeconomic Status

X₄-Level of Educational Aspiration   X₈-Mental Ability

Figure 49.1   Path Coefficients of Antecedents of Educational and Occupational Attainment Levels

experimental or other purposive interventions. This means that parts of it can be experimentally tested in future research and that practical policy agents can reasonably hope to use it in order to change educational and occupational attainments.

A Social Psychological Model

The model treats causal relationships among eight variables. X_1 is the occupational prestige level attained by the adult person, or *occupational attainment* (OccAtt); X_2 is the educational level he had previously attained, or *educational attainment* (EdAtt); X_3 is the occupational prestige level to which he aspired as a youth, or *level of occupational aspiration* (LOA); X_4 is his *level of educational aspiration* as a youth (LEA); X_5 is the influence for educational achievement exerted upon him by significant others while still in high school, or *significant others' influence* (SOI); X_6 is the quality of his *academic performance* in high school (AP); X_7 is the level of his family in the stratification system, or *socioeconomic status* (SES); and X_8 is his *mental ability* as measured while he was in high school (MA). Path models (Blau and Duncan, 1967:165–172; Wright, 1934; Wright, 1960; Heise, 1969) require a knowledge of the causal order among the variables. Beyond the causal arguments presented below, additional credibility is suggested by the existence of a plausible temporal order among variables. X_7 (SES) and X_8 (MA) precede everything else. X_5 (SOI) and X_6 (AP) precede both aspirations and attainments, and it can be assumed that for the most part X_6 precedes X_5. Youthful aspirations obviously precede later educational and occupational attainments. Pre-adult educational attainments precede adult occupational attainments.

By no means do all of the possible causal linkages seem defensible. The most likely ones are indicated in Figure 49.1. In it straight solid lines stand for causal lines that are to be theoretically expected, dotted lines stand for possible but theoretically debatable causal lines, and curved lines represent unanalyzed correlations among variables which cannot be assigned causal priority in present data.

Commencing from the left of the diagram, we assume, as has often been found before (Sewell and Shah, 1967; Sewell et al., 1957), that a low positive correlation, r_{78}, exists between the youth's measured mental ability (MA) and his parents' socioeconomic status (SES). This is the case: $r_{78} = .21$. We anticipate the existence of substantial effect of MA on academic performance (AP). We theorize that significant others' influence (SOI) is controlled by AP, and by socioeconomic status, as well as by exogenous factors, that they exert profound effects on aspiration, and that the latter in turn influences later attainments. A more detailed examination of the theory follows.

Working with partial conceptions of SOI (and using different terminology), Bordua (1960) and Sewell and Shah (1968) have shown that parents' expectations for the youths' attainments are important influences on later aspirations and attainment. Similarly, Cramer (1967), Alexander and Campbell (1964), Campbell and Alexander (1965), Haller and Butterworth (1960), and Duncan et al. (1968) have investigated peer influences on aspirations and attainments. Each of these sets of actors, plus some others, may be seen as a special case of reference group influence. Building on such

thinking, we have concluded that the key variable here is significant others' influence. Significant others are the specific persons from whom the individual obtains his level of aspiration, either because they serve as models or because they communicate to him their expectations for his behavior (Woelfel, 1967). The term "significant others" is more appropriate than that of "reference group" because it eliminates the implication that collectivities such as one's friends, or work groups, or parents are necessarily the influential agents for all individuals. Experimental research, beginning with Sherif's work (1935), has shown the importance of other persons in defining one's own situation. One obtains his social behavior tendencies largely through the influence of others. Herriott (1963) has carried this line of thinking into the present area of research. He has shown that one's conception of the educational behavior others think appropriate to him is highly correlated with his level of educational aspiration. Thus, significant others' influence is a central variable in a social psychological explanation of educational and occupational attainment. It is obviously important to discover the causal paths determining SOI, as well as those by which it exerts its effects on attainment. We hypothesize a substantial direct path (p_{57}) from socioeconomic status (SES) to SOI. We also hypothesize a substantial effect of mental ability on SOI. This is because we expect that the significant others with whom the youth interacts base their expectations for his educational and occupational attainments in part on his demonstrated abilities. In turn, this implies that the path from mental ability (MA) to SOI is indirect by way of academic performance (AP). Thus, we hypothesize the existence of a pronounced path from MA to

AP (p_{68}) and another from AP to SOI (p_{56}). So far we assume that one's grades in school are based on the quality of his performance. A strong undercurrent in the literature seems to have held, however, that the youth's family's SES has a direct influence on his grades (Havighurst and Neugarten, 1957:236–237). To our knowledge, this has not been adequately demonstrated, and in large high schools, often far removed from the youth's home and neighborhood, this may well be debatable. Nevertheless, since it is at least possible that school grades (the evidences of performance) are partly determined by teachers' desires to please prestigious parents or to reward "middle-class" behavior, we have drawn a dotted path (p_{67}) from SES to AP, allowing for the possibility of such an influence.

We hypothesize that the major effects of significant others' influence (SOI) on attainment are mediated by its effects on levels of aspiration. Thus, we have indicated a path (p_{35}) from SOI to level of occupational aspiration (LOA) and another (p_{45}) from SOI to level of educational aspiration (LEA). It is not inconsistent with this to suspect the possibility that SOI might have a direct influence on later educational attainment (EdAtt); we have thus included a dotted or debatable path (p_{25}) from SOI to EdAtt. Because we are here referring to SOI during late high school, it must necessarily refer largely to college education. There is, therefore, no reason to include such a path from SOI to occupational attainment.

Levels of educational aspiration (LEA) and occupational aspiration (LOA) are known to be highly correlated, since education is widely, and to some extent validly, considered to be a necessary condition for high occupational attainment (Haller and Miller, 1963:30, 39–42, 96). But LOA and LEA are not identical. (In these data, $r_{34.5} = r_{WX} = .56$.) We expect that LEA will have a pronounced effect on EdAtt (p_{24}), and that its entire effect on level of occupational attainment will be expressed through EdAtt. On the other hand, we do not hypothesize any effect of LOA on EdAtt which is not already contained in its correlation with LEA. Hence, there is no hypothetical path for LOA to EdAtt. A direct effect of LOA on OccAtt (p_{13}) is hypothesized, however.

There are 26 possible paths, given the sequence laid out above. As one can see by counting the paths (straight lines) in Figure 49.1, we hypothesize noteworthy effects for only eight of these—ten if the dotted lines are counted. If this were a rigorous theoretical model, path coefficients would be calculated only for these eight (or ten) supposed causal connections. We believe that because of the fact that it is not rigorous, and at this stage of our knowledge probably cannot be, it would be well to calculate all of the possible 26 path coefficients, using the calculated values as rough indicators of the influences operating in the system. If the theoretic reasoning is a fair description of the reality to which it is addressed, the path coefficients for the eight (or ten) predicted causal lines should be considerably greater than those for the remainder where no causal prediction was made. Also, it is entirely possible that some unhypothesized causal lines might turn out to be of importance. This, too, argues for calculating the whole set of 26. These data are presented in tabular form in Table 49.3.

Method

In 1957 all high school seniors in Wisconsin responded to an extensive questionnaire concerning their educational and occupational aspirations and a number of potentially related topics. In 1964 one of the authors (Sewell) directed a follow-up in which data on later educational and occupational attainments were collected from an approximately one-third random sample of the respondents in the original survey.

This study is concerned with those 929 subjects for whom data are available at both times, in 1957 and 1964, and who (a) are males and (b) whose fathers were farmers in 1957. Zero-order correlations are computed on all 929 cases, using a computer program which accepts missing data. All higher order coefficients are based on 739 cases for whom data on each variable were complete. (The matrices of zero-order correlations between all eight variables for those two sets of cases are practically identical.)

Variables

Level of occupational attainment (X_1—OccAtt) was measured by Duncan's (1961) socioeconomic index of occupational status.

Level of educational attainment (X_2—EdAtt) was operationalized with data obtained in 1964 by dividing the sample into those who have had at least some college education and those who have not had any at all.[1]

Level of occupational aspiration (X_3—LOA) was determined by assigning Duncan's (1961) socioeconomic index scores to the occupation indicated by the respondent as the one he desired to fill in the future.

Level of educational aspiration (X_4—LEA) is a dichotomous variable corresponding to the respondent's statement in 1957 of whether or not he planned to attend college after graduating from high school.

Index of significant others' influence (X_5—SOI) is a simple summated score (range: zero to three) of three variables: (a) The

youth's report of his parents' encouragement for college, dichotomized according to whether or not the respondent perceived direct parental encouragement for going to college. (b) The youth's report of his teachers' encouragement for college, dichotomized in a similar manner, according to whether or not direct teacher encouragement for college was perceived by the respondent. (c) Friends' college plans, dichotomized according to the respondent's statement that most of his close friends planned or did not plan to go to college. These variables, all emphasizing education, were combined because they reflect the same conceptual dimension, and that dimension is theoretically more relevant than any of its component parts. That the three components do in fact measure the same dimension is attested by the positive correlations among them and a subsequent factor analysis. These correlations and the correlation of each with the summated variable, significant others' influence, are shown in Table 49.1. It may be relevant to point out the composition of this significant others' index in the light of Kelley's distinction (1952). Clearly, the perceptions of direct parental and teacher pressures toward college conform to the classic case of normative reference groups. The educational plans of close friends, on the other hand, may be thought of as having mixed functions. First, close peer groups may exercise pressure toward conformity, and second, friends' plans also serve for the individual's cognitive comparison of himself with "people like himself." Therefore, though the main character of the dimension indicated by this index is clearly normative, it can be thought of as containing some elements of an evaluative function as well.

Quality of academic performance (X_6—AP) is measured by a reflected arc sine

Table 49.1   Zero-Order Correlations Between Indicators of Significant Others' Influence Regarding College

	Teachers' Influence	Friends' Influence	Index of Significant Others' Influence
Parental Influence	.37	.26	.74
Teachers' Influence	--	.32	.72
Friends' Influence	--	--	.68
Significant Others' Influence	--	--	--

transformation of each student's rank in his high school class.

Socioeconomic status (X_7—SES) is measured by a factor-weighted combination of the education of the respondent's father and mother, his perception of the economic status of the family, his perception of possible parental support should he choose to go to college and the approximate amount of such support, and the occupation of his father.[2]

Measured mental ability (X_8—MA) is indexed by Henmon-Nelson test scores (1942). The data were taken when the youths were in the junior year of high school. The scores, originally recorded as percentile-ranks, were treated with an arc sine transformation to approximate a normal distribution.[3]

Results

The zero-order correlation coefficients among eight variables are presented in Table 49.2. A complete path diagram would involve too many lines to be intelligible, because path coefficients presented in Figure 49.1 were calculated for all 26 possible lines implied in the causal order specified above. With the exception of the theoretically dubious direct path from SES to AP, which turned out to be $p_{67} = .01$, each of the path coefficients for causal lines hypothesized in Figure 49.1 is larger than

those not hypothesized. Both sets of standardized beta (or path) coefficients are presented in Table 49.3.

This table shows that the reasoning presented in the above section, offering a social psychological explanation for educational and occupational attainment, cannot be too far off the mark. We had hypothesized that SOI (significant others' influence) was of central importance. In fact, it has notable direct effects on three subsequent variables, each of which bears ultimately on prestige level of occupational attainment. Both theory and data agree that SOI has direct effects on levels of educational and occupational aspiration, as well as educational (i.e., college) attainment. In turn, each aspiration variable appears to have the predicted substantial effects on its respective attainment variable. Looking at its antecedents, we note theory and data again agree that SOI is affected directly by SES and indirectly by measured mental ability through the latter's effect on the youth's academic performance. The latter variable is crucial because it provides (or is correlated with) palpable evidence that significant others can observe and, thus to a degree, align their expectations for the youth with his demonstrated ability.

None of the unpredicted paths is very strong, but we must recognize that there may be more operating in such a system than we were able to anticipate from previ-

Table 49.2   Zero-Order Correlations

	X_1 Occupational Attainment (Prestige Scores: Duncan)	X_2 Educational Attainment (Years College)	X_3 Level of Occupational Aspiration	X_4 Level of Educational Aspiration	X_5 Significant Others' Influence	X_6 Academic Performance (Grade Point)	X_7 Socio-economic Status	X_8 Measured Mental Ability
X_1-Occ. Att.	--	.52	.43	.38	.41	.37	.14	.33
X_2-Ed. Att.	--	--	.53	.61	.57	.48	.23	.40
X_3-LOA	--	--	--	.70	.53	.43	.15	.41
X_4-LEA	--	--	--	--	.59	.46	.26	.40
X_5-SOI	--	--	--	--	--	.49	.29	.41
X_6-AP	--	--	--	--	--	--	.16	.62
X_7-SES	--	--	--	--	--	--	--	.21
X_8-MA	--	--	--	--	--	--	--	--

Table 49.3   Standardized Beta Coefficients for Hypothesized and Non-Hypothesized Causal Paths

Dependent Variables	Independent Variables						
	X_2 EdAtt	X_3 LOA	X_4 LEA	X_5 SOI	X_6 AP	X_7 SES	X_8 MA
X_6 AP	--	--	--	--	--	(.01)	.62
X_5 SOI	--	--	--	--	.39	.21	.13
X_4 LEA	--	--	--	.45	.18	.07	.08
X_3 LOA	--	--	--	.42	.12	−.02	.16
X_2 EdAtt	--	.07	.34	(.23)	.17	.05	.03
X_1 OccAtt	.38	.19	−.10	.11	.06	.00	.04

Figures in italics are coefficients for paths hypothesized in Figure 49.1.

Figures in parentheses refer to theoretically debatable causal lines.

ous thinking. There is a pair of perhaps consequential direct paths from academic performance to educational aspiration (p_{46} = .18) and to educational attainment (p_{26} = .17). There are several possibilities. The data might imply the existence of a mediating factor, such as one's self conception of his ability, a factor which could influence both educational aspirations and attainment. They also suggest that not all of the effect of ability on educational aspiration and attainments is mediated by SOI. Finally, one's ability may exert a continuing effect on his educational attainments quite apart from the mediation of either significant others or aspirations—and therefore apart from one's conception of his ability. Arguments such as these, however, should not be pressed too far because the figures are small. Another unexpected but noteworthy path links mental ability directly to level of occupational aspiration. We offer no speculation regarding it.

So far we have seen that a consistent and plausible social psychological position is at least moderately well borne out by the analysis of lines of apparent influence of its variables when they are arranged in causal order. How well does the total set of independent variables work in accounting for variance in the attainment variables? In brief, $R^2_{1.2345678}$ = .34 and $R^2_{2.345678}$ = .50. Thus, the variables account for 34 percent of the variance in level of occupational attainment and 50 percent of the variance in level of educational attainment. Obviously, variables X_3 through X_8 are much more effective in accounting for educational attainment than in accounting for occupational attainment. Indeed, educational attainment alone accounts for 27 percent of the variance in occupational attainment (from Table 49.3, r^2_{12} = .52² = .27). What we have here, then, is a plausible causal system functioning primarily to explain variation in educational attainment. This, in turn, has considerable effect on occupational attainment. The same set of variables adds a small but useful amount to the explanation of occupational attainment variance beyond that contributed by its explanation of educational attainment.[4]

Discussion and Conclusions

Using father's occupational prestige, the person's educational attainment, and his first job level, Blau and Duncan (1967:165–172) were able to account for 33 percent of the variance in occupational attainment of a nationwide sample of American men. Neither our sample nor our variables are identical with theirs; so it is impossible to assess the total contribution of this study to the state of knowledge as reflected in their work. Educational attainment is strategic in both studies and in this regard the studies are fairly comparable. The present model adds a great deal to the explanation of the social psychological factors affecting that variable. The prospects seem good, too, that if the present model were to be applied to a sample coming from a wider range of the American stratification system with greater age variation, it might prove to be more powerful than it appears with our sample of young farm-reared men. In general, the present take-off on the Blau-Duncan approach to occupational attainment levels seems worthy of further testing and elaboration.

Several comments are appropriate regarding the social psychological position and data presented here. (1) Clearly, the variable we have called significant others' influence is an important factor. The present evidence appears to show that once formed its effects are far-reaching. Also, besides being a powerful explanatory factor, significant others' influence should be amenable to manipulation. It thus suggests itself as a point at which external agents might intervene to change educational and occupational attainment levels. This means that at least part of the system is theoretically amenable to experimental testing. The parts of the present model which are hypothetically dependent upon this variable might be more securely tested if such experiments can be worked out. Also, practical change agents might be able to change levels of attainment, either by inserting themselves or others as new significant others or by changing the expectations existing significant others have for the individual. There may well be a substantial pay-off from more refined work with this variable.

(2) The results seem to indicate, too, that aspirations (a special class of attitudes) are in fact performing mediational functions in transmitting anterior factors into subsequent behaviors. This has been a subject of recent debate, much of which has in effect held that attitudinal variables are useless epiphenomena. This was recently discussed by Fendrich (1967).

Such encouraging results do not, however, mitigate the need for (a) general experimental determination of the supposed effects of attitudes on behaviors, and (b) specific experimental determination of the effects of aspirations on attainments.

(3) The question may be raised as to the extent to which this system is inherently culture-bound. One might wonder whether attainment behavior within an institutionalized pattern of "sponsored" rather than "contest" achievement (Turner, 1960) would change the path model. Besides this (and perhaps other institutionalized types of achievement patterns), there is also the question of the relevance of the model for ascribed occupational attainment systems. Obviously we do not have data bearing on these questions but we may at least discuss them. Let us suppose that the same eight variables are measured on youth in a "sponsored" achievement context. We speculate that if measured mental ability is the basis of selection of those who are to be advanced, then the direct path from mental ability to significant others' influence would increase because sponsors are significant others. (This would require a more general measure of significant others' influence than was used here.) If a variable other

than mental ability or socioeconomic status is important to the sponsors, then the residual effect of unmeasured variables on significant others' influence would increase. Since one's sponsors presumably influence one's aspirations and aspirations in turn mediate attainment, the rest of the model probably would not change much.

Consider the case of ascribed attainment. Here one's parents' position determines what one's significant others will expect of one; mental ability is either irrelevant or controlled by family position; and one's aspirations are controlled by the family. The importance of higher education may vary among basically ascribed systems: in one it may be unimportant, in another it may merely validate one's status, or in still another it may train ascribed elites to fulfill the key social roles in the society. If educational attainment is important within the social system, aspirations will mediate the influence of significant others upon it, and it in turn will mediate occupational attainment. If not, occupational aspirations will mediate occupational attainment and educational attainment will drop out of the path model. In short, by allowing for variations in the path coefficients, the same basic social psychological model might work well to describe attainment in stratification and mobility systems quite different from that of the present sample.

(4) The linear model used here seems to be an appropriate way to operationalize social psychological positions holding that the function of "intervening" attitudinal variables is to mediate the influence of more fundamental social structural and psychological variables on behavior. By assuming linear relations among variables and applying a path system to the analysis, we have cast the attainment problem in

such a framework. It seems to have worked quite well. We are sufficiently encouraged by this attempt to recommend that a parallel tack might be made on problems in which the overt behavior variables are quite different from educational and occupational attainment.

(5) Nonetheless, satisfactory as such a linear model and its accompanying theory seems to be, there is still the possibility that other techniques flowing from somewhat different social psychological assumptions might be better. It is possible that, in the action situation, enduring attitudes (such as educational and occupational aspirations) may function as independent forces which express themselves in relevant overt behaviors to the degree that other personality and situational variables permit. Linear models would thus be effective to the degree that the persons modify their aspirations to bring them in line with potentials for action offered by the latter variables. More importantly, the combined effects of aspirational and facilitational variables would produce nonlinear accelerating curves of influence on behavior variables. For the present types of data, this would imply that parental stratification position, mental ability, and significant others' influence not only produce aspirations, but also, to the extent to which these influences continue more or less unchanged on into early adulthood, they function as differential facilitators for the expression of aspirations in attainments. If this is true, a nonlinear system of statistical analysis handling interaction effects would be even more powerful than the one used in this paper.

(6) It should be remembered that the most highly educated of these young men had just begun their careers when the final data were collected. If the distance between

them and the less educated widens, the occupational attainment variance accounted for by the model may well increase. The direct relations of some of the antecedents to occupational attainment may also change. In particular, mental ability may show a higher path to occupational attainment.

(7) Finally, although the results reported in this paper indicate that the proposed model has considerable promise for explaining educational and early occupational attainment of farm boys, its adequacy should now be tested on populations with a more differentiated socioeconomic background. It is quite possible that in such populations the effects of socioeconomic status on subsequent variables may be significantly increased. The effects of other variables in the system may also be altered when the model is applied to less homogeneous populations.

The present research appears to have extended knowledge of the causal mechanism influencing occupational attainment. Most of this was accomplished by providing a consistent social psychological model which adds to our ability to explain what is surely one of its key proximal antecedents, educational attainment.

NOTES

Revision of paper originally prepared for delivery at the joint sessions of the Rural Sociological Society and the American Sociological Association, San Francisco, August 1967. The research reported here was supported by the University of Wisconsin Graduate School, by the Cooperative State Research Service, and the University's College of Agriculture for North Central Regional Research Committee NC–86, by funds to the Institute for Research on Poverty at the University of Wisconsin provided by the Office of Economic Opportunity pursuant to the provisions of the Economic Opportunity Act of 1964, and by a grant from the National Institute of Health, U. S. Public Health Service (M–6275). The writers wish to thank Otis Dudley Duncan for his careful reading and incisive criticisms and Vimal P. Shah for help in the statistical analysis. The conclusions are the full responsibility of the authors.

1. It is important to note that the timing of the follow-up was such as to allow most individuals to complete their education up to the bachelor's degree and beyond. It is unlikely that the educational attainment of the sample as a whole will change much in the years to come. On the other hand, while the span of seven years allowed those individuals who did not continue their education to find a stable position in the occupational structure and even improve upon it, there was not enough time for those who continued their education to do the same. A few of the latter were still in school; most had just begun their occupational careers. It is therefore possible that a follow-up taken five or ten years from now would show greater differentiation in attainments as the educated group gathers momentum and moves up in the occupational world.

2. Naturally, father's occupation is a constant in this subsample of farm-reared males. It is important to note that the SES mean and standard deviations for this subsample are considerably lower than for the total sample. The low and homogeneous SES levels of this subsample may yield atypical relations among the variables.

3. Our previous research (Sewell and Armer, 1966; Haller and Sewell, 1967) has led us to be skeptical of claims that local ecological and school class compositional factors influence aspirations and attainments. Nevertheless the zero-order intercorrelations of five such variables and their correlations with X_1–X_8 are available (although they are not presented here). Two of these pertain to the county in which the youth attended high school: county level of living and degree of urbanization. Three pertain to his high school senior class: average SES of the class, percentage of the class members whose fathers attended college, and percentage of the class members whose fathers had professional-level

occupations. Though substantially correlated with each other, the variables are uncorrelated with the variables in the above model.

4. Some readers will be interested in the path coefficients as calculated only for the lines hypothesized in the diagram. For this reason and because of the diagram's parsimony, we have calculated the values for each of its eight paths (or ten, including dubious ones). The restricted model explains 47 and 33 percent of the variance in X_2 and X_1, respectively. Data not presented here show that the model reproduces the zero-order correlation matrix quite well. For this reason and because the model is an effective predictor of X_2 and X_1, it may be considered to be fairly valid. Nonetheless, it seems more prudent to rest our case on the less presumptuous data already presented in Table 49.3. This is why the coefficients presented in the diagram are not discussed here.

REFERENCES

Alexander, C. Norman, Jr., and Ernest Q. Campbell. 1964. "Peer influences on adolescent educational aspirations and attainments." American Sociological Review 29 (August):568–575.

Blau, Peter M., and Otis Dudley Duncan. 1967. The American Occupational Structure. New York: Wiley.

Bordua, David J. 1960. "Educational aspirations and parental stress on college." Social Forces 38 (March):262–269.

Brookover, Wilbur B., Jean M. LePere, Don E. Hamachek, Shailer Thomas, and Edsel L. Erickson. 1965. Self-Concept of Ability and School Achievement. East Lansing: Michigan State University, Bureau of Educational Research Services.

Campbell, Ernest Q., and C. Norman Alexander. 1965. "Structural effects and interpersonal relationships." American Journal of Sociology 71 (November):284–289.

Cramer, M. R. 1967. "The relationship between educational and occupational plans of high school students." Paper presented at the meeting of the Southern Sociological Society, Atlanta (unpublished).

Duncan, Otis Dudley. 1961. "A socioeconomic index for all occupations." Pp. 109–138 in Albert J. Reiss, Jr. (ed.), Occupations and Social Status. New York: Free Press.

_____. 1968. "Ability and achievement." Eugenics Quarterly 15 (March):1–11.

_____. 1969. "Contingencies in the construction of causal models." Edgar F. Borgatta, (ed.), Sociological Methodology. San Francisco: Jossey-Bass.

Duncan, Otis Dudley, Archibald O. Haller, and Alejandro Portes. 1968. "Peer influences on aspirations: a reinterpretation." American Journal of Sociology 74 (September):119–137.

Fendrich, James M. 1967. "Perceived reference group support: racial attitudes and overt behavior." American Sociological Review 32 (December):960–970.

Gerth, Hans, and C. Wright Mills. 1953. Character and Social Structure. New York: Harcourt, Brace and World.

Gross, Neal, Ward S. Mason, and Alexander W. McEachern. 1958. Explorations in Role Analysis. New York: Wiley.

Haller, Archibald O. 1966. "Occupational choices of rural youth." Journal of Cooperative Extension 4 (Summer):93–102.

Haller, Archibald O., and Charles E. Butterworth. 1960. "Peer influences on levels of occupational and educational aspiration." Social Forces 38 (May):289–295.

Haller, Archibald O., and Irwin W. Miller. 1963. The Occupational Aspiration Scale: Theory, Structure and Correlates. East Lansing: Michigan Agricultural Experiment Station Bulletin 288.

Haller, Archibald O., and William H. Sewell. 1967. "Occupational choices of Wisconsin farm boys." Rural Sociology 32 (March):37–55.

Havighurst, Robert J., and Bernice L. Neugarten. 1957. Society and Education. Boston: Allyn and Bacon.

Heise, David R. 1969. "Problems in path analysis and causal inference." Edgar F. Borgatta, (ed.), Sociological Methodology. San Francisco: Jossey-Bass.

Henmon, V. A. C., and M. J. Nelson. 1942. The Henmon-Nelson Test of Mental Ability. Boston: Houghton Mifflin Company.

Herriott, Robert E. 1963. "Some social determinants of educational aspiration." Harvard Educational Review 33 (Spring):157–177.

Kelley, Harold H. 1952. "Two functions of reference groups." Pp. 410–414 in Guy E. Swanson et al. (eds.), Readings in Social Psychology. New York: Henry Holt and Company.

Kuvlesky, William P., and George W. Ohlendorf. 1967. A Bibliography of Literature on Status Projections of Youth: I. Occupational Aspirations and Expectations. College Station: Texas A&M University, Department of Agricultural Economics and Sociology.

Lipset, Seymour M., and Reinhard Bendix. 1959. Social Mobility in Industrial Society. Berkeley: University of California Press.

Merton, Robert K. 1957. Social Theory and Social Structure. New York: Free Press.

Miller, I. W., and Archibald O. Haller. 1964. "The measurement of level of occupational aspiration." Personnel and Guidance Journal 42 (January):448–455.

Ohlendorf, George W., Sherry Wages, and William P. Kuvlesky. 1967. A Bibliography of Literature on Status Projections of Youth: II. Educational Aspirations and Expectations. College Station: Texas A & M University, Department of Agricultural Economics and Sociology.

Parsons, Talcott. 1959. "The school class as a social system." Harvard Educational Review 29 (Summer):297–318.

Portes, Alejandro, Archibald O. Haller, and William H. Sewell. 1968. "Professional executive vs. farming as unique occupational choices." Rural Sociology 33 (June):153–159.

Sewell, William H. 1964. "Community of residence and college plans." American Sociological Review 29 (February):24–38.

Sewell, William H., and J. Michael Armer. 1966. "Neighborhood context and college plans." American Sociological Review 31 (April): 159–168.

Sewell, William H., Archibald O. Haller, and Murray A. Straus. 1957. "Social status and educational and occupational aspiration." American Sociological Review 22 (February):67–73.

Sewell, William H., and Alan M. Orenstein. 1965. "Community of residence and occupational choice." American Journal of Sociology 70 (March):551–563.

Sewell, William H., and Vimal P. Shah. 1967. "Socioeconomic status, intelligence, and the attainment of higher education." Sociology of Education 40 (Winter):1–23.

_____. 1968. "Social class, parental encouragement, and educational aspirations." American Journal of Sociology 73 (March):559–572.

Sherif, Muzafer. 1935. "A study of some social factors in perception." Archives of Psychology Number 187.

Super, Donald E. 1957. The Psychology of Careers. New York: Harper.

Turner, Ralph H. 1960. "Sponsored and contest mobility and the school system." American Sociological Review 25 (December):855–867.

Woelfel, Joseph. 1967. "A paradigm for research on significant others." Paper presented at the Joint Session of the Society for the Study of Social Problems and the American Sociological Association, San Francisco (unpublished).

Wright, Sewall. 1934. "The method of path coefficients." Annals of Mathematical Statistics 5 (September):161–215.

_____. 1960. "Path coefficients and regression coefficients: alternative or complementary concept?" Biometrics 16 (June):189–202.

50

Ain't No Makin' It

Leveled Aspirations in a Low-Income Neighborhood

JAY MACLEOD

"Any child can grow up to be president." So maintains the dominant ideology in the United States. This perspective characterizes American society as an open one in which barriers to success are mainly personal rather than social. In this meritocratic view, education ensures equality of opportunity for all individuals, and economic inequalities result from differences in natural qualities and in one's motivation and will to work. Success is based on achievement rather than ascription. Individuals do not inherit their social status—they attain it on their own. Because schooling mitigates gender, class, and racial barriers to success, the ladder of social mobility is there for all to climb. A favorite Hollywood theme, the rags-to-riches story resonates in the psyche of the American people. We never tire of hearing about Andrew Carnegie, for his experience validates much that we hold dear about America, the land of opportunity. Horatio Alger's accounts of the spectacular

mobility achieved by men of humble origins through their own unremitting efforts occupy a treasured place in our national folklore. The American Dream is held out as a genuine prospect for anyone with the drive to achieve it.

"I ain't goin' to college. Who wants to go to college? I'd just end up gettin' a shitty job anyway." So says Freddie Piniella,[1] an intelligent eleven-year-old boy from Clarendon Heights, a low-income housing development in a northeastern city. This statement, pronounced with certitude and feeling, completely contradicts our achievement ideology. Freddie is pessimistic about his prospects for social mobility and disputes schooling's capacity to "deliver the goods." Such a view offends our sensibilities and seems a rationalization. But Freddie has a point. What of Carnegie's grammar school classmates, the great bulk of whom no doubt were left behind to occupy positions in the class structure not much differ-

Jay MacLeod, *Ain't No Makin' It: Leveled Aspirations in a Low-Income Neighborhood* (Boulder: Westview Press, 1987), pp. 1–2, 4–5, 8, 60–63, 69–75, 78–79, 81, 137–141, 162. Copyright © 1987 by Westview Press, Inc. Reprinted by permission of Westview Press, Inc., a member of the Perseus Books Group. The postscript to this selection is taken from *Ain't No Makin' It: Leveled Aspirations in a Low-Income Neighborhood* (Boulder: Westview Press, 1995), pp. 155, 169–170, 196, 240–241. Copyright © 1995 by Westview Press, Inc. Reprinted by permission of Westview Press, Inc., a member of the Perseus Books Group.

ent from those held by their parents? What about the static, nearly permanent element in the working class, whose members consider the chances for mobility remote and thus despair of all hope? These people are shunned, hidden, forgotten—and for good reason—because just as the self-made man is a testament to certain American ideals, so the very existence of an "underclass" in American society is a living contradiction to those ideals.

Utter hopelessness is the most striking aspect of Freddie's outlook. Erik H. Erikson writes that hope is the basic ingredient of all vitality;[2] stripped of hope, there is little left to lose. How is it that in contemporary America a boy of eleven can feel bereft of a future worth embracing? This is not what the United States is supposed to be. The United States is the nation of hopes and dreams and opportunity. As Ronald Reagan remarked in his 1985 State of the Union Address, citing the accomplishments of a young Vietnamese immigrant, "Anything is possible in America if we have the faith, the will, and the heart."[3] But to Freddie Piniella and many other Clarendon Heights young people who grow up in households where their parents and older siblings are unemployed, undereducated, or imprisoned, Reagan's words ring hollow. For them the American Dream, far from being a genuine prospect, is not even a dream. It is a hallucination.

I first met Freddie Piniella in the summer of 1981 when as a student at a nearby university I worked as a counselor in a youth enrichment program in Clarendon Heights. For ten weeks I lived a few blocks from the housing project and worked intensively with nine boys, aged eleven to thirteen. While engaging them in recreational and educational activities, I was surprised by the modesty of their aspirations. The world of middle-class work was entirely alien to them; they spoke about employment in construction, factories, the armed forces, or, predictably, professional athletics. In an ostensibly open society, they were a group of boys whose occupational aspirations did not even cut across class lines. . . .

The male teenage world of Clarendon Heights is populated by two divergent peer groups. The first group, dubbed the Hallway Hangers because of the group's propensity for "hanging" in a particular hallway in the project [i.e., outside doorway #13], consists predominantly of white boys. Their characteristics and attitudes stand in marked contrast to the second group, which is composed almost exclusively of black youths who call themselves the Brothers. Surprisingly, the Brothers speak with relative optimism about their futures, while the Hallway Hangers are despondent about their prospects for social mobility. . . .

Before describing the boys' orientation toward work [in more detail], I would like to make an analytical distinction between aspirations and expectations. Both involve assessments of one's desires, abilities, and the character of the opportunity structure. In articulating one's aspirations, an individual weighs his or her preferences more heavily; expectations are tempered by perceived capabilities and available opportunities. Aspirations are one's preferences relatively unsullied by anticipated constraints; expectations take these constraints squarely into account.[4]

The Hallway Hangers: Keeping a Lid on Hope

Conventional, middle-class orientations toward employment are inadequate to describe the Hallway Hangers' approach to work. The notion of a career, a set of jobs that are connected to one another in a logical progression, has little relevance to these boys. They are hesitant when asked about their aspirations and expectations. This hesitancy is not the result of indecision; rather it stems from the fact that these boys see little choice involved in getting a job. No matter how hard I pressed him, for instance, Jinks refused to articulate his aspirations: "I think you're kiddin' yourself to have any. We're just gonna take whatever we can get." Jinks is a perceptive boy, and his answer seems to be an accurate depiction of the situation. Beggars cannot be choosers, and these boys have nothing other than unskilled labor to offer on a credential-based job market.

It is difficult to gauge the aspirations of most of the Hallway Hangers. Perhaps at a younger age they had dreams for their futures. At ages sixteen, seventeen, and eighteen, however, their own job experiences as well as those of family members have contributed to a deeply entrenched cynicism about their futures. What is perceived as the cold, hard reality of the job market weighs very heavily on the Hallway Hangers; they believe their preferences will have almost no bearing on the work they actually will do. Their expectations are not merely tempered by perceptions of the opportunity structure; even their aspirations are crushed by their estimation of the job market. These generalizations may seem bold and rather extreme, but they do not lack ethnographic support.

The pessimism and uncertainty with which the Hallway Hangers view their futures emerge clearly when the boys are asked to speculate on what their lives will be like in twenty years.

(all in separate interviews)

STONEY: Hard to say. I could be dead tomorrow. Around here, you gotta take life day by day.

BOO-BOO: I dunno. I don't want to think about it. I'll think about it when it comes.

FRANKIE: I don't fucking know. Twenty years. I may be fucking dead. I live a day at a time. I'll probably be in the fucking pen.

SHORTY: Twenty years? I'm gonna be in jail.

These responses are striking not only for the insecurity and despondency they reveal, but also because they do not include any mention of work. It is not that work is unimportant—for people as strapped for money as the Hallway Hangers are, work is crucial. Rather, these boys are indifferent to the issue of future employment. Work is a given; they all hope to hold jobs of one kind or another in order to support themselves and their families. But the Hallway Hangers believe the character of work, at least all work in which they are likely to be involved, is essentially the same: boring, undifferentiated, and unrewarding. Thinking about their future jobs is a useless activity for the Hallway Hangers. What is there to think about?

For Steve and Jinks, although they do see themselves employed in twenty years, work is still of tangential importance.

JM: If you had to guess, what do you think you'll be doing twenty years from now?

(in separate interviews)

STEVE: I don't fucking know. Working probably. Have my own pad, my own house. Bitches, kids. Fucking fridge full of brewskies. Fine wife, likes to get laid.

JINKS: Twenty years from now? Probably kicked back in my own apartment doing the same shit I'm doing now—getting high. I'll have a job, if I'm not in the service, if war don't break out, if I'm not dead. I just take one day at a time.

Although the Hallway Hangers expect to spend a good portion of their waking hours on the job, work is important to them not as an end in itself, but solely as a means to an end—money.

In probing the occupational aspirations and expectations of the Hallway Hangers, I finally was able to elicit from them some specific hopes. Although Shorty never mentions his expectations, the rest of the Hallway Hangers have responded to my prodding with some definite answers. The range of answers as well as how they change over time are as significant as the particular hopes each boy expresses.

Boo-Boo's orientation toward work is typical of the Hallway Hangers. He has held a number of jobs in the past, most of them in the summer. During his freshman year in high school Boo-Boo worked as a security guard at school for $2.50 an hour in order to make restitution for a stolen car he damaged. Boo-Boo also has worked on small-scale construction projects through a summer youth employment program called Just-A-Start, at a pipe manufacturing site, and as a clerk in a gift shop. Boo-Boo wants to be an automobile mechanic. Upon graduating from high school, he studied auto mechanics at a technical school on a scholarship. The only black student in his class, Boo-Boo was expelled early in his first term after racial antagonism erupted into a fight.

Boo-Boo was not altogether disappointed, for he already was unhappy with what he considered the program's overly theoretical orientation. (Howard London found this kind of impatience typical of working-class students in the community college he studied.[5]) Boo-Boo wanted hands-on training, but "all's they were doing was telling me about how it's made, stuff like that." Boo-Boo currently is unemployed, but he recently had a chance for a job as a cook's helper. Although he was not hired, the event is significant nevertheless because prior to the job interview, Boo-Boo claimed that his ambition now was to work in a restaurant. Here we have an example of the primacy of the opportunity structure in determining the aspirations of the Hallway Hangers. One job opening in another field was so significant that the opening prompted Boo-Boo to redefine totally his aspirations.

In contrast to the rest of the Hallway Hangers who are already on the job market, Steve wants to stay in school for the two years required to get his diploma. Yet he has a similar attitude toward his future work as do the other youths. He quit his summer job with the Just-A-Start program and has no concrete occupational aspirations. As for expectations, he believes he might enlist in the Air Force after graduation but adds, "I dunno. I might just go up and see my uncle, do some fuckin' construction or something."

Many of these boys expect to enter military service. Jinks and Frankie mention it as an option; Stoney has tried to enlist, but without success. Although Jinks refuses to think in terms of aspirations, he will say what he expects to do after he finishes school.

JM: What are you gonna do when you get out?

JINKS: Go into the service, like everybody else. The navy.

JM: What about after that?

JINKS: After that, just get a job, live around here.

JM: Do you have any idea what job you wanna get?

JINKS: No. No particular job. Whatever I can get.

Jinks subsequently quit school. He had been working twenty hours a week making clothes-racks in a factory with his brother. He left school with the understanding that he would be employed full-time, and he was mildly content with his situation: "I got a job. It ain't a good job, but other things will come along." Two weeks later, he was laid off. For the past three months he has been unemployed, hanging full-time in doorway #13.

Shorty has worked construction in the past and has held odd jobs such as shoveling snow. Shorty, an alcoholic, has trouble holding down a steady job, as he freely admits. He was enrolled in school until recently. Ordered by the court to a detoxification center, Shorty apparently managed to convince the judge that he had attended enough Alcoholics Anonymous meetings in the meantime to satisfy the court. He has not returned to school since, nor has he landed a job. Given that Shorty is often on the run from the police, he is too preoccupied with pressing everyday problems to give serious thought to his long-term future. It is not surprising that my ill-timed query about his occupational aspirations met with only an impatient glare. . . .

The definitions of aspirations and expectations given [earlier] suggest that an assessment of the opportunity structure and of one's capabilities impinge on one's preferences for the future. However, the portrait of the Hallway Hangers painted in these pages makes clear that "impinge" is not a strong enough word. But are the leveled aspirations and pessimistic expectations of the Hallway Hangers a result of strong negative assessments of their capabilities or of the opportunity structure?

This is not an easy question to answer. Doubtless, both factors come into play, but in the case of the Hallway Hangers, evaluation of the opportunity structure has the dominant role. Although in a discussion of why they do not succeed in school, the Hallway Hangers point to personal inadequacy ("We're all just fucking burnouts"; "We never did good anyways"), they look to outside forces as well. In general, they are confident of their own abilities.

(*In a group interview*)

JM: If you've got five kids up the high school with all A's, now are you gonna be able to say that any of them are smarter than any of you?

SLICK: (*immediately*) No.

JM: So how'd that happen?

SLICK: Because they're smarter in some areas just like we're smarter in some areas. You put them out here, right? And you put us up where they're living—they won't be able to survive out here.

SHORTY: But we'd be able to survive up there.

FRANKIE: See, what it is—they're smarter more academically because they're taught by teachers that teach academics.

JM: Not even streetwise, just academically, do you think you could be up where they are?

FRANKIE: Yeah.

CHRIS: Yeah.

SHORTY: Yeah.

JM: When it comes down to it, you're just as smart?

FRANKIE: Yeah.

SLICK: (*matter-of-factly*) We could be smarter.

FRANKIE: Definitely.

CHRIS: On the street, like.

FRANKIE: We're smart, we're smart, but we're just smart [inaudible]. It's fucking, y'know, we're just out to make money, man. I know if I ever went to fucking high school and college in a business course. . . .

SLICK: And concentrated on studying. . . .

FRANKIE: I know I could make it. I am a businessman.

JM: So all of you are sure that if you put out in school. . . .

FRANKIE: Yeah! If I went into business, I would, yeah. If I had the fucking money to start out with like some of these fucking rich kids, I'd be a millionaire. Fucking right I would be.

Although these comments were influenced by the dynamics of the group interview, they jibe with the general sense of self-confidence the Hallway Hangers radiate and indicate that they do not have low perceptions of their own abilities.

If their assessments of their own abilities do not account for the low aspirations of the Hallway Hangers, we are left, by way of explanation, with their perceptions of the job opportunity structure. The dominant view in the United States is that American society is an open one that values and differentially rewards individuals on the basis of their merits. The Hallway Hangers question this view, for it runs against the grain of their neighbors' experiences, their families' experiences, and their own encounters with the labor market.

The Clarendon Heights community, as a public housing development, is by definition made up of individuals who do not hold even modestly remunerative jobs. A large majority are on additional forms of public assistance; many are unemployed. Like most old housing projects, Clarendon Heights tends to be a cloistered, insular neighborhood, isolated from the surrounding community. Although younger residents certainly have external points of reference, their horizons are nevertheless very narrow. Their immediate world is composed almost entirely of people who have not "made it." To look around at a great variety of people—some lazy, some alcoholics, some energetic, some dedicated, some clever, some resourceful—and to realize all of them have been unsuccessful on the job market is powerful testimony against what is billed as an open society.

The second and much more intimate contact these boys have with the job market is through their families, whose occupational histories only can be viewed as sad and disillusioning by the Hallway Hangers. These are not people who are slothful or slow-witted; rather, they are generally industrious, intelligent, and very willing to work. With members of their families holding low-paying, unstable jobs or unable to find work at all, the Hallway Hangers are unlikely to view the job opportunity structure as an open one.

The third level of experience on which the Hallway Hangers draw is their own. These boys are not newcomers to the job market. As we have seen, all have held a variety of jobs. All except Steve are now on the job market year round, but only Stoney has a steady job. With the exceptions of Chris, who presently is satisfied with his success peddling drugs, and Steve, who is still in school, the Hallway Hangers are actively in search of decent work. Although they always seem to be following up on some promising lead, they are all unemployed. Furthermore, some who were counting on prospective employment have had their hopes dashed when it fell through. The work they have been able to secure typically has been in menial, dead-end jobs paying minimum wage.

Thus, their personal experience on the job market and the experiences of their family members and their neighbors have taught the Hallway Hangers that the job market does not necessarily reward talent or effort. Neither they nor their parents, older siblings, and friends have shared in the "spoils" of economic success. In short, the Hallway Hangers are under no illusions about the openness of the job opportunity structure. They are conscious, albeit vaguely, of a number of class-based obstacles to economic and social advancement. Slick, the most perceptive and articulate of the Hallway Hangers, points out particular barriers they must face.

SLICK: Out here, there's not the opportunity to make money. That's how you get into stealin' and all that shit.

(in a separate interview)
SLICK: That's why I went into the army—cuz there's no jobs out here right now

for people that, y'know, live out here. You have to know somebody, right?

In discussing the problems of getting a job, both Slick and Shorty are vocal.

SLICK: All right, to get a job, first of all, this is a handicap, out here. If you say you're from the projects or anywhere in this area, that can hurt you. Right off the bat: reputation.
SHORTY: Is this dude gonna rip me off, is he. . . .
SLICK: Is he gonna stab me?
SHORTY: Will he rip me off? Is he gonna set up the place to do a score or somethin'? I tried to get a couple of my buddies jobs at a place where I was working construction, but the guy says, "I don't want 'em if they're from there. I know you; you ain't a thief or nothing."

Frankie also points out the reservations prospective employers have about hiring people who live in Clarendon Heights. "A rich kid would have a better chance of getting a job than me, yeah. Me, from where I live, y'know, a high crime area, I was prob'ly crime-breaking myself, which they think your nice honest rich kid from a very respected family would never do."

Frankie also feels that he is discriminated against because of the reputation that attaches to him because of his brothers' illegal exploits. "Especially me, like I've had a few opportunities for a job, y'know. I didn't get it cuz of my name, because of my brothers, y'know. So I was deprived right there, bang. Y'know they said, 'No, no, no, we ain't havin' no Dougherty work for us.'" In a separate discussion, Frankie again makes this point. Arguing that he would have almost no chance to be hired as a fireman, despite ostensibly meritocratic hiring procedures, even if he scored very highly on the test, Frankie concludes, "Just cuz fuckin' where I'm from and what my name is."

The Hallway Hangers' belief that the opportunity structure is not open also emerges when we consider their responses to the question of whether they have the same chance as a middle- or upper-class boy to get a good job. The Hallway Hangers generally respond in the negative. When pushed to explain why, Jinks and Steve made these responses, which are typical.

(in separate interviews)
JINKS: Their parents got pull and shit.
STEVE: Their fucking parents know people.

Considering the boys' employment experiences and those of their families, it is not surprising that the Hallway Hangers' view of the job market does not conform to the dominant belief in the openness of the opportunity structure. They see a job market where rewards are based not on meritocratic criteria, but on "who you know." If "connections" are the keys to success, the Hallway Hangers know that they are in trouble.

Aside from their assessment of the job opportunity structure, the Hallway Hangers are aware of other forces weighing on their futures. A general feeling of despondency pervades the group. As Slick puts it, "The younger kids have nothing to hope for." The Hallway Hangers often draw attention to specific incidents that support their general and vague feelings of hopelessness and of the futility of nurturing aspirations or high expectations. Tales of police

brutality, of uncaring probation officers and callous judges, and of the "pull and hookups of the rich kids" all have a common theme, which Chris summarizes, "We don't get a fair shake and shit." Although they sometimes internalize the blame for their plight (Boo-Boo: "I just screwed up"; Chris: "I guess I just don't have what it takes"; Frankie: "We've just fucked up"), the Hallway Hangers also see, albeit in a vague and imprecise manner, a number of hurdles in their path to success with which others from higher social strata do not have to contend.

Insofar as contemporary conditions under capitalism can be conceptualized as a race by the many for relatively few positions of wealth and prestige, the low aspirations of the Hallway Hangers, more than anything else, seem to be a decision, conscious or unconscious, to withdraw from the running. The competition, they reason, is not a fair one when some people have an unobstructed lane. As Frankie maintains, the Hallway Hangers face numerous barriers: "It's a steeplechase, man. It's a motherfucking steeplechase." The Hallway Hangers respond in a way that suggests only a "sucker" would compete seriously under such conditions.

Chris's perspective seems a poignant, accurate description of the situation in which the Hallway Hangers find themselves.

CHRIS: I gotta get a job, any fucking job. Just a job. Make some decent money. If I could make a hundred bucks a week, I'd work. I just wanna get my mother out of the projects, that's all. But I'm fucking up in school. It ain't easy, Jay. I hang out there [in doorway #13] 'til about one o'clock every night. I never want to go to school. I'd much rather hang out and get high again. It's not that I'm dumb. You gimme thirty bucks today, and I'll give you one hundred tomorrow. I dunno. It's like I'm in a hole I can't get out of. I guess I could get out, but it's hard as hell. It's fucked up.

The Brothers: Ready at the Starting Line

Just as the pessimism and uncertainty with which the Hallway Hangers view their futures emerges when we consider what they perceive their lives will be like in twenty years, so do the Brothers' long-term visions serve as a valuable backdrop to our discussion of their aspirations. The ethos of the Brothers' peer group is a positive one; they are not resigned to a bleak future but are hoping for a bright one. Nowhere does this optimism surface more clearly than in the Brothers' responses to the question of what they will be doing in twenty years. Note the centrality of work in their views of the future.

(all in separate interviews)

SUPER: I'll have a house, a nice car, no one bothering me. Won't have to take no hard time from no one. Yeah, I'll have a good job, too.

JUAN: I'll have a regular house, y'know, with a yard and everything. I'll have a steady job, a good job. I'll be living the good life, the easy life.

MIKE: I might have a wife, some kids. I might be holding down a regular business job like an old guy. I hope I'll be able to do a lot of skiing and stuff like that when I'm old.

CRAIG: I'll probably be having a good job on my hands, I think. Working in an office as an architect, y'know, with my own drawing board, doing my own stuff, or at least close to there.

James takes a comic look into his future without being prompted to do so. "The ones who work hard in school, eventually it's gonna pay off for them and everything, and they're gonna have a good job and a family and all that. Not me though! I'm gonna have *myself*. I'm gonna have some money. And a different girl every day. And a different car. And be like this (*poses with one arm around an imaginary girl and the other on a steering wheel*)."

The Brothers do not hesitate to name their occupational goals. Although some of the Brothers are unsure of their occupational aspirations, none seems to feel that nurturing an aspiration is a futile exercise. The Brothers have not resigned themselves to taking whatever they can get. Rather, they articulate specific occupational aspirations (although these often are subject to change and revision).

Like all the Brothers, Super has not had extensive experience on the job market; he only has worked at summer jobs. For the past three summers, he has worked for the city doing maintenance work in parks and school buildings through a CETA-sponsored summer youth employment program. During the last year, Super's occupational aspirations have fluctuated widely. His initial desire to become a doctor was met with laughter from his friends. Deterred by their mocking and by a realization of the schooling required to be a doctor, Super immediately decided that he would rather go into business: "Maybe I can own my own shop and shit." This aspiration, however, also was ridiculed. "Yeah, right," commented Mokey, "Super'll be pimping the girls, that kinda business." In private, however, Super still clings to the hope of becoming a doctor, although he cites work in the computer field as a more realistic hope. "Really, I don't know what I should do now. I'm kinda confused. First I said I wanna go into computers, right? Take up that or a doctor." The vagueness of Super's aspirations is important; once again, we get a glimpse of how little is known about the world of middle-class work, even for somebody who clearly aspires to it. Of one thing Super is certain: "I just know I wanna get a good job."

Although Super does not distinguish between what constitutes a good job and what does not, he does allude to criteria by which the quality of a job can be judged. First, a good job must not demand that one "work on your feet," a distinction, apparently, between white and blue-collar work. Second, a good job implies at least some authority in one's workplace, a point Super makes clearly, if in a disjointed manner. "Bosses—if you don't come on time, they yell at you and stuff like that. They want you to do work and not sit down and relax and stuff like that, y'know. I want to try and be a boss, y'know, tell people what to do. See, I don't always want people telling me what to do, y'know—the low rank. I wanna try to be with people in the high rank." Although Super does not know what occupation he would like to enter, he is certain that he wants a job that is relatively high up in a vaguely defined occupational hierarchy. . . .

The Brothers display none of the cockiness about their own capabilities that the Hallway Hangers exhibit. Instead, they attribute lack of success on the job market exclusively to personal inadequacy. This is particularly true when the Brothers speculate about the future jobs the Hallway Hangers and their own friends will have. According to the Brothers, the Hallway Hangers (in Super's words) "ain't gonna get nowhere," not because of the harshness of the job market but because they are personally lacking. The rest of the Brothers share this view.

JM: Some of those guys who hang with Frankie, they're actually pretty smart. They just don't channel that intelligence into school, it seems to me.
CRAIG: I call that stupid, man. That's what they are.
JM: I dunno.
CRAIG: Lazy.

(*in a separate interview*)
SUPER: They think they're so tough they don't have to do work. That don't make sense, really. You ain't gonna get nowhere; all's you gonna do is be back in the projects like your mother. Depend on your mother to give you money every week. You ain't gonna get a good job. As you get older, you'll think about that, y'know. It'll come to your mind. "Wow, I can't believe, I should've just went to school and got my education."

(*in a separate interview*)
MOKEY: They all got attitude problems. They just don't got their shit together. Like Steve. They have to improve themselves.

In the eyes of the Brothers, the Hallway Hangers have attitude problems, are incapable of considering their long-term future, and are lazy or stupid.

Because this evidence is tainted (no love is lost between the two peer groups), it is significant that the Brothers apply the same criteria in judging each other's chances to gain meaningful employment. James thinks Mokey is headed for a dead-end job because he is immature and undisciplined. He also blames Juan for currently being out of work. "Juan's outta school, and Juan does *not* have a job (*said with contempt*). Now that's some kind of a senior. When I'm a senior, I'm gonna have a job already. I can see if you're gonna go to college right when you get out of school; but Juan's not doin' nothin'. He's just stayin' home." Juan, in turn, thinks that Mokey and Super will have difficulty finding valuable work because of their attitudes. He predicts that Derek and Craig will be successful for the same reason.

These viewpoints are consistent with the dominant ideology in America; barriers to success are seen as personal rather than social. By attributing failure to personal inadequacy, the Brothers exonerate the opportunity structure. Indeed, it is amazing how often they affirm the openness of American society.

(*all in separate interviews*)

DEREK: If you put your mind to it, if you want to make a future for yourself, there's no reason why you can't. It's a question of attitude.

SUPER: It's easy to do anything, as long as you set your mind to it, if you wanna do it. If you really want to do it, if you really want to be something. If you don't

want to do it . . . you ain't gonna make it. I gotta get that through my mind: I wanna do it. I wanna be somethin'. I don't wanna be livin' in the projects the rest of my life.

MOKEY: It's not like if they're rich they get picked [for a job]; it's just mattered by the knowledge of their mind.

CRAIG: If you work hard, it'll pay off in the end.

MIKE: If you work hard, really put your mind to it, you can do it. You can make it.

This view of the opportunity structure as an essentially open one that rewards intelligence, effort, and ingenuity is shared by all the Brothers. Asked whether their chances of securing a remunerative job are as good as those of an upper-class boy from a wealthy district of the city, they all responded affirmatively. Not a single member of the Hallway Hangers, in contrast, affirms the openness of American society. . . .

Reproduction Theory Reconsidered

This basic finding—that two substantially different paths are followed within the general framework of social reproduction—is a major challenge to economically determinist theories. Two groups of boys from the same social stratum who live in the same housing project and attend the same school nevertheless experience the process of social reproduction in fundamentally different ways. This simple fact alone calls into question many of the theoretical formulations of Bowles and Gintis.[6] If, as they argue, social class is the overriding determinant in social reproduction, what accounts for the variance in the process between the Brothers and Hallway Hangers? Bowles and Gintis, in considering a single school, maintain that social reproduction takes place primarily through educational tracking. Differential socialization through educational tracking prepares working-class students for working-class jobs and middle-class students for middle-class jobs. But the Hallway Hangers and the Brothers, who are from the same social class background and exposed to the curricular structure of the school in the same manner, undergo the process of social reproduction in substantially different manners. The theory of Bowles and Gintis cannot explain this difference.

Bourdieu's notion of habitus, however, can be used to differentiate the Hallway Hangers and the Brothers.[7] The habitus, as defined by Giroux, is "the subjective dispositions which reflect a class-based social grammar of taste, knowledge, and behavior inscribed in . . . each developing person."[8] According to Bourdieu, the habitus is primarily a function of social class. Bourdieu does not give an adequate sense of the internal structure of the habitus, but there is some precedent in his work for incorporating other factors into constructions of the habitus; for example, he differentiates people not only by gender and class, but also by whether they come from Paris or not. Although Bourdieu sometimes gives the impression of a homogeneity of habitus within the boundaries of social class, I understand habitus to be constituted at the level of the family and thus can include, as constitutive of the habitus, factors such as ethnicity, educational histories, peer associations, and demographic characteristics (e.g., geographical mobility, duration of

tenancy in public housing, sibling order, and family size) as these shape individual action. Although Bourdieu never really develops the notion along these lines, he does allude to the complexity and interplay of mediations within the habitus. "The habitus acquired in the family underlies the structuring of school experiences, and the habitus transformed by schooling, itself diversified, in turn underlies the structuring of all subsequent experiences (e.g. the reception and assimilation of the messages of the culture industry or work experiences), and so on, from restructuring to restructuring."[9] When understood along the lines I have indicated, the concept of habitus becomes flexible enough to accommodate the interactions among ethnicity, family, schooling, work experiences, and peer associations that have been documented [here].

Although we may accept the notion of habitus as a useful explanatory tool, we must reject the inevitability of its *function* in Bourdieu's theoretical scheme. According to Bourdieu, the habitus functions discreetly to integrate individuals into a social world geared to the interests of the ruling classes; habitus engenders attitudes and conduct that are compatible with the reproduction of class inequality. The outstanding example of this process is the development by working-class individuals of depressed aspirations that mirror their actual chances for social advancement.

The circular relationship Bourdieu posits between objective opportunities and subjective hopes is incompatible with the findings [presented here]. The Brothers, whose objective life chances probably were lower originally than those available to the Hallway Hangers because of racial barriers to success, nevertheless nurture higher aspirations than do the Hallway Hangers. By emphasizing structural determinants at the expense of mediating factors that influence subjective renderings of objective probabilities, Bourdieu presumes too mechanistic and simplistic a relationship between aspiration and opportunity. This component of his theory fails to fathom how a number of factors lie between and mediate the influence of social class on individuals; Bourdieu cannot explain, for instance, how ethnicity intervenes in the process of aspiration formation and social reproduction.

Thus, the theoretical formulations of Bowles and Gintis and the deterministic elements of Bourdieu's theory, although elegant and intuitively plausible, are incapable of accounting for the processes of social reproduction as they have been observed and documented in Clarendon Heights. These theories give an excellent account of the hidden structural and ideological determinants that constrain members of the working class and limit the options of Clarendon Heights teenagers. What the Hallway Hangers and the Brothers demonstrate quite clearly, however, is that the way in which individuals and groups respond to structures of domination is open-ended. Although there is no way to avoid class-based constraints, the outcomes are not predefined. Bowles and Gintis and Bourdieu pay too little attention to the active, creative role of individual and group praxis. As Giroux maintains, what is missing from such theories "is not only the issue of resistance, but also any attempt to delineate the complex ways in which working-class subjectivities are constituted."[10]

From Ethnography to Theory

Once we descend into the world of actual human lives, we must take our theoretical bearings to make some sense of the social landscape, but in doing so we invariably find that the theories are incapable of accounting for much of what we see. The lives of the Hallway Hangers and the Brothers cannot be reduced to structural influences or causes; although structural forces weigh upon the individuals involved, it is necessary, in the words of Willis, "to give the social agents involved some meaningful scope for viewing, inhabiting, and constructing their own world in a way which is recognizably human and not theoretically reductive."[11] We must appreciate both the importance and the relative autonomy of the cultural level at which individuals, alone or in concert with others, wrest meaning out of the flux of their lives.

The possibilities open to these boys as lower-class teenagers are limited structurally from the outset. That they internalize the objective probabilities for social advancement to some degree is beyond question. The process by which this takes place, however, is influenced by a whole series of intermediate factors. Because gender is constant in the study discussed in these pages, race is the principal variable affecting the way in which these youths view their situation. Ethnicity introduces new structurally determined constraints on social mobility, but it also serves as a mediation through which the limitations of class are refracted and thus apprehended and understood differently by different racial groups. The Brothers comprehend and react to their situation in a manner entirely different from the response the Hallway Hangers make to a similar situation; ethnicity introduces a new dynamic that makes the Brothers more receptive to the achievement ideology. Their acceptance of this ideology affects their aspirations but also influences, in tandem with parental encouragement, their approach to school and the character of their peer group, factors that in turn bear upon their aspirations.

If we modify the habitus by changing the ethnicity variable and altering a few details of family occupational and educational histories and duration of tenancy in public housing, we would have the Hallway Hangers. As white lower-class youths, the Hallway Hangers view and interpret their situation in a different light, one that induces them to reject the achievement ideology and to develop aspirations and expectations quite apart from those the ideology attempts to generate. The resultant perspective, which is eventually reinforced by the Hallway Hangers' contact with the job market, informs the boys' approach to school and helps us understand the distinctive attributes of this peer group. Thus, although social class is of primary importance, there are intermediate factors at work that, as constitutive of the habitus, shape the subjective responses of the two groups of boys and produce quite different expectations and actions.

Having grown up in an environment where success is not common, the Hallway Hangers see that the connection between effort and reward is not as clearcut as the achievement ideology would have them believe. Because it runs counter to the evidence in their lives and because it represents a forceful assault on their self-esteem, the Hallway Hangers repudiate the achievement ideology. Given that their parents are inclined to see the ideology in the same light, they do not counter their sons' rejection of the American Dream.

A number of important ramifications follow from the Hallway Hangers' denial of the dominant ideology: the establishment of a peer group that provides alternative means of generating self-esteem, the rejection of school and antagonism toward teachers, and, of course, the leveling of aspirations. In schematizing the role of the peer group, it is difficult not to appear tautological, for the group does wield a reciprocal influence on the boys: It attracts those who are apt to reject school and the achievement ideology and those with low aspirations and then deepens these individuals' initial proclivities and further shapes them to fit the group. But at the same time, the peer subculture itself, handed down from older to younger boys, is the product of the particular factors that structure the lives of white teenagers in Clarendon Heights.

In addition to the peer group, the curricular structure of the school solidifies the low aspirations of the Hallway Hangers by channeling them into programs that prepare students for manual labor jobs. Low aspirations, in turn, make the Hallway Hangers more likely to dismiss school as irrelevant. Once on the job market, the Hallway Hangers' inability to secure even mediocre jobs further dampens their occupational hopes. Thus although each individual ultimately retains autonomy in the subjective interpretation of his situation, the leveled aspirations of the Hallway Hangers are to a large degree a response to the limitations of social class as they are manifest in the Hallway Hangers' social world.

The Brothers' social class origins are only marginally different from those of the Hallway Hangers. Being black, the Brothers also must cope with racially rooted barriers to success that, affirmative action measures notwithstanding, structurally inhibit the probabilities for social advancement, although to a lesser degree than do shared class limitations. What appears to be a comparable objective situation to that of the Hallway Hangers, however, is apprehended in a very different manner by the Brothers.

As black teenagers, the Brothers interpret their families' occupational and educational records in a much different light than do the Hallway Hangers. Judging by the Brothers' constant affirmation of equality of opportunity, the boys believe that racial injustice has been curbed in the United States in the last twenty years. Whereas in their parents' time the link between effort and reward was very tenuous for blacks, the Brothers, in keeping with the achievement ideology, see the connection today as very strong: "If you work hard, it'll pay off in the end" (Craig). Hence, the achievement ideology is more compatible with the Brothers' attitudes than with those of the Hallway Hangers, for whom it cannot succeed against overwhelming contrary evidence. The ideology is not as emotionally painful for the Brothers to accept because past racial discrimination can help account for their families' poverty, whereas the Hallway Hangers, if the ideology stands, are afforded no explanation outside of laziness and stupidity for their parents' failures. The optimism that acceptance of the achievement ideology brings for the Brothers is encouraged and reinforced by their parents. Thus, we see how in the modified habitus ethnicity affects the Brothers' interpretation of their social circumstances and leads to acceptance of the achievement ideology, with all the concomitant results.

Postscript: The Hallway Hangers and Brothers Eight Years Later

"Hey, Jay, what the fuck brings you back to the Ponderosa?" Greeted by Steve in July 1991, I surveyed a Clarendon Heights that had changed considerably since 1983. Steve jerked his thumb over his shoulder at a group of African American teenagers lounging in the area outside doorway #13, previously the preserve of the Hallway Hangers. "How do you like all the new niggers we got here? Motherfuckers've taken over, man." I asked Steve about Frankie, Slick, and the other Hallway Hangers. "I'm the only one holding down the fort," he answered. "Me and Jinks—he lives in the back. The rest of 'em pretty much cut loose, man."

In their mid-twenties, the seven Hallway Hangers should be in the labor force full time. Most of them aren't: They are unemployed or imprisoned, or are working sporadically either for firms "under the table" or for themselves in the drug economy. . . . The Hallway Hangers have been trapped in what economists call the secondary labor market—the subordinate segment of the job structure where the market is severely skewed against workers. Jobs in the primary labor markets provide wages that can support families and an internal career structure, but the rules of the game are different in the secondary labor market. Wages are lower, raises are infrequent, training is minimal, advancement is rare, and turnover is high.

When the legitimate job market fails them, the Hallway Hangers can turn to the underground economy. Since 1984 almost all of the Hallway Hangers have at least supplemented their income from earnings in the burgeoning, multibillion-dollar drug market. The street economy promises better money than does conventional employment. It also provides a work site that does not demean the Hallway Hangers or drain their dignity. As workers in the underground economy, they won't have to take orders from a boss's arrogant son, nor will they have to gossip with office colleagues and strain to camouflage their street identities. . . .

Although they have certainly fared better than the Hallway Hangers, the Brothers have themselves stumbled economically in the transition to adulthood. Even more so than the Hallway Hangers, the Brothers have been employed in the service sector of the economy. They have bagged groceries, stocked shelves, flipped hamburgers, delivered pizzas, repaired cars, serviced airplanes, cleaned buildings, moved furniture, driven tow trucks, pumped gas, delivered auto parts, and washed dishes. They have also worked as mail carriers, cooks, clerks, computer operators, bank tellers, busboys, models, office photocopiers, laborers, soldiers, baggage handlers, security guards, and customer service agents. Only Mike, as a postal service employee, holds a unionized position. Although their experiences on the labor market have been varied, many of the Brothers have failed to move out of the secondary labor market. Instead, like the Hallway Hangers, they have been stuck in low-wage, high-turnover jobs. . . .

These results are depressing. The experiences of the Hallway Hangers since 1984 show that opting out of the contest—neither playing the game nor accepting its rules—is not a viable option. Incarceration and other less explicit social penalties are applied by society when the contest is taken on one's own terms. There is no escape: The Hallway Hangers must still generate income, build relationships, and establish households. Trapped inside the game, the Hallway Hangers now question their youthful resistance to schooling and social norms. Granted the opportunity to do it over again, the Hallway Hangers say they would have tried harder to succeed.

But the Brothers *have* always tried, which is why their experiences between 1984 and 1991 are as disheartening as the Hallway Hangers'. If the Hangers show that opting out of the contest is not a viable option, the Brothers show that dutifully playing by the rules hardly guarantees success either. Conservative and liberal commentators alike often contend that if the poor would only apply themselves, behave responsibly, and adopt bourgeois values, then they will propel themselves into the middle class. The Brothers followed the recipe quite closely, but the outcomes are disappointing. They illustrate how rigid and durable the class structure is. Aspiration, application, and intelligence often fail to cut through the firm figurations of structural inequality. Though not impenetrable, structural constraints on opportunity, embedded in both schools and job markets, turn out to be much more debilitating than the Brothers anticipated. Their dreams of comfortable suburban bliss currently are dreams deferred, and are likely to end up as dreams denied.

NOTES

1. All names of neighborhoods and individuals have been changed to protect the anonymity of the study's subjects.

2. Erik H. Erikson, *Gandhi's Truth* (New York: Norton, 1969), p. 154.

484 JAY MACLEOD

3. Ronald Reagan, "State of the Union Address to Congress," *New York Times,* 6 February 1985, p. 17.

4. Kenneth I. Spenner and David L. Featherman, "Achievement Ambitions," *Annual Review of Sociology* 4 (1978):376–378.

5. Howard B. London, *The Culture of a Community College* (New York: Praeger, 1978).

6. Samuel Bowles and Herbert Gintis, *Schooling in Capitalist America* (New York: Basic Books, 1976).

7. See Pierre Bourdieu, *Outline of a Theory of Practice* (Cambridge: Cambridge University Press, 1977).

8. Henry A. Giroux, *Theory & Resistance in Education* (London: Heinemann Educational Books, 1983), p. 89.

9. Bourdieu, *Outline of a Theory of Practice,* p. 87.

10. Giroux, *Theory & Resistance,* p. 85.

11. Paul E. Willis, *Learning to Labor* (Aldershot: Gower, 1977), p. 172.

51

The Pecking Order

Which Siblings Succeed and Why

DALTON CONLEY

Once upon a time a future president was born. William Jefferson Blythe IV entered the world one month premature but at a healthy six pounds and eight ounces. At twenty-three, his mother, Virginia, was young by today's standards, but perhaps a touch old for Arkansas in the 1940s. She was a widow, so times were tight during Bill's early years. In fact, times would be tough during all of Bill's childhood. Nonetheless, he seemed destined for great things. According to family lore, in second grade Bill's teacher "predicted that he would be President someday."

His mother eventually married Roger Clinton, but that didn't make life any easier for Bill. Roger was a bitterly jealous alcoholic who often became physically abusive to his wife. Bill cites the day that he stood up to his stepfather as the most important marker in his transition to adulthood and perhaps in his entire life. In 1962, when Bill was sixteen, Virginia finally divorced Roger, but by then there was another Roger Clinton in the family, Bill's younger half brother.

Though Bill despised his stepfather, he still went to the Garland County courthouse and changed his last name to Clinton after his mother's divorce from the man— not for the old man's sake, but so that he would have the same last name as the younger brother he cherished. Though they were separated by ten years, were only half siblings, and ran in very different circles, the brothers were close. The younger Roger probably hated his father more than Bill did, but he nonetheless started to manifest many of the same traits as he came of age. He was a fabulous salesman: at age thirteen, he sold twice as many magazines as any of his classmates for a school project, winning a Polaroid camera and a turkey for his superior effort. He also had an affinity for substance abuse: by eighteen, he was heavily into marijuana. During Bill's first (unsuccessful) congressional campaign in 1974, Roger spent much of his time stenciling signs while smoking joints in the basement of campaign headquarters.

As Bill's political fortunes rose, Roger's prospects first stagnated and then sank. He tried his hand at a musical career, worked odd jobs, and eventually got into dealing drugs. And it was not just pot; in 1984, then-governor Bill Clinton was informed that his brother was a cocaine dealer under investigation by the Arkansas state police. The governor did not stand in the way of a sting operation, and Roger was caught on tape boasting how untouchable he was as the brother of the state's chief executive. Then the axe fell. After his arrest, Roger was beside himself in tears, threatening suicide for the shame he had brought upon his family—in particular, his famous brother. Upon hearing this threat Bill shook Roger violently. (He, in truth, felt responsible for his brother's slide.)

The next January, Roger was sentenced to a two-year prison term in a federal corrections facility in Fort Worth, Texas. Bill describes the whole ordeal as the most difficult episode of his life. David Maraniss—the author of *First in His Class,* the most comprehensive biography of Clinton to date—summarizes the family situation as follows:

> How could two brothers be so different: the governor and the coke dealer, the Rhodes scholar and the college dropout, one who tried to read three hundred books in three months and another who at his most addicted snorted cocaine sixteen times a day, one who could spend hours explaining economic theories and another whose economic interests centered on getting a new Porsche? In the case of the Clinton brothers, the contrasts become more understandable when considered within the context of their family history and environment. They grew up in a town of contrast and hypocrisy, in a family of duality and conflict. Bill and Roger were not so much opposites as two sides of the same coin.

If asked to explain why Bill succeeded where Roger failed, most people will immediately point to genetic differences. After all, they were only half siblings to begin with. Others will pin it on birth order, claiming that firstborns are more driven and successful. But both of these accounts rely on individual explanations—ones particular to the unique biology or psychology of Bill and Roger—and both are incomplete. Was Bill more favored and more driven because he was a firstborn? My research shows that in families with two kids, birth order does not really matter that much. In fact, just under one-fourth of U.S. presidents were firstborns—about what we would expect from chance. The fact is that birth position only comes into play in larger families. But what about genes: was Bill simply luckier in the family gene pool? That may be so, but it still does not explain why sibling disparities are much more common in poor families and broken homes than they are in rich, intact families. In fact, when families have limited resources, the success of one sibling often generates a negative backlash among the others.

Sure, if one kid is born a mathematical genius and the other with no talents whatsoever, their respective dice may be cast at birth. But for most of us, how genes matter depends on the social circumstances around us. A child in one family may be born with innate athletic talent that is never nurtured because the parents in that family value reading ability over all else. Yet in another family, the fit between the individual talents of a particular child—say spatial reasoning—and the values of the parents may be perfect, and those abilities are realized. Finally, what kind of rewards talent brings depends entirely on the socioeconomic structure of the time. Fifty years ago, musical talent might have led to a decent living. Today—in an economy that rewards the most popular musicians handsomely at the expense of everyone else—innate musical ability is more often a route to financial struggle.

In Bill Clinton's case, he obviously had good genes—which contributed to his sharp mind, quick wit, tall stature, and verbal charisma—but there was not much advantage to being the firstborn. What really made a difference in his life was the good fit between his particular talents, the aspirations of those around him, and the political opportunities in a small state like Arkansas. This good fit combined with his family's lack of economic resources to generate an enormous sibling difference in success. However, had Virginia had money, she might not have had to put all her eggs—all her hopes and dreams—in Bill's basket. She might have been able to actively compensate for Bill's success by giving Roger extra financial and nonfinancial support—sending him, for example, to an elite private school when he started to veer off track. Instead, Bill's success seemed to come at the expense of Roger's—particularly when it led Roger to a false sense of invincibility.

On the surface, it may seem that the case of the Clintons is atypical. And, of course, a pair of brothers who are, respectively, the president and an ex-con is a bit extreme. But the basic phenomenon of sibling differences in success that the Clintons represent is not all that unusual. In fact, in explaining economic inequality in America, sibling differences represent about three-quarters of all the differences between individuals. Put another way, only one-quarter of all income inequality is between families. The remaining 75 percent is within families. Sibling differences in accumulated wealth (i.e., net worth) are even greater, reaching 90-plus percent. What this means is that if

we lined everyone in America up in rank order of how much money they have—from the poorest homeless person to Bill Gates himself—and tried to predict where any particular individual might fall on that long line, then knowing about what family they came from would narrow down our uncertainty by about 25 percent (in the case of income). In other words, the dice are weighted by which family you come from, but you and your siblings still have to roll them. For example, if you come from a family that ranks in the bottom 5 percent of the income hierarchy, then you have a 40 percent chance of finding yourself in the lowest 10 percent, a 21 percent chance of making it to somewhere between the 30th and 70th percentile, and only a one in a thousand chance of making it to the top 10 percent. If you come from the richest 5 percent of families in America, then your odds are flipped. And if you start at the dead middle of the American income ladder, then you are about 63 percent likely to end up somewhere in that 30th- to 70th-percentile range, with a 4 percent chance of ending up either in the top or the bottom 10 percent. A similar pattern holds for educational differences. For example, if you attended college there is almost a 50 percent chance that one of your siblings did not (and vice versa).

What do sibling disparities as large as these indicate? They imply an American landscape where class identity is ever changing and not necessarily shared between brothers and sisters. Taken as a whole, the above statistics present a starkly darker portrait of American family life than we are used to. We want to think that the home is a haven in a heartless world. The truth is that inequality starts at home. These statistics also pose problems for those concerned with what seems to be a marked erosion of the idealized nuclear family. In fact, they hint at a trade-off between economic opportunity and stable, cohesive families.

While it may be surprising to realize how common sibling inequality is on the whole, my analysis of national data shows that Americans are quite aware of sibling disparities within their own families. For instance, when given a choice of fourteen categories of kin ranging from parents to grandparents to spouses to uncles, a whopping 34 percent of respondents claimed that a sibling was their most economically successful relative. When the question is flipped, 46 percent of respondents report a sibling being their least successful relative. Both these figures dwarf those for any other category. When respondents were asked to elaborate about why their most successful relative got that way, their most common answer was a good work ethic (24.5 percent); when we add in other, related categories like "responsible, disciplined," "perseverance, motivation," or "set goals, had a plan," the total is well over half of all responses. Contrast that with the 22.6 percent that covers all categories of what might be called socioeconomic influences, such as "inheritance," "coming from a family with money," "marrying money," and so on. When accounting for the success of our kin, individual characterological explanations win out.

The pattern becomes even more striking when we flip the question to ask about the misfortune of the least successful relative. Only 9.6 percent of respondents cite social forces like poverty, lack of opportunity, or the pitfalls of a particular field as an explanation. Meanwhile, a whopping 82.4 percent cite individualistic reasons—having a "bad attitude" or "poor emotional or mental health." The single largest category was "lack of determination."

That shows us how harsh we are on our brothers and sisters. Are we fair when we pass this kind of judgment, or terribly biased? I think the latter. In my book *The Pecking Order*, I challenge the perceived split between individual personality-based explanations for success and failure, and sociological ones. I argue that in each American family there exists a pecking order between siblings—a status hierarchy, if you will. This hierarchy emerges over the course of childhood and both reflects and determines the siblings' positions in the overall status ordering in society. It is not just the will of the parents or the "natural" abilities of the children themselves that determines who is on top in the family pecking order; the pecking order is conditioned by the swirling winds of society, which envelop the family. Gender expectations, the economic cost of schooling in America, a rising divorce rate, geographic mobility, religious and sexual orientations— all of these societal issues weigh in heavily on the pecking order between siblings. In other words, in order to truly understand the pecking orders within American families, you cannot view them in isolation from the larger economy and social structures in which we live. The family is, in short, no shelter from the cold winds of capitalism; rather it is part and parcel of that system. What I hope you end up with is a nuanced understanding of how social sorting works—in America writ large, and in your family writ small. And just maybe— along the way—we will all have a little more sympathy for our less fortunate brothers and sisters.

Books about siblings debate why children raised by the same parents in the same house under the same circumstances turn out differently—sometimes very differently. They offer genetic explanations, or focus on birth order or the quality of parenting. The *Pecking Order* takes all these issues into account, but, based on years of research with three separate studies, it now moves us beyond those factors. Why is there a pecking order in American families, and how does it work? The reasons go way beyond relationships between family members. Americans like to think that their behavior and their destiny are solely in their own hands. But the pecking order, like other aspects of the social fabric, ends up being shaped by how society works.

In fact, siblings serve merely as a tool by which I hope to shed light on why some of us are rich and others poor; on why some are famous and others in America are anonymous. However, in figuring this all out, we do not gain much traction by comparing Bill Clinton with Joe Q. Public, Bill Gates with the average reader of this book, or any pair of randomly associated people. Some books tell you that the best way to understand why one person succeeds and another does not is to examine big amorphous categories like class or economics or race. I say the best way to do it is to examine differences within families, specifically to compare siblings with one another. Only by focusing in on the variety of outcomes that arise within a given family can we gain a real understanding of the underlying forces, of the invisible hands of the marketplace, that push each of us onto our chosen (or assigned) path in life. Siblings provide a natural experiment of sorts. They share much of their genetic endowment. They also share much of the same environment. So it's logical to ask: how and why is it that some siblings end up in radically different positions in life? If we find an answer to that question, I think we will understand something very fundamental to American life.

52

The Strength of Weak Ties

MARK S. GRANOVETTER

Most intuitive notions of the "strength" of an interpersonal tie should be satisfied by the following definition: the strength of a tie is a (probably linear) combination of the amount of time, the emotional intensity, the intimacy (mutual confiding), and the reciprocal services which characterize the tie. Each of these is somewhat independent of the other, though the set is obviously highly intracorrelated. Discussion of operational measures of and weights attaching to each of the four elements is postponed to future empirical studies. It is sufficient for the present purpose if most of us can agree, on a rough intuitive basis, whether a given tie is strong, weak, or absent.

Consider, now, any two arbitrarily selected individuals—call them A and B—and the set, $S = C, D, E, \ldots$, of all persons with ties to either *or* both of them. The hypothesis which enables us to relate dyadic ties to larger structures is: the stronger the tie between A and B, the larger the proportion of individuals in S to whom they will *both* be tied, that is, connected by a weak or strong tie. This overlap in their friendship circles is predicted to be least when their tie is absent, most when it is strong, and intermediate when it is weak.

The proposed relationship results, first, from the tendency (by definition) of stronger ties to involve larger time commitments. If A-B and A-C ties exist, then the amount of time C spends with B depends (in part) on the amount A spends with B and C, respectively. (If the events "A is with B" and "A is with C" were independent, then the event "C is with A and B" would have probability equal to the product of their probabilities. For example, if A and B are together 60% of the time, and A and C 40%, then C, A, and B would be together 24% of the time. Such independence would be less likely after than before B and C became acquainted.) If C and B have no relationship, common strong ties to A will probably bring them into interaction and generate one. Implicit here is Homans's idea that "the more frequently persons interact with one another, the stronger their sentiments of friendship for one another are apt to be" (1950, p. 133).

Mark S. Granovetter, "The Strength of Weak Ties," *American Journal of Sociology* 78 (May 1973), pp. 1361–1366, 1371–1373, 1378–1380. Copyright © 1973 by The University of Chicago Press. Used by permission of The University of Chicago Press and the author.

The hypothesis is made plausible also by empirical evidence that the stronger the tie connecting two individuals, the more similar they are, in various ways (Berscheid and Walster 1969, pp. 69–91; Bramel 1969, pp. 9–16; Brown 1965, pp. 71–90; Laumann 1968; Newcomb 1961, chap. 5; Precker 1952). Thus, if strong ties connect A to B and A to C, both C and B, being similar to A, are probably similar to one another, increasing the likelihood of a friendship once they have met. Applied in reverse, these two factors—time and similarity—indicate why weaker A-B and A-C ties make a C-B tie less likely than strong ones: C and B are less likely to interact and less likely to be compatible if they do. . . .

To derive implications for large networks of relations, it is necessary to frame the basic hypothesis more precisely. This can be done by investigating the possible triads consisting of strong, weak, or absent ties among A, B, and any arbitrarily chosen friend of either or both (i.e., some member of the set S, described above). A thorough mathematical model would do this in some detail, suggesting probabilities for various types. This analysis becomes rather involved, however, and it is sufficient for my purpose in this paper to say that the triad which is most unlikely to occur, under the hypothesis stated above, is that in which A and B are strongly linked, A has a strong tie to some friend C, but the tie between C and B is absent. This triad is shown in Figure 52.1. To see the consequences of this assertion, I will exaggerate it in what follows by supposing that the triad shown never occurs—that is, that the B-C tie is always present (whether weak or strong), given the other two strong ties. Whatever results are inferred from this supposition should tend to

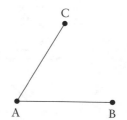

Figure 52.1   Forbidden Triad

occur in the degree that the triad in question tends to be absent.

Some evidence exists for this absence. Analyzing 651 sociograms, Davis (1970, p. 845) found that in 90% of them triads consisting of two mutual choices and one non-choice occurred less than the expected random number of times. If we assume that mutual choice indicates a strong tie, this is strong evidence in the direction of my argument. Newcomb (1961, pp. 160–65) reports that in triads consisting of dyads expressing mutual "high attraction," the configuration of three strong ties became increasingly frequent as people knew one another longer and better; the frequency of the triad pictured in Figure 52.1 is not analyzed, but it is implied that processes of cognitive balance tended to eliminate it.

The significance of this triad's absence can be shown by using the concept of a "bridge"; this is a line in a network which provides the *only* path between two points (Harary, Norman, and Cartwright 1965, p. 198). Since, in general, each person has a great many contacts, a bridge between A and B provides the only route along which information or influence can flow from any contact of A to any contact of B, and, consequently, from anyone connected *indirectly* to A to anyone connected indirectly to B. Thus, in the study of diffusion, we can expect bridges to assume an important role.

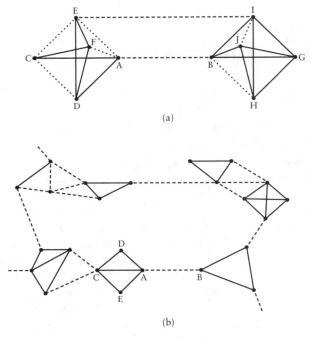

Figure 52.2   Local bridges. (a) Degree 3; (b) Degree 13.
Straight line = strong tie; dotted line = weak tie.

Now, if the stipulated triad is absent, it follows that, except under unlikely conditions, *no strong tie is a bridge.* Consider the strong tie *A-B:* if *A* has another strong tie to *C,* then forbidding the triad of Figure 52.1 implies that a tie exists between *C* and *B,* so that the path *A-C-B* exists between *A* and *B;* hence, *A-B* is not a bridge. A strong tie can be a bridge, therefore, *only if* neither party to it has any *other* strong ties, unlikely in a social network of any size (though possible in a small group). Weak ties suffer no such restriction, though they are certainly not automatically bridges. What is important, rather, is that all bridges are weak ties.

In large networks it probably happens only rarely, in practice, that a specific tie provides the *only* path between two points. The bridging function may nevertheless be served *locally.* In Figure 52.2a, for example, the tie *A-B* is not strictly a bridge, since one can construct the path *A-E-I-B* (and others). Yet, *A-B is* the shortest route to *B* for *F, D,* and *C.* This function is clearer in Figure 52.2b. Here, *A-B* is, for *C, D,* and others, not only a local bridge to *B,* but, in most real instances of diffusion, a much more likely and efficient path. Harary et al. point out that "there may be a distance [length of path] beyond which it is not feasible for *u* to communicate with *v* because of costs or distortions entailed in each act of transmission. If *v* does not lie within this critical distance, then he will not receive messages originating with *u*" (1965, p. 159). I will refer to a tie as a "local bridge of degree *n*" if *n* represents the shortest path between its two points (other than itself), and *n* > 2. In Figure 52.2a, *A-B* is a local bridge of degree 3, in 2b, of degree 13. As with bridges in a highway system, a local bridge in a social network will be more significant as a connection between two sectors to the extent that it is the only alternative for many people—that is, as its degree increases. A bridge in the absolute sense is a local one of infinite degree. By the same logic used above, only weak ties may be local bridges.

Suppose, now, that we adopt Davis's suggestion that "in interpersonal flows of most any sort the probability that 'whatever it is' will flow from person i to person j is (a) directly proportional to the number of all-positive (friendship) paths connecting i and j; and (b) inversely proportional to the length of such paths" (1969, p. 549). The significance of weak ties, then, would be that those which are local bridges create more, and shorter, paths. Any given tie may, hypothetically, be removed from a network; the number of paths broken and the changes in average path length resulting between arbitrary pairs of points (with some limitation on length of path considered) can then be computed. The contention here is that removal of the average weak tie would do more "damage" to transmission probabilities than would that of the average strong one.

Intuitively speaking, this means that whatever is to be diffused can reach a larger number of people, and traverse greater social distance (i.e., path length), when passed through weak ties rather than strong. If one tells a rumor to all his close friends, and they do likewise, many will hear the rumor a second and third time, since those linked by strong ties tend to share friends. If the motivation to spread the rumor is dampened a bit on each wave of retelling, then the rumor moving through strong ties is much more likely to be limited to a few cliques than that going via weak ones; bridges will not be crossed. . . .

I will develop this point empirically by citing some results from a labor-market study I have recently completed. Labor economists have long been aware that American blue-collar workers find out about new jobs more through personal contacts than by any other method. (Many studies are reviewed by Parnes 1954, chap. 5.) Recent studies suggest that this is also true for those in professional, technical, and managerial positions (Shapero, Howell, and Tombaugh 1965; Brown 1967; Granovetter 1970). My study of this question laid special emphasis on the nature of the *tie* between the job changer and the contact person who provided the necessary information.

In a random sample of recent professional, technical, and managerial job changers living in a Boston suburb, I asked those who found a new job through contacts how often they *saw* the contact around the time that he passed on job information to them. I will use this as a measure of tie strength. A natural a priori idea is that those with whom one has strong ties are more motivated to help with job information. Opposed to this greater motivation are the structural arguments I have been making: those to whom we are weakly tied are more likely to move in circles different from our own and will thus have access to information different from that which we receive.

I have used the following categories for frequency of contact: often = at least twice a week; occasionally = more than once a year but less than twice a week; rarely = once a year or less. Of those finding a job through contacts, 16.7% reported that they saw their contact often at the time, 55.6% said occasionally, and 27.8% rarely ($N = 54$). The skew is clearly to the weak end of the continuum, suggesting the primacy of structure over motivation.

In many cases, the contact was someone only marginally included in the current network of contacts, such as an old college friend or a former workmate or employer, with whom sporadic contact had been maintained (Granovetter 1970, pp. 76–80). Usually such ties had not even been very strong when first forged. For work-related ties, respondents almost invariably said that they never saw the person in a nonwork context. Chance meetings or mutual friends operated to reactivate such ties. It is remarkable that people receive crucial information from individuals whose very existence they have forgotten. . . .

From the individual's point of view, then, weak ties are an important resource in making possible mobility opportunity. Seen from a more macroscopic vantage, weak ties play a role in effecting social cohesion. When a man changes jobs, he is not only moving from one network of ties to another, but also establishing a link between these. Such a link is often of the same kind which facilitated his own movement. Especially within professional and technical specialties which are well defined and limited in size, this mobility sets up elaborate structures of bridging weak ties between the more coherent clusters that constitute operative networks in particular locations.

REFERENCES

Berscheid, E., and E. Walster. 1969. *Interpersonal Attraction*. Reading, Mass.: Addison-Wesley.

Bramel, D. 1969. "Interpersonal Attraction, Hostility and Perception." In *Experimental Social Psychology*, edited by Judson Mills. New York: Macmillan.

Brown, David. 1967. *The Mobile Professors*. Washington, D.C.: American Council on Education.

Brown, Roger. 1965. *Social Psychology*. New York: Free Press.

Davis, James A. 1969. "Social Structures and Cognitive Structures." In R. P. Abelson et al., *Theories of Cognitive Consistency*. Chicago: Rand McNally.

———. 1970. "Clustering and Hierarchy in Interpersonal Relations." *American Sociological Review* 35 (October): 843–52.

Granovetter, M. S. 1970. "Changing Jobs: Channels of Mobility Information in a Suburban Community." Doctoral dissertation, Harvard University.

Harary, F., R. Norman, and D. Cartwright. 1965. *Structural Models*. New York: Wiley.

Homans, George. 1950. *The Human Group*. New York: Harcourt, Brace & World.

Laumann, Edward. 1968. "Interlocking and Radial Friendship Networks: A Cross-sectional Analysis." Mimeographed. Ann Arbor: University of Michigan.

Newcomb, T. M. 1961. *The Acquaintance Process*. New York: Holt, Rinehart & Winston.

Parnes, Herbert. 1954. *Research on Labor Mobility*. New York: Social Science Research Council.

Precker, Joseph. 1952. "Similarity of Valuings as a Factor in Selection of Peers and Near-Authority Figures." *Journal of Abnormal and Social Psychology* 47, suppl. (April): 406–14.

Shapero, Albert, Richard Howell, and James Tombaugh. 1965. *The Structure and Dynamics of the Defense R & D Industry*. Menlo Park, Calif.: Stanford Research Institute.

53

Social Networks and Status Attainment

NAN LIN

Status attainment can be understood as a process by which individuals mobilize and invest resources for returns in socioeconomic standings. These resources can be classified into two types: personal resources and social resources. *Personal resources* are possessed by the individual who can use and dispose of them with freedom and without much concern for compensation. *Social resources* are resources accessible through one's direct and indirect ties. The access to and use of these resources are temporary and borrowed. For example, a friend's occupational or authority position, or such positions of this friend's friends, may be ego's social resource. The friend may use his or her position or network to help ego to find a job. These resources are "borrowed" and useful to achieve ego's certain goal, but they remain the property of the friend or his or her friends.

The theoretical and empirical work for understanding and assessing the status attainment process can be traced to the seminal study reported by Blau and Duncan (1967). Their major conclusion was that, even accounting for both the direct and in-direct effects of ascribed status (parental status), achieved status (education and prior occupational status) remained the most important factor accounting for the ultimate attained status. The study thus set the theoretical baseline for further modifications and expansions. All subsequent theoretical revisions and expansions must be evaluated for their contribution to the explanation of status attainment beyond those accounted for by the Blau-Duncan paradigm (Kelley 1990; Smith 1990). Several lines of contributions since then, including the addition of sociopsychological variables (Sewell and Hauser 1975), the recasting of statuses into classes (Wright 1979; Goldthorpe 1980), the incorporation of "structural" entities and positions as both contributing and attained statuses (Baron and Bielby 1980; Kalleberg 1988), and the casting of comparative development or institutions as contingent conditions (Treiman 1970), have significantly amplified rather than altered the original Blau-Duncan conclusion concerning the relative merits of achieved versus ascribed personal resources in status attainment.

Nan Lin, "Social Networks and Status Attainment," *Annual Review of Sociology* 25 (1999), pp. 467–470, 485–487. Copyright © 1999 by *Annual Review of Sociology*. Used by permission.

In the last three decades, a research tradition has focused on the effects on attained statuses of social resources. The principal proposition is that social resources exert an important and significant effect on attained statuses, beyond that accounted for by personal resources. Systematic investigations of this proposition have included efforts in (1) developing theoretical explanations and hypotheses, (2) developing measurements for social resources, (3) conducting empirical studies verifying the hypotheses, and (4) assessing the relative importance of social resources as compared to personal resources in the process of status attainment. . . .

Contributions of social network analysis to status attainment can be traced to the seminal study conducted by Mark Granovetter (1974), who interviewed 282 professional and managerial men in Newton, Massachusetts. The data suggested that those who used interpersonal channels seemed to land more satisfactory and better (e.g., higher income) jobs. Inferring from this empirical research, substantiated with a review of job search studies, Granovetter proposed (1973) a network theory for information flow. The hypothesis of "the strength of weak ties" was that weaker ties tend to form bridges that link individuals to other social circles for information not likely to be available in their own circles, and such information should be useful to the individuals.

However, Granovetter never suggested that access to or help from weaker rather than stronger ties would result in better statuses of jobs thus obtained (1995:148). Clues about the linkage between strength of ties and attained statuses came indirectly from a small world study conducted in a tri-city metropolitan area in upstate New York (Lin, Dayton, and Greenwald 1978).

The task of the participants in the study was to forward packets containing information about certain target persons to others they knew on a first-name basis so that the packets might eventually reach the target persons. The study found that successful chains (those packets successfully forwarded to the targets) involved higher-status intermediaries until the last nodes (dipping down in the hierarchy toward the locations of the targets). Successful chains also implicated nodes that had more extensive social contacts (who claimed more social ties), and yet these tended to forward the packets to someone they had not seen recently (weaker ties). The small world study thus made two contributions. First, it suggested that access to hierarchical positions might be the critical factor in the process of status attainment. Thus, the possible linkage between strength of ties and status attainment might be indirect: The strength of weak ties might lie in their accessing social positions vertically higher in the social hierarchy, which had the advantage in facilitating the instrumental action. Second, the study implicated behavior rather than a paper-and-pencil exercise, as each step in the packet-forwarding process required actual actions from each participant. Thus, the study results lend behavioral validity to those found in previous status attainment paper-pencil studies.

Based on these studies, a theory of social resources has emerged (Lin 1982, 1990). The theory begins with an image of the macro-social structure consisting of positions ranked according to certain normatively valued resources such as wealth, status, and power. This structure has a pyramidal shape in terms of accessibility and control of such resources: The higher the position, the fewer the occupants; and the higher the position, the better the view it has of the structure (especially down below). The pyramidal structure suggests advantages for positions nearer to the top, both in terms of number of occupants (fewer) and accessibility to positions (more). Individuals within these structural constraints and opportunities take actions for expressive and instrumental purposes. For instrumental actions (attaining status in the social structure being one prime example), the better strategy would be for ego to reach toward contacts higher up in the hierarchy. These contacts would be better able to exert influence on positions (e.g., recruiter for a firm) whose actions may benefit ego's interest. This reaching-up process may be facilitated if ego uses weaker ties, because weaker ties are more likely to reach out vertically (presumably upward) rather than horizontally relative to ego's position in the hierarchy.

REFERENCES

Baron, J. N., and W. T. Bielby. 1980. "Bringing the Firm Back in: Stratification, Segmentation, and the Organization of Work." *American Sociological Review* 45:737–65.

Blau, P. M., and O. D. Duncan. 1967. *The American Occupational Structure.* New York: Wiley.

Goldthorpe, J. H. 1980. *Social Mobility and Class Structure in Modern Britain.* New York: Oxford University Press.

Granovetter, M. 1973. "The Strength of Weak Ties." *American Journal of Sociology* 78: 1360–80.

Granovetter, M. 1974. *Getting a Job.* Cambridge, MA: Harvard University Press.

Granovetter, M. 1995. *Getting a Job.* Rev. ed. Chicago: University of Chicago Press.

Kalleberg, A. 1988. "Comparative Perspectives on Work Structures and Inequality." *Annual Review of Sociology* 14:203–25.

Kelley, J. 1990. "The Failure of a Paradigm: Log-Linear Models of Social Mobility." Pages 319–46, 349–57 in *John H. Goldthorpe: Consensus and Controversy,* edited by J. Clark, C. Modgil, and S. Modgil. London: Falmer.

Lin, N. 1982. "Social Resources and Instrumental Action." Pages 131–45 in *Social Structure and Network Analysis,* edited by P. V. Marsden and N. Lin. Beverly Hills, CA: Sage Publications.

Lin, N. 1990. "Social Resources and Social Mobility: A Structural Theory of Status Attainment." Pages 247–71 in *Social Mobility and Social Structure,* edited by R. L. Breiger. New York: Cambridge University Press.

Lin, N., P. Dayton, and P. Greenwald. 1978. "Analyzing the Instrumental Use of Relations in the Context of Social Structure." *Sociological Methods and Research* 7:149–66.

Sewell, W. H., and R. M. Hauser. 1975. *Education, Occupation & Earnings: Achievement in the Early Career.* New York: Academic Press.

Smith, M. R. 1990. "What Is New in New Structuralist Analyses of Earnings?" *American Sociological Review* 55:827–41.

Treiman, D. J. 1970. "Industrialization and Social Stratification." Pages 207–34 in *Social Stratification: Research and Theory for the 1970s,* edited by E. O. Laumann. Indianapolis: Bobbs-Merrill.

Wright, E. O. 1979. *Class Structure and Income Determination.* New York: Academic Press.

54

Structural Holes

RONALD S. BURT

Some people enjoy higher incomes than others. Some are promoted faster. Some are leaders on more important projects. The human capital explanation is that inequality results from differences in individual ability. The usual evidence is on general populations, as is Becker's (1975) pioneering analysis of income returns to education, but the argument is widely applied by senior managers to explain who gets to the top of corporate America—managers who make it to the top are smarter or better educated or more experienced. But, while human capital is surely necessary to success, it is useless without the social capital of opportunities in which to apply it.

Social capital can be distinguished in its etiology and consequences from human capital (e.g., Coleman, 1990; Bourdieu and Wacquant, 1992; Burt, 1992; Putnam, 1993; Lin, 1998). With respect to etiology, social capital is a quality created between people, whereas human capital is a quality of individuals. Investments that create social capital are therefore different in fundamental ways from the investments that create human capital (Coleman, 1988, 1990). I focus in this paper on consequences, a focus in network analysis for many years (Breiger, 1995). With respect to consequences, social capital is the contextual complement to human capital. Social capital predicts that returns to intelligence, education, and seniority depend in some part on a person's location in the social structure of a market or hierarchy. While human capital refers to individual ability, social capital refers to opportunity. Some portion of the value a manager adds to a firm is his or her ability to coordinate other people: identifying opportunities to add value within an organization and getting the right people together to develop the opportunities. Knowing who, when, and how to coordinate is a function of the manager's network of contacts within and beyond the firm. Certain network forms deemed social capital can enhance the manager's ability to identify and develop opportunities. Managers with more social capital get higher returns to their human capital because they are positioned to identify and develop more rewarding opportunities.

The Network Structure of Social Capital

Structural hole theory gives concrete meaning to the concept of social capital. The theory describes how social capital is a function of brokerage opportunities in a network (see Burt, 1992, for detailed discussion). The structural hole argument draws on several lines of network theorizing that emerged in sociology during the 1970s, most notably, Granovetter (1973) on the strength of weak ties, Freeman (1977) on betweenness centrality, Cook and Emerson (1978) on the power of having exclusive exchange partners, and Burt (1980) on the structural autonomy created by network complexity. More generally, sociological ideas elaborated by Simmel (1955) and Merton (1968), on the autonomy generated by conflicting affiliations, are mixed in the structural hole argument with traditional economic ideas of monopoly power and oligopoly to produce network models of competitive advantage. In a perfect market, one price clears the market. In an imperfect market, there can be multiple prices because disconnections between individuals, holes in the structure of the market, leave some people unaware of the benefits they could offer one another. Certain people are connected to certain others, trusting certain others, obligated to support certain others, dependent on exchange with certain others. Assets get locked into suboptimal exchanges. An individual's position in the structure of these exchanges can be an asset in its own right. That asset is social capital, in essence, a story about location effects in differentiated markets. The structural hole argument defines social capital in terms of the information and control advantages of being the broker in relations between people otherwise disconnected in social structure. The disconnected people stand on opposite sides of a hole in social structure. The structural hole is an opportunity to broker the flow of information between people and control the form of projects that bring together people from opposite sides of the hole.

Information Benefits

The information benefits are access, timing, and referrals. A manager's network provides access to information well beyond what he or she could process alone. It provides that information early, which is an advantage to the manager acting on the information. The network that filters information coming to a manager also directs, concentrates, and legitimates information received by others about the manager. Through referrals, the manager's interests are represented in a positive light, at the right time, and in the right places.

The structure of a network indicates the redundancy of its information benefits. There are two network indicators of redundancy. The first is cohesion. Cohesive contacts—contacts strongly connected to each other—are likely to have similar information and therefore provide redundant information benefits. Structural equivalence is the second indicator. Equivalent contacts—contacts who link a manager to the same third parties—have the same sources of information and therefore provide redundant information benefits.

Nonredundant contacts offer information benefits that are additive rather than redundant. Structural holes are the gaps between nonredundant contacts (see Burt, 1992: 25–30, on how Granovetter's weak ties generalize to structural holes). The hole

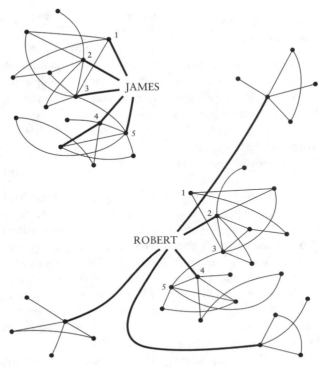

Figure 54.1   Illustrative Manager's Networks. Thick lines
represent a manager's direct contacts.

is a buffer, like an insulator in an electric
circuit. A structural hole between two clusters in a network need not mean that people in the two clusters are unaware of one
another. It simply means that they are so
focused on their own activities that they
have little time to attend to the activities of
people in the other cluster. A structural
hole indicates that the people on either side
of the hole circulate in different flows of information. A manager who spans the structural hole, by having strong relations with
contacts on both sides of the hole, has access to both information flows. The more
holes spanned, the richer the information
benefits of the network.

Figure 54.1 provides an example. James
had a network that spanned one structural
hole. The hole is the relatively weak connection between the cluster reached through
contacts 1, 2, and 3 and the cluster reached
through contacts 4 and 5. Robert took over
James's job and expanded the social capital
associated with the job. He preserved connection with both clusters in James's network but expanded the network to a more
diverse set of contacts. Robert's network,
with the addition of three new clusters of
people, spans ten structural holes.

Information benefits in this example are
enhanced in several ways. The volume is
higher in Robert's network simply because

he reaches more people indirectly. Also, the diversity of his contacts means that the quality of his information benefits is higher. Each cluster of contacts is a single source of information because people connected to one another tend to know the same things at about the same time. Nonredundant clusters provide Robert with a broader information screen and, therefore, greater assurance that he will be informed of opportunities and impending disasters (access benefits). Further, since Robert's contacts are only linked through him at the center of the network, he is the first to see new opportunities created by needs in one group that could be served by skills in other groups (timing benefits). He stands at the crossroads of social organization. He has the option of bringing together otherwise disconnected individuals in the network when it would be rewarding. And because Robert's contacts are more diverse, he is more likely to be a candidate for inclusion in new opportunities (referral benefits). These benefits are compounded by the fact that having a network that yields such benefits makes Robert more attractive to other people as a contact in their own networks.

Control Benefits

The manager who creates a bridge between otherwise disconnected contacts has a say in whose interests are served by the bridge. The disconnected contacts communicate through the manager, giving the manager an opportunity to adjust his or her image with each contact, which is the structural foundation for managerial robust action (Padgett and Ansell, 1993). Simmel and Merton introduced the sociology of people who derive control benefits from structural holes: The ideal type is the *tertius gaudens*

(literally, "the third who benefits"), a person who benefits from brokering the connection between others (see Burt, 1992: 30–32, for review). As the broker between otherwise disconnected contacts, a manager is an entrepreneur in the literal sense of the word—a person who adds value by brokering the connection between others (Burt, 1992: 34–36; see also Martinelli, 1994). There is a tension here, but not the hostility of combatants. It is merely uncertainty. In the swirling mix of preferences characteristic of social networks, where no demands have absolute authority, the *tertius* negotiates for favorable terms. Structural holes are the setting for *tertius strategies,* and information is the substance. Accurate, ambiguous, or distorted information is strategically moved between contacts by the *tertius*. The information and control benefits reinforce one another at any moment in time and cumulate together over time.

Networks rich in structural holes present opportunities for entrepreneurial behavior. The behaviors by which managers develop these opportunities are many and varied, but the opportunity itself is at all times defined by a hole in the social structure around the manager. In terms of the structural hole argument, networks rich in the entrepreneurial opportunities of structural holes are entrepreneurial networks, and entrepreneurs are people skilled in building the interpersonal bridges that span structural holes.

Predicted Social Capital Effect

Managers with contact networks rich in structural holes know about, have a hand in, and exercise control over the more rewarding opportunities. They monitor information more effectively than it can be monitored bureaucratically. They move information faster, and to more people, than memos. These entrepreneurial managers know the parameters of organization problems early. They are highly mobile relative to people working through a bureaucracy, easily shifting network time and energy from one solution to another. More in control of their immediate surroundings, entrepreneurial managers tailor solutions to the specific individuals being coordinated, replacing the boiler-plate solutions of formal bureaucracy. There is also the issue of costs: entrepreneurial managers offer inexpensive coordination relative to the bureaucratic alternative. Managers with networks rich in structural holes operate somewhere between the force of corporate authority and the dexterity of markets, building bridges between disconnected parts of the firm where it is valuable to do so. They have more opportunity to add value, are expected to do so, and are accordingly expected to enjoy higher returns to their human capital. The prediction is that in comparisons between otherwise similar people like James and Robert in Figure 54.1, it is people like Robert who should be more successful.

REFERENCES

Becker, Gary. 1975 Human Capital, 2d ed. Chicago: University of Chicago Press.

Bourdieu, Pierre, and Loïc J. D. Wacquant. 1992 An Invitation to Reflexive Sociology. Chicago: University of Chicago Press.

Breiger, Ronald L. 1995 "Socioeconomic achievement and social structure." In Annual Review of Sociology, 21: 115–136. Palo Alto, CA: Annual Reviews.

Burt, Ronald S. 1980 "Autonomy in a social topology." American Journal of Sociology, 85: 892–925.

_____. 1992 Structural Holes. Cambridge, MA: Harvard University Press.

Coleman, James S. 1988 "Social capital in the creation of human capital." American Journal of Sociology, 94: S95–S120.

_____. 1990 Foundations of Social Theory. Cambridge, MA: Harvard University Press.

Cook, Karen S., and Richard M. Emerson. 1978 "Power, equity and commitment in exchange networks." American Sociological Review, 43: 712–739.

Freeman, Linton C. 1977 "A set of measures of centrality based on betweenness." Sociometry, 40: 35–40.

Granovetter, Mark S. 1973 "The strength of weak ties." American Journal of Sociology, 78: 1360–1380.

Lin, Nan. 1998 Social Resources and Social Action. New York: Cambridge University Press (forthcoming).

Martinelli, Alberto. 1994 "Entrepreneurship and management." In Neil J. Smelser and Richard Swedberg (eds.), The Handbook of Economic Sociology: 476–503. Princeton, NJ: Princeton University Press.

Merton, Robert K. 1968 "Continuities in the theory of reference group behavior." In Robert K. Merton, Social Theory and Social Structure: 335–440. New York: Free Press.

Padgett, John F., and Christopher K. Ansell. 1993 "Robust action and the rise of the Medici, 1400–1434." American Journal of Sociology, 98: 1259–1319.

Putnam, Robert D. 1993 Making Democracy Work: Civic Traditions in Modern Italy. Princeton, NJ: Princeton University Press.

Simmel, Georg. 1955 Conflict and the Web of Group Affiliations. Trans. by Kurt H. Wolff and Reinhard Bendix. New York: Free Press.

55

Life at the Top in America
Isn't Just Better, It's Longer

JANNY SCOTT

Jean G. Miele's heart attack happened on a sidewalk in Midtown Manhattan in May 2004. He was walking back to work along Third Avenue with two colleagues after a several-hundred-dollar sushi lunch. There was the distant rumble of heartburn, the ominous tingle of perspiration. Then Miele, an architect, collapsed onto a concrete planter in a cold sweat.

Will L. Wilson's heart attack came four days earlier in the bedroom of his brownstone in Bedford-Stuyvesant in Brooklyn. He had been regaling his fiancée with the details of an all-you-can-eat dinner he was beginning to regret. Wilson, a Consolidated Edison office worker, was feeling a little bloated. He flopped onto the bed. Then came a searing sensation, like a hot iron deep inside his chest.

Ewa Rynczak Gora's first signs of trouble came in her rented room in the noisy shadow of the Brooklyn-Queens Expressway. It was the Fourth of July. Gora, a Polish-born housekeeper, was playing bridge. Suddenly she was sweating, stifling an urge to vomit. She told her husband not to call an ambulance; it would cost too much. In-

stead, she tried a home remedy: salt water, a double dose of hypertension pills, and a glass of vodka.

Architect, utility worker, maid: heart attack is the great leveler, and in those first fearful moments, three New Yorkers with little in common faced a single common threat. But in the months that followed, their experiences diverged. Social class— that elusive combination of income, education, occupation, and wealth—played a powerful role in Miele's, Wilson's, and Gora's struggles to recover.

Class informed everything from the circumstances of their heart attacks to the emergency care each received, the households they returned to, and the jobs they hoped to resume. It shaped their understanding of their illness, the support they got from their families, their relationships with their doctors. It helped define their ability to change their lives and shaped their odds of getting better.

Class is a potent force in health and longevity in the United States. The more education and income people have, the less likely they are to have and die of heart

---

disease, strokes, diabetes, and many types of cancer. Upper-middle-class Americans live longer and in better health than middle-class Americans, who live longer and better than those at the bottom. And the gaps are widening, say people who have researched social factors in health.

As advances in medicine and disease prevention have increased life expectancy in the United States, the benefits have disproportionately gone to people with education, money, good jobs, and connections. They are almost invariably in the best position to learn new information early, modify their behavior, take advantage of the latest treatments, and have the cost covered by insurance.

Many risk factors for chronic diseases are now more common among the less educated than the better educated. Smoking has dropped sharply among the better educated, but not among the less. Physical inactivity is more than twice as common among high school dropouts as among college graduates. Lower-income women are more likely than other women to be overweight, though the pattern among men may be the opposite.

There may also be subtler differences. Some researchers now believe that the stress involved in so-called high-demand, low-control jobs further down the occupational scale is more harmful than the stress of professional jobs that come with greater autonomy and control. Others are studying the health impact of job insecurity, lack of support on the job, and employment that makes it difficult to balance work and family obligations.

Then there is the issue of social networks and support, the differences in the knowledge, time, and attention that a person's family and friends are in a position to offer. What is the effect of social isolation? Neighborhood differences have also been studied: How stressful is a neighborhood? Are there safe places to exercise? What are the health effects of discrimination?

Heart attack is a window on the effects of class on health. The risk factors—smoking, poor diet, inactivity, obesity, hypertension, high cholesterol, and stress—are all more common among the less educated and less affluent, the same group that research has shown is less likely to receive cardiopulmonary resuscitation, to get emergency room care, or to adhere to lifestyle changes after heart attacks.

"In the last twenty years, there have been enormous advances in rescuing patients with heart attack and in knowledge about how to prevent heart attack," said Ichiro Kawachi, a professor of social epidemiology at the Harvard School of Public Health. "It's like diffusion of innovation: whenever innovation comes along, the well-to-do are much quicker at adopting it. On the lower end, various disadvantages have piled onto the poor. Diet has gotten worse. There's a lot more work stress. People have less time, if they're poor, to devote to health maintenance behaviors when they are juggling two jobs. Mortality rates even among the poor are coming down, but the rate is not anywhere near as fast as for the well-to-do. So the gap has increased."

Bruce G. Link, a professor of epidemiology and sociomedical sciences at Columbia University, said of the double-edged consequences of progress: "We're creating disparities. It's almost as if it's transforming health, which used to be like fate, into a commodity. Like the distribution of BMWs or goat cheese."

The Best of Care

Jean Miele's advantage began with the people he was with on May 6, when the lining of his right coronary artery ruptured, cutting off the flow of blood to his sixty-six-year-old heart. His two colleagues were knowledgeable enough to dismiss his request for a taxi and call an ambulance instead.

And because he was in Midtown Manhattan, there were major medical centers nearby, all licensed to do the latest in emergency cardiac care. The emergency medical technician in the ambulance offered Miele a choice. He picked Tisch Hospital, part of New York University Medical Center, an academic center with relatively affluent patients, and passed up Bellevue, a city-run hospital with one of the busiest emergency rooms in New York.

Within minutes, Miele was on a table in the cardiac catheterization laboratory, awaiting angioplasty to unclog his artery—a procedure that many cardiologists say has become the gold standard in heart attack treatment. When he developed ventricular fibrillation, a heart rhythm abnormality that can be fatal within minutes, the problem was quickly fixed.

Then Dr. James N. Slater, a fifty-four-year-old cardiologist with some twenty-five thousand cardiac catheterizations under his belt, threaded a catheter through a small incision in the top of Miele's right thigh and steered it toward his heart. Miele lay on the table, thinking about dying. By 3:52 P.M., less than two hours after Miele's first symptoms, his artery was reopened and Slater implanted a stent to keep it that way.

Time is muscle, as cardiologists say. The damage to Miele's heart was minimal.

Miele spent just two days in the hospital. His brother-in-law, a surgeon, suggested a few specialists. His brother, Joel, chairman of the board of another hospital, asked his hospital's president to call New York University. "Professional courtesy," Joel Miele explained later. "The bottom line is that someone from management would have called patient care and said, 'Look, would you make sure everything's okay?'"

Things went less flawlessly for Will Wilson, a fifty-three-year-old transportation coordinator for Con Ed. He imagined fleetingly that he was having a bad case of indigestion, though he had had a heart attack before. His fiancée insisted on calling an ambulance. Again, the emergency medical technician offered a choice of two nearby hospitals—neither of which had state permission to do angioplasty, the procedure Jean Miele received.

Wilson chose the Brooklyn Hospital Center over Woodhull Medical and Mental Health Center, the city-run hospital that serves three of Brooklyn's poorest neighborhoods. At Brooklyn Hospital, he was given a drug to break up the clot blocking an artery to his heart. It worked at first, said Narinder P. Bhalla, the hospital's chief of cardiology, but the clot re-formed.

So Bhalla had Wilson taken to the Weill Cornell Center of New York–Presbyterian Hospital in Manhattan the next morning. There, Bhalla performed angioplasty and implanted a stent. Asked later whether Wilson would have been better off if he had had his heart attack elsewhere, Bhalla said the most important issue in heart attack treatment was getting the patient to a hospital quickly.

But he added, "In his case, yes, he would have been better off had he been to a hospital that was doing angioplasty."

Wilson spent five days in the hospital before heading home on many of the same high-priced drugs that Miele would be taking and under similar instructions to change his diet and exercise regularly. After his first heart attack, in 2000, he quit smoking; but once he was feeling better, he stopped taking several medications, drifted back to red meat and fried foods, and let his exercise program slip.

This time would be different, he vowed: "I don't think I'll survive another one."

Ewa Gora's experience was the rockiest. First, she hesitated before allowing her husband to call an ambulance; she hoped her symptoms would go away. He finally insisted; but when the ambulance arrived, she resisted leaving. The emergency medical technician had to talk her into going. She was given no choice of hospitals; she was simply taken to Woodhull, the city hospital Will Wilson had rejected.

Woodhull was busy when Gora arrived around 10:30 p.m. A triage nurse found her condition stable and classified her as "high priority." Two hours later, a physician assistant and an attending doctor examined her again and found her complaining of chest pain, shortness of breath, and heart palpitations. Over the next few hours, tests confirmed she was having a heart attack.

She was given drugs to stop her blood from clotting and to control her blood pressure, treatment that Woodhull officials say is standard for the type of heart attack she was having. The heart attack passed. The next day, Gora was transferred to Bellevue, the hospital Jean Miele had turned down, for an angiogram to assess her risk of a second heart attack.

But Gora, who was fifty-nine at the time, came down with a fever at Bellevue, so the angiogram had to be canceled. She re-

mained at Bellevue for two weeks, being treated for an infection. Finally, she was sent home. No angiogram was ever done.

Comforts and Risks

Jean Miele is a member of New York City's upper middle class. The son of an architect and an artist, he worked his way through college, driving an ice-cream truck and upholstering theater seats. He spent two years in the military and then joined his father's firm, where he built a practice as not only an architect but also an arbitrator and an expert witness, developing real estate on the side.

Miele is the kind of person who makes things happen. He bought a $21,000 house in the Park Slope section of Brooklyn, sold it about fifteen years later for $285,000, and used the money to build his current house next door, worth over $2 million. In Brookhaven, on Long Island, he took a derelict house on a single acre, annexed several adjoining lots, and created what is now a four-acre, three-house compound with an undulating lawn and a fifteen-thousand-square-foot greenhouse he uses as a workshop for his collection of vintage Jaguars. . . .

His approach to his health was utilitarian. When body parts broke, he got them fixed so he could keep doing what he liked to do. So he had had disk surgery, rotator cuff surgery, surgery for a carpal tunnel problem. But he was also not above an occasional bit of neglect. In March 2004, his doctor suggested a stress test after Miele complained of shortness of breath. On May 6, the prescription was still hanging on the kitchen cabinet door.

An important link in the safety net that caught Miele was his wife, a former executive at a sweater manufacturing company who had stopped work to raise Emma but managed the Mieles' real estate as well. While Miele was still in the hospital, she was on the Internet, Googling stents.

She scheduled his medical appointments. She got his prescriptions filled. Leaving him at home one afternoon, she taped his cardiologist's business card to the couch where he was sitting. "Call Dr. Hayes and let him know you're coughing," she said, her fingertips on his shoulder. Thirty minutes later, she called home to check.

She prodded Miele, gently, to cut his weekly egg consumption to two, from seven. She found fresh whole wheat pasta and cooked it with turkey sausage and broccoli rabe. She knew her way around nutrition labels.

Lori Miele took on the burden of dealing with the hospital and insurance companies. She accompanied her husband to his doctor's appointments and retained pharmaceutical dosages in her head.

"I can just leave and she can give you all the answers to all the questions," Miele said to his cardiologist, Dr. Richard M. Hayes, one day.

"Okay, why don't you just leave?" Hayes said back. "Can she also examine you?"

With his wife's support, Miele set out to lose thirty pounds. His pasta consumption plunged to a plate a week from two a day. It was not hard to eat healthfully from the Mieles' kitchens. Even the "junk drawer" in Park Slope was stocked with things like banana chips and sugared almonds. Lunches in Brookhaven went straight from garden to table: tomatoes with basil, eggplant, corn, zucchini flower tempura.

At his doctor's suggestion, Miele enrolled in a three-month monitored exercise program for heart disease patients, called cardiac rehab, which has been shown to reduce the mortality rate among heart patients by 20 percent. Miele's insurance covered the cost. He even managed to minimize the inconvenience, finding a class ten minutes from his country house.

He had the luxury of not having to rush back to work. By early June, he had decided he would take the summer off, and maybe cut back his workweek when he returned to the firm.

"You know, the more I think about it, the less I like the idea of going back to work," he said. "I don't see any real advantage. I mean, there's money. But you've got to take the money out of the equation."

So he put a new top on his 1964 Corvair. He played host to a large family reunion, replaced the heat exchanger in his boat, and transformed the ramshackle greenhouse into an elaborate workshop. His weight dropped to 189 pounds, from 211. He had doubled the intensity of his workouts. His blood pressure was lower than ever. . . .

Lukewarm Efforts to Reform

Will Wilson fits squarely in the city's middle class. His parents had been sharecroppers who moved north and became a machinist and a nurse. He grew up in Bedford-Stuyvesant and had spent thirty-four years at Con Ed. He had an income of $73,000, five weeks' vacation, health benefits, a house worth $450,000, and plans to retire to North Carolina when he is fifty-five.

Wilson, too, had imagined becoming an architect. But there had been no money for college, so he found a job as a utility worker. By age twenty-two, he had two children. He considered going back to school, with the company's support, to study engineering.

But doing shift work, and with small children, he never found the time.

For years he was a high-voltage cable splicer, a job he loved because it meant working outdoors with plenty of freedom and overtime pay. But on a snowy night in the early 1980s, a car skidded into a stanchion, which hit him in the back. A doctor suggested that Wilson learn to live with the pain instead of having disk surgery, as Jean Miele had done.

So Wilson became a laboratory technician, then a transportation coordinator, working in a cubicle in a low-slung building in Astoria, Queens, overseeing fuel deliveries for the company's fleet. Some people might think of the work as tedious, Wilson said, "but it keeps you busy."

"Sometimes you look back over your past life experiences and you realize that if you would have done something different, you would have been someplace else," he said. "I don't dwell on it too much because I'm not in a negative position. But you do say, 'Well, dag, man, I should have done this or that.'"

Wilson's health was not bad, but far from perfect. He had quit drinking and smoking, but had high cholesterol, hypertension, and diabetes. He was slim, five foot nine, and just under 170 pounds. He traced his first heart attack to his smoking, his diet, and the stress from a grueling divorce.

His earlier efforts to reform his eating habits were half-hearted. Once he felt better, he stopped taking his cholesterol and hypertension drugs. When his cardiologist moved and referred Wilson to another doctor, he was annoyed by what he considered the rudeness of the office staff. Instead of demanding courtesy or finding another specialist, Wilson stopped going.

By the time Dr. Bhalla encountered Wilson at Brooklyn Hospital, there was damage to all three main areas of his heart. Bhalla prescribed a half-dozen drugs to lower Wilson's cholesterol, prevent clotting, and control his blood pressure.

"He has to behave himself," Bhalla said. "He needs to be more compliant with his medications. He has to really go on a diet, which is grains, no red meat, no fat. No fat at all."

Wilson had grown up eating his mother's fried chicken, pork chops, and macaroni and cheese. He confronted those same foods at holiday parties and big events. There were doughnut shops and fried chicken places in his neighborhood; but Wilson's fiancée, Melvina Murrell Green, found it hard to find fresh produce and good fish.

"People in my circle, they don't look at food as, you know, too much fat in it," Wilson said. "I don't think it's going to change. It's custom."

At Red Lobster after his second heart attack, Green would order chicken and Wilson would have salmon—plus a side order of fried shrimp. "He's still having a problem with the fried seafood," Green reported sympathetically. . . .

Ignoring the Risks

Ewa Gora is a member of the working class. A bus driver's daughter, she arrived in New York City from Kraków in the early 1990s, leaving behind a grown son. She worked as a housekeeper in a residence for the elderly in Manhattan, making beds and cleaning toilets. She said her income was $21,000 to $23,000 a year, with health insurance through her union.

For $365 a month, she rented a room in a friend's Brooklyn apartment on a street lined with aluminum-sided row houses and American flags. She used the friend's bathroom and kitchen. She was in her seventh year on a waiting list for a subsidized one-bedroom apartment in the adjacent Williamsburg neighborhood. In the meantime, she had acquired a roommate: Edward Gora, an asbestos-removal worker newly arrived from Poland and ten years her junior, whom she met and married in 2003.

Like Jean Miele, Ewa Gora had never imagined she was at risk of a heart attack, though she was overweight, hypertensive, and a thirty-year smoker, and heart attacks had killed her father and sister. She had numerous health problems, which she addressed selectively, getting treated for back pain, ulcers, and so on, until the treatment became too expensive or inconvenient, or her insurance declined to pay.

"My doctor said, 'Ewa, be careful with cholesterol,'" recalled Gora, whose vestigial Old World sense of propriety had her dressed in heels and makeup for every visit to Bellevue. "When she said that, I think nothing; I don't care. Because I don't believe this touch me. Or I think she have to say like that because she doctor. Like cigarettes: she doctor, she always told me to stop. And when I got out of the office, lights up."

Gora had a weakness for the peak of the food pyramid. She grew up on her mother's fried pork chops, spare ribs, and meatballs—all cooked with lard—and had become a pizza, hamburger, and french fry enthusiast in the United States. Fast food was not only tasty but also affordable. "I eat terrible," she reported cheerily from her bed at Bellevue. "I like grease food and fast food. And cigarettes." . . .

If Jean Miele's encounters with the health care profession in the first months after his heart attack were occasional and efficient, Ewa Gora's were the opposite. Whereas he saw his cardiologist just twice, Gora, burdened by complications, saw hers a half-dozen times. Meanwhile, her heart attack seemed to have shaken loose a host of other problems.

A growth on her adrenal gland had turned up on a Bellevue CAT scan, prompting a visit to an endocrinologist. An old knee problem flared up; an orthopedist recommended surgery. An alarming purple rash on her leg led to a trip to a dermatologist. Because of the heart attack, she had been taken off hormone replacement therapy and was constantly sweating. She tore open a toe stepping into a pothole and needed stitches. . . .

And Gora was gaining weight. To avoid smoking, she was eating. Her work had been her exercise and now she could not work. Jad Swingle, her doctor, suggested cardiac rehab, leaving it up to Gora to find a program and arrange it. Gora let it slide. As for her diet, she had vowed to stick to chicken, turkey, lettuce, tomatoes, and low-fat cottage cheese. But she got tired of that. She began sneaking cookies when no one was looking—and no one was.

She cooked separate meals for her husband, who was not inclined to change his eating habits. She made him meatballs with sauce, liver, soup from spare ribs. Then one day she helped herself to one of his fried pork chops, and was soon eating the same meals he was. As an alternative to eating cake while watching television, she turned to pistachios, and then ate a pound in a single sitting.

When the stress test was finally done, Dr. Swingle said the results showed she was not well enough to return to full-time work. He gave her permission for part-time work, but her boss said it was out of the question. By November, four months after her heart attack, her weight had climbed to 197 pounds from 185 in July. Her cholesterol levels were stubbornly high and her blood pressure was up, despite drugs for both.

In desperation, Gora embarked upon a curious, heart-unhealthy diet clipped from a Polish-language newspaper. Day 1: two hardboiled eggs, one steak, one tomato, spinach, lettuce with lemon and olive oil. Another day: coffee, grated carrots, cottage cheese, and three containers of yogurt. Yet another: just steak. She decided not to tell her doctor. "I worry if he don't let me, I not lose the weight," she said.

Uneven Recoveries

Nearly a year after his heart attack, Jean Miele was, remarkably, better off. He had lost thirty-four pounds and was exercising five times a week and taking subway stairs two at a time. He had retired from his firm on the terms he wanted. He was working from home, billing $225 an hour. More money in less time, he said. His blood pressure and cholesterol were low. "You're doing great," Dr. Hayes had said. "You're doing better than ninety-nine percent of my patients."

Will Wilson's heart attack had been a setback. His heart function remained impaired, though improved somewhat. At one checkup in the spring of 2005, his blood pressure and his weight had been a little high. He still enjoyed fried shrimp on occasion, but he took his medications diligently. He graduated from cardiac rehab with plans to join a health club with a pool. And he was looking forward to retirement.

Ewa Gora's life and health were increasingly complex. With Dr. Swingle's reluctant approval, she returned to work in November 2004. She had moved into the subsidized apartment in Williamsburg, which gave her her own kitchen and bathroom for the first time in seven years. But she began receiving menacing phone calls from a collection agency about an old bill her health insurance had not covered. Her husband, with double pneumonia, was out of work for weeks.

She had her long-awaited knee surgery in January 2005. But it left her temporarily unable to walk. Her weight hit two hundred pounds. When the diet failed, she considered another consisting largely of fruit and vegetables sprinkled with an herbal powder. Her blood pressure and cholesterol remained ominously high. She had been warned that she was now a borderline diabetic.

"You're becoming a full-time patient, aren't you?" Swingle remarked.

56

Health, Income, and Inequality

JOHN MULLAHY, STEPHANIE ROBERT, AND BARBARA WOLFE

The idea that income is associated with health goes back a long way in the literature. Perhaps the most influential work affecting contemporary work in this area was by Samuel Preston (1975), who observed, in comparing mortality rates across countries, that the impact of additional income on health (as measured by mortality) is greater on those with low income than on those with higher income. This effect is illustrated in Figure 56.1, which shows the health of individuals on the vertical axis, plotted against the income of the individual's family group on the horizontal axis. The concave shape of the curve conveys the idea that because a dollar transferred from the rich to the poor improves the health of the poor person more than it decreases the health of the rich person, this transfer increases the average level of health of the members of a community.

This is called the *absolute income hypothesis,* and in its simplest form it argues that if all that matters to health at the level of an individual is income, a community with more equal income will tend to have better average health than a community with more

inequality when comparing two communities with equal average income. In an international context, Angus Deaton (2001) points out that, according to the absolute income hypothesis, redistribution could improve health even if average income was not increased, and that redistribution from rich to poor countries would in principle improve worldwide average health.

A related concept is the *absolute deprivation* or *poverty hypothesis.* According to this hypothesis, those with the lowest incomes face poorer health and a greater risk of mortality owing to a variety of factors associated with extreme poverty, such as inadequate nutrition, lack of quality health care, exposure to a variety of physical hazards, and heightened stress. In this hypothesis, a dollar redistributed from rich to poor would improve the health of the poor and improve the average health of the entire population. The difference between the absolute income hypothesis and the absolute deprivation or poverty hypothesis is that in the former greater income improves the health of all persons, although in a nonlinear way, while in the latter only those who

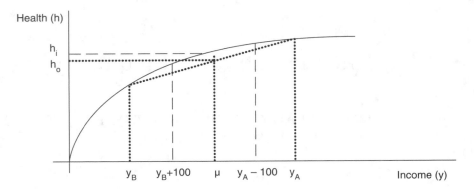

Source: Waqstaff and Van Doorslaer (2000, 546, fiq. 2).

Figure 56.1   Implications of the Concavity of the Health-Income Relationship

have low incomes are expected to see health improvements as a result of an increase in income.

The *relative income hypothesis* focuses on an individual's income relative to that of others in that individual's "group" rather than on his or her absolute income. According to this hypothesis, if the income of everyone but one in a group increases, that one person's health is expected to deteriorate. A related hypothesis is the *relative position* or *relative deprivation hypothesis*. According to this hypothesis, it is an individual's relative rank in society that is tied to health outcomes. This hypothesis encompasses the relative income hypothesis, but it extends the concept of relative position to measures of rank other than income, such as occupational rank or educational rank. These hypotheses are consistent with some research in the United States and the United Kingdom that demonstrates that the association between socioeconomic position and health occurs at all levels of the socioeconomic hierarchy, with even those in the highest socioeconomic groups having better health than those just below them in the socioeconomic hierarchy, which is referred to as a "gradient

effect" of socioeconomic position on health (Adler et al. 1994; Marmot et al. 1991).

The relative income and relative position hypotheses imply that it is not just the conditions experienced by those in absolute poverty that lead to poor health. Rather, there are psychosocial and other factors that remain unevenly distributed all the way up the income scale that perpetuate income inequalities in health. Perceptions of being relatively deprived ("keeping up with the Joneses"), stress, and other more psychosocial and behavioral than material factors may play a role in perpetuating income inequalities in health at the upper income levels. Health effects at the upper end of the income distribution may reflect relative position, whereas health effects at the lower end may reflect absolute deprivation (Adler and Newman 2002).

The hypothesis that focuses most directly on the tie between health inequality and income inequality is the *income inequality hypothesis*. According to the strong version of this hypothesis, societies with greater inequality produce worse health among their citizens, holding constant the average income of societies. Although these arguments were first made in comparisons of income inequality between countries, research has more recently examined whether regions, states, counties, and cities with greater income inequality have worse health than their more equal counterparts.

A Brief Review of the Evidence

Although all of these hypotheses initially seem testable, controversy arises because they are not always mutually exclusive. For example, tests of the income inequality hypothesis at the aggregate level may be empirically consistent with tests of the absolute poverty or relative income hypotheses at the individual level. Such overlap continues to obscure our understanding of the relationship between income, income inequality, and health. Without a clearer conceptual and empirical understanding of these relationships, program and policy recommendations about how to reduce income-related inequalities in health remain elusive and hotly debated.

In general, two empirical approaches have been taken to examine these hypotheses. Research examining the absolute deprivation, relative income, and relative position hypotheses has usually examined individual-level data on income and health or mortality to examine the existence and shape of the income-health relationship among individuals. Recent research has extended examination of these hypotheses by including aggregate measures of *community* socioeconomic level, such as the percentage of persons in poverty or community median family income, along with individual-level income data. In contrast, research examining the income inequality hypothesis has employed aggregate data either exclusively or at least at the level of measuring

income inequality. We divide our brief review of the literature into these two general types of studies, focusing particularly on the recent research testing the income inequality hypothesis.

Income and Health

Voluminous empirical studies and reviews demonstrate a robust association between income and morbidity and mortality, using various measures of both income and health across samples and at various time points (Adler et al. 1993, 1994; Antonovsky 1967; Feinstein 1993; Williams and Collins 1995; Robert and House 2000a). To date, most of the evidence demonstrates a nonlinear rather than linear gradient relationship between income and mortality (Backlund, Sorlie, and Johnson 1996; McDonough et al. 1997; Ettner 1996) and between income and morbidity (House et al. 1990, 1994; Mirowsky and Hu 1996).

Although most research on income and health is cross-sectional, there is some evidence that there may be widening socioeconomic inequalities in health in the United Kingdom (Black et al. 1982), the United States (Pappas et al. 1993), and other developed countries (Evans, Barer, and Marmor 1994; Marmot, Kogevinas, and Elston 1987). However, Deaton (2001, 60) suggests that the rapid increases in income inequality in the 1970s and 1980s in Britain and the United States "have not been associated with any slowdown in the rate of mortality decline." To date, datasets have been of insufficiently long duration or too incomplete in terms of longitudinal information on both income and health to explore the relationship between income, income inequality, and health over time.

Figure 56.2 reports on trends in family income from 1974 to 1996. It illustrates the

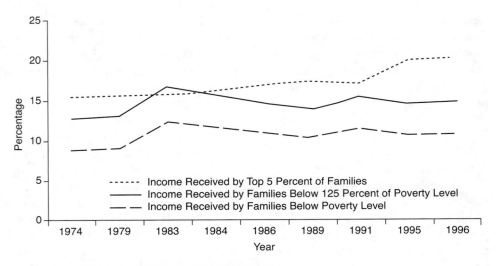

Source: U.S. Department of Commerce (2000, tables 745, 760).

Figure 56.2   Trends in Income of U.S. Families, 1974 to 1996

growing share of income received by the top 5 percent of families and shows the proportion of U.S. families below the official poverty line and the proportion who are near-poor (those below 125 percent of the poverty line). The growing share of the top 5 percent is indicative of growing inequality; the proportion poor and near-poor shows a more complicated picture—an increase from 1974 to 1983, a decline through 1989, followed by a smaller increase to 1991, with little change in the next few years.

Figure 56.3 reports the proportion of the population who reported poor or fair health by income group over these same years. Consistent with both the absolute income and deprivation hypotheses and the relative income and deprivation hypotheses, the health of the poor is always worse than that of the nonpoor, and the health of the near-poor is between the two. The trends over time show a continual improvement in the health of the nonpoor, but not among the poor and near-

poor: in both cases, after some improvement over the period 1974 to 1989, there was some deterioration in health from 1991 to 1996. Caution should be used in viewing these trends, however, since the way in which these health statistics are reported changed over this time period; hence the "jump" may be due to the reporting change. The increase after 1991, however, cannot be explained by the change in reporting, since there were no further changes.

Health status also differs systematically by race, and increasing attention is being paid to racial inequalities in health in the United States. There is a strong but far from complete overlap between racial and income inequalities in health (Williams 2002; Hayward et al. 2000; Williams and Collins 1995; Sorlie, Backlund, and Keller 1995; Ren and Amick 1996). Although this overlap is often acknowledged, it is not explicitly examined in much research on income and health.

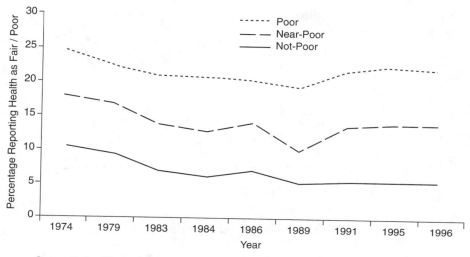

Source: National Center for Health Statistics (1998–1999).

Figure 56.3   Trends in Self-Reported Health of U.S. Families by Family Income, 1974 to 1996

Figures 56.4 and 56.5 present the trend in poverty and in poor and fair health for white and African American respondents. Figure 56.5 highlights the well-known higher poverty rates among African Americans and the higher proportion of African Americans with poor or fair health relative to the white population. The trends in health are of interest, for they are consistent with a tie between poverty and overall health for whites but not for African Americans. After 1983, the two lines track closely for whites. For African Americans, Figure 56.5 shows generally improving health, while the poverty rate fluctuates more. In this case, the figure does not illustrate or suggest a link between the two, although if the trend lines began in 1983, both would show some steady decline and hence improvement in health and reduction of poverty. Clearly, more attention should be paid to measuring trends in the relationship between income, race, and health and mortality over time in the United States.

Some recent research examines not only the relationship between individual or family income and health but also the impact of the neighborhood or community income level on individual health (see reviews in Robert 1999; Bond Huie 2001; Pickett and Pearl 2001; Robert and House 2000b; Diez-Roux 2000, 2001). This research finds evidence that living in communities with a higher proportion of poverty households, or with overall lower income (for example, low median family income), is associated with poor health and mortality over and above the effects of individual or family income in the United States (Haan, Kaplan, and Camacho 1987; Waitzman and Smith 1998a; Robert 1998; Diez-Roux et al. 1997; Anderson et al. 1997; Blakely, Lochner, and Kawachi 2002). Living in poorer communities may be detrimental to the health of all residents, regardless of their own income.

Most of this multilevel research, however, finds that individual- or family-level

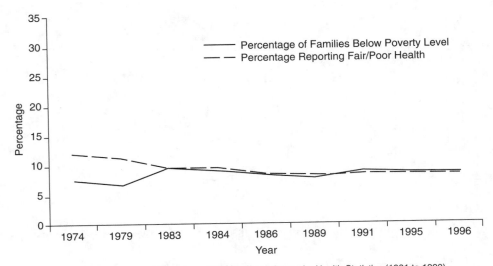

Source: U.S. Department of Commerce (2000) National Center for Health Statistics (1981 to 1999).

Figure 56.4   Comparing Self-Reported Health and Poverty Status of U.S. Families: White Families, 1974 to 1996

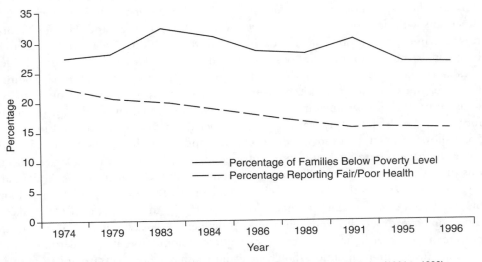

Source: U.S. Department of Commerce (2000) National Center for Health Statistics (1981 to 1999).

Figure 56.5   Comparing Self-Reported Health and Poverty Status of U.S. Families: African American Families, 1974 to 1996 socioeconomic characteristics are more significant correlates of health than are community variables (Robert 1998; Brooks-Gunn, Duncan, and Aber 1997; Elliott et al. 1996).

Combining multilevel research on the individual and community socioeconomic context and health with research on race, income, and health may be particularly important. For example, because the United States is residentially segregated by race (Jargowsky 1997; Massey and Denton 1993; Wilson 1987), African American and non-Hispanic white people of the same family income level live in very different neighborhoods. In a study by Stephanie Robert and Kum Yi Lee (2002), the disadvantaged health status of African American older adults that remains after controlling for individual SES is further explained after considering community socioeconomic characteristics. The higher number of chronic conditions experienced by African American older adults is explained only after considering both individual-level and community-level socioeconomic characteristics. Moreover, Robert and Lee demonstrate that African American older adults may even have slightly better self-rated health than non-African American older adults once the individual SES and the community socioeconomic context are controlled.

A number of researchers have also demonstrated the necessity of exploring more explicitly how the community racial context and individual race and ethnicity are related to community and individual income and health (Deaton and Lubotsky 2003; Collins and Williams 1999; Robert and House 2000b; Haan, Kaplan, and Camacho 1987; LeClere, Rogers, and Peters 1997, 1998; Robert 2002; Nazroo 2003; Krieger 2003; Acevedo-Garcia et al. 2003; Miller and Paxson 2001). What role do racial distribution, concentration, and segregation play in determining or explaining community-, family-, and individual-level income inequalities in health? We turn to these questions.

Income Inequality and Health

Whereas the evidence for a relationship between individual income and health is strong and relatively consistent, the evidence for a relationship between aggregate measures of income inequality and health is weak and controversial. There has been much focus in recent years on the latter research, with heated and excited debate about the importance to health and well-being of living in more or less unequal places. Ironically, the focus on this latter, more speculative, research may have unwittingly diverted attention from the former, more consistent, research.

The literature regarding the income inequality hypothesis must refer to Richard Wilkinson, given the influence of his writings on the field. In various writings over the last decade (see, for example, Wilkinson 1992, 1994, 1996), he has provided evidence of a relationship between income inequality in a country and life expectancy, both at a point in time and over time. However, other researchers have raised questions about this evidence, calling into doubt the reliability of the data Wilkinson uses to measure income inequality (Gravelle, Wildman, and Sutton 2002; Mellor and Milyo 2001). Using two more recent datasets considered to be of superior quality, two teams of researchers, Ken Judge, Jo-Ann Mulligan, and Michaela Benzeval (1998) and Hugh Gravelle, John Wildman, and Matthew Sutton (2002), find no significant relationship between income inequality and life expectancy across developed countries.

The idea that income inequality per se may influence health has caught the attention of many researchers, and a growing body of literature tests this hypothesis not only at the level of countries but across regions, states, counties, and cities within nations. For example, using states as the unit of comparison, George Kaplan and his colleagues (1996) and Bruce Kennedy, Ichiro Kawachi, and Deborah Prothrow-Stith (1996) find a significant relationship between several mortality rates and income inequality. Kennedy and his colleagues (1998) also find similar associations between self-rated health and income inequality. Kaplan and his colleagues find a tie between mortality rates and inequality in household income at the state level in the United States, even when median incomes are included. Kennedy and his colleagues (1996) use an alternative index of inequality, the "Robin Hood Index," also using state data for the United States. In their analysis of a variety of mortality rates, inequality is a statistically significant predictor. A follow-up study by Kawachi and Kennedy (1997) explores additional measures of inequality and mortality with similar results: a statistically significant link between measures of income inequality at the state level and health as measured by mortality rates. Examining 283 metropolitan areas as units of analysis rather than states, John Lynch, George Kaplan, and Elsie Pamuk (1998) similarly look at the relationships between multiple measures of inequality and mortality. The inequality measures predict mortality over and above other community-level factors, such as per capita income and the proportion of the population with incomes under 200 percent of the poverty level. Using county and tract-level data, Felicia LeClere and Mah-

Jabeen Soobader (2000) find independent income inequality effects primarily at the county level, but only for some specific subgroups by age, race, and gender. In these studies, various controls were added for median income, for proportion below the poverty line or near poverty, per capita income, and average household size.

Although most researchers accept this raw association between income inequality and health, even after controlling for median income levels or poverty, debate arises primarily over potential *explanations* for this relationship. Lynch and his colleagues (2000) describe three types of explanations for the association between income inequality and health: the individual income interpretation, the psychosocial environment interpretation, and the neomaterial interpretation. According to the *individual income interpretation,* aggregate associations between income inequality and health simply reflect the nonlinear (concave) relation between income and health at the individual level. According to the *psychosocial environment interpretation,* perceptions of inequality produce instabilities in social capital—perceived mistrust, lack of social cohesion, and so on—that work through behaviors and psychosocial responses that affect an individual's biological responses and ultimate health. The *neomaterial interpretation* suggests that places with the greatest income inequality are places that also have inequalities in human, physical, health, and social infrastructure that ultimately affect health.

The individual income interpretation suggests that, theoretically, if the relationship between individual income and health is nonlinear, then there should be an aggregate-level association between income inequality and health (Ecob and Davey Smith

1999; Gravelle 1998; Preston 1975; Rodgers 1979). Empirically, this has been tested in several studies that control for individual income while examining the association between income inequality and health. The association between income inequality and health or mortality sometimes remains after controlling for individual SES (Waitzman and Smith 1998b; Soobader and LeClere 1999; Fiscella and Franks 2000; Kennedy et al. 1998; LeClere and Soobader 2000; Lochner et al. 2001), and sometimes it does not (Fiscella and Franks 1997, 2000; Mellor and Milyo 1999; LeClere and Soobader 2000; Blakely, Lochner, and Kawachi 2002; Daly et al. 1998). For example, Tony Blakely, Kimberly Lochner, and Ichiro Kawachi (2002) use individual-level data from the 1996 and 1998 Current Population Survey in conjunction with 1990 Gini coefficient measures at the metropolitan area (MA) levels to look at self-rated health. They find no significant association between MA-level income inequality and health self-rated as poor or fair after controlling for sex, age, race, individual-level household income, and MA-level household income. In a recent review, Subramanian, Blakely, and Kawachi (2003) suggest that the only consistent associations between income inequality and health in multilevel studies may be seen at the state level in the United States, rather than at either smaller levels of aggregation within the United States or between or within other countries.

It seems crucial to explore further the extent to which the relationship between measures of inequality at the aggregate level and health reflects the nonlinear association between individual income and health. However, even if the aggregate relationship were fully explained by the individual-level

relationship, the interpretation of this finding would still be open for debate. Should the aggregate relationship then be seen as an artifact of the individual-level data, and therefore not meaningful, or does income inequality at more macro levels play a more causal role in producing or reproducing income inequalities in health?

Much of the heated debate in the literature on income inequality and health seems to stem from reactions to the so-called psychosocial environment interpretation. A number of researchers have explored the possibility that inequality per se produces a social environment that ultimately affects an individual's health (see, for example, Wilkinson 1996). For example, Kawachi and his colleagues (1997) suggest that high income inequality within states is associated with low social cohesion and disinvestment in social capital, which then affect mortality. Examples of this would be the relative income and deprivation hypotheses, which suggest that an individual's perceived relative income or position may affect health through psychosocial pathways (Adler et al. 1994).

Proponents of the neomaterial interpretation believe that more consideration should be given to factors that exist outside of, or as precursors to, psychosocial pathways. For example, Lynch and his colleagues (2000) point out that there are structural, political, and economic processes that generate inequality, and that these processes exist before individuals experience or perceive their effects. Therefore, focusing on the structural, political, and economic processes that both produce and result from inequality may be more appropriate than attending primarily to individual perceptions or experiences that occur downstream from these processes.

Examples of research exploring neomaterial interpretations of the link between income inequality and health include research that explores the potential intermediating role of public investment in, for instance, health care, public safety, education, and environmental quality. To the extent that such investments are concentrated in higher-income areas, or in less unequal areas, then an individual living in such areas gains more access to such goods and services (Kaplan et al. 1996; Lynch, Kaplan, and Pamuk 1998; Davey Smith 1996). The neomaterial interpretation implies that greater income inequality in society leads to greater differences in resources across communities that are associated with greater differences in health across communities. This finding highlights deprivation, but in this view deprivation at the individual level is compounded by deprivation at the community level as socioeconomic segregation and greater income inequality make the indirect costs of acquisition of health care and a healthy lifestyle more expensive to those with the lowest incomes. This suggests interaction effects between income inequality and individual income level. A number of studies suggest that income inequality may be a significant determinant of health, but only for those with the lowest incomes (Mellor and Milyo 1999; Soobader and LeClere 1999).

Critiquing the Literature on Income Inequality and Health

To summarize our primary understanding of the literature on income, income inequality, and health: there is a strong relationship between individual income and health that persists, and perhaps strengthens, over time. The shape of the relationship between income and health appears to be nonlinear, such that increases in income among those at the low end of the distribution should have greater positive consequences for their health than similar increases in income would have for the health of those at the top end of the income distribution. Much attention has been paid recently to the possibility that income inequality per se is related to health. The results of this research are still tenuous, though deserving of further study. However, it appears that the focus on this more tenuous research has unwittingly diverted attention from the former research on individual income and health. We conclude that (1) more research is needed to examine the relationship between income inequality and health, although (2) the greater advances in our understanding of the relationship between income and health will come from research that refocuses attention on the relationship between individual income level and health. Nevertheless, even if the primary relationship between income and health should be examined at the individual level, mediators of this relationship may very well operate at more aggregate levels such as households or neighborhoods.

REFERENCES

Acevedo-Garcia, Dolores, Kimberly A. Lochner, Theresa L. Osypuk, and Sukanya V. Subramanian. 2003. "Future Directions in Residential Segregation and Health Research: A Multilevel Approach." *American Journal of Public Health* 93(2): 215–21.

Adler, Nancy E., Thomas Boyce, Margaret A. Chesney, Sheldon Cohen, Susan Folkman, Robert L. Kahn, and S. Leonard Syme. 1994. "Socioeconomic Status and Health: The Challenge of the Gradient." *American Psychologist* 49(1): 15–24.

Adler, Nancy E., W. Thomas Boyce, Margaret A. Chesney, Susan Folkman, and S. Leonard

Syme. 1993. "Socioeconomic Inequalities in Health: No Easy Solution." *Journal of the American Medical Association* 269: 3140–45.

Adler, Nancy E., and Katherine Newman. 2002. "Socioeconomic Disparities in Health: Pathways and Policies." *Health Affairs* 21(2): 60–76.

Anderson, Roger T., Paul Sorlie, Eric Backlund, Norman Johnson, and George A. Kaplan. 1997. "Mortality Effects of Community Socioeconomic Status." *Epidemiology* 8: 42–47.

Antonovsky, Aaron. 1967. "Social Class, Life Expectancy, and Overall Mortality." *Milbank Memorial Fund Quarterly* 45: 31–73.

Backlund, Eric, Paul D. Sorlie, and Norman J. Johnson. 1996. "The Shape of the Relationship Between Income and Mortality in the United States: Evidence from the National Longitudinal Mortality Study." *Annals of Epidemiology* 6(1): 12–20.

Black, Douglas, J. N. Morris, Cyril Smith, and Peter Townsend. 1982. *Inequalities in Health: The Black Report.* New York: Penguin.

Blakely, Tony A., Kimberly Lochner, and Ichiro Kawachi. 2002. "Metropolitan-Area Income Inequality and Self-Rated Health: A Multilevel Study." *Social Science and Medicine* 54(1): 65–77.

Bond Huie, Stephanie A. 2001. "The Concept of Neighborhood in Health and Mortality Research." *Sociological Spectrum* 21: 341–58.

Brooks-Gunn, Jeanne, Greg J. Duncan, and J. Lawrence Aber, eds. 1997. *Neighborhood Poverty: Context and Consequences for Children,* vol. 1. New York: Russell Sage Foundation.

Collins, Chiquita A., and David R. Williams. 1999. "Segregation and Mortality: The Deadly Effects of Racism?" *Sociological Forum* 14(3): 495–523.

Daly, Mary C., Greg J. Duncan, George A. Kaplan, and John W. Lynch. 1998. "Macro-to-Micro Links in the Relation Between Income Inequality and Mortality." *Milbank Memorial Fund Quarterly* 76(3): 303–4, 315–39.

Davey Smith, George. 1996. "Income Inequality and Mortality: Why Are They Related?" *British Medical Journal* 313: 987–88.

Deaton, Angus. 2001. "Health, Inequality, and Economic Development." Working paper 8318. Cambridge, Mass.: National Bureau of Economic Research (June).

Deaton, Angus, and Darren Lubotsky. 2003. "Mortality, Inequality, and Race in American Cities and States." *Social Science and Medicine* 56(6): 1139–53.

Diez-Roux, Ana V. 2000. "Multilevel Analysis in Public Health Research." *Annual Review of Public Health* 21: 171–92.

_____. 2001. "Investigating Neighborhood and Area Effects on Health." *American Journal of Public Health* 91: 1783–89.

Diez-Roux, Ana V., F. Javier Nieto, Carles Muntaner, Herman A. Tyroler, George W. Comstock, Elad Shahar, Leslie S. Cooper, Robert L. Watson, and Moyses Szklo. 1997. "Neighborhood Environments and Coronary Heart Disease: A Multilevel Analysis." *American Journal of Epidemiology* 146(1): 48–63.

Ecob, Russell, and George Davey Smith. 1999. "Income and Health: What Is the Nature of the Relationship?" *Social Science and Medicine* 48(5): 693–705.

Elliott, Delbert S., William J. Wilson, David Huizinga, Robert J. Sampson, Amanda Elliott, and Bruce Rankin. 1996. "The Effects of Neighborhood Disadvantage on Adolescent Development." *Journal of Research in Crime and Delinquency* 33: 389–426.

Ettner, Susan L. 1996. "New Evidence on the Relationship Between Income and Health." *Journal of Health Economics* 15(1): 67–86.

Evans, Robert G., Morris L. Barer, and Theodore R. Marmor, eds. 1994. *Why Are Some People Healthy and Others Not? The Determinants of Health of Populations.* New York: Aldine de Gruyter.

Feinstein, Jonathan S. 1993. "The Relationship Between Socioeconomic Status and Health: A Review of the Literature." *Milbank Memorial Fund Quarterly* 71: 279–322.

Fiscella, Kevin, and Peter Franks. 2000. "Individual Income, Income Inequality, Health, and Mortality: What Are the Relationships?" *Health Services Research* 35(1): 307–18.

Gravelle, Hugh. 1998. "How Much of the Relationship Between Population Mortality and Unequal Distribution of Income Is a Statistical

Artifact?" *British Medical Journal* 316: 382–85.

Gravelle, Hugh, John Wildman, and Matthew Sutton. 2002. "Income, Income Inequality, and Health: What Can We Learn from the Aggregate Data?" *Social Science and Medicine* 54: 577–89.

Haan, Mary, George A. Kaplan, and Terry Camacho. 1987. "Poverty and Health: Prospective Evidence from the Alameda County Study." *American Journal of Epidemiology* 125(6): 989–98.

Hayward, Mark D., Toni P. Miles, Eileen M. Crimmins, and Yu Yang. 2000. "The Significance of Socioeconomic Status in Explaining the Racial Gap in Chronic Health Conditions." *American Sociological Review* 65: 910–30.

House, James S., Ronald C. Kessler, A. Regula Herzog, Richard P. Mero, Ann M. Kinney, and Martha J. Breslow. 1990. "Age, Socioeconomic Status, and Health." *Milbank Memorial Fund Quarterly* 68(3): 383–411.

House, James S., James M. Lepkowski, Ann M. Kinney, Richard P. Mero, Ronald C. Kessler, and A. Regula Herzog. 1994. "The Social Stratification of Aging and Health." *Journal of Health and Social Behavior* 35: 213–34.

Jargowsky, Paul A. 1997. *Poverty and Place: Ghettos, Barrios, and the American City.* New York: Russell Sage Foundation.

Judge, Ken, Jo-Ann Mulligan, and Michaela Benzeval. 1998. "Income Inequality and Population Health." *Social Science and Medicine* 46(4–5): 567–79.

Kaplan, George A., Elsie R. Pamuk, John W. Lynch, Richard D. Cohen, and Jennifer L. Balfour. 1996. "Inequality in Income and Mortality in the United States: Analysis of Mortality and Potential Pathways." *British Medical Journal* 312: 999–1003.

Kawachi, Ichiro, and Bruce P. Kennedy. 1997. "The Relationship of Income Inequality to Mortality: Does the Choice of Indicator Matter?" *Social Science and Medicine* 45: 1121–27.

Kawachi, Ichiro, Bruce P. Kennedy, Kimberly Lochner, and Deborah Prothrow-Stith. 1997. "Social Capital, Income Inequality, and Mortality." *American Journal of Public Health* 87(9): 1491–98.

Kennedy, Bruce P., Ichiro Kawachi, Roberta Glass, and Deborah Prothrow-Stith. 1998. "Income Distribution, Socioeconomic Status, and Self-rated Health in the United States: Multilevel Analysis." *British Medical Journal* 317: 917–21.

Kennedy, Bruce P., Ichiro Kawachi, and Deborah Prothrow-Stith. 1996. "Income Distribution and Mortality: Cross-sectional Ecological Study of the Robin Hood Index in the United States." *British Medical Journal* 312: 1004–7.

Krieger, Nancy. 2003. "Does Racism Harm Health? Did Child Abuse Exist Before 1962? On Explicit Questions, Critical Science, and Current Controversies: An Ecosocial Perspective." *American Journal of Public Health* 93(2): 194–99.

LeClere, Felicia B., and Mah-Jabeen Soobader. 2000. "The Effect of Income Inequality on the Health of Selected U.S. Demographic Groups." *American Journal of Public Health* 90(12): 1892–97.

Lynch, John W., George A. Kaplan, and Elsie R. Pamuk. 1998. "Income Inequality and Mortality in Metropolitan Areas of the United States." *American Journal of Public Health* 88: 1074–80.

Lynch, John W., George Davey Smith, George A. Kaplan, and James S. House. 2000. "Income Inequality and Mortality: Importance to Health of Individual Income, Psychosocial Environment, or Material Conditions." *British Medical Journal* 320(7243): 1200–4.

Marmot, Michael G., Manolis Kogevinas, and Mary Ann Elston. 1987. "Social/Economic Status and Disease." *Annual Review of Public Health* 8: 111–35.

Marmot, Michael G., G. Davey Smith, Stephen A. Stansfeld, C. Patel, F. North, J. Head, I. White, E. J. Brunner, and A. Feeney. 1991. "Health Inequalities Among British Civil Servants: The Whitehall II Study." *Lancet* 337(8754):1387–93.

Massey, Douglas S. 1990. "American Apartheid: Segregation and the Making of the Underclass." *American Journal of Sociology* 96: 329–58.

Massey, Douglas S., and Nancy A. Denton. 1993. *American Apartheid: Segregation and the Making of the Underclass.* Cambridge, Mass.: Harvard University Press.

McDonough, Peggy, Greg J. Duncan, David Williams, and James House. 1997. "Income Dynamics and Adult Mortality in the United States, 1972 Through 1989." *American Journal of Public Health* 87(9): 1476–83.

Mellor, Jennifer M., and Jeffrey D. Milyo. 1999. "Income Inequality and Individual Health: Evidence from the Current Population Survey." Working paper 8. Boston: Robert Wood Johnson Foundation Scholars in Health Policy Research Program.

———. 2001. "Reexamining the Evidence of an Ecological Association Between Income Inequality and Health." *Journal of Health Politics, Policy, and Law* 26(3): 487–522.

Miller, Douglas, and Christina Paxson. 2001. "Relative Income, Race, and Mortality." Working paper. Princeton, N.J.: Princeton University, Center for Health and Wellbeing.

Mirowsky, John, and Paul Nongzhuang Hu. 1996. "Physical Impairment and the Diminishing Effects of Income." *Social Forces* 74: 1073–96.

National Center for Health Statistics. Various years. *Health, United States.* Washington: U.S. Government Printing Office.

Nazroo, James Y. 2003. "The Structuring of Ethnic Inequalities in Health: Economic Position, Racial Discrimination, and Racism." *American Journal of Public Health* 93(2): 277–84.

Pappas, Gregory, Susan Queen, Wilbur Hadden, and Gail Fisher. 1993. "The Increasing Disparity in Mortality Between Socioeconomic Groups in the United States, 1960 and 1986." *New England Journal of Medicine* 329: 103–9.

Pickett, Kate E., and Michelle Pearl. 2001. "Multilevel Analyses of Neighborhood Socioeconomic Context and Health Outcomes: A Critical Review." *Journal of Epidemiology and Community Health* 55: 111–22.

Preston, Samuel. 1975. "The Changing Relation Between Mortality and Level of Development." *Population Studies* 29: 231–48.

Ren, Xinhua S., and Benjamin Amick. 1996. "Race and Self-assessed Health Status: The Role of Socioeconomic Factors in the United States." *Journal of Epidemiology and Community Health* 50: 269–73.

Robert, Stephanie A. 1998. "Community-Level Socioeconomic Status Effects on Adult Health." *Journal of Health and Social Behavior* 39: 18–37.

———. 1999. "Socioeconomic Position and Health: The Independent Contribution of Community Context." *Annual Review of Sociology* 25: 489–516.

Robert, Stephanie A., and James S. House. 2000a. "Socioeconomic Inequalities in Health: An Enduring Sociological Problem." In *Handbook of Medical Sociology,* edited by Chloe E. Bird, Peter Conrad, and Allen M. Fremont. New York: Prentice-Hall.

———. 2000b. "Socioeconomic Inequalities in Health: Integrating Individual-, Community-, and Societal-Level Theory and Research." In *Handbook of Social Studies in Health and Medicine,* edited by Gary L. Albrecht, Ray Fitzpatrick, and Susan C. Scrimshaw. London: Sage Publications.

Robert, Stephanie A., and Kum Yi Lee. 2002. "Explaining Race Differences in Health Among Older Adults: The Contribution of Community Socioeconomic Context." *Research on Aging* 24(6): 654–83.

Rodgers, Gerry B. 1979. "Income and Inequality as Determinants of Mortality: An International Cross-section Analysis." *Population Studies* 33: 343–51.

Soobader, Mah-Jabeen, and Felicia B. LeClere. 1999. "Aggregation and the Measurement of Income Inequality: Effects on Morbidity." *Social Science and Medicine* 48: 733–44.

Sorlie, Paul D., Eric Backlund, and Jacob B. Keller. 1995. "U.S. Mortality by Economic, Demographic, and Social Characteristics: The National Longitudinal Mortality Study." *American Journal of Public Health* 85: 949–56.

Subramanian, Sukanya V., Tony Blakely, and Ichiro Kawachi. 2003. "Income Inequality as a Public Health Concern: Where Do We Stand?" *Health Services Research* 38: 153–67.

U.S. Department of Commerce. U.S. Census Bureau. 2000. *Statistical Abstract of the United States: 2000.* Washington: U.S. Government Printing Office.

Wagstaff, Adam, and Eddy van Doorslaer. 2000. "Income Inequality and Health: What Does the Literature Tell Us?" *Annual Review of Public Health* 21: 543–67.

Waitzman, Norman J., and Ken R. Smith. 1998a. "Phantom of the Area: Poverty-Area Residence and Mortality in the United States." *American Journal of Public Health* 88(6): 973–76.

———. 1998b. "Separate but Lethal: The Effects of Economic Segregation on Mortality in Metropolitan America." *Milbank Memorial Fund Quarterly* 76(3): 341–73.

Wilkinson, Richard G. 1992. "Income Distribution and Life Expectancy." *British Medical Journal* 304: 165–68.

———. 1994. "The Epidemiological Transition: From Material Scarcity to Social Disadvantage?" *Daedalus* 123: 61–77.

———. 1996. *Unhealthy Societies: The Affliction of Inequality.* London: Routledge.

Williams, David R. 2002. "Racial/Ethnic Variations in Women's Health: The Social Embeddedness of Health." *American Journal of Public Health* 92(4): 588–97.

Williams, David R., and Chiquita Collins. 1995. "U.S. Socioeconomic and Racial Differences in Health: Patterns and Explanations." *Annual Review of Sociology* 21: 349–86.

Wilson, William Julius. 1987. *The Truly Disadvantaged: The Inner City, the Underclass, and Public Policy.* Chicago: University of Chicago Press.

57

The Social Stratification of Theatre, Dance, and Cinema Attendance

TAK WING CHAN
JOHN H. GOLDTHORPE

In current sociological literature the relationship between social inequality and patterns of cultural taste and consumption is the subject of a large and complex debate. This paper starts by outlining the leading positions that have been taken up in this debate, and then presents some illustrative findings from a research programme in which the authors are currently engaged. These findings are used chiefly as the basis for a critical evaluation of the rival positions that have been set out, although they may also be of interest in their own right. In addition, attention is drawn to the methodology on which the paper rests. Although this may appear somewhat daunting, at least to readers who lack a statistical background, it is, we would argue, only by following such an approach that the issues with which we are concerned can be adequately addressed.

In the sociological literature referred to, it is possible to identify three main lines of argument. In their essentials, these arguments can be stated as follows, although each has variant forms.

1. *The homology argument:* this claims that social stratification—that is, the prevailing structure of inequality within a society—and cultural stratification map onto each other very closely. Individuals in higher social strata are those who prefer and predominantly consume 'high' or 'elite' culture, and individuals in lower social strata are those who prefer and predominantly consume 'popular' or 'mass' culture—with, usually, various intermediate situations being also recognized. In some versions of the argument (e.g. Bourdieu, 1984) it is further claimed that the arrogation of 'distinction' in cultural taste and, conversely, processes of 'aesthetic distancing' are actively used by members of dominant social classes as means of symbolically demonstrating and confirming their superiority.

2. *The individualization argument:* this seeks in effect to relegate the homology argument to the past. In modern, relatively affluent and highly commercialized societies, it is held that differences

Tak Wing Chan and John H. Goldthorpe, "The Social Stratification of Theatre, Dance, and Cinema Attendance." *Cultural Trends* 14 (September 2005), pp. 194–201, 203–205, 207–208, 211–212.

in cultural taste and consumption are rapidly losing any clear grounding in social stratification: age, gender, ethnicity or sexuality, for example, all can, and do, serve as alternative social bases of cultural differentiation. And in more radical forms of the argument (e.g. Bauman, 1988; Featherstone, 1987), emphasis is placed on the growing ability of individuals to free themselves from social conditioning and influence of any kind and to choose and form their own distinctive identities and lifestyles—patterns of cultural consumption included.

3. *The omnivore–univore argument:* this in effect challenges both the homology and individualization arguments (see especially Peterson & Kern, 1996; Peterson & Simkus, 1992). As against the latter, it sees cultural differentiation as still mapping closely onto social stratification; but, as against the former, it does not see this mapping as being on 'elite-to-mass' lines. Rather, it claims that the cultural consumption of individuals in higher social strata differs from that of individuals in lower social strata in that it is *greater and much wider in its range.* It comprises not only more 'high-brow' culture, but also more 'middle-brow' and more 'low-brow' culture as well, while the consumption of individuals in lower social strata tends to be largely restricted to more popular cultural forms. Thus, the crucial distinction is not between elite and mass but rather between cultural omnivores and cultural univores.

In other work (Chan & Goldthorpe, 2005), we seek to evaluate these three argu-

ments by analysing data on musical consumption. Far stronger, even if still somewhat qualified, support is found for the omnivore–univore argument than for either the homology or individualization argument, as explained further below. However, it has to be noted that the omnivore–univore argument was initially developed with specific reference to musical consumption (Peterson & Simkus, 1992); and while, in this context, it has in fact received support additional to that of the present authors (see e.g. Coulangeon, 2003; Van Eijck, 2001), its wider application has been rather little studied. The present paper, therefore, aims to examine how well it fares in another domain of cultural consumption, that of theatre, dance and cinema. This differs from music in several ways, but perhaps most obviously for present purposes in that consumption generally requires attendance at some venue and, with the main exception of video film (which is discounted in what follows), there is no equivalent to the home consumption via various media that is of major importance in the domain of music.

Data and Concepts

As in the authors' work on musical consumption, data is used from the Arts in England survey which was carried out by the Office for National Statistics on behalf of Arts Council England. The survey was based on a stratified probability sample of individuals aged over 16 and living in private households in England in 2001. In all, 6,042 interviews were completed, representing a response rate of 64 per cent (for further details, see Skelton *et al.,* 2002). However, here attention is restricted to respondents aged 20 to 64. With this limitation, and after deleting all cases with missing values on variables of interest here, there is an effective sample of $N = 3,819$.

As regards theatre and cinema attendance, attention is concentrated on the results obtained in the survey from six questions. Respondents were asked whether or not, in the last 12 months, they had attended a performance of a play/drama, a musical, a pantomime, a ballet, some other form of dance (including contemporary dance, African People's dance and South Asian dance), or had seen a film at a cinema (or other venue rather than at home). It should be stressed that interest in these results lies not primarily in the answers given to each question taken separately, but rather in the possibility that the answers to the six questions *taken together* can reveal *patterns* of theatre and cinema consumption and in turn serve to identify *types of consumer* in this domain. As will be seen, this interest is reflected in the way in which the data are analysed.

As regards social stratification, we believe it important to do more than treat this through some single classification or scale of an essentially *ad hoc* kind—such as, say, the Market Research Society categories (AB, C1, C2, D) or the old Registrar General's Social Classes. Therefore information collected in the Arts in England survey on respondents' employment and occupation is drawn on in order to allocate them by both *social class* and *social status,* which are viewed, following a long-established tradition in sociology, as *conceptually separate forms of stratification.*

The class structure overall, and likewise individuals' positions within it, are seen as being defined in a quite objective way by economic relations or, more precisely, by relations in labour markets and production

units. To allocate individuals by class, the new National Statistics Socio-Economic Classification (NS-SEC) is used—in its seven-category version—which is specifically designed to capture differences in employment relations (Rose & Pevalin, 2003). The categories of the classification are shown in Table 57.4. In contrast, the status order is seen as reflecting inter-subjective assessments of individuals' social superiority, equality and inferiority as expressed most directly in relations of social intimacy. Such relations, where present among members of different social groupings, imply a basic equality of status and, where absent, a recognition of inequality. To allocate individuals by status, a 31-category occupationally based scale developed by the authors from analyses of patterns of close friendship in contemporary British society is used (Chan & Goldthorpe, 2004). The categories of this scale are shown in rank order, from high to low status, in Table 57.5. The closer together any two categories in the scale are, the more similar, occupationally, are their members' friends; the further apart they are, the less similar are their members' friends.

In any society, the positions of individuals within the class structure and the status order will tend to be correlated—but not perfectly so. Instances of discrepancy between class and status position are always likely to occur. For example, the authors' own results indicate that in present-day Britain salaried professionals and associate professionals tend to have higher status than do salaried managers, and especially managers in manufacturing, construction or transport, despite holding similar class positions as defined in terms of employment relations; or again that routine wage workers in services, especially personal services, tend to have higher status than even skilled manual workers. Since class and status are only imperfectly correlated, it is possible to ask whether it is the one or the other that exerts the greater influence on individuals' experience and action across different areas of social life. There is, for example, evidence that class is the dominant influence so far as individuals' economic life-chances are concerned—i.e. in determining their degree of economic security and their prospects—and also in shaping their political orientations and affiliations. But, in contrast, the expectation would be that in regard to cultural consumption it is status that will carry the greater weight. This is because differences in status are typically expressed in lifestyles, and cultural consumption is one important aspect of lifestyle through which status 'markers' can be readily laid down. In order to test whether this expectation holds good, it is of course essential that one should be able to distinguish class and status, conceptually and operationally.

In addition to treating class and status separately, we also draw on information available from the Arts in England Survey on respondents' incomes and on their educational qualifications. The latter are coded to the six National Vocational Qualification levels that range from 'no qualifications' to 'degree-level qualification or higher'. In sociological analyses of cultural consumption, income and education are often taken as substitutes or proxies for more direct measures of class or status of the kind to be used in the present study. However, income and education are here considered *along with* such measures of class and status, so that their independent effects, if any, can be established.

Finally, also included in the present analyses is socio-demographic information

Table 57.1   Percentage of Respondents Who Have Visited a Cinema or a Theatre for Various Kinds of Performance in the Past Twelve Months

Ballet	1.9
Other dance	12.7
Pantomime	14.6
Musical	25.4
Play/drama	29.0
Cinema	62.7

collected in the Arts in England survey, in particular regarding respondents' sex, age, marital status, family composition and region of residence. Given that the primary concern is with the social stratification of theatre, dance and cinema attendance, these socio-demographic variables are intended to serve primarily as 'controls': that is to say, they are brought into analyses chiefly in order to remove the possibility of any hidden confounding of their effects with those of class, status, income and education on which present interest centres.

Analytical Strategy

In Table 57.1 we show the percentage of respondents who in the last year had attended a theatre, for performances of the kinds previously indicated, or a cinema. As can be seen, there is some wide variation in the probabilities of attendance, although much on lines that might be expected. Cinema attendance is by far the most frequently reported, while, at the other extreme, going to the theatre for a ballet performance is at a very low level.

As earlier remarked, we wish to treat the data in question primarily as basis for obtaining an understanding of individuals' patterns of theatre and cinema attendance and of the different types of consumer in this cultural domain. To this end, a statisti-

Table 57.2   Latent Class Models Fitted to Data on Cultural Participation in the Domain of Theatre, Dance and Cinema

Model	Number of classes	G^2	df	p
1	1	1583.64	57	0.00
2	2	268.16	50	0.00
3	2[a]	53.22	49	0.31

[a]A local dependence term is included in this model to allow for an association between attendance at ballet and other dance events.

cal technique known as latent class analysis is employed, which can be intuitively understood as follows.

There are six questions that serve as indicators of theatre or cinema attendance. Since each question has a two-option (yes/no) answer, there are in fact 2^6 or 64 different possible response sets. The overall pattern of individuals' responses will therefore be complex. But the answers given by respondents to the six questions can be expected to show some degree of association. Thus, for example, those who say that they have been to a play are also likely to report having been to a cinema. Conversely, those who say that they have not been to a ballet are also likely to report that they have not been to other dance events, and so on. What the technique of latent class analysis aims to do is to simplify matters by exploiting this association among the six indicators. It seeks to identify a limited number of discrete classes, or categories, of respondents such that, *conditional on their belonging to one or other of these classes,* individuals' responses on the indicator items become independent of each other—i.e. there is no longer any association between them. Insofar as this can be done, it can be said that it is individuals' membership of the latent classes that is the *source* of the association initially found among their responses, and each latent class can be taken as representing a quite distinctive pattern of response.

Results

Latent Class Analysis of Theatre and Cinema Attendance

It turns out in fact that, as is shown in Table 57.2, a very simple latent class solution can be obtained for our data on theatre and cinema attendance. With the minor technical modification that is noted in Table 57.2, a model proposing just two latent classes fits the data satisfactorily: that is, just two latent classes prove sufficient to capture virtually all of the association that exists among responses on the six indicator items. Or, one could say, it emerges that underlying the results previously reported in Table 57.1 on these six different kinds of attendance, a clear, essentially dichotomous, patterning prevails.

On the basis of this solution we can then go on to assign each individual in the sample to one or other of the two latent classes that are identified—that is, to whichever he or she has the highest probability of belonging to, given his or her own set of responses on the six indicator items; in this way the respondents are divided into two types of consumer of theatre, dance and cinema. In Table 57.3 it is shown, first of all, that this process of assignment does not result in any major change in the relative size of the latent classes from that initially estimated under the model; or, in other words, no great degree of uncertainty appears to arise about the latent

Table 57.3   Estimated Size of the Latent Classes and Conditional Probabilities (Percent) of Attendance Under Our Preferred Model

	Latent class	
	1	2
Relative size (%), initial	62.5	37.5
Relative size (%), post-assignment	64.2	35.8
Probabilities of attendance (%)		
Ballet	0.1	5.0
Other dance	5.6	24.6
Pantomime	6.7	27.9
Musical	6.9	56.2
Play/drama	6.1	67.1
Cinema	48.0	87.1

class with which particular respondents should be affiliated. Second, the probabilities of individuals reporting each of the six different kinds of attendance considered are shown, given their latent class membership.

What, then, can be discovered about the two types of consumer that are derived from the latent class analysis? Our findings are in fact rather clear cut. As can be seen, latent class 1, which accounts for almost two-thirds of the sample, comprises individuals who have a very low probability— less than 10 per cent—of having attended a theatre in the year before the interview for any of the kinds of performance distinguished, and whose consumption is effectively limited to a fairly modest—48 per cent—probability of having visited a cinema. Latent class 2, in contrast, which accounts for somewhat over one-third of the sample, comprises individuals who have a relatively high probability (i.e. as compared to the overall rates shown in Table 57.1) of having attended a theatre for each of the kinds of performance covered and of having been to the cinema as well.

These findings would then, so far as they go, appear highly consistent with the omnivore–univore argument initially referred to. The latent Class 2 represents the theatre and cinema omnivores, and latent Class 1 the univores, whose consumption is in fact more or less restricted to the cinema. Certainly, we find no evidence of the kind that might be expected from the homology argument of a cultural elite who, in pursuit of 'distinction', attend the theatre for, say, drama and ballet performances but who at the same time display 'aesthetic distancing' in shunning musicals and pantomime. Members of latent Class 2 have the highest probability of attendance at not only drama and ballet but also all other kinds of theatre performance covered and the cinema. Furthermore, the very fact that the sample divides so readily into just two types of consumer is in itself sufficient to throw serious doubt on the individualization argument. There is no evidence here of the kind of individual diversity in cultural consumption that would, were it present, effectively defy latent class analysis or at all events require that an unmanageably large number of latent classes be distinguished, and ones to which individuals could be assigned only with great uncertainty.

Table 57.4   Distribution of Univores (U) and Omivores (O) Within NS Social Classes

NS social class	U (%)	O (%)	N
1 Higher managerial and professional occupations	43.9	56.2	488
2 Lower managerial and professional occupations	49.4	50.6	1023
3 Intermediate occupations	63.2	36.8	574
4 Small employers and own-account workers	72.7	27.3	275
5 Lower supervisory and technical occupations	77.7	22.3	359
6 Semi-routine occupations	77.1	22.9	620
7 Routine occupations	85.8	14.2	480
	64.2	35.8	3819

Theatre, Dance and Cinema Attendance and Social Stratification

As already noted, in our work on musical consumption (Chan & Goldthorpe, 2005), we also find, with some qualification, support for the omnivore–univore argument. Our latent class analyses in this case point in fact to three types of musical consumer: univores, whose consumption is largely restricted to pop and rock, and then two kinds of omnivore—'true' omnivores and omnivore listeners. The former have a high probability both of attending musical events and of listening to music across all the genres distinguished, while the latter are omnivorous only in their listening to broadcast or recorded music. Further analysis then reveals that the chances of being an omnivore, and especially a true omnivore, rather than a univore, increase with status, although—following the expectations earlier mentioned—the effects of class are negligible once status is included in the analysis. In addition, it is shown that even when the effects of status (and class) are controlled, the chances of being a musical omnivore rather than a univore still increase fairly steadily with level of educational qualifications, but that, in contrast,

these chances do not appear to be affected by income when other stratification variables are controlled. How far, then, are similar results obtained in regard to cultural consumption in the form of theatre and cinema attendance?

To begin with, we may examine the simple two-way relationships that exist between the chances of being in this regard an omnivore or a cinema-only univore (according to the previous analyses) and class and status respectively. In Table 57.4 we show the distribution of univores (latent Class 1) and omnivores (latent Class 2) within the seven classes of NS-SEC. It is evident that omnivores are most common in the professional and managerial classes, 1 and 2, where they are in fact in a slight majority, while univores dominate in Classes 5, 6 and 7, those of lower supervisory and technical, semi-routine and routine workers.

Figure 57.1 is then analogous to Table 57.4, but with the 31 categories of our status scale replacing the seven NS-SEC classes. An obvious 'status gradient' exists in the chances of being an omnivore rather than a univore.

These results are then consistent with the general idea that it is members of higher social strata who are more likely to be culturally omnivorous, and members of lower strata who are more likely to be univorous.

(a)   Theatre and Cinema Omnivores

(b)   Theatre and Cinema Univores

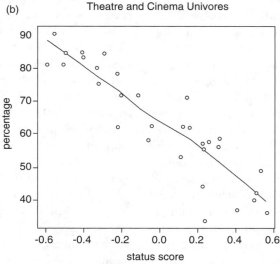

Figure 57.1   The Proportion of Respondents Being
Univores and Omnivores Within Status Categories by
Status Score

But to test this idea more rigorously against the data on theatre and cinema attendance, it is necessary to move on from merely two-way, or bivariate, analysis to analysis of a multivariate kind. That is to say, it is necessary to relate the chances of an individual being an omnivore rather than a univore to the full range of stratification variables referred to earlier and also to the socio-demographic variables of sex, age, marital status, family composition and region of residence that are introduced as controls. Only if the effects of all these variables are considered simultaneously can we hope to gain some reliable idea of their relative importance.

In Table 57.5 we report results from a binary logistic regression analysis. Such an analysis is appropriate where the 'dependent' variable—that on which our explanatory interest centres—has just two possible values, 'x' or 'not x': or, in our case, being an omnivore or not being an omnivore, and thus a univore. The β coefficients shown in the second column of the table represent the estimated effects of the variables listed in the first column. A positive coefficient implies that the higher the value of the explanatory variable, the higher the probability of being an omnivore rather than a univore, and a negative coefficient implies the opposite. Coefficients that are starred are statistically significant.

In assessing the results obtained from our regression analysis, we may begin with those relating to the socio-demographic control variables at the top of the table, since these turn out to be methodologically instructive. First, we may note a result that serves to confirm what several other investigators (e.g. O'Hagan, 1999; Quine, 1999) have previously reported: namely, that a highly significant gender effect exists in that women are more likely to be theatre goers than men; or, in our terms, women are more likely than men to be theatre and cinema omnivores rather than simply cinema-only univores. Second, though, the further finding of other investigators that the probability of theatre attendance increases with age cannot be confirmed. What we do find is that having a family that includes children below age 5, as compared with having no children, has a significant negative effect on the chances of being an omnivore. This would then suggest that where positive age

effects on theatre attendance do show up in two-way analyses, or indeed in multivariate analyses in which family composition variables are not included, they should be very cautiously interpreted, and with the possibility being kept in mind that they may well reflect life-cycle stage rather than generation.

A third result likewise brings out the advantage of multivariate analysis. It can be seen that the coefficients for living in regions outside London, although often negative in sign, in no case achieve significance (though that for the North comes close). Again, then, the implication is that where in two-way analyses living outside London (or the South East) appears to have a negative effect on theatre attendance, this finding could easily mislead. If stratification variables are not simultaneously considered, it could be that what region variables largely pick up is not any specifically geographical effects, such as the location of venues, travelling times, etc., but rather the (concealed) effects of stratification variables, on account of the populations of regions differing in their class and status composition and in their average levels of income and educational attainment.

Now turning to the effects of stratification variables in our own analysis, which is our main focus of interest, the following points stand out. First, it can be seen that when class and status are included in the analysis together, the effect of status is highly significant and positive—i.e. the chances of being an omnivore rather than a univore increase with status—while class effects are for the most part insignificant. Only membership of Class 7, that of routine, largely manual wage workers, has a significant—negative—effect on the chances of being an omnivore. In other words, our

Table 57.5　Coefficients from Binary Logistic Regression Analysis for Effects of Covariates on the Probability of Being an Omnivore Rather than a Univore

	$\hat{\beta}$	SE
Female[a]	0.615**	0.092
Married[b]	0.148	0.112
Separated	0.188	0.139
Age[c]	0.005	0.004
Child (0–4)[d]	−0.562**	0.113
Child (5–10)	0.070	0.100
Child (11–15)	0.088	0.105
The North[e]	−0.231	0.124
Midlands	−0.207	0.123
South East	0.083	0.135
South West	−0.189	0.153
Income	0.026**	0.005
CSE/others[f]	0.169	0.152
O levels	0.668**	0.128
A levels	1.130**	0.145
Sub-degree	1.027**	0.160
Degree	1.223**	0.151
Class 2[g]	0.078	0.126
Class 3	−0.161	0.160
Class 4	−0.205	0.203
Class 5	−0.134	0.218
Class 6	−0.199	0.195
Class 7	−0.507*	0.230
Status	0.631**	0.179
Constant	−2.118**	0.292

Notes: [a]Male is reference category. [b]Single is the reference category. [c]Centred at age 20. [d]Not having children is the reference category. [e]London is the reference category. [f]No qualifications is the reference category. [g]Class 1 is the reference category. * $p < 0.05$, ** $p < 0.01$.

results in the domain of theatre, dance and cinema do in this regard largely replicate those obtained in the domain of music, even if in the present case the preponderance of status over class effects is somewhat less marked, and thus our general theoretical expectation that status will be more closely associated with cultural consumption than will class, because such consumption represents an aspect of lifestyle through which status is readily expressed and displayed, is further borne out.

Second, Table 57.5 reveals that level of educational qualification tends also to have a significant and positive effect, over and above that of status (and class), on the chances of being an omnivore rather than a univore. Thus, in this regard, too, our findings in the case of music are broadly confirmed, although it should be noted that with theatre and cinema attendance, in contrast with musical consumption, the effects of education are not entirely 'monotonic'. That is to say, the effects of having some educational qualifications rather than none on the chance of being an omnivore do not consistently increase with level of qualification. As can be seen, having CSE-level qualifications rather than none has no significant effect, and having tertiary but sub-degree qualifications has a weaker effect than having only A levels.

Third, our regression analysis also shows that even when all other stratification variables are taken into account, a highly significant and positive effect of income on theatre and cinema attendance still remains: the higher an individual's income the more likely he or she is to be an omnivore rather than a univore. This result is then that which is most at variance with what we find in the analysis of musical consumption in which, as earlier noted, income proved to have no significant effect on the probability of being an omnivore rather than a univore, or in fact on the probability of being a true omnivore rather than an omnivore listener.

Conclusions

Three rival arguments concerning the relationship between social stratification and cultural consumption have been advanced and widely discussed in the sociological literature: what we have labelled as the homology, individualization and omnivore–univore arguments. In previous work on musical consumption in England, we have presented findings that broadly favour the omnivore–univore argument, while lending little support to its competitors. In the present paper, we turn to the domain of theatre, dance and cinema, and ask how far the results of the analyses of musical consumption can be replicated.

In one respect, it could be said that the case of theatre, dance and cinema provides a yet more straightforward confirmation of the omnivore–univore argument than that of music. Our latent class analyses indicate just two main patterns of attendance, and, in turn, two main types of consumer: those, around one-third of the sample, who do appear omnivorous in having a relatively high probability of attending theatre performances of *all* the kinds considered *and* of going to the cinema; and those, around two-thirds of the sample, who are univorous in being cinema-goers only, if indeed they are consumers in the domain of theatre and cinema at all. That it is these two types of consumer that are empirically identifiable, and only these types, does then in itself serve to call both the homology and the individualization arguments into question. Our latent class analyses fail to reveal a cultural elite who systematically discriminate among different kinds of theatre performance; but at the same time, theatre and cinema attendance clearly cannot be regarded as simply forms of individual expression, devoid of all social patterning. Moreover, when stratification variables are introduced into the analyses the results obtained are generally those that would be expected under the omnivore–univore argument. Higher status, higher educational qualifications and a higher income all increase individuals' chances of being an omnivore rather than a univore. In sum, theatre and cinema attendance, like musical consumption, is quite evidently socially stratified, but on omnivore–univore rather than elite–mass lines.

At the same time, though, some differences from our findings in the domain of music have also to be recognized. To begin with, while status effects do generally dominate class effects on theatre and cinema attendance, as would be expected to be the case, class is not so completely overshadowed as it is in relation to musical consumption. The chances of being a theatre and cinema omnivore significantly decrease for those holding the least advantaged class positions (Class 7), even when status is controlled for. Further, while education is clearly an important influence on theatre and cinema attendance, its effects would appear to be somewhat less consistent and also relatively less strong than they are on musical consumption. And finally, and most notably, income, which appears statistically non-significant in regard to musical omnivorousness, exerts a highly significant and fairly substantial effect on the probability of being a theatre and cinema omnivore, even when other stratification variables are included in the analysis.

REFERENCES

Bauman, Z. (1988). *Freedom*. Milton Keynes: Open University Press.

Bourdieu, P. (1984). *Distinction: A social critique of the judgement of taste*. London: Routledge & Kegan Paul.

Chan, T. W., & Goldthorpe, J. H. (2004). Is there a status order in contemporary British society? Evidence from the occupational structure of friendship. *European Sociological Review, 20*(5), 383–401.

Chan, T. W., & Goldthorpe, J. H. (2005). *Social stratification and cultural consumption: music in England*. Paper presented at a one-day workshop on 'The social bases of cultural consumption', Oxford, March 18.

Coulangeon, P. (2003). La stratification sociale des goûts musicaux. *Revue francaise de sociologie, 44*, 3–33.

Featherstone, M. (1987). Lifestyle and consumer culture. *Theory, Culture and Society, 4*(1), 55–70.

McCutcheon, A. L. (1987). *Latent class analysis*. Newbury Park, CA: Sage.

O'Hagan, J. (1999). Policy analysis of theatre in the UK. *Cultural Trends, 9*(34), 25–29.

Peterson, R. A., & Kern, R. M. (1996). Changing highbrow taste: from snob to omnivore. *American Sociological Review, 61*(5), 900–907.

Peterson, R. A., & Simkus, A. (1992). How musical tastes mark occupational status groups. In M. Lamont & M. Fournier (Eds.), *Cultivating differences: Symbolic boundaries and the making of inequality* (pp. 152–186). Chicago, IL: University of Chicago Press.

Quine, M. (1999). Audiences for live theatre in Britain: the present situation and some implication. *Cultural Trends, 9*(34), 1–24.

Rose, D., & Pevalin, D. J. (Eds.). (2003). *A researcher's guide to the National Statistics Socio-economic Classification*. London: Sage.

Skelton, A., Bridgwood, A., Duckworth, K., Hutton, L., Fenn, C., Creaser, C., & Babbidge, A. (2002). *Arts in England: Attendance, participation and attitudes in 2001* (Res. report 27). London: Arts Council England.

Van Eijck, K. (2001). Social differentiation in musical taste patterns. *Social Forces, 79*(3), 1163–1184.

Weber, M. (1922/1968). *Economy and society*. Berkeley, CA: University of California Press.

58

Unequal Childhoods

Class, Race, and Family Life

ANNETTE LAREAU

There are many studies that tell us of the detrimental effects of poverty on children's lives, but it is less clear what the mechanisms are for the transmission of class advantage across generations.

I suggest that social class has an important impact on the cultural logic of childrearing (see Lareau 2003 for details). Middle-class parents, both white *and* black, appear to follow a cultural logic of childrearing that I call "concerted cultivation." They enroll their children in numerous age-specific organized activities that come to dominate family life and create enormous labor, particularly for mothers. Parents see these activities as transmitting important life skills to children. Middle-class parents also stress language use and the development of reasoning. Talking plays a crucial role in the disciplinary strategies of middle-class parents. This "cultivation" approach results in a frenetic pace for parents, creates a cult of individualism within the family, and emphasizes children's performance.

Among white and black working-class and poor families, childrearing strategies emphasize the "accomplishment of natural growth." These parents believe that as long as they provide love, food, and safety, their children will grow and thrive. They do not focus on developing the special talents of their individual children. Working-class and poor children have more free time and deeper and richer ties within their extended families than the middle-class children. Some participate in organized activities, but they do so for different reasons than their middle-class counterparts. Working-class and poor parents issue many more directives to their children and, in some households, place more emphasis on physical discipline than do middle-class parents.

The pattern of concerted cultivation, with its stress on individual repertoires of activities, reasoning, and questioning, encourages an *emerging sense of entitlement* in children. Of course, not all parents and children are equally assertive, but the pattern of questioning and intervening among the white and black middle-class parents in the study contrasts sharply with the definitions of how to be helpful and effective observed among the white and black working-class and poor families. The pattern of the ac-

This is a commissioned chapter that draws heavily on material in a previous publication (Annette Lareau, *Unequal Childhoods: Class, Race, and Family Life*. Copyright © 2003 by the Regents of the University of California).

Table 58.1   Argument of Unequal Childhoods: Class Differences in Childrearing

	Childrearing Approach	
	Concerted Cultivation	*Accomplishment of Natural Growth*
Key Elements	Parent actively fosters and assesses child's talents, opinions, and skills	Parent cares for child and allows child to grow
Organization of Daily Life	*multiple child leisure activities orchestrated by adults	*child "hangs out" particularly with kin
Language Use	*reasoning/directives *child contestation of adult statements *extended negotiations between parents and child	*directives *rare for child to question or challenge adults *general acceptance by child of directives
Interventions in Institutions	*criticisms and interventions on behalf of child *training of child to take on this role	*dependence on institutions *sense of powerlessness and frustrations *conflict between childrearing practices at home and at school
Consequences	Emerging sense of entitlement on the part of the child	Emerging sense of constraint on the part of the child

complishment of natural growth, with its emphasis on child-initiated play, autonomy from adults, and directives, encourages an *emerging sense of constraint.* Members of these families, adults as well as children, tend to be deferential and outwardly accepting (with sporadic moments of resistance) in their interactions with professionals such as doctors and educators. At the same time, however, compared to their middle-class counterparts, the white and black working-class and poor families are more distrustful of professionals in institutions. These are differences with long-term consequences. In a historical moment where the dominant society privileges active, informed, assertive clients of health and educational services, the various strategies employed by children and parents are not equally valuable. In sum, differences in family life lie not only in the advantages parents are able to obtain for their children, but also in the skills being transmitted to children for negotiating their own life paths.

Methodology

Study Participants

The study is based on interviews and observations of children eight to ten years of age and their families. A team of graduate research assistants and I collected the data. The first phase involved observations in third-grade public school classrooms, mainly in a metropolitan area in the Northeast. The schools serve neighborhoods in a white suburban area and two urban locales—one a white working-class neighborhood and the other a nearby poor black neighborhood. About one-half of the children are white and about one-half are black. One child is interracial. The research assistants and I carried out individual interviews (averaging two hours each) with all of the mothers and most of the fathers (or guardians) of 88 children, for a total of 137 interviews. We also observed children as they took part in organized activities in the communities surrounding the schools. The most intensive part of the research, however, involved home observations of 12 children and their families. Nine of the 12 families came from the classrooms I observed, but the boy and girl from the two black middle-class families and the boy from the poor white family came from other sites. Most observations and interviews took place between 1993 and 1995, but interviews were done as early as 1990 and as late as 1997. This chapter focuses primarily on the findings from the observations of these 12 families since the key themes discussed here surfaced during this part of the fieldwork. I do include some information from the larger study to provide a context for understanding the family observations. All names are pseudonyms.

Intensive Family Observations

The research assistants and I took turns visiting the participating families daily, for a total of about 20 visits in each home, often in the space of one month. The observations were not limited to the home. Fieldworkers followed children and parents as they took part in school activities, church services and events, organized play, kin visits, and medical appointments. Most field observations lasted about three hours; sometimes, depending on the event (e.g., an out-of-town funeral, a special extended family event, or a long shopping trip), they lasted much longer. In most cases, there was one overnight visit. We often carried tape recorders with us and used the audiotapes for reference in writing up field notes. Families were paid $350, usually at the end of the visits, for their participation.

A Note on Class

My purpose in undertaking the field observations was to develop an *intensive*, realistic portrait of family life. Although I deliberately focused on only 12 families, I wanted to compare children across gender and race lines. Adopting the fine-grained differentiation of categories characteristic of current neo-Marxist and neo-Weberian empirical studies was not tenable. My choice of class categories was further limited by the school populations at the sites I had selected. Very few of the students were children of employers or of self-employed workers. I decided to concentrate exclusively on those whose parents were employees. Various criteria have been proposed to differentiate within this heterogeneous group, but authority in the workplace and "credential barriers" are the two most commonly used. I assigned the families in the study to a working-class or middle-class category based on discussions with each of the employed adults. They provided extensive information about the work they did, the nature of the organization that employed them, and their educational credentials. I added a third category: families not involved in the labor market (a population traditionally excluded from social class groupings) because in the first school I studied, a substantial number of children were from households supported by public assistance. To ignore them would have restricted the scope of the study arbitrarily. The final subsample contained 4 middle-class, 4 working-class, and 4 poor families.

Children's Time Use

In our interviews and observations of white and black middle-class children, it was striking how busy they were with organized activities. Indeed, one of the hallmarks of middle-class children's daily lives is a set of adult-run organized activities. Many children have three and four activities per week. In some families, every few days activities conflict, particularly when one season is ending and one is beginning. For example in the white middle-class family of the Tallingers, Garrett is on multiple soccer teams—the "A" traveling team of the private Forest soccer club and the Intercounty soccer team—he also has swim lessons, saxophone lessons at school, private piano lessons at home, and baseball and basketball. These organized activities provided a framework for children's lives; other activities were sandwiched between them.

These activities create labor for parents. Indeed, the impact of children's activities takes its toll on parents' patience as well as their time. For example, on a June afternoon at the beginning of summer vacation, in a white-middle-class family, Mr. Tallinger comes home from work to take Garrett to his soccer game. Garrett is not ready to go, and his lackadaisical approach to getting ready irks his father:

> Don says, "Get your soccer stuff—you're going to a soccer game!" Garrett comes into the den with white short leggings on underneath a long green soccer shirt; he's number 16. He sits on an armchair catty-corner from the television and languidly watches the World Cup game. He slowly, abstractedly, pulls on shin guards, then long socks. His eyes are riveted to the TV screen. Don comes in: "Go get your other stuff." Garrett says he can't find his shorts. Don: "Did you look in your drawer?" Garrett nods. . . . He gets up to look for his shorts, comes back into the den a few min-

utes later. I ask, "Any luck yet?" Garrett shakes his head. Don is rustling around elsewhere in the house. Don comes in, says to Garrett, "Well, Garrett, aren't you wearing shoes?" (Don leaves and returns a short time later): "Garrett, we HAVE to go! Move! We're late!" He says this shortly, abruptly. He comes back in a minute and drops Garrett's shiny green shorts on his lap without a word.

This pressured search for a pair of shiny green soccer shorts is a typical event in the Tallinger household. Also typical is the solution—a parent ultimately finds the missing object, while continuing to prod the child to hurry. The fact that today's frenzied schedule will be matched or exceeded by the next day's is also par:

> Don: (describing their day on Saturday) Tomorrow is really nuts. We have a soccer game, then a baseball game, then another soccer game.

This steady schedule of activity—that none of the middle-class parents reported having when they were a similar age—was not universal. Indeed, while we searched for a middle-class child who did not have a single organized activity we could not find one, but in working-class and poor homes, organized activities were much less common and there were many children who did not have any. Many children "hung out." Television and video games are a major source of entertainment but outdoor play can trump either of these. No advanced planning, no telephone calls, no consultations between mothers, no drop-offs or pickups—no particular effort at all—is required to launch an activity. For instance, one afternoon, in a black working-class family, Shannon (in

7th grade) and Tyrec (in 4th grade) walk out their front door to the curb of the small, narrow street their house faces. Shannon begins playing a game with a ball; she soon has company:

(Two boys from the neighborhood walk up.) Shannon is throwing the small ball against the side of the row house. Tyrec joins in the game with her. As they throw the ball against the wall, they say things they must do with the ball. It went something like this: Johnny Crow wanted to know. . . . (bounces ball against the wall), touch your knee (bounce), touch your toe (bounce), touch the ground (bounce), under the knee (bounce), turn around (bounce). Shannon and Tyrec played about four rounds.

Unexpected events produce hilarity:

At one point Shannon accidentally threw the ball and it bounced off of Tyrec's head. All the kids laughed; then Tyrec, who had the ball, went chasing after Shannon. It was a close, fun moment—lots of laughter, eye contact, giggling, chasing.

Soon a different game evolves. Tyrec is on restriction. He is supposed to remain inside the house all day. So, when he thinks he has caught a glimpse of his mom returning home from work, he dashes inside. He reappears as soon as he realizes that it was a false alarm. The neighborhood children begin an informal game of baiting him:

The kids keep teasing Tyrec that his mom's coming—which sends him scurrying just inside the door, peering out of the screen door. This game is enacted about six times. Tyrec also chases Shannon around the street,

trying to get the ball from her. A few times Shannon tells Tyrec that he'd better "get inside"; he ignores her. Then, at 6:50 [P.M.] Ken (a friend of Tyrec's) says, "There's your mom!" Tyrec scoots inside, then, says, "Oh, man. You were serious this time."

Informal, impromptu outdoor play is common in Tyrec's neighborhood. A group of boys approximately his age, regularly numbering four or five but sometimes reaching as many as ten, play ball games together on the street, walk to the store to get treats, watch television at each other's homes, and generally hang out together.

Language Use

In addition to differences by social class in time use, we also observed differences in language use in the home. As others have noted (Bernstein, 1971; Heath, 1983) middle-class parents used more reasoning in their speech with children while working-class and poor parents used more directives. For example, in observations of the African American home of Alex Williams, whose father was a trial lawyer and mother was a high level corporate executive, we found that the Williamses and other middle-class parents use language frequently, pleasurably, and instrumentally. Their children do likewise. For example, one January evening, Alexander is stumped by a homework assignment to write five riddles. He sits at the dinner table in the kitchen with his mother and a fieldworker. Mr. Williams is at the sink, washing the dinner dishes. He has his back to the group at the dinner table. Without turning around, he says to Alex, "Why don't you go upstairs to the third floor and get one those books and see if there is a riddle in there?"

Alex [says] smiling, "Yeah. That's a good idea! I'll go upstairs and copy one from out of the book." Terry turns around with a dish in hand, "That was a joke—not a valid suggestion. That is not an option." He smiled as he turned back around to the sink. Christina says, looking at Alex: "There is a word for that you know, plagiarism." Terry says (not turning around), "Someone can sue you for plagiarizing. Did you know that?" Alex: "That's only if it is copyrighted." They all begin talking at once.

Here we see Alex cheerfully (though gently) goading his father by pretending to misunderstand the verbal instruction to consult a book for help. Mr. Williams dutifully rises to the bait. Ms. Williams reshapes this moment of lightheartedness by introducing a new word into Alexander's vocabulary. Mr. Williams goes one step further by connecting the new word to a legal consequence. Alex upstages them both. He demonstrates that he is already familiar with the general idea of plagiarism and that he understands the concept of copyright, as well.

In marked contrast to working-class and poor parents, however, even when the Williamses issue directives, they often include explanations for their orders. Here, Ms. Williams is reminding her son to pay attention to his teacher:

> I want you to play close attention to Mrs. Scott when you are developing your film. Those chemicals are very dangerous. Don't play around in the classroom. You could get that stuff in someone's eye. And if you swallow it, you could die.

Alex chooses to ignore the directive in favor of instructing his misinformed mother:

Alex corrects her, "Mrs. Scott told us that we wouldn't die if we swallowed it. But we would get very sick and would have to get our stomach pumped." Christina does not follow the argument any further. She simply reiterates that he should be careful.

Possibly because the issue is safety, Ms. Williams does not encourage Alex to elaborate here, as she would be likely to do if the topic were less charged. Instead, she restates her directive and thus underscores her expectation that Alex will do as she asks.

Although Mr. and Ms. Williams disagreed on elements of how training in race relations should be implemented, they both recognized that their racial and ethnic identity profoundly shaped their and their son's everyday experiences. They were well aware of the potential for Alexander to be exposed to racial injustice, and they went to great lengths to try to protect their son from racial insults and other forms of discrimination. Nevertheless, race did not appear to shape the dominant cultural logic of child-rearing in Alexander's family or in other families in the study. All of the middle-class families engaged in extensive reasoning with their children, asking questions, probing assertions, and listening to answers. Similar patterns appeared in interviews and observations with other African American middle-class families.

A different pattern appeared in working-class and poor homes where there was simply less verbal speech than we observed in middle-class homes. There was also less speech between parents and children, a finding noted by other observational studies (Hart and Risley, 1995). Moreover, interspersed with intermittent talk are adult-issued directives. Children are told to do certain things (e.g., shower, take out the garbage) and not to do others (e.g., curse, talk back). In an African American home of a family living on public assistance in public housing, Ms. McAllister uses one-word directives to coordinate the use of the single bathroom. There are almost always at least four children in the apartment and often seven, plus Ms. McAllister and other adults. Ms. McAllister sends the children to wash up by pointing to a child, saying, "Bathroom," and handing him or her a washcloth. Wordlessly, the designated child gets up and goes to the bathroom to take a shower.

Children usually do what adults ask of them. We did not observe whining or protests, even when adults assign time-consuming tasks, such as the hour-long process of hair-braiding Lori McAllister is told to do for the four-year-old daughter of Aunt Dara's friend Charmaine:

Someone tells Lori, "Go do [Tyneshia's] hair for camp." Without saying anything, Lori gets up and goes inside and takes the little girl with her. They head for the couch near the television; Lori sits on the couch and the girl sits on the floor. [Tyneshia] sits quietly for about an hour, with her head tilted, while Lori carefully does a multitude of braids.

Lori's silent obedience is typical. Generally, children perform requests without comment. For example, at dinner one night, after Harold McAllister complains he doesn't like spinach, his mother directs him to finish it anyway:

Mom yells (loudly) at him to eat: "EAT! FINISH THE SPINACH!" (No response. Harold is at the table, dawdling.) Guion and Runako and Alexis finish eating and leave. I finish with Harold; he eats his spinach. He leaves all his yams.

The verbal world of Harold McAllister and other poor and working-class children offers some important advantages as well as costs. Compared to middle-class children we observed, Harold is more respectful towards adults in his family. In this setting, there are clear boundaries between adults and children. Adults feel comfortable issuing directives to children, which children comply with immediately. Some of the directives that adults issue center on obligations of children to others in the family ("don't beat on Guion" or "go do [her] hair for camp"). One consequence of this is that Harold, despite occasional tiffs, is much nicer to his sister (and his cousins) than the siblings we observed in middle-class homes. The use of directives and the pattern of silent compliance are not universal in Harold's life. In his interactions with peers, for example on the basketball "court," Harold's verbal displays are distinctively different than inside the household, with elaborated and embellished discourse. Nevertheless, there is a striking difference in linguistic interaction between adults and children in poor and working-class families when compared to that observed in the home of Alexander Williams. Ms. McAllister has the benefit of being able to issue directives without having to justify their decisions at every moment. This can make childrearing somewhat less tiring.

Another advantage is that Harold has more autonomy than middle-class children in making important decisions in daily life. As a child, he controls his leisure schedule. His basketball games are impromptu and allow him to develop important skills and talents. He is resourceful. He appears less exhausted than ten-year old Alexander. In addition, he has important social competencies, including his deftness in negotiating the "code of the street."[1] His mother has stressed these skills in her upbringing, as she impresses upon her children the importance of "not paying no mind" to others, including drunks and drug dealers who hang out in the neighborhoods which Harold and Alexis negotiate.

Still, in the world of schools, health care facilities, and other institutional settings, these valuable skills do not translate into the same advantages as the reasoning skills emphasized in the home of Alexander Williams and other middle-class children. Compared to Alexander Williams, Harold does not gain the development of a large vocabulary, an increase of his knowledge of science and politics, a set of tools to customize situations outside the home to maximize his advantage, and instruction in how to defend his argument with evidence. His knowledge of words, which might appear, for example, on future SAT tests, is not continually stressed at home.

In these areas, the lack of advantage is *not* connected to the intrinsic value of the McAllister family life or the use of directives at home. Indeed, one can argue raising children who are polite and respectful children and do not whine, needle, or badger their parents is a highly laudable childrearing goal. Deep and abiding ties with kinship groups are also, one might further argue, important. Rather, it is the specific ways that institutions function that ends up conveying advantages to middle-class children. In their standards, these institutions also permit, and even demand, active parent involvement. In this way as well, middle-class children often gain an advantage.

Intervention in Institutions

Children do not live their lives inside of the home. Instead, they are legally required to go to school, they go to the doctor, and many are involved in church and other adult-organized activities. In children's institutional lives, we found differences by social class in how mothers monitored children's institutional experiences. While in working-class and poor families children are granted autonomy to make their own way in organizations, in the middle-class homes, most aspects of the children's lives are subject to their mother's *ongoing* scrutiny.

For example in an African American middle-class home, where both parents are college graduates and Ms. Marshall is a computer worker and her husband a civil servant, their two daughters have a hectic schedule of organized activities including gymnastics for Stacey and basketball for Fern. When Ms. Marshall becomes aware of a problem, she moves quickly, drawing on her work and professional skills and experiences. She displays tremendous assertiveness, doggedness, and, in some cases, effectiveness in pressing institutions to recognize her daughters' individualized needs. Stacey's mother's proactive stance reflects her belief that she has a duty to intervene in situations where she perceives that her daughter's needs are not being met. This perceived responsibility applies across all areas of her children's lives. She is no more (or less) diligent with regard to Stacey and Fern's leisure activities than she is with regard to their experiences in school or church or the doctor's office. This is clear in the way she handles Stacey's transition from her township gymnastics classes to the private classes at an elite private gymnastic program at Wright's.

Ms. Marshall describes Stacey's first session at the club as rocky:

The girls were not warm. And these were little . . . eight and nine year old kids. You know, they weren't welcoming her the first night. It was kinda like eyeing each other, to see, you know, "Can you do this? Can you do that?"

More importantly, Ms. Marshall reported that the instructor is brusque, critical and not friendly toward Stacey. Ms. Marshall cannot hear what was being said, but she could see the interactions through a window. A key problem is that because her previous instructor had not used the professional jargon for gymnastic moves, Stacey does not know these terms. When the class ends and she walks out, she is visibly upset. Her mother's reaction is a common one among middle-class parents: She does not remind her daughter that in life one has to adjust, that she will need to work even harder, or that there is nothing to be done. Instead, Ms. Marshall focuses on Tina, the instructor, as the source of the problem:

We sat in the car for a minute and I said, "Look, Stac," I said. She said, "I-I," and she started crying. I said, "You wait here." The instructor had come to the door, Tina. So I went to her and I said, "Look." I said, "Is there a problem?" She said, "Aww . . . she'll be fine. She just needs to work on certain things." Blah-blah-blah. And I said, "She's really upset. She said you-you-you [were] pretty much correcting just about everything." And [Tina] said, "Well, she's got—she's gotta learn the terminology."

Ms. Marshall acknowledges that Stacey isn't familiar with specialized and technical gymnastics terms. Nonetheless, she continues to defend her daughter:

I do remember, I said to her, I said, "Look, maybe it's not all the student." You know, I just left it like that. That, you know, sometimes teaching, learning and teaching, is a two-way proposition as far as I'm concerned. And sometimes teachers have to learn how to, you know, meet the needs of the kid. Her style, her immediate style was not accommodating to—to Stacey.

Here Ms. Marshall is asserting the legitimacy of an individualized approach to instruction. She frames her opening remark as a question ("Is there a problem?"). Her purpose, however, is to alert the instructor to the negative impact she has had on Stacey ("She's really upset."). Although her criticism is indirect ("Maybe it's not all the student . . . "), Ms. Marshall makes it clear that she expects her daughter to be treated differently in the future. In this case, Stacey does not hear what her mother says, but she knows that her wishes and feelings are being transmitted to the instructor in a way that she could not do herself.

Although parents were equally concerned about their children's happiness, in working-class and poor homes we observed different patterns of oversight for children's institutional activities. For example in the white working-class home of Wendy Driver, Wendy's mother does not nurture her daughter's language development like Alexander Williams' mother does her son's. She does not attempt to draw Wendy out or follow up on new information when Wendy introduces the term mortal sin while the family is sitting around watching television. But, just like Ms. Williams, Ms. Driver cares very much about her child and just like middle-class parents she wants to help her daughter succeed. Ms. Driver keeps a close and careful eye on her Wendy's schooling. She knows that Wendy is having problems in school. Ms. Driver immediately signs and returns each form Wendy brings home from school and reminds her to turn the papers in to her teacher.

Wendy is "being tested" as part of an ongoing effort to determine why she has difficulties with spelling, reading, and related language-based activities. Her mother welcomes these official efforts but she did not request them. Unlike the middle-class mothers we observed, who asked teachers for detailed information about every aspect of their children's classroom performance and relentlessly pursued information and assessments outside of school as well, Ms. Driver seems content with only a vague notion of her daughter's learning disabilities. This attitude contrasts starkly with that of Stacey Marshall's mother, for example. In discussing Stacey's classroom experiences with fieldworkers, Ms. Marshall routinely described her daughter's academic strengths and weaknesses in detail. Ms. Driver never mentions that Wendy is doing grade-level work in math but is reading at a level a full three years below her grade. Her description is vague:

> She's having problems. . . . They had a special teacher come in and see if they could find out what the problem is. She has a reading problem, but they haven't put their finger on it yet, so she's been through all kinds of special teachers and testing and everything. She goes to Special Ed, I think it's two classes a day . . . I'm not one hundred percent sure—for her reading. It's very difficult

for her to read what's on paper. But then—she can remember things. But not everything. It's like she has a puzzle up there. And we've tried, well, they've tried a lot of things. They just haven't put their finger on it yet.

Wendy's teachers uniformly praise her mother as "supportive" and describe her as "very loving," but they are disappointed in Ms. Driver's failure to take a more active, interventionist role in Wendy's education, especially given the formidable nature of her daughter's learning problems. From Ms. Driver's perspective, however, being actively supportive means doing whatever the teachers tell her to do.

> Whatever they would suggest, I would do. They suggested she go to the eye doctor, so I did that. And they checked her and said there was nothing wrong there.

Similarly, she monitors Wendy's homework and supports her efforts to read:

> We listen to her read. We help her with her homework. So she has more attention here in a smaller household than it was when I lived with my parents. So, we're trying to help her out more, which I think is helping. And with the two [special education] classes a day at the school, instead of one like last year, she's learning a lot from that. So, we're just hoping it takes time and that she'll just snap out of it.

But Ms. Driver clearly does not have an *independent* understanding of the nature or degree of Wendy's limitations, perhaps because she is unfamiliar with the kind of terms the educators use to describe her daughter's needs (e.g., a limited "sight vocabulary," underdeveloped "language arts skills"). Perhaps, too, her confidence in the school staff makes it easier for her to leave "the details" to them: "Ms. Morton, she's great. She's worked with us for different testing and stuff." Ms. Driver depends on the school staff's expertise to assess the situation and then share the information with her:

> I think they just want to keep it in the school till now. And when they get to a point where they can't figure out what it is, and then I guess they'll send me somewhere else. . . .

Her mother is not alarmed, because "the school" has told her not to worry about Wendy's grades:

> Her report card—as long as it's not spelling and reading—spelling and reading are like F's. And they keep telling me not to worry, because she's in the Special Ed class. But besides that, she does good. I have no behavior problems with her at all.

Ms. Driver wants the best possible outcome for her daughter and she does not know how to achieve that goal without relying heavily on Wendy's teachers:

> I wouldn't even know where to start going. On the radio there was something for children having problems reading and this and that, call. And I suggested it to a couple different people, and they were like, wait a second, it's only to get you there and you'll end up paying an arm and a leg. So I said to my mom, "No, I'm going to wait until the first report card and go up and talk to them up there."

Thus, in looking for the source of Ms. Driver's deference toward educators, the answers don't seem to lie in her having either a shy personality or underdeveloped mothering skills. To understand why Wendy's mother is accepting where Stacey Marshall's mother would be aggressive, it is more useful to focus on social class position, both in terms of how class shapes worldviews and how class affects economic and educational resources. Ms. Driver understands her role in her daughter's education as involving a different set of responsibilities from those perceived by middle-class mothers. She responds to contacts from the school—such as invitations to the two annual parent-teacher conferences—but she does not initiate them. She views Wendy's school life as a separate realm, and one in which she, as a parent, is only an infrequent visitor. Ms. Driver expects that the teachers will teach and her daughter will learn and that, under normal circumstances, neither requires any additional help from her as a parent. If problems arise, she presumes that Wendy will tell her; or, if the issue is serious, the school will contact her. But what Ms. Driver fails to understand, is that the educators expect her to take on a pattern of "concerted cultivation" where she actively monitors and intervenes in her child's schooling. The teachers asked for a complicated mixture of deference and engagement from parents; they were disappointed when they did not get it.

Conclusions

I have stressed how social class dynamics are woven into the texture and rhythm of children and parents' daily lives. Class position influences critical aspects of family life: time use, language use, and kin ties. Working-class and middle-class mothers may express beliefs that reflect a similar notion of "intensive mothering," but their behavior is quite different. For that reason, I have described sets of paired beliefs and actions as a "cultural logic" of childrearing. When children and parents move outside the home into the world of social institutions, they find that these cultural practices are not given equal value. There are signs that middle-class children benefit, in ways that are invisible to them and to their parents, from the degree of similarity between the cultural repertoires in the home and those standards adopted by institutions.

NOTES

1. Elijah Anderson, *Code of the Street*, New York: W. W. Norton (1999).

BIBLIOGRAPHY

Anderson, Elijah. 1999. *Code of the Street.* New York, NY: W. W. Norton.

Bernstein, Basil. 1971. *Class, Codes, and Control: Theoretical Studies Towards a Sociology of Language.* New York, NY: Schocken.

Hart, Betty and Todd R. Risley. 1995. *Meaningful Differences in the Everyday Experiences of Young American Children.* New Haven: Yale University Press.

Heath, Shirley Brice. 1983. *Ways with Words: Language, Life, and Work in Communities and Classrooms.* Cambridge: Cambridge University Press.

Lareau, Annette. 2003. *Unequal Childhoods: Class, Race, and Family Life.* Berkeley, CA: University of California Press.

59

Digital Inequality

From Unequal Access to Differential Use

PAUL DIMAGGIO, ESZTER HARGITTAI,
CORAL CELESTE, AND STEVEN SHAFER

Social scientists and policymakers began worrying about inequality in Internet access as early as 1995 (Anderson et al. 1995), when just 3 percent of Americans had ever used the World Wide Web (Pew Center for the People and the Press 1995). At first most believed that the Internet would enhance equality of access to information by reducing its cost. As technoeuphoria wore off, however, observers noted that some kinds of people used the Internet more than others and that those with higher Internet access also had greater access to education, income, and other resources that help people get ahead (Hoffman and Novak 1998, 1999; Benton Foundation 1998; Strover 1999; Bucy 2000). Concern that the new technology might exacerbate inequality rather than ameliorate it focused on what analysts have called the "digital divide" between the online and the offline.

Since the mid-1990s researchers have found persistent differences in Internet use by social category (NTIA 1995, 1998, 1999, 2000, 2002; Lenhart et al. 2003). Although operational definitions of access

vary from study to study, most make a binary distinction between people who use the Web and other Internet services (especially e-mail) and people who do not. At first "access" was used literally to refer to whether a person had the means to connect to the Internet *if she or he so chose* (NTIA 1995). Later "access" became a synonym for use, conflating opportunity and choice. This is unfortunate, because studies that have measured both access *and* the extent of Internet use have found, first, that more people have access than use it (NTIA 1998 and Lenhart et al. 2003 report that 20 percent of residents of Internet households never go online), and second, that whereas resources drive access, demand drives intensity of use among people who have access. Thus, young adults are less likely to have home access than adults between the ages of twenty-five and fifty-four (NTIA 2000), but in Internet households teenagers spend more time online than adults (Kraut et al. 1998). . . .

Thanks to the NTIA's research program, we have a series of valuable snapshots (based on the Current Population Survey in 1994, 1997, 1998, 2000, and 2001) of intergroup differences in Internet use by:

1. *Region and place of residence:* Rates of Internet use are highest in the Northeast and far West and lowest in the Southeast. Of Americans age three or older (the NTIA reporting base for most purposes), state-level estimates range from 42 percent online in Mississippi to 69 percent in Alaska (NTIA 2002, 7–8). Suburbanites are most likely to use the Internet (57 percent), followed by rural dwellers (53 percent) and central-city residents (49 percent) (NTIA 2002, 19).

2. *Employment status:* In 2001, 65 percent of employed people age sixteen or older were Internet users, compared to just 37 percent of those who were not working (NTIA 2002, 12).

3. *Income:* Internet use rates rise linearly with family income, from 25 percent for persons with incomes of less than $15,000 to almost 80 percent for those with incomes above $75,000.

4. *Educational attainment:* Among persons age twenty-five or older, educational attainment is strongly associated with rates of Internet use. Proportions online range from fewer than 15 percent of those without a high school diploma to 40 percent of persons with a high school diploma, and more than 80 percent of college graduates (NTIA 2002, 17).

5. *Race-ethnicity:* Rates of Internet use are greater for Asian Americans and non-Hispanic whites (about 60 percent for each) than for non-Hispanic blacks (40 percent) and persons of Hispanic origin (just under 32 percent) (NTIA 2002, 21). Variation among these groups in income and education explains much of the difference, but even among those similar in educational attainment or income level, fewer African Americans than whites use the Internet (Hoffman, Novak, and Schlosser 2001; Lenhart et al. 2003).

6. *Age:* Rates of Internet use rise rapidly from age three to a peak around age fifteen, when nearly 80 percent of Americans are online; decline to around 65 percent at age twenty-five; then descend gently to just below 60 percent by age fifty-five. At that point rates decline rapidly with age (NTIA 2002, 13).

7. *Gender:* In early surveys men used the Internet at higher rates than women, but by 2001 women and men were equally likely to be online (Losh 2003). From the late teens to the late forties, women are *more* likely than men to use the Internet; men acquire an increasing edge after age fifty-five (NTIA 2002, 14).

8. *Family structure:* Families with children in the home are more likely to have computers and the Internet than are families without children (NTIA 2002, 14).

These patterns of inequality are similar to those observed in other countries. In Switzerland, for example, in 2000, 69 percent of university graduates but only 19 percent of high school graduates were online, and similar advantages were found for persons with high incomes, the young, and men (with the gender gap notably greater than in the United States) (Bonfadelli 2002, 75; see also De Haan 2003 on the Netherlands; Heil 2002 on the United Kingdom and Germany; and McLaren and Zappalà 2002 on Australia).

Persistent Disagreement

The availability of high-quality data has failed to dampen a hot debate over whether socioeconomic and racial divisions in Internet access warrant government action. During the Clinton administration the Commerce Department advanced an ambitious set of programs aimed at wiring schools, libraries, government offices, and community centers throughout the country. The second Bush administration has alternately treated the digital divide as something that was never a problem (Bush's FCC chair likened it to the "Mercedes divide") and a problem that has been solved. (The NTIA's 2002 report on Internet access is triumphantly titled *A Nation Online*.) Almost everyone agrees that the CPS data are reliable. But disagreement on how to interpret the trends persists. It centers on four questions:

1. *What do we mean by "access"?* If we mean an individual's ability to get on-line in some fashion at some location, then inequality is much diminished. If "access" means an individual's ability to use graphically complex websites from his or her home, differences among groups remain substantial.
2. *Which "digital divide"?* Some intergroup differences that were large at the onset of the digital revolution have diminished or disappeared. Others have persisted.
3. *How should we measure the difference?* It is simple to find measures that convey whatever impression an advocate prefers. But some measures are better than others.
4. *How should we interpret trends?* Can we count on the market to provide exten-

sive service soon enough in the future (and how extensive and how soon are "extensive" and "soon enough"?), or are current inequalities likely to persist indefinitely?

What Do We Mean by Access?

The original literal sense of "access" has gradually been replaced by a set of more concrete operational definitions. Different definitions yield somewhat different conclusions about inequality. We compare digital divides based on three increasingly demanding definitions of access: using the Internet anywhere; using the Internet at one's place of residence; and using the Internet at home through a high-speed connection. (The second criterion is meaningful because most people can surf more freely and spontaneously at home than at the office or in a public library. High-speed connections enable people to access streaming media or graphically complex websites.) For each criterion, Table 59.1 provides access rates for two contrasting groups and a measure of inequality—the ratio of the odds of access for the more- and less-privileged groups.[1]

Three features of this table deserve note. First, different criteria yield different estimates of inequality. For example, the disadvantage of people over age fifty-five relative to that of the young (age eighteen to twenty-five) is greater with respect to using the Internet anywhere than it is with respect to using the Internet at home and, especially, to having a high-speed home connection. (The difference reflects the fact that older people have higher incomes, more stable residences, and fewer other places to go online than the young.) Similarly, in 2001 women surpassed men in rates of Internet use, but men were still

Table 59.1 Internet Access of Americans Age Eighteen and Older, 2001

	Use Internet	Use Internet at Home	Use Internet at Home High-Speed
Black	39.09%	26.21%	5.57%
Non-black	57.89	46.54	10.87
Non-black/black			
Odds ratio	2.111	2.451	2.068
Women	56.33	44.23	9.71
Men	55.84	45.03	11.09
Male/female odds ratio	0.970	1.033	1.160
High school degree	54.61	42.71	9.53
College graduate	83.39	68.90	16.69
B.A./high school degree odds ratio	4.173	2.972	1.903
Income $20,000 to $29,999	40.02	28.04	4.79
Income greater than $67,500	68.24	57.01	14.91
Greater/lesser income odds ratio	3.220	2.991	3.484
Age eighteen to twenty-five	67.62	50.00	11.57
Age fifty-five and older	30.96	25.30	5.98
Younger/older odds ratio	4.657	2.952	1.837

Source: 2001 CPS.

ahead in access to the Internet at home, especially through high-speed connections.

Second, different criteria yield different impressions for different intergroup comparisons. Inequality with respect to age and educational attainment (comparing college graduates to high school graduates) is greatest for Internet use anywhere. Racial inequality, however, is greatest for at-home access, and income inequality (people with family incomes of $67,500 or more compared to those with incomes between $20,000 and $30,000) is greatest for high-speed connections at home.

Third, it follows that the size of intergroup "divides" depends on how we define "access." Inequality in Internet access anywhere between college and high school graduates dwarfs inequality between blacks and nonblacks, but racial inequality is slightly greater for access to high-speed connections at home. By the same token, the age and education "divides" exceed inequality between

income groups in use of the Internet at all, but income inequality slightly exceeds that associated with age and educational attainment for use of the Internet in one's home.

Which Divide?

In the few years that the Internet has been widely available, it has diffused widely. Some inequalities in access have already closed. Other gaps persist, however (see Figures 59.1 through 59.4).[2] Differences in rates of Internet use between men and women essentially disappeared between 1994 and 2001. (This descriptive conclusion is confirmed by Hiroshi Ono and Madeline Zavodny's [2003] logistic regression analyses with controls for income, age, educational attainment, and marital status.) Age remains strongly associated with Internet use, but the disadvantage of persons in their fifties and sixties has diminished. Regional differences and urban/rural differences also have declined (on the latter, see Bikson and Panis 1999).

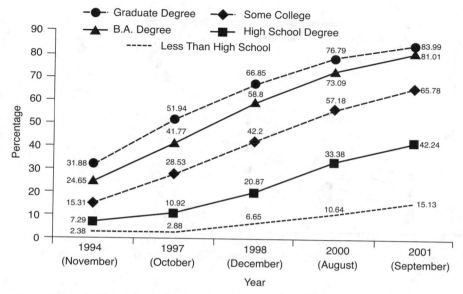

Figure 59.1   Internet Users in the United States, by Education (Age Eighteen and Older)
Source: CPS

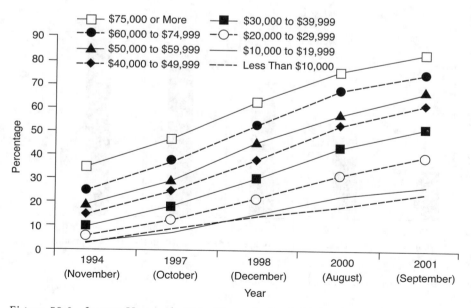

Figure 59.2   Internet Users in the United States, by Family Income (Age Eighteen and Older)
Source: CPS

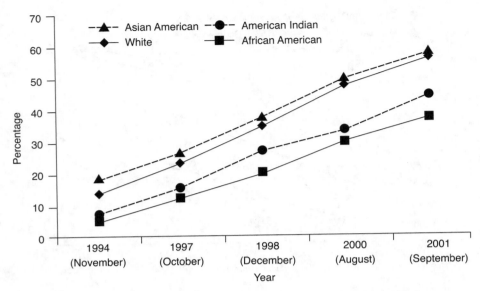

Figure 59.3   Internet Users in the United States, by Race (Age Eighteen and Older)
Source: CPS

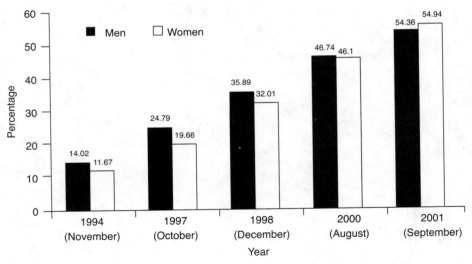

Figure 59.4   Internet Users in the United States, by Gender (Age Eighteen and Older)
Source: CPS

By contrast the absolute gap between Asian Americans and Euro-Americans, on one side, and African Americans and Native Americans, on the other, increased (though the ratio of the more-privileged to the less-privileged groups' rates declined; see also Hoffman, Novak, and Schlosser 2001). Most absolute differences based on educational attainment and income fanned out in the early years of rapid penetration, then remained stable (or in the case of differences among the topmost categories, declined) thereafter. Policy analysts particularly interested in disparities based on gender, age, or place of residence are likely to find reasons for cheer in the Internet's trajectory, whereas analysts especially concerned about racial or socioeconomic inequality will be far less satisfied.

Which Measures?

Interpretation of trend data is complicated by the fact that different measures of inequality yield diametrically different results. Observers measure over-time change in intergroup inequality in Internet use in many ways: absolute percentage differences; the ratio of the proportion online in the advantaged group to the proportion online in the less-advantaged group; the ratio of the proportion offline in the less-advantaged group to the proportion offline in the more-advantaged group; the odds ratios of adoption (or non-adoption) between two groups; and for forms of inequality that can be expressed ordinally, pseudo-gini coefficients expressing deviation from equality in the distribution of Internet users across income (or educational) strata. Some measure relative rates of change: ratios in the rate of increase of the less-advantaged to the more-advantaged group, or ratios of the rate of decrease of non-use of the more-advantaged to the less-advantaged use (both expressed

as change in either absolute rates or in odds ratios).

Figures 59.5 and 59.6 use CPS data to illustrate why this proliferation of measures is problematic, using a single type of inequality—that between blacks and whites age eighteen or older. Figure 59.5 compares the shares of each group online between 1994 and 2001. Those pointing with pride can emphasize a steady decline in the ratio of the percentage of white Americans online to the percentage of black Americans online. Those viewing with alarm may note that the absolute percentage difference between whites and blacks has increased slightly and that the ratio of the percentage of African Americans who are offline to the percentage of whites who are offline has risen steadily. In fact, the online and offline ratios are mirror images, for as the proportion of Internet users has increased from a very low base, the percentage of non-users has declined from a very high base. Other things being equal, groups that start at a disadvantage will increase their percentage of those online while constituting an ever-larger share (proportionately) of the disenfranchised.

We see the same thing if we compare rates of change (Figure 59.6). Whether inequality seems to be worsening or improving varies from measure to measure. Optimists may note that the rates of percentage increase in the proportion online have been greater for blacks than for whites. Pessimists can point out that the rates of absolute percentage increase for whites have outpaced those for blacks and that whites reduced their offline numbers at a higher rate than blacks throughout this period.

Steven Martin (2003) argues that there is something wrong with measures that yield opposite conclusions depending on whether

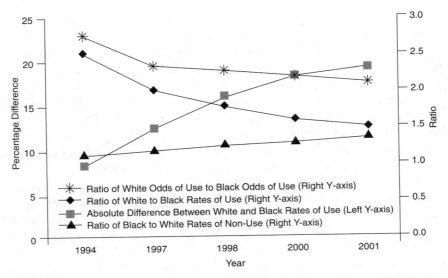

Figure 59.5 Measure of Inequality in Black and White Americans' Internet Use (Age Eighteen and Older)

Source: CPS

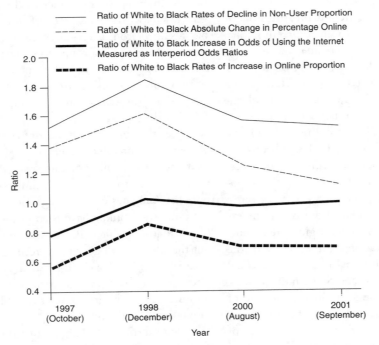

Figure 59.6 Measures of Inequality in Rate of Change in Black and White Americans' Internet Use (Age Eighteen and Older)

Source: CPS

one measures the proportion of two groups online or the complement of that proportion (intergroup ratios of use/non-use rates or rates of change in use/non-use, as well as quasi-gini coefficients for forms of inequality that can be represented ordinally), and he offers an attractive solution. Odds ratios do not have this problem, he notes: they are the same whether one focuses on the proportions of two groups who are users or the proportions who have been left behind. We include odds ratios in both Figure 59.5 (the ratio of the odds that a white American is online to the odds that a black American is online) and Figure 59.6 (the ratio of interperiod changes in odds for whites to changes in odds for blacks). Both demonstrate that the white advantage declined notably between 1994 and 1997 and remained stable or grew slightly from 1997 to 2001.

To understand the mechanisms that produce inequality it is helpful to identify the advantages and disadvantages that accrue to people as a consequence of their race (or gender or income) independent of other salient characteristics that travel in tandem with race (or gender or income). A good measure of a characteristic's net contribution to inequality in Internet use is its coefficient in a logistic regression equation with statistical controls for other factors associated with going online. One study that employed this technique, using CPS household data from 1994 to 2000, found that the net effects of education, race, and, to a lesser extent, income increased over this period (Leigh and Atkinson 2001). Another, using CPS data from 1993 and 1997, found constant income effects but increasing education effects on use of Internet services, as well as growing net differences between African Americans and non-Hispanic whites (Bikson and Panis 1999). A study of Internet use in fourteen European countries (Norris 2001) found growing effects of education, income, and occupation from 1996 to 1999. Such studies indicate that inequality grew modestly during the first years of diffusion.[3]

Interpreting the Trends

Andrew Leigh and Robert Atkinson (2001) argue that changing differences between groups in rates of Internet use simply reflect the position of those groups on an S-shaped diffusion curve that will culminate in full access for everyone. Groups that have reached the point of rapid ascent at the curve's midsection will always appear to be outpacing groups that are still in the takeoff stage. When the latter achieve takeoff and the former reach the "top" of the S, where rapid growth yields to slower increases, the less-advantaged groups will appear to be catching up (Norris 2001, 30–31).

This is a crucial analytic insight. But *can* we assume that different groups are merely at different points on the same curve? Perhaps the most important question facing policymakers is whether disadvantaged groups are simply a few paces behind or, by contrast, whether they are becoming marooned as the rest of the world moves ahead. If the former is true, we can count on time to bridge the divide; if the *trajectories* are different, public policy must play a larger role to reduce inequality (Leigh and Atkinson 2001).

We can make a good theoretical case for either scenario. Liberals, who set policy in the Clinton administration, tend to take the latter stance, whereas conservatives, like those in the Bush administration, embrace the former. The case for the optimistic scenario goes like this. In its rapid diffusion the Internet is traversing the path of such communication technologies as radio and television. At first access is restricted to an elite defined by wealth, institutional location, or both, but increasing penetration reduces gaps between rich and poor, urban and rural, old and young, the well educated and the unschooled (Compaine 2001).

Peter Blau's (1977) insights explain why purely structural factors may ensure that inequality in access declines with diffusion. The first people to gain access to a new technology usually occupy privileged positions on several dimensions—for example, income, white-collar work, educational level, race, rural residence, and gender. But many fewer people are privileged on all dimensions than on each. For example, there are a lot more white-collar workers than there are high-income, white, male, urban-dwelling, college-educated, white-collar workers. As penetration grows, access cascades beyond multiply privileged groups to people who are privileged in some ways but disadvantaged in others; the latter, in turn, become conduits to others with whom they share less-privileged characteristics. For example, when a rural, Latina, white-collar worker gains Internet access at her workplace, she may use the skills she acquires to help blue-collar family members go online, thus playing a role in reducing inequality between Hispanic and non-Hispanic Americans, and between urban and rural dwellers.[4]

An equally strong case can be made for the opposite scenario. When we examine technology diffusion, a distinction emerges between products and services. Even expensive products often reach high penetration levels when economies of scale reduce their prices (television sets, VCRs, computers) or less expensive secondary markets emerge (automobiles, refrigerators), or both. By contrast, the diffusion of services that entail continuing expense has been slower,

bumpier, and less complete (Schement 2003). As critical as telephone service would seem to be (especially to residents of rural areas), telephone penetration grew slowly and actually declined (markedly among farm families) during the Great Depression (Fischer 1992). Despite federal efforts, telephone service did not penetrate 90 percent of households until the 1970s, and the rate remains much lower than 90 percent in inner-city neighborhoods (Schement and Forbes 1999; Mueller and Schement 2001).

Evidence as well as theory can be mustered on behalf of both the optimistic and pessimistic points of view. Four arguments favor the former. First, as we have seen, some "divides" (gender, region, age, rural/urban) have already diminished. The trajectory of other gaps depends on the measures we use, but Internet use has undeniably expanded among all groups, so straight-line extrapolation (until recently at least) has suggested eventual convergence.

Second, surveys indicate that despite slowing growth after 2000, the market for Internet services is far from saturated. A spring 2000 survey by the Pew Center reported that 41 percent of Americans who did *not* use the Internet intended to do so (Lenhart 2000, 2); two years later, 44 percent of non-users predicted they would do so. If they did (and if those who said they probably or definitely would not go online did not), the proportion of Americans who are Internet users would rise above 70 percent.

Third, non-users' expectations are strongly correlated with age. In the Pew survey, 65 percent of non-users age fifty or younger expected to go online, compared to just 36 percent of non-users over age fifty, suggesting that generational succession will send Internet usage rates even higher. Based on these cohort differences, Lenhart (2000, 3) predicts that "in a generation, Internet penetration will reach the levels enjoyed by the telephone . . . and the television." Finally, late adopters come from less-privileged backgrounds than Internet pioneers. In both 1998 and 2000, surveys found that new users had lower incomes and less education than Americans who had been online longer (Horrigan 2000; Cummings and Kraut 2000; Howard, Rainie, and Jones 2001; Katz, Rice, and Aspden 2001).

Evidence in favor of the pessimistic scenario is equally strong. Inequality by race, income, and educational attainment has diminished little, if at all: Americans with few years of education and low incomes were still less likely to be online in 2001 as Americans with the most education and the highest incomes had been in 1994. Moreover, we can discount those divides that *have* been bridged as special cases: place of residence became less important because networks were built out and the technology became more flexible, and women and the elderly are usually slower technology adopters than men and the young, but both groups ordinarily catch up.

Second, the high diffusion rate of the 1990s did not represent a "natural" trajectory but rather the success of federal and state initiatives to encourage the Internet's rapid evolution and broad availability and the special benefits to the Internet of an extraordinary economic bubble (the eponymous "boom" of the late 1990s). The reversal of both public policy and macroeconomic fortune after 2000 has already belied projections made as recently as 1999 that income inequality in the use of Internet services would vanish by 2001 (Bikson and Panis 1999) and in 2001 that household Internet access would reach 90 percent by 2003 (Leigh and Atkinson 2001, 6). Instead, diffusion slowed as the bubble

popped (Lenhart et al. 2003). If curves plateau at or near 2001 rates, existing levels of inequality could be locked in for decades.

Third, although newer adopters are of lower socioeconomic status than longtime users, they may not *stay* online. In particular, loss of income during hard times may make consumers less able to pay monthly connection fees. Many people adopt the technology only to give it up later, and these Internet dropouts come disproportionately from groups with lower probabilities of going online in the first place. In surveys undertaken between 1995 and 2000, James Katz and his colleagues (Katz and Aspden 1997; Katz and Rice 2002) found that approximately 20 percent of those who had ever used the Internet no longer did so. In the fall of 2001, 3.3 percent of CPS households reported that they had discontinued Internet service (NTIA 2002, 77). Analyses prepared for this chapter reveal that about 10 percent of General Social Survey (GSS) respondents who used the Internet in the spring of 2000 no longer did so when they were reinterviewed eighteen months later. A 2002 study (Lenhart et al. 2003, 21) reports that 7 percent of U.S. adults are *former* Internet users and that between 27 and 44 percent of *current users* have gone offline for extended periods after becoming users. This study concludes that "the road to Internet use is so paved with bumps and turnarounds" (3) that the binary division of the population into "online" and "offline" is misleading. . . .

Online Inequality Compared to Inequality in the Use of Other Media

To understand the Internet's implications for equality of access to information, we must examine comparative evidence on access to and use of other communication media. Even if people with lots of money or education have privileged access to information online, whether or not an increasing role for the Internet exacerbates or ameliorates information inequality depends on whether access to and use of other media is more or less equally distributed. Socioeconomic status is ordinarily associated with access to communication media and, among those with access, with getting information (for evidence from the political domain, see Verba, Schlozman, and Brady 1995); it would be headline news if the Internet were an exception. As Pippa Norris (2001, 12) argues: "The interesting question is not whether there will be *absolute* social inequalities in Internet access [but] . . . whether *relative* inequalities in Internet use will be similar to disparities in the penetration rates of older communication technologies."

How might the Internet compare to mundane communication technologies like newspapers, magazines, the daily press, or even face-to-face conversation? Most online information is a free good. Economic theory tells us that if price elasticity is greater than zero, free information will be consumed at a faster rate than costly information, especially by people with little discretionary income. Thus, for those who have access to it, the Internet should make the distribution of information more equal. Yet this argument requires qualification in a number of ways. First, many competing information sources (network television news, interpersonal communication by telephone, daily newspapers) are either free or inexpensive. Second, online information is a "free good" only insofar as the user's time is without value. If lower-status Internet users take longer to find information

(because their search skills are poorer, their connections slower, or their domain knowledge less), then the Internet could be a more "expensive" form of information than the newspaper, television, or a phone call to a friend. If going online requires a drive to the library or the risk of getting caught surfing while at work, it may be more expensive still. Third, because of the vast amount of information online, the Internet may be most attractive to those whose demand for information is highest (in many domains, high-SES users). Others may be satisfied by more limited media. Heinz Bonfadelli (2002) argues that the heterogeneity and depth of Internet-based information (in comparison to the relative homogeneity of material in newspapers or news broadcasts) is likely to exacerbate information inequality. In other words, we could plausibly hypothesize that the Internet will lead to a more egalitarian distribution of information, *or* that it will reinforce or even exacerbate the usual inequalities.

We must distinguish analytically between *access* and *use* in this regard. With respect to access, we may ask what would happen (holding constant the way people distribute attention across media) if information *producers* took information currently transmitted by newspaper, television, or word of mouth and began distributing it through the Internet instead. For example, to what extent would low-income parents be hurt or helped if public schools used local newspapers less and websites more to distribute information about class assignments, policy changes, and extracurricular activities? With respect to use, the question is (given the current allocation of information across media) how would inequality be affected if information *consumers* shifted their attention from one medium to another? For example, would low-income parents learn more or less about their kids' schools if they spent more time online and less time reading the newspaper or talking with neighbors?

We know of only four studies that address such questions directly. Norris (2001, 90), using 1999 Eurobarometer data, found remarkably similar predictors of scores on a "new media index" (computer, CD-ROM, modem, and Internet) and an "old media index" (VCR, fax, satellite TV, cable TV, Teletext, and Videotext) in several European countries. Mariko Lin Chang (2003) used data from the 1998 Survey of Consumer Finances to investigate the impact of education, race, and other factors on where people get financial information. Education was more strongly associated with use of the Internet than with use of any other source of information; wealth (but not income) was significantly predictive of Internet use as well (but less so than of contact with financial professionals). African Americans favored financial professionals and advertisements over the Internet. Young people preferred the Internet and eschewed financial professionals; the elderly did the opposite. In a study of health information-seeking, Sanjay Pandey, John Hart, and Sheela Tiwary (2002) found that income and education significantly predicted Internet use. Compared to information sought from a doctor or in the newspaper, the Web was the only medium stratified by socioeconomic status. In a study of the use of media for political news, Bruce Bimber (2003) reported that African Americans were less underrepresented among Internet users than among newspaper readers and that young people were disproportionately likely to seek information online.

For this chapter, we analyzed data from the 2000 and 2002 General Social Surveys, which contained domain-specific questions about information-seeking in the areas of health (2000 and 2002), politics (2000), and jobs (2002). Respondents were first asked if they had "looked for information" at all during the past year; those who replied affirmatively were then asked which of several sources of information they employed.[5] Therefore, we can explore variation in search behaviors among people for whom we know that the knowledge domain is salient.

Here we focus on the association between median family income and the use of each source of information. Comparison of median incomes (reported in dollar ranges, to which we assigned values at the midpoint) indicates that respondents who sought information at all about health care or political candidates were financially better off than those who did not (see Table 59.2). No difference was evident for job information. Table 59.3 describes the search behavior of respondents who sought information in each domain. The results are striking: in each case, people who sought information on the Internet had notably higher incomes than people who searched through other means. The difference was least for employment information ($37,500 compared to $32,500), but the Internet was the *only* source for which users had higher incomes than non-users. The income advantage of those who sought political information online was greater than for any other source but general-interest magazines (both $55,000 for users and $37,500 for non-users). The differences were most marked in health care, where the Web users' income advantage was far greater than it was for any other information source.

To summarize, the little evidence we have is equivocal with respect to socioeconomic

Table 59.2   Median Income of Respondents Who Did or Did Not Search for Information

	Health Information (2000)	Health Information (2002)	Political Information (2000)	Employment Information (2002)
Sought information	$37,500	$45,000	$45,000	$37,500
Did not seek information	32,500	32,500	32,500	37,500

Data Source: 2000 and 2002 GSS.

Table 59.3   Median Family Income of Respondents Who Did or Did Not Use Specific Media for Information (Respondents Who Sought Such Information from Any Source Only)

	Panel A: Health Information Search (2000)						
	Doctor or Nurse	Friend or Relative	World Wide Web	Magazine (Health)	Magazine (General)	TV/Radio	Newspaper
Yes	$37,500	$45,000	$55,000	$37,500	$37,500	$32,500	$37,500
No	35,000	37,500	27,500	37,500	37,500	45,000	41,250

	Panel B: Health Information Search (2002)						
	Doctor or Nurse	Friend or Relative	World Wide Web	Magazine (Health)	Magazine (General)	TV/Radio	Newspaper
Yes	45,000	45,000	55,000	37,500	37,500	37,500	37,500
No	45,000	37,500	32,500	45,000	45,000	45,000	45,000

	Panel C: Political Information Search (2000)						
	Newspaper	TV/Radio	Magazine (General)	Friend or Relative	Political Campaign	World Wide Web	Magazine (Political)
Yes	45,000	45,000	55,000	45,000	45,000	55,000	45,000
No	37,500	55,000	37,500	37,500	45,000	37,500	45,000

	Panel D: Employment Information Search (2002)						
	Newspapter	Friend or Relative (Non-coworker)	Outside Contact	World Wide Web	Coworker	Publication	Counseling Service	TV/Radio
Yes	37,500	37,500	37,500	37,500	37,500	37,500	32,500	25,625
No	45,000	45,000	37,500	32,500	37,500	37,500	37,500	37,500

Data Source: 2000 and 2002 GSS.

inequality in the use of different media, but it suggests that for some purposes at least information would be more unequally distributed in a world in which the Internet played a greater role and other media a correspondingly smaller one. Insofar as we can judge from available studies, the level of socioeconomic inequality in access to information online is no less, and is probably greater, than the degree of inequality in access to information through other media. . . .

Conclusion

The digital divide paradigm served researchers and policymakers well during the opening years of Internet diffusion. Even though we know relatively little about the net effects of Internet access on educational attainment, labor market success, and life-course outcomes, the fact that public services and government information are increasingly migrating to the Internet makes access an important topic from the standpoint of public policy. Now that more than half of Americans go online, we should pursue a more differentiated approach to understanding the Internet's implications for social and economic inequality—one that focuses on the extent and causes of different returns to Internet use for different kinds of users. In particular, it is crucial to move beyond description and projection to understand the mechanisms, consequences, and institutional context of inequality in access to the Internet and use of the services it offers.

NOTES

Support from the Russell Sage Foundation, the National Science Foundation (grant IIS0086143), and the Markle Foundation is gratefully acknowledged, as is institutional support from the Princeton Center for Arts and Cultural Policy Studies and the Office of Population Research. This chapter reflects the impact on the first author's thinking of several helpful and provocative comments by participants at the Russell Sage Foundation Inequality Project's Harvard meeting in the summer of 2001.

1. The odds ratio, r_{jk}, equals $(p_j/[1 - p_j])/(p_k/[1 - p_k])$, where p_j is the probability that the more-advantaged group has access and p_k is the probability that the less-advantaged group has access.

2. Figures 59.1 to 59.4 were produced by Hargittai using CPS data. Comparable graphs for region, metropolitan residence, gender, and Hispanic ethnicity are available at http://www.eszter.com/netuse.html. Data for 1994 are on the presence of modems in the household. Data for subsequent years are on use of the Internet for any purpose.

3. Unfortunately, it is difficult to interpret these results with much confidence. The authors of the U.S. study chose a method (linear as opposed to logistic regression) that would tend to lead coefficients to become larger (other things being equal) as the Internet's penetration increased. The author of the European study describes her method as linear (OLS) regression in the text but as logistic regression in the notes to the table reporting results, complicating interpretation (Norris 2001, 86, 88).

4. This line of reasoning must make two assumptions, for both of which there is much empirical support. First, the parameters with respect to which advantage is accorded must be only moderately correlated with one another (Blau 1977); second, personal relationships must be characterized by bias toward homophily—that is, people must tend to have friends who are similar to themselves (Marsden 1987).

5. The text of the health item was: "In the past year . . . have you looked for information about a health concern or medical problem? If yes, please tell me if you tried to find such health information from [articles in a daily newspaper; articles in a general-interest magazine; special health or medical magazine or newsletter; a doctor, nurse, or other medical professional; friends or relatives; radio or television programs; the Internet or World Wide Web]." The text for the political item was: "In the past two years . . . have you looked for information about the views or background of a candidate for political office? If yes, please tell me if you tried to find such political information from [articles in a daily newspaper; articles in general newsmagazines like *Time, Newsweek,* or *U.S. News & World Report;* special magazine or newsletter with particular policy interest or perspective; radio or television programs; friends or relatives; campaign materials from campaign worker or candidate; the Internet or World Wide Web]." The text for the jobs item was: "In the past

year . . . have you searched for information about a new job or explored career opportunities? Please tell me how many times you tried to find such information from [classified ads in a daily newspaper; classified ads in an industry or professional publication; a fellow worker or human resources staff member at your workplace—that is, where you were working when you were searching; business or work contacts outside your workplace—that is, outside where you were then working; friends outside of work or relatives; any job placement or career counseling service; radio or television program; information posted on the Internet]." (The job responses were binarized as yes or no.) Note that respondents were asked these questions *before* being asked the series of items about their use of the Internet, so that they were *not* primed to think about the latter.

REFERENCES

Anderson Robert H., Tora K. Bikson, Sally Ann Law, Bridger M. Mitchell, et al. 1995. *Universal Access to E-mail: Feasibility and Societal Implications.* Santa Monica, Calif.: Rand Corporation.

Benton Foundation. 1998. *Losing Ground Bit by Bit: Low-Income Communities in the Information Age.* Washington, D.C.: Benton Foundation and National Urban League.

Bikson, Tora K., and Constantijn W. A. Panis. 1999. *Citizens, Computers, and Connectivity: A Review of Trends.* Santa Monica, Calif.: Rand Corporation. Available at: www.rand.org/publications/MR/MR1109. (Last accessed August 26, 2003.)

Bimber, Bruce. 2000. "The Gender Gap on the Internet." *Social Science Quarterly* 81: 868–76.

———. 2003. *Information and American Democracy: Technology in the Evolution of Political Power.* New York: Cambridge University Press.

Blau, Peter M. 1977. *Inequality and Heterogeneity: A Primitive Theory of Social Structure.* New York: Free Press.

Bonfadelli, Heinz. 2002. "The Internet and Knowledge Gaps: A Theoretical and Empirical Investigation." *European Journal of Communication* 17: 65–84.

Bucy, Erik P. 2000. "Social Access to the Internet." *Press/Politics* 5: 50–61.

Chang, Mariko Lin. 2003. "With a Little Help from My Friends (and My Financial Planner): How Socioeconomic Status and Race Influence the Search for Financial Information." Paper presented to the session on culture and economy at the 2003 annual meeting of the American Sociological Association, Atlanta (August 16–18, 2003).

Compaine, Benjamin M. 2000. "Re-examining the Digital Divide." Paper presented to the twenty-eighth Telecommunications Policy Research Conference, Alexandria, Va. (September 23–25).

———. 2001. "Information Gaps: Myth or Reality?" In *The Digital Divide: Facing a Crisis or Creating a Myth?*, edited by Benjamin M. Compaine. Cambridge, Mass.: MIT Press.

Cummings, Jonathon N., and Robert Kraut. 2000. "Domesticating Computers and the Internet." Unpublished paper. Carnegie-Mellon University, Pittsburgh.

De Haan, Jos. 2003. "IT and Social Inequality in the Netherlands." *IT and Society* 1 (4, Spring): 27–45. Available at: www.stanford.edu/group/siqss/itandsociety/v01i04/v01i04a04.pdf.

Fischer, Claude S. 1992. *America Calling: A Social History of the Telephone to 1940.* Berkeley: University of California Press.

Heil, Alexander. 2002. "The Information Society in the United Kingdom and Germany: Chances, Risks, and Challenges." Master's thesis, University of Leipzig. Available at: www.falling-through-the-net.de/analysis.pdf. (Last accessed September 1, 2003.)

Hoffman, Donna L., and Thomas P. Novak. 1998. "Bridging the Racial Divide on the Internet." *Science* 280: 390–96.

———. 1999. "Examining the Relationship of Race to Internet Access and Usage over Time." Working paper. Nashville: eLab Manuscripts, Vanderbilt University.

Hoffman, Donna L., Thomas P. Novak, and Ann E. Schlosser. 2001. "The Evolution of the Digital Divide: Examining the Relationship of Race to Internet Access and Usage over Time." In *The Digital Divide: Facing a Crisis or Creat-*

ing a Myth?, edited by Benjamin M. Compaine. Cambridge, Mass.: MIT Press.

Horrigan, John. 2000. New Internet Users: What They Do Online, What They Don't, and Implications for the Net's Future. Washington, D.C.: Pew Internet and American Life Project (September 25).

Howard, Philip, Lee Rainie, and Steve Jones. 2001. "Days and Nights on the Internet: The Impact of a Diffusing Technology." American Behavioral Scientist 45: 383–404.

Katz, James E., and Philip Aspden. 1997. "Motives, Hurdles, and Dropouts." Communications of the ACM 40: 97–102.

Katz, James E., and Ronald Rice. 2002. Social Consequences of Internet Use: Access, Involvement, and Interaction. Cambridge Mass.: MIT.

Katz, James E., Ronald Rice, and Philip Aspden. 2001. "The Internet, 1995–2000: Access, Civic Involvement, and Social Interaction." American Behavioral Scientist 45(3): 405–19.

Kraut, Robert, Michael Patterson, Vicki Lundmark, Sara Kiesler, Tridas Mukophadhyay, and William Scherlis. 1998. "Internet Paradox: A Social Technology That Reduces Social Involvement and Psychological Wellbeing?" American Psychologist 53: 1011–31.

Leigh, Andrew, and Robert Atkinson. 2001. "Clear Thinking on the Digital Divide." Washington, D.C.: Progressive Policy Institute (June 26, 1999). Available at: www.NDOL.org?Documents/DigitalDivide.PDF. (Last accessed October 21, 2003.)

Lenhart, Amanda. 2000. "Who's Not Online: 57 Percent of Those Without Internet Access Say They Do Not Plan to Log On." Washington, D.C.: Pew Internet and American Life Project (September 21).

Lenhart, Amanda, John Horrigan, Lee Rainie, Katherine Allen, Angie Boyce, Mary Madden, and Erin O'Grady. 2003. "The Ever-Shifting Internet Population: A New Look at Internet Access and the Digital Divide." Washington, D.C.: Pew Internet and American Life Project (April 16).

Losh, Susan Carol. 2003. "Gender and Educational Digital Chasms in Computer and Internet Access and Use over Time: 1983–2000." IT and Society 1(4, Spring): 73–86. Available at: www.stanford.edu/group/siqss/itandsociety/v01i04/v01i04a06.pdf.

Marsden, Peter V. 1987. "Core Discussion Networks of Americans." American Sociological Review 52: 122–31.

Martin, Steven P. 2003. "Is the Digital Divide Really Closing? A Critique of Inequality Measurement in A Nation Online." IT and Society 1(4, Spring): 1–13. Available at: www.stanford.edu/group/siqss/itandsociety/v01i04/html. (Last accessed June 12, 2003.)

McLaren, Jennifer, and Gianni Zappalà. 2002. "The 'Digital Divide' Among Financially Disadvantaged Families in Australia." First Monday 7(11). Available at: firstmonday.org/issues/issue7_11/mclaren/index.html. (Last accessed September 1, 2003.)

Mueller, Milton L., and Jorge Reina Schement. 2001. "Universal Service from the Bottom Up: A Study of Telephone Penetration in Camden, New Jersey." In The Digital Divide: Facing a Crisis or Creating a Myth?, edited by Benjamin M. Compaine. Cambridge, Mass.: MIT Press.

National Telecommunications and Information Administration (NTIA). 1995. Falling Through the Net: A Survey of the "Have-nots" in Rural and Urban America. Washington: U.S. Department of Commerce (July).

———. 1998. Falling Through the Net II: New Data on the Digital Divide. Washington: U.S. Department of Commerce (July).

———. 1999. Falling Through the Net: Defining the Digital Divide. Washington: U.S. Department of Commerce (November).

———. 2000. Falling Through the Net: Toward Digital Inclusion. Washington: U.S. Department of Commerce (October).

———. 2002. A Nation Online: How Americans Are Expanding Their Use of the Internet. Washington: U.S. Department of Commerce (February).

Norris, Pippa. 2001. Digital Divide? Civic Engagement, Information Poverty, and the Internet in Democratic Societies. New York: Cambridge University Press.

Ono, Hiroshi, and Madeline Zavodny. 2003. "Gender and the Internet." *Social Science Quarterly* 84: 111–21.

Pandey, Sanjay K., John J. Hart, and Sheela Tiwary. 2002. "Women's Health and the Internet: Understanding Emerging Trends and Implications." *Social Science and Medicine* 56: 179–91.

Pew Center for the People and the Press. 1995. *Technology in the American Household*. Washington, D.C.: Pew Center for the People and the Press.

Schement, Jorge Reina. 2003. "Measuring What Jefferson Knew and Tocqueville Saw: Libraries as Bridges Across the Digital Divide." *IT and Society* 1(4, Spring): 118–25. Available at: www.stanford.edu/group/siqss/itandsociety/v01i04/v01i04a10.pdf.

Schement, Jorge Reina, and Scott C. Forbes. 1999. "Approaching the Net: Toward Global Principles of Universal Service." Available at: www.benton.org/policy/schement/ptc99/home.html. (Last accessed November 16, 2001.)

Strover, Sharon. 1999. *Rural Internet Connectivity*. Columbia, Mo.: Rural Policy Research Institute.

Verba, Sidney, Kay Schlozman, and Henry E. Brady. 1995. *Voice and Equality: Civic Voluntarism in American Politics*. Cambridge, Mass.: Harvard University Press.

60

The Realignment of U.S. Presidential Voting, 1948–2004

MICHAEL HOUT
BENJAMIN MOODIE

Introduction

U.S. presidential elections since the 1960s have offered ample material for political scientists and political sociologists who have contended that the stable class politics of the industrial era—roughly 1932–1964 (or maybe as late as 1976)—gave way to new, "postmaterial" politics (e.g., Abramson and Inglehart 1995; Clark and Lipset 1991; Inglehart 1977, 1990; Lipset 1981). Scholars who subscribe to this view point to newer cleavages based on gender, identity, concern for the environment, and family values, which have, they argue, displaced class from its central place in U.S. politics. When Democrats appeal to middle-class voters and the British Labour party touts a "third way" in twenty-first century politics, some of these ideas ring true.

Other scholars have countered the postmaterialists. First, they note that although elections are zero-sum—an individual's vote for one candidate precludes her vote for another in the same election—cleavages are not. Voters can choose candidates based on a single dimension of their social identity, whether it be class, gender, religion, or something else, or they can balance a variety of considerations. Nothing in the political arithmetic of social cleavages mandates that a rise in the weight given to one factor lowers the weight given to others. In fact, research has shown that, to a first approximation, all the factors that were important for voting in U.S. presidential elections in the 1960s were more important in the 1990s (Greeley and Hout 2006, ch. 3). Second, the empirical evidence contradicts the postmaterialists. In Britain, class voting fluctuates without trend (Goldthorpe 1999; Heath, Jowell, and Curtice 1985). In the United States, classes realigned (Hout, Brooks, and Manza 1995; Hout, Manza, and Brooks 1999), and the effect of income on the vote increased (McCarty, Poole, and Rosenthal 2005).

Original article prepared for this book. We are updating the work of Hout, Manza, and Brooks (1999). We owe a huge debt to Jeff Manza and Clem Brooks, who established the research templates that we use in this work. We thank the participants of the Stanford-Berkeley Inequality Colloquium, especially Annette Lareau, for helpful discussion.

Class Voting and Class Politics

Interest in class voting goes back to the dawn of modern understandings of class; that is, back to the grand theorists of the nineteenth century. The roots of contemporary debates about class voting, however, are planted in data, not in class theory. The national election surveys that have accumulated in many countries since the 1960s and the World Values Surveys that began in the 1970s yielded a harvest of class-voting time series. Findings through the early 1970s showed a strong, if variable, relationship between class (as indicated by occupation) and voter's choices of candidates and parties (Alford 1963; Lipset 1960, 1981; Rose 1974). Lipset and Rokkan's (1967) influential synthesis of the empirical record pointed to two nineteenth-century revolutions—the National Revolution and the Industrial Revolution. Lipset and Rokkan argued that these two revolutions initiated everywhere processes of social differentiation and conflict. As democracy spread, the four axes of social differentiation—(1) church versus secular state, (2) dominant versus subject subcultures, (3) rural areas versus cities, and (4) employers versus workers—came to influence voting behavior. The details varied from country to country, depending on history, the presence and influence of churches and minority subcultures, and timing. But everywhere the advance of industrialization pushed the first three axes to the side and the fourth—class—to the fore.

In many Western European nations (and Australia) the cleavage structure was "frozen" in the dominance of class-based political parties (see Bartolini and Mair 1990; Lipset and Rokkan 1967; Mair 1999; and Rose and Urwin 1970). Where this happened, it makes sense to speak of "class politics" (Mair 1999).

Elsewhere the association between class and voting behavior is better thought of as "class voting." Without a party structure that freezes both classes and voters in place, there is the prospect of shifting alliances, new coalitions, and realignment. In the United States, the lack of explicit links between classes and parties frees voters to weigh each party's appeals and frees each party to revise its strategies from time to time.

This process has been explicit in U.S. presidential elections since 1992. First Bill Clinton and then John Kerry dropped the Democrats' familiar appeals to "working people" in favor of direct calls to the middle class. Al Gore made more traditional class appeals in his campaign, and the Republicans accused him of "inciting class warfare." At the same time, then-Governor Bush addressed the attendees at a high-priced fundraiser as the "haves and the have-mores," wisecracking that "some people call you the elites; I call you my base" (featured in Michael Moore's *Fahrenheit 911*). It is well known in the United States that many blue-collar workers identify with the middle class (Halle 1984). And, in any event, the working class is too small in the post-industrial United States to be an effective political base (Brooks and Manza 1999).

Even without a labor party, unions used to bind blue-collar Americans to the Democratic Party. From 1936 to 1968 (and again in 1984) Democrats gave unions an important voice in the selection of candidates. In exchange, the unions delivered their share of the working-class vote to the Democrats. That link was snapped by electoral reforms in the 1970s. The popular party primary system of selecting candidates moved politics from back rooms to TV screens. And unions lost out. They were, at the same time, losing membership and the trust of members and nonmembers alike (Hout, Manza, and Brooks 1999; Lipset and Schneider 1983). In the age of Jimmy Hoffa, identification with unions became more of a political liability than an asset, and unions never regained the clout they once had at the ballot box. Union members still lean strongly toward Democratic candidates (Hout, Manza, and Brooks 1999), but the heyday of identification between the Democrats and the labor movement is over.

The erosion of confidence in unions along with Republican appeals for "the right to work" and less industrial regulation seem to have had the greatest impact on the very people who had the most to lose in the new economy that emerged during the 1970s. As energy shocks and stagflation (inflation plus high unemployment) buffeted the economy and the Democrats seemed unable to deliver the economic prosperity and security that had been their hallmark midcentury, Republican candidates' promises of relief from regulations and taxes began to seem more appealing. In particular, lower taxes and less regulation had the greatest influence on small businesspeople and manual workers who were not in unions. To these people, Reagan's firing of striking air-traffic controllers in 1981 may have seemed like a dramatic rebuke of special pleaders who wanted to dodge the apparently inexorable economic changes that everyone else was facing. If we are reading these signs correctly, then the persistence of union membership as a factor in U.S. politics is as likely a reflection of a rightward tilt among people without union protection as it is a reflection of a leftward stance among those with it.

Following Hout, Brooks, and Manza (1995) and Hout, Manza, and Brooks (1999), we distinguish between "traditional" and "total" class voting and use statistical models appropriate to each. Traditional class voting hinges on the correspondence between the working class and parties of the left and the middle classes and parties of the center or right. This correspondence can be embedded in statistical models of class voting that identify a "natural" party for each class (Weakliem 1995). A slightly weaker version of the traditional approach arrays classes and parties as ordered points on latent continua and examines the strength of association between the two latent variables (Weakliem and Heath 1999). However the researcher approaches the data, the traditional model is really only appropriate to understanding the historically significant but specific identification of classes and parties.

Total class voting, on the other hand, is not tied to any specific correspondence of classes and parties. That trend is useful and informative when traditional class voting alliances may not be the strongest or most evident. For example, the recent emergence of affinities between Democrats and teachers may be as strong and significant as the former links between Democrats and blue-collar workers. Throw in trial lawyers, college professors, nurses, and half of the doctors, and the Democrats' courting of professionals starts to yield more votes than traditional appeals to blue-collar workers could. A traditional approach would miss this kind of class voting; a total approach can capture it. As long as traditional class voting is but one of several patterns of association between classes and parties, the total approach is preferable for its flexibility. In previous work, the total approach allowed us to see the class *realignment* in U.S. presidential politics, whereas the traditional approach miscast the same trends as *dealignment* (see Hout, Manza, and Brooks 1999).

Another advantage of the total class voting approach is that it incorporates the class differences in turnout as well as class differences in votes. Middle-class people are more likely to vote than working- or lower-class Americans (Verba, Brady, and Schlossman 1996). The class skew in participation is likely to affect the party system and public policy (Piven and Cloward 1986; Rosenthal 2004). Setting it aside, as the traditional class voting approach does, misses an important element of class politics.

Our distinction between traditional and total class voting is related to Mair's (1999) distinction between "class politics" and "class voting." According to Mair, class politics signifies the kind of institutionalized class alliances that we call traditional. Class voting, for Mair, signifies a tendency for classes to ally themselves with parties in a more ad hoc endorsement for a specific election. The deal, far from institutionalized in party structure, must be renegotiated each election cycle. Total class voting, as we have defined it, only requires class voting, not class politics.

The concept of traditional class voting is entrenched in the literature. It is unavoidable when class is conceived of or reduced to a dichotomy. Admitting to more than one class distinction (ergo more than two classes) opens the prospect of recombination. Contemporary theory elaborates several class distinctions, and history is full of examples of shifting class alliances. Thus the total class approach has the advantages of being both truer to theory and truer to history than the traditional class-voting approach is. Previous research (Hout, Brooks, and Manza [1995] and Hout, Manza, and Brooks [1999]) amply demonstrated the superiority of the total class voting model in accounting for trends in voting patterns from 1948 to 1992.

Data and Methods

We use data from the American National Election Surveys (ANES), a time series that stretches back to the 1952 presidential election (with a question in 1952 about the 1948 election). The ANES is a stratified random sample of the English-speaking adult population with sample sizes varying from approximately 1,200 to 2,500 respondents per election.

The dependent variable for our analysis is self-reported vote for president recoded in four categories, (1) the Democratic candidate, (2) the Republican candidate, (3) some other candidate, and (4) did not vote. Self-reports exaggerate turnout but reproduce the partisan split very well (e.g., Abramson, Aldrich, and Rhode 1994).

We include election, class, gender, age, region, education, and racial ancestry as independent variables. Age and education are coded in years; the other variables are coded in standard, obvious ways using dummy variables. Our class scheme involves six substantive classes (as in Hout, Brooks, and Manza 1995) plus separate categories for housewives and retired persons. The six substantive classes are (1) professionals, (2) managers, (3) routine white-collar workers (mostly clerical, sales, and white-collar service workers), (4) self-employed (other than professional), (5) skilled blue-collar workers, and (6) less-skilled blue-collar workers (including blue-collar service workers).

We test for changes across elections in the association between vote and the independent variables by generating interaction effects between the election and each of the independent variables. For statistical efficiency, we exclude interaction effects that fail to reach the conventional significance level (.05) from further calculations. For interaction effects involving class, Hout, Brooks, and Manza (1995) also investigated two intermediate forms, again to improve the statistical efficiency of tests. The first idea is the uniform differences model (see Hout, Brooks, and Manza 1995 for details); the second is a simple linear change. Both of these dramatically reduce the degrees of freedom used to detect change, and the second proved to be the preferred way of modeling class realignment. We fit the following, unrestricted model:

$$
\begin{aligned}
y_{ij} &= \ln\left(\frac{p_{ij}}{p_{i1}}\right) \\
&= \beta_0 + \sum_{k=1}^{14} \beta_k T_{ki} + \sum_{k=15}^{20} \beta_k X_{(k-14)i} + \sum_{k=21}^{P+20} \beta_k Z_{(k-20)i} \\
&\quad + \sum_{k=1}^{6}\sum_{k'=1}^{14} \gamma_{kk'} X_{ki} T_{k'i} + \sum_{k=1}^{P}\sum_{k'=1}^{14} \delta_{k,k'} Z_{ki} T_{k'i}
\end{aligned}
$$

for $i = 1, \ldots, N$ indexes persons; $j = 1, \ldots, 4$ indexes outcomes (1 = Republican, 2 = Democrat, 3 = other, 4 = did not vote); $T_1, \ldots T_{14}$ are dummy variables for elections, $X_1 \ldots X_6$ are dummy variables for classes, $Z_1 \ldots Z_p$ are dummy variables for other independent variables, $\beta_0 \ldots \beta_{P+21}, \gamma_1 \ldots \gamma_6$, and $\delta_{1,1} \ldots \delta_{14,P}$ are parameters to be estimated. For identification, we constrain $\sum_{k=1}^{14} \beta_k = \sum_{k=15}^{20} \beta_k = \sum_{k=1}^{6}\sum_{k'=1}^{14} \gamma_{kk'} = 0$. For our graph below, we obtained the points by summing the $\beta_k + \gamma_{kk'}$ for all possible combinations of $k = 1, \ldots, 6$ and $k' = 1, \ldots, 14$; to that we added a linear trend line (fit by unweighted OLS).

The Realignment of Class Voting

The traditional pattern of class voting held in U.S. presidential elections from 1948 to 1960. With the exception of the self-employed, middle-class voters supported

Republican candidates while working-class voters supported the Democrats. The self-employed split their votes between the two major parties. After 1964 professionals shifted rapidly toward the Democrats; routine white-collar workers followed at a slower pace. At about the same time, the self-employed and skilled blue-collar workers shifted toward the Republicans. For the self-employed this trend amounted to a shift from ambivalence to strong Republican support. For the skilled blue-collar workers, it was a shift from being part of the Democrats' base to ambivalence about the two parties by 1988. Less-skilled blue-collar workers moved about as much in the Republican direction as routine white-collar workers moved in the Democratic direction.

We summarize these trends in Figure 60.1. The dots show the year-by-year votes in detail; the lines show the expected percentages under the linear change model in the equation above. Statistical tests indicate that the lines fit the data well at conventional significance levels.

The most significant feature of these trends for political sociology is the realignment of the professions since the 1960s. This trend was first identified by Hout, Brooks, and Manza (1995) using data from 1948 to 1992. Brooks and Manza (1997) and Brooks (2000) show convincing evidence that professionals' rising commitments to civil rights for blacks (and maybe for other groups) prompted their shift from right to left. Professionals, when picking candidates, began to give greater weight to issues of equal opportunity than they had in the past, even bypassing their personal economic interests to do so. In extending the analysis onward by three more elections, we find that the trend that was already

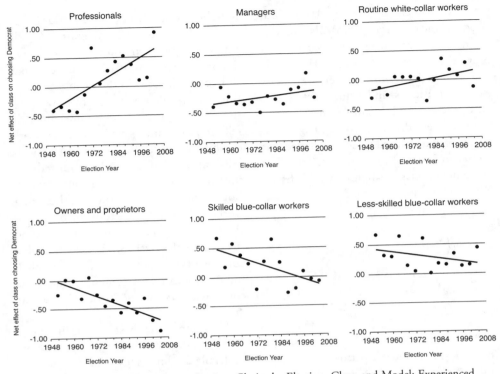

Figure 60.1   Net Effect of Class on Partisan Choice by Election, Class, and Model: Experienced Civilian Labor Force, 1948–2004

Note: Points and lines in these graphs represent multinomial logistic regression coefficients, normed to sum to zero within an election year. The models control for the effects of gender, race, region, age, education, and statistically significant changes in those effects.

significant by 1992 continued into the 1996, 2000, and 2004 elections. Comparing the dots and the lines in Figure 60.1, we see that the Democrats got less support from professionals in 1996 and 2000 but recouped it in 2004.

In one sense the triumph of civil rights movements (along with those for civil liberties and the environment) over personal material interests is a point in favor of postmaterialist accounts of electoral change. But the postmaterialists assert that class no longer correlates with vote. The correlation is evident here; it is just nontraditional (although it is by now forty years old). Here

we see one class moved from one party to another in response to these rising concerns and did so as a class. Furthermore, as we move through the rest of the class structure, we will see much more evidence of "traditional," that is, self-interested, class voting.

Managers voted in recent elections more or less as they did in the 1960s. They changed their attitudes toward civil rights through the 1970s, but their changing attitudes failed to influence their votes. Their personal interests (and perhaps the interests of the firms they managed) in cutting taxes and deregulating the economy proved to be more crucial to how they voted. Over time, the voting pattern of the self-employed became more and more conservative, eventually surpassing even managers' preference for Republicans. The self-employed were, in the 1950s, evenly divided between Democrats and Republicans. They moved strongly toward the Republicans and were their staunchest supporters by 1976 or perhaps 1980. We suspect that some of the change reflects issues and some reflects a shift from farming to small business within the ranks of the self-employed.

Skilled blue-collar workers moved from strong Democratic support to an even split between Republicans and Democrats (or perhaps a slight preference for Republicans, although their partisan split does not pass the statistical test for being significantly different from even). The evidence through 1992 was unclear on this point. Hout, Brooks, and Manza (1995) wrote of "volatility." The continued drift of the upper blue-collar voters in the last three elections makes it clear that they are moving toward the Republicans. Disaffection with the welfare state, a preference for a tougher approach to criminal justice, and support for the military are possible explanations for this shift.

Change among less-skilled blue-collar workers is more subtle but also, overall, favors Republican candidates. It is offset by a modest shift toward Democrats among routine white-collar workers.

All of these changes might suggest that total class voting has changed significantly. That is not the case, though. The summary measure of total class voting, *kappa*, introduced by Hout, Brooks, and Manza (1995), shows no net change from 1948 to 2004. Figure 60.2 shows that there are some up and down cycles in its value over a span of a few

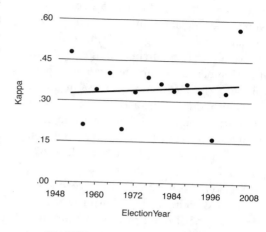

Total Effect of Class on Partisan Choice by Election:

Figure 60.2   Total Effect of Class on Partisan Choice by Election: Experienced Civilian Labor Force, 1948–2004

elections, but the experience of the 1996–2004 elections added here does not alter the conclusion Hout, Brooks, and Manza (1995) reached regarding 1952–1992—the long-term trend line is flat.

Conclusions

U.S. class coalitions realigned after the civil rights movement in the 1960s. Voters changed what they expect from presidential politics and parties changed what they promise. The Republican platform of lower taxes and deregulation deepened the loyalty of managers and won over the self-employed workers who used to back the Democrats. Blue-collar workers also prefer low taxes. Republicans courted and won their votes in most elections since 1972. But Democrats countered with strong plays for professionals' interests in many kinds of social spending and their commitment to civil rights. "New Democrats"—most notably

Clinton—appealed directly to middle-class voters and shored up support among professionals by balancing the budget in the 1990s. Overall, the Republicans gained and the Democrats lost among employed people. But the Democrats' defense of Social Security and Medicare allowed them to gain support among retirees and pensioners—people out of the labor force and, thus, out of this analysis. These changes helped balance the political arithmetic.

We do not have enough evidence to know if the class-voting realignment in U.S. politics is a general trend that extends to other Western democracies or another instance of "American exceptionalism." We note that English and German parties have started to adopt some American-style appeals. In Britain, "New Labour's" platform is known as "the third way;" Schröder moved the German Social Democrats in that direction, too. The statistical evidence makes us cautious. In Blair's first win, he drew proportionally higher support in each class, leading to no change in the association between class and vote in Britain (Goldthorpe 1999).

In this chapter we have shown that American social classes realigned: professionals replaced skilled blue-collar workers as the class base of the Democratic Party, whereas shopkeepers and proprietors joined managers as the class base of the Republican Party. This historical realignment coupled with no net change in total class voting shows how class can be important for elections without lining up in the traditional way.

REFERENCES

Abramson, P. R., and R. Inglehart. 1995. *Value Change in Global Perspective*. Ann Arbor: University of Michigan Press.

Abramson, P. R., J. H. Aldrich, and D. W. Rhode. 1994. *Change and Continuity in the 1992 Elections*. Washington, DC: Congressional Quarterly Press.

Alford, R. 1963. *Party and Society: The Anglo-American Democracies*. Westport, CT: Greenwood Press.

Bartolini, S., and P. Mair. 1990. *Identity, Competition, and Electoral Availability: The Stabilization of European Electorates, 1885–1985*. Cambridge: Cambridge University Press.

Brooks, C. 2000. "Civil Rights Liberalism and the Suppression of a Republican Political Realignment in the United States, 1972–1996." *American Sociological Review* 65: 483–505.

Brooks, C., and J. Manza. 1997. "Class Politics and Political Change in the United States, 1952–1992." *Social Forces* 76: 397–408.

Clark, T. N., and S. M. Lipset. 1991. "Are Social Classes Dying?" *International Sociology* 6: 397–410.

Goldthorpe, J. H. 1999. "Modelling the Pattern of Class Voting in British Elections, 1964–1992." In Geoffrey Evans, ed., *The End of Class Politics?*, pp. 59–83. Oxford: Oxford University Press.

Greeley, Andrew M., and Michael Hout. 2006. *The Trust About Conservative Christians: What They Believe and What They Think*. Chicago: University of Chicago Press.

Halle, D. 1984. *America's Working Man*. Chicago: University of Chicago Press.

Heath, A. F., R. Jowell, and J. Curtice. 1985. *How Britain Votes*. Oxford: Pergamon Press.

Hout, M., C. Brooks, and J. Manza. 1995. "The Democratic Class Struggle in U.S. Presidential Elections." *American Sociological Review* 60: 805–828.

Hout, M., J. Manza, and C. Brooks. 1999. "Classes, Unions, and the Realignment of U.S. Presidential Voting, 1952–1992." In Geoffrey Evans, ed., *The End of Class Politics?* pp. 83–95. Oxford: Oxford University Press.

Inglehart, R. 1977. *The Silent Revolution: Changing Values and Political Styles Among Western Publics*. Princeton: Princeton University Press.

———. 1990. *Culture Shift*. Princeton: Princeton University Press.

Lipset, S. M. 1960. *Political Man*. New York: Doubleday.

———. 1981. *Political Man*. 2nd, expanded ed. Baltimore: Johns Hopkins University Press.

Lipset, S. M., and S. Rokkan. 1967. "Cleavage Structures, Party Systems, and Voter Alignments." In S. M. Lipset and S. Rokkan, eds., *Party Systems and Voter Alignments*, pp. 1–64. New York: Free Press.

Lipset, S. M. and W. S. Schneider. 1983. *The Confidence Gap: Business, Labor, and Government in the Public Mind*. New York: Free Press.

Mair, P. 1999. "Critical Commentary." In Geoffrey Evans, ed., *The End of Class Politics?* pp. 308–312. Oxford: Oxford University Press.

McCarty, N., K. T. Poole, and H. Rosenthal. 2005. "Political Polarization and Income Inequality." Department of Politics, Princeton University Web site, available at http://www.princeton.edu/~nmccarty/ineqpold.pdf.

Piven, F. F., and R. A. Cloward. 1986. *Why Americans Don't Vote*. New York: Pantheon.

Rose, R., ed. 1974. *Electoral Behavior: A Comparative Handbook*. New York: Free Press.

Rose, R., and D. Urwin. 1970. "Persistence and Change in Western Party Systems since 1945." *Political Studies* 18: 287–319.

Rosenthal, H. 2004. "Politics, Public Policy, and Inequality: A Look Back at the 20th Century." In Kathryn Neckerman, ed., *Social Inequality*, 861–892. New York: Russell Sage Foundation.

Verba, S., H. Brady, and K. Schlossman. 1996. *Participation and Equality*. Cambridge, MA: Harvard University Press.

Weakliem, D. 1995. "Two Models of Class Voting." *British Journal of Political Science* 25: 254–270.

Weakliem, D., and A. F. Heath. 1999. "The Secret Life of Class Voting: Britain, France, and the United States since the 1930s." In Geoffrey Evans, ed., *The End of Class Politics?* pp. 97–136. Oxford: Oxford University Press.

61

Globalism's Discontents

JOSEPH E. STIGLITZ

Few subjects have polarized people throughout the world as much as globalization. Some see it as the way of the future, bringing unprecedented prosperity to everyone, everywhere. Others, symbolized by the Seattle protestors of December 1999, fault globalization as the source of untold problems, from the destruction of native cultures to increasing poverty and immiseration. In this article, I want to sort out the different meanings of globalization. In many countries, globalization has brought huge benefits to a few with few benefits to the many. But in the case of a few countries, it has brought enormous benefit to the many. Why have there been these huge differences in experiences? The answer is that globalization has meant different things in different places.

The countries that have managed globalization on their own, such as those in East Asia, have, by and large, ensured that they reaped huge benefits and that those benefits were equitably shared; they were able substantially to control the terms on which they engaged with the global economy. By contrast, the countries that have, by and large, had globalization managed for them

by the International Monetary Fund (IMF) and other international economic institutions have not done so well. The problem is thus not with globalization but with how it has been managed.

The international financial institutions have pushed a particular ideology—market fundamentalism—that is both bad economics and bad politics; it is based on premises concerning how markets work that do not hold even for developed countries, much less for developing countries. The IMF has pushed these economics policies without a broader vision of society or the role of economics within society. And it has pushed these policies in ways that have undermined emerging democracies.

More generally, globalization itself has been governed in ways that are undemocratic and have been disadvantageous to developing countries, especially the poor within those countries. The Seattle protestors pointed to the absence of democracy and of transparency, the governance of the international economic institutions by and for special corporate and financial interests, and the absence of countervailing democratic checks to

Joseph E. Stiglitz, *Globalization and Its Discontents,* pp. 78–80, 254. Copyright © 2003 by Norton Press. "Globalism's Discontents," *The American Prospect,* vol. 13, no. 1 (January 1, 2002–January 14, 2002), pp. A16–A21.

ensure that these informal and *public* institutions serve a general interest. In these complaints, there is more than a grain of truth.

Beneficial Globalization

Of the countries of the world, those in East Asia have grown the fastest and done most to reduce poverty. And they have done so, emphatically, via "globalization." Their growth has been based on exports—by taking advantage of the global market for exports and by closing the technology gap. It was not just gaps in capital and other resources that separated the developed from the less-developed countries, but differences in knowledge. East Asian countries took advantage of the "globalization of knowledge" to reduce these disparities. But while some of the countries in the region grew by opening themselves up to multinational companies, others, such as Korea and Taiwan, grew by creating their own enterprises. Here is the key distinction: Each of the most successful globalizing countries determined its own pace of change; each made sure as it grew that the benefits were shared equitably; each rejected the basic tenets of the "Washington Consensus," which argued for a minimalist role for government and rapid privatization and liberalization.

In East Asia, government took an active role in managing the economy. The steel industry that the Korean government created was among the most efficient in the world—performing far better than its private-sector rivals in the United States (which, though private, are constantly turning to the government for protection and for subsidies). Financial markets were highly regulated. My research shows that those regulations promoted growth. It was only when these countries stripped away the regulations, under pressure from the U.S. Treasury and the IMF, that they encountered problems.

During the 1960s, 1970s, and 1980s, the East Asian economies not only grew rapidly but were remarkably stable. Two of the countries most touched by the 1997–1998 economic crisis had had in the preceding three decades not a single year of negative growth; two had only one year—a better performance than the United States or the other wealthy nations that make up the Organization for Economic Cooperation and Development (OECD). The single most important factor leading to the troubles that several of the East Asian countries encountered in the late 1990s—the East Asian crisis—was the rapid liberalization of financial and capital markets. In short, the countries of East Asia benefited from globalization because they made globalization work for them; it was when they succumbed to the pressures from the outside that they ran into problems that were beyond their own capacity to manage well.

Globalization can yield immense benefits. Elsewhere in the developing world, globalization of knowledge has brought improved health, with life spans increasing at a rapid pace. How can one put a price on these benefits of globalization? Globalization has brought still other benefits: Today there is the beginning of a globalized civil society that has begun to succeed with such reforms as the Mine Ban Treaty and debt forgiveness for the poorest highly indebted countries (the Jubilee movement). The globalization protest movement itself would not have been possible without globalization.

The Darker Side of Globalization

How then could a trend with the power to have so many benefits have produced such opposition? Simply because it has not only failed to live up to its potential but frequently has had very adverse effects. But this forces us to ask, why has it had such adverse effects? The answer can be seen by looking at each of the economic elements of globalization as pursued by the international financial institutions and especially by the IMF.

The most adverse effects have arisen from the liberalization of financial and capital markets—which has posed risks to developing countries without commensurate rewards. The liberalization has left them prey to hot money pouring into the country, an influx that has fueled speculative real-estate booms; just as suddenly, as investor sentiment changes, the money is pulled out, leaving in its wake economic devastation. Early on, the IMF said that these countries were being rightly punished for pursuing bad economic policies. But as the crisis spread from country to country, even those that the IMF had given high marks found themselves ravaged.

The IMF often speaks about the importance of the discipline provided by capital markets. In doing so, it exhibits a certain paternalism, a new form of the old colonial mentality: "We in the establishment, we in the North who run our capital markets, know best. Do what we tell you to do, and you will prosper." The arrogance is offensive, but the objection is more than just to style. The position is highly undemocratic: There is an implied assumption that democracy by itself does not provide sufficient discipline. But if one is to have an external disciplinarian, one should choose a good disciplinarian who knows what is good for growth, who shares one's values. One doesn't want an arbitrary and capricious taskmaster who one moment praises you for your virtues and the next screams at you for being rotten to the core. But capital

markets are just such a fickle taskmaster; even ardent advocates talk about their bouts of irrational exuberance followed by equally irrational pessimism.

Lessons of Crisis

Nowhere was the fickleness more evident than in the last global financial crisis. Historically, most of the disturbances in capital flows into and out of a country are not the result of factors inside the country. Major disturbances arise, rather, from influences outside the country. When Argentina suddenly faced high interest rates in 1998, it wasn't because of what Argentina did but because of what happened in Russia. Argentina cannot be blamed for Russia's crisis.

Small developing countries find it virtually impossible to withstand this volatility. I have described capital-market liberalization with a simple metaphor: Small countries are like small boats. Liberalizing capital markets is like setting them loose on a rough sea. Even if the boats are well captained, even if the boats are sound, they are likely to be hit broadside by a big wave and capsize. But the IMF pushed for the boats to set forth into the roughest parts of the sea before they were seaworthy, with untrained captains and crews, and without life vests. No wonder matters turned out so badly!

To see why it is important to choose a disciplinarian who shares one's values, consider a world in which there were free mobility of skilled labor. Skilled labor would then provide discipline. Today, a country that does not treat capital well will find capital quickly withdrawing; in a world of free labor mobility, if a country did not treat skilled labor well, it too would withdraw. Workers would worry about the quality of their children's education and their family's health care, the quality of their environment and of their own wages and working conditions. They would say to the government: If you fail to provide these essentials, we will move elsewhere. That is a far cry from the kind of discipline that free-flowing capital provides.

The liberalization of capital markets has not brought growth: How can one build factories or create jobs with money that can come in and out of a country overnight? And it gets worse: Prudential behavior requires countries to set aside reserves equal to the amount of short-term lending; so if a firm in a poor country borrows $100 million at, say, 20 percent interest rates short-term from a bank in the United States, the government must set aside a corresponding amount. The reserves are typically held in U.S. Treasury bills—a safe, liquid asset. In effect, the country is borrowing $100 million from the United States and lending $100 million to the United States. But when it borrows, it pays a high interest rate, 20 percent; when it lends, it receives a low interest rate, around 4 percent. This may be great for the United States, but it can hardly help the growth of the poor country. There is also a high *opportunity* cost of the reserves; the money could have been much better spent on building rural roads or constructing schools or health clinics. But instead, the country is, in effect, forced to lend money to the United States.

Thailand illustrates the true ironies of such policies: There, the free market led to investments in empty office buildings, starving other sectors—such as education and transportation—of badly needed resources. Until the IMF and the U.S. Treasury came along, Thailand had restricted bank lending for speculative real estate. The Thais had seen the record: Such lending is an essential part of the boom-bust cycle

that has characterized capitalism for 200 years. It wanted to be sure that the scarce capital went to create jobs. But the IMF nixed this intervention in the free market. If the free market said, "Build empty office buildings," so be it! The market knew better than any government bureaucrat who mistakenly might have thought it wiser to build schools or factories.

The Costs of Volatility

Capital-market liberalization is inevitably accompanied by huge volatility, and this volatility impedes growth and increases poverty. It increases the risks of investing in the country, and thus investors demand a risk premium in the form of higher-than-normal profits. Not only is growth not enhanced but poverty is increased through several channels. The high volatility increases the likelihood of recessions—and the poor always bear the brunt of such downturns. Even in developed countries, safety nets are weak or nonexistent among the self-employed and in the rural sector. But these are the dominant sectors in developing countries. Without adequate safety nets, the recessions that follow from capital-market liberalization lead to impoverishment. In the name of imposing budget discipline and reassuring investors, the IMF invariably demands expenditure reductions, which almost inevitably result in cuts in outlays for safety nets that are already threadbare.

But matters are even worse—for under the doctrines of the "discipline of the capital markets," if countries try to tax capital, capital flees. Thus, the IMF doctrines inevitably lead to an increase in tax burdens on the poor and the middle classes. Thus, while IMF bailouts enable the rich to take their money out of the country at more favorable terms (at the overvalued exchange rates), the burden of repaying the loans lies with the workers who remain behind.

The reason that I emphasize capital-market liberalization is that the case against it—and against the IMF's stance in pushing it—is so compelling. It illustrates what can go wrong with globalization. Even economists like Jagdish Bhagwati, strong advocates of free trade, see the folly in liberalizing capital markets. Belatedly, so too has the IMF—at least in its official rhetoric, though less so in its policy stances—but too late for all those countries that have suffered so much from following the IMF's prescriptions.

But while the case for trade liberalization—when properly done—is quite compelling, the way it has been pushed by the IMF has been far more problematic. The basic logic is simple: Trade liberalization is supposed to result in resources moving from inefficient protected sectors to more efficient export sectors. The problem is not only that job destruction comes before the job creation—so that unemployment and poverty result—but that the IMF's "structural adjustment programs" (designed in ways that allegedly would reassure global investors) make job creation almost impossible. For these programs are often accompanied by high interest rates that are often justified by a single-minded focus on inflation. Sometimes that concern is deserved; often, though, it is carried to an extreme. In the United States, we worry that small increases in the interest rate will discourage investment. The IMF has pushed for far higher interest rates in countries with a far less hospitable investment environment. The high interest rates mean that new jobs and enterprises are not created. What happens is that trade liberalization, rather than moving workers from low-productivity jobs to high-

productivity ones, moves them from low-productivity jobs to unemployment. Rather than enhanced growth, the effect is increased poverty. To make matters even worse, the unfair trade-liberalization agenda forces poor countries to compete with highly subsidized American and European agriculture. . . .

An Unfair Trade Agenda

The trade-liberalization agenda has been set by the North, or more accurately, by special interests in the North. Consequently, a disproportionate part of the gains has accrued to the advanced industrial countries, and in some cases the less-developed countries have actually been worse off. After the last round of trade negotiations, the Uruguay Round that ended in 1994, the World Bank calculated the gains and losses to each of the regions of the world. The United States and Europe gained enormously. But sub-Saharan Africa, the poorest region of the world, lost by about 2 percent because of terms-of-trade effects: The trade negotiations opened their markets to manufactured goods produced by the industrialized countries but did not open up the markets of Europe and the United States to the agricultural goods in which poor countries often have a comparative advantage. Nor did the trade agreements eliminate the subsidies to agriculture that make it so hard for the developing countries to compete.

The U.S. negotiations with China over its membership in the WTO displayed a double standard bordering on the surreal. The U.S. trade representative, the chief negotiator for the United States, began by insisting that China was a developed country. Under WTO rules, developing countries are allowed longer transition periods in which state subsidies and other departures from the WTO strictures are permitted. China certainly wishes it were a developed country, with Western-style per capita incomes. And since China has a lot of "capitas," it's possible to multiply a huge number of people by very small average incomes and conclude that the People's Republic is a big economy. But China is not only a developing economy; it is a low-income developing country. Yet the United States insisted that China be treated like a developed country! China went along with the fiction; the negotiations dragged on so long that China got some extra time to adjust. But the true hypocrisy was shown when U.S. negotiators asked, in effect, for developing-country status for the United States to get extra time to shelter the American textile industry.

Trade negotiations in the service industries also illustrate the unlevel nature of the playing field. Which service industries did the United States say were *very* important? Financial services—industries in which Wall Street has a comparative advantage. Construction industries and maritime services were not on the agenda, because the developing countries would have a comparative advantage in these sectors.

Consider also intellectual-property rights, which are important if innovators are to have incentives to innovate (though many of the corporate advocates of intellectual property exaggerate its importance and fail to note that much of the most important research, as in basic science and mathematics, is not patentable). Intellectual-property rights, such as patents and trademarks, need to balance the interests of producers with those of users—not only users in developing countries, but researchers in developed countries. If we underprice the profitability of innovation to the inventor, we deter invention. If we overprice its cost to the research community and the end user, we retard its diffusion and beneficial effects on living standards.

In the final stages of the Uruguay negotiations, both the White House Office of Science and Technology Policy and the Council of Economic Advisers worried that we had not got the balance right—that the agreement put producers' interests over users'. We worried that, with this imbalance, the rate of progress and innovation might actually be impeded. After all, knowledge is the most important input into research, and overly strong intellectual-property rights can, in effect, increase the price of this input. We were also concerned about the consequences of denying lifesaving medicines to the poor. This issue subsequently gained international attention in the context of the provision of AIDS medicines in South Africa [see "Medicine as a Luxury" by Merrill Goozner, on page A7]. The international outrage forced the drug companies to back down—and it appears that, going forward, the most adverse consequences will be circumscribed. But it is worth noting that initially, even the Democratic U.S. administration supported the pharmaceutical companies.

What we were not fully aware of was another danger—what has come to be called "biopiracy," which involves international drug companies patenting traditional medicines. Not only do they seek to make money from "resources" and knowledge that rightfully belong to the developing countries, but in doing so they squelch domestic firms who long provided these traditional medicines. While it is not clear whether these patents would hold up in court if they were effectively challenged, it is clear that the less-developed countries may not have the legal and financial resources required to mount such a challenge. The issue has become the source of enormous emotional, and potentially economic, concern throughout the developing world. This fall, while I was in Ecuador visiting a village in the high Andes, the Indian mayor railed against how globalization had led to biopiracy. . . .

Trickle-Down Economics

We recognize today that there is a "social contract" that binds citizens together, and with their government. When government policies abrogate that social contract, citizens may not honor their "contracts" with each other, or with the government. Maintaining that social contract is particularly important, and difficult, in the midst of the social upheavals that so frequently accompany the development transformation. In the green eye-shaded calculations of the IMF macroeconomics there is, too often, no room for these concerns.

Part of the social contract entails "fairness," that the poor share in the gains of society as it grows, and that the rich share in the pains of society in times of crisis. The Washington Consensus policies paid little attention to issues of distribution or "fairness." If pressed, many of its proponents would argue that the best way to help the poor is to make the economy grow. They believe in trickle-down economics. *Eventually*, it is asserted, the benefits of that growth *trickle down* even to the poor. Trickle-down economics was never much more than just a belief, an article of faith. Pauperism seemed to grow in nineteenth-century England even though the country as a whole prospered. Growth in America in the 1980s provided the most recent dramatic example: while the economy grew, those at the bottom saw their real incomes decline. The Clinton administration had argued strongly against trickle-down economics; it believed that there had to be active programs to help the poor. And when I left the White House to go to the World Bank, I brought with me the same skepticism of trickle-down economics; if this had not worked in the United States, why would it work in developing countries? While it is true that sustained reductions in poverty cannot be attained without robust economic growth, the converse is not true: growth need not benefit all. It is not true that "a rising tide lifts all boats." Sometimes, a quickly rising tide, especially when accompanied by a storm, dashes weaker boats against the shore, smashing them to smithereens.

In spite of the obvious problems confronting trickle-down economics, it has a good intellectual pedigree. One Nobel Prize winner, Arthur Lewis, argued that inequality was good for development and economic growth, since the rich save more than the poor, and the key to growth was capital accumulation. Another Nobel Prize winner, Simon Kuznets, argued that while in the initial stages of development inequality increased, later on the trend was reversed.[1]

The history of the past fifty years has, however, not supported these theories and hypotheses. East Asian countries—South Korea, China, Taiwan, Japan—showed that high savings did not require high inequality, that one could achieve rapid growth without a substantial increase in inequality. Because the governments did not believe that growth would automatically benefit the poor, and because they believed that greater *equality* would actually enhance growth, governments in the region took active steps to ensure that the rising tide of growth did lift most boats, that wage inequalities were kept in bounds, that some educational opportunity was extended to all. Their policies led to social and political stability, which in turn contributed to an economic environment in which businesses flourished. Tapping new reservoirs of talent provided the energy and human skills that contributed to the dynamism of the region.

Elsewhere, where governments adopted the Washington Consensus policies, the poor have benefited less from growth. In Latin America, growth has not been accompanied by a reduction in inequality, or even a reduction in poverty. In some cases poverty has actually increased, as evidenced by the urban slums that dot the landscape. The IMF talks with pride about the progress Latin America has made in market reforms over the past decade (though somewhat more quietly after the collapse of the star student Argentina in 2001, and the recession and stagnation that have afflicted many of the "reform" countries during the past five years), but has said less about the numbers in poverty.

Clearly, growth alone does not always improve the lives of all a country's people. Not surprisingly, the phrase "trickle-down" has disappeared from the policy debate. But, in a slightly mutated form, the idea is still alive. I call the new variant *trickle-down-plus*. It holds that growth is necessary and *almost* sufficient for reducing poverty— implying that the best strategy is simply to focus on growth, while mentioning issues like female education and health. But proponents of trickle-down-plus failed to implement policies that would effectively address either broader concerns of poverty or even specific issues such as the education of women. In practice, the advocates of trickle-down-plus continued with much

the same policies as before, with much the same adverse effects. The overly stringent "adjustment policies" in country after country forced cutbacks in education and health: in Thailand, as a result, not only did female prostitution increase but expenditures on AIDS were cut way back; and what had been one of the world's most successful programs in fighting AIDS had a major setback.

The irony was that one of the major proponents of trickle-down-plus was the U.S. Treasury under the Clinton administration. Within the administration, in domestic politics, there was a wide spectrum of views, from New Democrats, who wanted to see a more limited role for government, to Old Democrats, who looked for more government intervention. But the central view, reflected in the annual Economic Report of the President (prepared by the Council of Economic Advisers), argued strongly against trickle-down economics—or even trickle-down-plus. Here was the U.S. Treasury pushing policies on other countries that, had they been advocated for the United States, would have been strongly contested *within the administration,* and almost surely defeated. The reason for this seeming inconsistency was simple: The IMF and the World Bank were part of Treasury's turf, an arena in which, with few exceptions, they were allowed to push their perspectives, just as other departments, within their domains, could push theirs. . . .

Global Social Justice

Today, in much of the developing world, globalization is being questioned. For instance, in Latin America, after a short burst of growth in the early 1990s, stagnation and recession have set in. The growth was not sustained—some might say, was not sustainable. Indeed, at this juncture, the growth record of the so-called post-reform era looks no better, and in some countries much worse, than in the widely criticized import-substitution period of the 1950s and 1960s when Latin countries tried to industrialize by discouraging imports. Indeed, reform critics point out that the burst of growth in the early 1990s was little more than a "catch-up" that did not even make up for the lost decade of the 1980s.

Throughout the region, people are asking: "Has reform failed or has globalization failed?" The distinction is perhaps artificial, for globalization was at the center of the reforms. Even in those countries that have managed to grow, such as Mexico, the benefits have accrued largely to the upper 30 percent and have been even more concentrated in the top 10 percent. Those at the bottom have gained little; many are even worse off. The reforms have exposed countries to greater risk, and the risks have been borne disproportionately by those least able to cope with them. Just as in many countries where the pacing and sequencing of reforms has resulted in job destruction outmatching job creation, so too has the exposure to risk outmatched the ability to create institutions for coping with risk, including effective safety nets.

In this bleak landscape, there are some positive signs. Those in the North have become more aware of the inequities of the global economic architecture. The agreement at Doha to hold a new round of trade negotiations—the "Development Round"—promises to rectify some of the imbalances of the past. There has been a marked change in the rhetoric of the international economic institutions—at least they talk about poverty. At the World Bank, there have been some real reforms; there has been some progress in translating the rhetoric into reality—in ensuring that the voices of the poor are heard and the concerns of the developing countries are listened to. But elsewhere, there is often a gap between the rhetoric and the reality. Serious reforms in governance, in who makes decisions and how they are made, are not on the table. If one of the problems at the IMF has been that the ideology, interests, and perspectives of the financial community in the advanced industrialized countries have been given disproportionate weight (in matters whose effects go well beyond finance), then the prospects for success in the current discussions of reform, in which the same parties continue to predominate, are bleak. They are more likely to result in slight changes in the shape of the table, not changes in who is *at* the table or what is on the agenda.

September 11 has resulted in a global alliance against terrorism. What we now need is not just an alliance *against* evil, but an alliance *for* something positive—a global alliance for reducing poverty and for creating a better environment, an alliance for creating a global society with more social justice.

NOTE

1. See W. A. Lewis, "Economic Development with Unlimited Supplies of Labor," *Manchester School* 22 (1954), pp. 139–91, and S. Kuznets, "Economic Growth and Income Inequality," *American Economic Review* 45(1) (1955), pp. 1–28.

62

The New Geography of
Global Income Inequality

GLENN FIREBAUGH

The new geography of inequality—not to be confused with the "new economic geography" that arose in economics in the 1990s (Fujita, Krugman, and Venables 1999)—refers to the new pattern of global income inequality caused by the recent phenomenon of declining inequality across nations accompanied by (in many places) rising inequality within nations. This phenomenon, which began in the last third of the twentieth century and continues today, results in a "new geography" because it represents the reversal of trends that trace back to the early stages of Western industrialization. Put in the perspective of an individual, the new geography of global income inequality means that national location—while still paramount—is declining in significance in the determination of one's income.

Despite a recent surge of interest in global inequality, researchers have largely overlooked its changing contour. Studies of global income inequality over the last decades of the twentieth century have been preoccupied with the problem of global divergence, that is, the presumed problem of worsening income inequality for the world as a whole (for example, Wade 2001; Milanovic 2002). This preoccupation with global divergence is misguided, first, because global income inequality almost certainly declined over this period and, second, because the focus on the level of global income inequality has diverted attention from the changing nature of global income inequality in recent decades. Global income inequality is no worse today than it was in the 1960s and 1970s, but global income inequality is nevertheless changing—it is gradually shifting from inequality across nations to inequality within nations. The rising importance of within-nation inequality and declining importance of between-nation inequality represents a historic change, since it involves the reversal of a trend that began with the uneven industrialization of the world that started more than two centuries ago.

This chapter contrasts the New Geography Hypothesis with the popular view that globalization—by which I mean the increased interconnectedness of localities, particularly the deepening of economic links between countries—has led to growing global income inequality:

Globalization ⟶ global inequality.

For short, I call this popular view the Trade Protest Model, because the protests against the World Trade Organization in Seattle and elsewhere were driven at least in part by the assumption that global trade is exacerbating global inequality. To place the New Geography Hypothesis in context, it is useful first to examine five myths that underlie the globalization ⟶ global inequality model.

Myths of the Trade Protest Model

Under the heading "Siege in Seattle," the December 13, 1999, issue of the U.S. magazine *Newsweek* gave this account of the protests surrounding the meeting of the World Trade Organization in Seattle, Washington:

> Until last week, not so many Americans had even heard of the WTO. Fewer still could have identified it as the small, Geneva-based bureaucracy that the United States and 134 other nations set up five years ago to referee global commerce. To Bill Clinton, it is a mechanism that can allow America to do well and good at the same time. But to many of the 40,000 activists and union members who streamed into Seattle—a clean, scenic city that has grown rich on foreign trade—the WTO is something else again: a secretive tool of ruthless multinational corporations. They charge it with helping sneaker companies to exploit Asian workers, timber companies to clear-cut rain forests, shrimpers to kill sea turtles and a world of other offenses.

Media accounts grappled with the sheer diversity of the protesters, from leaders of U.S. labor to members of environmental groups to a leading Chinese dissident. The common thread seemed to be, as the *New York Times* (1999) put it, the view that the WTO is a "handmaiden of corporate interests whose rulings undermine health, labor and environmental protections around the world." According to *The Economist* (1999), "The WTO has become a magnet for resistance to globalisation by both old-fashioned protectionists and newer critics of free trade."

Some of the protest groups emphasized rising inequality as among the most noxious consequences of increasing trade globalization. For example, Ralph Nader's Public Citizen group portrays the WTO as a tool of big business "which is harming the environment and increasing inequality" (*The Economist* 1999), and representatives of 1,448 nongovernmental organizations protesting the WTO signed a statement claiming that "globalisation has three serious consequences: the concentration of wealth in the hands of the multinationals and the rich; poverty for the majority of the world's population; and unsustainable patterns of production and consumption that destroy the environment" (*New Scientist* 1999). Note that two of the three consequences—concentration of wealth and impoverishment of the majority—tie globalization directly to growth in inequality.

Global income inequality is the result of the interplay of multiple causes, of course, so serious analyses are unlikely to give an unqualified endorsement to the notion that globalization has automatically resulted in an explosion in global income inequality. Global inequality existed before the recent growth in world trade, and it would persist if nations suddenly stopped trading. Nonetheless, popular literature on globalization has tended to fuel the belief in a globalization-led explosion in global income inequality by making claims that purport to be grounded in the findings of serious scholarly analyses. Upon closer inspection, however, many of the claims fly in the face of available empirical evidence. This section examines the key myths that underlie the globalization $\rightarrow$ global inequality model.

Myth 1. The Myth of Exploding Global Income Inequality. A steady drumbeat of reports and articles claims that the world's income is becoming more and more unequally distributed. Here is a sample:

- "Globalization has dramatically increased inequality between and within nations" (Jay Mazur, 2000, in *Foreign Affairs*).
- "The very nature of globalization has an inherent bias toward inequality. . . . One would have to be blind not to see that globalization also exacerbates the disparity between a small class of winners and the rest of us" (Paul Martin, Canada's prime minister, June 1998, quoted in Eggertson 1998).
- "Along with ecological risk, to which it is related, expanding inequality is the most serious problem facing world society" (Anthony Giddens, 1999).
- "Thus, overall, the ascent of informational, global capitalism is indeed characterized by simultaneous economic development and underdevelopment, social inclusion and social exclusion. . . . There is polarization in the distribution of wealth at the global level, differential evolution of intra-country income inequality, and substantial growth of poverty and misery

in the world at large" (Manuel Castells, 1998, p. 82, emphasis omitted).

What I have found (Firebaugh 2003) is that global income inequality has not exploded but in fact leveled off and then declined in the last part of the twentieth century. Although income inequality rose somewhat in the average nation, income inequality declined across nations. Since between-nation inequality is the larger component of global income inequality, the decline in between-nation income inequality more than offset the rise in within-nation income inequality. As a result, global income inequality declined in the last years of the twentieth century. Sherlock Holmes was right: it *is* a capital mistake to theorize in advance of the facts (Doyle 1955, p. 507). With respect to global income inequality, much mischief has been done by theorizing about global income inequality on the basis of the views expressed above. Theorizing based on the widespread view of exploding global income inequality is theorizing based on facts that aren't.

Myth 2. The Myth of Growing Income Inequality Across Nations, as Rich Nations Surge Ahead and Poor Nations Fall Further Behind. The first myth—exploding global inequality—is based on a second myth, the myth that inequality is growing across nations. The second myth is as widespread as the first, and it has been fueled by widely circulated reports of international agencies:

- "Figures indicate that income inequality between countries has increased sharply over the past 40 years" (World Bank 2000b, *World Development Report 2000/2001*, p. 51).

- "The average income in the richest 20 countries is 37 times the average in the poorest 20—a gap that has doubled in the past 40 years" (International Monetary Fund 2000, p. 50).
- "Gaps in income between the poorest and richest people and countries have continued to widen. In 1960 the 20% of the world's people in the richest countries had 30 times the income of the poorest 20%—in 1997, 74 times as much. . . . Gaps are widening both between and within countries" (United Nations Development Program 1999, *Human Development Report 1999*, p. 36).
- "It is an empirical fact that the income gap between poor and rich countries has increased in recent decades" (Ben-David, Nordström, and Winters 1999, World Trade Organization special study, p. 3).
- "In 1960, the Northern countries were 20 times richer than the Southern, in 1980 46 times. . . . [I]n this kind of race, the rich countries will always move faster than the rest" (Sachs 1992, *The Development Dictionary*, p. 3).

The myth of growing income inequality across nations is based in large part on a misinterpretation of the widely cited finding (for example, World Bank 2000b, p. 50) that income growth has tended to be slower in poor nations than in rich nations. As we shall see, this positive cross-country association between income level and income growth rate conceals the critical fact that the poor nations that are falling badly behind contain no more than 10 percent of the world's population, whereas the poor nations that are catching up (largely in Asia)

contain over 40 percent of the world's population. When nations are weighted by population size—as they must be if we want to use between-nation inequality to draw conclusions about global income inequality— we find that income inequality across nations peaked sometime around 1970 and has been declining since. This peaking of between-nation income inequality circa 1970 is particularly interesting in light of Manuel Castells's (1998, p. 336) well-known claim that a "new world" originated in the late 1960s to mid-1970s. Ironically, though, Castells characterizes the world born in this period as a world of sharply increasing global inequality, and many other globalization writers make the same error.

I have debunked myth number 2 first by replicating the United Nations/World Bank results and then by demonstrating how they have been misinterpreted (Firebaugh 2003). In addition to the weighting problem just mentioned, the claims of growing inequality often ignore nations in the middle of the income distribution, focusing instead on selected nations at the tails. When the entire income distribution is used, and when individuals are given equal weight, we find that—far from growing—income inequality across nations declined in the late twentieth century.

Myth 3. The Myth That Globalization Historically Has Caused Rising Inequality Across Nations. Contrary to this myth, the trend in between-nation inequality historically has not followed changes in the trend in world economic integration. First, although it is true that between-nation income inequality increased dramatically over the nineteenth and early twentieth centuries, Peter Lindert and Jeffrey Williamson (2000) argue that the period of rising inequality across nations began *before* the period of true globalization started, so globalization apparently did not cause the upturn. Second, the sharp decline in globalization between World War I and World War II did not result in declining inequality across nations (to the contrary, between-nation income inequality shot up rapidly over the period). Finally, income inequality across nations has declined in recent decades, during a period when globalization has presumably reached new heights. (I say "presumably" because globalization is itself a contentious issue: see Guillén 2001. Nonetheless virtually all agree that the world has become more economically integrated over recent decades, even if the degree of globalization is often overstated, as Chase-Dunn, Kawano, and Brewer 2000, among others, have noted.) In short, the rise in global inequality predates the rise in globalization, global inequality has risen while globalization was declining, and currently global inequality is declining while globalization is rising. It is hard then to make the case historically that globalization is the cause of rising income inequality across nations (O'Rourke 2001).

Myth 4. The Myth of a Postindustrial World Economy.   In reading the globalization literature it is easy to lose sight of the fact that, until recently, most of the world's people were engaged in agriculture. So the world's workforce is barely postagricultural, much less postindustrial. This book makes the point that the primary engine still driving the growth in world production is more manufacturing. A new information age might be on the way, but it is not here yet—at least it is not here for most of the world's people. It is important to look ahead, of course, and it

is hard to argue against the view that the world will eventually be postindustrial. The death of industrialization is nonetheless much exaggerated, as is the view that we are rapidly approaching an information-based global economy (Quah 1997). Estimates of the composition of global output, albeit rough approximations, rule out the claims of some globalization writers that we live in a new economic era quite unlike the era of the last generation. Industrialization was important in the nineteenth century, it was important in the twentieth century, and it remains important in most regions of the world in the twenty-first century. A preoccupation with postindustrialization in the face of the continuing diffusion of industrialization results in an incomplete and distorted story of global income inequality that deemphasizes the critical role of the continuing spread of industrialization to all regions of the world. Computers are important, but they are not all-important. In accounting for recent trends in global income inequality, the bigger story is industrial growth in Asia, not technological growth in the West.

Myth 5. The Myth of International Exchange as Inherently Exploitative.   Globalization involves increased exchange over national boundaries. One might posit that increased exchange worsens global inequality under some historical conditions and reduces it under other conditions. Until those historical conditions are identified and understood, the effect of globalization on global income inequality at any point in time is an open question to be settled empirically.

But if international exchange is inherently exploitative, as some theories of world stratification insist, then rising exchange implies rising exploitation, and the Trade

Protest Model is true virtually by definition. The Trade Protest Model then becomes:

> Globalization —→ more exploitation of poor nations by rich nations —→ greater global inequality

Note that this elaboration of the Trade Protest Model reveals how high the theoretical stakes are with regard to empirical tests of the globalization —→ global income inequality model, since the failure of globalization to lead to rising global income inequality would undermine exploitation theories (for example, dependency theories) as well as undermining the Trade Protest Model.

I have presented evidence that increasing international exchange over recent decades has been accompanied by declining—not rising—income inequality across nations (Firebaugh 2003). Other studies also document declining between-nation income inequality over recent decades. The decline in between-nation inequality has significant theoretical implications. The assumption of inherent exploitation favoring rich nations in international exchange is the linchpin of some theoretical schools. But if international exchange were inherently exploitative, we would not expect to observe declining inequality across nations during a period of rising international trade. Yet the assumption persists, suggesting that in some theories the notion of inherent exploitation is so essential that it enjoys creedal status as a doctrine to be believed rather than as a hypothesis to be tested.

Causes of the Reversal: An Overview

I argue that the world's spreading industrialization and growing economic integration in the late twentieth century and the early twenty-first have reversed the historical pattern of uneven economic growth favoring richer nations. The conventional view, just elaborated, is that globalization has exacerbated global income inequality. The evidence challenges that view. In reality globalization has offsetting effects—by spurring industrialization in poor nations, globalization raises inequality within many nations and compresses inequality across nations. The net effect has been a reduction in global income inequality in recent decades, since the reduction in between-nation income inequality has more than offset the growth in within-nation income inequality.

The new pattern of rising within-nation and falling between-nation income inequality has multiple causes. The most important cause is spreading industrialization—the diffusion of industrialization to the world's large poor nations. The diffusion of industrialization to poor regions compresses inequality across nations and boosts inequality within them. The effect of spreading industrialization on between-nation inequality is reinforced by the effect of the growing integration of national economies. Growing economic integration tends to dissolve institutional differences between nations. The convergence of institutional economic goals and policies compresses inequality across nations by (in some instances at least) removing impediments to growth in poor nations.

There are at least four other significant causes of the new geography of global inequality. The first is technological change that reduces the tyranny of space in general and more particularly reduces the effect of labor immobility across national boundaries. This technological change works to reduce inequality across nations. The second is a demographic windfall that has benefited some poor Asian nations in recent decades and promises to benefit other poor nations in the near future. This effect also operates to compress global income inequality, by reducing between-nation inequality. The third is the rise of the service sector, especially in richer nations. Growth in this sector has boosted income inequality within nations, and it is likely to do so in the future as well. The fourth is the collapse of communism, which also boosted within-nation inequality. This is a nonrecurring event, however, so its effect on within-nation inequality is limited to a specific point in history, the 1990s.

In short, the decline in between-nation income inequality that began in the late twentieth century was caused by deepening industrialization of poor nations, by growing economic integration that dissolves institutional differences between nations, by technological change that reduces the effects of labor immobility across national boundaries, and by a demographic windfall that has benefited some poor nations and promises to benefit others in the future. The growth in within-nation income inequality was caused by the deepening industrialization of poor nations, by the growth of the service sector, and by the collapse of communism.

The Inequality Transition

The industrialization of richer nations in the nineteenth century and first half of the twentieth caused income inequality across nations to explode. As a result, global income inequality shifted from inequality within nations to inequality across nations. Now, however, poorer nations are industrializing faster than richer ones are, and between-nation inequality is declining while within-nation inequality appears to be rising. If this turnaround continues, future historians will refer to an inequality transition that accompanied world industrialization. That transition is from within-nation inequality to between-nation inequality back to within-nation inequality, with the late twentieth century as the period when the shift back to within-nation income inequality began.

Phase 1 of the Transition: From Within- to Between-Nation Inequality

Phase 1 of the inequality transition coincides with the period of Western industrialization that began in the late eighteenth century and ended in the second half of the twentieth century. The first phase of the inequality transition was characterized by unprecedented growth in income inequality across nations. As Lant Pritchett (1996, p. 40) puts it, "the overwhelming feature of modern economic history is a massive divergence in per capita incomes between rich and poor countries." The evidence is incontrovertible. First, it is clear that current levels of between-nation income inequality would not have been possible earlier in human history. Again quoting Pritchett (1997, pp. 9–10): "If there had been no divergence, then we could extrapolate backward from present income of the poorer countries to past income assuming they grew at least as fast as the United States. However, this would imply that many poor countries must have had incomes below $100 in 1870 [in 1985 U.S. dollars]. Since this cannot be true, there must have been divergence."

Second, Pritchett's conclusion that "there must have been divergence" is supported by estimates of between-nation income inequality in the nineteenth century. Consider the recent estimates of Bourguignon and Morrisson (1999). Bourguignon and Morrisson use the Maddison (1995) data to estimate changes in the level of between-nation income inequality from 1820 to 1992. Because their objective is to estimate total world income inequality—not just between-nation income inequality—Bourguignon and Morrisson begin by disaggregating national income data into vintiles (5 percent groups, that is, twenty income groups per nation). National boundaries have changed over the past two centuries, of course, and nations have come and gone over the past two centuries. Even in nations where boundaries remained constant, we do not always have income data for the entire period. To overcome these problems, Bourguignon and Morrisson grouped the 199 nations with income data in 1992 into 33 homogeneous groups, each of which represented at least 1 percent of the world population or world GDP in 1950. The 33 groups include single nations (such as China and the United States) as well as large groups of small nations and small groups of medium-sized nations. From these 660 data points (33 nation groups x 20) it is a straightforward matter to apply the population-weighted formulas for the Theil index and the mean logarithmic deviation (MLD)—two measures of inequality—to calculate summary measures of the world's total inequality for different years. By collapsing the 199 nations into 33 groups, Bourguignon and Morrisson are able to extend their inequality series back to 1820. Note that, to the extent that their grouping strategy introduces bias, the bias is in the direction of underestimating between-nation inequality and inflating within-nation inequality, since some of the inequality within the nation groups is ac-

tually between-nation inequality. But that bias should not affect our basic conclusions about the relative growth in between-nation and within-nation income inequality over the past two centuries.

The results are striking (Figure 62.1). Two facts stand out. First, the B/W ratio—the ratio of between-nation to within-nation income inequality—is much higher now than it was in the early stages of Western industrialization. The increase in the B/W ratio reflects both a rise in between-nation income inequality and a decline in within-nation income inequality since 1820 (Table 62.1). By far the greater change is in between-nation income inequality, however. The Theil index for between-nation income inequality (actually, inequality between nation *groups*) shot up from 0.061 in 1820 to 0.513 in 1992, and the MLD shot up from 0.053 in 1820 to 0.495 in 1992. As anticipated, then, the Industrial Revolution of the past two centuries has increased income inequality across nations, but the magnitude of the increase is stunning. There has been a metamorphosis from a world where poverty was the norm in all nations to a richer world with much lower poverty rates (Bourguignon and Morrisson 1999, table 1) but also with much greater income inequality across nations. Because the steep rise in between-nation income inequality was not accompanied by an increase in inequality within nations, where you live—your nation—is much more important in determining your income in today's world than it was in the preindustrial world.

The second fact that stands out is that the growth in the B/W ratio stalled in the second half of the twentieth century. The B/W ratio stopped growing in the second half of the twentieth century because

The Reversal of Historical Inequality Trends

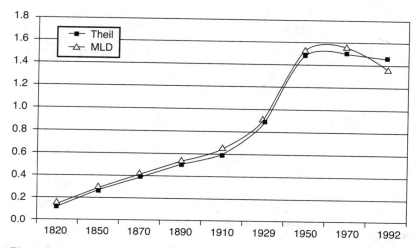

Figure 62.1   Ratio of Between-Nation to Within-Nation Income Inequality for
Thirty-three Nation Groups, 1820–1992.
Based on Table 62.1. Theil and MLD are measures of inequality

growth in inequality across the nation groups has slowed dramatically since 1950. In the four decades after 1950, income inequality across the nation groups increased by 6 percent using the Theil index and by 5 percent using the MLD. Over the four decades prior to 1950, the Theil had grown about 60 percent and the MLD had grown about 75 percent. Apparently the most dramatic effects of Western industrialization on between-nation inequality are over. After more than a century of sharp divergence in national incomes, the trend has been much more stable in recent years. This finding is in line with the findings of others (for example, Schultz 1998; Firebaugh 1999; Melchior, Telle, and Wiig 2000; Goesling 2001) who, drawing on data for individual nations instead of nation groups, find that between-nation income inequality is no longer rising. As we shall see later, between-nation income inequality declined in

the late twentieth century when income data for the 1990s are added to data for the 1970s and 1980s.

Finally, it should be emphasized that the results here are so strong that the historical story they tell of increasing inequality across nations and of a rising B/W ratio cannot be dismissed as due to error in the data. To be sure, income estimates for the nineteenth century are gross approximations for many nations. But even if we make the extreme assumption that incomes are so drastically overstated for poorer nations in 1820 (or so drastically understated for richer nations in 1820) that the Theil and the MLD estimates understate between-nation income inequality in 1820 by a factor of three, that would still mean that between-nation income inequality tripled from 1820 to 1992 (from 0.18 to 0.51 based on the Theil index and from 0.16 to 0.50 for the MLD), and the B/W ratio still

Table 62.1   Trends in Income Inequality Between and Within Thirty-three Homogeneous Nation Groups, 1920–1992

Year	Between nation groups		Within nation groups	
	Theil	MLD	Theil	MLD
1820	.061	.053	.472	.388
1850	.128	.111	.477	.393
1870	.188	.162	.485	.399
1890	.251	.217	.498	.408
1910	.299	.269	.500	.413
1929	.365	.335	.413	.372
1950	.482	.472	.323	.309
1970	.490	.515	.324	.330
1992	.513	.495	.351	.362

Source: Bourguignon and Morrisson (1999), table 3.

Estimates: Between nation groups: From Bourguignon and Morrisson (1999), based on Maddison (1995) data set. *Within nation groups:* From Bourguignon and Morrisson (1999), based on updating of Berry, Bourguignon, and Morrisson (1983a,b) for the post–World War II period and on various sources (for example, Lindert 1999; Morrisson 1999) for the pre–World War II period. Bourguignon and Morrisson (2002) published modestly revised estimates for inequality. By collapsing vintiles to deciles, they report slightly lower estimates of inequality within the nation groups, but the fundamental conclusions are the same.

Note: Income measures are adjusted for purchasing power parity, and inequality measures are based on income vintiles (see Bourguignon and Morrisson 1999 for elaboration).

would have more than tripled for both inequality measures.

Phase 2 of the Transition: From Between-Nation Back to Within-Nation Inequality

The second phase of the inequality transition began in the second half of the twentieth century, with the stabilization of between-nation income inequality in the 1960–1990 period and the decline in between-nation inequality beginning in earnest in the 1990s. Social scientists hardly have a stellar track record for predictions, especially with regard to sweeping predictions such as the one made here. Nonetheless there is sufficient theory and evidence that we can plausibly forecast that the *B/W* ratio will continue to decline in the twenty-first century.

The prediction of a declining *B/W* ratio is based on two separate conjectures. The first conjecture is that between-nation income inequality will decline, and the second conjecture is that within-nation income inequality will rise, or at least will not decline. These conjectures are based on the causes of the current trends, which I expect to continue and in some cases to intensify. (I am assuming that there will be no cataclysmic upheaval in the twenty-first century, such as a global war or a worldwide plague.) Recall the causes listed earlier for the inequality turnaround in the late twentieth century. I expect the major causes to continue, so between-nation income inequality will decline because of the continued industrialization of poor nations, because of the continued convergence of national economic policies and institutions arising from growing economic integration of national economies, because of the declining significance of labor immobility across national borders, and because of a demographic windfall for many poor nations. Within-nation income inequality will rise—or at least not decline—because of the continued industrialization of poor nations and because of continued growth in the service sector. Because between-nation inequality is the larger component, global income inequality will decline.

The conjecture of declining global income inequality is out of step with much of the globalization literature. A recurring theme in that literature is that we have entered a new information-based economic era where productive activity is becoming less dependent on physical space, as a rising share of the world's economic output is produced in electronic space that knows no national borders (Sassen 2000). This phenomenon is possible because of the emergence of a global economy where income—and hence income inequality—is becoming increasingly rooted in knowledge rather than in capital goods (Reich 1991). What do these developments imply for global income inequality? For many globalization writers, the answer is clear: global inequality is bound to worsen because of the growing "global digital divide" that enlarges the gap between the "haves" and the "have-nots" (Campbell 2001; Ishaq 2001; Norris 2001).

The theoretical argument that a shift to a knowledge-based global economy would worsen global income inequality is shaky. It is not hard to think of reasons why the shift from an industrial-based to a knowledge-based global economy would reduce, not increase, inequality across nations. Knowledge is mobile, especially with today's telecommunication technologies that permit virtually instant worldwide codification and distribution of knowledge. In addition, because knowledge can be given away without

being lost, the notion of property rights is more problematic in the case of knowledge, so it is harder to concentrate and monopolize knowledge across nations than it is to concentrate and monopolize capital goods across nations. Hence the switch to a knowledge-based global economy should mean that one's income is increasingly determined by how much knowledge one obtains and uses as opposed to where one lives. The tighter link between knowledge and income in turn implies declining income inequality across nations and rising inequality within nations since—absent institutional barriers . . . —the variance in individuals' ability to obtain and benefit from knowledge is greater within nations than between them.

The issue of how the new information age will affect global inequality in the near term is not as decisive as often imagined, since as already noted, the coming of the information age is often much exaggerated. What is still most important in today's world is industrialization for the many, not digitization for the few. Historically the spread of industrialization has been the primary force driving the growth in between-nation income inequality. The initially richer nations of the West were the first to industrialize, and the poorer nations of Asia and Africa lagged behind. The new geography of inequality is also driven by the spread of industrialization, but the effects are different today: now the spread of industrialization means the diffusion of manufacturing technology to the world's largest poor regions. In recent decades inequality has declined across nations as industrialization has been an engine of growth in the most populous poor regions of the world, especially East Asia. That growth has worked both to compress inequality across

Figure 62.2   Industrialization and Between-Nation Income Inequality:
Historically and in the Late Twentieth Century

nations (Figure 62.2) and to boost inequality within the industrializing nations.

The significance of this continuation of world industrialization has been lost in much of the literature on globalization, because of preoccupation with the idea that we are witnessing the emergence of a new knowledge-based technology regime. To be sure, in the categories used to classify world production, the output of the so-called service sector is estimated to exceed the output of the industrial sector for the world as a whole (World Bank 1997, table 12). Yet much of the service sector—an amorphous sector that includes wholesale and retail trade, the banking industry, government, the transportation industry, the commercial real estate industry, and personal services (including health care and education)—has arisen to grease the wheels of industry. Aside from the growth in personal services and government, much of the growth in the service sector has been for services for producers, not consumers—for example, the rise of an engineering industry to design better machines, and the growth of a banking industry and a commercial real estate industry for commercial transactions. In addition, many of the other so-called service industries—the transportation industry that distributes manufactured goods, for example,

and the specialized retailing industry that sells the goods—benefit producers as well as consumers. In short, a significant portion of the growth in service industries over the past century can be seen as ancillary to the industrialization process.

With regard to income inequality within nations, we expect the continuing spread of world industrialization to boost inequality along the lines of the classic argument, from Simon Kuznets (1955), that industrialization boosts inequality (at least initially) as workers move from the lower-wage but larger agricultural sector to the higher-wage industrial sector. Importantly, this argument suggests that income inequality increases in poor nations as they industrialize because of income gains, not income losses. In other words, inequality grows not because some people are becoming poorer but because some people are becoming richer, so the growth in income inequality in poor nations as they industrialize reflects rising rather than declining fortunes. If the industrialization of large poor nations does boost income inequality in those nations, at this juncture in history the continued spread of industrialization implies growth in income inequality in the average nation, because those nations are home to such a large fraction of the

world's population. And there are no obvious counterforces on the horizon. Although
the jump in income inequality following the
collapse of communism in Eastern Europe
and the former USSR is not likely to be repeated, there is no good reason to expect income inequality in those nations to fall in
the near future. Nor is there any good reason
to expect income inequality to decline notably in the West in the near future, either.
We lack reliable inequality data for many
African nations, but even if inequality were
falling rapidly (which is unlikely), the effect
of falling within-nation inequality in Africa
would not offset the effect of rising within-
nation inequality in Asia, given the relative
sizes of the two regions. Few expect within-
nation income inequality to decline sharply
in Latin America in the near future, even
though Latin America currently exhibits the
highest level of within-nation income inequality of the world's major regions. Indeed, because of the advantage enjoyed by
North American farmers with respect to
some types of produce, economic integration in the Americas could exacerbate inequality by removing protections for farmers
in Latin America. If that reasoning is correct,
there is merit in the concern of WTO protesters that globalization may exacerbate
income inequality within some poor nations by driving down incomes in the lower-
income agricultural sector. But the bigger
story is that industrialization (not the collapse of farm prices) will tend to drive up inequality within nations, at least initially.
Because many nations are still on the part of
the Kuznets (1955) curve where migration
from farm to factory boosts inequality, we
can anticipate further growth in within-
nation income inequality in the early decades
of the twenty-first century.

REFERENCES

Ben-David, Dan, Håkan Nordström, and L. Alan
Winters. 1999. *Trade, Income Inequality, and
Poverty.* WTO Special Study no. 5. Geneva:
World Trade Organization.

Berry, Albert, François Bourguignon, and Christian Morrisson. 1983a. "Changes in the world
distribution of income between 1950 and
1977." *Economic Journal* 93:331–350.

————. 1983b. "The level of world inequality:
How much can one say?" *Review of Income
and Wealth* 29:217–241.

Bourguignon, François, and Christian Morrisson.
1998. "Inequality and development: The role
of dualism." *Journal of Development Economics*
57:233–257.

————. 1999. "The size distribution of income
among world citizens: 1820–1990." Draft.
June.

————. 2002. "Inequality among world citizens:
1820–1992." *American Economic Review*
92:727–744.

Campbell, Duncan. 2001. "Can the digital divide be contained?" *International Labour Review* 140:119–141.

Castells, Manuel. 1998. *End of Millennium.*
Malden, Mass.: Blackwell.

Chase-Dunn, Christopher, Yukio Kawano, and
Benjamin D. Brewer. 2000. "Trade globalization since 1795: Waves of integration in the
world-system." Special millennium issue,
edited by Glenn Firebaugh, of the *American
Sociological Review* 65:77–95.

Doyle, Arthur Conan. 1955. *A Treasury of Sherlock Holmes.* Selected and with an introduction
by Adrian Conan Doyle. Garden City, N.Y.:
Hanover House.

The Economist. 1999. "The battle in Seattle."
U.S. edition. November 27.

Eggertson, Laura. 1998. "Rich-poor gap next
issue for Martin." *Toronto Star.* June 3, p. A6.

Firebaugh, Glenn. 1999. "Empirics of world income inequality." *American Journal of Sociology* 104:1597–1630.

————. 2003. *The New Geography of Global Income Inequality.* Cambridge: Harvard University Press.

Fujita, Masahisa, Paul Krugman, and Anthony J. Venables. 1999. *The Spatial Economy: Cities, Regions, and International Trade.* Cambridge: MIT Press.

Giddens, Anthony. 1999. "Globalization: An irresistible force." *The Daily Yomiuri,* June 7, p. 8.

Goesling, Brian. 2001. "Changing income inequalities within and between nations: New evidence." *American Sociological Review* 66:745–761.

Guillén, Mauro F. 2001. "Is globalization civilizing, destructive, or feeble? A critique of five key debates in the social science literature." *Annual Review of Sociology* 27:235–260.

International Monetary Fund (IMF). 2000. "How we can help the poor." *Finance and Development* (December). (http://www.imf.org/external/pubs.)

Ishaq, Ashfaq. 2001. "On the global digital divide." *Finance and Development* 38:44–47.

Kuznets, Simon. 1955. "Economic growth and income inequality." *American Economic Review* 45:1–28.

Lindert, Peter, and Jeffrey G. Williamson. 2000. "Does globalization make the world more unequal?" Paper presented at the "Globalization in Historical Perspective" preconference, National Bureau of Economic Research, Cambridge, Mass. November.

Maddison, Angus. 1995. *Monitoring the World Economy, 1820–1992.* Paris: OECD.

Mazur, Jay. 2000. "Labor's new internationalism." *Foreign Affairs* 79:79–93.

Melchior, Arne, Kjetil Telle, and Henrik Wiig. 2000. *Globalization and Inequality: World Income Distribution and Living Standards, 1960–1998.* Studies on Foreign Policy Issues. Oslo: Royal Norwegian Ministry of Foreign Affairs.

Milanovic, Branko. 2002. "True world income distribution, 1988 and 1993: First calculation based on household surveys alone." *Economic Journal* 112:51–92.

Morrisson, Christian. 1999. "Historical perspectives on income distribution: The case of Europe." In *Handbook of Income Distribution,* ed. A. B. Atkinson and F. Bourguignon. Amsterdam: Elsevier.

New Scientist. 1999. Editorial. December 4.

New York Times. 1999. "National guard is called to quell trade talk protests." December 1.

Norris, Pippa. 2001. *Digital Divide: Civic Engagement, Information Poverty, and the Internet Worldwide.* Cambridge and New York: Cambridge University Press.

O'Rourke, Kevin H. 2001. "Globalization and inequality: Historical trends." National Bureau of Economic Research. Draft. April.

Pritchett, Lant. 1996. "Forget convergence: Divergence past, present, and future." *Finance and Development* (June):40–43.

———. 1997. "Divergence, big time." *Journal of Economic Perspectives* 11:3–17.

Quah, Danny T. 1997. "Increasingly weightless economies." *Bank of England Quarterly Bulletin* (February):49–55.

Reich, Robert B. 1991. *The Work of Nations: Preparing Ourselves for Twenty-first-Century Capitalism.* New York: Knopf.

Sachs, Wolfgang, ed. 1992. *The Development Dictionary: A Guide to Knowledge as Power.* London: Zed Books.

Sassen, Saskia. 2000. "Territory and territoriality in the global economy." *International Sociology* 15:372–393.

Schultz, T. Paul. 1998. "Inequality in the distribution of personal income in the world: How it is changing and why." *Journal of Population Economics* 11:307–344.

United Nations Development Program. 1999. *Human Development Report 1999.* New York: Oxford University Press.

63

Does Poverty Cause Terrorism?

The Economics and the Education of Suicide Bombers

ALAN B. KRUEGER

JITKA MALEČKOVÁ

I

That investment in education is critical for economic growth, improved health, and social progress is beyond question. That poverty is a scourge that the international aid community and industrialized countries should work to eradicate is also beyond question. There is also no doubt that terrorism is a scourge of the contemporary world. What is less clear, however, is whether poverty and low education are root causes of terrorism.

In the aftermath of the tragic events of September 11, several prominent observers and policymakers have called for increased aid and educational assistance as a means for ending terrorism. "We fight against poverty," President George W. Bush has declared, "because hope is an answer to terror." But a careful review of the evidence provides little reason for optimism that a reduction in poverty or an increase in educational attainment would, by themselves, meaningfully reduce international terrorism. Any connection between poverty, education, and terrorism is indirect, complicated, and probably

quite weak. Instead of viewing terrorism as a direct response to low market opportunities or lack of education, we suggest it is more accurately viewed as a response to political conditions and long-standing feelings of indignity and frustration (perceived or real) that have little to do with economics.

An understanding of the causes of terrorism is essential if an effective strategy is to be crafted to combat it. Drawing a false and unjustified connection between poverty and terrorism is potentially quite dangerous, as the international aid community may lose interest in providing support to developing nations when the imminent threat of terrorism recedes, much as support for development waned in the aftermath of the Cold War; and connecting foreign aid with terrorism risks the possibility of humiliating many people in less developed countries, who are implicitly told that they receive aid only to prevent them from committing acts of terror. Moreover, premising foreign aid on the threat of terrorism could create perverse incentives in which some groups are induced to engage in terrorism to increase their prospects of receiving aid. In our view, allevi-

Alan B. Krueger and Jitka Malečková, "Does Poverty Cause Terrorism?" *The New Republic*, June 24, 2002, pp. 27–33.

ating poverty is reason enough to pressure economically advanced countries to provide more aid than they are currently giving. Falsely connecting terrorism to poverty serves only to deflect attention from the real roots of terrorism.

To make any headway investigating the determinants of terrorism, one must have a working definition of terrorism. This is a notoriously difficult task. More than one hundred diplomatic and scholarly definitions of the term exist. . . .

The State Department, which acknowledges that no single definition of terrorism has gained universal acceptance, seems to have captured what is considered terrorism by many governments and international organizations. Since 1983, it has employed this definition for statistical and analytical purposes: "The term 'terrorism' means premeditated, politically motivated violence perpetrated against noncombatant targets by subnational groups or clandestine agents, usually intended to influence an audience. The term 'international terrorism' means terrorism involving citizens or the territory of more than one country." The State Department also specifies that "the term noncombatant is interpreted to include, in addition to civilians, military personnel who at the time of the incident are unarmed and/or not on duty. . . . We also consider as acts of terrorism attacks on military installations or on armed military personnel when a state of military hostilities does not exist at the site, such as bombings against U.S. bases in the Persian Gulf, Europe, or elsewhere." The rub, of course, is that the definitions of "subnational" and "military hostilities" leave much latitude for disagreement.

The definitions of terrorism used by scholars, by contrast, tend to place more emphasis on the intention of terrorists to cause fear and terror among a targeted population that is considerably larger than the actual victims of their attacks, and to influence the views of that larger audience. The actual victim of the violence is thus not the main target of the terrorist act. Scholarly definitions often also include nation-states as potential perpetrators of terrorism.

Rather than dogmatically adhere to one definition, we have analyzed involvement in or support for activities that, at least when judged by some parties, constitute terrorism. Still, in the incidents that we have analyzed, the line between terrorism and resistance is often blurred. At the least, all of the cases we examine could be thought of as involving politically motivated violence. Moreover, it is reassuring that our main conclusions appear to hold across a varying set of circumstances, cultures, and countries. (We do not examine state terrorism because we suspect that the process underlying participation in state terrorism is quite different from the process underlying sub-state terrorism, and would involve a different type of analysis. We do not dispute that state terrorism exists, and that it has at times generated sub-state terrorism as a response.)

In economics, it is natural to analyze participation in terrorism in the framework of occupational choice. As is conventional in economics, involvement in terrorism is viewed as a rational decision, depending on the benefits, costs, and risks involved in engagement in terrorism compared with other activities. Not surprisingly, the standard rational-choice framework does not yield an unambiguous answer to the question of whether higher income and more education would reduce participation in terrorism.

In this context, we have also reviewed evidence on "hate crimes," which can be viewed as a close cousin to terrorism in that the target of an offense is selected because of his or her group identity, not because of his or her individual behavior, and because the effect of both is to wreak terror in a greater number of people than those directly affected by the violence. A consensus is emerging in the social science literature that the incidence of hate crimes, such as lynchings of African Americans or violence against Turks in Germany, bears little relation to economic conditions.

Most significantly, we have considered data from a public-opinion poll conducted in the West Bank and Gaza Strip by the Palestinian Center for Policy and Survey Research (PCPSR). In December 2001, Palestinians were asked whether they supported attacks on Israeli civilian and military targets, and about whether they considered certain incidents acts of terrorism. Breaking down the data by education and occupation indicates that support for violence against Israeli targets is widespread in the Palestinian population, and at least as great among those with higher education and higher living standards as it is among the unemployed and the illiterate. Similarly, a review of the incidence of major terrorist acts over time in Israel, and an analysis that relates the number of terrorist acts each year to the rate of economic growth in that year or in the recent past, yields the same skepticism about the idea that poverty is a cause of terrorism.

The data on participation in and support for political violence, militancy, and terrorism that we have examined are meager, often indirect, and possibly nonrepresentative. In addition, participation in terrorist activities may be highly context-specific, and we have examined terrorism, militancy, and politically motivated violence in a small

number of settings primarily in the Middle East. Consequently, our results must be considered tentative and exploratory. Yet we are not aware of compelling evidence that points in the opposite direction from what we have found. In light of our results, we would urge intellectuals and policymakers to exercise caution in presuming that poverty and education have a direct and causal impact on terrorism.

II

A simple view of terrorism is that participation in terrorism is akin to participation in crime in general. Economists have a well-developed and empirically successful theory of participation in criminal activities. As emphasized by Gary Becker, individuals should choose to allocate their time between working in the legal job market or working in criminal activities in such a way that maximizes their utility. After accounting for the risk of being caught and penalized, the size of the penalty, and any stigma or moral distress associated with involvement in crime, those who receive higher income from criminal activities would choose involvement in crime. According to this model, crime increases as one's market wage falls relative to the rewards associated with crime, and decreases if the risk of being apprehended after committing a crime, or the penalty for being convicted of a crime, rises. Available evidence suggests that individuals are more likely to commit property crimes if they have lower wages or less education; but the occurrence of violent crimes, including murders, is typically found to be unrelated to economic opportunities.

Some economists, notably William Landes, Todd Sandler, and Walter Enders, have applied the economic model of crime to transnational terrorism. They focus on how an increase in penalties and law enforcement influences the incentive to partake in terrorist activities. But the economic model yields few concrete predictions insofar as the relationship between market opportunities and participation in terrorism is concerned, because participation in terrorist acts by individuals with different characteristics depends on the probability that participation will bring about the desired political change, as well as the differential payoff for the various groups associated with achieving the terrorists' desired aims versus the penalties associated with failure. It is possible, for example, that well-educated individuals will disproportionately participate in terrorist groups if they think that they will assume leadership positions if they succeed, or if they identify more strongly with the goals of the terrorist organization than less-educated individuals.

Other important considerations include the relative pay of skilled and unskilled individuals for participation in terrorist organizations and how it compares to relative pay in the legal sector, and the selection of particular terrorists by terrorist organizations. Bill Keller recently reported in *The New York Times* that Iraq decided in March to increase the payment to families of suicide bombers in the West Bank and Gaza from $10,000 to $25,000. In the month after that decision, suicide bombings increased, though it is unclear whether the connection is causal.

Even before the increase in the payment to families of suicide bombers, there was a large supply of willing suicide bombers, as Nasra Hassan, a relief worker for the United Nations, reported last year in *The New Yorker*. Between 1996 and 1999, Hassan interviewed nearly two hundred fifty militants

and associates of militants involved in the Palestinian cause, including failed suicide bombers, the families of deceased bombers, and those who trained and prepared suicide bombers for their missions. One Hamas leader whom Hassan interviewed remarked: "Our biggest problem is the hordes of young men who beat on our doors, clamoring to be sent [on suicide missions]. It is difficult to select only a few." A senior member of the al-Qassam Brigades said: "The selection process is complicated by the fact that so many wish to embark on this journey of honor. When one is selected, countless others are disappointed." Thus, the demand side is also part of the equation.

With a queue of willing participants, how do terrorist or militant groups choose their suicide bombers? A planner for Islamic Jihad explained to Hassan that his group scrutinizes the motives of a potential bomber to be sure that the individual is committed to carrying out the task. Now, a high level of educational attainment is probably a signal of one's commitment to a cause, as well as of one's ability to prepare for an assignment and carry it out. For this reason, the stereotype of suicide bombers being drawn from the ranks of those who are so impoverished that they have nothing to live for may be wildly incorrect. This interpretation is also consistent with another of Hassan's observations about suicide bombers: "None of them were uneducated, desperately poor, simple-minded, or depressed. Many were middle class and, unless they were fugitives, held paying jobs. More than half of them were refugees from what is now Israel. Two were the sons of millionaires."

Suicide bombers clearly are not motivated by the prospect of their own individual economic gain, although it is possible that the promise of larger payments to their families may increase the willingness of some to participate in these lethal missions. We suspect their primary motivation instead results from their passionate support for the ideas and the aims of their movement. "Over and over," Hassan reported, "I heard them say, 'The Israelis humiliate us. They occupy our land and deny our history.'" The eradication of poverty and the attainment of universal high school education are unlikely to change these feelings. Indeed, it is even possible that those who are well-off and well-educated experience such feelings more acutely. . . .

III

The Palestinian Center for Policy and Survey Research (PCPSR) is an independent, nonprofit research organization in Ramallah that conducts policy analysis and academic research in the West Bank and Gaza. In December 2001, PCPSR conducted a public-opinion poll of 1,357 Palestinians eighteen years old or older in the West Bank and Gaza. The survey, which was conducted by in-person interviews, covered topics including the participants' views toward the September 11 attacks in the United States, the participants' support for an Israeli-Palestinian peace agreement, and their opinions about armed attacks against Israel. Under trying circumstances in the middle of one of the worst periods of the Israeli-Palestinian conflict, a researcher at the center kindly provided us with tabulations of key questions broken down by the educational level and the occupational status of the respondents.

Although public-opinion polls are subject to multiple interpretations, such data can provide indirect information about which segments of the population support terrorist or militant activities. The PCPSR poll reveals several things. First, the support for armed attacks against Israeli targets by the Palestinian population is widespread, though it is important to emphasize that there is a distinction between support for armed attacks expressed in a public-opinion poll at a particular point in time and participation in or active support for such attacks. Second, a majority of the Palestinian population believes that armed attacks against Israeli civilians have helped to achieve Palestinian rights in a way that negotiations could not have achieved. This finding raises obvious implications concerning the difficulty of ending the attacks, and may partially account for the Palestinian public's opposition to a United Nations initiative to fight terrorism, which was also found in the poll. If the Palestinian public believes the attacks are efficacious, they are unlikely to cease supporting additional attacks unless their demands are met. Another question asked was: "To what extent do you support or oppose the position taken by President Arafat and the [Palestinian Authority] regarding the U.S. campaign against terror?" Thirty-six percent supported or strongly supported the position of Arafat in this case, and 50.4 percent opposed it.

Moreover, a majority of the Palestinian population did not consider suicide bombings, such as the one that killed twenty-one Israeli youths at the Dolphinarium disco in Tel Aviv, terrorist events. Toward the end of the questionnaire, respondents were also asked whether they thought the international community considered the Dolphinarium bombing a terrorist event. Ninety-two percent responded yes. These results highlight important differences in interpreting the meaning of the word "terrorism."

Most important for our purposes, there is no evidence in these results that more highly educated individuals are less supportive of violent attacks against Israeli targets than are those who are illiterate or poorly educated. Consider the percentage of individuals who say they support or strongly support armed attacks against Israeli targets less those who say they oppose or strongly oppose such attacks. By a margin of 68 points, those with more than a secondary school education support armed attacks against Israeli targets, while the margin is 63 points for those with an elementary school education and 46 points for those who are illiterate.

A survey conducted by PCPSR in November 1994, before the current intifada, asked respondents whether they supported a dialogue between Hamas and Israel. Responses were reported by educational attainment. More highly educated respondents were less supportive of a dialogue with Israel: 53 percent of those with a B.A. and 40 percent of those with an M.A. or a Ph.D. supported a dialogue, compared with 60 percent of those with nine years of schooling or less. (Based on other questions, it is clear that supporters of dialogue generally favored a more peaceful coexistence with Israel.)

The PCPSR study in 2001 showed also that support for armed attacks against Israeli targets is widespread across all Palestinian occupations and groups, but particularly strong among students (recall that respondents are age eighteen or older) and merchants and professionals. Notably, the unemployed are somewhat less likely to support armed attacks against Israeli targets. If poverty was indeed the wellspring of support for terrorism or politically motivated violence, one would have expected the unemployed to be more supportive of armed attacks than merchants and professionals, but the public-opinion evidence points in the other direction. . . .

We also performed a detailed analysis of participation in Hezbollah in Lebanon, which has reportedly instructed Palestinian extremist groups on the use of suicide bomb attacks. We compared the background characteristics of 129 members of Hezbollah's militant wing who died in action mostly in the late 1980s to those of a random sample of 121,000 young people in the Lebanese population. Many of these militants died fighting Israeli occupation, while others died in suicide bomb attacks or while planting booby traps. The Hezbollah militants in this sample are likely to be representative of those who engaged in terrorist acts, and some were carrying out terrorist acts when they died. Compared to the general Lebanese population from the same age group and region, the Hezbollah militants were actually slightly less likely to come from impoverished households, and were more likely to have attended secondary school or higher. These results suggest that the militants were not particularly drawn from those with the least opportunities in society.

And this conclusion is ratified by political violence on the other side as well. In the late 1970s and early 1980s, numerous violent attacks against Palestinians were conducted by Israeli Jews in the West Bank and Gaza. These attacks included attempts to kill three Palestinian mayors of West Bank cities and attempts to blow up the Dome of the Rock mosque in Jerusalem. From 1980 to 1984, a total of twenty-three Palestinians were killed in attacks by what became known among Israelis as the Jewish Underground, and 191 Palestinians were injured. The *International Encyclopedia of Terrorism*

(1997) refers to these attacks as acts of terrorism. In a ruling in 1985, an Israeli court convicted three Israeli settlers of murder and found others guilty of violent crimes in cases involving attacks in the West Bank.

What were the biographical backgrounds of those involved in these violent attacks by Israeli Jewish extremists? A list may be compiled of the name, the age, the occupation, and the nature of underground activity for twenty-seven individuals involved in the Jewish Underground in the early 1980s, based mainly on a memoir of the Jewish Underground by Haggai Segal, one of its members. It is clear from such a chart that these Israeli extremists were overwhelmingly well-educated and in high-paying occupations. The list includes teachers, writers, university students, geographers, an engineer, a combat pilot, a chemist, and a computer programmer. As Donald Neff observed in 1999 about the three men convicted of murder, "all were highly regarded, well-educated, very religious." Although we have not statistically compared the backgrounds of these extremists to the wider Israeli population, these twenty-seven individuals certainly do not appear to be particularly underprivileged or undereducated.

IV

The evidence that we have assembled and reviewed suggests that there is little direct connection between poverty, education, and participation in or support for terrorism. Indeed, the available evidence indicates that compared with the relevant population, participants in Hezbollah's militant wing in the late 1980s and early 1990s in Lebanon were at least as likely to come from economically advantaged families and to have a relatively high level of education

as they were to come from impoverished families without educational opportunities. We should caution, however, that the evidence we have considered is tentative due to data limitations. In addition, our focus has been primarily on the Middle East, so our conclusions may not generalize to other regions or circumstances. . . .

While economic deprivation may not be associated with participation in terrorism and political violence at the individual level, it may nonetheless matter at the national level. If a country is impoverished, a minority of the relatively well off in that country may turn to terrorism to seek to improve the conditions of their countrymen. One might question, though, whether the goal of many terrorist organizations is to install a political regime that is likely to reduce poverty. In addition, there are well-documented cases of homegrown terrorism in economically advanced countries (remember Timothy McVeigh?), so it is far from clear that poverty at a national level is associated with support for terrorism. Of course, this question can only be addressed by cross-country analyses.

In addition, poverty may indirectly affect terrorism through the apparent connection between economic conditions and the proclivity for countries to undergo civil wars. James Fearon and David Laitin have found that GDP per capita is inversely related to the onset of civil war, and Paul Collier and Anne Hoeffler have found that the growth rate of GDP per capita and the male secondary-school enrollment rate are inversely related to the incidence of civil war. Lebanon, Afghanistan, and Sudan are high-profile examples of countries where civil war provided a hospitable environment for international terrorists to operate. But there are other situations in which countries undergoing a civil war did not provide a breeding ground for international terrorism, so it is unclear how much one should extrapolate from the relationship between economic development and civil war. And terrorism has arisen in many countries that were not undergoing a civil war.

Enough evidence is accumulating that it is fruitful to begin to conjecture why participation in terrorism and political violence is apparently unrelated—or positively related—to individuals' income and education. The standard economic model of crime suggests that those with the lowest value of time should engage in criminal activity. But we would hypothesize that in most cases terrorism is less like property crime and more like a violent form of political engagement. More-educated people from privileged backgrounds are more likely to participate in politics, probably in part because political involvement requires some minimum level of interest, expertise, commitment to issues, and effort, all of which are more likely if people are educated enough and prosperous enough to concern themselves with more than economic subsistence. These factors could outweigh the effect of opportunity cost on individuals' decisions to become involved in terrorism.

The demand side for terrorists must be considered as well as the supply side. Terrorist organizations may prefer highly educated individuals over less-educated ones, even for suicide bomb attacks. In addition, educated middle-class or upper-class individuals are better suited to carry out acts of international terrorism than are impoverished illiterates, because the terrorists must fit into a foreign environment to be successful. This consideration suggests that terrorists who threaten economically developed countries will disproportionately be drawn from the ranks of the relatively well off and highly educated.

On the whole, we must conclude that there is little reason to be optimistic that a reduction in poverty or increase in educational attainment will lead to a meaningful reduction in the amount of international terrorism without other changes. Jessica Stern has observed that many madrasahs, or religious schools, in Pakistan are funded by wealthy industrialists, and that those schools deliberately educate students to become foot soldiers and elite operatives in various extremist movements around the world. She further reported that "most madrasahs offer only religious instruction, ignoring math, science, and other secular subjects important for functioning in modern society." These observations suggest that, in order to use education as part of a strategy to reduce terrorism, the international community should not limit itself to increasing years of schooling, but should consider very carefully the content of education.

About the Editors

David B. Grusky is Professor of Sociology at Stanford University, Director of the Center for the Study of Poverty and Inequality at Stanford University, and coeditor (with Paula England) of the Studies in Social Inequality Series. He received his B.A. at Reed College, his M.S. and Ph.D. at the University of Wisconsin-Madison, and has held positions at the University of Chicago, Cornell University, and Stanford University. He is a Fellow of the American Association for the Advancement of Science, recipient of the 2004 Max Weber Award (with Maria Charles), founder of the Cornell University Center for the Study of Inequality, and a former Presidential Young Investigator. Although his research ranges widely, much of it examines whether and why gender, racial, and class-based inequalities are growing stronger or weaker, whether and why they differ in strength across countries, and how such changes and differences are best measured. His recent books are *Poverty and Inequality* (coedited with Ravi Kanbur, Stanford University Press, 2006), *Mobility and Inequality* (coedited with Stephen Morgan & Gary Fields, Stanford University Press, 2006), *Occupational Ghettos* (coauthored with Maria Charles, Stanford University Press, 2004), *The Declining Significance of Gender?* (coedited with Francine Blau and Mary Brinton, Russell Sage, 2006), and *Inequality: Classic Readings in Race, Class, and Gender* (coedited with Szonja Szelényi, Westview Press, 2006).

Szonja Szelényi has taught courses in poverty, inequality, and gender at the University of Wisconsin, Stanford University, and Cornell University. Her books are *Equality by Design* (Stanford University Press, 1998) and *Inequality: Classic Readings in Race, Class, and Gender* (coedited with David Grusky, Westview Press, 2006).

About the Book

The Inequality Reader and our
New Series of Inequality Anthologies

The publication of the *Inequality Reader* completes the recently undertaken expansion of our series of inequality anthologies into a full three-volume set. This expansion is a response to the burgeoning interest in poverty and inequality, the increasingly diverse research literature within the poverty and inequality field, and the increasingly diverse needs of consumers of this literature. The three books making up our series fill the following niches:

A comprehensive introduction. The *Inequality Reader* is intended for undergraduate and graduate readers requiring an introduction to the field as well as for scholars and general readers who would profit from a compilation of the most influential scholarship on poverty and inequality. This volume draws broadly from classic theoretical and conceptual pieces, qualitative and ethnographic studies, quantitative analyses of the sources of poverty and inequality, and "experiential pieces" that convey the lived experience of poverty and inequality. In assembling this volume, a special effort was made to include articles that cast light on recent changes in the structure of poverty and inequality, not only the spectacular takeoff in income inequality but also equally dramatic developments in contemporary race, class, and gender inequalities.

A compilation of the classics. Also just published in 2006, *Classic Readings in Race, Class, and Gender* is a slimmer volume of essential readings in poverty and inequality, readings that define the conceptual and empirical foundations of the field. This book, which represents the classical core alone, may be supplemented with contemporary articles that are tailored to the particular interests of the reader.

An advanced reader. The final book in our three-part series, the venerable *Social Stratification*, combines a full roster of classic readings with the most advanced, cutting-edge scholarship on poverty and inequality. Not for the faint of heart, *Social Stratification* is appropriate for anyone requiring full exposure to advanced scholarship in the field, including the most influential quantitative and technical pieces. The introductory graduate student should consider coupling this book with the new *Inequality Reader.*

Index

Aaronson, Daniel, 171
Absolute deprivation hypothesis, 511
Absolute income hypothesis, 511
Academic performance (AP), 456–458
Affirmative action, 252
African Americans: addresses of, 249; college drop-out rate of, 252; health status of, 515; job applications from, 248; in labor market, 251; middle class, 252; names of, 247, 249, 251; neighborhoods of, 168, 249, 517; prison population and, 192–193; skills of, 250; as students, 252. *See also* Blacks
Afrocentrism, 201
Alexander, C., 457
Altman, Drew, 26
"Ambient hazards," 171
American Civil War, 92, 231
An American Dilemma (Myrdal), 154
American Dream, 468–469
American Establishment, 116
American National Election Surveys (ANES), 570
Amsbary, Sarah McArthur, 293–294
Ancestry data, 205
ANES. *See* American National Election Surveys
Aneshensel, Carol, 171
Antipoverty devices, 139–141
AP. *See* Academic performance
Apartheid, 8, 159–163
Aronson, Joshua, 252–253, 255
Arrow impossibility theorem, 24
Arrow, Kenneth, 301
Ascription, 330, 374, 468
Aspden, Philip, 559
Aspirations: of Brothers, 476–478; educational, 458; expectations *v.,* 469; of Hallway Hangers, 469–476; in low-income neighborhoods, 468–483; occupational, 456, 458, 469

Assets: of groups, 7; human, 3; opportunities, 264
Assimilation, 204–205, 210–211
Atkinson, Anthony, 24
Atkinson, Robert, 557
Auditions: blind, 301–313; democratization of, 306; orchestral, 306–309
Autonomization, 70–71

Babbidge, A., 526
Bakunin, M., 108
Bakunin's doctrine, 107
Balance, 23, 28
Balfour, Jennifer L., 518
Baltzell, Digby, 117
Banfield, Edward, 156
Barnes, Brenda C., 292
Baron, James N., 323
Baumer, Eric, 171
Bechhofer, F., 70
Becker, Gary, 301, 498, 601
Begue, Brian, 197
Behavioral linkage, 70
Behrman, Jere, 29
Bell, Daniel, 108, 378
The Bell Curve (Herrnstein/Murray), 20, 252
Benabou, Roland, 27
Benson, John, 26
Benzeval, Michaela, 517
Bergmann, Barbara, 354
Berle, Adolph, 108
Bhagwati, Jagdish, 580
Bielby, William T., 323
Bimber, Bruce, 561
Biopiracy, 581
Biracials, 269, 271
Björklund, Anders, 29, 443
Black English, 161
Blacks: class stratification and, 235–236; isolation of, 161; middle class, 234, 239; poor, 241;

611